Table of Contents

Introduction

Welcome to the Denver Snuffer Podcast! When Denver began teaching about what God is doing today in continuing the Restoration of the Gospel that commenced in the days of Joseph Smith, it became obvious that sincere learners had many questions—and the same questions were often asked over and over. This podcast began early in 2018 as a simple way to provide answers to those common questions.

This volume includes transcripts of episodes 51-99, all of which were released during 2019. Episode 100 (which was released at the very end of 2019) was the first part of a series. As such, it is included in the next volume.

Each episode consists of one or more of the following kinds of recordings:

- Remarks made by Denver during various lectures, meetings, or Q&A sessions that had previously been recorded and released;
- Remarks by Denver that had previously been recorded but not released;
- Previously-published written material that Denver subsequently recorded for the podcast; and
- Recordings of new material for the podcast.

(Please see "Appendix 1: Episodes Containing New Material" for a list of those episodes that include previously unreleased, unrecorded, or new material.)

Readers with a keen eye will also note that, in some cases, Denver used an audio transcript as the basis for preparing an "expanded transcript" or paper, with clarifying comments or additional material added in that was not part of the original audio recording. This was particularly the case in lectures 5-10 of the "40 Years in Mormonism" lecture series where the original audio transcripts were greatly expanded into papers and, ultimately, into a book titled *Preserving the Restoration*, published by Mill Creek Press in 2015. In some cases, a podcast transcript may include these written additions even though they were not present in the audio version of the podcast. They provide additional depth and detail to the subject matter and may be of value to the reader.

Although these podcast episodes contain much information about the topics addressed, the reader should not assume they include everything there is to know or learn about these topics. The podcasts should rightly be considered as starting points or brief introductions that can *excite…inquiry and diligent search* and *[arouse your] minds to inquire after the knowledge of God* (Lectures on Faith 2:56). Readers are always encouraged to study the Scriptures with great care and use them as they were intended to be used: as a Urim and Thummim capable of revealing knowledge about the character and glory of God and to help one *obtain faith in God and power…to behold him face to face* (Lectures on Faith 2:55):

> The extent of any man's knowledge concerning the character and glory of God depends upon the diligence and the faithfulness of the individual until, *like Enoch, the brother of Jared, and Moses, they shall obtain faith in God, and power with him to behold him face to face. We have now clearly set forth how it is, and how it was, that God became an object of faith for rational beings; and also, upon what foundation the testimony was based which excited the inquiry and diligent search of the ancient saints to seek after and obtain a knowledge of the glory of God; and we have seen that it was human testimony, and human testimony only, that excited this inquiry, in the first instance, in their minds. It was the credence they gave to the testimony of their fathers, this testimony having aroused their minds to inquire after the knowledge of God; the inquiry frequently terminated, indeed always terminated when rightly pursued, in the most glorious discoveries and eternal certainty* (Lectures on Faith 2:55-56).

> And what is "the most glorious discovery"? It is the person of God. And what is the "eternal certainty" that you want? It is your own salvation. Because no man can give that to you—but God can. (Denver Snuffer Podcast, Episode 17: Prayer, Part 1)

We remain grateful for the opportunity to assist in some small way in the furtherance of God's great work. We hope that our efforts in this endeavor will be acceptable to our Lord, to whom all glory, praise, and honor rightly belong.

The Denver Snuffer Podcast Team
May 31, 2021

51. Discernment, Part 1

This is Part 1 of a special series on Discernment.

QUESTION: In a lengthy *Times and Seasons* article titled "Try the Spirits," published on April 1, 1842, Joseph Smith wrote:

> *A man must have the discerning of spirits before he can drag into daylight this hellish influence and unfold it unto the world in all its soul-destroying, diabolical, and horrid colors; for nothing is a greater injury to the children of men than to be under the influence of a false spirit when they think they have the Spirit of God. (T&C 147:9)*

What is discernment? How can I develop the gift and ability? What can be done to correctly discern true and false spirits? And how can I discern my own thoughts from those from God?

DENVER: The authenticity of God's message is not proven by the means of delivery. Even if an angel comes, an angel can come and mislead you. The only way to distinguish between what is and what is not of God is through the medium of sacrifice, because when you do this, the vessel is clean. And when the vessel is clean before God, then even an angel of light cannot mislead you. Because what they offer is darkness, and you can tell it, because they have not the power to mislead.

Everyone can be misled, unless the course in life that they pursue is according to God's will. I want to go to vs 27 of Mormon 9:27: "*O then despise not, and wonder not, but hearken unto the words of the Lord, and ask the Father in the name of Jesus for what things soever ye shall stand in need. Doubt not, but be believing, and begin as in times of old, and come unto the Lord with all your heart, and work out your own salvation with fear and trembling before him. Be wise in the days of your probation; strip yourselves of all uncleanness; ask not, that ye may consume it on your lusts, but ask with a firmness unshaken, that ye will yield to no temptation, but that ye will serve the true and living God.*" You don't acquire favor with God in order to consume what He gives to you on your lusts, to satisfy your ambition, to become someone great in the eyes of everyone else. It doesn't happen that way. And if you try to turn it in that way, you'll meet the same kind of unfortunate end that we see happening time and time again by the ambitious and the unscrupulous, the knavish and the foolish.

Be wise in the days of your probation. Strip yourselves of all uncleanness. Check your thoughts. Focus them on something that is light and true and pure. Because in the end, none of us have anything to be proud of. In the end, the only thing that matters is if God will vouch for us in the day of judgment. If He will and if He does, then it is a gift. I honestly believe—and I'm not saying this for rhetorical purposes, I honestly believe—

I have lived my life; I know the mistakes I've made. In the book *The Second Comforter*, the little vignettes taken out of my life illustrate how to make a mistake, how to do something wrong, how to fail. And what follows in the chapter is a description of how to do it right. I have learned all that I have learned as a consequence of my own failings, as a consequence of my own errors.

I genuinely believe that almost every person in this room (I say "almost" because I know there is a Marine here), almost every person in this room has lived a life that has been better, more pure, more decent, more honorable, and more noble than my own. I am unworthy of anything other than your pity. But I can bear testimony of someone who is pure, who is true, and who can save you. My belief is that every one of you have lived lives so much more worthy of the Lord's recognition than my own. For the life of me, I can't understand why you don't have the faith and confidence to realize that He loves you. And you are more lovable than am I. He probably finds it a lot easier to love you than me. I feel like I'm the idiot that's writing graffiti on the walls of heaven, and they really wish the guy would leave and wonder what he's doing here. I mean, I get that you're into forgiving the sinners, but you've got to be kidding me. I think if you were to arrive there, there would be a lot more propriety to that. Have faith. Be believing. Trust in Him.

Go to Moses 1:8: *"And it came to pass that Moses looked, and beheld the world upon which he was created..."* Moses beheld the world. To me, this is very interesting. He's describing a view that is very often in scripture referred to as "being caught up into an exceedingly high mountain." This is a view up and looking down. In any event, let's move to verse 18: *"And again Moses said..."* now he's talking because Satan has come during this interlude period as an angel of light, tempting him—vs 18: *"And again Moses said: I will not cease to call upon God, I have other things to inquire of him: for his glory has been upon me, wherefore I can judge between him and thee. Depart hence, Satan."*

The defect that Moses perceived in what Lucifer was saying, tempting him, did not consist merely in the presence. This is an angel. Go to Section 76, and read the description: an angel, in a position of authority in the presence of God, was cast down. That is not a being who, to look upon, would appear to be a vile creature. That would be someone who, to look upon, would appear to be a being of light, a being of glory, an angel of light. The reason Moses could discern between them had nothing to do with the appearance. It had to do with the content. It had to do with the Spirit. It had to do with what he radiated. And what Moses was able to discern was that this was not the source of something which he, Moses, chose to take in, as a consequence of which, he could judge between him and say, You—you I disprefer.

When you look at the Joseph Smith History, the thick darkness (I talked about this last time)—the Orson Hyde account of that talks about the thick darkness that gathered around him. It consisted of the adversary benighting his mind with doubts and brought to his soul all sorts of improper pictures. The reason why it is possible to do that, and more easily so with many of us, is because we have ingested into ourselves all kinds of improper images, which then can be summoned back up.

Look at 2 Nephi 9:9. This is one of the early sermons given by Jacob, "*And our spirits must have become like unto him, and we become devils, angels to a devil, to be shut out from the presence of our God, and to remain with the father of lies, in misery, like unto himself; yea, to that being who beguiled our first parents, who transformeth himself nigh unto an angel of light, and stirreth up the children of men unto secret combinations of murder and all manner of secret works of darkness.*" It is not the physical appearance, nor the transformation that takes place—it is the content—which is why you need to know that the course that you are pursuing is in accordance with the will of God, because once you have made the required sacrifice, you acquire the required knowledge.

Look at Alma 30. This is an explanation given at the bad end of Korihor. As the judgments were upon him, and he was writing his final confession before his death, Alma 30:53, "*But behold, the devil hath deceived me; for he appeared unto me in the form of an angel, and said unto me: Go and reclaim this people, for they have all gone astray after an unknown God. And he said unto me: There is no God; yea, and he taught me that which I should say. And I have taught his words; and I taught them because they were pleasing unto the carnal mind; and I taught them, even until I had much success, insomuch that I verily believed that they were true; and for this cause I withstood the truth, even until I have brought this great curse upon me.*"

You see, he was convinced by the devil who appeared to him in the form of an angel. It's not always that the adversary comes to you with murderous intent. Sometimes he comes to appeal to your vanity, to your pride. Pride is such a sinkhole that he can get most people there. "Oh, you could have acclaim, you could have wealth." No, you acquire what you need to acquire as a consequence of sacrificing for God. And in that process you will endure criticism, rejection, opposition, the world's hatred. You may even be cast out —but you obtain what you obtain from God by sacrifice.

MAN: What keys of knowledge, what tools do you use to help discern between truth and error?

DENVER: The most correct measuring stick, in my view, is the Book of Mormon. As long as you have the Book of Mormon, you have the ability to make a comparison, and if something reaffirms something I find there, then I regard that as having passed the test. If it contradicts that [the Book of Mormon], then I regard that as having failed the test. And if it harmonizes with it, but it extends it beyond anything known to me, then I've got something to pray about, because the ultimate arbiter of truth is God.

Within your family, within your marriage, are you and your wife learning to use persuasion? Within your marriage, are you and your husband learning to use gentleness in dealing with one another? Are the two of you, together, facing one another in all the difficulties that come as a result of being married, are you facing that together in meekness? Do you find that, in all the relationship troubles, turmoil, and challenges, what predominates is kindless? Is there a search for understanding that results in pure knowledge, when it comes to a dilemma? Look at verse 37:

> *"That they may be conferred upon us, it is true; but when we undertake to cover our sins, or to gratify our pride, our vain ambition, or to exercise control or dominion or compulsion upon the souls of the children of men, in any degree of unrighteousness, behold, the heavens withdraw themselves; the Spirit of the Lord is grieved; and when it is withdrawn, Amen to the priesthood or the authority of that man."* (D&C 121:37)

It has been my observation that as soon as the Spirit of the Lord withdraws, that quickly will another spirit step in to assure you that you're right, that you should be vindicated, that you ought to proceed on in the arrogance of your heart to feel yourself justified and vindicated. There are false spirits that go about, but there is no better an audience to receive the whisperings of those false spirits than the abusers who, having grieved the spirit and caused it to withdraw, then accept counsel from another spirit that says: "You are right; press on! Well done! You are good; you're right. You'll be vindicated. This is all God's work, and you're a great man because you're engaged in God's work! Do not back down; do not relent. Forget about persuasion—you should never be long-suffering; you should make those under your rule suffer. They should yield to your rule. There is no place for meekness. We believe in a God of strength, a God of power, a God whose work can be done despite the frailties of man! There is no need for men to be meek. And it's kind, in the end, after all, to punish and to force and coerce, because we have a good objective in mind." All of the lies and all the deceit that led, in turn, to Catholicism falling into the abyss that it fell into are presently in play with Spirits that worked this out long ago, taking the Restoration of the Gospel as yet another opportunity in which to whisper in once the Spirit is withdrawn.

And so does your marriage help you avoid covering your sins? Does your marriage— Because you are never going to solve this problem in a community of Zion, until you first begin to solve it in the walls within your own home. You are never going to have Zion that exists somewhere in a community, until first that community has been composed of those who have a marriage that is in the image of God.

Does your marriage help you to avoid "gratifying your pride?" Does it help hold down your "vain ambition?" Is your ambition to exalt the two of you, rather than the one of you? Does it bring you, time and time again, to not exercise control but to respect the freedom to choose? Your kids are going to make mistakes. It is not your job to force them to not make the mistake. It is your job to counsel them and to let them have the experience by which your counsel makes sense and is vindicated. You hope the mistakes they make are not too serious, but even if they are serious and they involve lifelong struggles, it is their right to choose. It is your obligation to teach and to persuade and then to rejoice when they return after they are tired of filling their bellies with the husks that the pigs are fed. It is your job to go and greet them and put a robe on their shoulder and put a ring on their hand and to the kill the fatted calf. It's not your job to beat them and chain them to the farm, so that they can't go away and behave foolishly. They need to know that your bonds of love towards them are stronger than death itself. They need to know that they will endure in your heart into eternity—not only your children, but one another. Because we all make mistakes.

Do not exercise dominion; do not exercise compulsion; but exercise long-suffering, gentleness, meekness, and kindness. Some of the biggest disasters come when you do not give people the right to choose freely, and you attempt to coerce them. Be wise, be prudent, be someone that they would respect and who they would listen to. (Your children will correctly measure you in the end, even if they do not do so at the beginning.)

When you submit to the rule of God and you place yourself in a position in which you must be dependent upon Him, every one of you realizes your own weaknesses. Every one of you has to grapple with the uncertainty of, "Is this right, or is this wrong?" Every one of you has to grapple with the fact that, in answer to some questions, there is silence, and you are forced to choose—if you choose right, you do not know you chose right, because He refused to answer you. Then you act in reliance on that, going forward—only later to be told, "If you'd made the mistake, I would have corrected you, but you needed that experience."

God answers prayers. And sometimes He forces you to make choices. And very often (I can't tell you how often, but very often), I make the wrong choice. It is almost like I've got a compass pointing south. I don't know what the deal is there. I choose wrong, and then I get an answer. But I got an answer, because I made a mistake. I have no clue why, other than the fact I was so converted and faithful to the LDS Church, why the Lord would have chosen me to accomplish what He's accomplished. Because I sincerely believe most of you here are just genuinely better people than I am. I have nothing but weakness to offer. Weak things are used by God because that requires faith. And faith requires that we have a correct belief and then that we take action. That's from the *Lectures on Faith*: A correct belief, and then we take action. But if you do take action, then you will receive the reward from your faith. Do not rely on man.

There is nothing special about us...YET. But there can be. We do not need numerous temples, but we will need one to which Christ can come. We do not need to perform endless work for the dead until after there has been a covenant made for us. We must be first connected. Only then can we do something to liberate them. I've written so much on that, I won't repeat it.

There are so many opportunities to go off the rails that I want to remind you of some of the early problems in Kirtland. In Doctrine and Covenants 50:2,

> Behold, verily I say unto you, that there are many spirits which are false spirits, which have gone forth in the earth, deceiving the world. And also Satan hath sought to deceive you, that he might overthrow you. Behold, I, the Lord, have looked upon you, and have seen abominations in the church that profess my name. But blessed are they who are faithful and

endure, whether in life or in death, for they shall inherit eternal life. But wo unto them that are deceivers and hypocrites, for, thus saith the Lord, I will bring them to judgment. Behold, verily I say unto you, there are hypocrites among you, who have deceived some, which has given the adversary power; but behold such shall be reclaimed [not the hypocrites; He's going to reclaim those that are deceived]. *But the hypocrites shall be detected and shall be cut off, either in life or in death, even as I will; and wo unto them who are cut off from my church, for the same are overcome of the world. Wherefore, let every man beware lest he do that which is not in truth and righteousness before me. And now come, saith the Lord, by the Spirit, unto the elders of his church, and let us reason together, that ye may understand; Let us reason even as a man reasoneth one with another face to face. Now, when a man reasoneth he is understood of man, because he reasoneth as a man; even so will I, the Lord, reason with you that you may understand. Wherefore, I the Lord ask you this question—unto what were ye ordained? To preach my gospel by the Spirit, even the Comforter which was sent forth to teach the truth. And then received ye spirits which ye could not understand, and received them to be of God; and in this are ye justified? Behold ye shall answer this question yourselves; nevertheless, I will be merciful unto you; he that is weak among you hereafter shall be made strong. Verily I say unto you, he that is ordained of me and sent forth to preach the word of truth by the Comforter, in the Spirit of truth, doth he preach it by the Spirit of truth or some other way? And if it be by some other way it is not of God. And again, he that receiveth the word of truth, doth he receive it by the Spirit of truth or some other way? If it be some other way it is not of God. Therefore, why is it that ye cannot understand and know, that he that receiveth the word by the Spirit of truth receiveth it as it is preached by the Spirit of truth? Wherefore, he that preacheth and he that receiveth, understand one another, and both are edified and rejoice together. And that which doth not edify is not of God, and is darkness. That which is of God is light; and he that receiveth light, and continueth in God, receiveth more light; and that light groweth brighter and brighter until the perfect day. And again, verily I say unto you, and I say it that you may know the truth, that you may chase darkness from among you; He that is ordained of God and sent forth, the same is appointed to be the greatest, notwithstanding he is the least and the servant of all.*

This is what we should be. This is how we should teach. This is how we should edify one another. This is how we should be preparing our children. This is what we should be laying hold upon: truth, light, understanding, edifying, growing in knowledge of the principles of truth. You should not waste another 3-hour block of time fiddling around with nonsense, because you don't have permission from God to do that. Preach the principles. And if you don't think you know enough to do anything else—get together, and read the scriptures out loud.

(**Transcribers Note:** This next paragraph (in italics) was intended to be included in the audio at this point in the podcast, but due to difficulties in the transcript that was used to identify the start and stop times of the audio segments, the paragraph didn't make it in—but it's highly relevant and has therefore been included here):

False spirits will be among you. Prideful and pretentious people will want to impress you to give them honor. Honor God instead. Do not let a new revelation displace your attention away from the scriptures. They are sufficient for our day, as these ten sessions have demonstrated, I hope. I have expounded the scriptures as Moroni did to Joseph and as Christ did on the road to Emmaus the day of His resurrection. We must first remember and observe. Preserving the Restoration requires us to be very familiar with the scriptures of the Restoration. At present, we should fear most our ignorance of the scriptures.

In the tenth talk, given in Phoenix two years ago, you were warned about false spirits, as happened in Kirtland, which you were warned would come among us. That warning has proven true. False spirits have mislead some into foolish errors. I am astonished at vain, foolish, and prideful ideas that are anti-Christ, degrading, and dark but have been welcomed by some. Remember Pharaoh's magicians also enchanted their rods to become snakes (Exo. 7:11-12) and conjured frogs to mimic the sign given by God through Moses and Aaron (Exo. 8:7). Pharaoh's heart was hardened by these imitations. Do not let yours become so likewise.

For two years I have watched, attended some of your meetings, gathered reports, and tried to let you stand and display your strength and understanding. Even God left Adam and Eve in the Garden and allowed Lucifer, the common enemy, to tempt and try them, promising to return again to visit them. They transgressed His commandment, and He provided the means to cover their shame, repent, and return. He also promised to later send messengers. But God did not "babysit" Adam and Eve, informing them that it was given unto them to choose, even when He forbids something. God is the same now as in the beginning. We are all required to display our strength, obedience, and prove our understanding.

People have come among you preaching falsehoods and inviting others to follow false spirits—adulterers and adulteresses who justify sins and mock the commandment, *"thou shalt not commit adultery"* (Exo. 20:14). False claimants are pretending to seal others up to eternal life, changing the ordinances, and introducing foolish and vain ideas borrowed from pagans and heathen who do not know Christ nor His righteousness. I do not oppose them directly by debate or counter-argument. I declare the truth and leave it for everyone to decide between clearly opposing teachings. If people cannot discern, then they will need to learn from sad experience to choose between good and evil, perhaps only coming to understand after their destruction in this world.

There are those who use well-reasoned arguments to expound their understanding of scripture who have declared with certainty it is impossible for what I say to be true. These voices come from both the fearful anonymous and proud academics. I do not respond to either.

In a letter on August 24, 1834, Joseph Smith described the only way falsehoods could be avoided. He wrote, "If the Saints are very humble, very watchful and very prayerful, that few will be deceived by those who have not authority to teach, or who have not the Spirit to teach according to the power of the Holy Ghost, in the scriptures" (JS Papers, Documents Vol. 4, p. 117).

Only the truth is at issue. Individuals other than Christ do not matter. The message I have and do preach is from the Lord. His sheep hear His voice. If they accept it as His, then deceivers, false spirits, and men's learning are powerless to destroy faith in Him. He promised He "will take care of our flocks" (D&C 88:72), and therefore, it will be Him, and not me, who will keep His flock shepherded.

Of course, a false spirit can project love. Of course. False spirits imitate. The great imitator, who is a liar from the beginning, begins by assuming the role that is designed to be a counterfeit. The only way that a counterfeit works is if it has the look and feel, sentiment, and everything that the real thing has. If the adversary is going to imitate, of course love can be one of those things that are imitated. The question—if you want to try and dial in yea/nay, good/bad, true/false—is whether or not the love that is being shown leads, in turn, to pride, to haughtiness, to thinking I'm great, I'm wonderful. If it has, as its objective, creating pride and haughtiness in the individual, then you have to question the content of the message, not the means by which it gets delivered. Because if the means by which it is delivered is a counterfeit, it will seem like the 'coin of the realm'—the real thing. Therefore, you have to question if the objective is prideful or if the objective is ultimately destructive.

———

In addition to the foregoing, Denver has addressed this topic extensively in several blog posts that may be worthwhile for you to review, including:

"False Spirits" posted January 19, 2012
"Gifts Come from God" posted June 2, 2010
"The Battle" posted January 13, 2011; and
"Faith Requires Correct Acts" posted August 7, 2016

The foregoing excerpts were taken from:

- Denver's *40 Years in Mormonism Series*, Talk #2 titled "Faith," given in Idaho Falls, ID on September 28, 2013;
- His talk titled "Other Sheep Indeed," given at the Sunstone Symposium in Salt Lake City, UT on July 29, 2017;
- Denver's *40 Years in Mormonism Series*, Talk #9 titled "Marriage and Family," given in St. George, UT on July 26, 2014;
- Denver's *40 Years in Mormonism Series*, Talk #10 titled "Preserving the Restoration," given in Mesa, AZ on September 9, 2014; and
- His conference talk titled "The Doctrine of Christ," given in Boise, ID on September 11th, 2016.

52. Discernment, Part 2

This is Part 2 of a special series on Discernment.

QUESTION: What is discernment? How can I develop the gift and ability? What can be done to correctly discern true and false spirits? And how can I discern my own thoughts from those from God?

―――――

DENVER: Then there is the weakness of mind and spirit of mankind. Moroni discussed the ministering of angels, and he described in these words:

> "Neither have angels ceased to minister unto the children of men. For behold, they are subject unto him, to minister according to the word of his command, showing themselves unto them of strong faith and a firm mind in every form of godliness. And the office of their ministry is to call men unto repentance, and to fulfil and to do the work of the covenants of the Father, which he hath made unto the children of men, to prepare the way among the children of men, by declaring the word of Christ unto the chosen vessels of the Lord, that they may bear testimony of him" (Moroni 7:29-31).

If you go through those verses and you look at what he's saying, it requires a firm mind in every form of godliness. A firm mind can be descriptive of a variety of things, including someone that's just stubborn. But it's not stubbornness—it's a firm grasp on the things that lead to godliness; not excesses, not foolishness—and we'll get more into that in a bit. Their purpose in ministering is to equip the person who has an audience and those who hear the message to be called to repentance; not a lot of flowery, fancy things but repentance, because essentially, without repentance—that is turning to face God in all you do—none of us are going to make it.

He goes on to say that the purpose of calling people to repentance is to *"fulfil and do the works of the covenants" (Moroni 7:31).* There is sort of a pattern here in what is happening. Angelic ministrants comes to people of a firm mind and every form of godliness, calls repentance in order to fulfil and in order to do the work of the covenants. *"To fulfil and to do the work of the covenants of the Father,"* that requires that people bear testimony of Him. These are the essential things that are needed. It doesn't require a fanciful or a flowery imagination. It does not require that we bear testimony of ourselves. It doesn't require us to do something other than to fulfil and do the work of the covenants. Therefore, I would suggest this is a pretty good guide to consider when you're evaluating all of the competing claims that are now being made by people (to having inspiration or revelation or the word of God to them).

We are vulnerable to being mislead, even as we claim to be inspired. I'm going to read from a recent study from the National Academy of Science. I read from it because it's a really interesting study result:

Religion appears to serve as a moral compass for the vast majority of people around the world. It informs whether same-sex marriage is love or sin, whether war is an act of security or of terror, [and] whether abortion rights represent personal liberty or permission to murder. Many religions are centered on a god (or gods) that has beliefs and intentions, with adherents encouraged to follow "God's will" on everything from martyrdom to career planning to voting.

Within these religious systems, how do people know what their god wills? When people try to infer other people's attitudes and beliefs, they often do so egocentrically by using their own beliefs as an inductive guide. This research examines the extent to which people might also reason egocentrically about God's beliefs. We predicted that people would be consistently more egocentric when reasoning about God's beliefs than when reasoning about other people's beliefs. Intuiting God's beliefs on important issues may not produce an independent guide, but may instead serve as an echo chamber that reverberates one's own beliefs. "The Jewish and Christian traditions state explicitly that God created man in his own image, but believers and nonbelievers alike have long argued that people seem to create God in their own image as well."

That's a problem that you find everywhere. "God wills this to be so, well, because God agrees with me that it ought to be so, and therefore, I'm comfortably in tune with God!" The greatest help given to us to solve the contradiction between praying to God and the answer being exactly what we wanted, exactly what we expected, and exactly what makes us right and everyone else wrong—the greatest guide is the scriptures. They provide us a lifeline for measuring any inspiration we think we obtain from God. But that's not enough if it's not coupled together with prayerful, ponderous thought and time and experience. I want to compare these statements from

Joseph Smith about this topic: "A person may profit by noticing the first intimation of the spirit of revelation; for instance, when you feel pure intelligence flowing into you, it may give you sudden strokes of ideas, so that by noticing it, you may find it fulfilled the same day or soon; (i.e.) those things that were presented unto your minds by the Spirit of God, will come to pass; and thus by learning the Spirit of God and understanding it, you may grow into the principle of revelation, until you become perfect in Christ Jesus" (*DHC* 3:381, June 1839).

That seems to suggest that answers can come suddenly, quickly, perhaps even easily. But Joseph also said this: "A fanciful and flowery and heated imagination beware of; because the things of God are of deep import; and time, and experience, and careful and ponderous and solemn thoughts can only find them out. Thy mind, O man! if thou wilt lead a soul unto salvation, must stretch as high as the utmost heavens, and search into and contemplate the darkest abyss, and the broad expanse of eternity—thou must commune with God" (*TPJS*, p. 137, March 1839).

That second quote is taken from a letter that Joseph Smith composed while he was in Liberty Jail, in which he had plenty of time to fashion the language. The first quote, sadly, is taken from a source which may not be reliable or accurate. The source for that first quote is *Willard Richard's Pocket Companion,* in which he quoted something which, **if** Joseph Smith said it, Joseph said it while Willard Richards was in England on a mission, and he could not possibly have heard it. He doesn't even attribute it to Joseph Smith. But when the documentary history was being compiled, they used the *Willard Richard's [Pocket] Companion* to take that language and attribute it to a talk given by Joseph in 1839 because most of the stuff in the Pocket Companion can be tracked to Joseph, and therefore they conclude this one likewise fit that same category. The second one is clearly, unambiguously from Joseph Smith and describes the process. Now, while Joseph was in the Liberty Jail on occasion he would have a friendly face show up, or he would have a letter arrive. On one of the occasions he got letters from other people and his wife, Emma. Joseph, who had been brooding at the time and longing for the companionship of some friends, describes what his mind was going through at the time of the letter and his response to it. He says his mind was frenzied, and any man's mind can be when contemplating the many difficult issues we are called upon to confront.

Just like Joseph, we have perpetual conundrums and contradictions. We all face them. Some are of our own making but others are just inherent in living in this existence. When we thoughtfully consider the challenges, just like

Joseph, it seizes the mind, and like Joseph in Liberty Jail, makes us reflect upon so many things with the "avidity of lightning." That was Joseph's word. The mind is in this frenzied state, and with the avidity of lightning he's jumping from subject to subject, a fence to a fence, from things that console to things that outrage you. From things you know to be true to things that offend you. Back and forth, and back and forth until, as Joseph puts it, "...finally all enmity, malice and hatred, and past differences, misunderstandings and mismanagements are slain victorious at the feet of hope; and when the heart is sufficiently contrite, then the voice of inspiration steals along and whispers...." It's almost poetry, the way Joseph describes what he went through there. But it is poetry describing the actual bona fides of Joseph receiving answers from God.

God's most important inspiration for the most challenging subjects is often not hasty, quick, and without effort at our end. Consider the advice to Oliver Cowdery that he must "study it out in his own mind first" before asking God to tell him the answer. Many people want a quick, perfunctory response from God with no forethought. What they receive in turn is a quick, perfunctory answer. God is almost always, for the most difficult challenges, not a "short order cook," although there are certainly false spirits who are willing to be just that.

I asked God in October what the term "mutual agreement" (as used in the Answer) meant. Before I asked, I hesitated and pondered the issue for two months. I discussed it with my wife and several others, and then discussed again the views of others with my wife. I read emails from people involved in an active discussion about the meaning of the term. It requires humility to approach God and ask Him for His answer and yet more humility to know it is from Him and not my own ego, presumptions, hopes, desires, wants, and conceit. It is for me, as it was for Joseph, only "when the heart is sufficiently contrite, then the voice of inspiration steals along and whispers" the truth that comes from a purer source, higher than myself, and more filled with light than any man. Certainly, greater light than I have. When the definition was given, it was accompanied by the realization the Lord could have disputed every day of His life with someone. He deliberately chose to not contend. He was not an argumentative personality.

The more we contend with others, the more we are taken captive by the spirit of contention. We become subject to the spirit we submit to follow. Those who are prone to contention become more contentious as they listen to that spirit. Eventually they are overcome by that spirit, and it is a great work involving great effort to subdue and dismiss that spirit from the heart and mind of the victim.

Let me give you a description of the *Prayer for the Covenant*: It took months of pondering, testing, questioning beforehand before I even dared to ask. The idea that presented itself to my mind was that Joseph's prayer at the dedication of the Kirtland Temple was a pattern to be followed when some great event involving God was to take place. The House of the Lord was one such event in Kirtland, but having a new volume of scripture was at least equally important to that. Therefore, a prayer to God asking for His acceptance was an idea that continued to press upon my mind.

But it concerned me that the idea of my offering that prayer may be based on my own will and not heaven's. Before proceeding, I questioned my motive, my desire, and why I would even ask. I was haunted by the continuing impression that it needed to be done and was required of me. Finally, when the idea could not be shaken from my mind, I determined it was not my own thought but God's beckoning voice telling me this was an obligation I needed to act upon and not suppress. I want you to think of Joseph's description that says, "Never did any passage of scripture come with more power to the heart of man than this did at this time to mine. It seemed to enter with great force into every feeling of [my] heart. I reflected on it again and again...."

Joseph did not act hastily when the impression came to him. He couldn't shake it. It persisted. He reflected upon it again and again. I don't know whether that's days, weeks, or months, but I can tell you before the *Prayer for the Covenant* was offered, for me it was months, because if it isn't of God, I have no right to step forward and do something. I ought not be volunteering for things of that nature. At length I determined that I should act on the impulse, and therefore, I ought to offer a prayer for the acceptance of the scripture. When I began to compose the prayer, the content was provided by inspiration from Heaven and not my own words. It took me nearly 200,000 words to write a history of the Restoration from the time of Joseph to the present in a book that's fairly lengthy. The *Prayer for the Covenant*, coming by inspiration, only took a few pages and stated in more concise terms, more correctly, the history of the Restoration from the beginning until now. The *Prayer for the Covenant*—the prayer for the Scriptures—is not me being clever and insightful and succinct. The words were given, and the words are God's view of what has happened.

There are those who have claimed inspiration on very important matters who make decisions quickly. Almost as soon as they finish a prayer asking for something, they assume the first thing that pops into their mind is God's infallible answer. I do not doubt that may happen. It has happened to me, but for the most important things I have found that careful, ponderous, and solemn thought and meditation over time produces God's will and word with clarity that does not happen in haste.

Plural marriage history is a very convoluted and difficult topic. It's easy to reach a decision without the labor of careful, solemn, ponderous, and searching thought to determine the truth. When the policy was announced publicly in 1852, the focus of the announcement that was made by Orson Pratt was on the Constitution of the United States. In fact, when he got up to deliver the announcement, one of the things that's stressed in the talk–and you can read it, it's in the Journal of Discourses; the talk is preserved—one of the things he stressed was that the Constitution protected religious practices and that if it is a bona fide part of your religion, then it is protected. In fact, there is more emphasis in that talk placed on the Constitutionality of the practice than there is on scriptural support or divine pattern of the practice. This is the first public announcement.

So one of the questions that presents to my mind—and should present to your mind—is why, if this is an eternal principle, why, when the first public explanation of it is given, was the focus upon the Constitutionality of the practice. It seems incongruent. The Constitution of the United States, at that time, was less than 75 years old, but this is a practice that often goes back—depending upon whether you accept what Brigham Young says or not—all the way to the Creation, but certainly by those who advocated it, back to the early patriarchal fathers. So why the focus on the Constitutionality of the practice? It was one of the dilemmas and one of the questions that occurred to me when I first encountered the subject. If it begins with Adam bringing "one of his wives," why isn't that much more important to relate? The practice, if it is of Divine origin, should have a great body of scripture and truth to back it. Why focus on something as comparatively trivial as the then 75-year-old U.S. Constitution? It took me several decades of searching before I felt qualified to reach a conclusion on the topic. 27 years of preparation and pursuit was involved before I found God, which then brings this point:

If a group of prayerful people spend months focused on a challenge; and then many hours together and individually discussing, searching, praying, and looking to heaven for guidance; and then reach a conclusion they can all individually and collectively testify came from heaven, how can I adequately test their outcome without giving it careful, solemn, ponderous thought and take the time to test and retest the answer they get? People who can make truly inspired snap decisions are far better at obtaining God's voice than am I. For gravely important matters, it takes me a great deal of wrestling with heaven before I can trust that I am humble enough before God to accept what He has to offer and to exclude all of what I want, all of what I hope, and all of what I expect. Those who have a "short order cook" for their God can do what I cannot.

There are many who dispute the inspiration others have received. I have two concerns with the decision a good person makes to dispute with others. First, the Lord's example is to refrain from disputing, as He did. When confronted, He would respond, but He did not go about picking a fight with others. He responded. The only exception was when He went up to Jerusalem to be slain. Then He went into the seat of Jewish power and authority to throw it down and provoke their decision to finally judge, reject and crucify Him. He, and not they, controlled that timing. His provocation at that time was a deliberate act on His part because His *"time had come,"* and His sacrifice needed to be made.

Second, there are the Lord's teachings. We have time and time again focused on the Doctrine of Christ. We have the doctrine of Christ on numerous websites, enshrined in numerous talks, and as a theme that has been adopted for conferences. Just before the doctrine of Christ He tells you what His doctrine is NOT. This is what Christ says immediately preceding His doctrine: *"neither shall there be disputations among you concerning the points of my doctrine, as there have hitherto been. For verily, verily I say unto you, he that hath the spirit of contention is not of me, but is of the devil, who is the father of contention, and he stirreth up the hearts of men to contend with anger, one with another. Behold, this is not my doctrine, to stir up the hearts of men with anger, one against another; but this is my doctrine, that such things should be done away" (3 Nephi 11:28-30).* And then He proceeds to declare His doctrine of Christ.

The more we contend and dispute with one another, the better we become at contention. We polish the rhetorical skills to oppose others. That spirit of contention can take possession of us, and when it does, we are hard-pressed to be a peacemaker with others. Christ said: *"Blessed are the merciful: for they shall obtain mercy. Blessed are the pure in heart: for they shall see God. Blessed are the peacemakers: for they shall be called the children of God" (Matthew 5:7-9).* But peace should not be made at the cost of truth. Truth must be the only goal. Truth, however, belongs to God. Our desires, appetites, and passions are prone to make us stray well beyond the bounds set by God.

- Therefore, when our pride is gratified, we should question if what we are advancing is truth.

- When our ambition is served, we should question if we are in the Lord's employ or our own.

- When we insist upon control, we should question if we are like our Lord or instead like His adversary.

- When we use any means for compelling others, we should wonder if we are mocking the God who makes the sun to shine and rain to fall on all His fallen children without compulsion.

- When we display unrighteous dominion, we should question whether we are worthy of any dominion at all.

Our tools must be limited to persuasion, gentleness, meekness, love unfeigned, pure knowledge—all of them mustered *"without compulsory means"* to persuade others to accept the truth. And if we fail to make the persuasive case, then the problem is not others; the problem is that we've yet to figure out how to be sufficiently knowledgeable so as to bring them aboard.

I believe every person we encounter down here, no matter who they are, wants to follow Christ. That's why we're here. The only reason they got here was because they want to follow Christ. Therefore, since they are predisposed to following Christ, the reason they are not doing so at present is because no one has taken the time, no one has taken the trouble of giving sufficient cause to them to change, to turn, to repent, and to follow Christ. And by the way, at this point, none of us know enough in order to be able to truly follow Christ, because we are all riddled with half truths, part understanding, and the need for constant repentance—all of us. But if you're further along and you accept Christ, and you understand His will better than your brother or sister, then you have the obligation to present—persuasively—to them the same reasons that touched their heart before they ever entered this world, when they elected to follow Christ into this dark abyss in the first place. They're here trying to find Him. If you can point to it and give them reason to believe, my view is that every single individual on earth has a native free disposition to turn and face Christ. We just have to figure out how to present that sufficiently persuasively so that it touches their heart, and it resonates with that truth—that light that they came down here in the first instance possessing.

The light of Christ illuminates every single being that is in this world. Therefore, Christ is in them already. You just have to animate that so that they realize the truth that you express, the testimony that you bear. The one whom you worship is God, indeed, and worthy of their worship, worthy of their acceptance, as well.

There is so much left to be done. I know that we can't jump hastily from point to point along the way and that we have to carefully proceed with every step. But it's astonishing to me the steps that people decide to get hung up on and to spend a great deal of time, when time could better be spent moving further along on the path. I don't know what it will take to get people to enthusiastically welcome and to move along with alacrity on the pathway that the prophecies foretell someone is going to achieve in the last days. Because it seems like all that murmuring that we read about in the Book of Exodus going on in the camp of Israel, when we scratch our heads and say, Why are they complaining about missing the fleshpots of Egypt when God is leading them with a pillar of smoke by day and a pillar of fire by night? One would think that you'd be happy eating manna in the wilderness, if you knew God was with you.

I also think that in our current state of technological development, it's possible for the discontent to magnify the voice electronically over the Internet and to make any level of discontent seem to be much greater than it really is. But if one person is discontent and 500 people are arguing with the one who is discontent, it appears that the argument includes at least half a thousand, maybe more. As between one another—that is, every one of us, because every one of us is involved in a relationship with one another—you choose. Mind you, Christ could have disputed, He could have corrected, he could have challenged every one of the ongoing religious and social conventions of His day. "You are doing that wrong. Oh, you should stop doing that. Would you quit it! And by the way, you're so dark in your mind that I don't know where it begins, except for him, he's worse...and then her." Oh!

How much of the gospel of Christ would not have been possible for Him to preach if He'd gone about contending? He chose not to. In that respect, perhaps His most godly example was the patience with which He dealt with those around Him; kindly, patiently correcting them when they, largely, came to Him with questions trying to trap Him, but affirmatively stating in the Sermon on the Mount how you could take any group of people and turn them into Zion itself, if we would live the Sermon on the Mount.

I figure that I'm not that good a teacher because it appears to me that there are a lot of mistakes being made that are perfectly avoidable. I don't take King Benjamin's statement that the number of errors that people can make— The number of sins that people can commit are endless; there is no way to possibly number them as— I don't take that as consoling words. I take that as a challenge to say, Okay, but your people did find peace among one another. And even Enoch's people found peace among one another. Melchizedek was called the Prince of Peace because he preached, but what he preached was repentance. The office of the ministering of angels is to spread the message of repentance. So then all of us have an obligation there to join in the same thing—repenting, turning to face God. The more we face Him, the more light we take in, the more differently we behave, individually and in connection with each other.

I am certain we will see Zion, because it's been promised, and it's been prophesied from the beginning of time. When father Adam prophesied, being overcome by the Spirit in the valley of Adam-ondi-Ahman, and foretold what would happen to his posterity down to the latest generations, Zion was pointed to. Therefore, from the days of Adam on, all the holy prophets have looked forward to that as the essential moment in the history of the world, because Christ will come and will redeem the world. It will be the end of the wicked; it will be the beginning of something far better. That's been the hope, that's been the promise, that's been what they've looked forward to. I wonder how many of us share that same longing, that same hope, that same desire that originated in the beginning, because if we don't subdue our desires, appetites, and passions enough to try and deal peaceably one with another, choosing deliberately to not contend, even when we know people are wrong — When Christ was confronted and He corrected the error, He corrected only that error; He didn't go on with a list of other weaknesses, failings, and challenges, He only addressed the one that was put to him.

———

The foregoing excerpts were taken from Denver's fireside talk titled "That We Might Become One," given in Clinton, UT on January 14, 2018.

In addition to the foregoing, Denver has addressed this topic extensively in several blog posts that may be worthwhile to review, including:

"False Spirits" posted January 19, 2012
"Gifts Come from God" posted June 2, 2010
"The Battle" posted January 13, 2011; and

"Faith Requires Correct Acts" posted August 7, 2016.

53. Discernment, Part 3

This is the final part of a special series on Discernment.

QUESTION: What is discernment? How can I develop the gift and ability? What can be done to correctly discern true and false spirits? And how can I discern my own thoughts from those from God?

———

DENVER: The battle we are all called upon to fight is not external. Some people spend their time stirring people up to alarm them about carnal security. They are usually trying to sell something. There are fortunes being made by proponents of fear. But the audience for such things are only being distracted from a much greater, more immediate, and more personal battle. Until the internal condition of the individual has been conquered and brought into alignment with heaven, there is no amount of political, social, economic, or military security which will matter in the long run.

It's more advisable to seek for and listen to the Lord—and secondarily, those teachers who will convert you to the Lord—rather than any other advice or movement advocated by those promoting causes. Teachers ought always to point to Him. Never to themselves. No one but the Lord is coming to rescue you; and no group will be able to overcome error apart from Him. Ultimately, the battle we each face is the Lord's. We must cooperate with Him for Him to be able to win it, in us. When He does, however, the victory is ours, for we are the ones that He redeems.

The path back to the Lord's presence is an individual one. It is not likely to be accomplished while in an audience. There is no "support group" needed. It is you—what goes on inside you; what you love most. He will one day associate with a group in a city, but that group will be comprised of individuals who have previously met Him.

It surprises me how little discernment there is among those claiming to seek truth. Many of them will take in ideas from foolish, vain, and proud sources with as much enthusiasm as from a true one. How is it that people cannot tell the difference between them? Does not a true message sound much different from a false one? Is merely associating some lesser virtue with a cause enough to have it have persuasive power and distract you? What is more plain than the admonishment to seek first the kingdom of God and His righteousness? Whenever there is an increase in spiritual manifestations, there is always an increase in both true and false spiritual phenomena. You do not get one without the other.

In Kirtland, new converts (who were overzealous to participate in the new heavenly manifestations coming as a result of Joseph Smith's claims) opened themselves up to receiving influences they could not understand and did not test for truthfulness. They were so delighted to have any kind of experience, they trusted anything "spiritual" was from God. As a result, there were many undignified things, degrading conduct, foolish behavior, and evil influences which crept in among the saints. Joseph received a revelation in May 1831 concerning this troubling development. In it the Lord cautioned there were *"many false spirits deceiving the world"* (D&C 50:2); that Satan wanted to overthrow what the Lord was doing (D&C 50:3). The presence of hypocrites and of people harboring secret sins and abominations caused false claims to be accepted (D&C 50:4,6-7). It is required for all people to proceed in truth and in righteousness (D&C 50:9) if they are going to avoid deception, meaning that unrepentant and unforgiven men will not be able to distinguish between a true and a false spirit.

All spiritual gifts, including distinguishing between true and false spirits, requires the Holy Ghost, given through obedience to the truth, which allows a person to distinguish between truth and error—or truth being light, and error being darkness (D&C 50:17-23). The truth is like light, and when you follow the light of truth it grows inside you until you have a "perfect day" in which there is no more darkness, but everything is illuminated by the light of the spirit within you (D&C 50:24). In that light you are able to see clearly the difference between light and darkness, the shadows, and the pitch black.

The revelation clarifies that a preacher of truth will become only a servant. He will not claim greatness but will seek only to give truth, as a result of which false spirits will be subject to him (D&C 50:26-27). But this only comes as a result of repenting of all sin, because the light of a perfect day cannot arise when men harbor evil desires and inappropriate ambitions within their hearts (D&C 50:28-29). Truth will not leave you confused but will enlighten your understanding (D&C 50:31).

From this you can see how necessary it is for each one of us to continually repent, conduct our lives in conformity with such truth as you presently understand, and avoid deliberate wrongdoing in order to be able to distinguish between a true and a false spirit. You must attract light into yourself. It is attracted by obedience to such light as you already have. When you proceed forward using the light you already possess to attract more light, it will grow in one consistent and truthful manner from a lesser to a greater light, all of it conforming to the teachings of Jesus Christ.

Ambition in spiritual gifts leads to acceptance of evil influences. As part of the same problem in Kirtland, in September of the previous year, Hiram Page wanted to be like Joseph and was able to attract a deceiving spirit to communicate with him through a seer stone. But the commandments he received were designed to lead him into error (D&C 28:11).

Truth will always testify of Christ and lead to repentance. It will lead you to do good, not evil; to serve God and to not seek and obtain ambition to have men follow you, to have men praise you; to repent and forsake darkness which appeals to the carnal mind is the effect that truth has (see Moroni 7:12-19).

Just because you have a "spiritual experience," you cannot trust it will invariably be from God. True spirits will:

- Testify of Christ.
- Lead to repentance.
- Be consistent with existing scripture.
- Lead you to be submissive to authority that comes from God—and God alone.
- Edify and enlighten your mind.
- Be understandable and not cause confusion.
- Cause light to grow within you.
- Turn you toward Christ, not toward men.
- It will never cause pride.
- It will make you a better servant. You will be able to bless the lives of others.
- It will increase your love of your fellow man.
- It will clothe you with charity for the failings of others, instead of making you judgmental and proud.
- It will conform to the true whisperings of the Holy Ghost you previously have received.
- It will leave you humble and grateful for God's condescension.
- It will make you want to bring others to that same light.
- It will be grounded in love toward God and all mankind.
- It will lead you to rejoice.

Contrariwise, false spirits will lead you to:

- Deny Chris or to diminish his importance; or to relegate him to a status other than the Redeemer, the Savior.
- False spirits will give you messages that bring about your pride.
- They will make you believe you are better because of the experience.
- They will contradict the scriptures.
- They will appeal to carnality and self-indulgence, tending to have you violate the ten commandments and to make your violation of the ten commandments something that is viewed as excusable or justified, reasonable, or that God approves it, when He does not.
- It will lead you to rebel against those who preach the truth.
- It will cause you confusion.
- It will lead to ambition to try to control others.
- It will make you intolerant of other people's failings, and you'll judge and dismiss them.
- False spirits cause people to seek self fulfillment rather than service to their fellow man.
- False spirits appeal to your vanity and assure you that you are a great person. In fact, part of the message that succeeds comes about from false spirits precisely because it reassures people that they are great, that they are better than others. This brings about darkness in your mind; it repulses the Holy Ghost; it prevents you from understanding your sins repenting and forsaking them. It interferes with your ability to serve others. It makes you focus on yourself rather than the needs of others.

You should never think that all spiritual experiences can be trusted. There is no difference between the activities of deceiving spirits today and those in Kirtland (as well as those in the New Testament times). If you follow the Lord, you must still test the spirits and only follow those which point to Christ (see 1 John 4:1). Even Joseph Smith had to ask God about some of the phenomena going on in Kirtland before he knew which were of God and which were deceiving.

There are those today who are enjoying some success, and they target, specifically, people that have accepted the new covenant. They tell you that you are great, you are chosen; and they can assure you and confer upon you even greater blessings. What follows in the wake of their ministry though is pride, self indulgence, disobedience, and in turn, their minds become darkened, and they wind up committing serious sins. I've had a number of them come and talk to me, confessing serious sins. But they were misled at the beginning because they thought that these phenomenal spiritual experiences that people boast of could be trusted.

I hardly mention the spiritual experiences that I have had. That's for a purpose. I do not want people pointing to me and saying, "There is a great man." I want people looking at the message, evaluating the content of the message; testing it against scripture, seeing whether it brings them closer to Christ; seeing whether their faith in Christ is increased, whether their trust in our Lord grows.

It doesn't matter that a weak and flawed instrument gets used. And I consider myself only that. What matters is the truth to be found through Christ. The people who are most vocal about their great spiritual enlightenment almost invariably quickly begin to teach things that are anti-Christ, that are opposed to Him and opposed to His teachings, opposed to the commandments that He has given.

There is no higher order of things that justifies disobedience to the ten commandments. There is no higher order of things that allows you to disregard the teachings to be found by Christ in the Sermon on the Mount, in which He elaborates on and extends what it requires in the heart to obey the ten commandments. If you find yourself following someone whose preaching and teaching and visionary experiences suggest to you that there is no need to obey the Lord, that there is no need to follow Christ, that you needn't look to the commandments given in the ten commandments (which Christ elaborated upon and made personal, as our individual challenges within our own hearts, in the Sermon on the Mount), then rest assured that message—if they are preaching against that—they are misled by a false spirit. I don't care how elaborate and how wonderful their message may be cloaked.

I've tried to preach from the scriptures and rarely mention anything of a personal experience. I only do so when I am constrained or commanded to do so. If people knew all that I had experienced— Well, they never will. At least not while I'm living. It just doesn't edify; it distracts. God has made His will known. God does appear to men today. The heavens are open for business. But hell is eager to jump into that same track. When you've opened up a conduit for spiritual communication, that conduit can be just as compromised by the evil as it can be used by the good, the pure, and the true. Therefore, try the spirits. Test them. Examine them and their message against the criteria I've just discussed.

———

The foregoing was recorded by Denver Snuffer in Sandy, Utah on January 6, 2019.

54. Abraham, Part 1

This is the first part of a special series on Abraham.

QUESTION: What do we need to understand about Abraham in order to understand our place in the last-days events? What is God's view of the book of Abraham, and what ought we to take from it as we look towards a continuation of the Restoration?

————

DENVER: There's a great gulf separating us from the first Fathers of mankind. At the very beginning, a book of remembrance was kept in the language of Adam. Enoch taught repentance and knowledge of God using that book of remembrance. Those records were passed down for generations until Abraham. He learned of the first Fathers, the Patriarchs, from those records. Abraham wrote: *But the records of the Fathers, even the Patriarchs, concerning the right of Priesthood, the Lord, my God, preserved in mine own hands* (Abraham 2:4).

At the time of Abraham, Egypt was the greatest civilization on earth. Egypt was great because it imitated the original religion of the first Fathers. Abraham explained:

> *Now the first government of Egypt was established by Pharaoh, the eldest son of Zeptah, the daughter of Ham, and it was after the manner of the government of Ham, which was Patriarchal. Pharaoh, being a righteous man, established his kingdom and judged his people wisely and justly all his days, seeking earnestly to imitate that order established by the fathers in the first generations, in the days of the first Patriarchal reign, even in the reign of Adam, and also Noah, his father, who blessed him with the blessings of the earth, and with the blessings of wisdom, but cursed him as pertaining to the Priesthood.* (Abraham 2:3)

Egypt began by imitating the pattern Adam, Seth, Enos, and their direct descendants through Noah used to organize the family of the faithful. Abraham calls it a "government," but it was a family. The title "Pharaoh" originally meant "great house" or "great family," because Pharaoh was the "father" over Egypt who taught and led them. Over time, however, the title "Pharaoh" came to mean "king" or "tyrant who controlled people."

The first Pharaoh—or founding father of Egypt—imitated the first Fathers of mankind. He could only imitate because he did not have the right to act as the patriarchal head of mankind. He nevertheless tried to be a shepherd who led by righteous example. Abraham knew more about the first Fathers than did the Egyptians because Abraham had the original book of remembrance written by the Fathers in the language of Adam.

Today, scholars are trying to understand ancient Egypt. The earlier or farther back in time you look, the closer Egypt's imitation is to the government of Adam and the Patriarchs down to Noah.

The records of Egypt from the very earliest time are lost. But we have some records. The oldest are the *Pyramid Texts*. Then a few centuries later there are *Coffin Texts*. Then much later are the *Book of the Dead* texts. Near the end, we have the *Book of Breathings* texts. There are thousands of years between the first *Pyramid Texts* and the last *Book of Breathings* texts. Within those thousands of years, the religion and knowledge of Egypt became more and more corrupted.

The earliest records of the Egyptian religion carved in the *Pyramid Texts* date from 2500 BC. That was before Abraham, before Joseph was sold into Egypt, before Moses, and before the exodus from Egypt. It was long before King David, King Solomon, and Elijah. These are their earliest records.

More than 2000 years later we have the last records, the *Book of Breathings* texts. These were written at about 300 years before Christ. They were written during the time when Greece and Rome controlled Egypt. After Alexander the Great subdued western Persia, Syria, and Tyre, he conquered Egypt and became an Egyptian Pharaoh. When he died, one of Alexander's generals, named Ptolemy, replaced Alexander as Pharaoh. The descendants of Ptolemy followed him as Pharaohs in what is called the Ptolemaic Dynasty of Egypt.

You've probably heard of Cleopatra. She was a descendant of Ptolemy and was Queen of Egypt at the time when Rome controlled Egypt. Rome fell into a civil war during Cleopatra's lifetime, and Mark Antony, one of the generals of Rome, fought against Octavian, hoping to become Emperor. Cleopatra sided with Mark Antony. Cleopatra and Mark Antony both died by suicide when Octavian defeated the Roman-Egyptian military controlled by Mark Antony. When Octavian won, he became the undisputed Roman Emperor and Egyptian ruler, and his name was changed to Caesar Augustus. Jesus was born while Caesar Augustus was the Roman Emperor and ruler of Egypt.

Beginning long before Abraham and ending just before Christ was born, the records of Egypt were carved, painted, or written. The religion of Egypt changed and became more elaborate in places and more vague in others over those thousands of years. The very first *Pyramid Texts* date from the 4th Dynasty. The next records, the *Egyptian Coffin Texts*, date from the 7th and 8th Dynasties. They show changes in the religion of Egypt from the earlier *Pyramid Texts*.

Abraham lived during the 9th or 10th Dynasty, at a time called the "First Intermediate Period." This was a period of significant change (or apostasy) for the Egyptian religion. But even before Abraham, the order established by the first Fathers (despite efforts to keep the faith) had been poorly preserved. The *Pyramid Texts* are the oldest records, but they were carved during the 4th and 5th Dynasties. By the time these records had been carved, six or more centuries had passed between the original and their preservation. This would be like us composing the history from the time Robert the Bruce gained Scottish independence through the death of Joan the Arc for the first time today.

After the First Intermediate Period came the Middle Kingdom, during the 11th and through the 14th Dynasties. It was during the First Intermediate Period that Joseph was sold into Egypt. The *Book of the Dead* dates from the New Kingdom or 18th Dynasty. Moses lived during the beginning of the 18th Dynasty, and Josephus dates the exodus from Egypt at that point.

Over the long time period of their history, Egyptian religion changed. It began emphasizing ascending to heaven following this life. But it later emphasized navigating the dangers of the underworld where the dead face perils, tests, and judgments. It's more accurate to say Egypt had "religions" rather than "a religion," because so much changed over their history.

Solomon dedicated the temple at Jerusalem during the 20th Dynasty, a little over 1000 years BC. An attempt to reconstruct the religions of Egypt requires the study of materials that date over nearly 3000 years. Over that time, a great deal of change, uncertainty, apostasy, and error crept in. Much was lost, but also much was added. Some things were amplified or extended and represent uninspired efforts to improve on the original. Even the most meticulous scholar, using the most inspired approach, will never be able to reconstruct the original religion, or *that order established by the Fathers in the first generations, in the days of the first Patriarchal reign, even in the reign of Adam* (Abraham 2:3).

Yet God demands that our hearts turn to the Fathers, or we will be wasted at His return. This requirement is not to turn to them in just a figurative way, where we do genealogical work to connect ourselves with our recently deceased forbearers. That work is a wrong-headed effort to seal people to those kept in prison. The return of our hearts will require us to have the same religion and the same beliefs in our hearts that the original Fathers had beginning with Adam. Only in that way will our hearts turn to the Fathers.

God declared to Abraham that the chosen descendants, the people of God, would call Abraham their father. They would need to have that same religion belonging to the first Fathers. God explained: *For as many as receive this gospel shall be called after thy name and shall be accounted thy seed, and shall rise up and bless thee, as unto their Father* (Abraham 3:1).

The term used by God, *this gospel,* is the original Holy Order the first Fathers, including Adam, possessed at the beginning. Our hearts must turn to the Fathers because their religion—not apostate Christianity or Judaism or apostate Mormonism or some remnant or relic of Adam's religion but the order of the first Fathers—must be fully restored before we have *this* gospel possessed by Abraham, who had the records of the Fathers and, therefore, knew the original.

Adam still presides and still holds the keys. Joseph Smith said: *Adam holds the keys of the dispensation of the fullness of times; i.e., the dispensation of all the times have been, and will be revealed through him, from the beginning to Christ, and from Christ to the end of all the dispensations that are to be revealed* (T&C 140:3).

Though the Egyptians tried to preserve the things that came down from the beginning, as we read in the book of Abraham, the Pharaoh sought earnestly to imitate the order that came down from the beginning. And the Pharaoh succeeded in large measure in doing that. And he was a righteous man. *Pharaoh, being a righteous man, established his kingdom and judged his people wisely and justly all his days, seeking earnestly to imitate that order established by the fathers in the first generations, in the days of the first patriarchal reign, even in the reign of Adam, and also of Noah, his father* (Abraham 2:3). Pharaoh was not out there freelancing; he was trying to imitate something. And Egypt did a good job of preserving some things that have fallen into decay elsewhere.

But the Restoration through Joseph Smith and the promises that were made to the Fathers and the statement that was made by Moroni to Joseph on the evening that he came to him and talked about and reworded the promise given through Malachi—all of these are pointing to something that is, at this moment, still incomplete; a work that is, at this moment, still undone; a project that remains for us, if we will receive it, to finally receive.

Joseph Smith was doing something which did not just put together a man and a wife. He was doing something that put together families. The Church of Jesus Christ of Latter-day Saints is a mockup of a family. It is a mockup of the family of Abraham, Isaac, and Jacob, with the First Presidency, and the 12 sons of Jacob in the Quorum of the Twelve, and the 70 descendants that went into Egypt when they migrated into Egypt when Joseph was counselor to Pharaoh (that you can read in [Exodus 1:1]). That's the church. It is a mockup; it is an imitation; it is a facsimile of the family of Abraham. It is not the family of Abraham, but it is a powerful evidence that the family of Abraham is, in fact, something Joseph Smith was interested in restoring. Eventually, that which is a mockery is going to give way that which *is* the family. First, you have a schoolmaster, and then you have the reality. Joseph was headed to the reality, but he didn't get there in his day.

The Book of Mormon begins with a title page that was on the very last plate of the plates that Joseph Smith translated, and it appears as the first page of the Book of Mormon.

> *AN ACCOUNT WRITTEN BY THE HAND OF MORMON UPON PLATES TAKEN FROM THE PLATES OF NEPHI Wherefore, it is an abridgment of the record of the people of Nephi and also of the Lamanites; written to the Lamanites who are a remnant of the house of Israel and also to Jew and gentile....*

The Book of Mormon was written for three groups. Three targeted audiences are identified right at the outset—the Lamanites, the Jews, and the gentiles. That's who the Book of Mormon was sent to.

In the Teachings and Commandments section 158, there is a covenant offered to the gentiles, to the remnant of the Lamanites, and to the remnant of the Jews. These are the words of that covenant:

> *Do you have faith in these things and receive the scriptures approved by the Lord as a standard to govern you in your daily walk in life, to accept the obligations established by the Book of Mormon as a covenant, and to use the scriptures to correct yourselves and to guide your words, thoughts and deeds?* (T&C 158:3)

It also goes on to say: *But if you do not honor me, nor seek to recover my people Israel...then you have no promise* (T&C 158:19).

The people that the Book of Mormon established as the target audience are the Lamanites, the Jews, and the gentiles. We have an obligation to try and reach out to the Lamanites, the Jews, and the gentiles.

The title page goes on to say:

> ...*written by way of commandment, and also by the spirit of prophecy and of revelation. Written, and sealed, and hid up unto the Lord, that they might not be destroyed; to come forth by the gift and power of God unto the interpretation thereof; sealed up by the hand of Moroni and hid up unto the Lord, to come forth in due time by the way of gentile; the interpretation thereof by the gift and power of God.*

Did you get that? Almost in rapid succession, twice we're told *to come forth by the gift and power of God unto the interpretation thereof,* and the *interpretation thereof by the gift and power of God.* Joseph Smith did not translate the Book of Mormon; God translated the Book of Mormon and told Joseph Smith what He wanted that interpretation to say.

I've read as many source documents as are currently available to review in print. There are some source materials I haven't looked at because they're in private collections, and you have to travel to see those. But we have this fanciful narrative about how the Book of Mormon was translated.

One of the things that went on in Kirtland was a Shouting Methodist tradition. People would go into the woods, and they would shout praises to God in hopes that they obtain some kind of spiritual manifestation. The typical manifestation that they were able to create in this tradition was to be seized upon, bound up, and unable to move, which was considered a sign of God's grace and redemption, because they were seized upon by some unseen power that had such marvelous power as to bind them up so they could not move. One of the other things that the Shouting Methodist tradition in Kirtland, Ohio encountered was the idea that as you're out and shouting praises, oftentimes standing on the stump of a tree that's been cut down, there would be a scroll or parchment that would flutter down from heaven, and when arrived, on the parchment there would be words written. And you would read the words, and after you'd read the words, the parchment would disappear. It would disintegrate. These were the kinds of manifestations that were the Shouting Methodist tradition, which (when Mormonism came to Kirtland) some of the Kirtland Mormon converts had similar experiences.

Well, one of the stories that gets told about the translation of the Book of Mormon is that Joseph Smith would look in a hat, a parchment would appear, he would read the words off the parchment, and then the parchment would disintegrate as soon as the translation was written up, and then a new parchment would appear. Okay?

At a conference in Kirtland, Hyrum Smith introduced his brother, Joseph, and as Joseph was coming up to talk, Hyrum said, "And Joseph is going to tell us about how the translation of the Book of Mormon took place." Joseph got up in front of the people, and he said, "It's not appropriate. It was translated by the gift and power of God." And then he went on. He refused to describe the process.

If you want to know how the Book of Mormon was translated, the Book of Mormon tells you how: by the gift and power of God. When pressed, after Joseph is dead and gone, and you want to sound like you know something, and you think back about the experiences of the Shouting Methodist tradition in the early days in Kirtland, well, why not say scrolls would appear, and then when you read them, they'd disintegrate?

There is so much that has crept into the reconstruction of events that are accepted by the LDS church, that are accepted by historians, that are accepted by the scholars. There's only two people— (I was going to say one person that knows how it was done, and that was Joseph, but there are two: the second one is God). How did God interpret the Book of Mormon? And, by the way, would— If you took only the etchings that are on the plates of the Book of Mormon and you rendered a word-for-word translation of that set of inscriptions, would it read exactly like the Book of Mormon that we have? Or did God, in His mercy, understanding the weaknesses of our day, give us an interpretation that helps us to understand things in our language maybe a little more clearly than if we had simply a word-for-word translation from the plates? These are things that Joseph may know, or he may not. But certainly God would know.

When people pretend to know everything there is to know about the translation of the Book of Mormon and then to mock the process, they're really inviting— They're putting their own foolishness on display, and they're inviting the ire of God. The fact is that the witness to how that process unfolded confined what he had to say to "It was translated by the gift and power of God." And the source of these other fanciful tales—Oliver Cowdery, Martin Harris (two of the three witnesses to the Book of Mormon)—they were commanded to bear testimony, and their testimony was to consist of "the interpretation thereof was by the gift and power of God." So when they go beyond that to give details that they probably have no way of knowing a thing about, they're actually violating the restriction that God put upon it for a wise purpose.

Well, Joseph Smith was not the translator; it plainly states that God was the translator. It does not mean that what was composed by Nephi, Jacob, Enos, Omni, and others on the small plates and by Mormon and Moroni on the rest (and their abridgement) is necessarily—exactly—what was composed by them, because God used the interpretation of the text that He provided to state what He intended, by His gift and power, to be the message that we receive today. It is literally God's statement to us about the content He wants us to understand, adapted to our needs.

It goes on to say in this title page:

> An abridgment taken from the book of Ether also, which is a record of the people of Jared, who were scattered at the time the lord confounded the language…which is to shew unto the remnant of the house of Israel what great things the Lord hath done for their fathers, and that they may know the covenants of the Lord, that they are not cast off forever. And also to the convincing of the Jew and gentile that Jesus is the Christ, the eternal God, manifesting himself unto all nations. And now if there be fault, it be the mistake of men; wherefore, condemn not the things of God, that ye may be found spotless at the judgment seat of Christ.

What are the covenants of the Lord that are supposed to be made known unto the remnant of the house of Israel that comes through the Book of Mormon? Well, the Book of Mormon tells you what they are:

> And it shall also be of worth unto the gentiles, and not only unto the gentiles but unto all the house of Israel, unto the making known of the covenants of the Father of Heaven unto Abraham, saying, In thy seed shall all the kindreds of the earth be blessed (1 Nephi 7:3).

So the purpose of the Book of Mormon is to alert the gentiles and the Jews of the covenants that were made—specifically the covenants that were made with Abraham. Okay?

One of the great things about the new set of scriptures is that the Teachings and Commandments are laid out chronologically. There's this tradition that the last great revelation that Joseph Smith received was in January of 1841 in which the Lord outlined the commandment to build the temple and the signs that would be given if the temple were completed in sufficient time and how the church would be accepted with their kindred dead or rejected with their kindred dead depending upon how they pursued this. That's supposedly his last great revelation. In the Teachings and Commandments, however, what you see in the layout of Joseph's revelations chronologically is that in 1842, the first installment of the Book of Abraham was published. And it appears in the Teachings and Commandments in it's chronological layout. And then a few months later, the next installment of the Book of Abraham appears. And so the last, largest revelation given to Joseph, although there are others that are included in this same timeframe, is the text of the Book of Abraham.

The Book of Mormon points to a recovery of knowledge and understanding about the covenants God made with Abraham. The Book of Abraham had to be revealed! It *had* to come forward! In order for us to understand the covenants that God made with Abraham, we had to get the Book of Abraham, which did not roll out until the 1842-and-beyond time period. Joseph's work culminated in attempting to get on the ground ordinances that would have reflected more fully the covenants made with Abraham. But the Book of Abraham is part of vindicating the promises that were made in the Book of Mormon.

So, as you read the Teachings and Commandments and you see it unfolding chronologically, you see where the Lectures on Faith fit in. You see where the Book of Abraham fit in. You see how Joseph's ministry was taking on a trajectory that, literally, fits the pattern of what the Book of Mormon was promising would come forth and be vindicated.

In the Book of Abraham: *I have purposed to take thee away out of Haran, and to make of thee a minister to bear my name* [this is God's great gift to Abraham; He's going to make of him a minister to bear His name] *in a strange land which I will give unto thy seed after thee for an everlasting possession.* Okay, this is cumbersome language, but I want you to ask yourself if the great gift that God gives to Abraham is to make of him a minister to bear His name, and then He mentions he's going to bear His name in a strange land, followed with *which I will give unto thy seed after thee for an everlasting possession.* Is the gift that He's giving to his descendants the land or the ministry? *I will give unto thy seed after thee for an everlasting possession, when they hearken to my voice* (Abraham 3:1). Does that sound like land, or does that sound like the ministry relating to hearkening to God's voice?

As He goes on to explain what his descendants are going to inherit:

> ...thou shalt be a blessing unto thy seed after thee, that in their hands they shall bear this ministry and priesthood unto all nations. And I will bless them through thy name; for as many as receive this gospel shall be called after thy name and shall be accounted thy seed, and shall rise up and bless thee, as unto their Father. And I will bless them that bless thee and curse them that curse thee. And in thee (that is, in thy Priesthood) and in thy seed, (that is, thy Priesthood) — for I give unto thee a promise that this right shall continue in thee and in thy seed after thee. (Abraham 3:1)

The seed of Abraham are the people that hearken to the same God that Abraham hearkened to. If you hearken to that same God, you're the seed of Abraham. And the ministry that you're supposed to bear is the testimony that *that God* lives, and that *that God* is *the God* over the whole earth, that His work began with Adam and won't wrap up until the second coming of Christ in judgment on the world, to save and redeem those that look for Him.

We have to have the record of Abraham in order to understand the covenant that God made with Abraham, in order to vindicate the promise that's made in the Book of Mormon.

One of the sharp edges of criticism of Mormonism is directed specifically at the Book of Abraham. There are a lot of intellectual arguments that are being made out there, a lot of challenges for why the Book of Abraham ought to be thrown out, and how the Joseph Smith papyrus that got recovered is really simply Egyptian *Book of Breathings* material that has very little to do with a record written by the hand of Abraham on papyrus, and so on. Well, if the Book of Mormon was translated by the gift and power of God, the Book of Abraham was translated no differently, except by the gift and power of God. And it includes information that's vital for us to understand—in order for us to know what the covenants were that were made with Abraham, in order for us to inherit the same gospel that was given to Abraham, so that we can lay hold upon the same blessings that were given to Abraham—so that the covenants that were made with the Fathers can be understood, activated, realized, and we can obtain the blessings of those here in the last days. All this stuff fits together, and Joseph's work had to necessarily include recovery of the covenants made with Abraham.

Now, you may regard yourself as a gentile, but the covenant that was made with Abraham makes you a descendant of Abraham if you hearken to that same God and receive that same gospel. And Nephi explains who the gentiles are in relation to the family of Father Abraham, also. This is Nephi:

> And it shall come to pass that if the gentiles shall hearken unto the Lamb of God in that day that he shall manifest himself unto them in word and also in power, in very deed, unto the taking away of their stumbling blocks, and harden not their hearts against the Lamb of God, they shall be numbered among the seed of thy father. Yea, they shall be numbered among the house of Israel; and they shall be a blessed people upon the promised land for ever. They shall be no more brought down into captivity. (1 Nephi 3:25)

Nephi is telling you, "If you are willing to receive what God has offered, then you're numbered among the house of Israel."

Jacob, the brother of Nephi, wrote about the gentiles. He said:

> He that fighteth against Zion shall perish, saith God, for he that raiseth up a king against me shall perish. For I the Lord [God], the King of Heaven, will be their king, and I will be a light unto them for ever... Wherefore, for this cause, that my covenants may be fulfilled which I have made unto the children of men, that I will do unto them while they are in the flesh, I must needs destroy the secret works of darkness, and of murders, and of abominations. Wherefore, he that fighteth against Zion, both Jew and Gentile, both bond and free, both male and female, shall perish; ...the gentiles shall be blessed and numbered among the house of Israel. Wherefore, I will consecrate this land unto [them and] thy seed. (2 Nephi 7:2-4)

So Jacob, likewise, says gentiles who are willing to receive this as their covenant— numbered among the house of Israel; no longer numbered among gentiles—they change identities, just like the promise that was made to Abraham. You receive it? You're his seed.

Christ picked up the same thing in 3 Nephi: *that the gentiles, if they will not harden their hearts, that they may repent, and come unto me, and be baptized in my name, and know of the true points of my doctrine, that they may be numbered among my people, O house of Israel* (3 Nephi 9:11).

The purpose of the Book of Mormon is to reveal that God made a covenant with Abraham in the beginning. And at the end, God intends to vindicate the covenant that God made with Abraham by changing gentiles into the house of Israel by covenant.

When the Restoration began, the people from the first publication in 1830 until September of 2015 in Boise—no one accepted the Book of Mormon as a covenant. It had not been done. The Lectures on Faith got accepted; the Doctrine and Covenants got accepted; the church leaders got accepted; a First Presidency, a High Council—all kinds of things got accepted; but *not* the Book of Mormon, as a covenant, until September… was it— what year was that?

MAN: 2017

DENVER: 2017. It was— It was an odd year. (But not '15). September of 2017—it was the very first time in history that the Book of Mormon was received as a covenant. And in the words that I read you just a moment ago, Nephi mentions covenant people. You have to receive it as a covenant. God only works to bring people into His good graces by covenants. They have to be made. Without covenants you cannot— You cannot participate in what the Lord sets out.

Well, the Book of Mormon was intended as a record for our day to restore our knowledge to make it possible for us to enter back into a covenant relationship with God, in order for the promises that were made to the Fathers to be vindicated. Abraham looked forward to having seed that would be countless. He had one son. But God told him, "Don't worry about that. The time will come when everyone who receives this gospel…"— That is the gospel that Abraham had in his possession, the gospel that is unfolding in front of your eyes today, that will continue to unfold until all of its covenants, rights, obligations, privileges, understandings will all roll out.

The Restoration will be completed. But the promise was made to Abraham that whenever *that* is on the earth, those who receive it will acknowledge him, Abraham, as their covenant Father—the Father of the righteous.

———

The foregoing excerpts are taken from:

- Denver's remarks titled "Keep the Covenant: Do the Work," given at the Remembering the Covenants Conference in Layton, UT on August 4, 2018;
- Denver's *40 Years in Mormonism Series*, Talk #4 titled "Covenants," given in Centerville, UT on October 6, 2013;
- A fireside talk on "Plural Marriage," given in Sandy, UT on March 22, 2015; and
- Denver's remarks titled "Book of Mormon as Covenant," given at the Book of Mormon Covenant Conference in Columbia, SC on January 13, 2019.

In addition to the foregoing, Denver has addressed this topic extensively in several blog posts, including:

"Ignorance Enshrined" posted February 22, 2013
"Questions from This Week" posted February 23, 2013
"Book of Abraham" posted February 24, 2011
"Egypt and Egyptian" posted April 18, 2010
"Book of Mormon" posted December 3, 2015

55. Abraham, Part 2

This is the second part of a special series on Abraham.

QUESTION: What do we need to understand about Abraham in order to understand our place in the last-days events? What is God's view of the book of Abraham and what ought we to take from it as we look towards a continuation of the Restoration?

————

DENVER: In the course of events, Melchizedek established a city—city of peace, city of righteousness. He was the king, and he was the priest, and he presided over his people in righteousness. And Abraham, who was converted to the truth, came to Melchizedek. They had a ceremonial get-together in which, among other things, there's a sacral meal. And Melchizedek, who has been waiting for this moment, "hands the football" to Abraham and says, "At last! Me and my people are gone!" And so, once again, Zion flees.

And when Zion flees again, now we have the people of Melchizedek. Now notice, if you will, that the Priesthood after the Order of the Son of God has been renamed the Priesthood of Enoch and then renamed, again, the Melchizedek Priesthood. And that name has become rather more enduring, because in each case they came, and they established Zion; and when they established Zion, they were taken with their people up into heaven.

And so now, now we have— you know, I was going to read this stuff about Melchizedek. You'll find it in the Joseph Smith translation of Genesis 14. It's a long enough section that it's back in the back of your Bible, beginning at verse 25:

> And Melchizedek lifted up his voice and blessed Abram. Now Melchizedek was a man of faith, who wrought righteousness; and when a child he feared God, and stopped the mouths of lions, and quenched the violence of fire. And thus, having been approved of God, he was ordained an high priest after the order of the covenant which God made with Enoch [Okay? He's got the same covenant as had been previously made with Enoch; that tells you something, if you're paying attention] it being after the order of the Son of God; which order came, not by man, nor the will of man; neither by father nor mother; neither by beginning of days nor end of years; but of God; And it was delivered unto

*men by the calling of his own voice, according to his own will, unto as
many as [received] his name.* (Genesis 7:17-18 RE)

"Again the doctrin [of the] sealing power of Elijah is as follows if you have
power to seal on earth & in heaven then we should be Crafty, the first thing
you do [is you] go & seal on earth your sons and daughters unto yourself, &
yourself unto your fathers in eternal glory" (*Wilford Woodruff Diary*, 10
March 1844).

"Unto your fathers in eternal glory"— that is *not* your kindred dead. They are
relying upon *you* to be redeemed. The connection that needs to be formed is
between you and the Fathers who dwell in glory.

And who are the Fathers who dwell in glory? Well, if we go back to the
revelation in which Joseph Smith received the sealing power—and he received
the sealing power some time before 1831, in that portion of the revelation
known as D&C 132:49: *I the Lord thy God will be with thee even unto the end
of the world and through all eternity for verily I seal upon your exaltation. Prepare
your throne for you in the kingdom of my Father, with Abraham your father* (vs.
49). *I say unto you whatsoever you seal on earth shall be sealed in heaven.
Whatsoever ye shall bind on earth in my name by my word, saith the Lord, it shall
be eternally bound in the heavens. Whosoever sins you remit on earth shall be
remitted eternally in heaven* (vs. 46) and so on.

Just before that portion of the revelation, in verse 37, he talks about
Abraham, he talks about Isaac, and he talks about Jacob. And then
concerning those three, the Lord says to Joseph: *Because they did none other
things than that which they were commanded, they have entered into their
exaltation, according to the promises, and sit upon thrones, and are not angels but
are Gods.* This is Abraham, Isaac, and Jacob. These are the ones who are Gods.

And so when Christ— And I think Christ is deliberate about everything He
says, about the analogies that He uses, and about the stories that He tells.
When Christ takes occasion in a parable to tell someone about the status of
heaven, the story that He tells is about Lazarus and a rich man. And it says
(concerning the beggar, Lazarus) when he died, he was *carried [by] the angels
into Abraham's bosom* (Luke 9:20 RE). Okay? So the dead man Lazarus, with
an angelic accompaniment, is taken to Abraham's bosom when he dies. And
so the definition of a reward in the afterlife is to go to the bosom of Abraham.

And see, the rich man is dead, and he cries. And the rich man, who is now in
a state of torment, he cries out. He does not cry out (in Jesus' story) to God.

He cries out to Abraham. So when Jesus is describing positions of authority in the afterlife, a person He puts into a position of authority in the afterlife, to answer the petition of the dead rich man for relief from his torment, is Abraham.

> *Father Abraham, have mercy on me, and send Lazarus, that he may dip the tip of his finger in water, and cool my tongue; for I am tormented in this flame. But Abraham said, Son, remember that thou in thy lifetime receivedst thy good things, and likewise Lazarus evil things: but now he is comforted, and thou art tormented.* (ibid)

There is an equation; everything will balance. The things that you suffer from, it is the Lord's intention to wipe away every tear. And if you are one that chooses to inflict tears, then that will be recompensed, as well—because what will be restored unto you is exactly (as we began with Alma) what you send out. It is an equation, after all.

Then the rich man cried out:

> *I pray thee therefore, father, that thou wouldest send him to my father's house* [send Lazarus to my father's house], *for I have five brethren, that he may testify unto them lest they also come into this place of torment. Abraham said unto him, They have Moses and the prophets, let them hear them. And he said, Nay, father Abraham, but if one went unto them from the dead, they will repent. And he said unto him, If they hear not Moses and the prophets, neither will they be persuaded though one should rise from the dead* [foreshadowing, of course, the rejection of the Lord's resurrection and testimony, as well]. (ibid.)

The promise made by Elijah is about reconnecting us to the Fathers. Joseph called them the "Fathers in heaven." These are not our kindred dead, because our kindred dead are required to be redeemed by us. These are the Fathers in heaven. Among them would be Abraham, Isaac, and Jacob, and (because of this dispensation being what it is) Peter, James, and John.

The purpose of the Holy Ghost is to allow you to see things in their true light with the underlying intent behind them and to allow you to do that without distortion and without confusion.

The temple is a ceremony designed to teach you about the path back to God —the very same thing that the Book of Mormon teaches repeatedly. The path back to God is so that you can meet with, and be instructed by, our Savior.

The purpose of our Savior is to prepare us in all things so that we can, at last, become Zion. Because if your heart is right and my heart is right—and if I'm looking to God and God only, and you're looking to God and God only—then the trivial things of having things in common are of so little import that they matter not. Because we ought to fear God more than we fear man. We ought to fear God more than we fear the loss of anything that is down here. We ought to fear God more than we fear the approval or disapproval, the criticism, the ostracism— We ought to love God and fear Him, because it's our relationship to Him, and Him alone, that matters.

This requires more than mere belief or supposition that he's doing the will of God, but actual knowledge, realizing that when these sufferings are ended, he will enter into eternal rest and be a partaker of the glory of God. It does require more than mere belief or supposition. But it's obtained in accordance with this set of principles. And it is purchased by the same price, paid by each of us, in turn, on the same conditions. And no one gets it on any other condition.

Your life may be uniquely situated. You may be inside an environment—a group of friends, a family, a neighborhood, an association—that is completely unique to you and has nothing in common with anyone else in this room. Inside of that, whatever the sacrifices are that are required, it will be exactly the same as it was for Moses who gave up everything, and then gave up everything again. It will be the same as for Abraham who gave up everything, and then gave up everything again. It will be the same. And you'll be called upon to make a sacrifice. Because knowing God requires obedience to Him and sacrifice to Him—and not to some man, certainly not to me; but not to a pope, not to a president, not to a priest—to Him. You're not trying to get to know me; or if you are, you're a damn fool. You're supposed to be getting to know the Lord. You're not supposed to be getting to know some local presiding authority.

The way to preserve yourself consists in having faith in God. And the conditions upon which faith in God is obtained are exactly the same for you as they were for Moses and Abraham and all of the those who have ever had faith—Joseph Smith being the latest great example of that.

So let's turn to a few scriptures and interrupt this for a moment, because we want to repent, after all. We want to change what we are. Let's go to Doctrine and Covenants 84, and let's look beginning at verse 33. Now I'm simply going to allow you to entertain your present views on some things for tonight, but we're going to have to deconstruct a bunch of junk later, and we'll do that down in Spanish Fork, I think. Beginning at verse 33 of section 84 of the Doctrine and Covenants: *For whoever is faithful unto the obtaining these two Priesthoods of which I have spoken, and the magnifying their calling, are sanctified by the Spirit unto the renewing of their bodies that they become the sons of Moses, and of Aaron, and the seed of Abraham, and the church, and Kingdom, and the elect of God* (D&C 84:33-34; see also T&C 82:16). *Sons...seed.* And it's necessary that you become that in order that you become *the church, and Kingdom...the elect of God.* Because, as we saw in the statements made to Joseph Smith, the hearts have to be turned to the Fathers because it's going to be reconstructing the Holy Family at some point.

And also all they who receive this priesthood receive me, saith the Lord (vs. 35). Now many of you read that verse 35, and you think that what that means is: If you fetch this priesthood by ordination, ipso facto you have fetched Jesus. Praise Jesus! (And by the way, Joel Olsteen is coming to the E Center. You're not going to want to miss that. It's a mega church! It's a mega church in transit! It's going to come to the E Center! SUNDAY, SUNDAY, SUNDAY! I'm sorry; I get worked up when the evangelicals show up on the horizon. He had some nice things to say about Mormons, though, so Joel Olsteen has kind of creeped a little more in the positive column for me of late.)

I want to suggest that verse 35 can also be read exactly as D&C 93:1 (that we were reading a moment ago) is read. And that is to say: If you're going to receive this priesthood you're going to get it from Him. That is, you enter into His presence, you receive Him, *if* you have it. Then when you have it, as a consequence of having it, you receive Him.

Oh! *For he that receiveth my servants receiveth me* (D&C 84:36). I want to suggest that throughout scripture, almost invariably the word *servants* is referring to angelic ministrants. And so angels minister—that would be Aaronic. And then Christ ministers—that would be "sons of Moses."

And he that receiveth me receiveth my Father (vs. 37). Because it is the purpose of the Son to bear record of the Father. It is the purpose of the Son to bring others to the Father so that there might be many sons of God. *And he that receiveth my Father receiveth my Father's kingdom* (vs. 38; see also T&C 82:17), because you can't go where the Father is without entering into and receiving an inheritance.

You know, one of the things that we tend to think is that if you get something (this is based upon statements made in 132)—but if you get something here and you get it by a covenant, that you are automatically entitled to take it into the next world. But what if the covenant that you are to receive in order to obtain that inheritance in the next world doesn't reckon merely from something handled by ordinance, but that the ordinance is pointing you to something higher and more holy? What if the thing that secures for you the inheritance in the next life is not the ordinance but what the ordinance testifies to—that is, embracing the Lord through the veil; and then, having conversed with Him, entering into His presence; and then having entered into His presence, being ministered to and taught? What if it means all that?

There is a law, irrevocably decreed in heaven before the foundations of this world, upon which all blessings are predicated— And when we obtain any blessing from God, it is by obedience to that law upon which it is predicated (D&C 130:20-21). Therefore, what is important for you to understand and to know is whatever it is that law consists of. Because the way in which you accept the covenant that has been offered to you is by learning the principle or the law upon which the blessing you seek is predicated. And then, having learned what law that is upon which it is predicated, obeying it. We learn all of this through the revelations given to us through Joseph Smith.

Before Joseph of Egypt, one of the Fathers that we need to look at is Abraham. And therefore, I want to turn to Abraham chapter 1, beginning at verse 2: *And, finding there was greater happiness and peace and rest for me, I sought for the blessings of the fathers.* Once again, now we have Abraham— We've gone all the way back to him, generations before Joseph of Egypt, and we encounter the same thing, that is: searching for the blessings which belong to the Fathers. Abraham, looking for the blessings of the Fathers, hoping to find thereby happiness, hoping to find peace and rest for himself.

And the right whereunto I should be ordained to administer the same; having been myself a follower of righteousness, desiring also to be one who possessed great knowledge (ibid). You know, when I spoke in Logan, I talked about repentance being related to knowledge and that it's our ignorance that damns us, most of all. Abraham perceived the same thing. And Abraham believed that redemption and possessing great knowledge went hand-in-hand.

And if he could obtain that great knowledge, then he wanted to be *a greater follower of righteousness* and, as a consequence of that, *to possess a greater knowledge.* Because this is one of those laws upon which blessings are predicated. Knowledge, light, truth, the glory of God— all of those things are obtained by obedience to law. And Abraham sought for and desired to possess more light and truth. And as a result of that he wanted inevitably to become *a father of many nations, a prince of peace,* and he desired most of all to receive instructions and to keep commandments of God. As a result of all that desire, he became *a rightful heir, a High Priest, holding the right belonging to the fathers. It was conferred upon me from the fathers; it came down from the fathers, from the beginning of time, yea, even from the beginning, or before the foundation of the earth, down to the present time, even the right of the firstborn, or the first man, who is Adam, or first father, through the fathers unto me* (ibid).

All of this ties back necessarily to Adam. *I sought for mine appointment unto the Priesthood according to the appointment of God unto the fathers concerning the seed* (Abraham 1:2-4; see also Abraham 1:1 RE). Everything about the original form of priesthood, everything about what it is that Abraham was seeking, all of this ties together because there is only one gospel.

In the Lectures on Faith, the second lecture, paragraphs 37 to 53, there is a chronology given. I'm not going to go through the chronology, and you needn't have brought it with you tonight. But that chronology is listed in the Lectures on Faith in order to save you the trouble of going through and tracking it yourself. But it was important enough to Joseph Smith to put it into the Lectures on Faith so that you know how to reconstruct the Fathers, who they were.

Noah was 502 years old when Shem was born. Ninety-eight years later, the Flood came. Noah was 600 years old when the Flood came; Shem was 98. You can see that in paragraph 45 of the second lecture. Shem lived to be 600. Shem was 448 years old when Noah died. Shem was acquainted with both Noah and Abraham.

Abraham lived to be 175 years old. And Shem was alive and a contemporary [with Abraham] for 150 of the 175 years of the life of Abraham. Shem knew Noah. And Shem knew those on the other side of the Flood, having lived with them for 98 years before the Flood.

Abraham had the records of the Fathers. Look at Abraham 1:31: *But the records of the fathers, even the patriarchs, concerning the right of Priesthood, the Lord my God preserved in mine own hands; therefore a knowledge of the beginning of the creation, and also of the planets, and of the stars, as they were made known unto the fathers, have I kept even unto this day, and I shall endeavor to write some of these things upon this record, for the benefit of my posterity that shall come after me* (Abraham 2:4 RE).

Since Abraham was acquainted with the priesthood that belonged to the Fathers—and since Abraham had a knowledge that was reckoned from priesthood that goes back to the time of the Patriarchs—he, as a consequence of possessing that, knew about the beginning of creation, knew about the planets, knew about the stars as they were made known unto the Fathers.

Go back to Doctrine and Covenants 121. It's talking about our dispensation. I want to look at beginning about verse 28: *A time to come in the which nothing shall be withheld, whether there be one God or many gods, they shall be manifest.* Because that's included within the knowledge that the first Fathers had. That's included with what was here at one time. *All thrones and dominions, principalities and powers, shall be revealed and set forth upon all who have endured valiantly for the gospel of Jesus Christ. And also, if there be bounds set to the heavens or to the seas, or to the dry land, or to the sun, moon, or stars— All the times of their revolutions, all the appointed days, months, and years, and all the days of their days, months, and years, and all their glories, laws, and set times, shall be revealed in the days of the dispensation of the fulness of times— According to that which was ordained in the midst of the Council of the Eternal God of all other gods before this world was, that should be reserved unto the finishing and the end thereof, when every man shall enter into his eternal presence and into his immortal rest* (vs. 28-32; see also T&C 138:21).

Abraham is not merely talking about something—both in this verse (Abraham 1:31), as well as what we encounter later on in the book of Abraham about the various stars that were shown to him and the relationship between them and his Facsimile 2, as I recollect—that is an effort to lay out a relationship in the heavens between certain positions of glory and authority, but Abraham is testifying that it was part of the original gospel that was entrusted to the Fathers, and that those records were handed down to him. In Doctrine and Covenants 121, we find out that that's part of what is supposed to have been included within and is ultimately scheduled for revelation to those that will receive the restoration of the Gospel when it is fully upon the earth in the dispensation of the fullness of times.

Abraham received his priesthood ordination through Melchizedek. You see that in Doctrine and Covenants 84:14: *Which Abraham received the priesthood from Melchizedek, who received it through the lineage of his fathers, even till Noah* (T&C 82:10).

Now Bruce R McConkie reads that verse, and he disagrees with what the Church had previously taught; that is, that Melchizedek was Shem. He takes the position that this means that Melchizedek received it *through the lineage of his fathers, even [until] Noah* means that there were Fathers between Melchizedek, on the one hand, and Noah, on the other; and therefore,

Melchizedek could not be Shem. I take the view instead that it was received *through the lineage of his fathers even [until] Noah*, meaning: from Adam down to the time of Noah, the priesthood was preserved and that Melchizedek—that is Shem—received it from Noah. In any event, it's clear in verse 14 that Abraham received it from Melchizedek.

But if you go to Abraham 2, in the book of Abraham, beginning at verse 6:

> But I, Abraham, and Lot, my brother's son, prayed unto the Lord, and the Lord appeared unto me, and said unto me: Arise, and take Lot with thee; for I have purposed to take thee away out of Haran, and to make of thee a minister to bear my name in a strange land which I will give unto thy seed after thee for an everlasting possession, when they hearken to my voice. For I am the Lord thy God; I dwell in heaven; the earth is my footstool; I stretch my hand over the sea, and it obeys my voice; I cause the wind and the fire to be my chariot; I say to the mountains—Depart hence—and behold, they are taken away by a whirlwind, in an instant, suddenly. My name is Jehovah, and I know the end from the beginning; therefore my hand shall be over thee. And I will make of thee a great nation, and I will bless thee above measure, and make thy name great among all nations, and thou shalt be a blessing unto thy seed after thee, that in their hands they shall bear this ministry and Priesthood unto all nations; And I will bless them through thy name; for as many as receive this Gospel shall be called after thy name, and shall be accounted thy seed, and shall rise up and bless thee, as their father. (vs. 6-10; see also Abraham 3:1 RE)

Ordination and *confirmation by the voice of God* are two separate events. We'll speak more about this in the next talk, which will be on Priesthood; but it's enough to simply take note of that here.

Jehovah, speaking directly to Abraham, tells him that from this moment, from the moment God spoke to Abraham before his departure, Abraham would now become the Father of all the righteous. Now you ought to ask yourself: Why would that be the case? Why is it that Abraham becomes the prototype of who will be saved and the Father of whomever is saved from that point going forward?

When you go back to the Fathers and you begin with Adam, although there were apostasies—and apostasies began immediately—it was generations before Eve bore Cain and thought she had a son that would at last be faithful. They were grandparents when Cain was born. And then Abel was born. And

Cain slew Abel. And Seth came as a replacement to the grandparents, Adam and Eve. And from Seth reckons, then, the seed of the righteous.

Father to son to grandson to great-grandson. When you look at the list of those that are gathered together into the valley of Adam-ondi-Ahman, in the first Zion, where the Lord came and dwelt among them: *And he rose up and he called Adam, Michael* ("El" being the name of God)— Jehovah appeared in the valley of Adam-ondi-Ahman, and you have, seventh from Adam being Enoch; you have a line of continuity from Adam, directly down all the way until you arrive at Shem.

But when you hit Shem, it interrupts. There is a complete falling away. There are no righteous fathers for Abraham. His fathers had turned to idolatry. Abraham is the prototype of the saved man and the Father of all who would be righteous thereafter because Abraham represents coming to the truth in a generation of apostasy. Abraham represents coming back to the light, despite the fact that his fathers taught him idolatry. Abraham represents the challenge that every man who would be saved from that point forward must find themselves within—and then overcome the idolatry of their fathers. Abraham is the prototype.

And so Abraham is acknowledged by that same Jehovah who visited with the Fathers in Adam-ondi-Ahman and identified Himself again to Abraham— who, after apostasy, becomes literally the first—the first to return to the righteousness of the first Fathers, the first to return to the religion that belonged in the beginning to mankind, the first to discover *a knowledge of the beginning of the creation, and also of the planets, and of the stars, as they were made known unto the fathers.*

Abraham was the one who desired to be *a follower of righteousness, ...one who possessed great knowledge, to be a greater follower of righteousness and to possess greater knowledge* still. It is this which made him a candidate the Lord could speak to. It's this that made him the prototype in his generation of what it takes to turn away from idolatry, to turn away from the kind of corrupt and degrading religions that were then in play on the earth—the fertility cults and the human sacrifices and the vileness that surrounded him. And then having done so, to be asked by God to slay his son, as if there was some legitimacy to the rites that were practiced all around him.

Now in the version that we have in the King James Bible, Isaac is not slain. There is an older tradition that you can find in the book of Hebrews (and you can find it in the Book of Mormon) where Isaac is slain, and he's brought back to life, rather like Lazarus is brought back to life. But it's clear that the Old Testament version that we have in King James, he raises his hand with a knife to commit the act, and then the ram is found in the thicket to deliver him. Sometimes as it turns out, rams are not found in thickets and the sacrifice will be required.

The Lord says: *And I will bless them that bless thee, and curse them that curse thee; and in thee (that is, in thy Priesthood)....* Because fundamentally, what distinguishes Abraham and what distinguishes the covenant is the knowledge that he has. Abraham is in possession of something because Abraham knows some things that are true that relate back to the very beginning. And as a consequence of that, those who are given the same knowledge necessarily have to belong to the same priesthood.

...in thy seed (that is, thy Priesthood).... Because you become a son of Abraham if you take upon yourself the requirements for the covenant, you inherit that just as Abraham inherited it. It comes down from the beginning from the fathers.

For I give unto thee a promise that this right shall continue in thee, and in thy seed after thee (that is to say, the literal seed, or the seed of the body) shall all the families of the earth be blessed, even with the blessings of the Gospel, which are the blessings of salvation, even of life eternal. Now, after the Lord had withdrawn from speaking to me, and withdrawn his face from me, I said in my heart: Thy servant has sought thee earnestly; now I have found thee (Abraham 3:1-2 RE). And there again, Abraham stands as the prototype of the saved man, the Father of the righteous, the example of all those who, coming out of apostasy, find themselves redeemed because all of the servants that will be acknowledged by Him must seek Him earnestly and will, as the Lectures on Faith promise, assuredly find Him.

Everyone who receives the gospel, *this gospel*—verse 10 of that Abraham 2—*as many as receive this Gospel shall be called after thy name* (Abraham 3:1 RE)— You ought to ask yourself what is *this gospel?* And are you yet in possession of it? Because it would appear that the promises made to the Fathers includes rather more than what we know about as yet.

But it is nevertheless the case that it is through Joseph and Jacob, Isaac, and Abraham that the promises remain. You can see that in Doctrine and Covenants 27. We only need to look at verse 10 of section 27: *And also with Joseph and Jacob, and Isaac, and Abraham, your fathers, by whom the promises remain.* That is, promises are still in play right now as a consequence of what

God did in covenant with Joseph and covenant with Jacob and covenant with Isaac and covenant with Abraham. Those promises are still in play. This is what Moroni was talking to Joseph Smith about. And verse 11: *And also with Michael, or Adam, the father of all, the prince of all, the ancient of days.* Promises that are in play today go all the way back to them.

The covenant which we receive will come as consequence of *them*. What *they* got secured for *us* promises which the Lord intends to honor. Therefore, when we are the beneficiaries of those covenants, we are going, like Abraham, to have restored to us a knowledge of the beginning of creation, the planets, the stars as they were made known unto the fathers, and (as section 121 tells us) is going to be the case in the dispensation of the fullness of time.

Go to Joseph Smith translation of Genesis 14, beginning at verse 25:

> *And Melchizedek lifted up his voice and blessed Abram. Now Melchizedek was a man of faith, who wrought righteousness; and when a child he feared God, and stopped the mouths of lions, and quenched the violence of fire. And thus, having been approved of God, he was ordained an high priest after the order of the covenant which God made with Enoch, It being after the order of the Son of God.* (Genesis 7:17-18 RE)

There is an order that is after the son of God. But there was a covenant that preceded even the days of Melchizedek—it came down as a consequence of what happened with Enoch.

> *And it was delivered unto men by the calling of his own voice, according to his own will, unto as many as believed on his name. For God having sworn unto Enoch and unto his seed with an oath by himself; that every one being ordained after this order and calling should have power, by faith, to break mountains, to divide the seas, to dry up waters, to turn them out of their course; To put at defiance the armies of nations, to divide the earth, to break every band, to stand in the presence of God; to do all things...according to his command, subdue principalities and powers; and this by the will of the Son of God which was from before the foundation of the world.* (ibid, vs. 18-19)

See, it's not your will. Even if you're given this ordination, it is by the will of the Son of God. That is to say, nothing gets broken; nothing gets held in defiance; nothing gets done except by the will of the Son.

> *And men having this faith, coming up unto this order of God, were translated and taken up into heaven. And now, Melchizedek was a priest of this order; therefore he obtained peace in Salem, and was called the Prince of peace. And his people wrought righteousness, and obtained heaven, and sought for the city of Enoch which God had before taken, separating it from the earth, having reserved it unto the latter days, or the end of the world; And hath said, and sworn with an oath, that the heavens and the earth should come together; and the sons of God should be tried so as by fire.* (ibid, vs. 19-20)

These are they who are coming, whose glory and brightness will burn them up (who are on the earth, who are unprepared to receive them). These are they about whom Moroni was speaking to Joseph Smith.

> *And this Melchizedek, having thus established righteousness, was called the king of heaven by his people, or, in other words, the King of peace. And he lifted up his voice, and he blessed Abram, being the high priest, and the keeper of the storehouse of God; Him whom God had appointed to receive tithes for the poor. Wherefore, Abram paid unto him tithes of all that he had, of all the riches which he possessed, which God had given him more than that which he had need. And it came to pass, that God blessed Abram, and gave unto him riches, and honor, and lands for an everlasting possession; according to the covenant which he had made, and according to the blessing wherewith Melchizedek had blessed him.* (ibid, vs. 20-22)

Joseph Smith restored this information—as he restored the rest he gave us—in order for us to understand that when God swears by Himself to the Fathers about what it is He intends to accomplish in the last days, and we get near enough to that event so that we're over the horizon and inevitably going to fall into that dark day, some few will take it seriously enough to say, like Abraham, "I would like to seek for the blessings of the Fathers. I would like, also, to have from God a covenant. I would like to inherit what it was that was given in the beginning."

God alone makes the covenant. We accept it by abiding the conditions. The only thing we can do on our own is attempt to make vows. And we can make vows, but Christ discouraged us from doing that in Matthew. Go back to Matthew 5—this is in the Sermon on the Mount. You can read the same thing in 3 Nephi 12. But look at Matthew 5:33:

Again, ye have heard that it hath been said by them of old time, Thou shalt not forswear thyself, but shalt perform unto the Lord thine oaths: But I say unto you, Swear not at all; neither by heaven; for it is God's throne: Nor by the earth; for it is his footstool: neither by Jerusalem; for it is the city of the great King. Neither shalt thou swear by thy head, because thou canst not make one hair white or black. [Well, cosmetically some of you women can.] *But let your communication be, Yea, yea; Nay, nay: for whatsoever is more than these cometh of evil.* (Matthew 3:24 RE)

He'll say the same thing in 3 Nephi 12:33-37 [LE].

The fact of the matter is that you can make a vow to God, but you can't make a covenant with God. God can make a covenant which you can fulfill by your performance. God can offer you something; it's up to you to accept it, and you accept it by what you do. It's not enough to say, "Yea Lord, I'll go out, and I'll do as I'm bidden." You have to do it. Because it's only in the doing that the covenant is kept. It's only in the doing that the covenant is able to be empowered sufficient to give you the blessing upon which a law has been established for the blessing to be predicated. You can't get there without God offering, and you accepting.

So now we should realize, I hope, that that city which Melchizedek, the King of Peace, was able to teach righteousness sufficiently so that it was taken up from the earth, reserved to the last days of the end of the world— The next time we have such an event on the earth, the next time there is this kind of a gathering and this kind of a population anywhere, it will not be for the purpose of going up; it will be for the purpose of permitting those who have gone up to come back down. It will be for the purpose of having those who can endure the presence of those who will come—because those who come will burn up all those who are unworthy, and therefore, some few need to be gathered, so that the earth is not utterly wasted at His coming.

As it was in the days of Noah, so it shall be also at the coming of the Son of Man (Matthew 11:11 RE). How many people were required in order to have the Ark be an acceptable place in which God could preserve all of humanity? It was a portable Ark of the Covenant in which the family was preserved.

And so, if it's going to be as it was in the days of Noah, there is this net that has been cast out to gather together all manner of fish. But as the Lord tells the parable, the angels are going to come, and they're going to pick through all manner of fish, and they're going to keep the good, and the rest are going to be scheduled for burning. And so the question is, how diligent ought the search be into the things of God? How carefully ought we to consider the things that have been restored to us through the Prophet Joseph Smith?

The fact is that this stuff is assigned to our dispensation. And I'm reading from the Book of Mormon, which the world does not have or accept. I'm reading from the book of Abraham, which the world does not have or accept. I'm reading from the Joseph Smith Translation, which the world does not have and accept. All of you have this information in front of you. All of this material has been restored through someone that we claim we honor and regard as a prophet. Well, they who come will burn up those who are unprepared. And therefore, what should we be doing in order to make sure that we are included among those who are prepared?

See, the angels were unwilling to receive what they might have received, and as a consequence of that, they could not go. Look in Doctrine and Covenants 132:16. *Therefore, when they are out of the world they neither marry nor are given in marriage; but are appointed angels in heaven, which angels are ministering servants, to minister for those who are worthy of a far more, and an exceeding, and an eternal weight of glory.* Angels—in this context, if you will hear it—are included within Joseph's description of "Angels desire to look into it, but they have set up too many stakes." As a consequence of their unwillingness to receive what God freely offers to all, and their hedging up their own way by their failure to develop that faith and confidence necessary to lay hold upon the blessings of heaven—because they believe that those blessings are reserved for others and not for them; because as the de-canonized-now Lectures on Faith suggest, they fear that they do not have the power to lay hold upon all the blessings which were entirely reserved and promised to them; because they have not that faith required—they become limited in what they seek for and, therefore, what they obtain.

> God cursed the children of Israel because they would not receive the last law from Moses. The sacrifice required of Abraham in the offering up of Isaac, shows that if a man would attain to the keys of the kingdom of an endless life; he must sacrifice all things. When God offers a blessing or knowledge to a man, and he refuses to receive it, he will be damned. (*TPJS*, p. 322)

Which is why when the Lord sets something in motion and begins to declare the truth again and He offers a message that needs to be received—and it is not received by those to whom it is offered—the results are, "they refused to receive the blessing or knowledge that is offered to them, and therefore they will be damned." Damned, in this sense, meaning that they hedge up the way, that they limit the ability of God to confer upon them what they might have received. They partake of, ultimately, the sufferings of the damned because the pain of the mind is exquisite when they realize that they have not laid hold upon what God freely offered to give unto them. And therefore, they are their own condemnor, and they are their own judge.

"The Israelites prayed that God would speak to Moses and not to them; in consequence of which he cursed them with a carnal law" (ibid). Can you imagine?! If the children of Israel in that day were cursed by God because they said, "Moses must talk to God and not us," how much greater must be the damnation upon those who say, "You must not talk to God because we have one who does so for you! And you're not entitled to receive anything beyond the bounds of your limited position in this beehive we've constructed!" Damnable heresy! Doctrines of devils, propounded by those who are purveyors of a false priestcraft, unauthorized by God; unsanctioned by Him! They suffer not themselves to enter in, and they will hedge up the way if you will heed them. There is no man— There is no man on his own errand in this world who can offer to you salvation. But if God sends a message, you'd better heed it, even if you find it difficult to hear.

"What was the power of Melchizedek? 'Twas not the Priesthood of Aaron which administers in outward ordinances, and the offering of sacrifices. Those holding the fulness of the Melchizedek Priesthood are kings and priests of the Most High God, holding the keys of power and blessings" (ibid), because the Aaronic holds and is given for judgments and destruction; the Melchizedek is given for blessing. And when someone claims to hold Melchizedek priesthood and they use it in order to offer up judgment and condemnation and control and compulsion and authority over the souls of men and they refuse to constrain themselves to use persuasion only and gentleness and meekness, then you know you're listening to an Aaronic and not a Melchizedek authority. Because the office and the authority and the keys of the Melchizedek is to bless; it's to enlighten; it's to raise and to bring to you light and truth.

"In fact, that Priesthood is a perfect law of theocracy, and stands as God to give laws to the people, administering endless lives to the sons and daughters of Adam" (ibid). Because once again, it is always genealogical. It is always familial. It has always been turning the hearts of the children back to the fathers, the final Father in that chain being Adam.

> Abraham says to Melchizedek, I believe all that thou hast taught me concerning the priesthood and the coming of the Son of Man; so

Melchizedek ordained Abraham and sent him away. Abraham rejoiced, saying, Now I have a priesthood. Salvation could not come to the world without the mediation of Jesus Christ. How shall God come to the rescue of this generation? He will send Elijah the prophet. The law revealed to Moses in Horeb never was revealed to the children of Israel as a nation. Elijah shall reveal the covenants to seal the hearts of the father to the children, and the children to the fathers. (ibid, pg 322-323)

Some people asked a question about God speaking to Cain as a result of the talk I gave in Idaho Falls, referring to your privilege of talking to God because He spoke to Cain. It doesn't say that God *appeared* to Cain; it says that God *spoke* to Cain. Cain heard the voice of God speaking to him. He didn't get caught up to the throne of God; he did not have a throne theophany; he was not brought back and redeemed from the fall, but he heard the voice of God. God spoke to Cain *after* the murder of Abel. The *angels* withdrew from him. The angels were grieved; they would have nothing to do. And yet the God still spoke to him. His words are endless.

I don't care what malignancy you think you carry around within you. The fact is, none of you have done the same crap that Cain did, because Cain possessed greater knowledge than you did at the time of the murder that he committed. And yet God spoke to him still. Therefore, have the confidence, even if you grieve angels, that God will talk to you.

...my words, for they never cease (Genesis 1:1 RE). Yeah, God is talkative. God desires us to know more than we know, if we will receive it. And the minute we tell Him to be quiet and withdraw and leave us alone, we are in the very act of damning ourselves. Because what we're saying is, That which you offered unto us we would prefer to be silence instead. Don't do that.

Abraham 3:12, we encounter God saying: *And he said unto me:* [Abraham saying] *My son, my son (and his hand was stretched out), behold I will show you all these. And he put his hand upon mine eyes, and I saw those things which his hands had made, which were many; and they multiplied before mine eyes, and I could not see the end thereof.* Once again, you have—at the same instance that he is being acknowledged as a son—the outpouring of the intelligence of God, the glory of God, light and truth, knowledge of things as they are, and as they were, as they are to come. Joseph Smith [said] in Doctrine and Covenants 121:7: *My son, peace be unto thy soul* (T&C 138:11).

Okay, if you view priesthood as a brotherhood or an association, then I want to suggest that the way in which you should parse the three orders of priesthood is to parse them this way:

- As among men, it's merely a brotherhood of men.
- As between mankind and the heavens:
  - the first order is an order in which there is an association between men and angels.
  - The second order is an order in which there is an association between mankind and the Son of God.
  - And the third order, the highest order, the Patriarchal order brings one into contact with the Patriarch, who—of all the names that He could choose to be called by—chooses to have us call Him "Our Father who art in heaven"—the third grand order being Sonship to the Father and association with Him who sits in the bosom of eternity and sustains all the creation.
  - The highest priesthood is an association with the Father, brought about as a consequence of the Father calling "My son." It is the Holy Order after the Son of God, because those who inherit that become, by definition, His Sons. They are the Church of the Firstborn because they are in association with, and made by the Father equal to, all those who rise up to be Firstborn.

Go to Moses 6:7. This is a prophecy given by Adam which constituted one of the covenants which I referred to in the talk given at Centerville. *Now this same Priesthood* [this is Adam speaking]— *Now this same Priesthood which was in the beginning, shall be in the end of the world also. Now this prophecy Adam spake, as he was moved upon by the Holy Ghost* (Genesis 3:14 RE). Therefore, it was by the power of the priesthood, animated by the holy ghost, which established—as a matter of right and, therefore, of covenant—the promise that this thing, this authority, this power, and this relationship which once existed in the beginning of the world is to exist again at the end of the world. And that that, too, arises as a consequence of the covenant given in the beginning.

So what kind of person receives that ordination? I'm going back to the Joseph Smith Translation of Genesis 14. This is the kind of person: *Melchizedek was a man of faith who wrought righteousness* (Genesis 7:18 RE). You have to have faith. You have to wrought (or perform) righteousness, which is not the same thing as virtue.

Virtue can be offended by righteousness. Virtue would never kill, okay? It just never would. But it is righteous in the case of Nephi—at the command of God—to slay Laban. Virtue would never do any number of things, say any number of things, or behave in any number of ways in which John the Baptist behaved. *You generation of vipers!* (Luke 3:7 RE). Look, we translate that as if what we're reading is some nicely phrased King James-ian version of an insult. If you were trying to put it into modern English— This is John the Baptist, a righteous man with whom the kingdom of God existed, essentially in the language of their day saying, "You sons of bitches!" Because in our vernacular, by saying "Sons of bitches," what you're saying is, Your mother is a female dog, and therefore, you are a dog; and since you're a dog, you are a cur, and you are unworthy. This is guttural language. We read, *You generations of vipers,* and we say, Oh isn't that a nice way to parse out that John's thinks he's talking to the bad guys. And yet, we look sometimes at righteousness, and we say it can never be so, because it is not virtuous. Because we overlay virtue atop righteousness, and it does not work, and never has worked that way. Righteousness controls, and virtue surrenders. And virtue yields every time to righteousness. Else Abraham could never have been commanded to slay his son, because that was not virtuous.

Therefore, Melchizedek was a man of righteousness. *And when a child he feared God* [not man], *and stopped the mouths of lions, and quenched the violence of fire. And thus, having been approved of God* [not man] (Genesis 7:18 RE)—in fact, to be approved of God, in many cases, will make you offensive to man. But the opinions and the vagaries and the fashions of men, the opinion polling, and the drifts of what is and what is not popular at one point or another are damnable. They ought not even be considered. Righteousness does not give any regard to such things. And yet it may be virtuous. It may be virtuous to be a limp-wristed, weepy, happy-go-lucky, "have a nice day" kind of chap. But righteousness will kick his ass everyday.

———

The foregoing excerpts are taken from:

- Denver's talk titled "The Mission of Elijah Reconsidered," given in Spanish Fork, UT on October 14, 2011;
- His fireside talk on "The Temple," given in Ogden, UT on October 28, 2012;
- Denver's *40 Years in Mormonism* Series, Talk #2 titled "Faith," given in Idaho Falls, ID on September 28, 2013;

- Denver's *40 Years in Mormonism* Series, Talk #3 titled "Repentance," given in Logan, UT on September 29, 2013;
- Denver's *40 Years in Mormonism* Series, Talk #4 titled "Covenants," given in Centerville, UT on October 6, 2013; and
- Denver's *40 Years in Mormonism* Series, Talk #5 titled "Priesthood," given in Orem, UT on November 2, 2013.

In addition to the foregoing, Denver has addressed this topic extensively in multiple blog posts that may be worthwhile for you to review. Some of them include, among many others:

"Abraham and Sarah" posted April 29, 2010
"Abraham's Gospel" posted January 17, 2012
"Alma 13:15" posted June 14, 2010
"1 Nephi 14:1-2" posted July 5, 2010
"3 Nephi 20:25-27" posted September 20, 2010
"Jos Smith Letter Sept 1833" posted February 22, 2015

56. Abraham, Part 3

This is the third part of a special series on Abraham.

QUESTION: What do we need to understand about Abraham in order to understand our place in the last-days events? What is God's view of the book of Abraham and what ought we to take from it as we look towards a continuation of the Restoration?

———

DENVER: The last-days Zion is connected with the rights of the Fathers. And I talked about covenants, and I talked about the preliminaries, and in Centerville there was some material that is relevant to this topic.

From Adam to Noah and then to Melchizedek, there was an unbroken chain of both priesthood, on the one hand, and father to son descent, on the other hand. There was literally "a family of God" that began with Adam as the son of God, and it descended, then, generation after generation until Melchizedek in an unbroken chain. But then there was an apostasy from that order. As a result of the apostasy from that order, the chain got broken. And because the chain got broken, like we looked at in Centerville, it was the hope of Abraham to reconnect that chain.

> *I sought for the blessings of the Fathers and the right whereunto I should be ordained to administer the same* [that is, the rights of the Fathers]. *Having been myself a follower of righteousness, desiring also to be one who possessed great knowledge...and to possess a greater knowledge [and to be a greater follower] and to be a...*

And this doesn't make much sense unless you comprehend what it was that he was looking at and you are convinced that what he was looking at is exactly that order that began with Adam. He was desiring to be

> *...a Father of many nations, a prince of peace, and desiring to receive instructions and to keep the commandments of God, I became a rightful heir, a high priest, holding the right belonging to the Fathers. It was conferred upon me from the fathers: it came down from the fathers, from the beginning of time, yea, even from the beginning or before the foundation of the earth, [down] to the present time, even the right of the first born, or the first man, who is Adam, or first Father, through the Fathers unto me* (Abraham 1:1 RE).

This is what Abraham sought. And the reason Abraham sought that was because he understood that once that connection had been broken, that he needed to turn his heart to the Fathers so that he, Abraham, would not be smitten with the curse of apostasy. Therefore, he sought for the "blessings of the Fathers."

Now, in this late moment in time, in this late period of the generations of humanity, I don't think we can much aspire to being one of the Fathers, because, well, they were established long ago. But we ought to be turning our hearts to the Fathers, and we ought to be seeking also for what it was Abraham was seeking for—not to become ourselves but to become connected, not as a father but as a descendent, as a son or daughter.

When Abraham reconnected into the Fathers, Abraham was again able to perpetuate an unbroken chain from himself to Isaac, and Isaac in turn to Jacob, and Jacob in turn to Joseph, and Joseph in turn to Ephraim, to whom passed the right of the Fathers, or the right of the Firstborn—even though Isaac wasn't first born, Jacob wasn't first born, Joseph wasn't first born, and Ephraim wasn't first born—and yet they were all the "Firstborn" because they received the inheritance by right, and it was conferred upon them by right. Therefore, they were the Firstborn. Five generations in which the ancient pattern through the faith of Father Abraham returned and took; it actually endured for five more generations.

Disapproval from God feels terrible. When we were looking at the reaction that people have in the last day of judgement to standing in the presence of a just and holy being and feeling awful, I pointed out to you that in that passage, God was doing nothing other than existing. But the disappointment in the mind of man is so exquisite that it is likened by Joseph Smith to a lake of fire and brimstone. Therefore, God in His wrath has simply withdrawn. He's taken a step back because we are not suited to be in His presence. Therefore, having God withdraw is a matter of feeling keenly that absence, that rejection.

This incident is being described in modern revelation in [D&C] 84, but the incident itself occurred back in the book of Exodus. This is Exodus chapter 20, beginning at verse 18:

> And all the people saw the thunderings, and the lightnings, and the noise of the trumpet, and the mountain smoking: and when the people saw it, they removed, and stood afar off. And they said unto Moses, Speak thou with us and we will hear: but let not God speak with us, lest we die. And

Moses said unto the people, Fear not: for God is come to prove you, and that his fear may be before your faces, that ye sin not. And the people stood afar off, and Moses drew near unto the thick darkness where God was. (Exodus 20:18-21; see also Exodus 12:14 RE)

They did not want to encounter Him—not because the presence of God is so terrible that it drives men from Him, because Moses approached Him; but because the evidence of His presence makes us internally evaluate who and what we are. And although we can lie to ourselves about how good we really are, when the measuring stick against which you compare yourself is God, all of us come short. Even when the Lord Himself testifies to you that your sins are forgiven, you still recognize that you fall short. To the extent that you have confidence in the presence of the Lord, it is wholly derivative from Him. He has to strengthen you, because if He does not, all of us would retire in shame.

Sanctify yourselves that your minds become single to God, and the days will come that you shall see him; for he will unveil his face unto you, and it shall be in his own time, and in his own way, and according to his own will (D&C 88:68; see also T&C 86:12). He is in charge. We don't dictate this. We prepare, and then we wait. We prepare, and we do everything we know to get ready for it. But He surely will come; and when He comes, He comes suddenly to His temple, which temple ye are. He will come to you. Have faith! Be believing! Seek for Him! This is that day in which these things need to happen.

Go to the book of John, chapter 14. Two verses—chapter 14:18, the Lord says: *I will not leave you comfortless: I will come to you* (see also John 9:8 RE). This is Christ talking to the Apostles about what He intends to do on the other side of His death, burial, and resurrection. He's saying, "I'm not going to leave you comfortless, I will come to you!"

And then verse 23: *Jesus answered and said unto him, If a man love me, he will keep my words: and my Father will love him, and we will come unto him, and make our abode with him* (John 9:8 RE). Christ is saying that's the intention.

And so that we can have the definition given through Joseph, go to Doctrine and Covenants section 130 discussing this verse. D&C 130:3: *John 14:23— The appearing of the Father and the Son, in that verse, is a personal appearance; and the idea that the Father and the Son dwell in a man's heart is an old sectarian notion, and is false.* The promise was designed to have this actually happen. This is why Doctrine and Covenants 93:1 says what it says. This is what the fullness of the Gospel consists of.

You can take all your rights and ordinances, you can take all your abidingly deep mysteries—Adam-God and the topography of Kolob…. And by the way, that whole thing about Kolob is so mangled. Kolob was a star. Kolob was a star within sight. From the vantage point of the earth, which is the entire astronomy revealed to Father Abraham, it's entirely earth-based, looking upward. From the vantage point of the earth, looking up at that day— because the precession of the equinoxes changes the alignment of the stars, okay?—Kolob was a star. Abraham knew the name of the star. God said to Abraham, "You see that star? From where you sit looking there…." It's like saying, "Okay, from where my thumb is looking that way, Shay is sitting by my thumb." That doesn't mean Shay is on my thumb; he's some considerable distance from my thumb, okay? "Tim is in the direction of my index finger." He's not on my index finger; he's some considerable distance there away from — That's the direction. So if you know the topography of Kolob, you still don't know where God resides. Because where He resides is in a place hidden in the north. If I were telling you where the throne of God is today, I could tell you that, but I would use a different star because in our day it has a different name, and in our day it has a slightly different alignment because of the precession of the equinoxes. He is out there, but He's in a place that is hidden in the north. And it will require the heavens to be rolled to like a scroll before you finally see past the veils that prevent us from seeing it. But by that time, if you're unprepared, it's too late because the glory will be such that you cannot abide it. And when the Lord appears, preliminary to the rolling together of the scrolls, He will appear in a hole that is unveiled in which the glory of God, in His return, is behind Him, along with concourses of angels.

(I hate this because I'm just getting ready to change subjects, and so now here we are.)

Now, if you can discover what that alignment is and you can figure out where the throne of God is, that's up to you. I've been given no such either obligation or permission. But I can tell you there is a location. God exists. And Abraham walked through the geography of heaven, reckoned from the vantage point or viewpoint of the earth. And when you leave here, one of the obligations that you have is to find your way back. And in finding your way back, you need to be able to avoid those who seek to bring you back into captivity. Because if you're brought back into captivity, you may find yourself in a telestial kingdom (or the world in which you presently reside, as the temple endowment puts it). And that's a rather unpleasant thing to think about. You may find yourself in a casino in Las Vegas.

In Romans chapter 4, he's talking about Father Abraham, and in verse 3 he talks about Abraham believed God; it was counted unto him for righteousness. Faith was reckoned to Abraham for righteousness. Verse 13— the promise that he should be an heir of the world was not to Abraham or to his seed through the law but through the righteousness of faith. Because Abraham believed in God; he trusted in Him; therefore, he inherited it all— the world. He's the Father of the righteous. Beginning with verse 17:

> *(As it is written, I have made thee a father of many nations,) before him whom he believed, even God, who quickeneth the dead, and calleth those things which be not as though they were. Who against hope believed in hope, that he might become the father of many nations, according to that which was spoken, So shall thy seed be. And being not weak in faith, he considered not his own body now dead, when he was about an hundred years old, neither yet the deadness of Sara's womb: He staggered not at the promise of God through unbelief; but was strong in faith, giving glory to God; And being fully persuaded that, what he had promised, he was able also to perform. (Romans 4:17-21; see also Romans 1:20 RE)*

There was no proof that an aged, "dead" (that is, now impotent), old man, could sire a child with a barren, post-menopausal Sarah. But Abraham doubted not; and you have before you promises spoken by the voice of an angel concerning the things God has in store for your day, and you doubt? And you question? And you think God not able to bring about what He has said He intends to do?

The very day that they have looked forward to from the beginning of the days of Adam down till now (as we looked at in Centerville)— You doubt that God can bring this to pass? You doubt that what I have been talking about since we began in Boise and have now arrived here— If God can send someone to declare these things to you, in the confidence and the faith and the knowledge that I'm speaking to you on His errand, and I can do it in this room, in this building, in this city—salvation comes to you today by the word of God. And you doubt that God cannot make a holy place somewhere that has not been trodden under the foot of the gentiles? You doubt that God cannot bring to pass His work in culminating the ages? Have the faith of a grain of mustard seed, because it is coming; it is going to happen; and if you lack the faith, you will not be invited.

This required Abraham to endure the test of his faith. It is not easy.

I'm talking about priesthood because I want to remind you of a few things about priesthood conceptually. The priesthood was restored by John the Baptist before there was any organized church. Therefore, it is before, and it is independent and has never required a church in order for priesthood to exist.

If you go to Doctrine and Covenants 84:6: *And the sons of Moses, according to the Holy Priesthood which he received under the hand of his father–in–law, Jethro* (see also T&C 82:3)—now just to remind you about this, Jethro was a Midianite. He was a descendent of Midian. Midian was the son of Keturah. Keturah was the wife of Abraham after Sarah. After Sarah died, Keturah bore him children, one of whom was Midian. The birthright had already been given to Isaac.

See, there is so much about the priesthood that has yet to be clarified (and I think that is a good thing, and I'm not going to clarify enough for mischief to ensue.) But the fact of the matter is that that priesthood which Abraham handed to Midian—which then descended down and came to Moses—did not possess the birthright. Didn't possess that. Therefore, it was not the same thing as the priesthood that had belonged previously to the Patriarchs. It was something less, and it was something different.

But Moses obtained *that* priesthood through Jethro, a Midianite (not even an Israelite, because Midian was named at the same time genealogically as Isaac; and it would be Isaac's son, Jacob, who would be named Israel; and it was Israel who possessed the birthright that descended down). And so Moses inherited a form of priesthood that was, by its very nature, lesser. It's one of the reasons why the prophets of the Old Testament all had to be ordained directly by heaven in order to obtain what they obtained.

In any event, this point is only this: Priesthood exists independent of Israel. It exists independent of a church; and while a church may be dependent upon priesthood, priesthood is not and never has been dependent upon a church—Period. I hope you understand that. Priesthood is not and never has been dependent upon a church! These are two entirely different topics.

Now we get to the point in the history of the world in which, after the days of Shem (who was renamed Melchizedek), people fell into iniquity. They fell into iniquity, and they lost the birthright. There was no continuation of this. It was broken by an apostasy, and it had to be restored again—which ought to give all of us great hope, because Abraham sought for this. He sought for a restoration of the kingdom of God. He sought for a restoration of this, which only one man on the earth can hold at a time. Abraham 1:2:

> *And, finding there was greater happiness and peace and rest for me, I sought for the blessings of the fathers, and the right whereunto I should be ordained to administer the same; having been myself a follower of righteousness, desiring also to be one who possessed great knowledge, and to be a greater follower of righteousness, and to possess a greater knowledge, and to be a father of many nations, a prince of peace, and desiring to receive instructions, and to keep the commandments of God, I became a rightful heir, a High Priest, holding the right belonging to the fathers.* (see also Abraham 1:1 RE)

When you are in possession of *that*, you have no problem asking God and getting an answer. It *is* the right belonging to the Fathers.

After a period of apostasy and the break of this line, Abraham received it by adoption. Therefore, this power has the ability to cure the break. This covenant-making-through-God has the ability to restore the family of God, even when wicked men kill in order to destroy it; even when a substitute needs to be made; even when the fathers turn from their righteousness. Yet God is able to cause it to persist. And Joseph Smith was doing something which no one else either understood or had the right to perpetuate.

This continued through ten generations from Adam to Melchizedek, but through Abraham it continued five generations. And it appeared again, once on the earth, in a single generation that included Joseph and his brother, Hyrum.

Now even the mockery of it has come to an end, because there is no such thing as a perpetuation "in honorable mention" of the descendants of Hyrum Smith in the office of Patriarch in the Church. There have been many signs that have been given by God that He was about to do something new from the time of the death of Joseph Smith till today. All that was left at the end was for a witness to be appointed to come and to say, "It now has come to an end."

In the last talk that I gave in the 10 lecture series, I said a witness has now come, and I am him. It has come to an end. One of the signs of it having come to an end was the passing of Eldred Smith. There are many other signs that have been given if you are looking for them. You can see them all along the line.

Emma Smith once said that without Joseph Smith, there is no church. And you know what? Emma Smith was right. Because as soon as you remove

Joseph Smith out of the picture, what you had, essentially, was a complete overthrow of the church by the Quorum of the Twelve. The Quorum of the Twelve substituted themselves in the place.

The First Presidency under Joseph Smith was a quorum that the Quorum of the Twelve may be equal in authority to, but there was never a single apostle taken out of the Quorum of the Twelve moved into the First Presidency by Joseph Smith. These were two independently existing bodies. The Quorum of the Twelve did not occupy the First Presidency, and the First Presidency filled itself without regard to the Twelve. Similarly, the Quorum of the Seventy formed a quorum equal in authority with the Quorum of the Twelve and, therefore, with the First Presidency, also.

None of this survived Brigham Young! *None* of this survived Brigham Young! The high councils of Zion, the standing high councils formed a quorum equal in authority with the First Presidency and the Quorum of the Twelve. All the "keys" to rule in Israel—100% First Presidency, 100% Quorum of the Twelve, 100% Quorum of the Seventy, 100% in the High Councils—after Brigham Young took over, that was destroyed, and it became an oligarchy in which the Quorum of the Twelve runs everything, even through today.

But they don't run *this*; and they *can't* run *this*. And for *this*, God alone is in charge.

There is more to this than you can even begin to imagine. In the last revelation I received on this subject I recorded:

> It has puzzled me how the Lord could go to visit the dead, the dead could greet the Son of God in the Spirit World where He, *declared their redemption from the bands of death. Their sleeping dust was to be restored unto its perfect frame, bone to his bone, and the sinews and the flesh upon them, the spirit and the body to be united never again to be divided, that they might receive a fulness of joy* (D&C 138:16-17), on the one hand; but Christ did not go to preach to the wicked, instead, *from among the righteous he organized his forces and appointed messengers clothed with power and authority and commission[ed] them to go forth.* Therefore, the very SAME spirits who rejoice at the deliverance from the grave were left in the grave and it was by them *was the Gospel preached to those who had died* (D&C 138: 30-32). I had wondered how they could be raised from the dead and remain yet to preach to the dead.

After inquiring about this matter diligently, I have learned that when the Lord declared the resurrection, He did not resurrect them. He assured them it would come, but comparatively few were resurrected with the Lord at the time He came forth from the grave.

This then puzzled me to know who, then, was taken from the grave, as recorded in Matthew 27:52 (*Many of the bodies of the Saints which slept, arose*) and prophesied by Samuel and confirmed by Christ (3 Nephi 23:9-13). Who arose that were called "many Saints" by both the New Testament and the Book of Mormon?

I was shown that the spirits that rose were limited to a direct line back to Adam, requiring the hearts of the fathers and the hearts of the children to be bound together by sealing, confirmed by covenant and the Holy Spirit of Promise. This is the reason Abraham, Isaac and Jacob *have entered into their exaltation according to the promises and sit upon thrones and are not angels but are gods* (D&C 132:37).

The coming of the Lord in the future will not bring an immediate resurrection—just as the resurrection of Christ did not empty the world of spirits of even the righteous dead. Those who will be prepared at His coming will remain comparatively few still. Hence, the great need to turn the hearts of the children to the fathers, and the fathers to the children—and this too by covenant and sealing through the Holy Spirit of Promise. (*Journal of Denver C. Snuffer, Jr.,* Vol. 8, pp. 93-95)

It was abundantly clear, according to Joseph, that the only way in which this kind of a welding link could be accomplished required a temple to be built—and not the temple that was built in Kirkland that was accepted by the Lord; but something different.

Only the organization through a temple and associated rites results in finishing the family of God in the house of order, following the results achieved—or allowing the results achieved by Abraham, Isaac, and Jacob, which are described in D&C 132:37: *Abraham, and Isaac, and Jacob they did none other things than that which they were commanded, they have entered into their exaltation according to the promises. And they sit upon thrones and are not angels, but are Gods.*

In D&C 138:41, Abraham (the father of the faithful), Isaac, and Jacob were also there. In verses 41 and 42 of 138, Abraham, Isaac, and Jacob were there.

But in the revelation given in 1843, they're sitting on thrones. They're not in the spirit world proselytizing. They're sitting on thrones. The difference between these two categories are the differences between individual salvation —which can come—and reorganizing the family of God—which must occur by an ordinance in a temple to be acceptable to God.

This was why the command was given to build the temple in Nauvoo and why God offered to restore to them the fullness that they did not achieve. We need to let God take the lead, and then we need to patiently await each step along the way.

This is the stuff of which the prophecies speak. And it is the stuff that will be fulfilled. But the rites and the ordinances necessary to accomplish that— People in this generation don't even have a clue how that necessarily has to roll forth. But rest assured, it will. It will.

Zion will be God's work. And in the end, it will be His and His alone. He will own it; He will bring it; He will be the author of it; and He is the one who says that He will take credit for it. When it happens, however, it will conform to a pattern.

This is a verse that gets attributed to Enoch who is, in turn, quoting a prophecy that was given by Adam. And so this is the original prophecy, given at the beginning of the world through Father Adam, who established in the beginning the covenant that God, Himself, intends to vindicate: *Now this same Priesthood, which was in the beginning, shall be in the end of the world also* (Genesis 3:14 RE).

Well, that authority gets explained a little more fully when Abraham sought for the blessing that began in the beginning. He describes what it was that he wanted:

> *I sought for the blessings of the fathers, and the right whereunto I should be ordained to administer the same; having been myself a follower of righteousness, desiring also to be one who possessed great knowledge, and to be a greater follower of righteousness, and to possess a greater knowledge, and to be a father of many nations, a prince of peace, and desiring to receive instructions, and to keep the commandments of God, I became a rightful heir, a High Priest, holding the right belonging to the fathers. It was conferred upon me from the fathers; it came down from the fathers, from the beginning of time, yea, even from the beginning, or before the foundation of the earth, down to the present time, even the*

right of the firstborn, or the first man, who is Adam, or first father, through the fathers unto me. (Abraham 1:1 RE)

There's some very bright, well-studied Latter-day Saints who think they know what the gospel and priesthood of Abraham was. I'm here today to declare to you the truth, whether you accept it or not, whether you understand it or not, whether you think you can parse the scriptures otherwise or not. I'm telling you what the truth is today: Abraham sought for the right that came down through the Fathers, from Adam, which was the right of the Firstborn, which is that priesthood which must be restored in order to bring about the purposes of God in the last days. Abraham 2:11—the Lord says that through him:

> *I will bless them that bless thee, and curse them that curse thee; and in thee (that is, in thy Priesthood) and in thy seed (that is, thy Priesthood), for I give unto thee a promise that this right shall continue in thee, and in thy seed after thee (that is to say, the literal seed, or the seed of the body) shall all the families of the earth be blessed, even with the blessings of the Gospel.* (see also Abraham 3:1)

Abraham's fatherhood reckons from priesthood. Although the right will continue through the literal seed, it reckons through priesthood. He sought for the right to be one of the Fathers. We're talking about a time in the last days, prophesied and repeated by Jacob as his testimony in the Book of Mormon, when the natural fruit is going to reappear upon the earth. "Natural fruit" is always genealogical. It is always familial. There's going to come a time in the last days when the family of God will return again to the earth. That same priesthood includes a function that is not well understood. Abraham knew what this was when he said he desired to be a "father of many nations." He's identifying one of the attributes and one of the roles that necessarily must return.

If you go to Moses chapter 5 there's an incident that takes place in which Mother Eve celebrated—because after the apostasy of son after son after son —she rejoiced because, well, I'll read it to you. This is Moses 5:16:

> *And Adam and Eve, his wife, ceased not to call upon God. And Adam knew Eve his wife, and she conceived and bare Cain, and said* [now this is her; she conceived; she bare Cain; and she said concerning this son]: *I have gotten a man from the Lord; wherefore he may not reject his words. But behold, Cain hearkened not, saying: Who is the Lord that I should know him?* (see also Genesis 3:6 RE)

That is to say, Mother Eve looked at Cain—in contrast to those that had rejected the gospel message that had been born by her previously—and Cain, apparently in answer to her supplication to the Lord, came as what she anticipated would be the son upon whom the birthright would be conferred, the one through whom the lineage would continue, the one through whom the government of God would continue upon the earth, the replacement for Adam.

But Cain, when he arrived at the age of accountability and beyond, *hearkened not, saying: Who is the Lord that I should know him? And she again conceived and bare his brother Abel. And Abel hearkened unto the voice of the Lord. And Abel was a keeper of sheep, but Cain was a tiller of the ground* (Genesis 3:6 RE).

Now mind you, there is no attempt to set out the chronology here other than by milestones. But Cain had determined to reject the Lord and not hearken to Him by the time the replacement, Abel, was born. And when Cain, who thought it his birthright, found that he could be displaced by his younger brother— As an act of overthrowing the government of God, Cain slew Abel in order to prevent the birthright, in order to prevent the promised Messiah, in order to prevent the work of God progressing through any lineage other than his own. This was an act of treason. This was an act of overthrowing the government of God. This was an attempt to force God to place the Messiah that should redeem all mankind into a position inferior to Cain, his father. But God replaced the slain Abel with Seth. And Seth was the one through whom, then, the promise would be realized.

As you go through the account in Moses chapter 6, at 10 and 11: *Adam lived one hundred and thirty years, and begat a son in his own likeness, after his own image, and called his name Seth.* So *in his own likeness, after his own image*— when Adam was created in God's own likeness after God's own image— makes Seth, like Adam, a godly man.

And the days of Adam, after he had begotten Seth, were eight hundred years, and he [that is Seth] *begat many sons and daughters.* There is no indication that any of them were as rebellious as were the descendents of Cain. *He begat many sons and daughters.* And yet, in the next verses, there is only one son who is identified.

Seth lived one hundred and five years, and begat Enos, and prophesied in all his days, and taught his son Enos in the ways of God; wherefore Enos prophesied also"(Genesis 3:15-16 RE). So although there are many sons and many daughters, there is only one named, and you can follow it through.

Seth—*many sons*, all of whom are unnamed other than one—and that one that is named is Enos. Enos has *many sons*, all of whom are also unnamed other than one: Cainan. And Cainan has *many sons*, all of whom are unnamed other than one; the one that's named is Mahalaleel. And although all of his predecessors had had *many sons*, Mahalaleel had *sons*. So the fertility rate is collapsing as we get closer to the Flood. There is only one named son of Mahalaleel, and that is Jared. And there is only one named son out of all the sons of Jared, and that is Enoch. And there is only one named son out of all of the sons of Enoch, and that's Methuselah.

This is not a genealogy. This is a description of the government of God as it descended down through each generation, so that upon the death of one, you then knew who stood next in line in order to be "the father of all, the father of many nations," the role that is occupied by the head of the human family, okay? It is a priesthood line in which only one in each generation stands at the head as the Father.

This one stands as "the father of all," and hence, Abraham's desire to become "a father of many nations," because if he stepped into the line, he necessarily stepped into the role of providing the government of God. Christ is the one to whom all generations belong. He is the Redeemer of all mankind, and as the Savior of mankind, He becomes the Father of all.

Christ was born a King. In fact, wise men from the East came inquiring saying: *Where is he that was born King of the Jews?* Because that was His status; that was what the prophecies said of Him; that was the role He occupied. And the person they approached to find out where they might identify the newborn king was the king of the land, who knew nothing about the matter and had to go to the scriptorians to ask them, who after some fumbling came up with Bethlehem. *Bethlehem of Judea, thou art not the least.*

Well, Christ was born as a King, but He explained how He discharged His Kingship. In John chapter 18 beginning at verse 36: *Jesus answered* [this is when He was on trial for His life]—

> *Jesus answered, My kingdom is not of this world: if my kingdom were of this world, then would my servants fight, that I should not be delivered to the Jews: but now is my kingdom not from hence. Pilate therefore said unto him, Art thou a king then? Jesus answered, Thou sayest that I am a king. To this end was I born, and for this cause came I into the world, that I should bear witness unto the truth. Every one that is of the truth heareth my voice.* (See also John 10:7 RE)

That's the King. And He suffered Himself to be surrendered into the hands of wicked men who despitefully used, abused, beat, and humiliated Him, and then killed Him publicly on a thoroughfare where the notoriety of His death would be on public display. And no one entering or leaving, on that day, the city of Jerusalem, could do so without noticing the humiliation of our Lord. That's our King.

He explained Himself further in contrasting who He, the King, the Almighty Father, the Wonderful, Counselor, of the end of His government there shall not be a failure of increase—He explained Himself and how He rules to his disciples. *And he saith unto them* [this is in Luke chapter 22 beginning at verse 25],

> *And he saith unto them, The kings of the Gentiles exercise lordship over them; and they that exercise authority upon them are called benefactors. But ye shall not be so: but he that is greatest among you, let him be as the younger; and he that is chief, as he that doeth service.* (See also Luke 13:6 RE)

The great King came, above all else, to serve.

Zion will come. It will come not because of the worthiness of any of us; it will come because of the repentance of us and the worthiness of those with whom God covenanted to bring it to pass, including Adam and Enoch and Abraham and Melchizedek. It will come as a consequence of the righteousness of those that went before and with whom God, who cannot lie in a covenant, made a covenant to cause it to happen in the last days. It will surely come.

Joseph's original instruction about sealing dealt with connecting the living faithful to the Fathers in heaven: Abraham, Isaac, and Jacob. The connection was to be accomplished through adoption sealings, not genealogy. Joseph was connected to the Fathers through his priesthood. He and his brother Hyrum were to become Fathers of all who would live after them. (Just read Abraham 1:2). Families were originally organized under Joseph as the Father of the righteous in this dispensation. Accordingly, men were sealed to Joseph Smith as their Father, and they as his sons. This was referred to as "adoption" because the family organization was not biological but priestly, according to the law of God. As soon as Joseph died, the doctrine began to erode, ultimately replaced by the substitute practice of sealing genealogical lines together. In between the original adoptive sealing to Joseph and the current practice of tracking genealogical or biological lines, there was an intermediate step when families were tracked back as far as research permitted, then the line was sealed to Joseph Smith. That practice is now forgotten and is certainly no longer practiced by any denomination within Mormonism.

When Joseph died, any understanding of the practice of "adoption" was quickly lost. Confusion over this subject once again confirms both the ever-changing nature of Mormonism and its failure to become complete during Joseph Smith's lifetime.

If the original Mormonism needed to recover the fullness that was lost, then to revive an original, it will require a recovery of what was lost and more. If recovered, believers will be able to receive a holy spot, accepted and defended by God. In that place, the religion of Adam will be taught. The promised original religion includes the revelation of everything; nothing shall be withheld. Today's Mormonism has a great deal withheld, but the religion of Abraham (and, therefore, the religion of Adam) included *a knowledge of the beginning of the creation, and also of the planets, and of the stars, as they were made known unto the fathers.* The original Mormonism must grow in ancient knowledge and understanding until their understanding reaches into heaven —not just spiritual understanding, but also physical understanding of the layout of the universe. The placement of the lights in the firmament was for "signs" to man, and therefore, were deliberately placed and contain information originally understood by Adam.

Because of prophecies made to the patriarchal Fathers, the right to found this future city of peace descends from a specific ancient line. There will be an heir descended from both Jesse and Joseph who will accomplish it. Occupants of the community will likewise have lineal qualification. The last-day's Zion is an accomplishment promised earlier to the patriarchal Fathers, and it is through their descendants God intends to vindicate the promises. The result of this alignment will be a priestly city of Zion that will "return to that power which she has lost."

———

The foregoing excerpts are taken from

- Denver's *40 Years in Mormonism Series,* Talk #6 titled "Zion," given in Grand Junction, CO on April 12, 2014;
- Denver's *40 Years in Mormonism Series,* Talk #8 titled "A Broken Heart," given in Las Vegas, NV on July 25, 2014;
- Denver's *40 Years in Mormonism Series,* Talk #10 titled "Preserving the Restoration," given in Mesa, AZ on September 9, 2014;

- A fireside talk on "Plural Marriage," given in Sandy, UT on March 22, 2015;
- A Q&A session titled "A Visit with Denver Snuffer," held on May 13, 2015;
- His talk titled "Zion Will Come," given near Moab, UT on April 10, 2016; and
- The presentation of Denver's paper titled "Was There an Original," given at the Sunstone Symposium on July 29, 2016.

In addition to the foregoing, Denver has addressed this topic extensively in multiple blog posts that may be worthwhile for you to review. Some of them include, among many others:

"Adam's Religion" posted December 21, 2015
"1, 2 or 3 Priesthoods?" posted February 28, 2016
"2 Nephi 29:14" posted August 14, 2010
"The Sacrifice" posted March 1, 2010
"Inquiry and Response" posted March 30, 2017
"Cycles of Truth" posted December 11, 2011
"Jacob 5:57-59" posted April 11, 2012

57. Abraham, Part 4

This is the final part of a special series on Abraham.

QUESTION: What do we need to understand about Abraham in order to understand our place in the last-days events? What is God's view of the book of Abraham and what ought we to take from it as we look towards a continuation of the Restoration?

———

DENVER: We face the same test as all others have ever faced from the days of Adam down to the present. Things never change. From the time of Adam the roles have been filled by different persons in different ages, but the conflict is perpetual. And the same battle continues from age to age. You can even lift the arguments that are made from one epoch and put them into the next, and they fit. It doesn't change.

Adam taught his posterity the gospel; and Satan, imitating an angel of light, declared himself to be a son of God and taught this doctrine: "Believe it not." And most of Adam's posterity did not believe.

Enoch received a message from God, and the record that Enoch left behind says, *and all men were offended because of him* (Genesis 4:4 RE).

Noah taught the same gospel as was taught in the beginning to Adam, but his audience claimed "we are the sons of God," and they would not hearken to the message that came through Noah.

Abraham obtained the same rights that were "belonging to the fathers"—or to Adam, in the beginning—including holding the right of the firstborn that came down from the first Father, Adam. And those who claim the gospel of Abraham is less than the gospel given to Adam are a false message borne by a false messenger. Mark it: If they don't repent for preaching that message in opposition to what the Lord declares both in scripture and by my voice, they will regret it. But, unfortunately, Abraham's own family—that is, his father(s), his uncles—utterly refused to hearken to his voice.

Moses saw God face to face, and he talked with Him. God gave Moses a work to do. Satan tempted Moses to instead worship him, even declaring to Moses, *I am the only begotten, worship me* (Genesis 1:4 RE). When Moses rejected this demand, his message from God was opposed by sorcerers and magicians who *did in like manner with their enchantments* (Exodus 4:6 RE), duplicating signs shown through Moses over and over again in the record in Exodus. Even after delivering Israel from Egypt, the Israelites wished they had died in Egypt rather than being delivered and freed. And of course, what might have happened, given the qualification of Moses to bring it about, did not happen because the people that he led were unwilling to rise up as they were invited.

Christ was opposed by Satan who demanded that He worship him, and then He was opposed by religious leaders of the people. The people He went to save conspired to kill Him and ultimately brought that about.

Joseph Smith was, and is, opposed by those who claim to follow him or to belong to a church that was founded by him. If you don't understand the extent to which the opposition to Joseph Smith arose out of those claiming to be Mormons, take a look at the book *A Man Without Doubt,* and you'll see that Joseph's greatest opposition came from those who claim to follow him.

Opposition in scripture seems clear. But when we struggle in our environment, it becomes much more difficult to make decisions about what is right, what is wrong, what is good, what is bad, what is of God, what is deception, what is truth, what is false. But that's not a correct understanding, because the scriptures may reveal the conflict in sharp contrast, but it was no different in that day than it is today. Deciding between the opposing sides was not any more clear to those living at the time the scriptures were written than the opposition you encounter every day of your life.

The scriptures were written by or about prophets who took clearly opposing positions from those who were deceived. The clarity you read in scripture is because the views and opinions of prophets were used to tell about the events. But as the events happened, those living at the time had to have faith to distinguish between truth and error, to believe or to ignore a message from the Lord. It is no different for them than it is for the dilemma that we face today.

Does the message invite or entice you to believe in Christ and to do His works? Does it get presented in a way that displays patience, long-suffering? Does it use gentleness and persuasion, meekness and love and consistency with the revelations and commandments found previously in scripture? Or does it appeal to your vanity, to your arrogance? Does it make you proud of yourself, or does it make you instead wish that you were a better person?

Humility is absolutely required to progress. The more we think we understand, the less willing we can become to receive more. Joseph said, "It is the constitutional disposition of mankind to set up stakes and bounds to the works and ways of the Almighty." He also said, "I never heard of a man being damned for believing too much, but they are damned for unbelief."

James 4:6 says: *God resisteth the proud but giveth grace unto the humble* (see also Epistle of Jacob 1:16 RE). Damnation is limiting progress or stopping progress. Setting up boundaries to what the Lord can do is voluntary damnation. No matter how much you believe you know, if you will be humble, you will learn a great deal more. We must continue progression, or if we don't, we accept damnation and that, too, voluntarily.

When Christ established and organized the New Testament dispensation, Christ patterned what He did as a reminiscence—as an homage—to the children of Israel. That was who He was serving with. It would not go out to the gentiles until after Christ's death. So during His immediate ministry, Christ was serving among the Jews who notoriously would claim repeatedly they're children of Abraham. And that children-of-Abraham-status gave them a credential with which they could pass into heaven. And so when He structures the incipient stage of the dispensation—

- Peter, James, and John = Abraham, Isaac, and Jacob;
- Twelve apostles = twelve tribes of Israel;
- The seventy (Exodus 1:5) = seventy descendants of Jacob that went into Egypt.
- Christ gives an homage, a send up, a mirror, a structure to resonate with the people to whom He was serving.

There are things that because I went to law school and I learned how to be a lawyer, that I can see in the record of the Old Testament that explains a legal system that they had back in those days.

Abraham's wife, Sarah, died. And Abraham wanted to bury his wife, but he was in a land, at that time, in which he owned no land; so he needed to acquire a burial site for his wife. Well, their system in that day required that whatever the bargain was that was struck between the people that were negotiating, it had to be witnessed by at least two people. And in order for that agreement to be binding, something had to be given in exchange. If you didn't give something in exchange, then whatever you got could be taken back. And Abraham wanted Sarah buried in a place where it could not be taken back— it would be hers as her burial spot forever.

So, he goes to the people of the city to try and find out who owns the field that has the cave that he would like to bury Sarah in. Well, the field has a crop in it. He wants the land, but he doesn't necessarily want the crop. And he wants the land because of the cave, and that's where he wants to bury Sarah.

So he approaches the fellow who owns the cave, in the presence of others, and he says, "I would like to purchase this for the burial spot." And the first response is, "Oh, you don't need to buy that from me. I'll give it to you. Go ahead, and use it as the burial spot." Which meant that he was really going to retain ownership and he could, in fact, disturb the gravesite of Sarah because nothing was being exchanged. And Abraham said, "No, no you can't give it to me. I want to purchase that," because he wants his wife's remains undisturbed.

And so now that he knows he can't give it to him and therefore take it back, Efron (that was the name of the fellow that owned the field) says, "Well what is it to me to give to you something that is worth [and I think it was] 200 shekels of silver?" I think that was the price he named. Said, "That's a small sum between you and I, and it's no problem." So now Abraham knows the price that's being asked for the property. And he was overcharging; it was an unfair amount. But he had a crop on it, so maybe he valued the crop. And Abraham, in the presence of the witnesses, paid the 200 shekels, secured the ground, and he acquired for himself the burial place for Sarah that could not now be taken back.

Well, there are a lot of little legal things that are going on in the process of getting an enforceable agreement so that Abraham owns the ground and Sarah's body will not be disturbed. And I learned about those things by going to law school.

> *Marriage was, in the beginning, between one man and one woman, and was intended to remain so for the sons of Adam and the daughters of Eve, that they may multiply and replenish the earth. I commanded that there shall not any man have save it be one wife, and concubines he shall have none. I, the Lord your God, delight in the chastity of women, and in the respect of men for their wives. Marriage was established at the beginning as a covenant by the word and authority of God, between the woman and God, the man and woman, and the man and God. It was ordained by my word to endure forever. Mankind fell, but a covenant established by my word cannot fail, and therefore in death they were not to be parted. It was my will that all marriages would follow the pattern of the*

beginning, and therefore all other marriages would be ordained as at the first. But fallen men refused my covenant, did not hearken to my word, nor receive my promise, and marriages fell outside my rule, disorganized and without me, therefore unable to endure beyond the promises made between the mortal man and the mortal woman, to end when they are dead. Covenants, promises, rights, vows, associations and expectations that are mine will endure, and those that are not cannot endure. Everything in the world, whether it is established by men, or by Thrones, or by Dominions, or by Principalities, or by Powers, that are not by my word and promise, shall be thrown down when men are dead and shall not remain in my Father's Kingdom. Only those things that are by me shall remain in and after the resurrection. Marriage by me, or by my word, received as a holy covenant between the woman and I, the man and woman, and the man and I, will endure beyond death and into my Father's Kingdom, worlds without end. Those who abide this covenant will pass by the angels who are appointed, and enter into exaltation. Concerning them it shall be said, You shall come forth in the first resurrection, and if they covenant after the first resurrection, then in the next resurrection, and shall inherit in my Kingdom their own thrones, dominions, principalities, powers, all heights and depths, and shall pass by the angels to receive exaltation, the glory of which shall be a fullness and a continuation of their posterity forever. Marriage is necessary for the exaltation of the man and woman and is ordained by me through the Holy Spirit of Promise, or in other words, by my covenant, my law, and my authority. Like the marriage in Eden, marriage is a sacrament for a sacred place, on holy ground, in my presence, or where the Holy Spirit of Promise can minister. But rebellion has kept mankind from inheriting what I ordained in the beginning, and therefore women and men have been left to marry apart from me. Every marriage established by me requires that I be part of the covenant for it to endure, for Endless is my name and without me the marriage cannot be without end: for so long as I endure it shall also endure, if it is made by my word and covenant. But know also that I can do my work at any time, for I have sacred space above, and can do my work despite earth and hell. The wickedness of men has not prevented my will, but only kept the wicked from what they might have received. Whenever I have people who are mine, I command them to build a house, a holy habitation, a sacred place where my presence can dwell or where the Holy Spirit of Promise can minister, because it is in such a place that it has been ordained to recover you, establish by my word and my oath your marriages, and endow my people with knowledge from on high that will unfold to you the mysteries of godliness, instruct you in my ways, that you may walk in my path. And *all the outcasts of Israel will I gather to my house, and the jealousy of Ephraim and Judah will end; Ephraim will not envy Judah and Judah will not provoke Ephraim. And again I say to you, Abraham and Sarah sit upon a Throne, for he could not be there if not for Sarah's covenant with him; Isaac and Rebecca sit upon a Throne, and Isaac likewise could not be there if not for Rebecca's covenant with him; and Jacob and Rachel sit upon a Throne, and Jacob could not be there if not for Rachel's covenant with him; and all these have ascended above Dominions and Principalities and Powers, to abide in my Kingdom. Therefore the marriage covenant is needed for all those who would likewise seek to obtain from me the right to continue their seed into eternity, for only through marriage can Thrones and Kingdoms be established.* (T&C 157:34-43)*

Christ is the means by which we lay hold upon the promises, but it is His intention to make of us all sons of God. Therefore, the Holy Order after the Son of God is—when the name is announced—self-identifying the person holding such a Holy Order as one of God's sons, even though they may be mortal, even though they may be in the flesh. The Holy Order is for that very purpose.

> ...and is after the Order of the Son of God. All other priesthoods are only parts, ramifications, powers and blessings belonging to the same, and are held, controlled and directed by it. It is the channel through which the Almighty commenced revealing His glory at the beginning of the creation of this earth, and through which He has continued to reveal Himself to the children of men to the present time, and through which He will make known His purposes to the end of time. (*History of the Church* 4:207)

Therefore, among other things, the purpose of the Holy Order is to put in place a mechanism by which God can reveal from heaven what is necessary for the salvation of man on earth in every generation, in order to fix what is broken; in order to restore what has been lost; in order to repair, heal, forgive, and reconnect those who are willing to give heed to the message sent from heaven, so that they can rise up to become sons of God.

The Holy Order descended from Adam, in turn. We're not going to do it, but if you take the time to go through and look at who got ordained, Seth was a replacement for the slain Abel. Cain was an elder brother. Cain would have qualified as the elder brother if he had been righteous for inheriting the Holy Order. And he had lived long enough, and he had been observed by his parents long enough so that Eve identified Cain as a man who had been gotten from God. Therefore, she knew he would not fail—which means that for at least some prolonged period of time after the sons and daughters of Adam and Eve had drifted into apostasy, Cain exhibited not only an interest but an adherence to what was being taught by the first parents. And so Eve celebrated that they had at last someone to whom the Holy Order could be passed. Cain was not the oldest son. He was the oldest *righteous* son, and as the oldest righteous son, it would have passed to him in due course.

Abel, his younger brother, was probably in his day righteous because of the positive example of his older brother, Cain. If you've got someone in the family who is on the right path, it's so much easier for the sibling to respect the example of someone similarly situated with them than it is to listen to the parents. And so Abel, likewise, followed in the path of righteousness.

Satan put it into the heart of Cain to view the inheritance that he was going to receive of the Holy Order as an opportunity to gratify his pride and to satisfy his ambition and to exert control and compulsion, because if he were the one in the line, then the Messiah would descend through him. And he would have a patriarchal position superior to the Messiah Himself. This was an important part of the plot of the adversary—because if the adversary could gain control over the inheritor under Adam of the Holy Order, then (as I just read a moment ago) before the Savior returns—

(When dominion was given to Adam, it was by God's word. And God cannot break His word. The right of dominion had been conferred; it has to be returned to Him.)

If Cain were the one in a position to exercise control, then he could exert whatever conditions Satan put into his heart before he would return the right of dominion back to the Savior. Thus, if a disciple of Satan were to be in possession of that Holy Order in that line holding dominion, all of the conditions that Satan had demanded in the preexistence—which were rejected by the Father and created the war in heaven, designed to destroy the agency of man—could become the condition for the redemption of this creation. Therefore, Cain's apostasy represented an enormous threat to the salvation of everyone who would live thereafter.

As a consequence of that, the offering by the younger brother was approved, and the older brother, Cain, was told, "You need to stop what you're doing. You need to repent and return. And if you do not, sin lieth at the door. The adversary is ready to enter into your house." This represented a serious frustration or threat to the second great conspiracy to destroy the souls of men and to capture this creation. And therefore, Satan put it into the heart of Cain to murder his brother, and Abel was slain so that (the theory was) by controlling the position, that necessarily meant that the Messiah would be a descendant of Cain's, the line would come through him, and he would have the authority, the control, the dominion, and the right to change the plan or the conditions for the salvation of the souls of men in this world.

At this point, we're at the very beginning; we haven't gotten very far. But it is essential when you begin to talk about the Holy Order that you start here. If you don't start here, if you want to start at the time of Moses and the Aaronic priests, if you want to start at the time of Joseph Smith and talk about ordinations in June of 1831, if you want to talk about the Three Witnesses identifying the Quorum of the Twelve and then ordaining them, you're not going to comprehend what the Holy Order is all about because the Holy Order has, as part of its implication, the right of dominion over all creation. That was what it was established for, and it came down to the beginning. It belonged to God. It is why God is God. In essence, the Holy Order is to create of flesh and blood a surrogate for the Father and Mother. That's what the Holy Order was designed to accomplish.

So in the beginning, when you're talking about this process, the reason why we have Seth as the next person is because Cain fell, Abel was murdered, and perhaps because of the example, Adam and Eve in their sorrow were able to inform Seth of things that secured his fidelity to God.

It descended in regular course down through these Fathers until you get to Shem, who was called Melchizedek: *Mulek*=King; *Zedek*=Priest. It's a new name for the man, Shem. And then it simply falls into disrepair or apostasy, and we encounter our first gap in the descent from the days of Adam down, which lasted several generations until we get to Abraham.

Abraham also happened to have a genealogical right, but that wasn't what was important. In the case of Abraham, *finding there was greater happiness and peace and rest for me, I sought for the blessings of the fathers* (Abraham 1:1 RE). The "blessings of the fathers" after which he was seeking was the Holy Order. He wanted to become one like those that had been in the beginning.

When God spoke to Cain, He called him to repent. So God speaks to Cain and tells him to repent. He didn't repent; he did forfeit. But he forfeited it by becoming the first murderer. So the first time that you do something wrong, would you want God to say, "There you go, you're done; you're cut off. You will never have an opportunity to become what I would like you to become, a son of God." Or would you want Him to call you to repentance? Because God called Cain to repent, and he didn't. He went out, and he murdered his brother. He just got more determined to accomplish what he wanted. And at that point, Cain did not die as a result of the murder of his brother. He was driven out, but he wasn't killed; and he did lose the right. So even though he was living and even though he was alive at the time of his brother Seth, the right went to his brother exactly for that reason. But the first instance of error—I mean, heavens, the Kirtland Safety Society may have been enough to get rid of Joseph's position.

> *I sought for the blessings of the fathers, and the right whereunto I should be ordained to administer the same; having been myself a follower of righteousness, desiring also to be one who possessed great knowledge, and to be a greater follower of righteousness, and to possess a greater knowledge* (Abraham 1:1RE)

When you think of the Holy Order after the Order of the Son of God, don't think of it exclusively as some sort of status. It's implicit that what that includes is possession of great knowledge and greater knowledge. "A man cannot be saved in ignorance," as Joseph put it. "A man is saved no sooner than he gets knowledge" (*History of the Church* 4:588). But implicit in those statements by Joseph Smith is that the purpose of the knowledge is so that you can be a greater follower of righteousness. It's not so that you can play spiritual Trivial Pursuit and win, because the knowledge has to be implemented into practice in order for it to have the desired effect. Without accompanying obedience to the things that are known, there is no salvation in that. It has to be as Abraham puts it: *To be a greater...and to possess a greater knowledge and to be a father of many nations, a prince of peace, and desiring to receive instructions, and to keep the commandments of God, I became a rightful heir* (ibid). Okay?

At this point in the creation, Adam would have all mankind descend from him, and Noah would have all mankind descend from him, and therefore they would be the Father of nations. Abraham knew that was part of what was involved. It's not merely knowledge for knowledge's sake. It's being put into a position in which there is a posterity involving nations that would look to him as they looked to Noah, as they had looked to Adam as their Father.

Think of fatherhood as an opportunity to nurture, to assist, to provide for, to care for, to bring along; to take what is innocent and malleable and turn it into something that is God-like, responsible, capable—something or someone who can stand on their own two legs and defend the truth when called upon to do so, someone that will themselves be a vessel of righteousness. Don't think of a father as a bully with a whip or a belt.

What Abraham desired was to be a servant; that was what his ambition to be a Father of nations involved. And so he *became a rightful heir, holding the right belonging to the fathers. It was conferred upon me from the fathers; it came down from the fathers, from the beginning of time... even from the beginning, or before the foundation of the earth, down to the present time, even the right of the firstborn, or the first man, who is Adam, or first father, through the fathers unto me* (ibid).

That's where it came from. A son of God descended through those Fathers to Abraham, because Melchizedek—after a period of apostasy lasting generations —reconnected Father Abraham into the Fathers, which is the issue raised a minute ago about this genealogical thing. This is non-genealogical. This is a righteous man in a world of apostasy, looking to reconnect to heaven. He becomes the Father of the righteous because he's the first example of a generation, a man in a world of apostasy, coming out of that apostasy and reconnecting to Heaven.

There were generations separating Abraham from Shem. But Abraham qualified to receive the rights belonging to the Fathers because he sought for his appointment, he possessed knowledge, he lived consistent with the knowledge he had, he wished to have greater knowledge so that he could obey more commandments, so that he could gain further light and knowledge by the things that he learned through obedience.

So when you get to what happens after he's connected up, the Lord talking to him says:

> *My name is Jehovah, and I know the end from the beginning; therefore my hand shall be over thee. And I will make of thee a great nation, and I will bless thee above measure, and make thy name great among all nations, and thou shalt be a blessing unto thy seed after thee, that in their hands they shall bear this ministry and [Holy Order] unto all the nations; And I will bless them through thy name; for as many as receive this Gospel shall be called after thy name, and shall be accounted thy seed, and shall rise up and bless thee, as their father.* (Abraham 3:1 RE)

That's non-genealogical. That's the same process through which Abraham went to become a descendant of the Fathers. It's reconnecting, and whoever does that, in whatever generation, is a descendant and can call Abraham their Father.

Abraham 2 (that one is verse 10, but I started at verse 9, and I'm going on to 11, so right in there):

> I will bless them that bless thee, and curse them that curse thee; and in thee (that is, in thy [Holy Order]) and in thy seed (that is, the [Holy Order]), for I give unto thee a promise that this right shall continue in thee, and in thy seed after thee (that is to say, the literal seed, or the seed of the body) shall all the families of the earth be blessed, even with the blessings of the Gospel, which are the blessings of salvation, even of eternal life. (ibid)

Abraham says: *Now, after the Lord had withdrawn from speaking to me, and withdrawn his face from me, I said in my heart: Thy servant has sought thee earnestly; now I have found thee* (Abraham 3:2 RE). So he's saying that whenever you receive the gospel, whenever you receive *this* gospel (and it's really hard to try and get *this* gospel back on the earth; there was still a great deal left to be recovered, restored, and returned when Joseph was killed at 38½), but when *this* Gospel (the one that Abraham had received) was on the earth at any time, then whoever receives *that* is a descendant of Abraham. They are part of the family of Abraham, and he is their Father.

And so he becomes the Father of many nations. He instructed and passed along the same birthright to Isaac and to Jacob and to Joseph and to Ephraim. And then it rather turns into the same sort of mess that we had previously, until the time of Moses.

The way in which I would suggest it would be best to understand is that they came, not for purposes of conferring priesthood that would occur in June of 1831, but for reconnecting the genealogical line that required someone to be designated as descendants from "the Fathers." Now, some folks have argued that that meant that Joseph Smith was like *the* birthright holder in the line from Ephraim.

Given the way in which genealogical lines run, if you kill Charles and William and George (and I think there's another one—the royal line of England), then it's all the way back to Andrew, okay? So you can have a line that goes on a long distance, but if you have the Thirty Years War, and you have World War I, and you have World War II, and you have the Black Plague, and you're following genealogical lines, there's no way to track who

God thinks holds the birthright. Then you have the added complication that Esau was older than Jacob, but Jacob was more righteous, and so Jacob got the birthright. Seth—he had older brothers who were grandfathers by the time he was born, but the birthright went to Seth because he was true and faithful.

I would suggest that it may be possible that in this room there is a lot of people who could qualify. And whether or not that ever happens depends upon being a son of Abraham, which requires you to receive *this* gospel, meaning the one to which Abraham had been exposed, which requires a great deal of correct information to be restored.

It's almost amusing for people in their arrogance to assume that they know enough to understand what God is doing or has done, because the things of God are of deep import, and careful and solemn and ponderous and prayerful thought can only find them out. Your understanding has to reach into heaven itself and search into and contemplate the darkest abyss if you're going to save any soul, including your own. And that's not accomplished casually, nor is it accomplished without sacrifice.

The government of God is the family. The government of God is not stakes and wards and districts and missions and areas and all that; it's family. The government of God is family. Therefore, the sealing is to put together a family.

Now one of the requests that the mother of John and his brother came and made of Christ was that when Christ got into His kingdom, the mother was asking if her boys could sit on His left and on His right. Okay? And Christ said that, "When I get my kingdom they can be there with me, but I don't have the right to assign who's going to sit on my right and who's going to sit on my left. That's left up to the Father."

The purpose of organizing the family on earth through the sealing process is to make sure you get into the kingdom. But it's kind of foolish to say, "I have ambition to be way up high in the organization of the family of God, because Christ told parables about people that are capable of ruling over a city will be put in that position...." People that aren't— I mean His parable of the talents, His parable of the laborer in the vineyard— That what you really want is to get into the kingdom. Once you get into the kingdom, then how the kingdom gets organized is going to be entirely up to the Father. How that will unfold will be on the permanent resolution of all issues involving salvation pertaining to this planet at the very end. And all those that have lived or come through here—and that organization at the end—is more relevant for what will come thereafter. It's permanent, until there is some further development that requires people to go out and develop.

Get into the kingdom, because like the talk down in Ephraim, the prototype of the saved man is Jesus Christ. And if any man will be saved, he must be precisely what Christ is and nothing else. Because Christ attained to the resurrection, we're going to be resurrected. Christ attained to the resurrection. On the other side of that, you won't hold the keys of death and hell; He will. He'll use them for your benefit, but ultimately, you're going to have to hold the keys of death and hell if you're going to be precisely what the prototype of the saved man is—or else not be saved.

Joseph would certainly have the right to lay claim upon not just himself and his wife, but certainly his children. It begins to become a little less certain and a little more tenuous when you get to his grandchildren and even more so when you get to his great-grandchildren, because—

The reason why Father Abraham had to go to Melchizedek in order to then rejoice and say, "I have gotten me a priesthood," was because, although the line may have had fatherly connections from Father Shem down to Abraham, the immediate ancestors of Father Abraham were idolaters. True enough, his father repented for a short period of time, but he didn't persist in that. And therefore, despite the fact that Melchizedek certainly held authority, there were members of the posterity of Melchizedek between him and Father Abraham who were lost. And then Abraham was required to come and reconnect because of the apostasy.

When you're talking about the greatest blessings that God offers for the salvation of His children, when you're talking about the family of God, if it could simply be put in one time forever, then putting it into Father Adam would have solved the problem all the way down to us today. It can and it has been broken. It can and it has been restored. It can and it has been reconnected after a period of apostasy. In fact, once you reconnect Abraham with Melchizedek, you actually have, then, a family of God beginning with Adam that runs in one continuous line right down to Ephraim.

Then you have Joseph's comment about the prophets of the Old Testament— I'm not sure that he means all of them, but he certainly means a number that are identifiable: "All prophets held Melchizedek priesthood and were ordained by God Himself." Joseph said that. Okay? So I don't think what Joseph is talking about is, like, you know, "I confer upon you something." I think he's talking about this very connection, where you have an isolated, faithful individual who honors the Fathers and is doing everything that he can in his day, but for whom there is no existing possibility for having it occur. God fixes that problem for that individual—not in order to establish a new dispensation in which salvation proceeds with a gathering of a people and a making of a people—but it's a dispensation to that individual for purposes of trying to call others to repentance, and if others were to repent, then God could do something with that.

The reason He led away Lehi and the family of Lehi was to try and establish a righteous branch in the vineyard of the Lord, and the only way to do that was to get them away from the people who were corrupt in Jerusalem—and maybe give them the potential for holding onto and becoming a people of promise. And they were on again, off again, and faithful. A number of troubling moments in their history; but in general, they were sufficiently intact by the time that the Lord came, that He visited with them, and He renewed that with them, and that connection was certainly fulsome at that point.

The only purpose behind the last-days work, both what was happening at the time of Joseph and what the Lord is offering to us today, is to accomplish that fulsome restoration of the family of God. I mean, Joseph talked about temples, and they were built incrementally, and they never reached the finish line, even on the second one, before he was killed. But he laid a fabulous foundation and pointed in a direction that the Restoration necessarily must go to and complete. Because if we don't have the tabernacle of God where He comes to dwell with His people (which He does when He has a family on earth), then the prophecies are not going to be fulfilled. Then the promises that were made to Enoch will not be realized. Then the statements of what will happen in the last days through Moses will not be vindicated. Then Adam's prophecy concerning his descendants to the end of time will not be realized. All of these things point—so we know it is going to happen. The question is not, is it going to happen? The question is, Will we rise up, or will we not? Because what He's offering is, in fact, a legitimate opportunity for that to indeed happen.

The "hearts of the children turning to the Fathers so that the earth in not smitten with a curse" means that the purpose of the Restoration, ultimately, is to turn us back to something that was here in the beginning, the way in which it once was—the dispensation of Adam, the dispensation of Enoch, the dispensation of Noah, all of which were running simultaneously at the time of the Flood. *As it was in the days of Noah so also shall it be at the time of the coming of the Son of Man* (Matthew 11:11 RE). We're going to have three different kinds of remnants operating at the same time at the coming of the Lord:

- A dispensation that will reflect somewhat of the Christian era;
- A dispensation that will reflect somewhat of Joseph Smith's era; and
- A dispensation that will reflect somewhat of the original, the one in which man stood in the presence of God.

And of course, we've got a couple of those functioning, after a fashion. What we lack yet, and what necessarily will involve the presence of Son Ahman to achieve, is something that He must bring about. When He said, "I will bring again Zion," He literally means that; because you can't have it without His presence. *That* dispensation, that's the one that needs to occur. Joseph gave a talk where he referred to the spirit of Elias and the spirit of Elijah and the spirit of Messiah—because there are really three great spirits that are involved, with three great stages.

Abraham is the Father of the righteous because, at the time that Abraham lived, the connection back to the government of God that began with Adam —to whom dominion was given over the earth—had been broken. It had been broken for generations. It had existed at one time for ten generations, continuously and uninterrupted from the days of Adam to the days of Shem. But when Abraham lived, it had been broken for generations.

Now Shem, who had lived on the other side of the Flood and who could have fled with Enoch's people into Zion (because people were taken up into Zion continuously, right up until the flood, and Shem did not need to remain on the earth), but he remained on the earth to perpetuate what was there in the beginning. And so Shem, who would be called Melchizedek—*Melek Zadok*: King, Priest, the Prince of Peace, the King of Salem, the King of Peace, the Teacher of Righteousness—he remained through the Flood, but he held onto the covenant that would allow him to lay hold upon that. And he waited through generations of apostasy.

And Abraham represents every man, because Abraham came into the world in a state of apostasy, disconnected from the Fathers, incapable of laying hold upon the promises that go back through Adam and Seth and Enos and Jared and Mahalalel and the other descendants, right down until the days of Shem. Abraham was disconnected from that. And he went, and he looked, and he searched because the records belonging to the Fathers had come down into his possession, and he knew there was something to that. He knew there was something more to be obtained, and he longed for his appointment unto that —that which was in the beginning.

He obtained a connection for himself into that. That's why he had to connect up with Melchizedek, because the bond had to be formed, the covenant had to be established, the connection had to be made. And when it was made, the same right that belonged to Adam in the beginning—that right that belonged to Adam as the one to whom dominion over all the earth had been given— had been passed to Abraham. And Abraham became the rightful heir, the holder of that right belonging to the Fathers, even the first Father, or Adam, that came down from the beginning. That's what Joseph Smith sought to have be restored. That's something that cannot be done apart from the direct, personal involvement of God. That's something that, when it's restored, returns us back to a state in which Eden is again possible.

It was a year ago that a renewed covenant was given to all willing to accept it by God. New covenant people sprang into existence when a few accepted that gift. Until that moment, there were only lost and scattered remnants who (although the object of God's earlier covenants) lived in ignorance of God's renewed labor in His vineyard. Now, in addition to other remnants, there is a new covenant remnant aware of God's renewed labor—a remnant who has been asked to labor alongside the Master of the Vineyard as He sends His final invitation to come to His wedding feast. Christ spoke of this very thing when He taught the Nephites. He foretold that the barren gentiles would eventually produce more children for His Kingdom than the remnants on this land and at Jerusalem. Christ said:

> And then shall that which is written come to pass: Sing, O barren, thou that didst not bear; break forth into singing and cry aloud, thou that didst not travail with child; for more are the children of the desolate than the children of the married wife, saith the Lord. Enlarge the place of thy tent and let them stretch forth the curtains of thy habitations; spare not, lengthen thy cords and strengthen thy stakes, for thou shalt break forth on the right hand and on the left, and thy seed shall inherit the gentiles and make the desolate cities to be inhabited. Fear not, for thou shalt not be ashamed, neither be thou confounded, for thou shalt not be put to shame, for thou shalt forget the shame of thy youth and shalt not remember the reproach of thy widowhood anymore. For thy maker, thy husband, the Lord of Hosts is his name, and thy Redeemer, the Holy One of Israel, the God of the whole earth shall he be called. (3 Nephi 10:2 RE)

We can see a new and different meaning in Christ's Book of Mormon prophecy to the Nephites. Before, Christ's words seemed to foretell that the lost and scattered remnants would build the Lord's house in the New Jerusalem. Now it appears that there are covenant-receiving gentiles who are included. Gentiles who repent and hearken to Christ's words and do not harden their hearts will be brought into the covenant as His people.

Christ mentions three distinct bodies:

- First, those who have accepted the covenant and are numbered among the remnant of Jacob, to whom Christ gave this land for their inheritance.

- Second, the lost descendants of the remnant of Jacob on this land who will repent and return.

- Third, as many from the House of Israel who will repent and return.

These three will build a city that shall be called the New Jerusalem. All three of those will come to know God in gathering and laboring to build the New Jerusalem. Then they will go out to assist all of God's people in their lost and forgotten state, to be awakened to the work of God and gathered as if one body of believers. Then all who have any of the blood of Abraham, who are scattered upon the face of the land, will come to be taught in the New Jerusalem. There the Power of Heaven will come down to be among them. The angels and Enoch (with his ten thousands) will come down; the Ancient of Days, or Adam our first Father, and Christ also will be in the midst of His people.

———————

The foregoing excerpts are taken from

- Denver's conference talk titled "Things to Keep Us Awake at Night," given in St. George, UT on March 19, 2017, including a question and answer session;
- His remarks at "A Day of Faith and Connection" youth conference in UT on June 10, 2017;
- The presentation of "Answer and Covenant," given at the Covenant of Christ Conference in Boise, ID on September 3, 2017;
- A fireside talk titled "The Holy Order," given in Bountiful, UT on October 29, 2017;

- A fireside talk titled "Cursed, Denied Priesthood," given in Sandy, UT on January 7, 2018;
- His remarks given at the Joseph Smith Restoration Conference in Boise, ID on June 24, 2018; and
- Denver's remarks titled "Keep the Covenant: Do the Work," given at the Remembering the Covenants Conference in Layton, UT on August 4, 2018.

58. Nephi, Part 1

QUESTION: In our day, what can we learn from the example of Nephi, son of Lehi, and from the legacy he left us in scripture?

––––––

DENVER: Look, we're enacting ancient events. We're part of a process that began a long time ago and is going on still. You read (what is it, Genesis chapter 49?) the patriarchal blessings of the various patriarchs, you look at the lives of those men in the flesh—we're just reenacting them on a grander scale and with more of us, to be sure, but the patterns are there.

The records of the prophets are not just history. As the Book of Mormon demonstrates very ably, it's not history—it's highly edited, very limited, highly selected. At one point, they estimate less than one percent of their history even gets alluded to—material that has been selected on account of prophetic foreknowledge of our circumstance. And so it constitutes not merely a history, but a prophetic pattern in which they try to get us to see the process that we ought to be reenacting in our lives to do the things that they did that brought them to know the Lord.

Nephi couldn't have been more plain if he had said, "Here's my guidebook. Here's my rule book. Here's my pattern recognition sequence. You go and do likewise." He's trying to get us to get our hands around, as Joseph Smith put it, the fullness of the gospel of Jesus Christ. And the fullness of the gospel of Jesus Christ involves the path to and through the veil into the presence of God, becoming joint heir, becoming a son of God.

Teachings of the Prophet Joseph Smith page 375, he refers to (and I don't have a copy of it with me, but I think I can quote it) "sons of God who exalt themselves to be God even before they were born, and all can cry Abba, Father." Joseph wanted us to take the religion that he restored to the earth rather seriously and to search into and contemplate both the heavens and the darkest abyss.

As Nephi paraphrased Isaiah in the concluding chapter of Nephi's use of Isaiah in his material, he left out a phrase that appears in Isaiah 29, and I believe he did it very wittingly. I believe he did it so that as you look at the material, you'll ask yourself, "Why did he leave that out?" And you'll think about the omission: *And the vision of all is become unto you as the words of a book that is sealed* (Isaiah 29:11). He left out "the vision of all" (see also T&C

Appendix,"A Prophet's Prerogative"). Well, you're talking about Zion here, yesterday and today, and as is usual any time you get to a substantive topic that's worth paying a lot of attention to, the Book of Mormon has something to say. In fact, while it doesn't comment at extraordinary length, the substance of what it has to say on this subject is really quite startling.

I think anyone who is unwilling to entertain a thoroughgoing examination of the life and the ministry of Joseph Smith is demonstrating fear, which is the opposite of love. We don't have details about the life of Moses. We don't have details about the life of Peter. We have an extraordinarily limited vantage point from which to examine either one of them. We don't have much in the way of detail about the life of Nephi. In fact, everything that we have about him is autobiographical. Therefore, to some extent, Nephi is going to tell us a narrative about himself that doesn't give a full and fair and impartial accounting of why it was his brothers continually found themselves not persuaded by the message that Nephi was delivering.

I understand there are those who are hard-hearted, and I understand there are those who resent and envy the younger brother when the younger brother supplants the older brother—particularly when the supplanting takes place very early on in a difficult life's journey, when he returns with the emblems of kingship, with the possession of the sword of Laban, with the brass plates, with all of the indicia that he's the leader. And then during the trek in the wilderness, he actually assumes the role. And by the time they get to the coast now, he is the one (and not his father) to whom the revelation is coming about the construction of the boat. And so the supplanting has been complete by the time they get to the coast. And when Lehi dies in the new world, you've now taken off the one governing, rallying point, and the rebellion is in full swing. But what might have been done in the way of a list of legitimate criticisms of Nephi by Laman and Lemuel, if we were willing to hear their side of the story? We don't know; we don't have that.

Joseph Smith, as they're translating the Book of Mormon, encounters the topic of baptism; and he goes, and he inquires, and John the Baptist appears to him. And it's translating the Book of Mormon that is the trigger for the inquiry. He translates the Jacob chapter 2 material. Now, keep in mind, he began with the record of Lehi, abridged by Mormon, and he went all the way through 116 pages, at which point he entrusted Martin Harris. The 116 pages were lost, and Joseph commenced the translation (from the point that it stopped after the 116 pages) to the end. And when he got to the end, then he was told, "Go back and take the small plates of Nephi that had been included for a wise purpose, and translate them." So he translated the small plates of

Nephi, in which we find from 1 Nephi to the Words of Mormon. Therefore, in translation, you pick up after that period—King Mosiah, King Benjamin, to the end of the Book of Mormon, and then you move to the beginning of 1 Nephi.

When you walk through the lives of all these men whose lives have some import— Even Nephi's brother, Jacob, who was ordained by Nephi, talks about his ordination by his brother and then later confirms, "I got my errand from the Lord" (see Jacob 1:4 RE). There's a difference between the invite that is extended by ordination and the blessing that comes when the authority is conferred, when the power is conferred. And you're seeing that dichotomy, because *Enoch was twenty-five years old when he was ordained under the hand of Adam, and he was sixty-five and Adam blessed him. And he saw the Lord, and he walked with him, and was before his face continually; and he walked with God three hundred and sixty-five years, making him four hundred and thirty years old when he was translated* (T&C 154:15).

We have a tendency, all of us, to take concepts or pictures or ideas and to put them in our heads and then to rely upon those pictures as we go forward learning new things—the object being to fit what we learn that is new into the framework of what we already know, or we are already familiar with. That can be handicapping.

In the 28th chapter of 2 Nephi, Nephi cautioned us about permitting what he calls *the traditions of men* to override what he calls *the whisperings of the spirit.* And he suggests that you run into mistakes, you run into errors—some of them terrible errors—when you permit those traditions or those pictures that you already have inside your head to be the framework from which you reconstruct new information that you learn. It's hard to do so, but when it comes to the gospel of Jesus Christ, you would be best advised to start with a blank slate and to allow it to inform you as if you're hearing it for the first time, because those words in scripture don't necessarily mean what the picture in your head suggests that they mean.

Our Savior was, and is, first and foremost a teacher. *By His knowledge,* Isaiah and Nephi wrote, *[he] shall justify many* (Isaiah 19:2 RE; Mosiah 8:4 RE)—by His knowledge. He possesses things which we do not yet comprehend. He possesses things which He would like us *to* comprehend. How then are we to comprehend the things which only He can teach? By permitting Him to do so, by coming to Him.

1 Nephi 13—there's a series of verses in there that's giving the prophetic foreshadowing, the foretelling of what was going to happen when the gentiles became the inheritors of this land. And beginning at verse 12: *And I looked and [I] beheld a man among the Gentiles, who was separated from the seed of my brethren by...many waters; and I beheld the Spirit of God, that it came down and wrought upon the man; and he went forth upon the many waters, even unto the seed of my brethren, who were in the promised land.*

There's your answer to the question of whether people got the Holy Ghost without the laying on of hands. At some point, I mean, Columbus was inspired by... Well, anyway...

It came to pass that I beheld the Spirit of God, that it wrought upon other Gentiles; and they went forth out of captivity, upon the many waters (vs. 13). So it wasn't just Columbus; it was your own ancestors who were wrought upon by the Holy Ghost to come and occupy this land.

Even though two of my ancestors were children in the Liverpool area who accepted a free afternoon boat ride from a captain who was loading the boat up with children, and then proceeded to sail from Liverpool to the United States—well, to the colonies—where he sold the children off as indentured servants. And one of those was a boy, and another one was a girl who were sold to the same family as indentured servants. And when they worked their way through the indentured servitude and they were free, they married one another. And so I guess the Spirit works directly on some and through captains on others. In any event...

> *And it came to pass that I beheld many multitudes of the Gentiles upon the land of promise; and I beheld the wrath of God, that it was upon the seed of my brethren; and they were scattered before the Gentiles and were smitten. And I beheld the Spirit of the Lord, that it was upon the Gentiles, and they did prosper and obtain the land for their inheritance; and I beheld that they were white, and exceedingly fair and beautiful, like unto my people before they were slain* (vs. 14-15) —

Which tells you that what he's talking about is the ones who were the designated inheritors match a specific description and fit within a certain ethnicity called "gentile."

> *And it came to pass that I, Nephi, beheld that the Gentiles who had gone forth out of captivity did humble themselves before the Lord; and the power of the Lord was with them. And I beheld that their mother*

Gentiles were gathered together upon the waters, and upon the land also, to battle against them. And I beheld that the power of God was with them, and also that the wrath of God was upon all those that were gathered together against them to battle. And I... beheld that the Gentiles that had gone out of captivity were delivered by the power of God out of the hands of all other nations. (vs. 16-19; see also 1 Nephi 3:20 RE)

Well, you'd have to know a lot about our early history to know just how very true that is. Sometime you ought to look into the battle of New York and how Washington managed to escape. And he was the last one to leave that morning. He wanted all of the troops withdrawn before he would leave and enter the boat himself. But for the intervening fog bank, the American Revolution would've ended that day. The hand of God was throughout it. In fact, Washington talked about the hand of Providence ruling throughout.

Then we have Jacob's teaching in 2 Nephi 10. And Jacob—the one that Nephi thought so much of as a teacher that he gave chapters of his own writing over to his younger brother, Jacob— Jacob, teaching in chapter 10 beginning at verse 10, says:

But behold, this land, said God, shall be a land of thine inheritance, and the Gentiles shall be blessed upon the land. And this land shall be a land of liberty unto the Gentiles, and there shall be no kings upon the land, who shall raise up unto the Gentiles. And I will fortify this land against all other nations. And he that fighteth against Zion shall perish, saith God. For he that raiseth up a king against me shall perish, for I, the Lord, the king of heaven, will be their king, and I will be a light unto them forever, that hear my words. (see also 2 Nephi 7:2 RE)

Joseph said, "Knowledge saves a man; and in the world of spirits no man can be exalted but by knowledge" (*TPJS* p. 357). He also said in another talk:

When you climb up a ladder, you must begin at the bottom, and ascend step-by-step, until you arrive at the top; and so it is with the principles of the Gospel— you must begin with the first, and go on until you learn all the principles of exaltation. But it will be a great while after you have passed through the veil before you will have learned them. It's not all to be comprehended in this world; it will be a great work to learn our salvation and exaltation even beyond the grave. (*TPJS*, p. 348)

Now, if you go back and you reread that quote, and you comprehend that it is possible to pass through the veil before you leave here, "it will be a great while after you pass through the veil before you will have learned them. It's not all to be comprehended in this world" — you begin to say, "Ah, I think I understand why, after 40 years of reflection, Nephi commented about how it was his constant meditation to think upon the things which he had seen and heard. And knowledge obtained from heaven is dynamic.

Another place, Joseph said:

> A man is saved no faster than he gets knowledge, for if does not get knowledge, he will be brought into captivity by some evil power in the other world, as evil spirits will have more knowledge, and consequently more power than many men who are on the earth. Hence it needs revelation to assist us, and give us knowledge of the things of God. (*TPJS*, p. 217)

The fact of the matter is that Nephi did not compose what he composed until about 40 years after the event, because it was time and distance and reflection that gave him the ability to put into words the truth of what it was he experienced.

In fact, it's really sort of an interesting study. If you take and you look at what the Lord does in 3 Nephi, He has this agenda that He's been assigned by the Father, and Christ discharges the agenda. And He goes through, and as you read the chapters in 3 Nephi, it's really structured; it's really orderly. And then He announces, "Now I've finished what the Father told me to deliver to you," and He just begins to talk. And as He begins to talk, what unfolds is non-chronological; it's topical, but it's past, present, and future. His thoughts are not like our thoughts; they aren't. They're nonlinear. And sometimes, it's not easy.

We are so situated that we have the inability to do two things at once. No matter who you are, you are only doing one thing at a time. Your entire life you are either focusing on one thing or on something else. And whatever it is upon which you dwell, that's what you've chosen. Hence the saying: *Let virtue garnish thy thoughts unceasingly then shall thy confidence wax strong in the presence of God* (T&C 139:6).

Is the power of godliness related to that? Is the power of godliness related to the presence of God? Well, the Book of Mormon continually declares that to be the case. And anyone that suggests otherwise is flatly contradicting the message of the Book of Mormon. It is all about the ascent back to the presence of God. Testimony after testimony, experience after experience— that's what the Book of Mormon stands for. That is the fullness of the gospel of Jesus Christ. You encounter it almost immediately in the first chapter when Lehi rises up; and you encounter it in Nephi; and you encounter it in Jacob; and you encounter it in Enos and in Alma and in Mosiah. You just continually get the same message.

Let's go to 2 Nephi chapter 30. I want to remind you that it is knowledge which defines the millennial glory of man. Begin at verse 8 of 2 Nephi chapter 30:

> *And it shall come to pass that the Lord God shall commence his work among all nations, kindreds, tongues, and people, to bring about the restoration of his people upon the earth. And with righteousness shall the Lord God judge the poor, and reprove with equity for the meek of the earth. And he shall smite the earth with the rod of his mouth; and with the breath of his lips shall he slay the wicked. For the time speedily cometh that the Lord God shall cause a great division among the people, and the wicked will he destroy; and he will spare his people, yea, even if it so be that he must destroy the wicked by fire. And righteousness shall be the girdle of his loins, and faithfulness the girdle of his reins. And then shall the wolf dwell with the lamb; and the leopard shall lie with the kid, and the calf, and the young lion, and the fatling, together; and a little child shall lead them. And the cow and the bear shall feed; their young ones shall lie down together; and the lion shall eat straw like the ox. And the sucking child shall play on the hole of the asp, and the weaned child shall put forth his hand on the cockatrice's den. They shall not hurt nor destroy in all my holy mountain; for the earth shall be full of the knowledge of the Lord as the waters cover the sea.* (see also 2 Nephi 12:13 RE)

Would you like to stand in that day? Would you like to survive that burning which is to come? Then the way to obtain that—and the means to preserve yourself through that—is to obtain that knowledge which saves.

Why is it possible? Beginning at verse 16:

> *Wherefore, the things of all nations shall be made known; yea, all things shall be made known unto the children of men. There is nothing which is secret save it shall be revealed; there is no work of darkness save it shall be made manifest in the light; and there is nothing which is sealed upon the*

earth save it shall be loosed. Wherefore, all things which have been revealed unto the children of men shall at that day be revealed; and Satan shall have power over the hearts of the children of men no more, for a long time. And now, my beloved brethren, I make an end of my sayings (see also 2 Nephi 12:13 RE)

Why is it possible for such things to be revealed in that day? Why do *they* have such faith? What must *you* do in order to qualify to be among *them*? Does anyone other than you have the ability to prepare you? This is your dispensation. This. What are you going to do with it?

Joseph, writing from Liberty Jail in a passage that belongs somewhere between Section 121 and 123 but never made its way in— I mean, if we're going to take out by fiat the Lectures on Faith, why can't we put this in, at least? Here's where we are:

> *the things of God are of deep import; and time, and experience, and careful and ponderous and solemn thoughts can only find them out. Thy mind, O man! if thou wilt lead a soul unto salvation, must stretch as high as the utmost heavens, and search into and contemplate the darkest abyss, and the broad expanse of eternity— thou must commune with God. How much more dignified and noble are the thoughts of God, than the vain imaginations of the human heart! None but fools will trifle with the souls of men. How vain and trifling have been our spirits, our conferences, our councils, our meetings, our private as well as public conversations—too low, too mean, too vulgar, too condescending for the dignified characters of the called and chosen of God.* (T&C 138:18-19)

That's Joseph's lament. What are *you* doing with *your* time? What are you doing when you are called upon to teach? What are you doing when your teacher abuses yours and everyone else's time with something that is too low, too mean, too vulgar, too condescending for those called of God? The gospel is delicious! And we ought to return to it. The glory of God is intelligence, and we are absolutely unintelligent and dumber, I might add, with our curriculum year-by-year. I don't know how we endure it, unless you, like me, bring a very good book to church with you each week.

When Nephi—2 Nephi 9:14-ish—about how the things that he had seen and heard, he constantly meditated upon that, writing some 40 years after the fact. The revelations that Joseph Smith received, including that one that he received in the sacred grove, was not all to be comprehended in the first pass through.

The things of God are of deep import. Why did God reveal what He revealed when He revealed it? Why did He reveal it in the order in which He revealed it? What was He building upon? Why, in the first revelation, did He go there? Why, in the next, did He go to that point? If you think Joseph's mind wasn't caught up in the things that he had seen and heard (just as yours should be about the things that you have seen and heard), then you need to think again, because "the things of God are of deep import; and time, and [care], and careful and solemn and ponderous thoughts" are the only way in which you, or anyone, can find them out. And that applies especially to you, because you control you. You determine how much light and truth you will receive, and it's predicated upon a law that was ordained before the foundation of the world. Any one of you can obey it. God is no respecter of persons, and you are authorized to exercise faith in Him unto salvation. *You* are authorized to exercise faith in Him, until you know Him. You are authorized to see His face and know that He is—everyone of you.

Chapter 4 of 2 Nephi talks about— This is Nephi now interjecting: *He* [that is, Joseph—verse 2 of chapter 4—He, Joseph of Egypt] *truly prophesied concerning all his seed.* "All his seed" include not just the folks that were included in the tribe of Manasseh and (through others that joined the party) Ephraim—descendants of Joseph in the Book of Mormon—but it includes, as well, other portions of the tribe of Joseph, scattered wherever they were throughout the world, many of whom may be here among us tonight in your bloodlines.

Prophecies, as I've said before, revolve around two and primarily two events only—one being the first coming of the Lord; the other one being the coming of the Lord in judgment at the end of the world. Now there are plenty of prophecies that reckon to other events that are intermediate; however, the primary focus is the first and the second coming of the Lord:

- The vindication of the promise that the Father made in the beginning that He would redeem us all from the grave, and

- The vindication of the promise that at some point the world would come to an end as to its wickedness, and there would be peace again on the earth.

- Everything revolves around those two prophetic events.

The seed that's to be preserved—and the effort that the Lord has made to try and preserve the seed that He needs to have in order to establish a population on the earth at His coming—is a topic about which Zenos prophesied, an allegory that was picked up by Jacob; and Jacob preserves it in his testament —the book of Jacob—in chapter 5.

Nephi wrote the first books in the small plates of Nephi, and in there is his testimony, is his prophecy. What he did was he adopted the words of Isaiah in order to explain what it was that he, Nephi, had seen. But he used Isaiah's words as the means to do that. And Jacob does the same thing.

Jacob says, "I want everyone to come up to the temple. I'm going to deliver to you a prophecy." And when they get there and he delivers his prophecy, he reads them the allegory that's taken from Zenos, which goes on and on about the history of God's chosen people. And when he finishes reading this lengthy chapter from Zenos, he says, "Here's the words of my prophecy, because I told you I was going to give it. Here it is, it's coming: What I just told you is true."

And that's Jacob's testimony. Jacob adopts the words of Zenos in order to bear testimony of the things which he, Jacob, had been taught by the Lord when the Lord spoke to him face-to-face. Jacob didn't invent a new allegory. Jacob didn't invent a new narrative; he didn't invent a new story; and he didn't invent new scriptures. He simply took the words of prophets that went before and he said, "Here they are. The words of my prophecy are: They are true." Nephi had done the same thing. Jacob does the same thing. And so in Nephi, Jacob saw the example which he chose to follow.

> For God, having sworn unto Enoch and unto his seed, with an oath by Himself, that everyone being ordained after this order and calling, should have power, by faith, to break mountains, to divide the seas, to dry up waters, to turn them out of their course, to put at defiance the armies of nations, to divide the earth, to break every band, to stand in the presence of God [now take that impressive list of things, and read it in light of this] to do all things according to His will, according to His command: subdue principalities and powers, and this by the will of the Son of God, [which] was from before the foundation of the world. (Genesis 7:19 RE)

See, such persons holding such power are not freelancing. And in fact, evidence of the possession of this power does not come as a consequence of someone displaying every one of these things, but if they display *any* one of these things— For example: Nephi, when he was bound in the desert and left to die by his brothers, broke every band that bound him, having been strengthened by God. And that same Nephi, bound to the mast when the storm came that threatened the survival of the ship, not only could not break the band, but when they finally got around to relieving him, he said his hands were much swollen, as a consequence of the trauma that he'd suffered. Nephi, who had power given to him by God to break the bands that would've cost him his life, was left subject to the bands because it was not according to the Father's will or the word of the Son when he was bound to the mast. And so, had Nephi called upon that power and not suffered, Nephi would've been offending, and not conforming, to the will of God, and he would have had to suffer some loss.

If you go to Moses chapter 1 beginning at verse 1:

> *The words of God, which he spake unto Moses at a time when Moses was caught up into an exceedingly high mountain, And he saw God face to face, and he talked with him, and the glory of God was upon Moses; therefore Moses could endure his presence. And God spake unto Moses, saying: Behold, I am the Lord God Almighty* [threefold, three titles] *and Endless is my name; for I am without beginning of days or end of years; and is not this endless? And, behold, thou art my son.* (see also Genesis 1:1 RE)

And so he was ordained by man, and he was ordained by heaven.

You can see it in the case of Jacob (we'll look at that, and then we'll stop). Jacob— Go to 2 Nephi 5:26: *And it came to pass that I, Nephi, did consecrate Jacob and Joseph, that they should be priests and teachers over the land of my people* (see also 2 Nephi 4:5 RE). And if you go to Jacob chapter 1, and you look at verse 17 of Jacob chapter 1, you see Jacob saying: *Wherefore I, Jacob, gave unto them these words as I taught them in the temple, having first obtained mine errand from the Lord* (see also Jacob 1:4 RE), because Jacob didn't go out and commence a ministry of teaching, even to his own people over whom he had been consecrated as a priest, until he had first obtained that second ordination.

So what kind of person receives that ordination? I'm going back to the Joseph Smith Translation of Genesis chapter 14. This is the kind of person: *Melchizedek was a man of faith who wrought righteousness* (see also Genesis 7:18 RE). You have to have faith. You have to wrought (or perform) righteousness, which is not the same thing as virtue. Virtue can be offended by righteousness. Virtue would never kill, okay? It just never would. But it is righteous in the case of Nephi, at the command of God, to slay Laban.

Moses saw Zion. If you go to Moses 1:8 it tells you that: *And it came to pass that Moses looked, and beheld the world upon which he was created; and Moses beheld the world and the ends thereof, and all the children of men which are, and which were created; of the same he greatly marveled and wondered* (see also Genesis 1:2 RE).

It's actually— It's amusing to me when I encounter Moses dealing with what he just told you about in one verse. Nephi made a valiant effort to hint around it, and then he defaulted back to the words of Isaiah to try and convey what it was that he saw. Isaiah made an enormous effort to put into epic poetry what it was he saw. And Moses, when he's given that same opportunity, his response in his record is that he *beheld the world and the ends thereof, and all the children of men which are, and which were created.* Well put, Moses. I get why you did it that way. Another one of the prophets: *[I] saw and [I] heard much* (1 Nephi 1:3 RE). I get why they do that, and there's a reason for that.

Turn to 2 Nephi chapter 10 beginning at verse 11:

> *And this land shall be a land of liberty unto the gentiles, and there shall be no kings upon the land who shall raise up unto the gentiles, and I will fortify this land against all other nations. And he that fighteth against Zion shall perish, saith [the Lord], for he that raiseth up a king against me shall perish. For I the Lord, the King of Heaven, will be their king, and I will be a light unto them for ever that hear my words.* (see also 2 Nephi 7:2 RE)

We, if we're going to have Zion, must reject even the idea of a king. I know that embedded in the doctrine of the Restoration is the notion that we're going to become "Kings and Queens, Priests and Priestesses." I want to suggest to you when Christ said, *My kingdom is not of this world* (John 10:7 RE) and He gird himself with a towel and He knelt down and He washed the feet of those that He was ministering to, that implicit within that is the kind of conduct that the real King—and those who are His kings and priests—put on display. If He said, *My kingdom is not of this world,* here He came merely to be a servant. How much more should we gratefully look at the opportunity to kneel and to serve, rather than to say, "I want the chief seats;" rather than to say, "I want to be upheld and sustained and lauded and praised; and if you can, would you mind throwing a big musical celebration my next birthday?" Christ is our only King, and His kingdom is not of this world (see John 18:36). He said: *If I...have washed your feet; ye also ought to wash one another's feet. For I have given you an example...The servant is not greater than his lord....* That is John 13:14,16 (see also John 9:3 RE).

The twin of kingship is priestcraft. In 2 Nephi 26:29— By the way, the denunciation of kingship came from the same prophet who denounces priestcraft; he hit them both! 2 Nephi 26:29: *He commandeth that there shall be no priestcrafts; for, behold, priestcrafts are that men preach and set themselves up for a light unto the world, that they may get gain and praise of the world; but they seek not the welfare of Zion* (see also 2 Nephi 11:17 RE).

Do you lay on hands? Yes, I would follow everything that has been given to this point. We're "adding to"—we're not throwing away. We're trying to preserve, and we're trying to return, and we're trying to renew. We are not trying to tread under our feet anything that is useful, laudable, worthy, desirable, or that came down from the Restoration. It is not God's purpose to abandon the Restoration, but it is His purpose to preserve it.

There are changes presently underway that are going to jar the LDS community more and more in the coming years. If you are not prepared to preserve what has been given, everything will be lost in what will soon happen. It's necessary that there be someone who seeks for some community that tries to preserve, in its purity, what is rapidly becoming, at an accelerating pace, more and more corrupted. It has to be preserved.

Every one of you have some issue that you would say to yourself, "If 'this,'" then I would no longer follow." All of the "if this's" are in the wings. Inexorably, they are coming. It has to be preserved, and it has to be preserved in a manner in which it can remain pure.

In modern revelation, once again the Lord clarified in D&C 10:67-68 exactly what He said to the Nephites. *Behold this is my doctrine: Whosoever repenteth and cometh unto me, the same is my church. Whosoever declareth more or less than this, the same is not of me, but is against me. Therefore he is not of my church* (JSH 10:21 RE).

So, if the LDS Church chooses to do more or chooses to do less (and they are choosing to do both), then His church will consist of those who choose instead to do what He says. It's what He said to the Nephites; it's what He said in modern revelation. It is exactly the same.

Not only does it appear there, as if that were not enough witnesses, Nephi taught it, as well. In 2 Nephi he explained the doctrine of Christ. 2 Nephi chapter 31, beginning at verse 5, he talks about the need of baptism. The Lamb of God being holy, He needed to be baptized; therefore, don't we, likewise, need to be baptized? And then after baptism:

> *If ye shall follow the Son with full purpose of heart, acting no hypocrisy and no deception before God, but with real intent, repenting of your sins, witnessing unto the Father that ye are willing to take upon you the name of Christ by baptism — yea, by following your Lord and Savior down into the water according to his word — behold, then shall ye receive the holy ghost. Yea, then cometh the baptism of fire and of the holy ghost, and then can ye speak with the tongue of angels and shout praises unto the Holy One of Israel. But behold, my beloved brethren, thus came the voice of the Son unto me, saying, After ye have repented of your sins, and witnessed unto the Father that ye are willing to keep my commandments by the baptism of water, and have received the baptism of fire and of the holy ghost, and can speak with a new tongue — yea, even with the tongue of angels — and after this should deny me, it would have been better for you that ye had not known me. And I heard a voice from the Father saying, Yea, the words of my beloved are true and faithful. He that endureth to the end, the same shall be saved. And now my beloved brethren, I know by this that unless a man shall endure to the end in following the example of the Son of the living God, he cannot be saved.* (see also 2 Nephi 13:2-3 RE)

Then He goes on to talk about all the way through *the way; there is none other way nor name given under Heaven...this is the doctrine of Christ, and the only and true doctrine of the Father, and of the Son, and of the holy ghost, which is one God without end. Amen* (ibid).

It was what the doctrine of Christ consisted of at the time of Nephi. It was what the doctrine of Christ consisted of at the the time of the Restoration. It was what the Lord taught in His own voice to the Nephites in 3 Nephi. That is the doctrine.

All the scattered remnants will be brought back again. The original unified family of God will be restored again. The Fathers will have our hearts turned to them, because in that day, once it's permitted to get that far, we will be part of that family again.

Our day is filled with darkness and deception. Our day is the day about which Nephi wrote. If you turn to 2 Nephi chapter 28, beginning halfway through verse 4: *and they shall teach with their learning, and deny the Holy*

Ghost, which giveth utterance (see 2 Nephi 12:1 RE). This is why the ordinance has to be renewed. This is why the pattern has to be followed. This is why the light has to be turned on. Because the Holy Ghost has not assisted with the kind of robust assistance that it can, if you're penitent. God cannot dwell in unclean vessels, and so He remedies that by cleaning the vessel, cleaning it in accordance with the pattern that He's given; thereby making it possible that the Holy Ghost can give to you utterance.

> *And they deny the power of God, the Holy One of Israel. And they say unto the people, Hearken unto us and hear ye our precept, for behold, there is no God today, for the Lord and the Redeemer hath done his work, and he hath given his power unto men* [you can hear that every Sunday if you want but] *...Behold, hearken ye unto my precept. If they shall say there is a miracle wrought by the hand of the Lord, believe it not; for this day he is not a God of miracles; he hath done his work.* (ibid)

See, God doesn't do miracles, but if there is a miracle done then that's the devil. So the only ones responsible for anything miraculous is necessarily the devil, and you're following the devil.

Yea, and there shall be many which shall say, Eat, drink, and be merry, for tomorrow we die. Indulge yourself, you needn't be caring for the poor, you needn't be attentive to their needs, you don't need to minister to those who are in want. Eat, drink, and be merry! It is going to be well with us!

There shall also be many which shall say: Eat, drink, and be merry; nevertheless, fear God—he will justify in committing a little sin; yea, lie a little, take the advantage of one because of his words, dig a pit for thy neighbor; there is no harm in this; and do all these things, for tomorrow we die [And that's, by the way, how you get ahead—digging a pit for your neighbor); *and if it so be that we are guilty, God will beat us with a few stripes, and at last we shall be saved in the kingdom of God* (ibid). "Don't worry— there is no hell. There is no hell, no awful pit. There's just degrees of glory. Don't worry about it."

...which suffering caused myself...the greatest of all, to [shrink]...to bleed at every pore...how sore you know not, how hard to bear you know not, how exquisite you know not (T&C 4:5). There is no hell. There is no need for repentance. There is no need to come to Him to be redeemed, and to seek to remove from us the awful burden of sin.

There shall be many which shall teach after this manner false, and vain, and foolish doctrines, and shall be puffed up in their hearts, and shall seek deep to hide their counsels from the Lord (2 Nephi 12:1 RE).

How might one better "hide their counsels from the Lord" than to conceal all the money that's gathered from the tithes, all the revenues that are paid to the authorities of the Church, and even admonish the paid mission presidents that they must never disclose the revenue benefits that they are receiving? How better to hide your counsel, than to conceal it from the very sheep that are being shorn by the people who sit in positions of authority, claiming they have the right to come to the stake that I lived in, as a member of the Quorum of the Twelve, and to hand my membership record to the stake president and insist that there be disciplinary council held against me? (Now I know, President Hunt, that I told you I wouldn't mention that. But I have no intention from coming back again. Therefore, for us, it's over).

The Church seeks deep to hide their counsels. I participated in that conspiracy when I agreed that I would conceal that Elder Russell M. Nelson of the Quorum of the Twelve came on the day that he called my new stake president and handed to him my membership record and instructed him that I was to be excommunicated. And to his credit, President Hunt took 18 months fighting that decision—because he knew I was an innocent man—before he submitted. I will no longer participate in concealing the counsels that are kept from the public! It's wrong! President Hunt shouldn't do it, Elder Ballard, Elder Russell Nelson should not do it. None of them should do it. They should come clean.

When Elder Neal Maxwell (with whom I had correspondence) died, shortly after the funeral Elder Dallin Oaks showed up at the widow's home and demanded the journals that [Maxwell] had kept—because one of conditions of the agreement that general authorities must sign is that all of their diaries become the property of the Church once they become a general authority. And Elder Oaks went and gathered back the personal diaries of Elder Maxwell, because a great deal of information about what goes on spilled out into the public when the diaries became public.

"Seeking deep to hide their counsels from the Lord, and their works shall be in the dark," is exactly what the authorities of the LDS Church now do! It is exactly a description of the hierarchy of Mormonism. Put your budgets online! Disclose your revenue! Show us what you do with the poor! Don't hide— We don't even know what revenue is!

...seek deep to hide their counsels from the Lord; and their works shall be in the dark [indeed]. *And the blood of the saints shall cry from the ground against them. Yea, they have all gone out of the way; they have become corrupted. Because of pride, and because of false teachers, and false doctrine, their churches have become corrupted, and their churches are lifted up; because of pride they are puffed up. They rob the poor because of their fine sanctuaries; they rob the poor because of their fine clothing; and they persecute the meek and the poor in heart, because in their pride they are puffed up. They wear stiff necks and high heads; yea, and because of pride, and wickedness, and abominations, and whoredoms, they have all gone astray save it be a few, who are the humble followers of Christ; nevertheless, they are led, that in many instances they do err because they are taught by the precepts of men.* (2 Nephi 12:1-2 RE)

The dedication of the first book I wrote, *The Second Comforter, Conversing with the Lord Through the Veil*, was dedicated to "the few who are the humble followers of Christ," and it cited this verse. Some people say, "Well, he was, you know, enlightened at one point, and then he fell victim to a dark and evil spirit, and now he's an apostate!" I'm closer to the Lord at this moment than I've been at any time when I was a member of the Church. I know His will more today, and I understand it better than I have ever understood it before. It is not a different spirit than the one that brought me into the Church, and it is not a different spirit than the one that animated *The Second Comforter, Conversing with the Lord Through the Veil*. At the time I wrote that, I was keenly aware of the fact that from among *us*, there were only a few who were the humble followers of Christ. And I understood that we were, nevertheless, led that in many instances we err.

Working within the system, I did everything I could to preserve the doctrine, to preserve the truth, to testify of Christ, to teach the precepts, to remember the covenant. I would still do that today if I were left alone by them.

Clearly, those of you who think I am a rebel don't get it. God knew exactly what He was doing. I would have taken a bullet for Spencer Kimball. I was among the most devoted of Latter-day Saints. I viewed the Church as a source that had rescued me from a life that was headed into something terrible. I had friends I grew up with who became alcoholics, drug abusers, whose lives were in tattered ruins. One of my good friends in elementary, junior high, and high school died—stopped his heart with cocaine abuse when he was 26.

The LDS Church introduced me a to a form of cleanliness in living that I have nothing but high regard for. And if every one of you choose to remain active in the LDS Church while you do these other things, you won't hear me complaining or criticizing. You'll hear me praising. It's a community trying to do good. But "they are led, that in many instances *they do err*," and you should not go partake of that. Accept whatever is good, and hold onto whatever is good, but continually seek for something higher and better.

These are the kinds of precepts: "Hearken to our precept;" "hear my precept;" "hear my precept." This is where we get into all of the mischief—the precepts, if they're not true, are not worth having. And it is the doctrine, above all, that saves.

The foregoing excerpts are taken from:

- Denver's talk titled "Christ's Discourse on the Road to Emmaus," given in Fairview UT on April 14, 2007;
- His talk given at the "Zion Symposium" in Provo, UT on February 23, 2008;
- His talk titled "The Mission of Elijah Reconsidered," given in Spanish Fork, UT on October 14, 2011;
- A fireside talk on "The Temple," given in Ogden, UT on October 28, 2012;
- A fireside talk titled "Constitutional Apostasy," given in Highland, UT on June 7, 2013;
- Denver's *40 Years in Mormonism Series*, Talk #1 titled "Be of Good Cheer," given in Boise, ID on September 10, 2013;
- Denver's *40 Years in Mormonism Series*, Talk #3 titled "Repentance," given in Logan, UT on September 29, 2013;
- Denver's *40 Years in Mormonism Series*, Talk #4 titled "Covenants," given in Centerville, UT on October 6, 2013;
- Denver's *40 Years in Mormonism Series*, Talk #5 titled "Priesthood," given in Orem, UT on November 2, 2013;
- Denver's *40 Years in Mormonism Series*, Talk #6 titled "Zion," given in Grand Junction, CO on April 12, 2014; and
- Denver's *40 Years in Mormonism Series*, Talk #10 titled "Preserving the Restoration," given in Mesa, AZ on September 9, 2014.

59. Nephi, Part 2

QUESTION: In our day, what can we learn from the example of Nephi, son of Lehi, and from the legacy he left us in scripture?

———

DENVER: It's not appropriate that someone should collect money from the flock nor lord it over the flock. Priestcraft is one of those toxic failures of the last-day Gentiles that we have to guard against it appearing among us as well. Nephi wrote:

> For...the time speedily shall come that all churches which are built up to get gain, and all those who are built up to get power over the flesh, and those [that] are built up to become popular in the eyes of the world, and those who seek the lusts of the flesh and [of] the things of the world, and to do all manner of iniquity; yea, in fine, all those who belong to the kingdom of the devil are they who need fear, and tremble, and quake; they are those who must be brought low in the dust; they are those who must be consumed as stubble; and this is according to the words of the prophet. (1 Nephi 22:15; see also 1 Nephi 7:5 RE)

Nephi supplies us with a definition of priestcraft: *He commandeth that there shall be no priestcraft, for behold, priestcrafts* **are** *that men preach and set themselves up for a light unto the world that they may get gain and praise of the world, but they seek not the welfare of Zion* (2 Nephi 26:29, emphasis added; see also 2 Nephi 11:17 RE).

The difference between persuasion and contention: Persuasion largely does not happen because you overcome the resistance with argument and contention. Persuasion comes by opening up an idea and letting it enter into the heart of the man or the woman, and then letting God take over and get the growth inside them. But *contention is not of me, but is of the Devil, who is the father of contention; ...stirreth up the hearts of men to contend with anger, one with another. Behold, this is not my doctrine, to stir up the hearts of men with anger, one against another, but this is my doctrine, that such things should be done away* (3 Nephi 11:29-30; see also 3 Nephi 5:8 RE).

So He's saying, "Don't contend, don't make people mad, don't confront them; take a step back from that, and I'll tell you what my doctrine is." And then: *This is my doctrine...I bear record of the Father, and the Father beareth record of me, and the Holy Ghost beareth record of the Father and me* (3 Nephi

11:32; see also 3 Nephi 5:9 RE). Every bit of that is internal to the proselyte. Every bit of that.

Preach, teach, exhort, expound, contend, bitch them into conversion—you've ignored what His doctrine is. It's internal to them. It goes on with Him and them. We facilitate, but He's the one that ultimately becomes the object of their worship, the object of their adoration. It's like God lights a candle inside of you. You can hold the candle up, and you can give people light, but if they don't get their own candle, get their own flame, they're still dead. They aren't alive.

There's this description that's given in 1 Nephi 14, beginning at verse 12:

> And it came to pass that I beheld the church of the Lamb of God, and its numbers were few, because of the wickedness and abominations of the whore who sat upon many waters; nevertheless, I beheld that the church of the Lamb, who were the saints of God, were also upon all the face of the earth; and their dominions upon the face of the earth were small, because of the wickedness of the great whore whom I saw. (See also 1 Nephi 3:28 RE)

I mean, we're not going to get 15 million people. But it's not necessary that we get 15 million people; it's only necessary that the invitation be extended. If the invitation is extended and if the hearts of people respond, there is a resilience, there is a power; there is something inside of them that cannot be broken. And we're not looking for anything other than the few.

The scriptures do not foretell any great numbers will repent. Christ said: *I will take you one of a city and two of a family and I will bring you to Zion* (Jeremiah 3:14; see also Jeremiah 2:3 RE)—too few, perhaps, to impress the world, but the Lord does not view things as do men. The Lord describes those who respond to His invitation as His elect. He explained: *[Mine] elect hear my voice and harden not their hearts* (D&C 29:7; see also T&C 9:3).

Nephi foresaw how few believers there would be in the last days.

> He *beheld the church of the Lamb of God, and its numbers were few, because of the wickedness and abominations of the whore who sat upon many waters; nevertheless, I beheld that the church of the Lamb, who were the saints of God, were also upon all the face of the earth; and their dominions upon the face of the earth were small, because of the*

wickedness of the great whore whom I saw. (1 Nephi 14:12; see also 1 Nephi 3:28 RE)

The Lord requires us to invite the world to repent but not to expect large numbers to do so. Numbers matter to man, but the hearts of men matter to the Lord. It is the quality of conversion, not the quantity. He always spoke of having few sheep. Of the likely billions living at the time of Enoch, only some few thousand were saved—and only eight by Noah. The end times will be like those days.

Now, I need to address the subject of what is appropriate to be explained and what is appropriate not to be explained. Why does the Book of Mormon draw lines and say, "At this point in the record it's not permitted for me to cover this. I was about to write this, but I'm forbidden from doing so." Or Nephi saying, "I was about to give you the rest of this story, but the Lord said, 'You can't do that.'"

There is a very good reason why information gets withheld (there's actually more than one, but there's one that ought to be front and center): the more information that becomes available that ought to be held in sacred solitude, the more you equip the pretenders and the deceivers to improve their false act —the more equipment you hand to them with which to develop an illusion and a mirage that will deceive and take people from the Lord. But more importantly, when you get to the end of the actual process of what the Lord was teaching to the Nephites, there is power in the government of God that when it got hijacked in the beginning, by the time you get down to the time of Noah, the earth was so corrupted, Lucifer (or Satan) has this great chain on the earth. He's chained the earth, and he's looking up at heaven—this is in the Book of Moses in the Pearl of Great Price (see Moses 7:26; see also Genesis 4:15 RE)—He's got the whole earth wrapped in a chain, and he's looking up at heaven, and he's laughing. How did he manage to get the whole earth bound down into a great chain? He did so by imitating the government of Adam. He did so by binding together, in a false way, things that God would put together in a Godly way.

Right now the struggle—*the* struggle on this earth—is over the agency of man. I don't care if you're looking at economic difficulties, governmental difficulties, business, religion, society, entertainment— It's all about destroying the agency of man. In order to prevent Zion, the adversary knows he has now but a little time. The only way to make sure that it doesn't spill out and accomplish the objective that God wants it to accomplish is by curtailing the ability of people to choose. Take away the right to say, the right to speak, the right to preach—take away and categorize, or if you can, criminalize. And if you can't do that, then simply murder in order to prevent the agency of man. Because men must, women must, come willingly to the Lord, have to voluntarily accept the invitation from Him. Compulsory means cannot be used. Everywhere you look right now, the struggle is over the agency of men. And some things are absolutely essential and needful, more than the mysteries of God. Right now what is most important is to preach the Doctrine of Christ and baptize people so that we at least have someone living at the Lord's return.

Nephi was told recovering the scriptures for his people was essential, otherwise they would dwindle and perish in unbelief. When the record that Nephi was able to obtain on the brass plates was studied, it included an account of the creation—Adam and Eve—and God's dealings with mankind down to the time of Lehi, including their genealogy and prophecies of Joseph of Egypt.

When Christ visited with the Nephites, He asked them to bring to Him their scriptural record so that He could review it. He reviewed the things that they brought that constituted their scriptures, and He commanded them to fix omissions that had been made in the record. Christ then dictated two chapters of additional scripture to be added to the Nephite record. Only then did He expound all things to them using the scriptures.

When it comes to scripture, corruption happens, and each new dispensation is responsible for fixing the canon of scripture to reclaim truths, to correct errors, and to adopt guiding principles applicable to their day. Again, remember the statement Joseph Smith made at the conference: "God had often sealed up the heavens because of covetousness in the church. Said the Lord would cut his work short in righteousness and except the church receive the fullness of the scriptures that they would yet fall" (*Joseph Smith Papers*, "Documents," Vol. 2: July 1831-January 1833, p. 85).

Sustaining is planned to happen at the next conference, after a chance has passed for review of the material. This is necessary for the Gentiles to claim they have accepted a covenant and the law.

> For behold, I say unto you, [that] as many of the Gentiles as will repent are the covenant people of the Lord, and as many of the Jews as will not repent shall be cast off. For the Lord covenanteth with none [such] save it be with them that repent and believe in his Son, who is the Holy One of Israel....For the time speedily cometh that the Lord...shall cause a great

division among the people, and the wicked will he destroy. And he will spare his people, yea, even if it so be that he must destroy the wicked by fire.

That's in 2 Nephi 30 (see also 2 Nephi 12:11,13 RE).

Zion will include people who are willing to receive revelations from God and obey commandments. God does this to bless His people.

> *Blessed are they whose feet stand upon the land of Zion, who have obeyed my gospel, for they shall receive for their reward the good things of the earth, and it shall bring forth in its strength. And they shall also be crowned with blessings from above, yea, and with commandments not a few, and with revelations in their time, they that are faithful and diligent before me.*

That's from Doctrine and Covenants Section 59 (see also T&C 46:1).

If you want Zion, you'd necessarily must want commandments. And you must necessarily be willing to receive revelations. And you must set aside your covetousness and receive the fullness of the scriptures if you plan to not fall. Remember that there are more scriptures that are coming. 2 Nephi 29:11-13 tell us that there are records that are out there that have been kept by yet other parts of the ten tribes that are yet to be gathered in. The Book of Mormon itself has significant omissions that are intended to come forth at some future date. But the record that has been given is given to test and to try the people to see if they will accept it.

Mormonism announced in its founding book of scripture that it is an incomplete, markedly unfinished religion, searching for more truth to achieve its destiny. The completion is to be accomplished primarily by two means: restoring lost scripture and continuing revelation. But even the concept of "continuing revelation" has been institutionally curtailed. The only institutionally authorized source for revelation is a single leader.

Of all faiths, Mormonism has the greatest canonical incentive to search for and embrace truth known to others. The keystone of Mormonism is the Book of Mormon. That book alerts its readers that there are many others from vastly different places with vastly different scriptures who are, nonetheless, Christ's sheep. Book of Mormon readers are expected to search for, welcome, and learn from them. In contrast, institutional Mormonism of all stripes confine trustworthy new religious ideas to their authorized leaders.

Early in the text we learn that our faith, like our scriptures, is unfinished and to anticipate a flood of additional sacred texts to help remove our ignorance. The portion of the Book of Mormon translated by Joseph Smith is carefully censored, with its greatest content withheld.

2 Nephi 29:11-12 states: *For I command all men, both in the east and in the west, and in the north, and in the south, and in the islands of the sea, that they shall write the words which I speak [to] them...* (see also 2 Nephi 12:10 RE). Obviously, the Gods of Mormonism view Their role as all-inclusive. The entire world and all mankind belong to Them. Their global audience has received and recorded sacred words directly from the Gods' *one* mouth. We have no way to define the extent to which that has happened. Nor do we have any concept of the number of sacred records that exist somewhere among unknown others, nor any idea what truths they were given that we lack.

Mormonism cannot, or at least should not, consider itself the exclusive possessor of *the* sacred canon or that there is only one canon containing God's teachings—the Gods' teachings. There are words from heaven spread throughout our world by deliberate planting of the Gods.

Continuing: *For out of the books which shall be written I will judge the world, every man according to their works, according to that which is written* (2 Nephi 29:11; see also 2 Nephi 12:10 RE). These books hold terrible importance for Mormons because we are going to be judged by the Gods based on a comparison between our "works" and "that which is written." With such a warning, we Mormons ought to be humble about our claims to know more than other faiths. We should be modest in thinking we are especially graced by the Gods' words and should be anxious to scour the globe to discover the sacred texts of other cultures. In humility, we should invite *them* to share the truths they value most with *us* because we have shown that we will respect what they regard as sacred.

To clarify this further, the record continues: *For behold, I shall speak unto the Jews and they shall write it; and I shall also speak unto the Nephites and they shall write it; and I shall also speak unto the other tribes of the house of Israel, which I have led away, and they shall write it* (2 Nephi 29:12; see also 2 Nephi 12:10 RE). So far, this describes a welcome Judeo-Christian boundary because the ancient Israelites are the backbone of God's dealings with mankind. The lost ten tribes continue to compose scripture, and their records will, in time, be recovered.

This passage continues by including yet others who are disconnected from any disclosed connection to Israel: *And I shall also speak unto all nations of the earth and they shall write it* (2 Nephi 29:12; see also 2 Nephi 12:10 RE). Who? When? And what was said?

The Book of Mormon foretold how the Gentiles would react to new scripture:

> *Many of the Gentiles shall say: A Bible! A Bible! We have got a Bible, and there cannot be any more Bible....Thou fool, that shall say: A Bible, we have got a Bible, and we need no more Bible....Because that I have spoken one word ye need not suppose that I cannot speak another; for my work is not yet finished; neither shall it be until the end of man, neither from that time henceforth and forever. Wherefore, because...ye have a Bible ye need not suppose that it contains all my words; neither need ye suppose that I have not caused more to be written.* (2 Nephi 29:3,6,10; see also 2 Nephi 12:8-10 RE)

The Book of Mormon gives an extended description of Mary, the Mother of God. In the original translation text, the words "Mother of God" were used, but that was changed by Joseph Smith in 1837 to "Mother of the Son of God." Here is how it reads following that change:

> *And it came to pass that I looked and beheld the great city of Jerusalem, and also other cities. And I beheld the city of Nazareth; and in the city of Nazareth I beheld a virgin, and she was exceedingly fair and white. And it came to pass that I saw the heavens open; and an angel came down and stood before me; and he said unto me: Nephi, what beholdest thou? And I said unto him: A virgin, most beautiful and fair above all other virgins. And he said unto me: Knowest thou the condescension of God? And I said unto him: I know that he loveth his children; nevertheless, I do not know the meaning of all things. And he said unto me: Behold, the virgin whom thou seest is the Mother of the Son of God, after the manner of the flesh. And it came to pass that I beheld that she was carried away in the Spirit; and after she had been carried away in the Spirit for [a] space of a time the angel spake unto me, saying: Look! And I looked and beheld the virgin again, bearing a child in her arms. And the angel said unto me: Behold the Lamb of God, yea, even the Son of the Eternal Father! Knowest thou the meaning of the tree which thy father saw? And I answered him, saying: Yea, it is the love of God, which sheddeth itself abroad in the hearts of the children of men; wherefore, it is the most*

desirable above all things. And he spake unto me, saying: Yea, and the
most joyous to the soul. (1 Nephi 11:13-23; see also

1 Nephi 3:8-9 RE)

Most who read this passage interpret the condescension reference solely as
Christ's. They view it as Christ alone who descended by being born of Mary
here in mortality. However, when leading up to the angel's question—
Knowest thou the condescension of God?—the text focuses exclusively on Mary.
When the angel clarified the "condescension," he again focused, primarily, on
Mary and, secondarily, on Her Son. The angel explained:

> *Behold, the virgin whom thou seest is the **Mother of the Son of God,***
> *after the manner of the flesh. And it came to pass that I beheld that **she***
> *was carried away in the Spirit; and after **she** had been carried away in*
> *the Spirit for the space of a time the angel spake unto me, saying: Look!*
> *And I looked and **beheld the virgin** again, bearing a child **in her***
> ***arms**. And the angel said unto me: Behold the Lamb of God.* (1 Nephi
> 11:18-21, emphasis added; see also 1 Nephi 3:8-9 RE)

Who would you reasonably expect to be the woman chosen before the world
was organized to become the mortal Mother of the Lord? Who would you
expect Heavenly Father would want to bear His child, if not His Spouse?
Together, God the Father and Mary can be acknowledged as the Parents of
Christ. The scriptures shift the focus of the "condescension" from Christ to
His Mother and then back to Her Son—the seed of the woman.

Lectures on Faith describe Christ as the prototype of the saved man (see
Lectures on Faith 7:9). Lecture seven focuses attention on Christ as the Savior
and Redeemer. But the Lecture extends the requirement met by Jesus Christ
to also apply for every saved man. In other words, for any man to be saved,
they must attain to the resurrection, like Christ. Shifting attention for a
moment from Jesus Christ as our Redeemer and Savior to His Mother, we
could acknowledge Her as the prototype of the saved woman. In other words,
we could consider what She did a divine pattern to be followed by women.

When a female deity has been worshiped in past cultures, more often than
not the result is a gradual degeneration into fertility cults and sexual excesses.
Ritual prostitution was often practiced by ancients who believed in a Divine
Mother. Even Israel fell into sexual deviancy as part of their worship of a
female god.

At a pivotal time for ancient Israel, Jeremiah condemned worship of *the queen of heaven* (Jeremiah 44:17; see also Jeremiah 16:15 RE). Because some scholars want a divine female to be authentic, Jeremiah's condemnation is considered problematic. His words can be interpreted to denounce altogether a female god. In part because of this, in current scholarship Jeremiah has become a controversial figure—even his existence is now questioned.

Margaret Barker recently wrote the following:

> This assumes that a person of that name existed, since scholars cannot begin to agree if Jeremiah even existed, nor on the process by which the present texts of Jeremiah were formed. Many have resorted to other ways of dealing with the text. A recent volume on the latest trends in Jeremiah studies was introduced thus: "Jeremiah is an intractable riddle. ...Taken together, the essays in this volume press for an end to 'innocent' readings of Jeremiah. ...And the turn to Jeremiah as a social semiotic discourse presses for an end to 'innocent biblical theology readings that have companioned historical-critical orthodoxy in one fashion or another.' No help there in our quest for reconstructing what happened in the time of Josiah!" (Qtd. in Barker, Margaret. *The Mother of the Lord.* Vol. 1: The Lady in the Temple. London, Bloomsbury Publishing, 2012. Quoting A.R.P. Diamond, K.M. O'Connor and L. Stulman, editors. *Troubling Jeremiah.* Introduction, pp. 15,32. Sheffield, Sheffield Academic Press, 2001)

But **we** know Jeremiah was real, and he was a prophet, because Nephi mentions him in his description of what had been preserved on the brass plates of Laban. The description includes the following:

> And also a record of the Jews from the beginning, even down to the commencement of the reign of Zedekiah, king of Judah. And also the prophecies of the holy prophets, from the beginning, even down to the commencement of the reign of Zedekiah; and also many prophecies which have been spoken by the mouth of Jeremiah. (1 Nephi 5:12-13; see also 1 Nephi 1:22 RE)

The Book of Mormon confirms Jeremiah's existence and status as a prophet. We can accept him today, even if scholars doubt. Revelation remains more reliable than mere scholarship and opinion.

Joseph Smith, in retelling the story when the angel (correctly identified as Nephi by Joseph; incorrectly identified by everyone else as Moroni)—and by the way, before the three witnesses to the Book of Mormon saw the plates shown them by the angel (and they never identified the name of that angel—they referred to him as "an angel"; so the three witnesses never weigh in on the identity), David Whitmer's mother encountered the angel, and she identifies him with the same name that Joseph Smith identifies him with—Nephi.

The angel who appeared to Joseph in September 1823 said:

> *He called me by name, and said unto me that he was a messenger sent from the presence of God to me and that his name was Nephi, that God had a work for me to do, and that my name should be had for good and evil among all nations, kindreds, and tongues, or that it should be both good and evil spoken of among all people.* (Joseph Smith History 3:3 RE)

In the Book of Mormon, there's an early visionary encounter before they migrate very far from Jerusalem in which Nephi is shown the whole sweep of history, and he begins to record the account of what it was he saw. And he's interrupted and told, You can't write a record of what I'm going to show you hereafter because this record is going to be entrusted to another person who is going to write it; his name is John—and the account that John would record the Book of Mormon doesn't recite, but we can all identify it as the Book of Revelation. And so Nephi is told, Don't write about this visionary material; someone else is going to do that. So Nephi is told he cannot write that; a fuller account is going to be given by John. But Nephi is also told that this same kind of material has been shown to others.

Nephi, later—in the second book that he composes—by that time 40 years has passed from the time of the visionary encounter near Jerusalem. He's now on another continent, a new world, a promised land given to them, and he's had 40 years of reflection on what he saw and what he heard. And from that 40 years of reflection, he realizes that he can bear testimony of what he saw (without infringing upon the right of John to write the fuller account) simply by quoting Isaiah, who wrote about much of the same material. And so Nephi adopts as his text, in large measure, the text that came from Isaiah as it appeared on the brass plates—slightly different than the version that we have in our Bibles that descend from the Masoretic text—but he preserves as his testimony words that were composed by Isaiah, in the form that he had them, as his testimony.

Then as his entire account is winding down at the end of the second book that Nephi composed, he begins (at about—in the standard LDS published version, its chapter 27)—he begins to change from quoting the Isaiah text to paraphrasing the Isaiah text in order to adapt it to a very specific prophetic foretelling of the coming forth of the Book of Mormon in the last days—in order to make the Isaiah text fit exactly what would be happening with the Book of Mormon coming forth. Then he gives his interpretive key from that point, explaining exactly why it was that he put those Isaiah materials in—in order to have people understand that it is his testimony of what he knows and what he was shown and to convert the language of Isaiah into the prophecy of Nephi to convey Nephi's message.

There's a bunch of scholarly effort to talk about the content of the Book of Mormon, but the Book of Mormon itself explains how the translation process was done. This is in 2 Nephi 27. Nephi has used the Isaiah material to testify about Nephi's experience. He does not have a Jewish intent, an Isaiah intent, in using Isaiah's words. Nephi has been prohibited from writing about the vision that he has had, but the angel tells him others have seen this. And so Nephi, intending to express his own testimony of what God has shown him, uses Isaiah's words to tell you Nephi's visionary experience. When he gets to chapter 27 of 2 Nephi, he begins to transition. He ceases to be directly quoting Isaiah, and he begins to paraphrase Isaiah in a transitional chapter 27 before he then gives you an explanation for why he said all of the Isaiah materials that went on before. And chapter 27 begins to be the transition from Isaiah quotes, Isaiah paraphrase, Isaiah meaning in the words of Nephi, in the experience of Nephi.

So in 27 we get to the Isaiah material where he talks about the words of a book that's going to be delivered to someone who's learned who says he can't read a sealed book. And then he's going to go from there when the learned won't do it—and God tells you how the Book of Mormon was translated: *I am able to do mine own work; wherefore, thou shalt read the words which I shall give unto thee...I will show unto the children of men that I am able to do mine own work* (2 Nephi 27:20, emphasis added; see also 2 Nephi 11:20 RE).

The translation of the Book of Mormon was not done by Joseph Smith; it was done *through* Joseph Smith. The translator of the text of the Book of Mormon was God. God told Joseph what was in the text of the Book of Mormon. You want to know who translated it? God.

Last night as I was listening to Jeff and others who spoke, one of the things that struck me is that almost all revelation—going back to the days of Adam and coming right down to today—come as a consequence of understanding scripture. That was true even of Enoch, because Enoch had a record that had been handed down from Adam. And in the case of Abraham, the records belonging to the Fathers fell into his hands, and he studied them to gain the understanding that he had. Micah quotes Isaiah. Isaiah quotes Zenos and Zenock. Jacob quotes the allegory of Zenos. Nephi quotes Isaiah. All of them study scripture in order to get an understanding. And revelation is largely based upon expanding your understanding of scripture.

The Book of Mormon is really the keystone of the religion but also the keystone to revelation itself. It was intended to open our eyes to things that we couldn't see before. The Book of Mormon is really a giant Urim and Thummim intended for our benefit.

I was also struck by something that I went and found this morning. This is a passage in which Nephi is describing the saints at the very end, at the end of time just before the scene wraps up:

> And it came to pass that I beheld the church of the Lamb of God, and its numbers were few because of the wickedness and abominations of the whore who sat upon many waters. Nevertheless, I beheld that the church of the Lamb, who were the saints of God, were also upon all the face of the earth; and their dominions upon the face of the earth were small because of the wickedness of the great whore whom I saw. And it came to pass that I beheld that the great mother of abominations did gather together in multitudes upon the face of all the earth, among all the nations of the gentiles, to fight against the Lamb of God. And it came to pass that I, Nephi, beheld the power of the Lamb of God, that it descended upon the saints of the church of the Lamb and upon the covenant people of the Lord, who were scattered upon all the face of the earth. And they were armed with righteousness and with the power of God in great glory. And it came to pass that I beheld that the wrath of God was poured out upon that great and abominable church, insomuch that there were wars and rumors of wars among all the nations and kindreds of the earth. And as there began to be wars and rumors of wars among all the nations which belonged to the mother of abominations, the angel spake unto me, saying, Behold, the wrath of God is upon the mother of harlots, and behold, thou seest all these things. (1 Nephi 14:12-16; see also 1 Nephi 3:28-29 RE)

These words don't say that the coming conflict is against the covenant people of God or the Church of the Lamb. Nor does it say that the wrath of God consists of God picking a fight with the wicked. In the case of the wrath of God, people are stirred to anger against each other. They decide— The wicked destroy the wicked because the wicked decide that they cannot put up with peaceful coexistence anymore. Their hearts are so angry with one another that they manage to inflict violence and death and destruction upon one another.

Like the judgment that Mormon describes in Mormon 9 of the old set, God is a bystander. The wrath of God is manifest by the rejection of God and the violence that people turn upon one another. And the power of God and the glory of God—meaning the peace of God and the ability to live with one another in harmony without this raging conflict—that power is manifest among the people of God, the church of God, and the covenant people that belong to God.

So if you can maintain peaceful coexistence with one another as you worship God in the coming days, the power and glory of God will descend and be with you because you manage to extract yourself from the coming conflict, rage, hatred, polarization. And if you don't think those days are not commencing, then, well, you're not watching the news. It's just an ongoing political battle escalating continually.

Well, the Book of Mormon—this is the "Book of Mormon Covenant Conference"—the Book of Mormon tells you what it's for.

Oh, one last thought about the Church of the Lamb of God. At the time that these words were being written by Nephi—and he had seen the vision, and he's talking about what he saw—at the time that he's writing that prophecy, the earliest stages of the Nephite civilization had just begun. Nephi is still living—he has a wife; he has some children; he has brothers. The total group that are involved is not much larger than the group that we have right here today. He's looking down through history prophetically, and he's saying the saints—the covenant people of God, the people that the Lamb of God's church—that group is few. Now if it was 16 million people scattered globally, in the reality of Nephi's context, he would not describe them as few. He's not making a comparative analysis; he's simply describing what he saw. He said they're all around the world, but there's only very few of them. Okay?

If you go to the fellowship locator, and you look at what you see among those that have identified themselves with the last-days covenant, they're all over the world, but there's really very few of them.

The foregoing excerpts are taken from:

- His talk titled "Zion Will Come," given near Moab, UT on April 10, 2016;
- Denver's comments during an assembly on "Missionary Work" in Eden, UT on July 2, 2016;
- His conference talk titled "The Doctrine of Christ," given in Boise, ID on September 11, 2016;
- Denver's conference talk titled "Things to Keep Us Awake at Night," given in St. George, UT on March 19, 2017;
- His talk titled "Other Sheep Indeed," given at the Sunstone Symposium in Salt Lake City, UT on July 29, 2017;
- Denver's *Christian Reformation Lecture Series*, Talk #2, given in Dallas, TX on October 19, 2017;
- Denver's conference talk titled "Our Divine Parents," given in Gilbert, AZ on March 25, 2018;
- His remarks given at the Joseph Smith Restoration Conference in Boise, ID on June 24, 2018;
- The presentation of Denver's paper titled "The Restoration's Shattered Promises and Great Hope," given at the Sunstone Symposium in Salt Lake City, UT on July 28, 2018;
- Denver's *Christian Reformation Lecture Series*, Talk #6, given in Sandy, Utah on September 8, 2018;
- Denver's remarks titled "Remember the New Covenant," given at Graceland University in Lamoni, IA on November 10, 2011; and
- Denver's remarks titled "Book of Mormon as Covenant," given at the Book of Mormon Covenant Conference in Columbia, SC on January 13, 2019.

60. Third Root

In this episode, Denver teaches us about the three roots of scripture and how these efforts to recover lost information compare with the Book of Remembrance that contained the gospel, as originally revealed to Adam.

————

DENVER: At the beginning, in the first generations, there was a book of remembrance that was kept contemporaneous with Adam. Enoch was one of those who helped preserve the records from the early days, but a book of remembrance began; and so, the first scripture that ever existed began at the time when Adam was still living. That record of the first fathers got preserved all the way down to the time of Abraham because Abraham writes that the records of the fathers at the beginning—the first fathers, even Adam—all that came down into his possession. I could tell you exactly how that came to pass, but that's of no moment.

He inherited the records, and he was able to look at the records and learn about things that were around in the beginning, including the religion as it had been preached in the days of Adam. And Abraham says *Therefore, a knowledge of the beginning...and...the stars...*(Abraham 2:4 RE)—those things came into his possession. So part of the religion that went back to the beginning was something that tells you about the organization of the heavens and the signs that are put up there and things that are going on. After the days of Abraham, the records of the fathers disappear from the scene, and we don't have any mention of them—although it's probably safe to assume that Isaac and Jacob had access to that same record.

By the way, it's never "the God of Abraham, Isaac, and Jacob"—it's *the God of Abraham, and the God of Isaac, and the God of Jacob* (see Exodus 2:3,6 RE; Matthew 10:22 RE; and 1 Nephi 2:1 RE). There's a reason why it is stated *the God of Abraham, and the God of Isaac, and the God of Jacob*, because each one of them, in turn, separately held a covenant with God, and therefore, He was their God; they were His son, in effect—certainly a member of His family. And so the way the scriptures refer to it is to acknowledge the covenantal existence, and from that I think it's probably safe to conclude that Abraham passed the records down to Isaac, who passed the records down to Jacob.

So reading between the lines of the Old Testament (because the record doesn't make it clear), we can assume that the garment that was given to Adam in the beginning was handed down through each of those, just like the records were handed down through each of those; and it was that garment that came into the possession of Joseph that the jealous brothers took and destroyed—well, damaged; a remnant of it remained, all of which proved to be an allegory to what history would show about that family.

We don't know if, at the time of destroying the relic of the garment, they destroyed the relic of the records of the fathers, because the record is silent about that. But it's pretty clear that if they couldn't *share* in the prize, if they couldn't *share* in the artifact, if they couldn't share (and from their perspective, this is probably the correct way to categorize it) in the *talisman*—

See, when Abraham received the records of the fathers, he got it from his father who was an idolater. He regarded those records as nothing more than a talisman, a good luck charm. Abraham regarded it as something different, and he worshipped the God of Heaven, and through them he connected to the God of Heaven. Well, the brothers who were jealous of this passing down of a relic (that's more "talisman" than "meaningful source of inspiration and knowledge about God") may well have destroyed it. They may have *copied* it; there may have been other versions of it that were made available or parts of it, if they were interested in it. But I think the original of that may, just like the garment that was given to Adam, have been destroyed at that point.

But when we get down to the end of the hundreds of years of captivity in Egypt, Moses comes into possession of an ordination from Reuel who was (also had a new name of Jethro) the priest of Midian, who would ordain him. He handed down some kind of (at least oral) tradition, at the time that Moses was ordained by Jethro, and so he fell into possession of *something*—however distant that may have been from the records of the fathers at the beginning. When Moses established prophetically the religion that had been lost in a more pure form, Moses actually *wrote* the scriptures. So whether what he did was rely upon oral traditions or scraps, whatever it was that Moses had in his possession, he wrote the five books of Moses as an attempt to re-create the scriptural record that goes back to the beginning—because it's always an attempt to restore the original religion; it's never an attempt to start something new. We have been in a state of apostasy and restoration ever since the original Patriarchs died, and so the tension is always between apostasy and restoration of what was here at the beginning. Moses attempted, in part, to restore that; and we know from fairly-reliable history that Moses wrote five books. We can't be certain that the five books that Moses wrote are the five books that have been handed down to us, but he wrote five books. So Moses is one root of scripture.

There is a concept in the law called "root of title." If you can trace back — depending upon what state you're in; the state we're in right now looks at the root of title back fifty years—if you can track the title that you have to your property back for fifty years, than you have a good root of title. In some places, people can track the title to their property back to the Spanish and before the United States gained possession of the property in the western United States.

But there is such a thing as a root of *scripture*, as well; and the root of all the scriptures that were subsequently inherited by the various Judeo-Christian-Muslim traditions— when you reach Moses, that's a starting point. Everything that happened before that is largely obliterated, with one exception I'll get to in a minute. And Moses is the commencement of the scriptural canon as a new work, as a new restoration. What Moses did, then got handed down for generations—got added to, got supplemented—until we get to the point where the Babylonian captivity takes place. (And I'm setting aside, for a moment, the party of Lehi and the Book of Mormon record; we'll backtrack to that in a bit.)

After the Babylonian captivity, the remnant returned back to Jerusalem, and whatever records they may have had before they went into Babylon—doesn't appear from our scriptural record that it was well- preserved or intact—and Ezra rewrote the scriptures. And so the second root of all scripture that we have, that goes back into antiquity, is Ezra's recovery and restoration of what had once been a scriptural record that began with Moses and had been added to; and so the second root of all scriptures becomes Ezra. And the Old Testament, largely, was reconstituted, rewritten, restored, and recovered by Ezra when they returned from the Babylonian captivity.

Now, we have reason to believe that at the time that they went into the Babylonian captivity, there was an active conflict underway. The Book of Mormon record begins in the middle of the conflict immediately preceding the Babylonian captivity, and the tension that you see is over the concept of a Messiah. A group of people (we have, in common vernacular today, begun to refer to those people as the Deuteronomists—"deutero" meaning "a second" —and they wanted to create a *second* kind of interpretation of the law that had been handed down from Moses), the Deuteronomists were decidedly opposed to the idea of a Messiah—so much so that there are people today who are Jewish who claim that the concept of a Messiah, the concept of a Redeemer came very late to Judaism—post-Babylonian- captivity late. And so they, as followers of the Deuteronomist tradition, have been successfully taught of a faith that purged the idea of a Savior—of a Redeemer—out of the religion; which means that by the time you get to Ezra re-establishing the root that originally went back to the days of Adam, the recovery was so complete, at that point, of the Deuteronomist point of view, that you now have a second root to your scriptures that is purged of Messianic information.

Now, the Deuteronomists couldn't get away with everything they wanted to get away with. They couldn't thoroughly purge every indication of a coming Messiah. They could only get away with eradicating the most radical information that testified bluntly and directly of a Messiah. The one who had done a tremendous job of bluntly disclosing a Messiah was coming was Zenos. Zenos tells plainly about the coming of Christ, of His sacrifice, of His death, of His resurrection, of witnesses that will know about this on a global scale because there will be earthquakes; that the islands of the sea are going to know about (and the islands of the sea, in the Book of Mormon vernacular, includes America)—are going to know about it because there will be these tremendous signs in nature, testifying to the birth and testifying to the death.

In the Book of Mormon, Zenos is generally referred to as "*the* prophet." When we think of "*the* prophet," we think of Moses, or we think of Isaiah. When the Book of Mormon is referring to "*the* prophet"—as an unidentified "the prophet"—it's Zenos. The Book of Mormon preserves something over 3000 words—(I cut and pasted, one time, all the words that you could attribute to Zenos into one MS Word document; my recollection is about 3400 words. I don't know what happened to the document. I don't have it anymore)—but 3400 words of Zenos makes him one of the most quoted authorities in the entire Old Testament record. Lehi's party departed from Jerusalem before the Babylonian captivity, in possession of a brass-plates-version of the Old Testament, in which you find Zenos talking plainly, openly, and blatantly about the coming of a Messiah.

As the opening scenes of the Book of Mormon begin, Lehi—who is praying —gets a vision, is shown a book, and Lehi begins to prophesy. He joins in with others, and he testifies that the Jews are wicked (which causes them to laugh at the man because they think that's a ridiculous proposition—that they're not righteous), and he testifies of a Messiah; and it's that second testimony of the Messiah that provokes them to want to kill him. So the coming of a Messiah was so controversial—at the time that the party of Lehi departed from Jerusalem—that to testify openly about the Messiah had become so divisive (because of the effort of the Deuteronomists) that you risked your life to testify about it. They were—they were militant, they were motivated, and they were determined to eradicate the concept of a Messiah out of the religion that they had inherited from the days of Moses down.

You might ask: Well, why—why would the Messiah be so controversial? Messianic hopes and dreams had proven to be a kind of plague on Jerusalem and the Jews. Surrounding cultures opposed it; fools made claims that they *were it*; bad luck ensued every time you had someone out there claiming to be a Messiah; and it was troubling to conquerors to think that these Jews were one day going to be liberated by a Deliverer. And so, that part of the religion made a Jewish population continuously a political threat to whoever held dominance over them. Babylonians didn't want to hear that they were going to have a Deliverer; the Assyrians didn't want to hear that; the Greeks wouldn't want it; and the Romans, later, wouldn't want it.

And so, the Deuteronomists were taking a more pragmatic approach to the religion and said, "We can improve this thing by getting rid of the idea, because if we've got a Messiah coming, we're continuously a threat. Let's get rid of this part of the religion." So because Zenos is so blatantly Messianic—is so blatantly a writer filled with Christology or notions about Christ—that book simply got decanonized. It was removed from scripture. *Isaiah* is Messianic, but his poetry, his imagery, his vagueness, his poetic structure allowed for different interpretations to be made; and it was a lot less successful in getting rid of Isaiah because, in many respects, Isaiah can be interpreted in a variety of ways: the "suffering servant" can be Israel itself or the remnant of the Jews itself. It needn't be a single individual—there are a lot of things you can do to manipulate that text.

So Zenos is gone from the Deuteronomist canon when they succeed, but a bunch of material got preserved when Ezra restored it. You can ask yourself, how much mischief can they do with a text when they're rewriting it, and how true is it the original? There's a—there's Sirius XM radio that will play for you (if you want it) channels wholly devoted to the 1950s or the 1960s or the 1970s, 80s, and so on. You can just choose the era—and there's even a Beatles channel on Sirius XM. You can hear the opening chord of songs that go back to the 1960s and you can start singing right along with it because you grew up hearing these tunes. You grew up familiar with this music. I don't know how many songs you have in your head as a library of material, but if someone picks up *Please Please Me* and starts singing it and substituting new words, you'll be able to pick up the error that quickly because they're not singing it the way that the song was written and sung by the Beatles. K? Scriptures with the Deuteronomists posed exactly the same problem. People could quote them—they were their songs; they were their literature; they were their folklore; they were their everyday conversational stuff.

I don't know how many times I hear people quoting *Ferris Bueller's Day Off*, and you just instantly [Denver snaps] identify with the context of the comment. "I'll bet you've never smelled a real bus before." Okay? (I didn't realize how obscene *Ferris Bueller's Day Off* was until my daughter was sick, stayed home, watched it, and reported: in the first fifteen minutes, there were over, I think, twenty-five obscenities in the show—she's a junior-high kid at the time, home sick from school, and I didn't realize there was that much. It's not a kid's show, as it turns out, at all!)

The Deuteronomists were confronting exactly the same problem. ([Quoting *Ferris Bueller's Day Off*.] "He'll keep calling and calling!" I mean Ferris is just gonna bug Cameron until he finally comes around.) When you've got a culture that knows how the language ought to go and you try to introduce complete alterations of the text, you're gonna run into a brick wall because the people are gonna detect it. They're gonna call you out on it; and they're gonna reject your work. So while Ezra could do some things—like throwing out Zenos, like altering marginally the text—what we got in the recovery (the second root of our scripture), we can have some level of confidence that they didn't make a wholesale, complete alteration of what Ezra was doing. It was more clipping, cutting, eliminating, curtailing; it was more of that sort of thing than it was complete rewrite. If you can throw it out, throw it out. And so what we've got is probably true and faithful to what had been here earlier, it was just the *Reader's Digest* abridged version of what had once existed. But it's a second root of title, a root of scripture, root of the record. So whatever it was that Moses did *originally* got replaced in the recovery at the time of Ezra.

Well, *if* you believe in the restoration of the gospel—from our perspective, in our day, we have a *third* root of scripture in the work that was done by Joseph Smith. Joseph was commanded, very early on, to go through the scriptures and to make inspired corrections, additions, emendations into the record, in order to clarify, in order to make the record more complete; and repeatedly, revelations given through the Prophet Joseph Smith affirmed that the church itself would fail if it did not have possession of that record that he was supposed to produce.

In the process of doing that, there were revelations that were inspired by inquiries into the meaning of certain passages of the scriptures. While working on the book of John, for example, there was an inquiry made about the afterlife. Doctrine and Covenants section 76 (which is now part of the Teachings and Commandments with a new section number on it that I haven't memorized yet) is a revelation about the afterlife that came about as a result of the work on recovering and correcting the scriptures. Joseph Smith worked on that but never published it. He expressed the intent to publish it in a single volume with the Book of Mormon, but that never got done in his lifetime.

When Joseph Smith died—when he was murdered—the record that he had been working on remained in the possession of his widow. When Brigham Young led a group of people out west, they left without having access to or the ability to read and recover the Joseph Smith version of the scriptures. And so Mormonism—in its predominant form, in the largest single and most successful version of Mormonism (the Church of Jesus Christ of Latter-day Saints)—never had possession of the Joseph Smith work on the Old- and the New Testament. Emma Smith turned the manuscript over to her son, Joseph Smith III. Joseph Smith III eventually let the Reorganized Church of Jesus Christ of Latter Day Saints get custody of it, and it was eventually published by Harold House in Missouri (the publication arm of the RLDS Church) as what is called the Joseph Smith Translation—or we call it the Inspired Version.

However [Denver chuckles], the Inspired Version (published by the RLDS Church) got put into print by a committee, and the committee felt at liberty to make changes to the text that *they* thought were important to have included, and they also failed to be faithful to all of the changes that Joseph had made; and therefore, many of the things that Joseph had done with the scriptures were not included in that publication. In fact, a fully-complete version of the new root of scripture that we have in Joseph Smith did not get published at all in a correct form until the recent work of the scripture committee that has been laboring with the original manuscripts, now available in photograph-photostatic copies, so that you can actually look at the appearance of the text that Joseph worked on.

We also have—rolling out at the same time—transcripts prepared by note-takers who are present in Nauvoo, listening to Joseph Smith give talks in which he mentions a passage of scripture, and then he'll say, "I could render a plainer translation," or he says, "This should be read this way instead of being read that way." And so, by the time you get down to the late Nauvoo talks and Joseph is including new changes or additions or corrections to the scripture, he did not go back to the actual manuscript and insert some of *those* changes into the actual manuscript copy that you can see in photographs available today. But he made the information available *publicly*. So if you're following what Joseph is saying, you can go and see whether or not that change exists in the Joseph Smith Translation.

Well, in the last few years, it has become possible, for the first time, to get access to all of that kinds of information. At the same time, just within the last few years, technological advances have made it possible for document preparation to occur through cooperation between people that are widely separated, even continents apart. They can all access and contribute to the same document, so that work that would have taken hundreds of people thousands and thousands of days to go through, exchange, and look at it (in copies that are passed back and forth), the technological advances allowed for —at almost the same time that the material becomes available to look at—a technological method for those (who are interested in looking at it) to faithfully cooperate in a recovery effort.

So while the *third* root of scripture was created or given to us by Joseph Smith —who made an inspired effort to recover, correct, and make the scriptures state what they should have stated—no one was interested in preserving that or publishing that, in order to overcome condemnation that had been pronounced by God upon the people that pretended to be His. And so the work of doing that remained *undone*, until a group of people cooperatively— all moved upon independent—began the effort of trying to gather together not only what Joseph Smith had done with the Old Testament and the New Testament, but also to do the same thing with the text of the Book of Mormon and do the same thing with the text of the revelations (the revelations that came through Joseph Smith).

And so what we wind up with is, for the first time since Joseph Smith died, an effort to find the most correct version of Joseph Smith's changes to the Old Testament, changes to the New Testament, what his revelations actually said before other people began to interliniate and alter it—some of which was done long after the fact—and an effort to look at the Book of Mormon and make it a more faithful translation of what had come out through Joseph, including the fact that the punctuation was never supplied by a believer. Punctuation was done by a printer that was hired by EB Grandin because he was competent in book layout and knew how to do that. But he certainly wasn't a believer in the Book of Mormon; he was a believer in type-setting and type-printing and how to lay it out and cut it so that you had front and back, the pages laid out correctly.

Well, so we have a new root of scripture at the time of Joseph Smith, and *no one's interested in it*. No one wants to have it—until now; until the project reached its incipient completion and was presented and accepted as a volume, binding upon the people (the Book of Mormon as a covenant; the rest of it as a guide to your life, your belief, your faith), adopted at a conference in Boise,

Idaho in September of 2017. And for the first time, the scriptures become a faithful—as much as is possible, despite the neglect and the foolishness of people that have been involved with this—it is as accurate a third root of scripture as can be, at this point, recovered.

In the process of doing that, we know that Joseph Smith intended to do some things to fix the text of the Book of Mormon and that he was actually in the process of making corrections to the Book of Mormon. Most of them were done in order to make it more faithful to the first translation. We still have about 22% of the first manuscript—rest of it rotted away in a cornerstone, but we still have about 22% of that. We have 100% of the printer's manuscript. We can do a comparison between those two and see that the copyist who copied from the original to the one given to EB Grandin to type-set made about 1 ½ mistakes in copying every page. Much of what Joseph Smith did in the second addition of the Book of Mormon was to go back to the first one, compare the original translation to the type-set copy, and fix the mistakes to bring it back into conformity with the original translation.

So Joseph was interested in being faithful to the original revelation. Likewise, the scripture recovery people have tried to be faithful to exactly what Joseph Smith was doing or did, including the revelations to eliminate the additions, the changes, the alterations that people made to the revelations—after they had come out through Joseph Smith—trying to recover the original.

The condemnation that the LDS church (and the people that believed in the restoration) fell under in 1831, in the words of God, *condemned* the people because they had failed not only to *say* but to *do* that which they'd been commanded. Most people have read that revelation as being a failure of *conduct*— they're not *doing* what they're supposed to do. It's been during the process of recovering the scriptures that it has become apparent that the defect was not just in the failure to do, it was also in the failure to *say*; that is, the *text* had not been faithfully preserved and faithfully cared for, cultivated, curated, and kept in print.

So with the new scriptures (that we're hoping to see in leather-bound, onion skin, highly-portable, and very durable print format soon—they're available online, electronically, for anyone in the world to read right now at the scriptures.info website, and they will continue to be so. They are available in a paperback version through Amazon called The Old Covenants, which is the Old Testament; The New Covenants, which is the—as Joseph Smith always planned it to be—the New Testament and the Book of Mormon; and then the Teachings and Commandments, which comprises the revelations of

Joseph Smith—along with a number of letters, editorials, statements that Joseph had made that should have been canonized and never were—all of those are gathered in and included, along with some of what God has been up to in our day in this final Teachings and Commandments)—

The result of that is that we now have available to us, in the third root of scripture, a more faithful and more complete restoration of scripture (to give us a more clear picture of the original religion that belonged to the first fathers) then we have ever had available to us at any time, since the days of Abraham. We have recovered—in addition to a better Old Testament—a book that was originating with Abraham, restored by revelation through Joseph Smith. *Unlike* the way in which the book of Abraham has been preserved in the LDS tradition (with some typographical misspellings and some name changes that shouldn't have crept into the text), in the Teachings and Commandments, the book of Abraham is fit in chronologically, right where it belongs.

I think a lot of the criticism of the book of Abraham that has come about by publishing it as a separate text—and making people look at it as a dubious document because it may or may not be a faithful interpretation of facsimiles, and it may be more appropriately regarded as something from the *Book of the Dead*, a very late Egyptian text—if instead, it had always been fitted into the scriptures in the way it is in the Teachings and Commandments (in the Teachings and Commandments, it simply looks like another revelation through the Prophet Joseph Smith, fitted in chronologically in about that 1842 time frame, when a number of other things are canonized; it's *another* revelation), had it been packaged in that format all along, I think much of the criticism would probably never even been thought of. Joseph's revealing something. He revealed something from a parchment that had been written on by *John*—and we don't have *that parchment*. So if we accept a revelation that was written by John on parchment (that Joseph Smith gave as a revelation in the Doctrine and Covenants, now in the Teachings and Commandments), the book of Abraham becomes no different. It's just another revelation tumbling out through the inspiration given to a prophet by God.

The scriptures, in the format that they appear in the new publication, is not only a new root—it's a *more accurate root*. And it originates directly from God's active intervention, in order to try and recover the religion as a witness to all the world.

———

The foregoing was recorded by Denver Snuffer in Sandy, Utah on March 2nd, 2019.

61. Witness in All the World

QUESTION: Who or what is the Witness spoken of by John the Revelator, about which Joseph Smith prophesied on May 12, 1844 (just before his death) saying, That Witness would be "ordained and prepared" to "preach the everlasting gospel to all nations in the last days"?

> ...all the testimony is, that the Lord in the last days would commit the keys of the Priesthood to a witness over all people—has the Gospel of the Kingdom commenced in the last days? and will God take it from the man, until he takes him, himself? I have read it precisely as the words flowed from the lips of Jesus Christ—John the Revelator saw an angel flying thro' the midst of heaven, having the everlasting Gospel to preach unto them that dwell on the earth, &c. the Scripture is ready to be fulfilled when great wars, famines, pestilence, great distress, judgements, &c are ready to be poured out on the Inhabitants of the Earth—John saw the angel having the holy Priesthood who should preach the everlasting gospel to all nations,—God had an angel, a special messenger, ordained, & prepared for that purpose in the last days—Woe! Woe! be to that man, or set of men, who lift up their hands against God and his Witness in these last days. —for they shall deceive almost the very chosen ones—my enemies say that I have been a true prophet—& I had rather be a fallen true prophet, than a false prophet. (Thomas Bullock Report, 12 May 1844)

Who is the angel that is flying through the midst of heaven to have the everlasting [Gospel to preach unto them that dwell on the earth]? Who was this Witness in the last days?

———

DENVER: Um yeah, here's the problem. We tend to look at events as having a singular fulfillment and that it um, it's an on/off switch, K? The fact is, that Christ has a lamentation that appears in scripture a number of times, which is: *How oft would I have gathered you as a hen gathereth her chicks under her wings...and ye would not* (3 Nephi 4:9 RE). Um, the Lord can't make that lamentation unless He extends a bonafide opportunity for that gathering to take place. The prophecies about the last days—from the New Testament and Old Testament perspective—generally, are pointing you to the actual accomplishment and fulfillment. The Book of Mormon, on the other hand, is pointing to the last days in which offering is made, and it's rejected.

The allegory in now-Jacob chapter 3 of The New Covenants (Jacob chapter 5 in the traditional way of numbering it) suggests that the process of that labor of the master in the vineyard in the last days with servants includes an extended period of work in which there's activity going on—dunging, digging, and then pruning—and that this labor occurs over a long-enough period of time for natural fruit to begin to appear. And then as it begins to appear, then there's an ongoing process of cutting and discarding, pruning away, and development.

The prophecy that you've got, that Joseph is referring to (and probably, at that time, the expectation that Joseph had about what was gonna happen was it was gonna be a complete culmination, vindication, and fulfillment in his generation), it's very clear that when the fulfillment of the prophecies occurs, it will occur in a single generation. It's not gonna be one generation building upon the work of a prior generation, which built upon the work of yet another prior generation, that culminates in the work. It happens with a single generation. That's what the prophecies all say. And because Joseph was there, because the opportunity was actually bonafide, in existence, and God was working with them, from Joseph's perspective the fulfillment of that prophecy could happen right then. From the Lord's perspective, *How oft would I have gathered you as a hen [gathers her chicks], and ye would not*, He was saying, I will do this; I will do this now and with you; or if not, I will do it three and four generations from now when the condemnation of your rejection has been sufficiently long-endured to justify making another offering.

If you ask specifically who will rise up and fulfill that prophecy, I don't think anyone has the right to claim that they are going to do it. I think the only claim that can be made is: I have done it. Until you can say, in the past tense, that it is a real accomplishment, all it is is vanity and foolishness and pride— because men are literally not going to bring about Zion. The Lord takes credit. Everywhere you see this future prophesied—Zion accomplishing— It's **God's** accomplishment; it's not men doing it. The Lord says, "I will bring again Zion." It's more than foolhardy; it's prideful, it's vanity, and it's just likely to provoke the ire of Heaven for someone to claim that they are going to accomplish something without having first accomplished it. Because that then moves from the Lord asserting that it's Him, and Him alone, that is going to bring again Zion down to the level of some mere mortal—that they're going to accomplish some great thing. And mortals simply aren't going to accomplish it.

If God is willing to gather and if God is willing to bring the purposes about, then men cooperating with Him—the Lord of the Vineyard laboring alongside—is really the reason why the work gets done. It's the Lord of the Vineyard that agreed that the work would be done. It's the Lord of the Vineyard who owns all of the trees that determines that they're going to take the approach of cutting and grafting and in restoring, in laboring, because the Lord of the Vineyard had the right to just burn the whole thing down. And He elected not to do so. So when you get to the fulfillment of the work, the only one that gets to accept the credit is the Lord of the Vineyard. The only credit that we can take, assuming that we are actually involved, is that we were meek and humble enough to cooperate with Him and to do what He said; and He lifted us out of a state of condemnation and decay, and so we cooperated. But the only appropriate reaction is gratitude to Him and not, you know, boasting about our own wisdom and strength, 'cause we don't have much of that—none of us.

Now the question that you asked a few minutes ago, Paul, about that witness to all the world is actually Joseph Smith correcting a misapprehension about what that witness is. Because the way that the New Testament in the King James Version is worded, it suggests that the gospel itself has to be preached everywhere in the world, as a witness, before the end come. Joseph changed that in his commentary and in his alterations of the text to say the world, everywhere, is going to be put on notice by God calling someone to stand as a witness. Whether they heed the witness, whether they're interested in the witness, it doesn't matter; because it's like Amos says: *Surely the Lord God will do nothing [save] he [reveal His] secret unto his servants the [prophet]* (Amos 1:9 RE). It doesn't matter that you don't like the prophet. It doesn't matter you won't listen to the prophet. The world is still bound by the words that God entrusts, and therefore, like 'em, don't like 'em; listen, don't listen! It's not necessary to fulfill Christ's prophecy and promise that every single door get knocked on and that every single person get confronted on their front porch by someone that says, I'm a witness, and you have to follow my religion! What is necessary, instead, is exactly what has now become possible.

We have a new root of scripture. They are available as a witness to the whole world online; you don't have to spend one cent. You can read every word of them, online, for free. For a modest amount of money, you can hold them in your hands by ordering them through Amazon. And in fairly short order, they'll be available in a very portable, leather-bound, thin-paper version that'll be available as soon as we can get the printer identified and the order placed. That witness—that witness that a whole group of people stand behind and labored to produce—is coming out at a very time when it has, for the first time, become technologically possible to produce it. As soon [as] it was possible, it exists. That's one of the signs that the moment has arrived, when —in a single generation—a whole lot of things are prophesied to occur.

All the prophecies in scripture are primarily about two generations of time— and only two generations of time. The first is a generation to which Jesus Christ came, and not much of the world took note of that. Inside the Western-European world, Rome was largely oblivious to the Savior's coming. In other places—islands of the seas—the Book of Mormon testifies there were still those who got a witness of it. But His sermon at Bountiful was to about twenty-five hundred people, and so the rest of the continent in North and South America, word may have leaked out over time, but it was comparatively few. That first generation, that all those prophecies focused on, a small group of people heard about 'em; Christ came; He ministered; He lived; He performed His sacrifice; He was resurrected; and then He taught in Jerusalem and in various other places as a resurrected being, and the world took very little note of it.

The Second Coming is the other generation about which all the prophecies are focused, and like that first generation, it really isn't necessary that the world sit up and take note and say, Oh my word—look—it's all happening; His words are being vindicated; the signs are being given! The world is perfectly entitled to remain oblivious to what's going on. The only thing that needs to happen is that the Savior be born, and that He come into the world as a descendant (genealogically and legally) through David, and that He be exactly who and what He was—modest though the notice was taken of Him, in the world at large.

The Second Coming is going to be just as inconsequential to those who say, *Eat, drink, and be merry, for tomorrow we die* (2 Nephi 12:1), because this world provides plenty of distractions. You do not have to be focused upon the fulfillment of the prophecies. The only thing that's necessary is that the prophecies be fulfilled. And I think it's a mistake to always assume that we should have a macro view of the fulfillment when, in fact, so much of the first coming of the Lord was fulfilled in micro, fulfilled in the modest. I mean, they who sit in darkness shall see a Great Light—Jesus gets up in an obscure synagogue and preaches a lesson based upon the text of Isaiah to a small congregation of people that weren't particularly impressed with Him, and when He finishes His sermon, His commentary on the passage that is read, He says, *This day [has] this scripture [been] fulfilled in your ears* (Luke 4:3 RE).

That doesn't seem like much. And it certainly didn't seem like much to many of the people who were present that day. It seems so fabulously pretentious and unlikely to be true that they threw Him out of the synagogue, and they tried to kill Him because they thought it was blasphemous for Him to apply such a passage to Himself.

So we don't have to accept the witness. We don't have to notice the witness. It's only required that God send the witness. If He sends the witness, God's done His part. In a perfect world—with perfect people whose ideals were based upon finding and following every word that proceeds forth from the mouth of God—in that world, everyone would take note. Everyone would be eagerly looking, eagerly waiting, instead of having this profound indifference to what's happening in our day.

———

The foregoing was recorded by Denver Snuffer in Sandy, Utah on March 2nd, 2019.

62. Every Word, Part 1

QUESTION: Some people believe that re-baptism, receiving the new Covenant, and so forth are not necessary for them because of their bloodlines, race, previous ordination or religion, affiliation with a tribe of Israel, etc. Some believe that they do not need to obey all of the ten commandments or other teachings of Christ or that some parts of the restoration, now underway, are not necessary for them to accept or live by. Are there some parts that don't apply to some people, or must every person accept every part of what is now being offered, in order to be right with God?

———

DENVER: The specific question here, which is a long question, comprehends an issue—and it's more the issue I want to address, than it is the lengthy question. Problems present themselves when there are those who are participants in a fellowship or have aligned themselves with people that are trying to faithfully worship and continue the process of the restoration, and among the group of people there are those who think that parts of what one person believes is not essential or important, or they outright reject the other portion of what's going on. Here's the purpose of the restoration: It is to return and reestablish on earth, again, a religion that existed and was taught to Adam in the first generation. The purpose is not to create a New Testament church. It's not to revive and revitalize Judaism. All of the Judeo-Christian religions are relics, and they are incomplete relics. They are not what existed before.

When Moses went up on the mount to meet with God and receive from him an initial revelation, he came down from the mount bringing with him a more fulsome restoration than what the children of Israel were willing to receive at that time. And so, the initial revelation to Moses got destroyed, and it was replaced by something else. That "something else" was intended to point to the coming of the Messiah. The Messiah was symbolized in every one of the rites of the law of Moses—from the Passover that occurred before the law of Moses right down to all of the observances in the books of Exodus and Leviticus, where you are making specific sacrifices for specific problems. Each one of those involved a covenantal representation, type, and shadow of a Messiah that would come to offer a sacrifice that would count. It's like the apostle Paul wrote to the Hebrews, trying to get it through their tradition, that the shedding of the blood of oxen and sheep and rams—that shedding of blood by these things cannot remove anyone's sin. They're simply pointing to something—some sacrifice—that actually could remove people's sin. And then he testifies to the Hebrews, in that letter, that that great sacrifice was Jesus Christ, whom they rejected. It was expected that they would reject Him. The chief cornerstone would be set at naught. Just like it's expected that the Gentiles will reject the fullness of the gospel, it was expected that the Jews would reject the Messiah. And so, the fact that someone thinks that there is a religion they would like to participate in, short of the fulsome restoration of the religion that goes back to the time of Adam—they are really behaving like the Jews (who rejected the Messiah) or the Gentiles (who rejected the fulness of the Restoration). What they're saying is, We will go thus far but no further. And, therefore, they're really not interested in the work that God is attempting to complete.

When Christ said, Thou shalt *live by every word which proceedeth forth [from] the mouth of God* (D&C 98:11; see also T&C 82:18), He wasn't talking merely about whatever the canon of scripture was in their day; He wasn't talking about His own sermons. He was talking about the work that God has to do. That work, in every generation, has remained incomplete, from the days of Adam until now. It's still incomplete. That doesn't mean that you can't pick up the Old Testament and find a way that is enriching and, perhaps, even deeply satisfying in worshiping God through what you learn in the Old Testament. It doesn't mean that you can't take both the Old Testament and the New Testament and find a[n] empowering, rewarding, richly edifying religion in accepting that. It also doesn't mean that you can't be someone that accepts the Book of Mormon, in addition to all of the foregoing— you can find yourself a satisfying, delightful religion by being a Latter-day Saint, by being a member of the Community of Christ. Any number of religions can give to you something that's satisfying. The purpose that is underway right now, however, is to do what Christ admonished be done; that is, *to live by every word that proceedeth forth [from] the mouth of God.*

We cannot see the fulfillment of the covenants and the promises that were given in the prophecies without [*living*] *by every word that proceedeth forth [from] the mouth of God* today. There is an enormous amount of work to be done. You can have your individual religious connection with God, but you are not aligning yourselves with the complete restoration that was interrupted by the deaths of Joseph and Hyrum Smith. There's work left to be done. Part of the work of rebuilding the restoration—and remembering and honoring what went before—was an act of penitence; an act of group repentance; an act of sincere, devoted, deliberate confession of the failure, acknowledging the failure, preliminary to the act of repenting and returning and recovering. That is an effort that—

An individual can always repent of their sins. But God wants a **people** to repent, **as a people**, of their sins. Covenants don't get given out, generally, one-on-one with God when He is trying to create a people. Covenants get given out to **people**. The purpose of the extending of the Covenant in Boise was God acknowledging and recognizing this confession of the sins, the confession of the failure, the desire to repent and return. And what we had in the record, in the scriptures, had been altered, had been corrupted, had been manipulated—just like the New Testament canon underwent alterations during the third and fourth century. And the Christological debates of the third and fourth century, in order for one side to win their argument about the nature of Jesus Christ, they changed the content of the New Testament, so that the New Testament supported their view of Jesus Christ. Like that, there were those in the early days of Mormonism who felt that they had the right to make sure that revelations through Joseph Smith conformed to their view of what they thought would be the right way.

And so changes and alterations and insertions got made, not only into scripture, but also into historical documents. Letters were changed; journal entries were changed; duplicate journals were put together, in order to replace journals that did not corroborate. And so, that the corruption that happened in the New Testament era has been mirrored in the Restoration through Joseph Smith in our era.

All the world's religions, basically, are created in a single generation. Between Moses and Joshua and Caleb and Aaron, Judaism was created in one generation. Now, some things got added later through subsequent prophets, but the root of that religion was in one generation. Christianity got created in a single generation that included Zacharias and John and Jesus and Peter and the twelve and Paul—and then Barnabas and a few outliers. But a single generation created Christianity. In Islam, you have Muhammad, and you have Omar, and you have the creation of the Islamic text in a single generation.

And every one of them underwent issues of others meddling in the content of what had been delivered in that single generation. In the case of Moses, that took a form (just prior to the Babylonian captivity) that was—it had become violent. The disagreements of the Deuteronomists with the Traditionalists had become violent, at that point. It was the threat of violence by the Revisionists (the folks that wanted to change the view of the Messiah) that drove Lehi and his family out of Jerusalem. And so that Lehi party preserves a tradition that is really the old religion in the Book of Mormon. In the New Testament, the texts of the New Testament—

One of the researchers who's done a very good job of laying out the problem is Bart Ehrman. He wrote—I know the main title of the book—it's *The Orthodox Corruption of Scripture:* —And then what follows the colon, I can paraphrase; I can get pretty close; *The Orthodox Corruption of Scripture:* ~~How the~~ *[The Effect of Early] Christological* ~~Debates~~ *[Controversies]* ~~of the Third and Fourth Century altered the Christian Canon~~ *[on the Text of the New Testament].* That's pretty close: Bart Ehrman, E-H-R-M-A-N. He was, one time, a believing, Christian theologian. He is now agnostic. He's lost his faith because his deep look into how the Christian canon was developed and altered affected his ability to trust the canon itself.

One example of alteration that you can see from the Deuteronomist era is that the sacrifice of Isaac (in the canon that we have) did not get completed. Isaac was not actually killed, but the ram was found in the thicket that saved his sacrifice. There was another tradition that Isaac actually was killed, and that he was able to be brought back to life. That older tradition—that involved the killing of Isaac and him making it back to life—is preserved in the Book of Mormon, and it's also preserved in Paul's letter to the Hebrews, in which he mentions that Abraham proceeded with what he did because he believed that God was able to bring Isaac back to life. And that tradition got altered, in part, by the Deuteronomists.

Well, there is— what is it? Where that the statement is made that *Thou art my Son; this day have I begotten thee* (Psalm 2:7; see also Psalm 2:2 RE)? That statement was Messianic and prophetic, and it was, at one point, in some—if not all—of the gospel accounts. At the baptism of Jesus Christ, the statement quoted from Psalms appears there, *Thou art my Son this day have I begotten thee.* That statement is also used by Paul in the letter to the Hebrews, as posing the question, *Unto [whom has God said], Thou art my Son, this day have I begotten thee?* (Hebrews 1:5; see also Hebrews 1:2 RE). Meaning, he's arguing that the Hebrews ought to believe in Jesus Christ, because that's what heaven did for Jesus Christ.

During the Christological debates, there was a group of people who denied that Christ was conceived miraculously to a virgin mother, by God's intervention to create the pregnancy that resulted in the divine birth of Christ. They contended that Jesus was just an ordinary guy—like any other guy—and that there was no difference between Him and the man on the street. However, the destiny of Jesus changed, and His status altered when, at the time of His baptism, He was told, *Thou art my Son, this day have I begotten thee,* at which point He became adopted into God's family and the Son of God.

And so the adoptionists (that's what they called themselves) interpreted the statement in scripture, *Thou art my Son, this day have I begotten thee* to mean that Jesus was just a chap, like any other chap out there, and on the day of His baptism, God adopted Him, and that's how He became the Messiah. Whereas others said, No, there's this other material we have to respect—He wasn't like you and me; He was divinely conceived by a virgin mother, and He fulfilled a lot of prophecy in the process of coming into this world.

And Bart Ehrman, in his book, shows how some of the ante-Nicene (the A-N-T-E—the "before" Nicene) fathers—the early Christian fathers, in the generation that followed the Apostles, up til the Council of Nicea, 324 [AD] —how many of those writers referred to the baptism of Jesus and, in fact, quoted the words differently than, *This is my beloved Son in whom I am well pleased.* They quoted the words, instead, to be *Thou art my Son, this day have I begotten thee.* Ehrman argued that this is one of many clear-cut examples of how the text got altered, in part because they were debating a doctrinal issue of how to understand Jesus Christ. Bart Ehrman has done great work with that.

In the case of the Islamic canon, there are those—generally, it's the consensus —some will disagree that Muhammad himself did not read or write; that he was functionally illiterate, in the sense that he didn't compose the text of the book of the Quran. Instead, he memorized it; he recited it. And that the correct way to perpetuate the Islamic tradition is by recitation and memorization. In fact, people use memorization as an act of devotion within the Islamic faith, in order to prove that you can, in fact, perpetuate the entirety of the text, intact, through an oral tradition. Omar reduced it to writing; the writing got preserved. But as happens with any written record in its preservation, there were different versions of the Quran that existed for a period of time.

But Islam has embedded within it the possibility that if there is a religious disagreement about something that is considered sacred, then violence can be employed in order to establish the correct view. Because you can denounce, and even kill, a heresy and heretics.

That culminated, after a couple of hundred years in Islam, with various versions of the Quran floating around, in a purge—in which different versions, belonging to weaker believers— numerically weaker, militarily weaker—got conquered, and the text got burned. And so we have a version of the Quran today that's considered Orthodox, because they managed to destroy competing versions of what was out there. There are still Islamic scholars that recognize that there are some parts of the Quran that may suitably read differently than they do today, whether they believe themselves Orthodox, Heterodox, or heretical, that's something that those that believe in the faith would have to figure out. But they had the same kind of problem.

I think anyone who is interested in understanding how a religion—any religion—came about should study Mormonism. Because Mormonism has available, in real-time, the exact same process and phenomenon that happened in every one of the world's great religions. (I left out Buddhism, but the same thing would be applicable to Buddhism; the same thing would be applicable to Hinduism—although when you get to the Vidas, you're going so far back into history, there are debates about over how long a period of time some of those were developed.) But all religions share similarly. They get founded, for the most part, [in a]single generation. Then they go through a metamorphosis process, in which you're trying to get it into a stable form that can be perpetuated. That initial period (between founding and assuming a stable form), involves a whole lot of textual manipulation, textual destruction, competing arguments. Arrogant people—who think they have something valuable to contribute—will insert themselves into the process. Sincere people—who may be meek and humble in their own right but who devoutly, earnestly believe that something's wrong—will use that conviction, that heart-felt conviction, that the wrong thing needs to be fixed, to go out and make their own changes to what's going on, out of the goodness of their heart. It doesn't mean that they're vile people; it just means that this is what people do.

————

The foregoing was recorded by Denver Snuffer in Sandy, Utah on March 4th, 2019.

63. Every Word, Part 2

QUESTION: Some people believe that re-baptism, receiving the new Covenant, and so forth are not necessary for them because of their bloodlines, race, previous ordination or religion, affiliation with a tribe of Israel, etc. Some believe that they do not need to obey all of the ten commandments or other teachings of Christ or that some parts of the restoration, now underway, are not necessary for them to accept or live by. Are there some parts that don't apply to some people, or must every person accept every part of what is now being offered, in order to be right with God?

———

DENVER: In the case of the restoration through Joseph Smith, he started a work that had an objective. Along the way, many, many things were done that got added. You take a look at Mormonism at the time of the publication of the Book of Mormon, and it has a look and feel in one direction. A few years later, by the time you get to Kirtland, the look and the feel of Mormonism is fairly different than what it was at that incipient stage—in part because onboard to the Mormon movement had come Campbellites, with a lot of Campbellite concerns and Campbellite beliefs that needed to be dealt with. To the extent that it's possible to accept them, Joseph was willing to accept them. To the extent that they wanted something and God would indulge that something, Joseph would do whatever needed to be done.

You get a few years later in Mormonism, and you look at what it looked like in the 1838 time frame. And Mormonism is different than what it was back in the halcyon days of Kirtland, and it's beginning to have a lot of internal conflicts. And some people who had been given status, standing, office, opportunity so that they became bonafides—they became authorities within the movement—

For example, the presidency in Zion considered themselves to be just as important, just as capable of exercising authority and control, and just as endowed with blessings from on high as anyone else. In fact, jurisdictionally, at that point—arguably, whenever you came within the boundaries of an organized stake (like the presidency that sat in Zion was at that time), then *they*—not the Quorum of the Twelve—*they*—not the First Presidency—*they* — not bishops from elsewhere—*THEY* were the supreme authority at that point on the land. And what happened in 1838, among other things, was a power struggle over who gets to define what. The presidency included David

Whitmer, who got excommunicated in 1838. It included Oliver and others—members of the Twelve.

The power struggle that resulted in 1838 shook the nascent Mormon movement to its core, because now you are in the middle of a struggle over power, authority, control, jurisdiction—issues that had come about as a consequence of the formal organization of a church with a hierarchy, a church with a hierarchy that was divided into separate hierarchies, all of which had equal authority with the other hierarchy; an organization in which the equality that existed was not because every person stood on the same level—the equality that existed was because one body (that is, high councils) was equal to the First Presidency. And another body (that is, the Quorum of the Twelve) was equal in authority with the high council and with the First Presidency. And another body, the Quorum of the Twelve, was equal in authority to the high councils and to the First Presidency. And another body, the Seventy, was equal to them all. None of these were preeminent. And so, the concept of this equality didn't exist because every member stood on the same ground; it is because within the body there were organizational groups that operated as a check on one another. *All* of them could look at the other and say, "You're not the boss of me." And so that precipitated a crisis in 1838 that resulted in internal division—members that were disaffected signing affidavits to implicate Joseph Smith in some wrongdoing; a wayward Sampson Avard engaging in gratuitous violence; a talk by Sidney Rigdon that threatened all the neighbors, the neighbors having enough of it, and they were basically frontiersmen that were refugees from arrest and the eastern states—all of which turns into this cultural stew that results in violence and the Mormon War.

So, you have the Mormon War in Missouri in 1838 and '39 with the expulsion of the Mormons, largely growing out of an internal power struggle and a lot of people trying to assert the right to have control, dominion, compulsion, power. Joseph Smith gets arrested; he spends half a year in Liberty Jail; and just before he's allowed to escape (because he was allowed to escape; that was the most politically savvy way to deal with the mess that Missouri had created for itself—just let him run away), just before he was allowed to escape, in the Liberty Jail, Joseph composed a two-part letter (that's in the new scriptures; it's not in the old one, although an excerpt of this part of the letter does appear in the LDS Doctrine and Covenants), in which Joseph Smith backtracks on the whole idea of power, authority, and control by *anyone* who's holding *any* priesthood *anywhere*. And he denounces that as men get a little authority, as they suppose, they *immediately* begin to exercise unrighteous dominion. And so while many may be called, very few wind up being chosen. And *why* are they not chosen? Because they aspire to the honors of men, and their hearts aren't right, they seek to have dominion and control. And so, the letter explains that *no power or influence can or **ought** to be maintained by virtue of the priesthood* (T&C 139:5-6). The only way it's to be exercised is by pure knowledge, by love, by meekness, by gentleness, by persuasion.

Well, that lesson also informed how Joseph proceeded, and by the time you get into the Nauvoo era, Mormonism has morphed, once again, into something very different than what it was in *any* of the prior periods. And Joseph Smith begins talking about other very ancient things.—things that look a lot like they could go back to Egypt or before; things that refer to Abraham and lay out a book by revelation of father Abraham. He's beginning to talk about things like pre-earth existence of personalities or spirits or intelligences and how that they were organized and gradated before the world began.

A passage (in the traditional Alma chapter 13) about this priesthood order that existed *from the first place* or *before the world wa*s begins to assume a great deal more clarity. Now Joseph is not talking about or attempting to restore New Testament organization. He's attempting to restore *very* ancient understanding about the very nature of man, the very nature of God, the very nature of why this creation came into existence. The "what God is up to in bringing us to this spot" issue is confronted squarely in the Nauvoo era by Joseph Smith. It's a new look and feel for Mormonism. It's edging its way backward to earlier periods of time.

Then you get into the last (about) year of Joseph's life, and he is, more or less, graduating from the church itself; and instead, he's talking about something *different* than the church—he's talking about the *kingdom*. The kingdom that Joseph will begin to organize just very shortly before his death is different from—and distinct altogether from— the church that had been organized with this hierarchy. Joseph Smith begins to move from Church President to *co*-Church President, with Hyrum being given the church as his problem. And Joseph moves over into the "kingdom of God" and announces that it is his ambition within the kingdom of God to begin to create what he calls "kings" and "priests." He wants to organize kings and priests, not as part of a church organization but something separate. And that body of kings and priests are going to then have what they need to go out and establish their own kingdom. And he wants a group of *those* people to be sufficiently well-equipped with everything they need, so that they can go out into the West.

Because by 1844, now the Indians that had been concentrated through the Indian Relocation Act of 1830 and were sitting right next to Independence, Missouri in 1830 are gone, and they're somewhere in the West. They are in the Black Hills of South Dakota; they're in the Great Western Plains before you reach the Rockies; they're all over the Rocky Mountains. They've scattered all the way out to Oregon. Joseph wants to organize a group of kings and priests who can go out and live among these people and, ultimately, establish the kingdom of God in the West with these people. He's talking in these terms in the last months of his life, but it never gets far enough to be acted on.

When he leaves Nauvoo, just before the summer solstice in 1844, he crossed the river; he was heading out to the West. He was going to go attempt to implement—even if he was the only king and priest that went out there—he intended to implement the plan and program of God and to look for a group of people, natives in the West, in which he could establish the city of the New Jerusalem and, ultimately, have Zion come to exist. He gets persuaded to return to Nauvoo, and he turns back to go to Nauvoo and surrender himself, because if his life is of no value to his friends, then it's no value to himself. And with that, ultimately, the Restoration was doomed to come crashing to a halt. Because no one understood what Joseph was doing or possessed the capacity to continue that Restoration process among the people that were *still* vying for power, control, and authority inside a hierarchy, as opposed to lifting their eyes up and realizing that something more was intended.

Now, Joseph used the words "king" and "priest." And there are those who say that that desire, that ambition, is exactly in conflict with the Book of Mormon statement that *there shall be no kings upon [**this**] land* (2 Nephi 7:2 RE), the Americas, and fault Joseph for defying the restriction on kings on this land and attribute the martyrdom to that. However, you'd have to understand what Joseph believed a king and a priest *was* in order to understand what he was trying to restore. The king and the priest is not the strong hand that rules over all; he's the servant that kneels to lift. Christ was the King of the Jews, but His Kingdom is not of this world. Joseph's kingdom would not have been for him to rule and reign and to be the boss; the purpose would be to teach and educate. In fact, arguably, the better word—instead of king and priest—would be **teacher**. Because if he knows more, he has an obligation to teach and, therefore, bring about God's purposes. And if you've got a kingdom, the kingdom itself belongs to God. If you want to have God acknowledge it as the Kingdom of God on earth, God has to be the one who is exclusively in control over the Kingdom. Therefore, you actually need a Revelator, in order to have the Kingdom—because it's dependant upon direction from the King, the *real* King—that is, God—in order to have the proper order exist on earth.

Well, those who say, "I want to have some religious experience, but I don't want to be part of a covenant community," are perfectly well entitled to say that. But they have no *right*, before God, to be on the land—because a covenant is required in order to receive a land inheritance. If you reject the Covenant—in the eyes of God, in the tradition of the religion that you think you're following— If you study your Old Testament, if you study your New Testament, you're going to realize, and if you read your Book of Mormon, you're going to realize, you have no legal right to be on the land that belongs to God if you're not a Covenant-holder who honors the Covenant. Therefore, at His coming, He will evict you. That is, you will be gathered in bundles and burned (as the allegories go, as the Lord's own parable went) because you don't belong here. You're going to be evicted. Anyone who is teaching that is saying, "I like a rather incomplete religion; I cherish something that is *part*, but I don't cherish something that is *more*." It's like the presidency of Zion rebelling in 1838, because things had so changed in the course of events that they did not appreciate how the Restoration was a project that was in motion, and it was not completed.

Well, the Restoration was a process in motion while Joseph was alive. It never reached the finish point. It was always intended to be a work in motion. It has resumed forward motion now. It has not acquired its final developmental stage, nor will it, until the Restoration reaches its culmination. Those who want to fight against it, reject it, depart from it, accept only part of it, not move forward as the thing moves forward are like the people that rebelled when Moses was here. They're like the people that wouldn't accept what Christ was doing. They're like those that said, "I'll go thus far, but no further in the Restoration." They're saying they want a static religion. They want to know that they've got their hands around it all. And the truth is: *no one* has their hands around it *all*. Because it *all* has not yet been returned.

If we're not willing to accept every word that proceeds forth from the mouth of God, then we're not willing to accept the religion that Jesus Christ was advocating. Because *that* religion has never been completed, and it isn't complete now. And if we harden our hearts and if we darken our minds and say, "We will go thus far and no further," you can have a religion; you can have *something*; in fact, you may have something really, really good, but that doesn't mean you are on board with the religion of Jesus Christ—because *it* is seeking for the completion of the entire return, back to the beginning—a great chiasm, returning back to the starting point—the religion that was here once at the time of Adam.

When someone comes along and advocates in a fellowship that you can do some, but not all, of what the Restoration now includes, what they are really saying is: they want to have their religion reach a dead end. They want a dead religion—and one that makes them feel rather good and become self-satisfied —but they don't want what God would urge them to accept. They don't want to have the prophecies fulfilled. They don't want to have the Covenant that will ensure that they will be around at the Lord's return. They don't want what God offers.

There is a statement in the Book of Mormon—it is a remarkable statement because it's spoken from God's vantage point. But it's a harrowing—it's a pathetic—comment. It instills pathos in the person that hears it. I think Nephi wrote it: "God loveth all who will have him to be their God." Because anytime you draw a line—anytime you set a mark and say, "I will go thus far and no further" with a God who wants to walk with you from Jerusalem to Emmaus and spend the day conversing with you and opening to your mind how in Moses (and all the prophets) everything testified of Him, and you say, "No, I'm not willing to go to Emmaus; you got 300 yards, and at the end of 300 yards I'm turning back, because I will go thus far and no further"—they will *never* have the opportunity to break bread and have their eyes opened and realize that they are walking alongside the Savior as they go on this journey.

You don't interrupt it. The religion of Christ is *living*. A living God has a living religion. And a living religion makes us all insecure, 'cause we don't know what's coming next. We have to be humble enough *and* nimble enough to respond to whatever it is that comes next. That makes every one of us uncomfortable. That's who God is; that's what His religion is; that's what we're expected to accept. So, when a false spirit comes along and preaches, "thus far and no further"—or you have to take a detour because the religion is not attempting to accumulate in a restoration fully of all things that go back to the beginning—

We have to become "Jewish Mormons," or we have to become "Christian Mormons," or we have to become "Evangelical Mormons," or we have to become "Buddhist Mormons." Well, Mormonism includes all of those things, but it isn't *that*. We should believe in a Restoration that is going to culminate in a return of *everything*, including things that we right now don't know about (and will never know about if we don't stay on task with God, welcoming every word that "proceedeth forth from the mouth of God").

Once the Restoration is set in motion, everyone has to come and enter through the same door. It doesn't happen any other way. All of the men that were called into Jesus's initial quorum had to be baptized. They were already Jews; they had to be baptized. They were already Jews; they had to be commissioned by Him. They were already Jews. I mean, Matthew was a Levite—why did Matthew need Jesus to ordain him? For goodness sake, he already had what he needed to have. All of the brethren who were called within the Nephite group had been practicing baptism, and Jesus comes and says, "Ok, I give you authority to baptize," and now the people who have been baptized now have to go be baptized. Every time there is a new beginning, it's mandatory that everyone submit to the new beginning, and it doesn't matter who you are: Jew or Gentile, bond or free, black or white, male or female—you have to submit. If you don't, then you're rejecting— you're refusing—to allow Him to be your God. You're saying, "My God is an idol, and that idol is my ancestry."

There was a time when, had the order been respected, descendancy from Hyrum Smith mattered a lot. At this point, it doesn't matter one whit. It's just a historical nicety. It died. Actually, it didn't die—it was killed. The act of apostasy requires deliberate activity, and it was deliberate. The activity resulted in the killing off of what might have been, and therefore, God has to start anew; and He has, and what started anew stands on it's own and requires that we respond to it on its own.

———

The foregoing was recorded by Denver Snuffer on March 4th, 2019.

64. Noah

QUESTION: Christ said in Matthew 11:11 RE: *As it was in the days of Noah, so it shall be also at the coming of the Son of Man, for it shall be with them as it was in the days which were before the flood.* What was happening in the days of Noah?

———

DENVER: There are two models that you can consider from the scriptures as possibilities for Zion in the last days. The one model is the Book of Mormon model, in which Zion gets introduced after destruction and after the return of the Lord and after folks have a season to incorporate the information and the teachings—the ordinances that Christ restores at His coming. Under *that* model, we will not see Zion until sometime post-Second Coming. There's a second model that we find in the scriptures, however, and that model is the one that Christ suggests. He says: *As it was in the days of Noah, so [also shall it be at the time of] the coming of the Son of Man* (Matthew 24:37; see also Matthew 11:11 RE). And what was it that was going on contemporaneous with Noah? It was the city of Enoch, in which a people separated themselves, and they found Zion. Melchizedek was able to do the same thing. The people of the Nephites were able to do the same thing. Whether the model that will actually apply is the model that Christ suggested about the city of Enoch and a righteous people ready to meet the Lord or the model that the Book of Mormon suggests (post Holocaust, post-Second Coming establishment of Zion), is *your* choice. And that ought to be the most sobering comment of all.

So now we should realize, I hope, that that city which Melchizedek, the King of Peace, was able to teach righteousness sufficiently so that it was taken up from the earth, reserved to the last days of the end of the world—the *next* time we have such an event on the earth, the *next* time there is this kind of a gathering and this kind of a population anywhere, it will not be for the purpose of going up—it will be for the purpose of permitting those who have gone up to come back down. It will be for the purpose of having those who can endure the presence of those who come, because those who come will burn up all those who are unworthy, and therefore, some few need to be gathered so that the *earth is not utterly wasted at His coming* (D&C 2:3; see also JSH 3:4 RE).

As it was in the days of Noah so [also shall it be at the time of] the coming of the Son of Man (Matthew 24:37; see also Matthew 11:11 RE). How many people were required in order to have the ark be an acceptable place in which God could preserve all of humanity? It was a portable ark of the covenant in which the *family* was preserved. And so, if it's going to be as it was in the days of Noah—

There is this net that has been cast out to gather together *all* manner of fish, but as the Lord tells the parable, the angles are going to come, and they're going to pick through all manner of fish, and they're going to keep the good, and the rest are going to be scheduled for burning (see Matthew 13:47-50; see also Matthew 7:12 RE).

And so the question is, how diligent ought the search be into the things of God? How carefully ought we to consider the things that have been restored to us through the prophet Joseph Smith? The fact is that this stuff is assigned to our dispensation. And I'm reading from the Book of Mormon, which the world does not have or accept. I'm reading from the Book of Abraham, which the world does not have or accept. I'm reading from the Joseph Smith Translation, which the world does not have and accept. All of you have this information in front of you. *All* this material has been restored through someone that we claim we honor and regard as a prophet. Well, they who come will burn up those who are unprepared. And therefore, what should we be doing in order to make sure that we are included among those who are prepared?

Though the Egyptians tried to preserve the things that came down from the beginning, as we read in the Book of Abraham, the Pharaoh sought earnestly to imitate the order that came down from the beginning, and the Pharaoh succeeded in large measure in doing that. And he was a righteous man.

> *Pharaoh being a righteous man established his kingdom...judged his people wisely...justly all his days, seeking earnestly to imitate that order established by the fathers in the first generations, in the days of the first patriarchal reign, even the reign of Adam, [as] also [Noah's father]...* (Abraham 1:26; see also Abraham 2:3 RE)

Pharaoh was not out there freelancing; he was trying to imitate something, and Egypt did a good job of preserving *some* things that have fallen into decay elsewhere. But a Restoration through Joseph Smith and the promises that were made to the fathers and the statement that was made by Moroni to Joseph on the evening that he came to him and talked about and re-worded the promise given through Malachi—all of these are pointed to something that is, at this moment, still incomplete; a work that is, at this moment, still undone; a project that remains for us—if we will receive it—to finally receive.

Let's look at Doctrine and Covenants section 107, and go to verse 52: *Noah was ten years old when he was ordained under the hand of Methuselah* (T&C 154:18). Okay? So Moses got priesthood, as a consequence of the hand of Methuselah having ordained him. *That* is a priesthood or fellowship or brotherhood on *this* side of the veil. Now go back to Moses chapter 8. In Moses chapter 8 verse 19, it says: *And the Lord ordained Noah after his...order, and commanded him that he should go forth and declare his Gospel unto the children of men, even as it was given unto Enoch* (Genesis 5:8 RE). Or in other words, in the case of Noah, the fellowship that originated as a relationship between him and his older brethren, here, extended by God ordaining him, also, to a fellowship on the other side. Therefore, he belonged not merely to the priesthood held by men but to the priesthood held by the immortals.

Moses chapter 7—this is the Lord speaking to Enoch in a vision (recorded subsequently by Moses by revelation), but it is a restoration of the Book of Enoch, and the conversation speaker is the Lord. Beginning in Moses chapter 7 verse 60: *And the Lord said unto Enoch: As I live, even so will I come in the last days, in the days of wickedness and vengeance, to fulfill the oath which I have made unto you concerning the children of Noah* (Genesis 4:22 RE). This is the Lord's oath to Enoch: He's going to come; He's going to come in the last days.

> *And the day shall come that the earth shall rest, but before that day the heavens shall be darkened, and a veil of darkness shall cover the earth; and the heavens shall shake, and also the earth. And great tribulations shall be had among the children of men, but my people will I preserve. And righteousness will I send down out of heaven....Truth will I send forth out of the earth, to bear testimony of mine Only Begotten, his resurrection from the dead, yea, and also the resurrection of all men. And righteousness and truth will I cause to sweep the earth as...with a flood....* (Moses 7:61-62; see also Genesis 4:22 RE)

The thing that is possible now by you sitting at a keyboard anywhere in the world—you can cause the truth to flood the earth.

> *To gather out mine elect from the four quarters of the earth, unto a place which I shall prepare, an Holy City, that my people may gird up their loins, and be looking forth for the time of my coming; for there shall be my tabernacle,* [in this context the tabernacle to be built is his house] *and it shall be called Zion, a New Jerusalem. And the Lord said unto Enoch: Then shalt thou and all thy city meet them there, and we will receive them into our bosom, and they shall see us; and we will fall upon*

their necks, and they shall fall upon our necks, and we will kiss each other.... (ibid, vs 62-63)

This is the second return of Enoch as well—first His house, then Enoch.

> *And there shall be mine abode, and it shall be Zion, which shall come forth out of all the creations which I have made; and for the space of a thousand years the earth shall rest. And it came to pass that Enoch saw the day of the coming of the Son of Man, in the last days, to dwell on the earth in righteousness for the space of a thousand years.* (ibid, vs 64-65)

Zion exists before these things can happen. If Zion does not exist, these things will be delayed. They will not be prevented because the Lord has, by a covenant, insured that they will happen. But the fact that the Lord has, by a covenant, insured that it will happen is no guarantee that *we* will see it. Because *we* will only see it if *we* undertake to abide the conditions by which *He* can accomplish His work. This is the Joseph Smith translation of Genesis chapter 9:

> *And the bow shall be in the cloud; and I will look upon it, that I may remember the everlasting covenant, which I made unto thy father Enoch; ...that, when men should keep all my commandments, Zion should again come on the earth, the city of Enoch which I have caught up unto myself and this is mine everlasting covenant, that when thy posterity shall embrace the truth, and look upward, then shall Zion look downward, and all the heavens shall shake with gladness, and the earth shall tremble with joy; and the general assembly of the church of the firstborn shall come down out of heaven and possess the earth, and shall have place until the end come. And this is mine everlasting covenant, which I made with thy father Enoch.* (JST Genesis 9:21-23; see also Genesis 5:22 RE)

The covenant that God made again with Noah, the covenant that He made originally with Adam, the covenant which *some* generation will rise up to receive—whether that's you or whether you go to the grave without realizing or not is entirely up to you.

The scriptures do not foretell any great numbers will repent. Christ said: *I will take you one of a city, and two of a family, and I will bring you to Zion* (Jeremiah 3:14; see also Jeremiah 2:3 RE)—too few perhaps to impress the world, but the Lord does not view things as do men. The Lord describes those who respond to His invitation as His elect. He explained: *Mine elect hear my voice and harden not their hearts* (D&C 29:7; see also T&C 9:3).

Nephi foresaw how few believers there would be in the last days:

> *[He] beheld the church of the Lamb of God, and it's numbers were few, because of the wickedness and abominations of the whore who sat upon many water; nevertheless, I beheld that the church of the Lamb, who were the saints of God, were also upon all the face of the earth; and their dominions upon the face of the earth were small, because of the wickedness of the great whore whom I saw* (1 Nephi 14:12; see also 1 Nephi 3:28 RE)

The Lord requires us to invite the world to repent but not to expect large numbers to do so. Numbers matter to men, but the hearts of men matter to the Lord. It is the quality of conversion, not the quantity. He always spoke of having few sheep. Of the likely billions living at the time of Enoch, only some few thousand were saved—and only eight by Noah. The end times will be like those days.

We face the same test as all others have ever faced, from the days of Adam down to the present. Things *never* change. From the time of Adam, the roles have been filled by different persons in different ages, but the conflict is perpetual, and the same battle continues from age to age. You can even lift the arguments that are made from one epoch and put them into the next—and they fit. It doesn't change.

Adam taught his posterity the gospel, and Satan, imitating an angel of light, declared *himself* to be a son of God and taught this doctrine: Believe it not. And most of Adam's posterity did not believe. Enoch received a message from God, and the record that Enoch left behind says: *And all men were offended because of him* (Moses 6:37; see also Genesis 4:4 RE).

Noah taught the same gospel as was taught in the beginning to Adam—but *his* audience claimed, *We* are the sons of God. And they would not hearken to the message that came through Noah. Abraham obtained the same rights that were belonging to the Fathers or to Adam in the beginning, including holding the right of the firstborn that came down from the first father, Adam. And those who claim the gospel of Abraham is less than the gospel given to Adam are a false message born by a false messenger. Mark it. If they don't repent for preaching that message in opposition to what the Lord decares, both in scripture and by my voice, *they will regret it.* But unfortunately, Abraham's own family—that is, his fathers, his uncles—utterly refused to hearken to his voice.

Moses saw God face to face, and He talked with him. God gave Moses a work to do. Satan tempted Moses to instead worship him, even declaring to Moses: *I am the only begotten, worship me* (Moses 1:19; see also Genesis 1:4 RE). When Moses rejected this demand, his message from God was opposed by sorcerers and magicians who did, in like manner, with their enchantments, duplicating signs shown through Moses, over and over again in the record in Exodus. Even after delivering Israel from Egypt, the Israelites wished they had died in Egypt rather than being delivered and freed. And, of course, what *might* have happened, given the qualification of Moses to bring it about, did *not* happen because the people that he led were unwilling to rise up as they were invited.

Christ was opposed by Satan who demanded that He worship him. And then He was opposed by religious leaders of the people. The people He went to save conspired to kill Him and, ultimately, brought that about.

Joseph Smith *was* and *is* opposed by those who claim to follow him or to belong to a church that was founded by him. If you don't understand the extent to which the opposition to Joseph Smith arrose out of those claiming to be Mormons, take a look at the book *A Man Without Doubt,* and you'll see that Joseph's greatest opposition came from those who claimed to follow him. Opposition in scripture seems clear, but when *we* struggle in *our* environment, it becomes much more difficult to make decisions about what is right, what it wrong, what is good, what is bad, what is of God, what is deception, what is truth, what is false—but that's not a correct understanding, because the scriptures may reveal the conflict in sharp contrast, but it was no different in that day than it is today. Deciding between the opposing sides was not any more clear to those living at the time the scriptures were written than the opposition you encounter every day of your life. The scriptures were written by or about prophets who took clearly opposing positions from those who were deceived. The clarity you read in scriptures—because the views and opinions of prophets were used to *tell* about the events, but as the events *happened,* those living at the time had to have faith to distinguish between truth and error, to believe or to ignore a message from the Lord—it is no different for them than it is for the dilemma that we face today.

In the beginning there was a unitary priesthood. It was the Holy Order after the Order of the Son of God, but in order to prevent the too frequent repetition of the name of the Son of God, it got renamed, first, after Enoch and then, later, after Melchizedek—but it is referring to *one* original, unitary priesthood, which is the Holy Order after the Order of the Son of God. Yet, Joseph spoke about three great divisions.

In the beginning, because the first patriarchs had that original, unitary fullness of the priesthood after the Order of the Son of God, and because Abraham acquired the rights of the Fathers (or the first father, Adam), and therefore, like Adam, held the Holy Order after the Order of the Son of God, I use the term "Patriarchal" priesthood to refer to that original fullness and to nothing else. And I divide them up into three categories and three nomenclatures using those terms.

There is the Spirit of Elias; there is the Spirit of Elijah; and there is the Spirit of Messiah. These three great spirits unfolded in the work of God in the generations of man in a steady *descent*. And they will be, likewise, inverted like a chiasm and return in an *ascent*. So that at the end, it will be as it was in the beginning. That *same Priesthood which was in the beginning, shall [at the end of earth be] also* (Moses 6:7; see also Genesis 3:14 RE) was the prophecy that father Adam gave—Enoch quoting Adam; Moses quoting Enoch—the prophecy being contained in the Book of Moses (or soon, in the Book of Genesis).

The first spirit was the Spirit of Messiah. Adam dwelt in the presence of God. Adam represents that original fullness. Adam was the first man. Adam received instructions and spoke to God face-to-face. He dwelt in a temple—from which he was cast out—but he dwelt in a temple. And therefore, Adam represents the Spirit of Messiah.

The Spirit of Elijah is represented by Enoch who—when the earth was threatened with violence and men were to be destroyed because of the wickedness upon the face of the earth—was able to gather a people into a city of peace and to have the Lord come to *their* city of peace and remove *them* from the coming violence and destruction. He is a type of the Spirit of Elijah because Elijah would, likewise, later ascend in the fiery chariot into heaven. He is a type of the Spirit of Elijah because it is the Spirit of Elijah and that ascent into heaven that must *prefigure* the return of the Spirit of Messiah in the last days, in order to gather a people to a place that God will acknowledge, will visit, and will shield from the coming violence that will involve the destruction of the world. And so Enoch becomes the great type of the Spirit of Elijah—although the name, Elijah, is associated with a man who lived later still but who duplicated, among a hardened people in a fallen world, the same achievement as Enoch had accomplished—albeit Enoch did so with a city, and Elijah did it as a solitary ascending figure. Yet, it will be Elijah and his spirit which, in the last days, will, likewise, prepare a city for salvation and preservation.

And then there is the Spirit of Elias, which is represented by Noah—in which everything that had gone on before was lost, things begin anew, and Noah begins a ministry of attempting to preserve what was before by preaching repentance. And so Noah—as the messenger or the Elias—bears testimony of what once was.

Well, in the end, before the Lord's return, these same three spirits need to have been brought into the world, in order for the completion of the plan that Adam prophesied about and that was in the heart of the Lord from before the foundation of the world:

- The Spirit of Elias, declaring the gospel has to come again into the world—and it did in the person of Joseph Smith and in the message that he brought and in the scriptures that he restored and in the message and the practices that he was able to bring about—however short-lived *that* success may have been. Elias and the Spirit of Elias came through Joseph Smith into the world. We have yet to take the Spirit of Elias seriously enough to move on to receive something further, but we're now facing a crossroads in which it may be possible to restore again and continue the work and move forward.

- Moving forward successfully, however, will require the Spirit of Elijah. This time, the Spirit of Elijah is *not* to prepare a people so that they might ascend into heaven but instead to prepare a people so that those who come will not utterly destroy them. There must be a people prepared to endure the burning that is to come. Just as Enoch's people were prepared, shielded, and brought worthy to ascend, so as not to be destroyed by the flood, the Spirit of Elijah must prepare a people, in order for them to *endure* the day that is coming that shall burn the wicked as stubble. That will be people living in a place of peace, and they will be the *only* people who are not at war one with another. They will be people who will accept a body of teachings and allow them to govern their daily walk, both with each other and with God, so that they receive commandments, not a few, and revelations in their day—because that is what the people of Zion must necessarily be willing to do. We're promised that one *will* come who will be part of Jesse and part of Ephraim who will set in order—whose identity will be established by the work accomplished and *not* by the foolishness of prideful claims made by someone who's *done* nothing. If the work is done, once it's completed, you might be able to guess—but any fool can run around claiming themselves to be whatever their peculiar schizophrenia allows them to claim.

- The third spirit that is to return is that Spirit which was in the beginning. It is the Spirit of Messiah—this time, the Messiah himself. This time *He* will come to His house. He will dwell there. Everything must be prepared in order for Messiah to return. And so—in the end, as it was in the beginning, Adam being a type who represents dwelling in the presence of God or the Spirit of Messiah—in the end it will be Messiah, Himself, who returns to dwell among a people who are prepared.

- This is a chiasm. It's returning to the beginning, as a work of the last days walks backward in time to the point where it all began. Elias goes before to prepare for a greater work that is coming after, just as the Aaronic ordinances go before. Joseph Smith said the Spirit of Elias was revealed to him. But the Spirit of Elijah holds something more—it holds the revelations, ordinances, endowments, and sealings necessary to accomplish *[turning] the heart[s] of the fathers to the children* (Malachi 4:6; see also Malachi 1:12 RE) by securing an unbroken thread between the living and the Fathers in heaven. *This* can only be done in a temple prepared for that purpose. (I'm reading Joseph): "Without sealing of living children to the fathers in heaven (who dwell in glory and who sit upon thrones), the return of the Lord with Enoch and the other thousands who will accompany him would result in none escaping the judgments to come."

Those who've entered faithfully into the covenant this day are going to notice some things. The Spirit of God *is* withdrawing from the world. Men are increasingly more angry without good cause. The hearts of men are waxing cold. There is increasing anger and resentment of gentiles—in political terms, its rejection of white privilege. Language of scriptures (description of the events now underway) calls it the end of the times of the gentiles (see Luke 21:24; see also Luke 12:16 RE). This process, with the spirit withdrawing, will end on *this* continent as two prior civilizations ended—in fratricidal and genocidal warfare. For the *rest* of the world, it will be as in the days of Noah, in which as that light becomes eclipsed, the coldness of men's hearts is going to result in a constant scene of violence and bloodshed. The wicked will destroy the wicked. The covenant, if it is kept, will prevent *you* from losing light and warmth of heart as the spirit now steadily recedes from the world. The time will come when you will be astonished at the gulf between the light and truth *you* will comprehend and the darkness of mind at the world. Be charitable and patient, and labor to reach others. They *will* judge you harshly, but nevertheless, be kind to them. They're going to grow to fear you, but that's only part of how darkness responds to light. Give them no reason to fear you. The time will come for us to gather, but between now and then, be leaven. Preserve the world. Be salt. Preserve the world, even if it hates you.

In the Book of Matthew chapter 24 is Christ's most extensive prophesy about the future events including the time of his Second Coming. While He gives some details in Matthew chapter 24, there's a statement that He makes about: *As the days of Noah were, so shall also the coming of the Son of Man be* (Matthew 24:37; see also Matthew 11:11 RE). He makes an analogy between the events that occured during Noah's time and what we will see on the earth at the time of His return. Let me read you a description of the events at the time of Noah (and these are the kinds of events with which we typically associate the days of Noah):

> *And God saw that the wickedness of men had become great in the earth; and every man was lifted up in the imagination of the thoughts of his heart, being only evil continually... The earth was corrupt before God, and it was filled with violence. And God looked upon the earth, and behold, it was corrupt, for all flesh had corrupted its way upon the earth. And God said unto Noah: The end of all flesh is come before me, for the earth is filled with violence, and behold I will destroy all flesh from off the earth.* (Moses 8:22, 28-30; see also Genesis 5:12 RE)

Ominous. Terrible. Reason for concern—and that's what we generally think of—but there's another side to that. That other side includes, *obviously,* Noah. You can't have the days of Noah without having a Noah. Another contemporary who lived at the same time with Noah was Enoch—who built a city of righteousness; where people gathered together to worship the only true God; who were then, in turn, taken up to heaven. That group of people taken up to heaven are going to return with the Lord when He comes again in glory. Book of Jude (there's only one chapter in there): *Enoch also the seventh from Adam, prophesied of these, saying, Behold, the Lord cometh with ten thousands of his saints* (Jude 1:14; see also The Epistle of Judas 1:3 RE). There were those that were taken up into the heavens, numbering in the tens of thousands, who will return with Him. So if there is reason for pessimism when Christ predicts that *as was in the days of Noah so shall it be at the time of his return* (ibid), there's also *extraordinary* reason for optimism, because we're going to see things like Noah and his family (that included Shem, who would be renamed Melchizedek—about whom the apostle Paul had a great deal to say in the Book of Hebrews, comparing that man, the son of Noah, to the Lord Himself—actually, we ought to flip that; he compares the Lord Himself to that man), and then there is Enoch.

And so, while we tend to look at the prophecy Christ gave concerning His coming negatively—about how far degenerate the world is going to go—*those* are the *tares* ripening. Christ said we're not going to uproot the tares, bind them in bundles, and burn them, until the wheat also becomes ripe. You're here. You're Christian—and God would like *you* to be wheat. He would like you to ripen in righteousness while the world ripens in iniquity.

As I mentioned, the days of Noah *have* to include Noah, *have* to include Enoch, or in other words, in addition to all of the wretchedness that we look forward to—the world disintegrating and devolving into—there will be an opposition to that, a hand sent from God in the form of prophets, apostles— someone with a message. When I use the word "apostle," I mean the word in the same sense in which it is used in the New Testament; that is, someone with a message, coming to deliver a message from God to those to whom he speaks. I'm not talking about some officious chap claiming a title as his rightful inheritance, as is done in Mormonism. I'm not talking about someone who calls *themselves*. I'm talking about someone to whom God speaks and says, "Go tell the people thus." We believe we are approaching a moment in which the Lord is about to return. Read that chapter Matthew 24 [see also Matthew 11 RE]. All of the signs that he speaks of will occur in **one single generation**. If you've not noticed, the signs have begun to appear. It means you're living within a generation in which a great deal is to occur. *As it was in the days of Noah* (ibid), so it is about to be. That means dreadful things are coming, on the one hand, and it means prophets are going to be among us again—people with messages that come from the Lord.

The purpose of the Restoration is to return the *heart[s] of the children to [the] fathers* (Malachi 4:6; see also Malachi 1:12) because everything that is going to happen in the last days God established at the beginning, by a covenant that was made three years previous to the death of Adam, when he gathered together his posterity in the valley of Adam-ondi-Ahman, and he prophesied *whatsoever should befall [them] unto the latest generation* (D&C 107:56-57; see also T&C 154:20). And the Lord appeared and administered comfort unto Adam, and the gathering there rose up and called him Michael, the Prince. Right there, at that moment, at the beginning of the history of the family of Adam, he prophesies by the power of the Holy Ghost what should befall his descendants unto the latest generation in the presence— Adam-ondi-Ahman —Adam in the presence of Son Ahman. (See D&C 107:53-56; see also T&C 154:19-20.)

Adam-ondi-Ahman was an event. It's like the Super Bowl—it doesn't matter where you play it; wherever it is, it's the Super Bowl. Adam-ondi-Ahman is an event. When Adam is there in the presence of Son Ahman, that *is* Adam-ondi-Ahman—and you can say Springhill, Missouri is Adam-ondi-Ahman, but it doesn't matter where it happens, when it happens, and it will happen again, in fulfillment of that original prophecy that was made in the valley of Adam-ondi-Ahman when Adam was before Son Ahman the first time. When it happens again, it doesn't matter if that's in Mesa, Arizona or Springfield (I don't know... where do the Simpsons live? Springfield, USA) or Bogus Basin. Wherever it is that that occurs, that *is* Adam-ondi-Ahman. And it will certainly happen. The hearts of the children turning to the fathers so that the earth is not smitten with a curse means that the purpose of the Restoration, ultimately, is to return us back to something that *was* here in the beginning— the way in which it once was.

The dispensation of Adam, the dispensation of Enoch, the dispensation of Noah—all of which were running simultaneously at the time of the flood— *As it was in the days of Noah so also shall it be at the time of the coming of the Son of Man* (Matthew 24:37; see also Matthew 11:11 RE). We're going to have three different kinds of remnants operating at the same time at the coming of the Lord. A dispensation that *will* reflect somewhat of the Christian era; a dispensation that *will* reflect somewhat of Joseph Smith's era; and a dispensation that *will* reflect somewhat of the original—the one in which man stood in the presence of God—and of course, we've got a couple of those functioning, after a fashion. What we lack yet (and what necessarily will involve the presence of Ahman—Son Ahman—to achieve) is something that *He* must bring about. When He said: *[I will] bring again Zion* (Isaiah 52:8, Mosiah 12:22, 3 Nephi 16:18; see also Isaiah 18:8 RE, Mosiah 7:17 RE, 3 Nephi 7:6 RE), He literally means *that*, because you can't have it without His presence. *That* dispensation—that's the one that needs to occur. Joseph gave a talk where he referred to the Spirit of Elias and the Spirit of Elijah and the Spirit of Messiah—because there are really three great spirits that are involved with three great stages.

There's a great gulf separating us from the first Fathers of mankind. At the very beginning, a book of remembrance was kept in the language of Adam (Genesis 3:14; see also Genesis 3:14 RE). Enoch taught repentance and knowledge of God using *that* book of remembrance. Those records were passed down for generations until Abraham. He learned of the first Fathers, the Patriarchs, from those records. Abraham wrote: *But the records of the Fathers, even the patriarchs, concerning the right of Priesthood, the Lord, my God, preserved in mine own hands* (Abraham 1:31; see also Abraham 2:4 RE).

At the time of Abraham, Egypt was the greatest civilization on earth. Egypt was great because it imitated the original religion of the first Fathers. Abraham explained:

> *Now the first government of Egypt was established by Pharaoh, the eldest son of [Zeptah] the daughter of Ham, and it was after the manner of the government of Ham, which was patriarchal. Pharaoh, being a righteous man, established his kingdom and judged his people wisely and justly all his days, seeking earnestly to imitate that order established by the fathers in the first generations, In the days of the first patriarchal reign, even in the reign of Adam, and also Noah, his father, who blessed him with the blessings of the earth, and with the blessings of wisdom, but cursed him as pertaining to the Priesthood.* (Abraham 1:25-26; see also Abraham 2:3 RE)

Egypt began by imitating the pattern Adam, Seth, Enos, and their direct descendants, through Noah, used to organize the family of the faithful. Abraham calls it a "government," but it was a family. The title "Pharaoh" originally meant "great house" or "great family," because Pharaoh was the "father" over Egypt who taught and led them. Over time, however, the title "Pharaoh" came to mean "king" or "tyrant" who controlled people. The first Pharaohs—or founding father of Egypt—imitated the first Fathers of mankind. He could only imitate because he did not have the right to act as the patriarchal head of mankind. He, nevertheless, tried to be a shepherd who led by righteous example. Abraham knew more about the first Fathers than did the Egyptians because Abraham had the original book of remembrance written by the fathers in the language of Adam.

———

The foregoing excerpts are taken from:

- Denver's talk given at the "Zion Symposium" in Provo, UT on February 23, 2008;
- Denver's *40 Years in Mormonism Series*, Talk #4 titled "Covenants," given in Centerville, UT on October 6, 2013;

- Denver's *40 Years in Mormonism Series*, Talk #5 titled "Priesthood," given in Orem, UT on November 2, 2013;
- Denver's *40 Years in Mormonism Series*, Talk #6 titled "Zion," given in Grand Junction, CO on April 12, 2014;
- His conference talk titled "The Doctrine of Christ," given in Boise, ID on September 11, 2016;
- Denver's conference talk titled "Things to Keep Us Awake at Night," given in St. George, UT on March 19, 2017;
- His "Closing Remarks," given at the Covenant of Christ Conference in Boise, ID on September 3, 2017;
- Denver's *Christian Reformation Lecture Series*, Talk #1, given in Cerritos, CA on September 21, 2017;
- His remarks given at the Joseph Smith Restoration Conference in Boise, ID on June 24, 2018; and
- Denver's remarks titled "Keep the Covenant: Do the Work," given at the Remembering the Covenants Conference in Layton, UT on August 4, 2018.

In addition, Denver has written extensively about this topic. If you are interested in learning more, please review the following blog posts:

https://denversnuffer.com/2012/03/it-will-be-again/
https://denversnuffer.com/2010/05/blessed-are-the-peacemakers/
https://denversnuffer.com/2012/02/zion/
https://denversnuffer.com/2012/02/interview-by-my-wife/
https://denversnuffer.com/2010/07/1-nephi-14-14/

You may also find it helpful to review the scriptural record of Enoch and Noah, found in the Restoration Edition of Genesis, chapters 4-6, especially when compared with the King James version of Genesis 5-9.

65. Discernment, Epilogue

QUESTION: As an epilogue to our series on Discernment, Denver provides additional information and insight into false spirits and how we can avoid being overtaken by them.

————

DENVER: In addition to varying forms of ignorance and study, diligence and sloth, interest and indifference that separates each of us in our religious beliefs, there are also false spirits that mislead and confuse. The term "false spirit" is not limited to the idea of a devil, imp, or mischievous personage, but includes the much broader attitude, outlook, or cultural assumptions that people superimpose atop religion. False spirits—in the form of ignorant, incomplete, or incorrect ideas—are easily conveyed from one person to another. People convey false spirits every time they teach a false idea and the student accepts the idea. False spirits infect every religious tradition on earth. This is not limited to Eastern religions that *deny* Christ but also include Christianity *and* Mormonism. So long as there is anything false or any error, a false spirit prevails.

Different religious structures lend themselves to be overtaken by false spirits through different means. If you have a hierarchy, only the top needs to be taken captive by a false spirit. If it is a diffused religion, then all you have to do is take captive the theological seminaries in order to spread the false spirit. But if the religion is individual, and each person is standing on their own—accountable for their relation to God; accountable to learn, to pray, to reach upward, and to have God connect with them individually—then the only way to corrupt a ~~diffused~~ [individual] religion is to corrupt every single believer, every single practitioner.

In the new scriptures there is a section in which Joseph Smith discusses, at length, the topic of false spirits. It's an editorial he published in the *Times and Seasons* on April the 1st of 1842. This new section 147 in the Teachings and Commandments is worth careful study—the Teachings and Commandments being the new volume of scripture, recovering and restoring the text as it was originally—available, if you're interested, either for free online to read at scriptures.info; or if you want to purchase a copy, it's available through Amazon. This new section of the Teachings and Commandments is worth careful study.

Keep in mind the meaning of several words: "Priesthood" means a fellowship. You could have a priesthood that is a fellowship of men; you can have a priesthood that is a fellowship between men and angels; you can have a priesthood that is a fellowship between man and Christ; and you can have a priesthood that is a fellowship between man and God the Father. In section 147, Joseph Smith ties discerning of false spirits to priesthood, and therefore, when a person has an association with **heavenly** angels, they are not apt to be misled by fallen, **false** spirits. Joseph Smith also uses the term "keys" in section 147. Joseph used the term to mean "understanding," the greatest key being the ability to ask God and receive an answer. In the T&C 10:1: *I have given him* [referring to Joseph] *the keys of the mysteries of the revelations which are sealed.* In section 141, Joseph (speaking about his ordination of Hyrum and endowing and in blessing him): *Joseph, who shall show unto him the keys whereby he may ask and receive* (T&C 141:32 RE). And then a reference again in that same section to another servant: *Let my servant William [Law] also receive the keys by which he may ask and receive blessings* (ibid, vs. 33).

Joseph used the term "keys of the kingdom" to mean: when a person can ask and receive and answer each time he asks—they hold the keys of the kingdom because the kingdom belongs to God, and God must direct its affairs for it to be His. Here are some excerpts from Joseph's editorial, section 147: *One great evil is that men are ignorant of the nature of spirits: their power[s], laws, government, intelligence, [and so on], and imagine that when there is anything like power, revelation, or vision manifested, that it must be of God* (T&C 147:6 RE). That is a great evil.

After criticizing the experiences of Methodists, Presbyterians, and others, Joseph inquired about manifestations of false spirits: *They consider it to be the power of God and [the] glorious manifestation from God—a manifestation of what?* (ibid). He's just described what these people take as glorious manifestations. And he says—despite their supernatural appearance—it's *a manifestation of what? Is there any intelligence communicated? Are the curtains of Heaven withdrawn, or the purposes of God developed? Have they seen and conversed with an angel—[and] have the glories of futurity burst upon their view? No!* (ibid) In other words, nothing has advanced that is of God: edifying, instructing, and providing greater intelligence. It's simply spiritual voyeurism, and it's evil. *Nothing is [a] greater injury to the children of men than to be under the influence of a false spirit when they think they have the spirit of God* (ibid, vs. 9). Then he extends this outward, as he continued: *The Turks, the Hindus, the Jews, the Christians, the Indian[s]—in fact all nations have been deceived, imposed upon, and injured through the mischievous effects of false spirits* (ibid vs. 10). Then he, close to the end, says:

*And we shall at last have to come to this conclusion, whatever we may think of revelation, that without it we can neither know nor understand anything of God, or the devil; ...it is equally as plain that without a divine communication they must remain in ignorance. The world **always** mistook false prophets for true ones, and those that were sent of God they considered to be the false prophets, and hence they killed, stoned, punished and imprisoned the true prophets, and [these] had to hide themselves in deserts, and dens, and caves of the earth, and though the most honorable men of the earth, they banished them from their society as vagabonds, [whilst] they cherished, honored, and supported knaves, vagabonds, hypocrites, imposters, and the basest of men.* (ibid vs. 11)

Read that section. False spirits are actively involved whenever God begins a work. And there are many false spirits, vying for your acceptance now at work among us. That having been said—it's time to stop dividing and to begin uniting. There are enough divisions in Christianity and in Mormonism. This does not need to continue. The restoration is intended to bring unity, not division. Division needs to end.

The vineyard that the Lord began the restoration in was cumbered with all sorts of strange fruit. I mean... I've spent a lifetime referring to it as the Jacob 5; in the new Book Mormon layout, it's one of the very few chapters that I can actually point you to from memory—it's Jacob 3 in the new layout. So, I'm becoming familiar with it.

Talking about the condition of this vineyard—and it's cumbered with all sorts of strange fruit. None of it worth harvesting; none of it worth keeping; none of it worth laying up and preserving against the harvest. The allegory says:

This is the last time that I shall nourish my vineyard, for the end is nigh at hand and the season speedily cometh. And if ye labor with your mights with me, ye shall have joy in the fruit [with] which I [shall] lay up unto myself against the time which will soon come. And it came to pass that the servants did go and labor with their mights, and the Lord of the vineyard labored also with them. And they did obey the commandments of the Lord of the vineyard in all things. (Jacob 3:26-27 RE)

Well, *that's* fairly critical. The Lord's gonna labor with ya, but he's gonna expect you to obey his commandments in all things. Have you recently read the Answer to the Prayer for Covenant? Are you determined to obey the Master of the vineyard and His commandments in all things? Maybe we oughta read that twice before we berate one another, belittle one another, argue with one another, dismiss one another, otherwise we're really *not* laboring *with* the Lord of the vineyard to help for the coming harvest. Instead, we're embracing a false spirit, and we're dividing one another, and we're trying— Our ambition, whether we are willing to acknowledge it or not, our ambition is to set this into the same sort of divisive factions as the Lord condemned to Joseph in 1820: *[they have] a form of godliness, but they deny the power thereof...they teach for commandments the doctrines of men* (JSH 1:19; see also JSH 2:5 RE). They're *all* corrupt.

And there began to be the natural fruit again in the vineyard. And the natural branches began to grow and thrive exceedingly, and the wild branches began to be plucked off and to be cast away... (Jacob 3:27 RE). Some of the plucking and some of the casting away is voluntarily done by those who submit to false spirits that stir them up to anger against one another, and they depart from fellowship, thinking themselves justified before God when, in fact, all they're doing is being plucked and cast away.

And so, I took the Book of Mormon seriously. I entertained no doubts. I employed no apologetics. I just accepted the book and tried to understand it. As I did so—going through the text of the Book of Mormon—there were moments when there were glints, where something leapt off the page to me as if someone had flashed the reflection of the sun off a windshield passing down the street, and it aligns with the right angle of the sun. The text itself seemed to spark to me. As I took it seriously, I could breath the spirit of the writers. I beheld more as I went through that text than the text will yield to the cautious and wary reader. The Book of Mormon—like the spirits I referred to earlier—the Book of Mormon also has a spirit, and that Spirit is Christ. If you want to relate to the Spirit of Christ and not a false spirit, drop all your apprehensions, lower your guard, and see if the Book of Mormon does not yield the Spirit of Christ. It was a better text than any other I had encountered in conveying the Spirit of Christ. It *is* in fact the most correct book, and a man *can* get closer to God by abiding it's precepts than any other book. It can be trusted as a source of direct information in our language. We don't have to encounter uncertainties and hurdles in trying to manage the language and understand the vocabulary, as is always the challenge when you're looking at a New Testament or an Old Testament text.

The New Testament text has a statement that was made by Christ:

> *Think not that I have come to destroy the law or the prophets. I am not come to destroy, but to fulfill; for truly I say unto you, heaven and earth*

must pass away, but one jot or one tittle shall by no means pass from the law until all shall be fulfilled. [Whosoever] therefore shall break one of [the] least [of these] commandments and [shall] teach men so to do, he shall by no means be saved in the kingdom of Heaven. But [whosoever] shall do and teach these commandments of the law until it shall be fulfilled, the same shall be called great and shall be saved in the kingdom of Heaven. For I say unto you, except your righteousness shall exceed that of the scribes and Pharisees, you shall in no case enter into the kingdom of Heaven. (Matthew 3:17 RE)

That's a text from Joseph Smith's Translation—or Joseph Smith's Inspired Version—of the New Testament. He's added a few words in there, including the word "until."

The English word that gets used in this text about "fulfilled" was translated from the Greek word "pleroo." Pleroo can be interpreted: "to make fully known, proclaim fully" instead of "to accomplish." In that sense, a scholar might conclude from the Greek that Christ's statement has nothing to do with "ending" or with "completing" the law of Moses. And there are scholars who have taught that—Christians. So, there's an ambiguity about whether Christ intended for the law of Moses to come fully to an end or if He was simply establishing it firmly by fulfilling it or adhering to it. Any ambiguity about what Christ intended is removed when His declaration to the Nephites is added to your understanding:

And it came to pass that when Jesus had said these words he perceived that there were some among them who marveled, and wondered what he would concerning the law of Moses; for they understood not the saying that old things had passed away, and that all things had become new. And he said unto them: Marvel not that I said unto you that old things [had] passed away, and that all things had become new. Behold, I say unto you that the law is fulfilled that was given unto Moses. Behold, I am he that gave the law, and I am he who covenanted with my people Israel; therefore, the law in me is fulfilled, for I have come to fulfill the law; therefore it hath an end. The covenant which I have made with my people is not all fulfilled; but the law which was given unto Moses hath an end in me. (3 Nephi 15:2-5,8; see also 3 Nephi 7:2 RE)

Those who teach the law of Moses has not come to an end are led by a false spirit. That having been said, someone that has been misled by a false spirit does not necessarily mean that they are an evil person. It only means they have been misled. Recall Christ rebuking Peter and calling Peter "Satan" because Peter was advising the Lord against the determined trip to Jerusalem where he would be crucified. And Peter told him, advised him, counselled him, and objected *far be it from you, Lord* (Matthew 9:2 RE). Don't do this thing. And the Lord, responding to Peter, called him "Satan." There are many people who are only kept from the truth because they do not know where to find it.

The obligation of those who can teach truth is to teach it. Overcoming most false spirits is to be done by gentleness, meekness, pure knowledge, and persuasion; not by rebuking, condemning, and dismissing the honest seeker for truth. At some point every one of us has emerged from a cloud of falsehoods into acceptance of some truth. We're no better than others who remain under that cloud but we have an obligation to invite them to join in receiving light and truth. Likewise, we have an obligation to continue to search for truth. Until you have an understanding of *all* things, you're still mislead, at least in part.

The prophets are not all fulfilled, and there will yet be many things returned and restored—this will include holy days—when we have a holy place to observe in proper order the things practiced between the time of Adam until the time of Abraham.

So the list goes on:

- The *mountains* is the first thing.

- *To divide the seas*: We have an example of that with Moses.

- *To dry up waters*: We have an example of that with Joshua when they reached the river Jordan.

- *To turn them out of their course*—which was done again at the time of Enoch.

- *To put at defiance the armies of nations*: Elijah.

- *To divide the earth, to break every band, to stand in the presence of God, to do all things according to **his** will, according to **his** command.* When it comes to "breaking every band," keep that in mind, because we are going to return to that in a moment. And then it says,

- To *subdue principalities and powers*. **These** are in the spiritual realm. Commanding devils? Subduing principalities and powers? These are rebellious spirits, cast down from heaven. These are those that pretend to be—and often are—false ministering spirits or angels.

- Have any of you ever witnessed the miracle of healing? Because I have. I've participated in some of those. But there are people I know who I would loved to have healed, who I begged God for the blessing that they *be* healed. I've gotten answers. I've been told why they will not be healed. But I don't have the ability to require God to heal at *my* insistence. Nor do any of you. Nor has any man *ever* in all the account of scripture. Christ could not heal some people in some instances, and he was the son of God. In all of scripture, there is only one moment when it appears that anyone could be healed no matter what their condition was—only one time—and at that moment, Christ was resurrected; and he was appearing as a resurrected being, not still as a mortal. As a mortal, Christ could not heal some. As a mortal, Christ could not persuade the Father to change the Father's will. Some of you, like the antagonists of Job, have said to others of you that you don't have enough faith to be healed. You're Worm-tongue. You're a false spirit. You're an accuser of the brethren. You have absolutely no right to make that assertion. Would you tell Christ when He could not perform a healing, "Jesus, your problem is you don't have enough faith." Because that's essentially what you are saying. You're saying, "Men ought to be sovereign, not God." You're saying, "Signs, which surely are given, signs follow people of faith incessantly."

There is a great deal left to be done. And there is no one seriously entertaining the possibility of constructing a city of holiness, a city of peace, a people that are fruit worthy to be laid up against the harvest. No one has made the effort until now. And while you may look at us and say, "You've done a crude job. You've done a rudimentary job. It needs improvement." Then help us improve it! Stop sitting back and throwing rocks. This is a time to gather, not to disperse. The same garbage that existed at the beginning—when Joseph looked around and saw confusion and disharmony—wants to creep in among us. Recognize that's a false spirit. If you'll cast it out of yourself and if you'll look at the words of the covenant that was offered in September of 2017, what you'll find is that Christ wants us—like the Book of Mormon explains —to be meek, to be humble, and to be easily intreated. And therefore, entreat one another to honor God, and recognize that all of us aspire to be equal.

Whether you're at the top or at the root, the aspiration is the same—to be equal.

There's a statement in the Book of Mormon—it's a remarkable statement because it's spoken from God's vantage point, but it's a harrowing, it's a pathetic comment; it instills pathos in the person that hears it—I think Nephi wrote it: *[God loveth all] who will have him to be their God* (1 Nephi 17:20; see also 1 Nephi 5:20 RE). Because anytime you draw a line, anytime you set a mark, and say, "I will go thus far and no further" with a God who wants to walk with you from Jerusalem to Emmaus and spend the day conversing with you and opening to your mind how in Moses and all the prophets—everything —testified of Him, and you say, "Ummm, no, I'm not willing to go to Emmaus. You got three hundred yards, and at the end of three hundred yards, I'm turning back. Because I'll go thus far and no further." They will *never* have the opportunity to break bread and have their eyes opened and realize that they're walking alongside the Savior as they go on this journey.

You don't interrupt it. The religion of Christ is living. A living God has a living religion. And a living religion makes us *all* insecure, because we don't know what's coming next. We have to be humble enough and nimble enough to respond to whatever it is that comes next. That makes every one of us uncomfortable. That's who God is; that's what His religion is; that's what we're expected to accept.

So when a false spirit comes along and preaches, "Thus far and no further," or "You have to take a detour"—because the religion is not attempting to culminate in a restoration fully of all things that go back to the beginning—we have to become Jewish-Mormons, or we have to become Christian-Mormons, or we have to become Evangelical-Mormons, or we have to become Buddhist-Mormons. Well, Mormonism includes all of those things—but it isn't *that*. We should believe in a restoration that is going to culminate in a return of everything—including things that we, right now, don't know about and will never know about, if we don't stay on task with God, welcoming every word that proceedeth forth from the mouth of God.

———

The foregoing excerpts are taken from:

- Denver's lecture titled "Signs Follow Faith," given in Centerville, UT on March 3, 2019; and

- Podcast 63 titled "Every Word - Part 2," recorded March 4, 2019, in Sandy, UT.

66. Allegory of the Olive Tree

In this episode, Denver discusses the Allegory of the Olive Tree (Jacob 3 RE).

———

DENVER: I mentioned that one of the criticisms of the Book of Mormon is the prevalent Christology—as a criticism, because people don't believe that Christ was so openly known, openly talked about, openly *expected* in the pre-Babylonian captivity of the people in the Bible. But in the Book of Mormon we learn that there were some prophets who had left a testimony and a record, before we get to Isaiah, who clearly influenced Isaiah and who spoke openly about the coming of Christ.

One of those prophets was named Zenos. In the Book of Mormon—I forget the total number of words—I went through and I copied and I pasted every quote of the prophet Zenos in the Book of Mormon into a single Word document one time; and I'm going from memory and my memory could be off, but it was in excess of 3,000 words—and I think it was about 3,200 words—that are from the record of Zenos quoted in the Book of Mormon.

From the vernacular within the Book of Mormon, the references there about "the prophet" appear to identify Zenos. When we talk about "the prophet" of the Old Testament, we think of Isaiah; they thought of Zenos. Zenos and Isaiah talk about the same topic. Zenos went before, and Isaiah came after. Zenos was apparently a Northern Kingdom prophet, and Isaiah was a Southern Kingdom prophet. Isaiah's record about Christ is poetic and, like most poetry, tends to be obscure—beautifully crafted language with difficult allegories to understand. Zenos, on the other hand, was pretty blunt and pretty straightforward; you could not miss the point of Zenos. Whereas it's very possible to take the Isaiah text and you can construe it, because of its vague allegories, to mean just about anything, Zenos could not be reformed to eliminate Christology. It was blatantly present in the Zenos text, therefore Zenos got dropped from the Old Testament.

Isaiah, on the other hand, could be used to obscure the Christology because —although he points forward to, in magnificent ways, the coming of the Savior and His sacrifice—the suffering-servant passages could be interpreted to not mean an individual Savior, Jesus Christ, but rather the people of God (or Israel)—who went through so much persecution because they preserved a religion that testified of the true God. And therefore, the language of Isaiah was susceptible of interpretation to construe it away from pointing to Jesus

Christ. Zenos could not be so handled or interpreted. He clearly spoke about this coming Savior.

As a result, in the reconstitution of the scriptures, the references contained in Zenos were too plentiful to allow it to get into the canon of scriptures; and it got obliterated from the scriptures that were re-gathered at the time of Ezra and Nehemiah. But the record of Zenos was included within what that planting of people in the Book of Mormon took with them. They didn't lose the prophecies of Zenos, and so it informed them about Christ in very specific ways.

The presence of Christology in the Book of Mormon are the inevitable result of possessing scriptures that speak candidly, openly, and frankly about the coming of this Messiah. And so, when you pick up the Book of Mormon and read it, you literally are reading a text that has not been corrupted by these other influences. And the abundant presence of a Christological theology in the Book of Mormon is not evidence that the Book of Mormon is false, but it is evidence that the traditions that surrounded the religion of the Jews—as it came to be understood when Christ came to earth—*that* was what was corrupted. *That* was what was incomplete. *That* was what failed to preserve the original religion that began all the way back with the first fathers, when they learned of a promised Messiah who would save us from the fall of Adam and death entering the world, by reversing that as the "second Adam"—as the apostle Paul described Him—the "second Adam" who would plant a restored family, brought back to life through the power of the resurrection, so that *as in Adam all die, ...so in Christ shall all be made alive* (1 Corinthians 15:22; see also 1 Corinthians 1:63 RE).

Prophecies, as I've said before, revolve around two, and primarily two events only. One being the first coming of the Lord, the other one being the coming of the Lord in judgment at the end of the world. Now there are plenty of prophecies that reckon to other events that are intermediate; however, the primary focus is the first and the second coming of the Lord. The vindication of the promise that the Father made in the beginning that He would redeem us all from the grave, and the vindication of the promise that, at some point, the world would come to an end as to its wickedness, and there would be peace again on the earth—everything revolves around those two prophetic events.

The seed that's to be preserved, and the effort that the Lord has made to try and preserve the seed that He needs to have, in order to establish a population on the earth at His coming, is a topic about which Zenos prophesied—an allegory that was picked up by Jacob, and Jacob preserves it in his testament, the book of Jacob, in chapter 5 (see also Jacob 3:7-28 RE). Nephi wrote the first books in the small plates of Nephi, and in there is his testimony, is his prophecy. What he did was he adopted the words of Isaiah in order to explain what it was that he, Nephi, had seen. But he used Isaiah's words as the means to do that. And Jacob does the same thing.

Jacob says, I want everyone to come up to the temple; I'm going to deliver to you a prophecy (Jacob 4:15; see also Jacob 3:6 RE). And when they get there and he delivers his prophecy, he reads them the allegory—was taken from Zenos—which goes on and on about the history of God's chosen people. And when he finishes reading this lengthy chapter from Zenos, he says, Here's the words of my prophecy—'cause I told ya I was gonna give it—here it is, it's coming: "What I just told you is true." And that's Jacob's testimony. Jacob adopts the words of Zenos in order to bear testimony of the things which he, Jacob, had been taught by the Lord, when the Lord spoke to him face-to-face.

Jacob didn't invent a new allegory. Jacob didn't invent a new narrative. He didn't invent a new story, and he didn't invent new scriptures. He simply took the words of prophets that went before and said, "Here they are. The words of my prophecy are: they are true." Nephi had done the same thing. Jacob does the same thing. And so, in Nephi, Jacob saw the example which he chose to follow; and he did follow. And we're going to look at this prophecy, which—delivered by Zenos—is reaffirmed, ratified, renewed; and a second witness is given to us in the form of Jacob, in the fifth chapter of Jacob. (But as I understand it, we're going to take a two minute break while you change discs, so...).

Alright, so, I want to skip to the time period that is relevant to our day—in Jacob chapter 5, beginning at verse 48—because all the rest of that stuff is past history. And what we're trying to do now is to figure out—from where we are—how we get to the spot in which we might not be burned up, root *and* branch.

Beginning at verse 48: *And it came to pass that the servant said unto his master: Is it not the loftiness of [the] vineyard—have not the branches thereof overcome the roots which are good?* That is to say, the roots—the original covenant, the original stock from which we reckon—they were good. But we've become lofty in the way in which *we* approach things, and as a consequence of that, *we* have done something that has so cumbered the construct of where we find ourselves that we've essentially destroyed the ability of the roots to do us any good.

And because the branches have overcome the roots thereof, behold they grew faster than the strength of the roots, taking strength unto themselves. That is their pride, their haughtiness. They decided that *they* were driving this, and not the covenants that were originally made in the beginning.

> *Behold, I say, is this not the cause that the trees of [the] vineyard have [all] become corrupted? And it came to pass that the Lord of the vineyard said unto the servant: Let us [go down, let us] go to and hew down the trees of the vineyard and cast them into the fire, that they shall not cumber the ground of my vineyard, for I have done all. What could I have done more for my vineyard? But, behold, the servant said unto the Lord of the vineyard: Spare it a little longer. And the Lord said: [Yeah, we'll] spare it a little longer, for it grieveth me that I should lose the trees of my vineyard.* (Jacob 5:48-51; see also Jacob 3:23 RE)

See, the Lord, despite the fact that He can't think of anything else that He's left undone in all of His preparations—and it is only that, it is only His preparations— Go to Doctrine & Covenants section 19 and look at what it is that the Lord did for us in the atonement. In describing what He went through, in verse 19 of section 19 of the Doctrine & Covenants, the Lord says: *Glory be to the Father, I partook and finished my preparations unto the children of men.* That's what He did! And He has finished that. He finished His preparations.

But [verse] 20 now is us: *Wherefore, I command you again to repent, lest I humble you with my almighty power* (D&C 19:19-20; see also T&C 4:5-6). That's us. He's done His part. What more could He do? Well, the only other thing He could do is rob us of our agency, and He's not prepared to do that because our existence then would come to an end. Because without the freedom to choose, we don't have existence. Therefore, what more could He have done?

But it does grieve Him that He's going to lose the trees of His vineyard. *Wherefore* [the Lord says], *let us take of the branches of these which I have planted in the nethermost parts of my vineyard* [that's where we find ourselves], *and let us graft them into the tree from whence they came* [that is, let's restore the covenant, or at least make it possible for it to be so]; *and let us pluck from the tree those branches whose fruit is most bitter* [that's coming], *and graft in the natural branches of the tree in the stead thereof. And this will I do that the tree may not perish, that, perhaps* [perhaps, on the off chance that—that without the ability to control the outcome, that depending upon what you decide to do—perhaps], *[the Lord] may preserve unto [Himself] the roots thereof for mine own purpose* (Jacob 5:52-53; see also Jacob 3:23 RE). That is some of the promises that were made back to the fathers, that their seed would not be utterly destroyed, might be fulfilled—perhaps.

How great a number is required in order for the Lord to vindicate His promise? It's not numerosity; it's never been about a big volume. It's the quality of the salvation. Because if you can save but one, what you have saved is infinite and eternal. And therefore it continues on forever.

Behold, the roots of the natural branches of the tree which I planted whithersoever I would are yet alive. Those promises remain. They are still in play. What the Father promised, what the covenants that were established did, remain in play. It is yet possible for the Lord to vindicate everything that has been given. *Wherefore, that I may preserve them also for mine own purpose, I will take of the branches of this tree, and I will graft them in unto them.* This is the process by which the house of Israel is restored—not in the way that you mass-produce, but in the way in which some rise up and lay hold upon that original religion that belonged to the fathers, that came down from the beginning, that existed one time, that is to exist again. *Yea, I will graft [into] them the branches of their mother tree, that I may preserve the roots also unto mine own self.* Notice the word "mother" appears in there, too—the mother tree. *When they may be sufficiently strong perhaps they may bring forth good fruit unto me that I may yet have glory in the fruit of my vineyard.*

And then they go through things. Verse 61: *Call servants, that we may labor diligently with our might in the vineyard, that we may prepare the way, that I may bring forth again the natural fruit.* That's the whole purpose of the endeavor. And when they call servants in order to help them, the labor of the servants is confined to trying to make the vineyard finally produce fruit again. Verse 62:

> Let us go to and labor with our might this last time, for behold the end draweth nigh, and this is for the last time that I shall prune my vineyard. [He tells them again in verse 64:] ...the last time, for the end draweth nigh. And if it be so that these last grafts shall grow, and [shall] bring forth natural fruit, then [ye shall] prepare the way for them, that they may grow. [Again in verse 71:] For behold, this is the last time that I shall nourish my vineyard; for the end is nigh...the season speedily cometh...if ye labor with your might with me ye shall have joy in the fruit which I shall lay up unto myself against the time which will soon come. And it came to pass...the servants did go and labor with their mights; and the Lord of the vineyard labored also with them.

Because the Lord, in the last effort, is not going to leave the servants that he sends unattended to by *His* ministration. This is why in the verses we've been reading, and every location we've been at, we find the personal ministry of the Lord Jesus Christ direct, immediate, and involved. He continues to remain personally in charge of what is going to happen. But as it begins to happen, they have to sit back and watch. Because the question isn't "Is the labor any less, any (less) well prepared, any less capable, any less complete?" The question is: "What are the branches going to do?"

You can minister all you want to the tree, but the tree has to respond— sometimes to what they view as offensive pruning, offensive digging, offensive conduct of cutting, and moving, and grafting, and saying, "What you have here is error; what you have here is a bundle of false traditions that will damn you."

You can plant the doctrine; you can restore the truth; you can have the Prophet Joseph Smith declare to you that he wants to be held to account for every word of the testimony that he delivers to you in a canonized set of scripture. But if you decide that you're going to throw that away, and you will not allow it to graft in and inform you about the nature of God, and the nature of the religion that God is seeking to deliver to you; then the ministration, and the pruning, and the care does not result in fruit. It simply results in a rather damaged vineyard continuing to produce precious little, other than what is suitable to be gathered in bundles and burned—the loftiness of the people.

Grafting is to restore, to reconnect, to return; or in other words, to *plant in the hearts of the children the promises made to the fathers. And the hearts of the children shall turn to [the] fathers.* That's what Moroni said. That's why Moroni reworked the language of Malachi in verse 39 of the Joseph Smith History: *He shall plant in the hearts of the children the promises made to the fathers, and the hearts of the children shall turn to their fathers* (see also T&C JSH 3:4). The work has been for one purpose. Joseph Smith began it; and he laid out all the information necessary for you to be able to identify who the fathers are. And he laid out all the information necessary for you to be able to identify what the covenants were.

And now, the question is, are we able at this point to preserve the roots— which is the Lord's purpose—by producing fruit in our day. The vineyard, that the Lord began the restoration in, was cumbered with all sorts of strange fruit. I mean, I've spent a lifetime referring to it as the Jacob chapter 5. In the new Book of Mormon layouts, it's one of the very few chapters that I can actually point you to from memory. It's Jacob chapter 3 in the new layout. So, I'm becoming familiar with it.

Talking about the condition of this vineyard, and it's cumbered with all sorts of strange fruit—none of it worth harvesting; none of it worth keeping; none of it worth laying up and preserving against the harvest—the allegory says:

> *This is the last time that I shall nourish my vineyard; for the end is nigh at hand, and the season speedily cometh; and if ye labor with your [mights] with me ye shall have joy in the fruit [with] which I shall lay up unto myself against the time which will soon come. And it came to pass that the servants did go and labor with their mights; and the Lord of the vineyard labored also with them; and they did obey the commandments of the Lord of the vineyard in all things.* (Jacob 5:71-72; see also Jacob 3:26-27 RE)

Well, that's fairly critical! The Lord's going to labor with you, but He's going to expect you to obey His commandments in all things. Have you recently read the Answer to the Prayer for Covenant? Are you determined to obey the Master of the vineyard and His commandments in all things? Maybe we ought to read that *twice* before we berate one another, belittle one another, argue with one another, dismiss one another. Otherwise, we're really not laboring with the Lord of the vineyard to help for the coming harvest. Instead, we're embracing a false spirit, and we're dividing one another, and we're trying— Our ambition, whether we're willing to acknowledge it or not, our ambition is to set this into the same sort of divisive factions as the Lord condemned to Joseph in 1820. They have *a form of godliness, but they deny the power thereof. They teach for commandments the doctrines of men. They're* **all** *corrupt* (see JSH 1:19; see also T&C JSH 2:5).

And there began to be the natural fruit again in the vineyard; and the natural branches began to grow and thrive exceedingly; and the wild branches began to be plucked off and to be cast away (Jacob 5:73; see also Jacob 3:27 RE). Some of the plucking and some of the casting away is voluntarily done by those who submit to false spirits that stir them up to anger against one another, and they depart from fellowship thinking themselves justified before God—when, in fact, all they're doing is being plucked and cast away.

And they did keep the root and the top thereof equal, according to the strength thereof. We are seeking to keep it equal. Every one of us is on the same plain. No one's getting supported by tithing money. If they are, that's done by a local fellowship that has voluntarily determined that they have one among them in need, because the tithes are gathered and used to help the poor. There's no general fund being accumulated, and there's no one who does anything that they get compensated for.

This is the only group of people whose religion requires, *incessantly*, sacrifice. No one gets paid. No one gets remunerated. Everything that's done is done at a price of sacrifice. If you're a person in need among a fellowship, the tithes are appropriately used because that's what they're for. They're for the poor. They're not for a leader.

You have to keep the root and you have to keep the top equal. If you allow inequality to creep in at the beginning, the end result is lavish palaces—in which some fare sumptuously. And others ask to eat the crumbs that fall from the table because they're treated so unequally; and their despair, and their poverty, and their need goes ignored. Among us, it can't go ignored because the money is gathered at a fellowship level. And if there is someone in need among you, and you don't minister to their needs, **you're cruel**.

And thus they labored, with all diligence, according to the commandments of the Lord of the vineyard, even until the bad had been cast away (Jacob 5:74; see also Jacob 3:27 RE). If you can't tolerate equality; if you can't tolerate the top and the root being equal; if you can't tolerate peace among brethren; then go ahead and be bad and cast yourself away. If you feel moved upon to do that, well that's the Lord of the vineyard getting rid of you.

Even until the bad had been cast away out of the vineyard, and the Lord had preserved unto himself that the trees had become again the natural fruit; and they became like unto one body; and the [fruit] were equal. That word "equal" shows up so often in the labor that the Lord of the vineyard is trying to accomplish with the people, that you ought to take note. We ought to probably typeset it **EQUAL**—in double-sized font. We're not going to do that, so you have to underline the word, or circle the word, or pay attention to it. The purpose is to go and become equal with one another. As soon as you set out to create rank, and position, and hierarchy— Admittedly, within the parable there is a top and there is a root, admittedly, but the objective is to achieve equality. If you start out saying the one is greater or better than the other, you're never going to arrive at the point that is the purpose of the parable. The purpose of the labor of the Lord of the vineyard and the fruit were equal.

The greatest instruction (that I know of) given by God—at any time to any generation—is a rule of community found in the Sermon on the Mount and in the Sermon at Bountiful. *Now* we have the Answer to the Prayer for

Covenant, that not only resonates with the message of those two sermons, but applies it directly to us in our peculiar circumstances—to fix our peculiar defects and urge us to become more like Him.

The Lord revealed His plan for our day approximately 3,000 years ago. We now begin fulfilling that ancient prophecy. Our current struggles were foreseen and foretold. The Lord of the whole earth considered destroying all the wicked, but His servant pled for him to grant more time (see Jacob 5:49-50; see also Jacob 3:23 RE). The Lord of the whole earth hearkened to His servant and decreed that He would spare it, and would labor within His vineyard a final time in our day (verse 51).

The Lord determined long ago He would use a covenant to graft back people who had become wild and bitter, and connect them to the original roots of the Tree of Life; or in other words, restore people in our day to His covenant. The covenant offered today is from God, and is the first step required to restore the family of God, or Tree of Life, on the earth. It will change the lost, wild, and bitter fruit, and begin to recover them and turn their hearts to the fathers. This will connect those who are living today with the natural roots, or those fathers who still hold rights under the original covenant (verses 52-54).

Work for this grafting began years ago, and it took a great leap forward approximately two years ago with the effort to recover, as near as possible, the text of the Book of Mormon and Joseph Smith revelations. The initial graft happens today.

Although the Book of Mormon has remained in print continuously since its first publication in 1830, Latter-day Saints did not respect it as scripture until the 1950s. The book has been a test and not the fulsome revelation of all God's dealings, even with the Nephites. *And when they shall have received this, which is expedient that they should have first, to try their faith, and if it so be that they shall believe these things then shall the greater things be made manifest unto them* (3 Nephi 26:9; see also 3 Nephi 12:1 RE).

From its founding until 1937, Brigham Young University did not offer a single course on the Book of Mormon. Only in 1961 did it become mandatory for incoming BYU freshmen to take a class on the Book of Mormon.

Hugh Nibley defended the Book of Mormon in a debate with Sterling McMurrin in 1955. Nibley offended nearly all those who were in attendance because of his serious defense, some of whom declared flatly that the Book of

Mormon needed to be abandoned because it was driving the best minds out of the church (Peterson, Boyd Jay, *Hugh Nibley: A Consecrated Life*. SLC: Greg Kofford Books, 2002, p.160). Although Hugh Nibley advocated taking the Book of Mormon seriously in the 1950s, the Saints only began to take it seriously after Ezra Taft Benson's General Conference talk in 1986.

The church was underwhelmed with the Book of Mormon until late in the 20th century. Noel B. Reynolds wrote about this Church-wide neglect in his article *The Coming Forth of the Book of Mormon in the Twentieth Century*, found at BYU Studies, Volume 38. He wrote, "Book of Mormon was largely overlooked throughout the nineteenth and early twentieth centuries. A handful of Church leaders appealed for more serious attention to the book, however the Church as a whole did not respond in any dramatic way to any of these urgent messages until after President Benson's emphatic messages in 1986."

Within 18 months of the restoration through Joseph Smith, the Saints were condemned for unbelief. By January 1841, the Saints were warned they would be rejected, with their dead, if they failed to repent and keep God's commandments (see D&C 84:54-57; see also T&C 82:20). They did not repent, and so, the restoration has been in a pause for four and five generations, waiting for God to begin it anew. Today marks a moment when the stirrings that have been underway for years result in God's offering to establish His people, on earth, by a covenant He ordains.

The few ready to receive the Lord's offer today are scattered to the nethermost parts of His vineyard (Jacob 5:52; see also Jacob 3:23 RE). Despite this, a live broadcast on the Internet allows them to be grafted in at the same moment this is happening in Boise, Idaho. Correspondingly, those who utterly refuse to accept the offered covenant are plucked from the restoration's Tree of Life because they are bitter fruit, unable to meet the Lord's requirements. The Lord is taking this step to preserve part of humanity, not to destroy it (that's verse 53).

A few descendants of the covenant fathers have the natural gift of faith. That gift belongs to the natural branches (that's verse 54). When grafted, we are connected to the natural roots, or covenant fathers, as heirs of the promises made to them. Even after the covenant, there will still be those who are bitter and wild, who will be unable to produce natural fruit despite the covenant. These will remain for a time despite their bitterness (verses 56 and 57). Today, only the "most bitter" who refuse to be grafted in will be trimmed away (verse 57).

We look forward to more "nourishing"— or restoring of truths, light, and commandments— which will bless those who receive. But for those who will not, the continuing restoration will prune them away (verse 58). These bitter and wild branches must still be cut off and cast away. These steps are necessary to preserve the opportunity for the natural fruit to fully return (verse 59). The *good* must overcome the evil. This takes time, and it means that the Lord's patience is extended to give time to develop and further improve.

We are not expected, and cannot become natural fruit in a single step. But we are expected to accept the initial graft today. The Lord is taking these steps so that "perhaps"—and that's a deliberate word—perhaps we may become natural fruit worthy to be preserved in the coming harvest (that's verse 60). "Perhaps" is the right word. Some who were grafted will still be plucked away and burned. But others will bear natural fruit and be preserved.

Accepting the covenant is not the final step. Our choices will determine whether we are bitter or natural fruit—*that* will decide our fate. Just as the ancient allegory foretold, the covenant makes us servants and laborers in the vineyard (verse 61). We are required to—this is from the covenant—*Seek to recover the lost sheep remnant of this land and of Israel and no longer forsake them. Bring them unto [the Lord] and teach them of [His] ways, to walk in them* (T&C 158:11). If we fail to labor to recover them, we break the covenant.

We must labor for this last time in the Lord's vineyard. There is an approaching, final pruning of the vineyard (verse 62). The first to be grafted in are gentiles, so that the last may be first. The lost sheep remnant next, and then Israelites, so that the first may be last (verse 63). But grafting is required for all, even the remnants, because God works with His people through covenant making.

There will be more grafting and further pruning. As more is revealed, and therefore more is required, some will find the "digging" and "dunging" too much to bear and will fall away; or in other words will be pruned despite the covenant (that's verse 64). The covenant makes it possible for natural fruit to return. The bad fruit will still continue, even among the covenant people, until there is enough strength in the healthy branches for further pruning.

It requires natural fruit to appear before the final pruning takes place (verse 65). The good and bad will co-exist. It will damage the tree to remove the bad at once; therefore the Lord's patience will continue for some time yet. The rate of removing the bad is dependent wholly upon the rate of the development of the good.

It is the Lord's purpose to create *equality* in His vineyard. In the allegory, equality in the vineyard appears three times—in verses 66, 72, and 74. We cannot be greater and lesser, nor divide ourselves into an hierarchy to achieve the equality required for Zion. When a group is determined to remain equal (and I am personally determined to be no greater than any other), then it faces challenges that never confront unequal people. A religion of bosses and minions never deals with any of the challenges of being equals. Critics claim we will never succeed—because of our determined desire for equality. None of our critics can envision what the Lord has said in verses 66, 72, and 74 about His people. But equality among us is the only way prophesied for us to succeed. That does not mean we won't have a mess as we learn how to establish equality.

Similarly, Zion cannot be established by isolated and solitary figures proclaiming a "testimony of Jesus" from their home keyboard. The challenge of building a community must be part of a process. Zion is a community, and therefore, God is a God of community; and His people must learn to live together with one heart, one mind, with no poor among us. Isolated keyboardists proclaiming their resentment of community can hardly speak temperately of others. How could they ever live peacefully in a community of equals? *We must become precious to each other.*

Although the laborers in this final effort are "few," you will be the means used by the Lord to complete His work in His vineyard (verse 70). You're required to labor with your might to finish the Lord's work in His vineyard (verse 72). But *He* will labor alongside you. *He*, not a man or a committee, will call *you* to do work. When He calls, do not fear—but do not run faster than you have strength. We must find His people in the highways and byways; invite them to join in. Zion will include people from every part of the world. This conference is broadcast worldwide as part of the prophecy to Enoch that God would send:

> *Righteousness and truth will [He] cause to sweep the earth as with a flood, to gather out mine elect from the four quarters of the earth, unto a place which I shall prepare, an Holy City, that my people may gird up their loins, and be looking forth for the time of my coming; for there shall be my tabernacle, and it shall be called Zion, a New Jerusalem.* (Moses 7:62; see also Genesis 4:22 RE)

We must proclaim this to the world.

Do not despair when further pruning takes place, it must be done. Only through pruning can the Lord keep His Tree of Life *equal*, without those who are lofty overcoming the body (verse 73). The lofty branches have always destroyed equality to prevent Zion. The final result of the Lord's labor in His vineyard is declared by the ancient prophet in unmistakable clarity: *The trees have become again the natural fruit; and they became like unto one body; and the fruits were equal; and the Lord of the vineyard had preserved unto himself the natural fruit, which was most precious unto him from the beginning.* Mark those words (that's verse 74).

When the Lord explained this to me I realized how foolish it was to expect "natural fruit" worthy of preservation in an instant. The Lord works patiently, methodically, and does not require any to run faster than they have strength (see Mosiah 4:27; see also Mosiah 2:6 RE).

We cannot allow ourselves to be drawn in to inequality when the result of this labor is to make us one body, equal with one another. We cannot imitate the failures of the past by establishing an hierarchy—elevating one above another and forgetting that we must be of one heart, one mind, and no poor among us.

The restoration was never intended to just restore an ancient Christian church. That is only a halfway point. It must go back further. In the words of the ancient prophet, God intends to do ...*according to [His] will; and [to] preserve the natural fruit, that it is good, even like as it was in the beginning* (verse 75). This means the beginning, as in the days of Adam, with the return of the original religion and original authority. Everything must be returned as it was in the beginning.

Civilization began with the temple as the center of learning, law, and culture. The temple was the original university because it taught of man's place with God in the universe. God will return the right of dominion, once held by Adam, to man on earth—to make us humble, servant-gardeners laboring to return the world to a peaceful Paradise. The covenant received today restores part of that right. There is a land inheritance given to us as part of the covenant; and therefore, if we keep the covenant, we have the right to remain when others will be swept away.

Ultimately, all rights given to us must be turned back to the fathers who went before; who will likewise return them to Adam; who will surrender them to

Christ. When Christ returns, He will come with the right to exercise complete dominion over the earth, and exercise judgment over the ungodly. Things set into motion today are part of preparing the way for the Lord's return in glory.

———

The foregoing excerpts are taken from:

- Denver's *Christian Reformation Lecture Series*, Talk #5 given in Sandy, Utah, on September 7, 2018;
- Denver's *40 Years in Mormonism Series*, Talk #4 titled "Covenants" given in Centerville, Utah, on October 6, 2013;
- Denver's lecture titled "Signs Follow Faith" given in Centerville, Utah, on March 3, 2019; and
- His "Opening Remarks", given at the Covenant of Christ Conference in Boise, Idaho, on September 3rd, 2017.

In addition, Denver has written extensively about this topic. If you are interested in learning more, please review the following blog posts:

https://denversnuffer.com/2012/03/nephis-brother-jacob-conclusion/
https://denversnuffer.com/2012/03/jacob-chapter-5/
https://denversnuffer.com/2012/03/jacob-5-3-6/
https://denversnuffer.com/2012/03/jacob-5-7-9/
https://denversnuffer.com/2012/03/jacob-5-10-13/
https://denversnuffer.com/2012/03/jacob-5-14-18/
https://denversnuffer.com/2012/03/jacob-5-19-26/
https://denversnuffer.com/2012/04/jacob-5-27-33/
https://denversnuffer.com/2012/04/jacob-5-34-37/
https://denversnuffer.com/2012/04/jacob-5-38-41/
https://denversnuffer.com/2012/04/jacob-5-42-47/
https://denversnuffer.com/2012/04/jacob-5-48-51/
https://denversnuffer.com/2012/04/jacob-5-52/
https://denversnuffer.com/2012/04/jacob-5-53-56/
https://denversnuffer.com/2012/04/jacob-5-57-59/
https://denversnuffer.com/2012/04/jacob-5-60-63/
https://denversnuffer.com/2012/04/jacob-5-64-65/
https://denversnuffer.com/2012/04/jacob-5-66-70/
https://denversnuffer.com/2012/04/jacob-5-71-73/
https://denversnuffer.com/2012/04/jacob-5-74-75/
https://denversnuffer.com/2012/04/jacob-5-76-77/

https://denversnuffer.com/2012/04/themes-from-jacob-5/
https://denversnuffer.com/2012/04/themes-from-jacob-5-part-2/
https://denversnuffer.com/2012/04/themes-from-jacob-part-3/

67. Calling & Election, Part 1

In this episode, Denver answers the question: Regarding Calling & Election, in various blog posts, talks, *Beloved Enos*, and so forth, you explain that if we can receive the Second Comforter, then our Calling & Election will take care of itself. In an email this week you stated:

> In the beginning there was one unified priesthood. It was called "The Holy Order after the Order of the Son of God." The division of that single unity into other divisions occurred later and was the result of limitations on those involved. I'd recommend looking at the Holy Order paper and using some of the information there.

How is that Unified Priesthood related to having your Calling & Election Made Sure?

———

DENVER: So,

> Elijah shall reveal the covenants to seal the hearts of the fathers to the children and the children to the fathers. The anointing and sealing is to be called, elected, and made sure. Without father, without mother, without descent, having neither beginning of days nor end of life, but made like unto the Son of God, abideth a priest continually. The Melchizedek Priesthood holds the right from the eternal God, and not by descent from father and mother; and that priesthood is as eternal as God Himself, having neither beginning of days nor end of life. (*TPJS*, p. 323)

That is not to say that because one receives that priesthood, that they cannot fall from that, because while you are in this world, as Paul put it, [*you*] *stand...in jeopardy every hour* (1 Corinthians 15:30; see also 1 Corinthians 1:64 RE). Here is the place in which the trial, the test, the temptation, the burden of mortality exists; and it exists for so long as you have the flesh. You do not—

Even if you possess the authority, you do not have that abide with you continually on into eternity until you have finished the course; until you have resisted the temptation; until you have completed the race and finished the work (2 Timothy 4:7-8). Only when you lay down the burden *here*— successfully having completed it—are you permitted then to take it up *there* as a matter of right. But here, although the priesthood is endless, although the covenant of God is eternal, a man may fall from it; and therefore, you proceed recognizing that you proceed with eternal peril.

And then, this is the place where Joseph says—he's talking about Elijah, he's talking about the seals being on the earth, and he's talking about preparing for Zion; and in this context, in January of 1844, this is where Joseph says:

> There has been a great difficulty in getting anything into the heads of this generation. It has been like splitting hemlock knots with a corn-dodger for a wedge, and a pumpkin for a beetle. Even the Saints are slow to understand. I have tried for a number of years to get the minds of the Saints prepared to receive the things of God; but we frequently see some of them, after suffering all they have for the work of God, will fly to pieces like glass as soon as any thing comes that is contrary to their traditions: they cannot stand the fire at all. How many will be able to abide a Celestial law, and go through and receive their exaltation, I am unable to say, [but] many are called, [and] few are Chosen. (*TPJS*, p. 331)

Then in March of 1844, he picks up the subject again—the 10th of March, 1844. And this time, when he's talking about Elijah, he says;

> The spirit...and calling of Elijah is,...[to] have [the] power to hold the [keys] of the revelations, ordinances, oracles, powers...endowments of the fulness of the Melchizedek Priesthood and of the kingdom of God on the earth; and to receive, obtain, and perform all the ordinances belonging to the kingdom of God, even unto the [sealing] of the hearts of the fathers unto the children, and the hearts of the children unto the fathers, *even those who are in heaven.* (*TPJS*, p. 337, emphasis added)

The hearts of the Fathers *who are in heaven*; that's the mission of Elijah. If you will receive it, this is the spirit of Elijah—that we redeem our dead and connect ourselves with *our Fathers which are in heaven.* Our dead—through us—us to our Fathers in heaven. Who are our Fathers in heaven? Who are our Fathers in heaven to whom we are to be connected? We want the power of Elijah to seal those who dwell on earth to those which dwell in heaven. Those who are in the spirit world, our dead—the ones that need redemption from us—are not redeemed. They cannot be in heaven because they need *us* to be redeemed. We need to be redeemed by *our* connecting to the Fathers who are in heaven. The dead have to be redeemed. The Fathers are in heaven. Joseph understood this doctrine.

Joseph spoke of three divisions of priesthood. He entitled these: the Aaronic, the Melchizedek, and the Patriarchal; and Joseph defined the greatest of these as Melchizedek priesthood because it comprehended all others. I'm not using, and have not used, and have explained before—since Melchizedek has acquired a definition in the heads of Latter-day Saints, I'm not going to try and extract for the bull, the line of thought that reckons from that. I'm just leaving that alone and saying, "Okay, let me re-define the terms." And so, in my re-definition of the terms, Aaronic refers to the least of these; Melchizedek refers to the next level of these; and Patriarchal refers to the greatest of these, in *my* nomenclature—not Joseph's.

I do this, as I have explained, because in the beginning there was a unitary priesthood. It was the Holy Order after the Order of the Son of God. But in order to prevent the too frequent repetition of the name of the Son of God, it got renamed; first after Enoch and then later after Melchizedek—but it is referring to one, original, unitary priesthood which is the Holy Order after the Order of the Son of God. Yet Joseph spoke about three great divisions. In the beginning, because the first patriarchs had that original unitary fulness of the priesthood after the Order of the Son of God, and because Abraham acquired the rights of the Fathers—or the first father, Adam—and therefore, like Adam, held the Holy Order after the Order of the Son of God; I use the term "Patriarchal" priesthood to refer to that original fulness and to nothing else. And I divide them up into three categories and three nomenclatures using those terms.

There is the Spirit of Elias; there is the Spirit of Elijah, and there is the Spirit of Messiah. These three great spirits unfolded in the work of God in the generations of man in a steady descent, and they will be, likewise, inverted like a chiasm and return in an ascent so that at the end, it will be as it was in the beginning. *[That] same Priesthood, which was in the beginning, shall...at the end of the [earth be] also* (Moses 6:7), was the prophecy that Father Adam gave; Enoch quoting Adam—Moses quoting Enoch; the prophecy being contained in the Book of Moses or, soon, in the Book of Genesis.

So if we turn to the oath and covenant of the priesthood that's contained in Doctrine and Covenants 84 (and that's something about which we all think we know because, as parents, we've heard our kids go through this; as adults, we've had it parsed through)—but if you look at it with the idea that all priesthood is singular and that there are merely different portions or degrees of it—starting at verse 33 of section 84: *For whosoever is faithful unto the obtaining of these two priesthoods...* (see also T&C 82:16).

Now I want to pause there for a moment because here in revelation, given through Joseph Smith, is a statement by the Lord, in revelation to Joseph, in which he calls it two priesthoods—and yet Joseph explains there's only one. There's only one, and the one is Melchizedek, but there's different portions of it. Here in the revelation it's dividing it into two. Therefore, there are two portions of it or two distinctions. And the possibility that those two distinctions are significant enough that they warrant treatment in the plural—instead of the singular—shows up right here in the revelation. I think Joseph knew what he was talking about; I think the Lord knows what He's talking about because they're trying to get ideas across into our minds that we tend to resist.

Now, I should mention, as a footnote, that there were discussions in the leadership of the Church about what was required in order to pass along priesthood. And during the administration of Heber J. Grant, for a period of over two decades, he ceased the practice of conferring priesthood upon people; but he had them only ordained to an office in the Church. Therefore, whenever someone was ordained to priesthood during that two decade-plus time period, they were ordained to an office. After the death of Heber J. Grant, the practice was reverted again, and they began to confer priesthood in addition to ordain into office. But that is something that Heber J. Grant, at least, did not think occupied any significance. So when I tell you there is a difference between an office in the Church and the priesthood, Heber J. Grant, at least, would say that I'm dead wrong on that point, and I don't know what I'm talking about. But entertain the idea, and see where it takes you.

There are in the church— Well, *whoso is faithful unto the obtaining these two priesthoods of which I have spoken, and the magnifying their calling...* (ibid). See, priesthood is not simply yadda yadda yadda, ipso-facto, canorus mundorum, there you are. It requires—

See, you get it—but then, faithful to obtain; and then, faithful to magnify; and faithful to magnify it as a calling—*calling* being an operative word there that means service.

Are sanctified by the Spirit unto the renewing of their bodies (ibid). Sanctified by the Spirit. Renewing their bodies. These things have meaning. Perhaps we'll get to that at some point.

*They **become** the sons of Moses, and of Aaron, and the seed of Abraham; and the church and kingdom, and the elect of God* (ibid, vs. 34, emphasis added). So they *become*—but they *become* as a consequence of having been sanctified. They become sanctified because they magnified their calling. They had to first obtain the priesthood, and the obtaining of the priesthood requires something that is *faithful*. And you ought to ask yourself, faithful to what? And always it is faithful to *Him*, to our Lord; the One who redeems. All of these things flow together as one continuum. It's not just: I got ordained! It doesn't matter that you got ordained. There's a process that's involved after ordination in which you follow these steps. We read it as one sentence and say; "There it is; he was faithful. I mean, he passed the Bishops interview; he obtained it. That is, he sat down there, and they got a certificate." I mean, when I was on the High Council, I was the one responsible for fetching the Melchizedek priesthood certificates and delivering it to them. And that was a definite point in time at which we can point and say, On this day this person gave this authority to this guy on this occasion; and when that happened, he also got a line of authority.

I'd like to suggest that the Holy Order after the Order of the Son of God includes the fact that those who inherit the Holy Order *are* sons of God. Therefore, in a way, calling it the Holy Order after the Order of the Son of God is a way of identifying the recipient as someone who has become one of God's sons. Now, I think it's appropriate to regard the primary identifier— that is the subject of who the Son of God is—to be Jesus Christ and Jesus Christ alone, because quite frankly, He's the only one that attained to the resurrection; and it is through the power of the resurrection that we're gonna come forth. We do not have the power in ourselves to rise from the dead. The wages of sin are death. We've earned those wages; we will die—we all will die. The Savior did not earn those wages. He died, and therefore, His death was unjust, and the law of justice got broken when He died. And therefore, whenever justice makes a claim on any of us, He can point to the fact that justice extracted from Him eternal life, and that is an infinite price for Him to have paid. Therefore, He has compensated for all of mankind's shortcomings, failures—and Christ is the means by which we lay hold upon the promises; but it is His intention to make of us all, sons of God.

Therefore, the Holy Order after the Son of God is—when the name is announced— self-identifying the person holding such a Holy Order as one of God's sons; even though they may be mortal, even though they may be in the flesh. The Holy Order is for that very purpose.

And is after the Order of the Son of God, and all other Priesthoods are only parts, ramifications, powers and blessings belonging to the same, and are held, controlled, and directed by it. *It* is the channel through which the Almighty commenced revealing His glory at the beginning of the creation of this earth, and through which He has continued to reveal Himself to the children of men to the present time, and through which He will make known His purposes to the end of time. (*TPJS*, p. 167, emphasis added)

Therefore, among other things, the purpose of the Holy Order is to put in place a mechanism by which God can reveal, from heaven, what is necessary for the salvation of man on earth, in every generation—in order to fix what is broken; in order to restore what has been lost; in order to repair, heal, forgive, and reconnect those who are willing to give heed to the message sent from heaven—so that they can rise up to become sons of God.

Abraham chapter 3 verse 12; we encounter God saying:

> *And he said unto me* [Abraham, saying]: *My son, my son (and his hand was stretched out), behold I will show you all these. And he put his hand upon mine eyes, and [he] saw those things which his hands had made, which were many; and they multiplied before mine eyes, and I could not see the end thereof.* (see also Abraham 5:3 RE)

Once again, you have at the same instance that he is being acknowledged as a son, the outpouring of the intelligence of God—the glory of God; light and truth; knowledge of things as they are, and as they were, and as they are to come.

Joseph in— Joseph Smith in Doctrine and Covenants section 121, verse 7, *My son, peace be unto thy soul.*

Okay, if you view priesthood as a brotherhood or an association, then I want to suggest that the way in which you should parse the three orders of priesthood is to parse them this way:

- As among men—it's merely a brotherhood of men.
- As between mankind and the heavens—
  - The first order is an order in which there is an association between men and angels.
  - The second order is an order in which there is an association between mankind and the Son of God.

- o   And the third order, the highest order—the patriarchal order —brings one into contact with the Patriarch who, of all the names that He could choose to be called by, chooses to have us call Him "our Father who art in heaven"—the third grand order being Sonship to the Father and association with Him who sits in the bosom of eternity and sustains all the creation.
- o   The highest priesthood is an association with the Father, brought about as a consequence of the Father calling, "My Son." It is the Holy Order after the Son of God, because those who inherit that become, by definition, His Sons. They are the Church of the Firstborn because they are in association with, and made by the Father equal to, all those who rise up to be Firstborn.

Go to Moses chapter 5. This is a prophecy given by Adam which constituted one of the covenants which I referred to in the talk given at Centerville. Moses, Oh excuse me— It's chapter 6, verse 7: *Now this same Priesthood* [this is Adam speaking]— *Now this same priesthood which was in the beginning, shall be in the end of the world also. Now this prophecy Adam spake, as he was moved upon by the Holy Ghost* (see also Genesis 3:14 RE). Therefore, it was the power of the priesthood, animated by the Holy Ghost, which established—as a matter of right and, therefore, of covenant—the promise that this thing, this authority, this power, and this relationship which once existed in the beginning of the world, is to exist again at the end of the world. And that that, too, arises as a consequence of the covenant given in the beginning.

Well, if you go to Doctrine and Covenants section 68, first verses 3 and 4:

> *This is the ensample unto them, that they shall speak as they are moved upon by the Holy Ghost. And whatsoever they shall speak when moved upon by the Holy Ghost shall be scripture, shall be the will of the Lord, shall be the mind of the Lord, shall be the word of the Lord, shall be the voice of the Lord, and the power of God unto salvation.* [Then go over to 12:] *And...as many as the Father shall bear record, to you shall be given power to seal them up unto eternal life. Amen.* (see also T&C 55:1-2 RE)

So this is talking in the context of someone having authority to seal when moved upon by the Holy Ghost. And that is authority which any one of you —and the prophetess Anna in the temple at Jerusalem when Christ came into the temple—a woman can use when moved upon by the power of the Holy

Ghost; and it is the word of God, and it is the power to seal if it originates from God. That doesn't mean it's the same thing as a dispensation head. It doesn't mean it's the same thing as an ordinance. And it doesn't mean that it's the same thing as the control of the elements given in those rare cases. But what it does mean is that the word of God will always be respected, both in time and in eternity, if it is given by God; if it is the power of the Holy Spirit.

There are those who have heard that their calling and election is made sure, and they've heard that as a witness from God. Don't doubt the word of God given to you. However, don't think for one moment that's the end of the matter. Remember that in the cases that we looked at before, that one of the purposes of ascending up into the presence of the Father is to be endowed with knowledge, with light and truth and with intelligence to possess a God-like mind and a God-like understanding. Therefore, no matter what you receive, you ought to always search deeper and deeper into the mysteries of God. Indeed, we're commanded to do so, as I reminded you in Boise and won't repeat again here. I've also read you previously and won't repeat it again here, Doctrine and Covenants section 1, verse 8 through 10—the sealing power manifested in an Aaronic setting, in which it is sealed up unto condemnation.

I want to mention that beyond there being a fellowship of man or males and a brotherhood, there is also a fellowship that is extended, as well, to women. If you find a woman in scripture who has had the ministry of angels, you have a sister who has joined in that association. I won't take time to do so, but if you look in Judges chapter 13, verses 2 to 5, you have Samson's mother being ministered to by an angel, promising the coming of the one who would be a judge in Israel. You have in Genesis chapter 18, verses 9 to 15, Abraham's wife with angelic ministrants. And the most obvious case being Mary in the book of Luke chapter 1, verses 26 to 31, in which Mary is ministered to by Gabriel, one of the Elohim, who came to announce that she would conceive and bear a child, though she knew no man.

I do want to talk about sealing authority, because there have been questions asked about sealing. I intended to address that, in any event, and I want to suggest to you that there are three kinds of sealing authority which are given.

There is a first form of sealing power; and I'm talking about the kind of power not that can seal you up unto condemnation or judgment. I'm talking, instead, about Melchizedek sealing power; the kind that was designed to bless and to preserve.

The first kind of sealing power is that kind which is given to someone when there is a dispensation of the gospel being founded. An example of that, you can find in Exodus chapter 34, involving Moses as a dispensation head, where in verses 27 and 28 the Lord says: *And the LORD said unto Moses, Write thou these words: for after the tenor of these words I have made a covenant with thee and with Israel. And he was there with the LORD forty days and forty nights* (see also Exodus 18:15 RE), and so on. And so, as a dispensation head, a form of sealing power is given to that person which establishes a covenant that was intended to go beyond that individual alone.

Take a look in Second Nephi chapter 1; and in Second Nephi chapter 1, we find Lehi speaking:

> *Notwithstanding our afflictions, we have obtained a land of promise, a land which is choice above all other lands; a land which the Lord God hath covenanted with me should be a land for the inheritance of my seed. Yea, the Lord hath covenanted this land unto me, and to my children forever, and also all those who should be led out of other countries by the hand of the Lord.* (2 Nephi 1:5; see also 2 Nephi 1:1 RE)

This is a covenant made by God with Lehi as a dispensation head, the beneficiaries of whom are beyond merely that dispensation head. It includes all those who come thereafter. They are beneficiaries of that. The covenant gets established through one; it is intended for others.

Joseph, in Doctrine and Covenants section 22: *BEHOLD, I say unto you that all old covenants have I caused to be done away in this thing; and this is a new and everlasting covenant, ...that which was from the beginning* (D&C 22:1; see also JSH 18:8 RE). So, through Joseph, there was a covenant formed, which would be binding beyond the person with whom God covenanted directly.

Dispensation heads are given the power—the sealing power, the authority, the ability to use the power to seal up; by embodying the covenant that is given to them by God into an ordinance. And that ordinance remains in effect after the death of Moses, after the death of Lehi, after the death of Joseph Smith, so long as it remains embodied within the ordinance. This kind of ordinance or this kind of sealing authority then requires and gives rise to the second kind.

And the second kind is a sealing power that is embodied within authoritative ordinances. All dispensations of the gospel follow the covenant giver's ordinances. For so long as the ordinances that were handed to you through the dispensation head are kept intact, the covenant is kept intact. And the second form of sealing power is a sealing power which is not dependent upon the persistent presence of a dispensation head. It is only dependent upon keeping faithfully the ordinance that has been established and handed down by God through covenant.

This second form of sealing power is the sealing authority which the Church claims to possess. It is the sealing authority that was referred to by Henry B. Eyring in the General Conference talk he gave in April of 2012, *Families under Covenant*, in which he proclaimed that the Church has the authority to seal families together by using the ordinances that have been handed down. I'm quoting from his talk:

> The Holy Spirit of Promise through our obedience and sacrifice, must seal our temple covenants in order to be realized in the world to come. The Holy Ghost is one who reads the thoughts and hearts of men and gives his sealing approval to the blessing pronounced upon their heads. Then it is binding, efficacious and of full force (unquote)..

I agree with what he has said. I believe that is a correct way to explain the limited authority to seal—enjoyed by the Church—and the condition that remains, even in the ordinance, requiring the faithfulness and the subsequent sealing by the Holy Spirit of Promise in order for those ordinances to endure. Nevertheless, the Church possess that second kind of sealing authority, and it uses it in the temples of the Church of Jesus Christ of Latter-day Saints.

The second form of sealing authority, however, has conditions upon it; because God is not bound by anything that differs one iota from His word. And that doesn't matter who it is. God is bound by His word, not by man's. Therefore, when you handle such ordinances, you need to keep in mind the admonition that was given in the prophecy of Isaiah:

> *The earth also is defiled under the inhabitants thereof; because they have transgressed the laws, changed the ordinance, broken the everlasting covenant. Therefore hath the curse devoured the earth, and they that dwell therein are desolate: therefore the inhabitants of the earth are burned, and few men left.* (Isaiah 24:5-6; see also Isaiah 7:1 RE)

It's talking about a future time at *His* coming. But it's lamenting a condition that you have to decide about it's currency. That's Isaiah chapter 24, verses 5 and 6.

So when you have possession of that second form of sealing authority, you have to recognize that the covenant, handed down from the dispensation head, can be broken. It was broken rather abruptly in the case of the covenant given to Lehi when, at the death of Lehi, his family fragmented into two groups—one of whom desired to preserve the covenant, and one of whom rejected it and walked away from it. Therefore, it was not to the ones that had rejected the covenant that the Lord would subsequently come to appear. But they, by and large, would have been destroyed. So, handling the second form of the covenant, after the dispensation head has established it, is a matter of fidelity to the word of God, and faithfulness to the word of God, and faithfulness in preserving and practicing the ordinance that has been established.

There is a third kind of sealing power, and this third kind of sealing power goes beyond either of the first two; and it has absolutely unique application, and it is given only in rare circumstances and for highly specific purposes. **That third form involves giving the authority to control the elements.** This was authority that was possessed by Enoch. This was authority that was possessed by Melchizedek. This was authority that was possessed by Christ. This was the authority that Christ had to suspend (or not employ) in order to permit those who would kill Him *to* kill Him. This is the kind of authority which, in the case of every such individual, they give their lives up willingly. Their lives cannot be taken.

An example (and it's a good example, because it gives you insight into why such authority would ever be given to a man) is found in Helaman chapter 10, beginning at verse 5. This is the Lord speaking to Nephi, son of Helaman, son of Helaman. To Nephi He says: *And now, because thou hast done this with such unwearyingness*—and the "unwearyingness" is described in verse 4; that is, Nephi has gone and he's declared what the Lord has asked him to declare. And he hasn't feared them, nor has he sought to protect his own life, but he's instead sought to keep the commandments of God. Therefore, because he has done this with such unwearyingness, *behold, I* [this is God speaking to Nephi] *will bless thee forever; and I will make thee mighty in word and in deed, in faith and in works; yea, even that all things shall be done unto thee according to thy word, for* **thou shalt not ask that which is contrary to my will** (see also Helaman 3:19 RE, emphasis added).

That's not a commandment. That's a description of the character and the nature of Nephi. That's not saying, "I'm giving this to you, but be careful how you use it. Please don't do anything that isn't according to my will." That's the Lord saying, "I, God, have faith in you, Nephi; that you, Nephi, will not do anything other than my will." You see, the whole thing turns on its head at this point. You see, this is God having faith in a man. What manner of man then does God have faith in?

Behold, thou art Nephi, and I am God. Behold, I declare it unto thee in the presence of mine angels (ibid, vs. 6), because this decree, in this circumstance, may require those who are watching to obey the word of the man. Therefore, the angels—the Powers of Heaven— must give heed because God is declaring it in the presence of the hosts who are standing before Him. *I declare it unto thee in the presence of mine angels, that ye shall have power over this people, and shall smite the earth with famine, and with pestilence, and destruction, according to the wickedness of this people* (ibid). *Behold...* [That is a rather Aaronic behavior.]

Behold, I give unto you power, that whatsoever ye seal on the earth shall be sealed in heaven; whatsoever ye shall loose on earth shall be loosed in heaven; and thus shall ye have power among this people (ibid, vs. 7). This is rather Melchizedek, because you can seal up unto eternal life. This is the positive side. This is the thing which those who are given this authority seek earnestly to do.

Thus, if ye shall say unto this temple it shall be rent in twain, it shall be done (ibid, vs 8), because the temple is subordinate to the word of God. The temple is not the place that controls the word of God, the temple is the place which, most of all, ought be subject to the word of God. It's not a place to innovate in ordinances. It's a place to obey, to follow, to give strict heed unto and to not vary.

And if ye say unto this mountain, Be thou cast down and become smooth, it shall be done. And behold, if thou shalt say that God shall smite this people, it shall come to pass (ibid, vs. 9-10). And then because he knows the nature and the character of the man involved in giving this authority, God commands him. He has to go out and deliver the message: *Except ye repent ye shall be smitten, even unto destruction* (ibid, vs. 11). He didn't want to do that because that's not in the character of the person who, with unwearyingness, would go out and declare the word of God; because such people have in their heart one and only one objective—and that is the salvation of the souls of men. But now this troubling message has to be given. And when he goes and he delivers it, he doesn't even use the authority that he's been given. He simply asks the Lord if the Lord will smite.

Look at Enoch in the book of Moses chapter 6 because, once again, we're looking at someone to whom this authority was given. Moses chapter 6, verse

34, God speaking to Enoch: *Behold my Spirit is upon you, wherefore all thy words will **I** justify; and the mountains **shall** flee before you, and the rivers **shall** turn from their course; and thou shalt abide in me, and I in you; therefore walk with me* (see also Genesis 4:2 RE, emphasis added) because it was Enoch's purpose to abide in God. Therefore, when he speaks and the elements obey, they obey precisely because it is the word of God which Enoch is speaking. It is not Enoch out there innovating. Enoch would have forfeited his life before he would have said or done anything that was not in accordance with the will of God, as would have Nephi. Therefore, they are trustworthy.

And then we looked at Joseph Smith; the translation of Genesis chapter 14.

As to these three kinds of authority, the first authority: given unto a dispensation head. Only God can pass that to man. Man cannot pass that to man.

The second kind of sealing authority that we talked about can be passed from man to man, from generation to generation, remains in full force and effect for so long as the covenant is not broken.

The third kind not only cannot be given by man to man, but is given as a consequence of that extraordinary combination of mortality and immortality, in which you find a person on the earth that God has faith and confidence in. *You* be that kind of person.

————

The foregoing excerpts are taken from:

- Denver's *40 Years in Mormonism* Series, Talk #5 titled "Priesthood," given in Orem, UT on November 2nd, 2013;
- His talk titled "The Mission of Elijah Reconsidered," given in Spanish Fork, UT on October 14th, 2011;
- His conference talk titled "Things to Keep Us Awake at Night," given in St. George, UT on March 19th, 2017; and
- Denver's fireside talk titled "The Holy Order," given in Bountiful, UT on October 29th, 2017.

In addition, Denver has written extensively about this topic. If you are interested in learning more, please review the following blog posts:

Follow-up Question, published January 3, 2012

<u>Last Week's Comments</u>, published May 19, 2012

You may also find value in reviewing the following Glossary Entries:

<u>Sealed in Their Foreheads</u>
<u>Called or Calling</u>
<u>Calling and Election</u>
<u>Elect</u>
<u>Sealing Power</u>

68. Calling & Election, Part 2

In this episode, Denver answers the question: Regarding Calling & Election, in various blog posts, talks, *Beloved Enos* and so forth, you explain that if we can receive the Second Comforter, then our Calling & Election will take care of itself. In an email this week, you stated:

> In the beginning there was one, unified priesthood. It was called "The Holy Order after the Order of the Son of God." The division of that single unity into other divisions occurred later, and was the result of limitations on those involved. I'd recommend looking at the Holy Order paper, and using some of the information there.

How is that Unified Priesthood related to having your calling & election made sure?

———

DENVER: Melchizedek (and the order of priesthood he obtained) is described in the book of Genesis—chapter 7 in the current set of scriptures, the Old Covenants: *For God... [swore] unto Enoch and unto his seed, with an oath by Himself, that everyone being ordained after this order and calling, should have power, by faith, to break mountains* (Genesis 7:19 RE). We have no direct account of when the mountains have been broken by those after that order. We have one indirect reference in the book of Genesis referring to Enoch: *And he spoke the word of the Lord, and the earth trembled, and the mountains fled even according to his command, and the rivers of water turned out of their course* (Genesis 4:13 RE).

You need to be careful how you parse that scripture. Enoch spoke the word of the Lord. The word of the Lord is spoken, and in response to the word of the Lord having been spoken, the earth trembled and the mountains fled, even according to His—the Lord—His command. And the rivers of water turned out of their course. Enoch preached, earthquakes followed, mountains moved. In Jacob 3:2 [RE], there's another reference: *We obtain a hope and our faith becometh unshaken, insomuch that we truly can command in the name of Jesus and the very trees obey us, or the mountains, or the waves of the sea.*

That's Jacob illustrating that the faith they have has this effect. He doesn't describe that effect having occurred, simply that it's there. Nephi explained this is the power that God entrusted him with in Helaman:

214   The Denver Snuffer Podcast, Volume 2: 2019

> For behold, the dust of the earth moveth hither and thither, to the
> dividing asunder, at the command of our great and everlasting God. Yea,
> behold, at his voice doth the hills and the mountains tremble and quake,
> and by the power of his voice are broken up and become smooth, yea,
> even like unto a valley. (Helaman 4:10 RE)

He was given the sealing power. He was told that the earth will obey you,
because He knew that he would not do anything with that power other than
what God willed. And shortly after being entrusted by God to this, Nephi
prays to God and asks God to send a famine to stop the people from killing
one another. So here's someone who can speak the word of God, and the
earth itself will obey him, and he uses that to get on his knees and pray and
ask God. He doesn't command anything.

That kind of endowment of priestly authority is done because God expressed
His faith in the man. Can God have faith in you? Can God trust you?

So the list goes on:

- The mountains is the first thing.

- *To divide the seas.* We have an example of that with Moses.

- *To dry up waters.* We have an example of that with Joshua when they
  reached the river Jordan.

- *To turn them out of their course,* which was done again at the time of
  Enoch.

- *To put at defiance the armies of nations*—Elijah.

- *To divide the earth, to break every band, to stand in the presence of God,
  to do all things according to his will, according to his command* (Genesis
  7:19 RE).

When it comes to breaking every band, keep that in mind because we're
gonna return to that in a moment. And then it says *to subdue principalities
and powers* (ibid). These are in the spiritual realm. Commanding devils,
subduing principalities and powers—these are rebellious spirits cast down
from Heaven; these are those that pretend to be and often are false
ministering spirits or angels.

And this by the will of the Son of God, who was from before the foundation of the world. And men having this faith, coming up unto this order of God, were translated and taken up into Heaven (ibid). Not always the case. The only reason translation occurred is because a mission was assigned to them, but that's outside of this.

Any one of the foregoing signs is a confirming sign. It's not required for all these signs to be given before faith is confirmed. And because these are gifts from God, it is God who decides when the sign will be given. God determines if, when, what, and how often a sign will be given—not the will of men.

Notice that the Brother of Jared's moving of the Mount Zerin is not recorded in his record or Moroni's abridgment of that record. It is only mentioned in passing as an illustration (see Ether 5:6 RE). Even if we have faith to participate, the signs are Gods. We are only witnesses. God sent Moses to deliver signs to Egypt, but the signs were God's. There is only one way in which a mortal can have discretion to invoke God's power, which involves one of the three kinds of sealing power I've previously discussed. That third kind is described in the book of Helaman and involves Nephi, and I've previously talked about that.

The reason Nephi was granted this authority was explained by God when he said, *Thou shalt not ask that which is contrary to my will* (Helaman 3:19 RE). When Nephi used that authority shortly afterward, he deferred to God, prayed, and asked God if He would cause a famine to stop the violence of the degenerate people of his generation.

The most righteous man who ever lived was allowed to be killed by the wicked. In fact, it was indispensable that the wicked get to kill the righteous because otherwise, there could not have an Atonement then made. Therefore, Christ was slain at the hands of wicked men.

But we have a problem with Zion—because when the Lord sets about to destroy, the Lord cannot destroy the righteous; and He's going to obliterate life on the earth except for those who are in the Ark—or those in Zion. The wicked can't come against them, and all are going to be destroyed.

So what do you do? Well, we've got a new status for humanity. And the new status is: you take them into heaven. But you don't take people into heaven without an associated calling. There is no reason—ever—to take a person off the earth, even if they're righteous. Abraham died and was buried. Christ died, and He was more righteous than any who ever lived. You don't take them off the earth unless they have a calling to **minister**—so we have a calling to minister. Enoch and his city (who could not be destroyed when the Lord was going to destroy)—and his city were called, and they were given two callings. Their first assignment is as ministering angels, not only here but elsewhere. And their second calling—I don't want to appear irreverent, but they're really—they're the crowd; they're the cheering group backing up the Lord at His Coming. They are the ones (when He comes in the clouds with the angels)—that group is Enoch's people. They are the certifiers; they are the testifiers; they are the chorus; they are the entourage.

Ya know, there is a reason why our tin-horn dictators and our phony idols have an entourage. It's to mimic the real deal, because when the Lord comes again in His glory, He's gonna come with an entourage. So they got the job— Enoch and his folk.

Consider how these ideas affect religion. A calling to priesthood does not accomplish anything if the individual is not "chosen" by God. We can ordain men, but heaven must ratify and elect that man. No one is permitted to function on God's behalf without God's personal imprimatur of approval.

Priesthood is connected to heaven. Without a connection to heaven, there's no priesthood. The "Powers of heaven" are, of course, the angels themselves. Priests must have angelic accompaniment to claim priesthood. And angels cannot be manipulated by the ambition, self-will, or worldly ambition of men.

The called but unchosen use office and position to cover their sins or to gratify their pride and vain ambition. They are like the Jews who persecuted Christ, while sitting in the chief seats. Likewise, there is no priesthood in the possession of any man who exercises control, dominion, or compulsion upon the souls of the children of men in the current sects of Mormonism. Christ's gentle example of kneeling to serve presents a neon-bright example of how priesthood is to be used. He came to **serve**, not to **be** served.

He taught, invited, bid others to repent, and clarified a better understanding of the scriptures for others. He did not demand support. He ministered light and truth for all who would listen. Any other kind of conduct antagonizes the heavens, which then withdraw themselves. The Spirit of the Lord is grieved, and when it's withdrawn, that's the end of the Priesthood.

So, let's turn to a few scriptures and interrupt this for a moment, because we want to repent, after all. We want to change what we are. Let's go to Doctrine and Covenants section 84, and let's look, beginning at verse 33. (Now I'm simply going to allow you to entertain your present views on some things for tonight. But we're gonna have to deconstruct a bunch of junk later, and we'll do that down in Spanish Fork, I think.) Beginning at verse 33 of section 84 of the Doctrine and Covenants:

> *For whoso is faithful unto the obtaining of these two priesthoods of which I have spoken, and the magnifying their calling, are sanctified by the Spirit unto the renewing of their bodies. They **become** the sons of Moses and of Aaron and the seed of Abraham, and the church and kingdom, and the elect of God.* (See also T&C 82:16, emphasis added)

"Sons." "Seed." And it's necessary that you become that in order that you become "the church and kingdom...the elect of God"—because as we saw in the statements made to Joseph Smith, the hearts have to be turned to the Fathers because this is going to be reconstructing a holy family at some point.

And also all they who receive this priesthood receive me, saith the Lord (D&C 84:35). Now, many of you read that verse 35 and you think that what that means is; if you fetch this priesthood by ordination, *ipso facto*, you have fetched Jesus. Praise Jesus! (And by the way, Joel Olsteen is coming to the E Center. You're not gonna want to miss that. It's a mega church. It's a mega church in transit. It's going to come to the E Center. SUNDAY, SUNDAY, SUNDAY. I'm sorry. I get worked up when the evangelicals show up on the horizon. He had some nice things to say about Mormons, though, so Joel Olsteen has kind of creeped a little more on the positive column for me, of late.)

I want to suggest that verse 35 can also be read exactly as D&C section 93, verse 1—that we were reading a moment ago—is read. And that is to say, if you're gonna receive this priesthood, you're gonna get it from Him. That is, you enter into His presence; you receive Him—*if* you have it. Then when you have it, as a consequence **of having it**, you receive Him.

Oh! *For he that receiveth my servants receiveth me* (vs. 36); I want to suggest that throughout scripture, almost invariably, the word "servants" is referring to angelic ministrants. And so angels minister (that would be Aaronic), and then Christ ministers (that would be sons of Moses).

And he that receiveth me receiveth my Father (vs. 37), because it is the purpose of the Son to bear record of the Father. It is the purpose of the Son to bring others to the Father so that there might be many sons of God.

And he that receiveth my Father receiveth my Father's kingdom (vs. 38), 'cause you can't go where the Father is without entering into and receiving an inheritance. You know, one of the things that we tend to think is that if you get something (this is based upon statements made in 132)— But if you get something here (and you get it by a covenant), that you are automatically entitled to take it into the next world. But what if the covenant that you are to receive, in order to obtain that inheritance in the next world, doesn't reckon merely from something handled by ordinance; but that the ordinance is pointing you to something higher and more holy? What if the thing that secures for you the inheritance in the next life is not the ordinance but what the ordinance testifies to—that is, embracing the Lord through the veil; and then having conversed with Him, entering into His presence; and then having entered into His presence, being ministered to and taught—what if it means all that?

> *This is according to the oath and covenant which belongeth to the priesthood. Therefore, all those who receive the priesthood, receive this oath and covenant of my Father, which he cannot break, neither can it be moved. But whoso breaketh this covenant after he hath received it, and altogether turneth therefrom, shall not have forgiveness of sins in this world nor in the world to come. [Oh,] and wo unto all those who come not unto this priesthood which ye have received, which I now confirm upon you who are present this day, by mine own voice out of the heavens; and even I have given the heavenly hosts and mine angels charge concerning you.* (Doctrine and Covenants 84: 39-42)

You know, that verse 42 of the oath and covenant of the priesthood—you ought to take a look at Joseph Smith Translation of Genesis chapter 14, verse 29, talking about the priesthood that was given after the Order of the Son of God; it says it was delivered unto men by the calling of His own voice, according to His own will, unto as many as believed on His name.

And so, we have—in section 76—a testimony given and justification for the translation Joseph rendered of Genesis chapter 14, dealing with the priesthood and qualifying it as coming from the voice of God.

The covenant which we receive will come as a consequence of *them*—what *they* got secured for *us* promises which the Lord intends to honor. Therefore, when we are the beneficiaries of those covenants, we are going, like Abraham, to have restored to us a knowledge of the beginning of creation; the planets; the stars, as they were made known unto the fathers; and—as Section 121 tells us—is going to be the case in the dispensation of the fullness of time.

Go to Joseph Smith Translation of Genesis chapter 14, beginning at verse 25:

> *Melchizedek lifted up his voice and blessed Abram. Now Melchizedek was a man of faith, who wrought righteousness; and when a child he feared God, and stopped the mouths of lions, ...quenched the violence of fire. ...thus, having been approved of God, he was ordained [a] high priest after the order of the **covenant** which God made with Enoch, It being after the order of the Son of God.* (JST Genesis 14:25-28; see also Genesis 7:17-18 RE, emphasis added)

There's an order that is after the son of God, but there was a covenant that preceded even the days of Melchizedek. It came down as a consequence of what happened with Enoch.

> *It was delivered unto men by the calling of his own voice, according to his own will, unto as many as believed on his name. For God having sworn unto Enoch and unto his seed with an oath by himself; that every one being ordained after this order and calling should have power, by faith, to break mountains, to divide the seas, dry up the waters, turn them out of their course; To put at defiance the armies of nations, to divide the earth, break every band, to stand in the presence of God; to do all things according to his command, subdue principalities and powers; and this by the will of the Son of God which was from before the foundation of the world.* (JST Genesis 14:29-31; see also Genesis 7:19 RE)

See, it's not your will; even if you're given this ordination, it is by the will of the Son of God. That is to say, nothing gets broken, nothing gets held in defiance, nothing gets done except by the will of the Son.

> *Men having this faith, coming up unto this order of God, were translated and taken up into heaven. And now, Melchizedek was a priest of this order; therefore he obtained peace in Salem, and was called the Prince of peace. His people* [His people] *wrought righteousness, and obtained heaven, and sought for the city of Enoch which God had before taken, separating it from the earth, having reserved it unto the latter days, or the end of the world; And hath said, and sworn with an oath, that the heavens and the earth should come together; and the sons of God should*

be tried so as by fire. (JST Genesis 14:32-35; see also Genesis 7:19-20 RE)

These are they who are coming—whose glory and brightness will burn them up who are on the earth who are unprepared to receive them. **These** are they about whom Moroni was speaking to Joseph Smith.

> *And this Melchizedek, having thus established righteousness, was called the king of heaven by his people, or, in other words, the King of peace. He lifted up his voice, he blessed Abram, being the high priest, and the keeper of the storehouse of God; Him unto whom God had appointed to receive tithes for the poor. Wherefore, Abram paid unto him tithes of all he had, of all the riches which he possessed, which God had given him more than that which he had need. And it came to pass, that God blessed Abram, and gave unto him riches, and honor, and lands for an everlasting possession; according to the covenant which he'd made, according to the blessings wherewith Melchizedek had blessed him.* (JST Genesis 14:36-40; see also Genesis 7:21 RE)

Joseph Smith restored this information as he restored the rest of what he gave us—in order for us to understand that when God swears by Himself to the Fathers about what it is He intends to accomplish in the last days and we get near enough to that event so that we're over the horizon and inevitably going to fall into that dark day, some few will take it seriously enough to say, like Abraham, "I would like to seek for the blessings of the Fathers. I would like also to have from God a covenant. I would like to inherit what it was that was given in the beginning."

God alone makes the covenant. We accept it by abiding the conditions. The only thing we can do on our own is attempt to make vows—and we can make vows, but Christ discouraged us from doing that in Matthew. Go back to Matthew chapter 5. This is in the Sermon on the Mount. (You can read the same thing in 3 Nephi chapter 12.) But look at Matthew chapter 5, verse 33:

> *[And] again, ye have heard it hath been said by them of old time, Thou shalt not forswear thyself, but [thou] shalt perform unto the Lord thine oaths: But I say unto you, Swear not at all; neither by heaven; for it is God's throne: Nor by the earth; for it is his footstool: neither by Jerusalem; for it's the city of the great King. Neither shalt thou swear by thy head, because thou canst not make one hair white or black.* [Well, cosmetically, some of you women can.] *But let your communication*

be, Yea, yea; Nay, nay: for whatsoever is more than these cometh of evil.
(See also Matthew 3:24 RE)

He'll say the same thing in 3 Nephi 12:33-37 (see also 3 Nephi 5:29 RE).

The fact of the matter is that you can make a vow to God, but you can't make a covenant with God. God can make a covenant which you can fulfill by your performance. God can offer you something—it's up to you to accept it; and you accept it by what you do. It's not enough to say, "Yea Lord, I'll go out, and I'll do as I'm bidden." You have to do it, because it's only in the doing that the covenant is kept. It's only in the **doing** that the covenant is able to be empowered sufficient to give you the blessing upon which a law has been established for the blessing to be predicated. You can't get there without God offering and you accepting.

So now we should realize, I hope, that that city which Melchizedek, the King of Peace, was able to teach righteousness sufficiently so that it was taken up from the earth, reserved to the last days of the end of the world—the next time we have such an event on the earth, the next time there is this kind of a gathering and this kind of a population anywhere, it will not be for the purpose of going up. It will be for the purpose of permitting those who have gone up to come back down. It will be for the purpose of having those who can endure the presence of those who come—because those who come will burn up all those who are unworthy. And therefore, **some few** need to be gathered, so that the earth is not utterly wasted at His coming.

For His atonement and sacrifice to have the greatest effect, we must preach the Doctrine of Christ. The scriptures do not foretell any great numbers will repent. Christ said, *I will take you one of a city, and two of a family, and I will bring you to Zion* (Jeremiah 3:14; see also Jeremiah 2:3 RE)—too few, perhaps, to impress the world, but the Lord does not view things as do men. The Lord describes those who respond to His invitation as "His elect." He explained, *Mine elect hear my voice and harden not their hearts* (D&C 29:7; see also T&C 9:3).

Nephi foresaw how few believers there would be in the last days. He—

> *beheld the church of the Lamb of God, and its numbers were few, because of the wickedness and abominations of the whore who sat upon many waters; nevertheless, I beheld that the church of the Lamb, who were the saints of God, were also upon all the face of the earth; and their dominions upon the face of the earth were small, because of the*

wickedness of the great whore whom I saw. (1 Nephi 14:12; see also 1 Nephi 3:28 RE)

The Lord requires us to invite the world to repent but not to expect large numbers to do so. Numbers matter to man, but the hearts of men matter to the Lord. It is the quality of conversion, not the quantity. He always spoke of having "few" sheep. Of the likely billions living at the time of Enoch, only some few thousand were saved (see Jude 1:14; see also Judas 1:3 RE) and only eight by Noah (see 1 Peter 3:20; see also 1 Peter 1:14 RE). The end times will be like those days (see Matthew 24:37; see also Matthew 11:11 RE).

The Lord charges us as He did Ezekiel:

> *I have made you who have received these tidings to be watchmen unto the scattered house of Israel; therefore **you** shall hear the words of my mouth, and warn **them** from me. When I say unto the wicked, O wicked man, thou shalt surely die; if **you** do not speak to warn the wicked from his way, that wicked man shall die in his iniquity; but his blood will I require at **your** hand. Nevertheless, if you warn the wicked of his way to turn from it; if he does not turn from his way, he shall die in his iniquity; but **you** have delivered your soul.* (See Ezekiel 33:7-9; see also Ezekiel 16:3 RE, emphasis added)

The Lord said in 1832 and again now, *Behold, I sent you out to testify and warn the people, and it becometh every man who hath been warned to warn his neighbor. Therefore, they are left without excuse, and their sins are upon their own heads.* (D&C 88:81-82; see also T&C 86:15)

We are to warn and invite but not expect many to respond. We have no obligation to dispute, contend, and debate with others to overcome their resistance. The Lord warned us about using "contention" to advance the truth about His Gospel: *And according as I have commanded you...* And by the way, these words were spoken by the Lord immediately preceding the Doctrine of Christ.

> *And according as I have commanded you thus shall ye baptize. And there shall be no disputations among you, as there have hitherto been; neither shall there be disputations among you concerning the points of my doctrine, as there have hitherto been. For verily, verily I say unto you, he that hath the spirit of contention is not of me, but is of the devil, who is the father of contention, and he stirreth up the hearts of men to contend with anger, one with another. Behold, this is not my doctrine, to stir up*

*the hearts of men with anger, one against another; but this is my
doctrine, that such things should be done away.* (3 Nephi 11:28-30; see
also 3 Nephi 5:8 RE)

We mustn't argue about our faith but declare it and leave it for the Lord to
confirm our testimony.

Similarly, Zion cannot be established by isolated and solitary figures
proclaiming a testimony of Jesus from their home keyboard. The challenge of
building a community must be part of a process. Zion is a community, and
therefore, God is a god of community; and his people must learn to live
together with one heart, one mind, with no poor among us. Isolated
keyboardists proclaiming their resentment of community can hardly speak
temperately of others. How could they ever live peacefully in a community of
equals? **We** must become precious to **each other.** Although the laborers in
this final effort are few, you will be the means used by the Lord to complete
his work in His vineyard (verse 70). You're required to labor with your might
to finish the Lord's work in his vineyard (verse 72), but He will labor
alongside you (see Jacob 5:70-72; see also Jacob 3:26-27 RE). He—not a man
or a committee—will call you to do work. When He calls, do not fear; but do
not run faster than you have strength. We must find His people in the
highways and byways and invite them to join in. Zion will include people
from every part of the world. This conference is broadcast worldwide as part
of the prophecy to Enoch that God would send

> *...righteousness and truth will [He] cause to sweep the earth as with a
> flood, to gather out mine elect from the four quarters of the earth, unto a
> place which I shall prepare, an Holy City, that my people may gird up
> their loins, and be looking forth for the time of my coming; for there shall
> be my tabernacle, and it shall be called Zion, a New Jerusalem.* (Moses
> 7:62; see also Genesis 4:22 RE)

The foregoing excerpts are taken from:

- Denver's talk titled "The Mission of Elijah Reconsidered," given in
  Spanish Fork, UT on October 14, 2011;
- His lecture titled "Signs Follow Faith," given in Centerville, UT on
  March 3, 2019;

- The presentation of Denver's paper titled "The Restoration's Shattered Promises and Great Hope," given at the Sunstone Symposium in Salt Lake City, UT on July 28, 2018;
- Denver's *40 Years in Mormonism Series* , Talk #3 titled "Repentance," given in Logan, UT on September 29, 2013;
- Denver's *40 Years in Mormonism Series*, Talk #4 titled "Covenants," given in Centerville, UT on October 6, 2013;
- His conference talk titled "The Doctrine of Christ," given in Boise, ID on September 11, 2016; and
- His talk titled "Opening Remarks," given at the Covenant of Christ Conference in Boise, ID on September 3, 2017.

In addition, Denver has written extensively about this topic. If you are interested in learning more, please review the following blog posts:

Follow-up Question, published January 3, 2012; and
Last Week's Comments, published May 19, 2012.

You may also find value in reviewing the following Glossary Entries:

Sealed in Their Foreheads
Called or Calling
Calling and Election
Elect
Sealing Power

69. Effective Study, Part 1

QUESTION: How do I get the most out of gospel study? Where do I begin? It can be frustrating to read and not really get much out of a text, aside from the most obvious and superficial reading. What can I do, or what skills or approaches do I need to utilize in order to make my study effective, so I can both understand *and* experience the gospel, as well as prepare for Zion?

————

DENVER: We have a tendency, all of us, to take concepts or pictures or ideas and to put them in our heads, and then to rely upon those pictures as we go forward learning new things. The object being to fit what we learned, that is new, into the framework of what we already know or we're already familiar with. That can be handicapping.

In the twenty-eighth chapter of Second Nephi, Nephi cautions us about permitting what he calls the "traditions of men" to override what he calls the "whisperings of the spirit." And he suggests that you run into mistakes, you run into errors—some of them terrible errors—when you permit those traditions, or those pictures that you already have inside your head, to be the framework from which you reconstruct new information that you learn. It's hard to do so, but when it comes to the gospel of Jesus Christ, you would be best advised to start with a blank slate and to allow it to inform you as if you're hearing it for the first time—because those words in scripture don't necessarily mean what the picture in your head suggests that they mean.

Let me pull an example. (If you've got your scriptures, you're welcome to pull them out, and turn the pages, and make all the noise you want finding the Joseph Smith History. You are NOT in a Sacrament meeting, and therefore, your scriptures are welcome to be used.) In the Joseph Smith History, it's the eighth verse, he says, about halfway through that eighth verse: *In process of time my mind became somewhat partial to the Methodist sect, and I felt some desire to be united with them* (Joseph Smith History 1:8; see also JSH 2:2 RE). Once again, this is high praise for Margaret Barker, a Methodist scholar.

But laying that aside, during the time of this period there was a (particularly in the revivalist part of Methodism)—there was a group called the Shouting Methodists; and the Shouting Methodists had a tradition. That tradition was to go into the woods alone to pray; and when they prayed alone in the woods, they were looking for some experience that would bind them up. And when they got bound up, they knew that they'd had an experience with God and the Holy Ghost, and they came back converted.

The miracle of The First Vision of Joseph Smith does not consist in the fact that he went in the woods alone to pray. Nor does it consist in the fact that when he's in the woods alone and praying, that he got bound up by some darkness which entirely overcame him. The miracle of Joseph Smith is that when that happened, he rejected it as the source of conversion. He did not allow his fears to control him. He did not allow the tradition to control him. But calling upon God, he then pressed through to receive what lays on the other side of the fears and of the darkness and of the things that put you off the trail to God. And he tells us about the vision of the Father and the Son telling him that he was to join none of them.

He goes on for some space of years; and during that space of years, he talks about how he frequently fell into many foolish errors—displayed by the weaknesses of youth and the foibles of human nature. And then he talks about he was guilty of levity and sometimes associating with jovial company. One of the pictures I think you have in your head about me (if you've read what I've written and you've read my blog) is that you may entirely misapprehend:

> #1—How difficult it is for me to get up here and do THIS, and

> #2—How incredibly irreverent I am by my native nature.

I am not a stoic religious person. I undertake to do what the Lord asks—what I think pleases Him—at the cost of personal inconvenience. I don't like being up here, and it's being recorded—by my voice and not by a camera—because I don't want people recognizing me. I don't want to be a celebrity. I want my privacy. And when it comes to a native, cheery temperament, I have, I suppose, a wicked sense of humor.

Well, he called upon, and he had confidence because he had previously received an answer. In verse 29, he had confidence that he would have an answer and a divine manifestation, as he had previously had one (see also JSH 3:1 RE). Then he gives the account, in some detail, of the appearance of the angel Moroni, how it occupied the night. And he passes through the events of his life until we get to the time in which, during the translation of the Book of Mormon (beginning in verse 68), they come upon the ordinance of baptism. They went into the woods. They prayed, in May of 1829, and John the Baptist appears and confers authority upon them. And immediately after conferring the authority upon Joseph Smith, the angel says to him: *He said [that] this Aaronic Priesthood had not the power of laying on hands for the gift of the Holy Ghost, but that this should be conferred on us hereafter* (Joseph Smith History 1:70; see also JSH 14:1 RE).

And then we get to verse 73, which is a description of what happened after being baptized:

> *Immediately on our coming...out of the water after we had been baptized, we experienced great and glorious blessings from our Heavenly Father. No sooner had I baptized Oliver Cowdery, than the Holy Ghost fell upon him...he stood up and prophesied many things which should shortly come to pass. And again, [as] soon as I had been baptized by him, I also had the spirit of prophecy, when, standing up, I prophesied concerning the [rising the] Church, and many other things connected with the Church, and this generation...We were filled with the Holy Ghost, and rejoiced in the God of our salvation. Our minds [now being] enlightened, we began to have the scriptures laid open to our understandings, and the true meaning and intention of their more mysterious passages revealed unto us in a manner which we [could never] attain to previously, nor ever before had thought of.* (Joseph Smith History 1:73-74; see also JSH 14:3-4)

Now, here are the questions: He saw God the Father and he saw Jesus Christ in a vision. And if you read all of the accounts, you find out it was a vision that included a view into Heaven, for he saw the Heavenly hosts—because the Father does not appear without a host. The Son can appear alone, but the Father never does. If you see the Father, you are going to see a host.

And thereafter, he's visited by the angel Moroni, and he's tutored—not merely through the one night, but in successive, annual occurrences for four years. AND YET, the first time his testimony mentions the Holy Ghost is after baptism. And after baptism using authority (which the angel told him HAD NOT the right to confer the gift of the Holy Ghost—that would happen at some *subsequent* occasion), why then—without the laying on of hands by one having authority—did Joseph Smith receive the Holy Ghost? Not merely as a visitation, mind you. Read the words. It lingered. It persisted. Because after they were baptized: *we began to have the scriptures laid open to our [understanding], and the true meaning and intention of their more mysterious passages revealed [to] us* (ibid). That required scripture study—over the ensuing weeks, months, years.

There we encounter a word: "mysterious" passages. You know that Peter, in Second Peter chapter 1, (I don't know) verse 16, maybe? You look it up. He says that the scriptures are not *of any private interpretation...but holy men...spake as they were moved [upon] by the Holy Ghost* (2 Peter 1:20-21; see also 2 Peter 1:5 RE).

The scriptures were given by the power of the Holy Ghost, and now Joseph Smith is explaining that he could *unravel* their *mysteries* by the power of the Holy Ghost. And things that did not make sense before, began to make sense. If you've read *The Second Comforter*, in the chapter about becoming as a little child there is an excerpt taken from a book: *Godel, Escher, Bach*—a brilliant mathematical book about Bongard problems. Bongard problems are designed to test a certain kind of reasoning, using symbols in order to test the person evaluating them. And invariably, Bongard problems are solved by children. And they confuse adults because the children's minds have not become cluttered by the kind of mathematical complexity that we have bouncing around in our heads, as a consequence of which, they look at it simply, and they see things simply, and they can solve the Bongard problems in a way in which adults fail to grasp.

The gospel is adapted to the simple mind. The statements that are contained in scripture are given in simplicity and in plainness. So when we encounter Joseph Smith speaking to us, now, about having the mysteries of the gospel laid open to his mind—as a consequence of having the Holy Ghost—I'm reminded of a statement that he made that you find in the *Teachings of the Prophet Joseph Smith* about the Holy Ghost, on pages 149 and 150, which I'm going to read an excerpt from:

> There are two Comforters spoken of. One is the Holy Ghost, the same as given on the Day of Pentecost, and that all Saints receive after faith, repentance, and baptism. This first comforter..." [And by the way, Joseph Smith is saying this at a time when the authority for the laying on of hands had been restored, but his list is faith and repentance and baptism; and that produces the same effect as on the Day of Pentecost. If you listen to the words of the ordinance that's performed in the church, the words of the ordinance are an admonition to **you** to receive the Holy Ghost. It's telling **you** to do something. Well, this first comforter] or Holy Ghost has no other effect than pure intelligence. [It's] more powerful in expanding the mind, enlightening the understanding, and storing the intellect with present knowledge. (*TPJS*, p. 149)

Did you get that list of things? The effect of the Holy Ghost is pure intelligence.

I can watch *Lawrence of Arabia*, and when they've successfully knocked the train off the track, and the group he is leading has charged and overcome the enemy, and Lawrence is walking on the top of the trains with the flowing robes, I can get goose bumps. It is moving. It is stirring. That's **not** the Holy Ghost. I can have that same effect with *Les Miserables*. I can have that same effect with some of the scenes in *Joseph's Amazing Technicolor Dreamcoat*. Moving and stirring things can delight your senses. That's **not** the Holy Ghost. It "has no other effect than pure intelligence...expanding the mind, enlightening the understanding, ...storing the intellect with present knowledge."

I'm not here to entertain you. I'm trying to inform you of doctrine that will save you. I don't care if any of you are stirred or (like one of our MSNBC folks) had a tremor run up his leg at the president's speaking. I don't care about that. I care about your salvation; I care about your souls; and I care about you understanding the things that will save you. Joseph Smith gave the list: pure intelligence, expanding the mind, enlightening the understanding, storing the intellect with present knowledge.

In the translation of the Book of Moses (which was Joseph correcting the Book of Genesis), he gives a list there of the Holy Ghost as well. Let me read you that list: *The Comforter; the peaceable things of immortal glory*— This is Moses chapter 6, verse 61: *The Comforter; the peaceable things of immortal glory; the truth of all things; that which quickeneth all things, which maketh alive all things; that which knoweth all things, and hath all power according to wisdom, mercy, truth, justice, and judgment* (Moses 6:61; see also Genesis 4:9 RE). This is the Holy Ghost.

Joseph Smith returned from the First Vision and didn't talk about the Holy Ghost because that incident, quite frankly, was not understood by Joseph Smith at the time it occurred. When he explained to his mother, he said, *Never mind...I'm well enough off. [I've] learned for myself that Presbyterianism [isn't] true* (Joseph Smith History 1:20; see also JSH 2:6 RE). And I think that is a candid description of what Joseph got out of it that day, at that time. He had been converted, and he knew now not to join the Presbyterians.

What Joseph Smith learned from the angel Moroni, also, did not confer upon him the Holy Ghost. Faith, repentance, baptism, and *then* he notes the Holy Ghost. And what are the effects that he reports? Immediately?

- Number one: prophecy, one of the hallmark signs. Paul lists it in Corinthians. Mormon and Moroni list it in Moroni's book—the list of what the gifts are. You can find it in the Doctrine and Covenants —section 46, if I'm remembering that correctly—the list of the gifts. Prophecy is always included as one of the hallmark signs of what it is that the Holy Ghost does.

- And then secondly: allow Joseph to understand the real intent of what is in the scriptures. How much of a blank slate was Joseph at the time that the Holy Ghost allowed him the "pure spirit of intelligence"?

- Well, I would suggest that if Joseph Smith can pass through the First Vision and can pass through the incident of the visits of the angel Moroni, and if he can even translate the Book of Mormon—which was then underway at the time this occurred—by the gift and power of God, but not attribute anything to the Holy Ghost until after he is baptized—that it is equally possible for you good people to go through everything you've gone through in your life, and yet not have experienced the thing that Joseph is talking about—which comes as a consequence of faith, repentance, and baptism.

In Revelation chapter 3, verses 20 and 21, there's a promise that John records — Well, the 20 is where He stands at the door and knocks: *Behold, I stand at the door, and knock.* See, in this description, it's almost a flip. It's not **you** knocking to get in; it's the **Lord** knocking to come to you. It's the Lord who is the eager One—the One who would like to have this relationship take up. He's the One knocking. He's the One trying to get into your life. And so, in this account: *I stand at the door* [the Lord speaking], *and knock: if any man hear my voice...* See, His sheep hear His voice. Do you **hear** His voice? *If any man hear my voice, and open the door*—because you're the one that shut it. You're the one that's saying:

- "Yeah, no thanks; I'll pass. I mean, I've got a skeptical mind now. I've been to college and have received training to practice law;"

- "I'm an engineer, and I understand formulas and equations;"

- "I'm a mathematician, and I know some things add up and some things don't;" and

- "I also know that I've been leading a reasonably decent life, and I've never had Jesus in **my** car."

- Our minds are skeptical. **We** have to open the door because, almost invariably, the door that **we** configure to keep him out, from our construct, is something that has come about as a consequence of what happened in **your** life—from the time you left that state of innocence, as a child in the Garden, until today. Every painful experience you've been through; every humiliation you've suffered; everything that has gone on in your life that has led to where you now construct a door—some of oak, some of iron—whatever it is that's happened to you, you use **that** to keep Him out. "Well, if He really cared, He would… " You know, the **notion** that He doesn't care is the greatest lie of all. If you knew what He suffered, you would **never** say, "If He cared." But if you'll open the door, He says: *I will come in to him, and will sup with him, and he with me* (Revelation 3:20; see also Revelation 1:20 RE).

Verse 8, once again: *So great were the confusion and strife among the different denominations, [that] it was impossible for a person young as I was, and so unacquainted with men and things, to come to any certain conclusion who was right and who was wrong* (Joseph Smith History 1:8; see also JSH 2:2 RE). See, that's the way it is. In verse 10—

There's always this ~~war of worlds~~ war of **words** (*War of Worlds*—that's what your kids play)—*war of words and tumult of opinions.* And so Joseph is confused. How do you resolve this?

Verse 11: *While I was laboring…* While-I-was-labor—

Folks, in general, have your skulls so junked up with the crap of the Internet that you don't even **have** the capacity to labor the way it needs to be labored; to solve the questions that need to be solved. It is labor. It is labor over the scriptures. It is labor. *Under the extreme difficulties caused by… these parties of religionists, [he] was one day reading the Epistle of James, first chapter…fifth verse, which reads: If any of you lack wisdom, let him ask of God, that giveth to all men liberally, and upbraideth not; and it shall be given him.*

"Let him ask of God." God gives "to **all** men liberally, and upbraideth not; **and it shall be given him**" (emphasis added). I can ask God. God will give to **me**. God will give to me **liberally**. God will not tell me, "There are lines here you mustn't cross. There are things about which you must not inquire. There are things your heart is not yet prepared to receive. You don't have standing!" He gives liberally. He can let **you** know what you **need** to know from **your** study and inquiry into the truth. And no man can stop that! Because this is a matter between you and God. It has **always** been a matter between you and God. There is no friar with a brown frock that you need to bend the knee to, in order to please God. If Joseph had known that (the friar with the frock), he would never have achieved the revolution that he achieved.

Well, when you're laboring, as verse 11 suggests, and when you hit the right verse, as verse 11 recites, **then** verse 12 confirms how you get answers to these kinds of inquiries: *Never did any passage of scripture come with more power to the heart of man than this did at this time to mine. It seemed to enter with great force.*

Turn back to Doctrine and Covenants section 76, and look at verse 18. This is the Vision of the Redemption of the Dead, that gave us the three degrees of glory. They're reading in John; and he gives you the verse in John that they were reading, in verses 16 and 17. And look at 18: *Now this caused us to marvel, for it was given unto us of the Spirit* (D&C 76:18; see also T&C 69:4).

The Spirit cannot lean upon you and cannot focus your mind upon the revelation that you are entitled to receive unless you use the scriptures as they were intended to be used—as a Urim and Thummim—as the basis from which you draw out the truths of God. And the best version of that is, of course, the Book of Mormon.

You can look at D&C section 138, and you'll find that Joseph F. Smith sat in his room **pondering** over the scriptures. He's near death—it's about eight weeks before the death of Joseph F. Smith. The Church had a lot of challenges going on at that time. Fortuitously for us, the man who sat at home—infirm and worried about death—happened to happily be the president of the Church of Jesus Christ of Latter-day Saints. And so, when he got an answer—not to his inquiry about leading the Church—when he got an answer to an inquiry that had nothing to do with his position or budgets or anything else that manages an organization; it had to do with his **own** concern, about his **own** deepest apprehensions: his impending death, which would follow about eight weeks after this, the scriptures opened like a Urim and Thummim to his view, and we get a Vision of the Redemption of the Dead, which we've now canonized.

It [entered]— This is back— Verse 12 of the Joseph Smith History: *It [entered into his heart] with great force into every feeling of my heart. I reflected on it again and again* (Joseph Smith History 1:12; see also JSH 2:3 RE).

Now **that's** an interesting statement—because it doesn't appear that this "labor" was a one-off event but that it occurred over and over as he sought more understanding, searching deeper and deeper into trying to understand what it was he ought to do and how it is he ought to accomplish it. *Again and again, knowing… if any person needed wisdom from God, I did.*

You should be asking God so that you can understand scripture. You shouldn't be trusting the expositions of **anyone**, myself included. These scriptures have a message for you. God has a message for you. God would like to talk to **you**—not through me or any other man. God would like to talk with **you**. You'll be saved by knowledge, and the things you need to know are uniquely situated. The things you have the right to get from God are uniquely situated.

I got an answer from God. That's why, 40 years ago today, I went in, and I got baptized. Elder Brian Black baptized me. During the baptismal service, because it was approaching twilight, the sun was beginning to set, the moon had emerged, and the first stars began to shine. And Brian Black commented in the talk that was given by him, before laying on hands, that all of the signs of heaven—the sun, the moon, and the stars—had been visible during my baptismal ceremony. I have felt the presence of God with me from that moment through today. Just this morning I checked into my office before coming here, and when I arrived at my office there was a dove on the lawn to meet me, and she stayed there as I went by. Now, it's a small thing, but if you're acquainted with the scriptures, you understand what such a symbol **can** mean, and to me, **did** mean.

Your lives should be **filled** with wonder. Be not faithless, but be believing—and be of good cheer! He knows you better than you know yourself. I was belly-aching about an idiot (friend), and as I am wont to do, it was prayerful. (The Stake President asked me, a few weeks ago, about whether I was praying at the time that I had one of the encounters he and I discussed. And I said, "It's not a fair question. I wake up in the morning, and I start to pray. Throughout the day, I will take care of a thousand things; and whenever I am free, my mind will revert back to the prayer, and we'll continue the dialogue. And it goes on all day. There's not a moment in my life in which I am not being prayerful. And so, the answer to the question is, I suppose, Yes, I was praying. Because there's hardly a moment—when I'm idle—when I am not praying.")

Well, God intends to speak to each of us—about us and about what matters to us and about what matters to **you**. He, unlike us, is not bounded by the linear existence that we have. All things past, present, and future are continually before the Lord. In fact, it's really sort of an interesting study.

If you take and you look at what the Lord does in Third Nephi, He has this agenda that He's been assigned by the Lord—or by the Father—and Christ discharges the agenda. And He goes through; and as you read the chapters in Third Nephi, it's really structured; it's really orderly. And then He announces: Now I have finished what the Father told me to deliver to you. And He just begins to talk. And as He begins to talk, what unfolds is non-chronological. It's topical; but it's past, present, and future. His thoughts are not like our thoughts. They aren't. They're nonlinear. And sometimes that's not easy.

At length—he says, in verse 13—*I came to the conclusion...I must either remain in darkness and confusion, or else I must do as James directs, that is, ask of God* (Joseph Smith History 1:13; see also JSH 2:3 RE). And so it is for all of us. You want to know the truth of a proposition? You ask God. And **don't be fearful**. If you ask, He'll answer. But you better be prepared for the answer. Because the battle that is already upon us is going to require valiance. Cowardly, effeminate, hen-like behavior can never, never obtain the promises of God. Christ asked: *What went [you forth]...to see? A reed [shaking in] the wind?* (Matthew 11:7; see also Matthew 6:2 RE). **That's** what you want?! I don't think John the Baptist cried on demand. And Zion isn't a bank.

> *So [it is] in accordance with this, my determination to ask of God, I retired to the woods to make the attempt. It was on the morning of a beautiful, clear day, early in the spring of eighteen hundred and twenty. It was the first time in my life...I had made such an attempt, for amidst all my anxieties I had never as yet made the attempt to pray vocally. After I had retired to the place where I had previously designed...finding myself alone, I kneeled down and began to offer up the desires of my heart to God. I had scarcely done so, when immediately I was seized upon by some power which entirely overcame me...had such an astonishing influence over me as to bind my tongue so that I could not speak. Thick darkness gathered around me...seemed to me for a time as if I were doomed to sudden destruction.* (Joseph Smith History 1:14-15; see also JSH 2:3-4 RE)

You know, we have Orson Hyde's account of this thick darkness, and I want to read it to you. This is Orson Hyde writing about the incident we just looked at:

> He, therefore, retired to a secret place, in a grove, but a short distance from his father's house, and knelt down and began to call upon the Lord. At first, he was severely tempted by the powers of darkness, which endeavored to overcome him. The adversary benighted his mind with doubts, and brought to his soul all kinds of improper pictures and tried to hinder him in his efforts and the accomplishment of his goal. However, the overflowing mercy of God came to buoy him up. (Orson Hyde, Published in a German Pamphlet, 1842)

You know, if salvation consists in obtaining knowledge, you can't afford to clutter your mind with the kinds of things which can readily summon up improper images, improper thoughts, improper ambitions. In fact, it doesn't matter what you **want** . There's only one thing that matters. And that is: What is the Lord's will **for** you, **with** you. And that will is always the same— to bring about your happiness; ultimately, to bring about your joy. He tells you that His burden is light. Because however it may seem in the direful circumstances of 1838 in the life of Joseph Smith, **this** statement of faith, **this** testimony of truth was worth the price that Joseph was called upon to pay to obtain it.

The things of God are infinitely preferable to anything that can be offered to you here in this world. You may indeed be able to buy anything in this world for money, but don't let that ever be the case with your heart or your soul. Zion will not have an economy—because they have all things in common.

So Joseph, in verse 16, tells you that it is some marvelous power from the unseen world. Let me take you back to that statement: "A man is saved no faster than he gets knowledge, for if he does not get knowledge, he will be brought into captivity by some evil power in the other world, as evil spirits will have more knowledge, and consequently more power" (*TPJS*, p. 217). Well, apply that quote in the context of what Joseph is experiencing there, and realize this is not merely something that will happen after you depart this world. It's something that, in fact, does happen here. I mean, being blinded here is part of being captured by the captivity of the adversary of your soul.

Awake and arise! Shake off the scales that blind you. Scales which [are] like contact lenses, on the one hand; but scales like judging wrongly, on the other hand. You have to judge a matter aright. And if the judgment that you judge is not just, then the scales of **your** eyes are darkness, indeed.

And so he called upon God to escape this being from the unseen world, and:

> *[He] saw a pillar of light exactly over [his] head, above the brightness of the sun, which descended gradually until it fell upon me. It no sooner appeared than I found myself delivered from the enemy which held me bound. When the light rested upon me I saw two Personages.* (Joseph Smith History 1:16-17; see also JSH 2:4 RE)

We'll get into this more in Idaho Falls. He saw two "Personages." Note the word. Joseph **knows** what he's talking about. He was in the presence of these Beings. He will later describe them, as a doctrinal exposition (which the Church accepted as doctrine, and which was, for a season, in your scriptures). That's why you need to bring your ~~Articles of~~ [Lectures on] Faith to Idaho Falls.

One of them spake unto me, calling me by name (ibid). I've mentioned this on a number of occasions, and I want to mention it again here. When God calls a person by name, it is not your full legal name. "Joseph Smith, Jr." (I mean, that's my Cecil B. Demille version of *The Ten Commandments* voice of God— "Moses.") The casual friendship— I don't know what Joseph was called at this point in his life. I don't know if it was Joey. I don't know if it was Junior. I don't know what the name was that he went by. Whoever his most intimate companion was, that was what the Lord called him. If it was Joey, it was "Joey." God doesn't call you by whatever your driver's license says.

So, He called him by name. Do you know how comforting it is to have God call you by a familiar name? Instead of recoiling in horror, He's drawing you in. Instead of stiff-arming you, like "I am the Great and Powerful," He wants you comfortable in His presence, so much so that, when you enter into His presence, it is a matter of course that God invariably forgives your sins.

In 1921, the Lectures on Faith were dropped from the scriptures by a committee that was comprised of George F. Richards, Anthony W. Ivins, Melvin J. Ballard, James E. Talmage, John A. Widstoe, and Joseph Fielding Smith. That committee dropped the Lectures on Faith from the scriptures because, they said,

> Certain lessons, entitled Lectures on Faith, which were bound...with...Doctrine and Covenants in some of its former issues,

are not included in this edition. Those lessons were prepared for use in the School of Elders...but they were never presented...nor accepted by the Church as being otherwise than theological lessons or lectures." (Explanatory Introduction, Doctrine and Covenants, 1921 edition, p. V)

That's a lie. And the *Joseph Smith Papers*, if you will read them today, tell you that that's not at all the truth. And part of what I hope to get to tonight—and if not tonight then in Logan—is the reasons why. Joseph Smith called this "doctrine—important doctrine;" "leading items of the religion;" and that he would answer to every principle that's advanced in the document.

Now to his credit, Joseph Fielding Smith, who was on that [committee] said (this was in 1966)—he said: *"I suppose that the rising generation knows little about the Lectures... In my own judgment these Lectures are of great value and should be studied... I consider them to be of extreme value in the study of the gospel of Jesus Christ"* ("The School of the Prophets", BYU Leadership Week, June 18, 1956).

And then in a talk given by Elder Bruce R. McConkie at Brigham Young University (the son-in-law to the one of the committee members, whose words I just read), in January the 4th of 1972 (that would have been before I was there), Elder McConkie said (every time I read Bruce R. McConkie [impersonating Bruce R. McConkie's voice] "I am tempted to read it in the voice of Elder McConkie, which echoes still in my skull." I won't do that. And I'm reading him now):

> In my judgment, it is the most comprehensive, intelligent, inspired utterance that now exists in the English language—that exists in one place defining, interpreting, expounding, announcing, and testifying what kind of being God is. It was written by the power of the Holy Ghost, by the Spirit of Inspiration...it is, in effect, eternal scripture, [it is] true. (BYU Speeches, 4 January, 1972)

Which brings us, then, to the Third Lecture on Faith. Now we're starting really to get into some important stuff, so I hope your chair's painful enough to keep you awake. Personally, I'd rather stand up here than sit in one of those things. That's it! You could get this over with a lot quicker if you put me in one of those chairs and said, "Talk until you're sick of that!"

Verse 2 of Lecture 3: *Let us here observe, that three things are necessary in order that any rational and intelligent being may exercise faith in God* [**faith in God**] *unto life and salvation* (Lectures on Faith 3:2). Faith in **God**, not in man, not in men, not in an institution, not in some magic talisman—*faith in God.* Faith in God unto life and salvation. Faith in **God**, not in man, not in men, not in an institution, not in some magic talisman—*faith in God.*

To the extent that anyone is trying to displace your faith in God and attract attention to themselves, **myself included**, that is a perversion. It will not save you. It is a distraction. It is evil. It is wrong. It is damnable. Anyone that tries to attract your worship, myself included, ought to be sent to hell. It's why I continually remind you: talking about me is a waste of time. Talking about the things I'm saying; talking about the content of these scriptures; talking about the doctrines that will save you; that's **very** important. But you can leave me out of that. You don't ever need to mention my name again in your life. But pay attention to the **doctrine** that we're talking about. Pay attention to the message that comes to us through scripture. You will never be saved because you relied upon some guy to elevate you. The only way in which that will happen is when you connect with God. You have to *exercise faith in God unto life and salvation.*

There are three things:

- *First, the idea that he actually exists.* You can get that from someone else.

- *Secondly, a **correct** idea of His character, perfections and attributes.* Any error in that prevents you from having faith. Therefore, in order to get *that* right, it's going to require something of you in the way of study and effort. Because if you're making—well, look at the word, they italicized it—a **correct** idea of His character perfections and attributes, that's what you need to study to show what it is you're going to have faith in.

- *Thirdly: an actual knowledge that the course of life which he is pursuing is according to His will.* (Lectures on Faith 3:3-5)

- **You** must know this. And **you** cannot cover the gap by lying to yourself. You can't lie to yourself, pretending that you are on God's course, and then have **actual** knowledge that the course of life that you are pursuing is according to His will. Nor can you depend entirely upon what other people are telling you. You're supposed to be asking and getting answers from God. And the answers from God are going to tell you what you need to do. And the sacrifices that He will require of you are unique to you, because the contribution that you can make for the salvation of yourself and others is unique to you.

There are things that you and only you can do. And if you will sign up with God, He will have you do them. You may find yourself doing things you would rather prefer not doing. It doesn't matter. If you have faith in Him, and you do what He asks, you'll **know** that the course you're pursuing is according to His will. And doing things He asks of you, according to **His** will, invariably produce faith. And they produce faith unto salvation. Because it always grows. Light grows or dims; it never stays static. Therefore, when you set on this course, you never turn back. If you turn back, you lose everything that you've gained up to that point. Look at verse 5 (this is third):

> *An actual knowledge that the course of life which he is pursuing is according to His will. For without an acquaintance with these three important facts, the faith of every rational being must be imperfect and unproductive, but **with** this understanding it can become perfect and fruitful, abounding in righteousness unto the praise and glory of God the Father and the Lord Jesus Christ.* (Lectures on Faith 3:5, emphasis added)

Therefore, these three things you need to know: God exists; you need to study until you have a correct understanding of his character, perfections, and attributes; and then you have to live your life so that you actually know that the course you're leading in your life conforms to what He would have. Turn to verse 23:

> *But it is also necessary that men should have an idea that he is no respecter of persons, for with the idea of all the other excellencies in his character, and this one wanting, men could not exercise faith in him; because if he were a respecter of persons, they could not tell what their privileges were, nor how far they were authorized to exercise faith in him, or whether they were authorized to do it at all, but all must be confusion; but no sooner are the minds of men made acquainted with the truth on this point, that he is no respecter of persons, than they see that they have authority by faith to lay hold on eternal life, the richest boon of heaven, because God is no respecter of persons, and that every man in every nation has an equal privilege.* (Lectures on Faith 3:23)

That's you. **That's you.** God has done nothing for Joseph Smith He will not do for you. I understand all of the doctrinal arguments. I can make them all. I

have made them all. And I've made them to the Lord. I've argued with Him on every point of doctrine that any of you— I've quoted to Him every scripture that any of you have advanced, and many more besides. And the Lord has always borne testimony back, consistently. This stuff is true! You're hedging up the way of your own salvation and of the salvation of others when you say, "No one has the privilege in our day, **yet**, to lay hold on salvation." You're hedging up the way; you are damning yourself. And you're damning those that will listen to you when you say people in our time are not yet authorized to exercise faith in God unto salvation—because you **are** authorized.

I have done so. I have spoken with Him as a man speaks to another. He speaks in plain humility, reasoning as one man does with another. He will reason with you. The first night I got a testimony, I was in the middle of an argument with God—I thought with myself—until when I got down to the final question in my mind, which was, "How do I even know there is a God?" To which the response came, "Who do you think you've been talking to the last two hours?" I didn't realize that that Still Small Voice, which will talk with any and all of you, was God. When you exercise the required faith to permit Him to step out from behind the veil, like the brother of Jared, He'll do that, too. He's no respecter of persons. You should not question what your privileges are, nor how far you are authorized to exercise faith in Him, or whether you're authorized to do it at all. Don't have doubts about your privileges.

And then verse 24, twice: *He is love...he is love.* He **is** love.

In verse 3, it talks about:

> *Having the assurance that they were pursuing a course which was agreeable to the will of God, they were enabled to take, not only the spoiling of their goods, and the wasting of their substance, joyfully, but also to suffer death in its most horrid forms; knowing (not merely believing) that when this earthly house of their tabernacle was dissolved, they had a building of God, a house not made with hands, eternal in the heavens.* (Lectures on Faith 6:3)

That's why Joseph could say, as he did, that he left with a conscience void of offense against God or any man—going as a sheep to the slaughter (see *TPJS*, p. 379). But he was okay with it. He was okay with it: *Such was, and always will be, the situation of the saints of God, that unless they have an actual knowledge that the course they are pursuing is according to the will of God, they will grow weary in their minds, and faint* (Lectures on Faith 6:4).

That's the problem with many of us. We grow weary in our minds and faint because we don't know that the course we're pursuing is according to God. Don't grow weary. Stay on that course. I have the absolute conviction that much of the stuff that we plague ourselves with, and think is such a heavy burden of sin, is because our minds are occupied with the wrong stuff. Study the things of God and fill yourself with light—and how quickly it is that all the rest of that stuff will simply dissolve away and evaporate. President Boyd Packer said you can fix behavior a lot more quickly by studying doctrine than you can by studying behavior (see '*Little Children,*' Ensign, Nov. 1986, p. 17).

And you'll be called upon to make a sacrifice, because knowing God requires obedience to Him and sacrifice to Him, and not to some man—certainly not to me; but not to a pope, not to a president, not to a priest—to Him. You're not trying to get to know me (or if you are, you're damn fool). You're supposed to be getting to know the Lord. You're supposed to be getting to know the Lord—you're not supposed to be getting to know some local presiding authority.

———

The foregoing excerpts are taken from:

- Denver's fireside talk on "The Temple," given in Ogden, UT, on October 28th, 2012;
- Denver's 40 Years in Mormonism Series, Talk #1, titled "Be of Good Cheer," given in Boise, ID, on September 10th, 2013; and
- Denver's 40 Years in Mormonism Series, Talk #2, titled "Faith," given in Idaho Falls, ID, on September 28th, 2013.

In addition, Denver has written extensively about this topic. If you are interested in learning more, please review the following blog posts:

Gospel Study, posted November 17, 2011
Christians Should Study Mormonism, posted January 12, 2017
How I Study the Scriptures, posted March 18, 2010
3 Nephi 11: 36, posted September 29, 2010
Scriptures, Not Traditions, posted February 24, 2014

70. Effective Study, Part 2

QUESTION: How do I get the most out of gospel study? Where do I begin? It can be frustrating to read and not really get much out of a text aside from the most obvious and superficial reading. What can I do, or what skills or approaches do I need to utilize in order to make my study effective so I can both understand *and* experience the gospel as well as prepare for Zion?

————

DENVER: When Moroni— Excuse me, when Nephi (Second Nephi chapter 9, verse 14-ish, about how the things that he had seen and heard)— He constantly meditated upon that, writing some 40 years after the fact. The revelations that Joseph Smith received, including that one that he received in the sacred grove, is not all to be comprehended in the first pass-through.

The things of God are of deep import. Why did God reveal what He revealed when He revealed it? Why did He reveal it in the order in which He revealed it? What was He building upon? Why in the first revelation did He go there? Why in the next did He go to that point?

If you think Joseph's mind wasn't caught up on the things that he had seen and heard (just as *yours* should be about the things that *you* have seen and heard), then you need to think again because the things of God are of deep import—and time and care and careful and solemn and ponderous thoughts are the only way in which you or anyone can find them out; and that applies especially to you because you control you.

You determine how much light and truth you will receive, and it's predicated upon a law that was ordained before the foundation of the world. Any one of you can obey it. God is no respecter of persons, and you are authorized to exercise faith in Him unto salvation. *You* are authorized to exercise faith in Him until you know Him. *You* are authorized to see His face and know that He is, every one of you, because if you intend to survive His return, you're going to *have* to be able to bear His presence—hence the need to now talk about this stuff and hence the agenda that we're on. We introduced it; we talked about faith; we talked about repentance; we're going to talk about covenants next.

I know not all of you come to all of these. I don't expect you to. I don't even expect you to get the disks and listen to them. But I'm trying to transcribe them and fill in the things that I'm thinking about even if I don't give you the scriptures—and they're up, and they'll be on the internet and available for you to read.

I'm introducing things. I'm trying to provoke you to study. I'm trying to provoke you to go look into this stuff. But I can't babysit you and shouldn't. I'll only make you weak and not strong if I attempt to do that. *You* need to take this as the beginning point and go on and discover for yourself *how* great things the Lord intends to do, and one of the neglected volumes of scripture you need to spend some time with is the Lectures on Faith. They remain scripture.

I told you how the Lord vouched for Joseph Smith. The Lord vouches for Joseph Smith again, and if no one else will say it, I'll declare it to you: If you ignore Joseph's words, you ignore it at your peril, and if you allow any man or men; if you allow any committee, any institution, or organization to claim that they have the right to alter, neglect, or discard the words of revelation given by God through the Prophet Joseph Smith, they will damn you if you listen to them. And they will surely be damned for doing so because *no one* has the right to do that.

God's work is *the same* yesterday, today, and forever, and those who would like to throw you about by every whim of doctrine are teaching you merely the commandments of men as if they *were* doctrine, and they aren't!

When God speaks through Joseph, and we forget him, we have no right to expect collectively that He's going to move anything forward for us. The first order of repentance is to remember what God gave to us through Joseph. You do *that*, and then you'll find God's perfectly willing to pick it up and move it forward. You don't do that, and God will simply wait for you to get around to discharge the duty that's devolving upon you.

God vouched for Joseph Smith. God spoke through him, and I don't have the right to move one of his words; but I do have the right to listen to him, to follow what came through him, and to lay hold upon the blessings that were promised as a consequence of remembering him—because to remember the words of Joseph is to remember your Lord. Remember Him, and don't let anyone tell you that they hold some authority that allows them to neglect, change, discard, veto, forget, or contradict what God told *you* through the voice of a prophet.

In verse 12, it talks about how there's going to be this restoration of *knowledge of their fathers in the latter days…also to the knowledge of my covenants, saith the Lord* (2 Nephi 3:12; see also 2 Nephi 2:4 RE).

And then in 15, it says: *His name shall be called after me…it shall be after the name of his father* [*after me* being Joseph of Egypt—so, the name should be Joseph; that will also be the name of his father]; *he shall be like unto me; for the thing, which the Lord [God] shall bring forth by his hand, by the power of the Lord shall bring my people unto salvation* (ibid, vs. 15; vs. 5 RE).

And then he goes on, and he tells— Lehi tells his son in verse 23: *Because of this covenant* [that is, the one that was done with Joseph of Egypt], *he* [the son of Lehi] *is blessed, for his* [the son of Lehi's] *seed shall not be destroyed…they shall hearken unto the words of the book. And there shall rise up one mighty among them* (ibid, vs. 23; vs. 7 RE). I talked about that in Boise.

And so, if Joseph Smith fulfills the prophecy that was delivered to Joseph that is recovered in part in the Book of Mormon (in this third chapter of Second Nephi), then Joseph Smith should give to us the ability to know something about these covenants that were made with the Fathers.

Well, we do not have to rely upon merely what we have in Second Nephi chapter 3. Nor do we have to have the brass plates, as it turns out, because Joseph Smith restored the prophecy of Joseph of Egypt, and you can read it right now in the Joseph Smith Translation beginning in Genesis chapter 50 at verse 24. It reads slightly different than Lehi's summation given and Lehi's choice of what he adds in and what he selects out. And what Joseph says has some interesting things. It's absolutely worth your time to study out all the differences and to pick apart what it is that Lehi did because it tells you much about Father Lehi—what he chose to include and what he chose to pass over.

The work of salvation is not achieved by your ignorance and indifference, and the gospel of Christ is not limited to making you *feel* better about yourself.

Quite frankly, my wife and I marvel all the time at how unprepared and unworthy she and I feel in *everything* that has gone on. *But*—I know God; and therefore, because I know God, I am confident that you can know Him, too—*absolutely* confident that you can know Him, too, and that He *will* speak to any one of you, just as He spoke to Joseph Smith, and that He will answer any earnest seeker. No one is sent away disappointed.

You think the Lord who would not turn away the blind, and the halt, the crippled, and the leprous—

You think the Lord who, seeing the widow whose only son was being carried away dead and was moved with compassion to restore the life of that young man so that she (in that circumstance, in that culture, in that environment)— she now had future security because she had a son to look out for her—

Do you think that *that* Lord *doesn't* intend to answer the prayers of the earnest seeker?

My suspicion is that God has answered, and you've turned a deaf ear to much of what you have looked for because you want something other than the answers He's already given in the material that sits in front of you unexamined. My suspicion is that if you would spend time looking into the revelations given us by the Prophet Joseph Smith and studying the history (however perilous that may prove to be to you), that you will conclude that God's already had an answer to the inquiry that you've made and that with a little effort, you can find it. And when you find it, you'll hear the voice of God saying, "There it is. Now was *that* so hard? Why don't you keep going and see what else is in there for you?"—because this stuff was given to us at the price of the life of a 38½-year-old young man and his older brother whose blood was shed in order to restore what we now have in our possession. And we take it lightly? And we look away?

I could write my own gospel. I could bear my own testimony. I could invent a new narrative about our Lord if it were necessary to do so. But I'll tell you, the only thing that is necessary is to open the scriptures and read them and to tell you the things that we looked at tonight are true—like Jacob. In fact, if you go all the way back to Jacob chapter 6:

And now, behold, my brethren, as I said unto you that I would prophesy, behold, this is my prophecy—that the things which this prophet Zenos spake, concerning the house of Israel, in the which he likened them unto a tame olive tree, must surely come to pass (Jacob 6:1; see also Jacob 4:1 RE).

So, here's the words of *my* prophecy—that the things that we have looked at this evening restored through the Prophet Joseph Smith (the seer named Joseph, the son of a father named Joseph) fulfilled the promise of Joseph of Egypt; and they are all true, and I know them to be true. And you can know them to be true, too, but the price you have to pay in order to gain that knowledge is to pay some attention to what it was that was restored through the Prophet Joseph Smith. Otherwise, they're just something gathering dust on a shelf.

Don't read them as if you're trying to vindicate the religion that you think you already understand. Don't read them as if you're trying to defend your current group of preferred doctrines. Read them as if you are as ignorant of the will of God as the convert is that you hope to make (living somewhere in Florida or New Guinea or Guatemala) because the truth of the matter is that we have been devolving in our understanding from the day of Joseph Smith until today at an *ever-accelerating* rate. And what we have left, Enoch called *gross darkness*.

As we get to sealing power—and we will get there before the day is up—there are some things about that you need to have parsed, and you need to understand. But the fact of the matter is that when we talk about priesthood, we throw about *lavish* claims among ourselves because we have a vocabulary; and as a consequence of possessing that vocabulary, we think, then, that we have understanding when, in fact, the scriptures are telling us a whole different story. And that whole different story is what we're pursuing here today. Hopefully, when we get to the end of this today, you'll walk away saying, "I need to go back and study my scriptures 'cuz it sounds like there's a whole lot in there about priesthood that makes distinctions which I had not heretofore appreciated."

As you read Section 76, remember that the things of God are not to be taken lightly. Nor are they given to you *merely* by study. You must also *receive* revelation in order to *understand* revelation. The scriptures are a launching point to take your mind *upward*. You must commune with God to understand the things of God. Do not be fooled by man's pretentions into sloth. No man, or committee, or organization will ever save you. *Nothing* some financial institution (managed by lawyers, bankers, managers, businessmen, and professors) offers will matter in the afterlife. The only things which will matter at *that* place will be what you secure for yourself from the Powers of Heaven while you live here.

This is a probation. Act like the choices you make are the choices a God-in-the-making would choose. Be responsible for your life's outcome. When the Day of Judgment comes, you'll not be able to hand a temple recommend to your Divine Judge and have Him respect a mere man's judgment of you. All that document proves objectively is that you paid money to the church. It's a *receipt*. And you don't even know what your money got used for because you do not even dare to ask the question of your leaders about how the money was spent. For the rest of the temple recommend questions, they're merely subjective in nature and allow the vain, the misled, and the blind to announce their purported worthiness. All of that is a mirage which will pass away when you depart this life.

It is not that God loves one more than another. It's that some of you love Him, and others do not. And by this He knows whether you love Him: It's whether your heart is soft and willing to receive, or you deliberately choose to be blinded by the false traditions that you've studied through and hold fast to —*because* you have not faith.

Religion is intended to be between you and God—deeply personal, individually redemptive. Christ is as accessible to you as He was to Moses on the mount. And what was Moses' ambition? It was to bring everyone up on the mount to see God, too. And what did the children of Israel say? "You go talk to Him. We don't want to." And why don't we want to? Because *I* can study about God, and *I* can develop a set of authorities, and *I* can expound upon the history of the church, and *I* can parse through the vocabulary of the restoration, and *I* can *prove*— *I* can *prove* what God is going to do next and that what's going on right now today in Ephraim, Utah, isn't it. And in the pride of your heart and in the blindness of your mind and in the *hardness* of your *soul*, you will not receive God saying, "Ignore the man with the microphone and come to Me." You will not say, "Perhaps the words of scripture mean something different and more intensely personal than I have ever taken them to mean before."

I'm not the best messenger. I wish I had the voice of an archangel. I wish I could do something to soften the heart. Christ is, in fact, holy, and I'm deeply aware of the fact that I am not. I can't redeem any of you, but He can. I can *testify* of Him. But when it comes down to it, at the end of the day, you can feel faith, and you can feel that something important is being communicated by God to you.

But if you read in the Doctrine and Covenants, look at the process: the wicked one comes, and he takes away the light from you, and he does this through your disobedience—and what is your disobedience? *That wicked one cometh and [take] away light and truth, through disobedience, from the children of men,* **and** *because of the tradition of their fathers* (D&C 93:39; see also T&C 93:11).

My voice is going to fall silent in your ears in a few moments, and you're going to leave here, and you're going to go on, and there are going to be a thousand voices and traditions that intervene. And come the morrow, you're going to attend meetings in which you're going to hear a lot of things expounded that just aren't true—and the traditions will take over; and your families are going to impose upon you the traditions that they have handed down; and you're going to sing about *blessed, noble pioneer,* and the cacophony of voices will rise; and the critics will chirp up—and the wicked one will come and take away light and truth. And I cannot be with you always, and if I were, it would only cripple you; and I'm not here to cripple you.

I hate the fact that these are ten talks given by me. I wish they were ten talks given by ten different people. That way you wouldn't say, "Well, he's, you know, something." I'm *nothing.* I'm keenly aware of my own limitations—but I am keenly aware of our Lord.

When I have had discussions with Him, they have invariably been parsing through the scriptures, explaining things. When I have inquired and gotten answers, it has been because of things that are in the scriptures that I do not understand.

I bear witness of Christ. I have seen Him. I know He lives. I know He is coming in judgment, and I know that before His coming, He has wanted some things to be declared. I have been as faithful as I can be in declaring the things that I've been asked to declare. I sense keenly my own inadequacy. I beg you to overlook all that. Look at the scriptures; look at the words of Christ; look at the explanations we got from Joseph; look at the things that are true—and go to Him in faith believing.

When I started out, I gave you a description of Him. I want to repeat that. The Lord is affable, but He is not gregarious. He is approachable; He is not aloof. He is patient, and He is willing to guide, and He is willing to teach. He is intelligent, but He is not overbearing. He is humble and approachable in His demeanor even though His power is absolutely undeniable. Therefore, He is both a Lamb and a Lion, and if you come to Him in the day that He offers redemption, you will be coming to the Lamb. But if you wait for His coming in judgment, you are waiting on the Lion, and you will not like what it is that you will see.

I asked you to remember He is quick to forgive sin. He allows all to come to Him. He is no respecter of persons. I said that when I began. I'm saying it again as we end today.

He is *real!* He *lives!* His work of redemption continues right now, just as it continued throughout His mortal life; just as it continued as He hung on the cross; just as it continued in His resurrection in Palestine and as He came to visit with the Nephites.

He ministered to other sheep (3 Nephi 16:1; see also 3 Nephi 7:3 RE), and for the life of me, I can't understand why the Nephites didn't ask Him about those other sheep. It's one of the things about which mankind has had absolutely no *curiosity* for some reason. He's ministered to other sheep. He's called other people, and there are, in fact, *holy men [whom] ye know not of* (D&C 49:8; see also T&C 35:3) that still remain.

If there was anything more I could do or say that I thought would convince or persuade you to believe in Him, I would do it, or I would say it. But despite it all, I realize some of you are going to walk out of here thinking that I'm just another one of these latter-day blowhards, and that's all good and well. Please, however, give heed to the scriptures I've read, the words of Joseph I've quoted, and the fact that I do have a witness that He's approachable and that He's every bit as much alive today as He was when He walked on the road to Emmaus. And He's every bit as much willing to come and redeem you from the Fall as He is willing to redeem anyone.

His work and His glory is culminated in *you.* His success is redeeming *you.* If you think that, well, He's aloof, He's distant, and this is an impossibly high thing to achieve, the fact of the matter is it is a greater achievement on *His* end to redeem you than it is at your end to *be* redeemed. There is more anxiety; there's more desire; there's more *rejoicing in heaven* when He redeems someone from the Fall than there is here.

> *Because of the many great works which the Lord [God]…showed unto him* [This man *knew* he was God.]…*And [then] because of the knowledge of this man he could not be kept from beholding within the veil; and he saw the finger of Jesus, which, when he saw, he fell with fear; for he knew that it was the finger of the Lord; and he had* **faith no longer**, *for he* **knew**, *nothing doubting. Wherefore, having this perfect knowledge of God, he could not be kept from within the veil; therefore he saw Jesus; and he did minister unto him.* (Ether 3:18-20; see also Ether 1:14 RE, emphasis added)

God is known by his many works. Faith gives way to knowledge. He ministers to him. Notice that—verse 18: *ministered unto him even as he ministered unto the Nephites…* [Verse 20:] *he did minister unto him* (ibid, vs.

18-20; vs. 14 RE). Christ has a ministry. His ministry is not yet complete. His ministry includes coming and bearing testimony, and that ministry continues, as we've looked at. Turn to chapter 4, verse 7:

> And in that day that they shall exercise faith in me, saith the Lord, even as the brother of Jared did, that they may become sanctified in me, then will I manifest unto them the things which the brother of Jared saw, even to the unfolding unto them all my revelations, saith Jesus Christ, the Son of God, the Father of ...[heaven] and of...earth, and all things that in them are. (Ether 4:7; see also Ether 1:17 RE)

This is the ministry of the Lord. *This* is the *comfort* that He would have—that He promises to bring to us.

This text that we're looking at in Ether chapter 3 is probably the best single text in existence to study about gaining the knowledge of God and the process by which it is gained. But most importantly, it exposes the attitude that is possessed by the person who comes back to be redeemed. It tells you, not directly— It tells you *indirectly* by telling you what he did. Go thou, and do likewise.

Everything that you have been put through, and every challenge that you have been given, and every weakness that you possess have been given to you in a studied way to bring you, hopefully, to your knees—to bring you, hopefully, to feel the chastening hand of God so that you, in your day, in your circumstance, can look upon that as a gift—because it *surely* is.

I give unto men weakness that they may [come unto me, and if they'll humble themselves and come unto me, I'll make weak things strong] (Ether 12:27; see also Ether 5:5 RE). That's also in the Book of Ether, and that's in an aside in which Moroni is complaining that the Gentiles aren't going to believe this book. The Gentiles aren't going to believe this record. They're going to say, "This stinks!"

Ether chapter 12, verse 26: *And when I had said this, the Lord [God] spake unto me, saying: Fools mock, but they shall mourn...my grace is sufficient for the* **meek**, *that they shall take no advantage of your weakness; And if men come unto me I will show unto them their weakness* (Ether 12:26-27, emphasis added; see also Ether 5:5 RE). That's an unavoidability. That's an inevitability. You stand in the presence of a just and holy being, you're going to realize your weaknesses. You're going to recognize what you lack.

I give unto men weakness that they may be humble; and my grace is sufficient for all men that humble themselves before me; for if they humble themselves before me, and have faith in me, then will I make weak things become strong unto them (ibid, vs. 27; vs. 5 RE).

How do weak things become strong? Not by fighting the battle that you're going to lose. It's by appreciating, as the brother of Jared did, the fact that none of us can come into the presence of God without feeling keenly this scripture: *Fools mock...they shall mourn. I* [this is Christ speaking] *[I] give unto men weakness* [for one purpose; I give unto them weakness] *that they may be [strong]* (ibid, vs. 26-27; vs. 5 RE).

The anvil that you're dragging around?— That anvil was given to you. Don't curse it. Pray for God to come and lift it. You're never going to be able to get far carrying it anyway. You may not even be able to lift it, but in the economy of God, *that* is a *gift*. It's a gift, not for you to act upon and surrender to but for you to fight against in humility and meekness and to say, "I'm not winning. I haven't won. It goes on and on, and yet *still*, I fight against it."

When will you finally come to Him and cry out? When, in the bitter anguish of your soul— like Joseph Smith in Liberty Jail— How long must I endure this? How long do I have to suffer from the abuse of the guards? How long do I have to sit inside a gated room in a dungeon to hear stories about the rape of the people who followed me and the murder of the people that believed what I was teaching?

How long did Joseph's heart break in Liberty Jail? He emerged from that ordeal a fundamentally different man than the man who went in. People who say, "Ah yeah, in Nauvoo he got carried away with all kinds of things." We'll talk more about that tomorrow. We'll talk more about this whole idea of marriage, and we'll touch upon the notion of plurality of wives. We'll brush up against that tomorrow.

Look, these scriptures, these invitations, these prophecies, and *this message* that began in Boise and will conclude in Phoenix— *This* message is inviting you to do what was originally prophesied as this dispensation began that we looked at at the beginning in Boise, Idaho. The game's afoot. The challenge is underway. The opportunity is here.

There's some eagerness that Father Hyrum had to get busy (before the Book of Mormon was even done) preaching repentance because he believed it, and the Lord held Hyrum back. If you go to Doctrine and Covenants section 11 beginning at verse 13, there's a revelation given to Hyrum that says:

> *Verily, verily, I say unto you, [I'll] impart unto you of my Spirit, which shall enlighten your mind, which shall fill your soul with joy; And then shall ye know, or by this [you shall] know, all things whatsoever you desire of me, which are pertaining unto things of righteousness, in faith believing in me that you shall receive. [But], I command you that you need not suppose that you are called to preach until you are called. Wait a little longer, until you shall have my word, my rock, my church, and my gospel, that you may know of a surety my doctrine.* (D&C 11:13-16; see also Joseph Smith History 14:13-14 RE)

See, Hyrum was being told, "It's good to be eager, but don't go out and try to preach something because you're not yet qualified. You don't have enough knowledge in order to do so." Likewise, Adam and Eve—not because the Lord held back and told them, "Don't do it! Don't do it!"—but because the circumstances of their lives did not prepare them to do it until there were generations already alive on the earth. *Then* they were given the gifts that were necessary in order to begin their preaching. Hyrum was told in verse 21:

> *Seek not to declare my word, but first seek to obtain my word, and then shall your tongue be loosed; then, if you desire, you shall have my Spirit and my word, yea, the power of God unto the convincing of men. But now hold your peace; study my word which hath gone forth among the children of men, and also study my word which shall come forth among the children of men, or that which is now translating, yea, until you have obtained all [that] which I...grant unto the children of men in this generation, and then shall all things be added thereto.* (D&C 11:21-22; see also JSH 14:15 RE)

Hyrum Smith who would eventually become co-president with Joseph; Hyrum Smith to whom the Lord would command that he be ordained not only to priesthood but to become the one possessing the sealing power over the Church; Hyrum Smith who would be the successor to Joseph (though he was killed before Joseph); Hyrum Smith who *was* the prophet of the Church, and Joseph rebuked the Church because they weren't giving heed to Hyrum's words; Hyrum Smith whose letter to the Church ought to be in the Doctrine and Covenants because he was a president, and he issued a general epistle admonishing people; Hyrum Smith whose name is omitted from the list of Church presidents even though it should be there—Hyrum Smith is told by the Lord, "Don't go out and start preaching yet. You need to learn something first. You need to be qualified first." In the revelation to Hyrum given in 1829 (and in the lives of Adam and Eve), God is in no great hurry to get people running around preaching before they're qualified.

There's this comment that Joseph Smith made. He said, "I am learned, and know more than all the world put together. The Holy Ghost does, anyhow, and He is within me, and comprehends more than all the world: and I will associate myself with Him. " (That's in *Teachings of the Prophet Joseph Smith* on page 350.) *This* is what qualified Adam and Eve to go declare repentance to their children. *This* is what qualified them to know the truth of all things and have the wisdom with which to impart it so that they could persuade their children to believe in Christ. *This is* the fullness of the gospel of Jesus Christ.

You, to be competent in teaching *your* children, *must* first have the Holy Ghost as your guide. Then, once you have that, you ought to have command of the scriptures (just as Hyrum was told) to learn what's in them. *Then* you are qualified to go and to teach your children, and you have an obligation to do that. Children are the means to preserve Zion. Without the conversion of children, Zion has no chance of surviving.

I read this before, and it belongs again right here. This is Joseph Smith writing from confinement in Liberty Jail. This is after Joseph has been confined in the Liberty Jail and had months of opportunity to reflect upon what it was that had gone on among the Saints while he was still free and living among them:

> *The things of God are of deep import; and time, and experience, and careful and ponderous and solemn thoughts can only find them out. Thy mind, O man! if thou wilt lead a soul unto salvation, must stretch as high as the utmost heavens, and search into and contemplate the darkest abyss, and the broad expanse of eternity—thou must commune with God. How much more dignified and noble are the thoughts of God, than the vain imaginations of the human heart! None but fools will trifle with the souls of men. How vain and trifling have been our spirits, our conferences, our councils, our meetings, our private as well as public conversations—too low, too mean, too vulgar, too condescending for the dignified characters of the called and chosen of God.* (*TPJS*, p. 137; see also T&C 138:18-19)

Don't waste your time when you're with one another! Learn; study; testify; search the scriptures; worship God. If you are still LDS, use whatever good you find there. This is what we should lay hold upon—truth, light, understanding, edifying, growing in knowledge of the principles of truth. You should not waste another three-hour block of time fiddling around with nonsense because you don't have permission from God to do that. Preach the principles, and if you don't think you know enough to do anything else, get together and read the scriptures out loud.

In the early church in this dispensation, when they got together, one of the things that they regularly did was they got together, and everyone prayed in turn. *Everyone* prayed. And the meeting would last until all had prayed. They called it a *prayer meeting*, oddly enough. One of the early brethren didn't like that. He didn't feel like he could pray vocally around other people (and there's a section in the Doctrine & Covenants admonishing him in a revelation that he needs to pray). If you don't have any wisdom to impart to one another, get together and pray. Get together and read the scriptures—but don't get together and read out loud out of any recent publication from Deseret Book.

If we are going to begin again, it must be in conformity with the doctrine of Christ. It must be taught by the Spirit of truth, and it must follow the pattern that was given in Kirtland for us to follow.

God could, does, and will work through anyone who awakens and then pays attention. There's an army of witnesses and awakened individuals that are being assembled by God.

It's required to know Him, and I know Him. I've been taught and understand His gospel. The first task is to assure people that He lives, and His gospel exists as an authentic method for saving souls. The second task is to remember the restoration Joseph gave his life to begin. We're ungrateful when we fail to remember and practice *it*.

At the moment, there is almost no clear understanding of that gospel. I'm working to set that out in a comprehensive way. It's never been completed. There's a great deal prophesied to roll out as part of the restoration that has not even commenced! Do we have Zion? What about the lost teachings of the brass plates? Do we have the rest of the Book of Mormon? Do we have the testimony of John? Do we have restored knowledge of the Jaredites? The list could be very long. But the fact that there *is* a list tells us that the restoration *must resume* at some point in order to be completed. We don't have it on the table; but we've *forgotten* what we once had.

So, the first job is to show that we're grateful enough to remember and to remember it in a fulsome, comprehensive way before God is going to say, "Now I will permit it to move forward." We haven't gotten to the point of remembering yet—which is why we ought to be studying a lot more diligently the material we got in the restoration. We ignore it at our peril.

Mormonism is true, but it is possible for people to believe in Mormonism and have a whole bundle of ideas in their head that I don't share with them. But the difference between the views that I have of Mormonism and the views that *that* person has of Mormonism can largely be accounted for based upon how much study, effort, review, thoughtfulness has gone into where they are and where I am. The effort to uncover the story of the restoration is still left undone; it's still incomplete.

I have been working as diligently as I can in every spare minute that I have, but I have to tell you, there is still a monumental pile of material yet to be reviewed before I get to the end of what's out there. And you know, I work full-time for a living. I don't have the luxury of doing this as a profession. I do it as a hobby, and these things are expensive to acquire and require months to review and get through and find. But let me tell you, the search is worth it.

No matter how shallow the pool is that you've drunk out of in trying to figure out what the history of Mormonism is, let me assure you that if you uncover a question, there is an answer to your question. There is something out there that will give you the truth of the matter.

I get so tired of reading these silly, inane, anti-Mormon rants like that Grant Palmer book. *An Insider's View of Mormon Origins* is silly. It's trite. That letter to the CES thing that has caused a crisis? I read it, and I laugh out loud at how superficially silly it is.

But in my view, there is a great work left to be done, and I have to stay focused on some things that are important, some things that still never got completed in Joseph's day that God promised would be completed at some point.

We may yet see the restoration take on a power and a glory that it hardly attained to at the beginning. The easiest way to hijack that is to spend all of your time dealing with—refuting arguments about our history. I have given up any ambition of either refuting critics or refuting my own critics.

The only thing I'm interested in doing is trying to at last state truthfully, based upon the work that God had Joseph do, what it was that God accomplished through him. Historians can go back and take everything I've written, and they can fill in all the gaps, and they can defend everything I've written. I'm going to keep pressing on, and I'm going to keep plowing new ground in order to try and construct what it was the restoration was intended to accomplish.

I would encourage every one of you to take seriously the restoration of the gospel. I would encourage every one of you to realize that Joseph Smith was exactly what he said he was and *probably* a whole lot more than he was ever willing to disclose.

Well, I haven't said for many, many, many years that the Church is true, but I have said, and I say again, the gospel's true; the restoration's true; Joseph was what he claimed to be and probably a lot more. *And*, if you stumble into questions in LDS Church history that raise some doubts in your mind about the restoration itself, *trust* me. If you'll just study the matter out and take the time to look into it, you're going to find an answer, and very often those answers are quite glorious—glorious beyond anything that you could imagine. If anything, Joseph Smith *understated* what he did. That list I read you (which is found in Doctrine & Covenants section 128) doesn't tell you what *divers angels from [Adam or Michael] down to the present* (D&C 128:21; see also T&C 151:15) who came and declared their keys, their rights, their honors—doesn't tell you what was involved there. Joseph Smith left out more than he put on the table.

Joseph's original Mormonism was inclusive, not exclusive. All truth belonged to Mormonism, but it never pretended to have it all. Mormonism was the search for truth. It was originally the search to discover truth without fear of finding something new. To Joseph, Mormonism did not possess all truth. His religion was not based on *conceit* but on *humility*—the willingness to continue to search, pray, study, and hope for newly revealed additions. It was understood there was a great deal more *yet* to be discovered. The claim that Mormonism was the only true and living church *presumed* the *willingness* to hear God's voice and receive new truth. It was not because it already had all truth. It was *living* during Joseph's life because it continued to grow and expand. Living organisms grow; dead ones decay.

———

The foregoing excerpts are taken from:

- Denver's *40 Years in Mormonism Series*, Talks 3, 4, 5, 7, 8, 9, and 10, given during 2013 and 2014;

- A Q&A session titled "A Visit with Denver Snuffer," held on May 13, 2015;
- A fireside talk on "Mormon History," given in Bountiful, Utah, on November 22, 2015; and
- The presentation of Denver's paper titled "Was There an Original," given at the Sunstone Symposium on July 29, 2016.

In addition, Denver has written extensively about this topic. If you are interested in learning more, please review the following blog posts, among others:

Gospel Study, posted November 17, 2011;
Christians Should Study Mormonism, posted January 12, 2017;
How I Study the Scriptures, posted March 18, 2010;
3 Nephi 11:36, posted September 29, 2010;
Scriptures, Not Traditions, posted February 24, 2014.

71. Effective Study, Part 3

This is Part 3 of a multi-part series, where Denver continues addressing the question: How do I get the most out of Gospel study? Where do I begin? It can be frustrating to read and not really get much out of a text, aside from the most obvious and superficial reading. What can I do or what skills or approaches do I need to utilize in order to make my study effective, so I can both understand and experience the Gospel, as well as prepare for Zion?

———

DENVER: But if you go and you study mathematics, or geology, or you study music—there are a lot of things in the Old Testament that are based upon music. There's incidents in the Book of Mormon in which there's singing and dancing going on, in a private place among only the daughters, and then the wicked priests of Noah come and abduct them, and the story goes on from there. It doesn't matter what you study in school. Everything you learn can help you better understand what's in the scriptures. So don't think that education doesn't matter. And don't think that you're wasting time in getting an education, because it's not focused in upon directly understanding better the volume of scriptures. That'll come. And everything should be done in its season, in its time.

In fact, there is an opening set of words in the Book of Ecclesiastes, which Bob Dylan turned into a folk song, which the Birds then fixed because Bob Dylan has a horrible voice. The name of the song is "Turn, Turn, Turn," and it talks about: *To everything there is a season and a time for every purpose under heaven: A time to be born, a time to die… A time to cast away stones…a time to gather stones together* (Ecclesiastes 3:1-5; see also Ecclesiastes 1:10 RE).

In your life there will be time for everything. And as you go through phases of life, at each interval, take advantage of that. Learn when it's time to learn. Play when it's time to play.

What I have learned by sad experience that the best way to approach someone is by your example and not by your mouth. And they can really hate what they're hearing you say, but if what they see you do is admirable, eventually they will reach the conclusion that what you are doing is the result of what you're believing. And if what you're believing is on display in what you do, that will touch them in ways that can't be opposed—can't be argued against.

But if all you're going to do is try to argue someone into agreement with you, well ,heavens! There are people that make a living arguing against Mormonism. Well, they've had to spend a lifetime studying it in order to come up with the arguments against it. If information alone was going to persuade, some of our biggest critics would now be converted. But they're not, because their hearts are hard. The way to get through to them is with kindness, is with the example. Christ, in the Sermon on the Mount said: *Blessed are [you] when men shall...say all manner of evil against you falsely, for my [name's] sake. Rejoice, and be exceedingly glad...for so persecuted they the prophets [beforehand]* (Matthew 5:11-12; see also Matthew 3:14 RE).

Most people have encountered "religious" folk (and I put religious in quotes), who talk a good fight but who will not sacrifice to benefit others. If, instead, you stay the course and you live the example, they're going to (at first) assume that you're just another religious hypocrite, because that's what we've all encountered. When, however, that example persists, and it persists against mocking, against ridicule, against criticism—when that example persists—

I mean, one of the questions that it was a vision, it was a dream, and therefore, we didn't finish the story—but fill that great and spacious building with a bunch of real people who are mocking and ridiculing and laughing at the people that are at the Tree of Life, and let them see the great example of the people who are at the Tree of Life. And before long, there will be some who leave the building and go and join the people at the Tree of Life, because that's what persuades, that's what convinces, that's what touches the heart. So I would say, less preaching and more self-sacrifice and example, and even the hard-hearted people will find themselves touched by what they see being done.

We study the Old Testament to learn about individual salvation from God. We study the New Testament to learn about individual salvation through Christ. We read the Book of Mormon to reassure ourselves that like those who lived before us, we can be individually saved in our day. We study the revelations of Joseph Smith to learn about individual salvation. Historic Christianity and the various Mormon traditions have all focused on individual salvation. Christians have been born-again and found salvation through God. Mormons have had their calling and election made sure and claimed God has saved them. Throughout the Judeo-Christian landscape, individual salvation is the great quest, the overarching yearning, and the religious end to be obtained. Salvation is individual. There is only individual salvation and no such thing as collective salvation. While I accept this as true, there is something else that is equally true. God wants people to collectively be His. There are remarkable similarities between the struggle from 1,900 years ago until 1,550 years ago in the Christian tradition, before it adopted a settled—although corrupted—form, and the last 160 years of Mormonism following the death of Joseph Smith. Christians could profit from the study of the more recent events involving Joseph Smith, to gain insight into the earlier Christian experience.

I believe that there is tension, if not outright hostility, between charity as a priority, on one hand, and knowledge as priority, on the other hand—and that as between the two, it is more important to acquire the capacity for charity or love of your fellow man, than it is to gain understanding. It's like what Paul said: *If I have all gifts and know all mysteries but have not charity, I'm nothing* (1 Corinthians 13; see also 1 Corinthians 1:51-53 RE). Charity, or the love of your fellow man is the greater challenge and the more relevant one, and when you've acquired that, you can add to it knowledge. But knowledge has the ability to render the possessor arrogant and haughty, whereas charity renders the possessor humble. If you want the greatest challenge in life, try loving your fellow man unconditionally and viewing them as God would view them and then behaving according to that view. And out of that you will learn a great deal more about Christ than you can simply by studying. Walking in His path is a greater revelation of who He is than anything else that's provided.

Joseph Smith once remarked that if you could gaze into heaven for five minutes you would know more about it than if you read every book that has ever been written on the subject. (*TPJS*, p. 324) Likewise, if you live charitably for five minutes in the presence of what you would normally condemn—what you would normally find repugnant—if you can deal with that charitably, you will understand Christ better than if you spend a lifetime reading books written about Him.

God's most important inspiration for the most challenging subjects is often not hasty, quick, and without effort at our end. Consider the advice to Oliver Cowdery that he must study it out in his own mind first before asking God to tell him the answer (see D&C 9:8; see also Joseph Smith History 13:30 RE). Many people want a quick, perfunctory response from God, with no forethought. What they receive, in turn, is a quick, perfunctory answer. God is almost always, for the most difficult challenges, not a short-order cook; although there are certainly false spirits who are willing to be just that.

The Father is the source of glory and likened to the sun. The Mother reflects and shares this glory and is likened to the moon. She reflects God's glory, endures within it, and is empowered by it. She can participate with Him in all that is done wielding that glory. Knowledge is the initiator or force, and Wisdom is the regulator, guide, apportioner, and weaver of that power. If not tempered and guided by Wisdom, Knowledge can be destructive. Wisdom makes the prudent adaptation required for order. The Father and Mother are One. But the Mother bridges the gulf between the Throne of the Father and fallen man. She made it possible for the Son of God to enter this fallen world for the salvation of everything in it.

A great deal of reflection and study is needed to understand all this implies. This is an introduction of some basic information about the Mother of God, or *the Mother of the Son of God after the manner of the flesh* (1 Nephi 11:18; see also 1 Nephi 3:8 RE). More will be given in a Temple where mankind's understanding of things kept hidden from the world will be greatly increased, when God directs one be built to His name.

There was a time when Christians recognized that the stars of heaven bore witness of the significance of Mary, Christ's earthly mother. Few Christians now look at the constellations as signs set in the firmament of God as His testimony. The light that was meant to shine on the earth was to illuminate both the eyes **and** mind of man. Man in the first generations understood this, and *a knowledge of the beginning of the creation, and also of the planets, and of the stars, as they were made known unto the Fathers* was written by Abraham, who received that same understanding (Abraham 1:31; see also Abraham 2:4 RE).

The Book of Mormon is filled with ascension lessons and example. There is one verse that captures Joseph Smith's ascent theology. That verse compresses into a single sentence. It explains why the Book of Mormon contains the fullness of the gospel. And it's perhaps Joseph's most inspired declaration:

> *Verily thus saith the Lord: It shall come to pass that every soul who forsakes their sins, and comes unto me, and calls on my name, and obeys my voice, and keeps my commandments, shall see my face and know that I Am, and [that] I am the true light that lights every man who comes into the world...* (D&C 93:1; see also T&C 93:1)

"Every soul" includes you and me. Every one of us has equal access to the Lord. The conditions are the same for all. Forsake sins; come to Christ; call on His name; obey His voice; keep his commandments. This is far more challenging than obedience to a handful of "thou shalt nots" because so much is required to be **done**, so much required to be **known**. A great deal of study and prayer is required to stand in the presence of the Lord. Once done, we shall see His face and know that He is the true light that enlightens every one. He is the God of the whole world.

Well, the more I began to take in the truths of the content in the Book of Mormon, the greater the gap grew between the lip-service paid to the Restoration by the Mormon church—the LDS church—and the practice of the institution itself. In fact, the Book of Mormon, used as a guide or measuring stick, condemns all of the institutions of Christianity. In fact, it condemns everyone except the few who are the humble followers of Christ, and points out, despite that few being *humble followers of Christ; nevertheless, they are led, that in many instances they do err because [they're] taught by the precepts of men* (2 Nephi 28:14; see also 2 Nephi 12:2 RE).

If you want precepts that come from God, the best place to look at this point is the Book of Mormon text. The closer you look, the more you'll see. The more you see, the more you'll find that, right now, the religion of Jesus Christ is hardly practiced anywhere on this earth. If it's going to be practiced at all, it needs to be done by **you**, by someone who is eagerly searching for and trying to find words that come from Jesus Christ as your guide, as something to lead you back to Him, as the message intended for the last days, and as the means by which you can interpret the earlier New Testament, the earlier Old Testament, to find out exactly what they mean—because the key to unlocking all of what God has been, is presently, and will ultimately be involved with to fulfill all the prophecies is contained primarily in the text of the Book of Mormon.

And so, if you want to escape before the ultimate destruction of that great image with the head of gold beforehand, to be prepared for the coming of the Lord—if you're a sincere Christian, you don't need to go and join another denominational institution, but you better take seriously the Book of Mormon and study it, and take its interpretations/its meaning/ its guidance seriously, because it is the standard that has been planted in the last days as the ensign of truth to which all Christians—if they believe in Christ—need to rally, in order to be part of His great latter-day work.

I say that to a Christian audience because the Book of Mormon has largely been so neglected by the people who are nicknamed "Mormons," that if Christians were to take that book up and to examine it through the eyes of a devoted Christian believer, I believe that Christians are going to find treasures within the Book of Mormon, an understanding (as a result of their Christian background) from the Book of Mormon that the Mormons themselves have never been able to harvest, have never noticed, and do not have the eyes with which to even see its presence. The Book of Mormon remains a Christian treasure that has yet to yield its greatest results, having only been taken seriously—

In 1950 there were leaders in the church who had never read the Book of Mormon—Mormon church leaders who did not read the Book of Mormon, much less understand it. It was quite some time after that before the Book of Mormon became something in which there was some regular study among Latter-day Saints.

Because the Book of Mormon was published before there was an LDS church and because the Book of Mormon stands as an independent witness, there is no reason why accepting the Book of Mormon requires you to be institutionally loyal to anyone. You can be a Baptist and believe in the Book of Mormon, and there is at least one minister out there who is doing that right now. There is no reason why Catholics and Presbyterians and other mainstream Christian denominations can't pick up the Book of Mormon and make use of it, without pledging allegiance to any institution that claims ownership over the Book of Mormon.

In fact, the most accurate edition of the Book of Mormon currently in print is one that was prepared independent of any institution and is available for purchase on Amazon. It's part of two books, combined in a single volume, called the New Covenants. The first half of the book is the New Testament, and the second half of the book is the Book of Mormon. They were intended to go together, as a witness by people who—on one side of the world and on the other side of the world—both witnessed the ministry of a resurrected Lord, who showed the prints of the nails in His side and in His hands and in His feet. And had people bear testimony that it was Him who was sacrificed, that rose again from the grave, and who is the Savior prophesied of by Isaiah —He uses Malachi in the Book of Mormon—He uses other texts to demonstrate and to teach His identity as the Son of God and the Redeemer of mankind.

And I believe if the Presbyterians and the Baptists and the Catholics were to pick up the Book of Mormon and treat it seriously, it would yield truths to them, which they could then preach independent of the LDS church or the people who are nicknamed "Mormons," and they would find themselves growing closer to Christ, as a consequence of having this material available to their study.

It's been too long that the Book of Mormon has been neglected. It's been too shoddily handled by the people to whom it was originally given. The copyright has expired. The book is now available to the public. The institution that got it originally has made precious little use of it. And if you find yourself not only disbelieving the LDS church, but because of your institution's native hostility towards the LDS church, you will find in the Book of Mormon a great deal of ammunition to use to condemn, to criticize, to censure the LDS institution; because the Book of Mormon spares very little ink in criticizing, condemning, and judging harshly the people to whom the Book of Mormon would be delivered, including the LDS Church.

The use to which the Book of Mormon can be put by Christians is so relevant to the Christian belief system, that if Christians will soften their heart and consider it and allow for the record that is latest in time to be used to help understand the records that are earlier in time—because God's latest word clarifies and governs the interpretation of His earlier word—Christians are going to reap a fabulous reward in doing so.

And unlike the texts that we have in the New Testament, many of which are copies of copies of copies that we know have been altered in the process of transmission—

Bart Ehrman (a one-time believer—now agnostic) parsed through the texts of the New Testament, compared it to quotes in the Ante-Nicene (the pre-Nicene) Fathers and to internal evidence in the New Testament itself and reached the conclusion that the New Testament text deserves a great deal of skepticism, because the method and manner of its transmission has been demonstratively shown to be inaccurate and the record to be muddled. In one place, the less-altered text of Hebrews preserves the words that are drawn right out of the 7th chapter of Proverbs: *This is my son; today I have begotten you*—a statement that was made prophetically about Christ. The book of Hebrews preserves it in that form. The Gospels, however, were altered, and the statement that was made at the time of the baptism of Christ, when John the Baptist was baptizing the Lord, was changed to be, *This is my beloved Son, in whom I am well pleased* (Matthew 3:17; see also Matthew 2:4 RE), because of a controversy that erupted over the nature of Christ during the Christological debates of the 3rd and 4th Century—and it's one of the illustrations that Bart Ehrman points to in his book, *The Orthodox Corruption of Scripture*. That title tells you something about the transmission of the New Testament: *The Orthodox Corruption of Scripture*. Bart Ehrman isn't the only scholar, but his books are fairly easily available (if you're interested in the topic) through Amazon.

Another scholar who has done essentially the same thing in picking apart the Old Testament and the integrity of the transmission of the Old Testament text is a Methodist scholar in England named Margaret Barker, whose works demonstrate that there was an earlier (an older) religion that got defeated at about the time that the Jews were taken captive into Babylon—and on the return from the exile, a new religion (that had been altered) emerged. Christians generally view information like that as threatening the very core of their religion, because if their Bible is flawed and not inerrant, if their Bible has been poorly transmitted and is inaccurate, then the basis upon which they seek salvation is itself threatened.

The Book of Mormon, on the other hand, bears witness of the very same Lord in essentially the very same kinds of terms, identifying Him as having accomplished the work of the redemption by the sacrificing of His sinless life in order to defeat death and to restore mankind back to life. But unlike the transmission of the Bible record, the Book of Mormon record was preserved for generations by a singular transmission through a line of record holders. At the end of that line, a prophet named Mormon—hence the name for the book— did a summary explanation, excerpting from all of the prior records a final and inspired, God-commanded, and prophetically-infused record-summary of the preceding nearly- millennium of history, giving us the truths that God wanted preserved. He turned that record over to his son; his son finished it up and then buried it up. And when it came forth out of the ground it was translated by the person who accomplished the translation through the means he called *the gift and power of God* (see Title Page of the Book of Mormon). And the original language in which the Book of Mormon was first published in the last days was English.

The original of the first transcription has been preserved in part; it was put into a cornerstone and water damaged it, and so we only have about 28% of that original, but the original was hand-copied before it was taken to the printer for the first printing. And all of that printer's manuscript still exists. And then the one who was responsible for the translation of the Book of Mormon had the opportunity to review it for another edition in 1837, and to review it and again publish it in 1840.

We do not have the transmission issues with the Book of Mormon that are existing with the current Bible. Christians hear this criticism about the Book of Mormon—that there's been 9,000 changes made to the text. Those 9,000 changes have been located and largely dealt with, every single one, in that New Covenants edition of the Book of Mormon that is currently in print and available through Amazon. Most of those purported changes are punctuation changes. Many of them come from the fact that when it was first printed, it was printed like a book, but it later became versified and divided into chapters, and footnotes were added—and in the tally of changes, many of the changes also are superficial changes to versification and chapter divisions and other such things. There were some errors made. There were some lines that were dropped out between the original manuscript and the printer's manuscript that have been located and have been put back in. But even with every one of the identified changes to the Book of Mormon, the fact is that it is—demonstrably, on a whole other order of magnitude—more faithfully preserved and more reliably a text attesting to Jesus Christ than anything that we have transmitted in the Bible.

In short, if you are a Christian who feels some insecurities as a consequence of the criticism leveled at the Bible because of its clear transmission issues (its very demonstrably true problems of conveying the text from the original authors down to what we get printed) and the vagaries of how you convert some Greek lettering into other languages—

At the time the New Testament was written, the form of Greek that was used didn't have lower case; it only had uppercase—didn't have punctuation. And in almost every text there's no separation from the end of one word and the beginning of another. Dividing it up into words, upper and lower-casing the alphabet that was used, all of that was accomplished by monks hundreds of years after the original text had been handed down.

Well, the Book of Mormon has far greater integrity. So if you're insecure about the reliability of the content of the Bible, none of those insecurities should attach to the text of the Book of Mormon. The Book of Mormon is not only a testimony of Jesus Christ, but it is perhaps the most reliable testimony of Jesus Christ that exists in available print right now, today, in the English language.

So, if you're a Christian and you're sincere about your faith, I think you neglect the Book of Mormon at your peril. If God has sent to you a message, a testimony about His Only Begotten Son—in order to bring you closer to Him, to prepare you for the day of His coming to judge the world—and you decide that you're simply going to dismiss that message that came from God, then what kind of a Christian are you, really? Have you no faith? Do you think that God cares less about the generation of people who will be on the earth at the time of His returning to judge the world, cares less about them, than He did about the people to whom He came and ministered when He came here to sacrifice His life to redeem mankind?

Institutional, formal churches invest in programs and productions to help their members believe in God. Institutions pre-package what is taught so their members will agree with them on religious worship. God has provided you scriptures and given you the ability to read and think. You need to find God directly and let your religion include your individual search for truth. Joseph Smith defined Mormonism in this way: "One of the grand fundamental principles of Mormonism is to receive truth, let it come from whence it may" (*Discourses of Joseph Smith*, p. 199, Kindle Book). We all want to freely search for truth, and when we find it, we want to be free to accept it. That is Mormonism. That is us.

There is a new edition of scriptures available in paperback and online. They will soon be available in a leather-bound edition. These new scriptures are the most accurate and complete volumes of Joseph Smith's work made available. If you study them, your understanding of the Restoration will exceed all others. Make them something you review daily, even if you only have a few minutes.

While Joseph Smith was alive, he taught that the Restoration would fail if the Saints did not have the new translation of the Bible published as part of their scriptures. Joseph said, "God had often sealed up the heavens, because of covetousness in the Church. Said the Lord would cut his work short in righteousness and except the church receive the fulness of the scriptures, that they would yet fall" (*Joseph Smith Papers*, "Documents Volume 2: July 1831-January 1833," p. 85).

After that warning on July 17, 1840, two men were assigned to go on a mission for the purpose of raising money to publish the scriptures. These included a new edition of the Book of Mormon and the Joseph Smith Translation of the Bible. In October 1840, a letter to all the Saints was published in the *Times and Seasons*, asking for their full support in the effort to publish "the new translation of the Scriptures" (*Times and Seasons*, Vol. 1, October 1840). That effort failed to put the Joseph Smith Translation in print, and Joseph died without it ever being published. Excerpts, with edits done by others, were published by the Reorganized Church of Jesus Christ of Latter Day Saints, but it failed to include all of Joseph's work.

The new edition of the scriptures is the first time the full work Joseph accomplished, without additions and including hundreds of punctuation changes previously omitted, have been made available in print. You are the first generation to have these scriptures available. Do not neglect them.

There are two things that will bring you closer to God than anything else; start this in your youth:

- First, personal scripture study. Learn from them when you have time. Your private study will be more important than what others tell you about the scriptures.

- Second, personal prayer. Your private time spent in prayer will have the power to shape your life.

- If you study the scriptures when you're alone and you pray in private, these two things, more than anything else, will draw you to God.

Joseph Smith once said that a man can get closer to God by heeding the Book of Mormon than any other book and that it was the most correct book that there is; and that if you will abide its precepts you will come closer to understanding God (see "Introduction to the Book of Mormon").

I started out with the Book of Mormon as a pedestrian looking at the book and saying, "Yeah, it's something. And it's part of the religion." If I had not been called to be a Gospel Doctrine teacher and left in that position—I moved again into a third location. I taught Gospel Doctrine in Pleasant Grove, UT; Alpine, UT; and Sandy, UT in two different places there. I was this guy going through this material. It took between 10 and 20 hours of study and preparation each week for a 50 minute class, as I went deeper and deeper into the text of all these materials, but deepest of all into the Book of Mormon.

One of the things that I have—and I want to point out to you these features of the new scriptures in hopes that you'll take note of the same kinds of things —one of the things that I have found is that when you get a new set of scriptures, everything is laid out differently than the way that it used to be laid out in the set that you're accustomed to reading and using. As a result, what used to be in the top left-hand side is now on the bottom right-hand side. Everything is re-oriented. And the new scriptures do not have versification. They're divided into paragraphs in order to have complete thoughts gathered together. (Now the paragraphs are numbered in order to cite them, but the purpose was to divide it into paragraphs so that you got a complete thought.) Therefore, when you're reading something that you're used to seeing out of context—

Some verses in the scriptures are a phrase; they're not even a sentence. They're just a phrase, but the phrase belongs inside a sentence, and the sentence belongs inside a paragraph, and when you pick up the new scriptures and you read them in this current layout, everything changes. You begin to see things —

I have read one way, a passage in a January 1841 revelation—the entire time, over 40 some years, I read it the same way. I got the new scriptures with the new layout, and I read the same material, and all of a sudden, it has a different meaning. I'm not going to take the time to read it, but I want you to find it. It's the January 1841 revelation. When you have time, read it. And read the words about *they shall not be moved out of their place* (D&C 124:45; see also T&C 141:13), which I've always read to mean, the people who are in Nauvoo. And if they're faithful, the people who are in Nauvoo shall not be moved out of their place. In the new scriptures, I read that and I believe it is referring to Joseph and Hyrum Smith—that **they** would be preserved and not moved out of their place if the people were faithful. And if they were not, they were going to lose Joseph and Hyrum. Now it doesn't matter whether the words are referring to the people living in Nauvoo or to Joseph and Hyrum. The sign was that they would be moved out of their place, and both were. We lost Joseph; we lost Hyrum; and we lost Nauvoo. So, things like that happen when you've got the new scriptures.

Last night, as I was listening to Jeff and others who spoke, one of the things that struck me is that almost all revelation—going back to the days of Adam and coming right down to today—come as a consequence of understanding scripture. That was true even of Enoch, because Enoch had a record that had been handed down from Adam. And in the case of Abraham, the records belonging to the Fathers fell into his hands, and he studied them to gain the understanding that he had. Micah quotes Isaiah. Isaiah quotes Zenos and Zenoch. Jacob quotes the allegory of Zenos. Nephi quotes Isaiah. All of them study scripture in order to get an understanding, and revelation is largely based upon expanding your understanding of scripture. The Book of Mormon is really the keystone of the religion but also the keystone to revelation itself. It was intended to open our eyes to things that we couldn't see before. The Book of Mormon is really a giant Urim and Thummim intended for our benefit.

By studying the scriptures and plumbing the depths of the message that we have in the scripture record that's in front of us, you can arrive at a point in your understanding in which it really doesn't matter if an angel appears to you or not. The angel's purpose is never going to be to produce faith in you.

If the angel is going to produce faith in you because of their appearance, then the angel ought not appear. Because they'll turn you into a sign-seeker. On the other hand, if you have developed faith by the careful study of what we've been given in the scriptures, and the presence or absence of an angel will have no effect on your faith—you will believe, you will have confidence, your understanding reaches the same depth with or without the angel's presence—then there's no reason for the angel to withhold. There's no reason for him not to appear.

People that are brought into God's presence are convicted of their own inadequacies because, you see, here at last, now, is a complete being—is a pure, just, and holy being. And in comparison, we all lack. We all lack. When Isaiah was caught up to the presence of the Lord, he's shouting, *Woe is me! ...I am undone; ...I am a man of unclean lips...I dwell among people of unclean lips* (Isaiah 6:5; see also Isaiah 2:2 RE). He recognizes the enormity of the gulf, the gap between him and God. And so God purges it. It's because of the faith and the confidence that he has in God that Isaiah afterwards says, *Here am I, Lord, send me* (Isaiah 6:8; see also Isaiah 2:2 RE). It's not because Isaiah is suddenly a greater being than he was before. It's because Isaiah had faith that this Being can indeed make one as flawed as we are, cleansed, holy, pure, confidence in him. If I were to make one recommendation about the process, I would say: forget about asking for signs; study the depths of the scriptures, and you'll find yourself in company with angels who will come help you to understand what is in these scriptures—and in particular, above all, the Book of Mormon. The Book of Mormon is a giant Urim and Thummim; used in the correct way, you'll find yourself in company with angels who are helping to tutor you, in a conversation, as you look into an understanding of what's written in the scriptures. And then there's no reason for them to withhold their presence from you. "Adam, having conversed with the Lord through the veil, desires now to enter into His presence" (LDS Temple Endowment). There's no reason, after you've conversed through the veil, for that presence to be denied you. But it follows an order. It follows a pattern.

QUESTION: The question is, Do you run any risks by studying? That you can just as easily study your way out of belief as you can study your way into belief.

DENVER: The way that I think that works is—

Everyone wants to understand, because of how proximate—how close—Joseph Smith is, everyone wants to understand how Joseph Smith did it. So, if we think we can figure out how Joseph Smith did it, then presumably, that will equip us to understand or put it into context. But most people who are studying to figure out how Joseph Smith did it are only interested in debunking it—"I want to know how he pulled this off because I'm a little skeptical that what he pulled off is actually genuine; and maybe, if I can understand how Joseph Smith pulled that off, then I can understand how Jesus pulled it off. Then I can understand how Moses pulled it off. Then I can put it all to rest because I needn't worry about it." Or, "I want to understand how Joseph Smith pulled it off, so I can pull it off—and when I get that and I figure it out, and I try it, and it doesn't work for me, then I can say Joseph made it up because it didn't work for me." I mean, there are a lot of pitfalls along the course of study.

The first and primary question you have to ask is—

Take a look around this world and ask yourself if—in this world—it makes sense to you that there is no Creator? Does it make sense to you that everything that's going on here, simply is a haphazard accident, that there is no Creation? There's no Creator? There's no Divine plan? There's nothing here that operates on any other basis than random chance? If you reach the conclusion that everything that's going on here could possibly be by random chance, then read Darwin's *Black Box*. There's a little over 200 different things that have to line up perfectly, in order for your blood to clot. If any one of those 200 things don't happen simultaneously—it's a little over 200—if any one of those don't happen simultaneously, you will die. For some of those, if you get a cut and they're not present, you'll bleed out. You'll simply die, because you will exsanguinate. For others of those, if you get a cut, your entire blood system will turn solid, and you will die because clotting knows no end. Darwin's *Black Box* makes the argument that it is evolutionarily impossible for trial and error to solve the problem of blood clotting because every one of the steps that are required, if nature simply experiments with it, kills the organism. And that ends that. You don't know that you are going to succeed until you've lined them all up and you've made them all work. It's an interesting book—Darwin's *Black Box*. In essence, it's saying that the evolutionists require more faith, really, than do people that believe in God, because the theory upon which they base their notion requires far too many things to occur by trial and error than is conceivably possible.

Well, if there is a Creation, then there is a Creator. If there is a Creator, then the question is—

I assume all of you have had a father or a grandfather—someone that you respected—a mother or a grandmother, an aunt or an uncle that over the course of a lifetime developed skills and talents and humor and character—someone that you admire. And then they pass on. How profligate a venture is it to create someone that you—a Creation that you view as noble, as worthy, as admirable, as interesting, as fascinating—some person that you love—take that, and just obliterate it. God, who can make such a Creation, surely doesn't waste a Creation. He's not burning the library at Alexandria every day by those who pass on. God had to have a purpose behind it all.

I don't know how many of you have had a friend or a loved one or a family member who passed on, who subsequent to their death, appeared to you, had a conversation with you, in a dream, in a thought. I can recall going to my father's funeral, and his casket with his body was in the front of the little chapel we were in, but his presence was not there—that may have been the hull he occupied while he was living and breathing—I had no sense at all that my father was there. I did have a sense that he was present, but he wasn't in the coffin. He was elsewhere in the room. I couldn't see him, but I could have pointed to him and said, "He's here." In fact, I made a few remarks at my father's funeral, and I largely directed them at him.

Nature testifies over and over again. It doesn't matter when the sun goes down; there's going to be another dawn. It doesn't matter when all the leaves fall off the deciduous trees in the fall; there's going to come a spring. There's going to be a renewal of life. There are all kinds of animals in nature that go through this really loathsome, disgusting, wretched existence, and then they transform. And where they were a pest before, now they're bright, and they're colorful, and they fly, and they pollinate. Butterflies help produce the very kinds of things that their larvae stage destroyed. These are signs. These are testimonies. Just like the transformation of the caterpillar into the butterfly—the pest into the thing of beauty; the thing that ate the vegetables that you were trying to grow into the thing that helps pollinate the things that you want to grow—that's the plan for all of us.

So when you study the scriptures, the objective should not be: Can I trust the text? Can I evaluate the text? Can I use a form of criticism against the text in order to weigh, dismiss, belittle, judge? Take all that you know about nature, take all that you know about this world and the majesty of it all; take all that you know that informs you that there is hope, there is joy, there is love—

Why do you love your children? Why do your children love you? These kinds of things exist—they're real, they're tangible, and they're important. And they're part of what God did when He created this world. Keep that in mind when you're studying, and search the scriptures to try and help inform you how you can better appreciate, how you can better enjoy, how you can better love, how you can better have hope. What do they have to say that can bring you closer to God? Not, can I find a way to dismiss something that Joseph said or did? As soon as Joseph was gone off the scene, people that envied the position that he occupied took over custody of everything, including the documents; and what we got, as a consequence of that, is a legacy that allowed a trillion dollar empire to be constructed. Religion should require our sacrifice. It should not be here to benefit us. We should have to give, not get. And in the giving of ourselves, what we get is in the interior; it's in the heart. It's the things of enduring beauty and value. If your study takes you away from an appreciation of the love/the charity/the things that matter most, reorient your study.

QUESTION: So you spoke of the need to plumb the depths of the scriptures, particularly the Book of Mormon, and how it becomes a Urim and Thummim to us. And the Book of Mormon itself informs us that this is the lesser things. It's intentionally withholding much. And it specifically states the purpose is to try our faith. The faith having been so tried, those who plumb the depths can expect more to come forth at some point—in terms of scripture; in terms of record. I guess the question there is—and not to minimize what we've already been given, because it's clearly enough for our present state and more—but does that sort of thing, those sorts of records that are promised, is that a Millennial sort of thing, after the Lord returns? Is that the sort of thing that, if we finally take seriously enough what's been given now, can we expect more to come forth before the Lord comes?

DENVER: I believe that how we respond to what we are given will drive that entirely, and whether we get it before the Millennium or after is dependent upon us. But I also think that—

Look, the people who prepared the summaries on the plates—the abridgment —and the Lord, who provided the translation of that, both know what's being withheld. They abridged what they abridged with what was being withheld in front of their eyes. So they can't tell you the abridged story without the content of what's being withheld present in their mind. If you go through the text carefully, you'll begin to see that there are patterns that start fitting together. I don't think that when the rest of what has been withheld is suddenly brought out into the light—if you've carefully looked at what's in the scriptures already, you're not going to say, "Wow! That is shockingly different!" You're going say, "I always suspected that. And that fits in with this, and this fits in with that, and the picture begins to emerge a bit more clearly. And, yeah, that just—I've always sort of suspected that to be the case."

When we read the scriptures, keep in mind that the people writing them have in their mind the rest of the picture, and it leaks through; a great deal leaks through because you can't—

If you know the rest of the story, and you're telling the tale (but you're leaving out some of the big punch lines, but they're present in your mind), the punch lines are going to leak through. There's a lot that comes through in the Book of Mormon. The character and the nature of God is probably better understood by what we have in the Book of Mormon, and it is perfectly consistent with the testimony the Gospel writers who knew Christ in mortality. And if you take what we got in a fairly battered New Testament record and the Book of Mormon together and what happened in the life of Joseph Smith, and you weave them all together, you begin to understand that God is a very patient, loving, kindly Being—and that the mysteries of God largely consist in developing the attributes of godliness in us. The things that matter the most are the things that make us more like Him—better people, more kindly. You want to know more of the mysteries of God? Serve your fellow man, and be of more value to them. In the process of blessing the lives of others, you find out that you know more of the character of God as a consequence of that.

In the new scriptures, there is a section in which Joseph Smith discusses at length the topic of false spirits. It's an editorial he published in the *Times and Seasons* on April the 1st of 1842. This new section 147 in the Teachings and Commandments is worth careful study—the Teachings and Commandments being the new volume of scripture recovering and restoring the text as it was originally; available (if you're interested) either for free online to read at www.scriptures.info, or if you want to purchase a copy, it's available through Amazon.

This new section of the Teachings and Commandments is worth careful study. Keep in mind the meaning of several words. Priesthood means a fellowship. You can have a Priesthood that is a fellowship of men. You can have a Priesthood that is a fellowship between men and angels. You can have a Priesthood that is a fellowship between man and Christ. And you can have a Priesthood that is a fellowship between man and God the Father.

> *You pray each time you partake of the Sacrament to always have my Spirit to be with you; and what is my spirit? It is to love one another as I have loved you. Do my works and you will know my doctrine. For you will uncover hidden mysteries by obedience to these things that can be uncovered in no other way. This is the way I will restore knowledge to my*

people. If you return good for evil, you will cleanse yourself and know the joy or your Master. You call me Lord and do well to regard me so, but to know your Lord is to love one another. Flee from the cares and longings that belong to Babylon, obtain a new heart for you have all been wounded. In me you will find peace and through me will come Zion, a place of peace and safety. Be of one heart and regard one another with charity. Measure your words before giving voice to them and consider the hearts of others. (T&C 157:51,53)

Although a man may err in understanding concerning many things, yet he can view his brother with charity and come unto me and through me, he can with patience overcome the world. I can bring him to understanding and knowledge. Therefore, if you regard one another with charity, then your brother's error in understanding will not divide you. I lead to all truth. I will lead all who come to me to the truth of all things. The fullness is to receive the truth of all things and this too, from me, in power by my word and in very deed. For I will come unto you, if you will come unto me. Study to learn how to respect your brothers and sisters, and to come together by precept reason and persuasion, rather than sharply disputing and wrongly condemning each other causing anger. Take care how you invoke my name. Mankind has been controlled by the adversary, through anger and jealousy which has led to bloodshed and the misery of many souls, even strong disagreements should not provoke anger, nor to invoke my name in vain, as if I had part in your every dispute. Pray together in humility, and together meekly present your dispute to me, and if you're contrite before me I will tell you my part. (T&C 157:53-54)

QUESTION: We're separated from the first Fathers, to whom our hearts must turn, by a vast expanse of time, language, and culture. How can we best reach out in our hearts and our minds to these successful mortals?

DENVER: You know, it's a great question. There is an enormous advantage that you'll find in reading the new scriptures and all of the things that have been added that focus upon that, both in the Old Covenants and in the Teachings and Commandments—in particular those two, where our knowledge of what the Fathers were up to is enormously expanded—and then in parts of the New Covenants that have been added through the Joseph Smith Translation. I think the scriptures equip us to accomplish something that—

Study them. Look there.

The time is now far spent, therefore labor with me and do not forsake my covenant to perform it; study my words and let them be the standard for your faith, and I will add thereto many treasures. Love one another and you will be mine, and I will preserve you, and raise you up, and abide with you for ever and ever. Amen. (T&C 158:20)

———————

The foregoing excerpts are taken from:

- Denver's remarks at *A Day of Faith and Connection Youth Conference* in UT on June 10th, 2017;
- Denver's conference talk titled "Civilization," given in Grand Junction, CO on April 21st, 2019;
- Denver's *Christian Reformation Lecture Series*, Talk #1, given in Cerritos, CA on September 21st, 2017;
- Denver's *Christian Reformation Lecture Series*, Talk #3, given in Atlanta, GA on November 16th, 2017;
- A fireside talk titled "That We Might Become One," given in Clinton, UT on January 14th, 2018;
- Denver's conference talk titled "Our Divine Parents," given in Gilbert, AZ on March 25th, 2018;
- The presentation of Denver's paper titled "The Restoration's Shattered Promises and Great Hope," given at the *Sunstone Symposium* in Salt Lake City, UT on July 28th, 2018;
- Denver's *Christian Reformation Lecture Series*, Talk #5, given in Sandy, UT on September 7th, 2018;
- Denver's *Christian Reformation Lecture Series*, Talk #6, given in Sandy, UT on September 8, 2018;
- Denver's remarks titled "Keep the Covenant: Do the Work," given at the *Remembering the Covenants Conference* in Layton, UT on August 4th, 2018;
- Denver's remarks titled "Remember the New Covenant," given at Graceland University in Lamoni, IA on November 10th, 2018;
- Denver's remarks titled "Book of Mormon as Covenant," given at the *Book of Mormon Covenant Conference* in Columbia, SC on January 13th, 2019;
- Denver's lecture titled "Signs Follow Faith," given in Centerville, UT on March 3rd, 2019;
- Denver's Q&A session held in Grand Junction, CO on April 21st, 2019; and

- The presentation of "Answer and Covenant," given at the *Covenant of Christ Conference* in Boise, ID on September 3rd, 2017.

In addition, Denver has written extensively about this topic. If you are interested in learning more, please review the following blog posts:

Gospel Study, posted November 17, 2011;
Christians Should Study Mormonism, posted January 12, 2017;
How I Study the Scriptures, posted March 18, 2010;
3 Nephi 11:36, posted September 29, 2010;
Scriptures, Not Traditions, posted February 24, 2014.

72. As a Little Child

In this episode, Denver addresses the question: What is it about little children that led Christ to say that we must become *as a little child* and that *of such is the kingdom of God*? What practical things can we do to become as little children? What are the most hindering traditions, mindsets, attitudes, or beliefs of adults that prevent us from doing as Christ taught?

———

DENVER: Christ made a comment about those that would be able to enter into the Kingdom of God, and He said that except you become *as a little child*, you shall not be able to enter into that kingdom. And I—

That thought about what it means to be as a little child is one worth considering. It's one worth puzzling over.

> *Therefore, whoso repenteth and cometh unto me as a little child, him will I receive, for of such is the kingdom of God. Behold, for such I have laid down my life, and have taken it up again; therefore repent, and come unto me ye ends of the earth, and be saved* .(3 Nephi 9:20; see also 3 Nephi 4:7 RE)

The scriptures were given by the power of the Holy Ghost, and now Joseph Smith is explaining that he could unravel their mysteries by the power of the Holy Ghost; and things that did not make sense before began to make sense.

If you've read *The Second Comforter,* in the chapter about "Becoming as a Little Child" there is an excerpt taken from a book, *Godel, Escher, Bach*—the brilliant mathematical book about Bongard problems. Bongard problems are designed to test a certain kind of reasoning using symbols in order to test the person evaluating them. And *invariably*, Bongard problems are solved by children, and they confuse adults—because the children's minds have not become cluttered by the kind of mathematical complexity that we have bouncing around in our heads, as a consequence of which, they look at it simply; and they see things simply; and they can solve the Bongard problems in a way in which adults fail to grasp. The gospel is adapted to the simple mind. The statements that are contained in scripture are given in simplicity and in plainness.

That's the purpose of the baptism and the gift of the Holy Ghost. The doctrine of Christ is connected to this so that once baptized, you can have the testimony of the Father concerning His Son shed upon you by the power of the Holy Ghost.

> *And again I say unto you, ye must repent, and become as a little child, and be baptized in my name, or ye can in nowise receive these things. And again I say unto you, [you] must repent, and be baptized in my name, and become as a little child, or [you] can in nowise inherit the kingdom of God. Verily, verily, I say unto you, that this is my doctrine, and whoso buildeth upon this buildeth upon my rock, and the gates of hell shall not prevail against them. And whoso shall declare more or less than this, and establish it for my doctrine, the same cometh of evil, and is not built upon my rock; but he buildeth upon a sandy foundation, and the gates of hell stand open to receive such when the floods come and the winds beat upon them. Therefore, go forth unto this people, and declare the words which I have spoken, unto the ends of the earth.* (3 Nephi 11:37-41; see also 3 Nephi 5:9 RE)

This is Christ's doctrine—nothing more and certainly nothing less. This is His doctrine. This is the power of redemption. This is the means by which the Holy Ghost is given. And it is the Holy Ghost which, when given, *bears record* of all things. It is the Holy Ghost by which you learn.

Believe in Christ, repent, be baptized, receive the Holy Ghost, and become as a little child. There is no more inquisitive a creature on the planet than a little child. That's who you're to become. You should hunger and search for understanding. This is *all* of the doctrine. There is no more doctrine. This is not all of the teachings; this is not all the tenets; these are not all of the precepts; this is not all of the covenants; this is not all of the commandments; and this is not all of the principles—but it's all of the doctrine. There is no more doctrine than this.

We have this absolutely schizophrenic set of pictures in our heads about the Lord. On the one hand, He is this limp-wristed, happy-go-lucky, permissive chap who sashays about, blessing everyone with fairy dust. And on the other hand, we have this stern, unapproachable, ~~distance~~ [distant], galactic ruler who just can't be troubled by any of us; and He *says* this is His work and His glory—to save *you*—not merely to save and preserve you but to bring about your eternal life and your exaltation. *That's* what He's about.

Get rid of the junk in your heads, and let the scriptures speak to you. As Joseph said—

Look, everything in them can be a mystery if what you have done is barred the information from getting through to you by the door that you have erected from the traditions that you have been handed. Many of you were handed traditions from very good and very well-meaning and very honorable Latter-day Saint parents who ought to be commended and praised for the effort that they made with you.

However, I don't care if your parents were nigh unto God or the devil himself. The fact of the matter remains that we all have the freedom to choose to leave behind whatever it is that becomes the door against which the Savior has to knock, hoping that you'll hear His voice.

We have to become as a little child because it's only the little children who are willing to open themselves up and become vulnerable enough to believe; and then hopeful enough to act on that belief so that they develop faith; and then persistent enough to ask again and again and again—are we there yet; are we there yet?

In the parable that Joseph was given in the Doctrine and Covenants about the unjust judge and the aggrieved woman, it was a *constant* petitioning. Little children not only don't know a lot of things, they *know* that they don't know, and they ask persistently, incessantly— because they desire to know what they don't know. They're like sponges, and we're like rocks. You can throw a rock into the water and pull it out again, and it's still a rock. But you throw a sponge in, and you pull it out, and it is *greatly* increased. Children are like the sponge. They're porous, and we are not.

Well—Doctrine and Covenants section 93, verse 1—you probably all can recite that in your head—I hope. I'm not going to read it. Oh, I'm looking in Mormon, and I'm trying to find a verse in Moses. Moses 6, verse 57:

> *Wherefore teach it unto your children, that all men, everywhere, must repent, or they can in nowise inherit the kingdom of God, for no unclean thing can dwell there, or dwell in his presence; for, in the language of Adam, Man of Holiness is his name, and the name of his Only Begotten is the Son of Man, even Jesus Christ, a righteous Judge, who shall come in the meridian of time.* (Moses 6:57; see also Genesis 4:9 RE)

Institutional forms of Mormonism want to claim that God has finished His work for our day and has given His authority to a select group of professional clergy. Their jealousy and envy keep them out of the kingdom, and those under their control are prevented from entering in. What an odd outcome this is for institutional Mormonism when the religion was founded on the relentless search for truth anywhere it can be found.

What, then, ought to be done? Can we still embrace an original once the original has been so deformed and disfigured? Can Mormonism, whose visage has been so marred by its adherents, yet bring Jacob again to God? Can Mormonism provide a covenant of the people for a light of the Gentiles? Can it again be a marvelous work among the Gentiles, of great worth to both them and the House of Israel? Are there any with the inclination or desire to deal prudently with the marred visage of Mormonism so that some believers will yet see and consider the depth and breadth of the religion hidden from them? Will Mormonism ever arise from the dust and become evidence that the work of the Father has begun to prepare mankind for the glorious return of His Son?

It cannot be done unless those who accept the challenge of Mormonism become as a little child. We must return to the innocent, childlike quest for the truth where others are not dreaded but welcomed with curiosity. We should attract, not repel others by the interest we have for discovering truth—whatever truth they have to offer. Plato observed, "We can easily forgive a child who is afraid of the dark; the real tragedy is when men are afraid of the light." How can Mormonism ever achieve its destiny if it fears both the light and the dark, insisting that it knows only *it* can be true?

There's a banner up there that says, "What unites us is greater than what divides us." As I think about what unites us and focus on the word *unite*, the things that—the *only* things that I know that are possible to unite us is if we are *open*. If I *know*... If I *know* the truth... I *know* the Church is true. Yeah... Churches are true? Well, what does that mean? Correctly organized as a legal entity? How can a church *be* true? I mean, *you* are true in that I see you sitting there, and you're breathing and moving. You're true. But what does that mean? Is truth capable of being embodied in an organization?

We have to be open, not to organizational forms but to truth. But, if we're gonna be united, it's not enough to just say, "I'm open." We need to be willing to search because whatever it is we have, it's not enough. It doesn't matter who we are. Whatever we have is not enough. Blessed are they who *hunger* and *search*. I mean, Christ didn't say, "Blessed are they who are content and closed-minded, for they shall be stubborn." He wants us to hunger and search after righteousness so that we can be filled. Well, if you're filled, wait a few hours. You ought to be hungry again, and therefore, you should begin the search yet again. The hungering in mortality does not end until life itself comes to an end. If you're alive, you need to engage in the search. *You don't have enough.* None of us do. And we have to be willing to accept. It doesn't do you any good to sit out at a banquet after you've hungered and thirst if you won't take it in. You have to be willing to *allow* it to come into you.

Christ said we all need to repent and *become* as a little child. Repenting at the fundamental level means to stop whatever it is you're doing in whatever direction you're heading and change directions to face God. That's the first thing—repent. Come to face God. And secondly, become as a little child. There is no more relentlessly inquisitive a creature on earth than a little child. They hunger, and they thirst. They not only don't know things—they *know* they don't know things. Why? What? When? Where? Relentlessly, they want to be filled. They know they're ignorant. The problem with us is we don't appreciate the enormity of the ignorance that we walk about with.

Hearts of people get hard the older they get, although there is at least one exception 'cuz I ran into a guy at my office who was like 85 years old, and he's still as young and as nimble and as open and as flexible as a child. That's why we have to become childlike—because we have to be willing to consider these things.

I have a theory that underlies the reason why we find this pattern that appears over and over. And this pattern appears: it's a *progression,* and then it's a *regression.* And if you take those and you close them in, what you wind up with are two triangles—one pointing upward, the other pointing downward—with the suggestion that if this relates to the heavens and God, then it suggests the notion that God is actively in the process of reaching down to man. And if this suggests mortality, then implicit in that is that it's the obligation of man to reach upward to God. And then implicit in this may be embedded a message about the point at which—the contact at which—the "X" (Kai [chiasmus]) crosses one another is at *that* moment or *that* instant of revelation *that* point in which we get perfectly aligned with heaven. And heaven is able, because of that alignment, to reach down and make contact with us. And perhaps implicit in the message of why this would appear is the suggestion that it's the obligation of man to reach upward because God is *permanently* in a state of reaching downward in order to make the contact with man.

The *progression* and the *regression*:—if you look at the pattern that you find in the menorah, ABCDCBA, what you're seeing in the pattern of menorah (which was a deliberate symbol located within the holy place of both the tabernacle and later the temple of Solomon and down from there) this symbol is suggesting in another way the exact same pattern of progression and regression and convergence in the center. See, those that take the chiastic literary form and explore why it was done—in addition to the ease of memorization—they say the point that you locate in the center of the chiasm is the point at which the central theme of the idea is presented.

And if you go into Alma chapter 36, and you look at Alma chapter 36's suggestion of what the center point is, it's that moment which the conversion occurs; it's the moment which the contact between the man and God occurs; it's the conversion point. And so, it would also be consistent with there being an underlying *why* to chiasmus that's perhaps more important than detecting its presence elsewhere. Because if Alma (or Mormon, and I think the greater light is that it was Alma and not Mormon that wrote that chapter because of its literary form—that's beyond this, but I think it was Alma that wrote it) experienced it and understood the underlying *why*, then of course, the central theme would be the point of contact between God and man because that is the point at which redemption occurs, the point at which the process goes on.

Well, the other thing that this does is, particularly here, this progression and this regression is the process of walking you backwards. It's the process of *returning* you to somewhere as opposed to *going* somewhere. You're already somewhere—you need to get away from where it is you are and back to something which was better and preferable and earlier. And so, the regression is a question about, well, What is it that regression would deliver to you, would fetch for you, if you were to take it seriously?

Matthew chapter 18 has this little incident in it:

> At the same time came the disciples unto Jesus, saying, Who is the greatest in the kingdom of heaven? And Jesus called a little child unto him, and set him in the midst of them, And said, Verily I say unto you, Except ye be converted, and become as little children, ye shall not enter into the kingdom of heaven. (Matthew 18:1-3; see also Matthew 9:10 RE)

And so the idea of progression and regression, and becoming something converted from what you are today (where you find yourself at this extremity) back to where you once were (at the other end of the scale) may also be a reminder that although your mind is currently filled with all of the issues and all of the experiences of adulthood, there was a time when, previously in childhood, you were capable of much more and much different kinds of things. Christ's comment that you—

The question that drove the answer was the question about who's the greatest in the kingdom of heaven. So, the issue on the plate was, "Where do we find something that is great? Show us one of these. Tell us." And I suppose they were hoping for some mention of themselves, but instead, what Christ did was He asked for a little child. And the narrative suggests that this is quite a young child, a toddler (and the younger that can toddle over, the better). So, He has the little child, and He puts the child in front of Him, and He says, "This—here is an example—this is what the greatest in the kingdom of heaven is like."

Well, why is the greatest in the kingdom of heaven something that has regressed from the complexity and the sophistication, particularly of *our* kind of thinking, back into a point at which there is this childlike faith; there is this childlike approach to whatever is out there? We put away childish things. In fact, Paul, in one of his passages (see 1 Corinthians 1:53 RE), makes a comment about childish things and putting them away.

King Benjamin had something to say about the character of a child, and he gives this in his big talk, beginning in Mosiah where they're all together for his farewell address. This is Mosiah chapter 3, verse 19:

> *The natural man is an enemy to God, and has been from the fall of Adam, and will be, forever and ever, unless he yields to the enticings of the Holy Spirit, and putteth off the natural man and becometh a saint through the atonement of Christ the Lord, and becometh as a child.* (See also Mosiah 1:16 RE)

Then, he elaborates what it is about the child that is so useful in yielding to the enticings of the Holy Spirit, putting off the natural man, becoming a saint through the atonement of Christ. All of those are driven by these kinds of characteristics which are childlike: *submissive, meek, humble, patient, full of love, willing to submit to all things which the Lord seeth fit to inflict upon him, even as a child doth submit to his father* (ibid, vs. 19; vs. 16 RE). Those are the characteristics of a child that manages to change their mind or to facilitate their development.

I heard again— People keep trying to calculate this and come up with a new number all of the time, but I'm sure all of you have heard said that most of what you're gonna learn in your entire life, you learn by the time you're five years old. The personality of a person is fully developed at five. There's another study that came out and said almost all of the education that a person is going to receive in their lifetime has been completed by the time they're in fourth grade. Then, they simply reapply and reapply the same techniques as they had acquired by the fourth grade repetitively thereafter to increasing levels of complexity; but nevertheless, it's the same tools.

Well, why is it, then, that at the early front end, there is this capacity for absorbing everything there is from the universe around them, and then that begins to quiet down, or slow down or to become resistant thereafter? It's because, by its very nature, the mind of a child is open.

Submissive is a characteristic that says: I am open to, will submit to, am looking forward to something you can give to me. I don't come here with a hard attitude. I don't come here with my predisposition. I don't come here with a bundle of things that, if you're going to present a truth to me, it must fit within the boxes that I have constructed.

[Speaking as a hard-headed adult]: "I... If you want, I... Wait a minute; wait a minute... How do you reconcile *that* with... Well, wait a minute, I... Now, Elder McConkie wrote in this book... We have to have a bibliography, ok?"

Here's an idea: It's a truth, but it is truth that you must relax, open your heart, open your mind, and accept and see if it contains light and truth.

[Speaking as a hard-headed adult again]: "No, no, no, no, no, no, no, I want a bibliography. If you don't fetch a bibliography for me (and I want footnotes), then—"

See, I have been *so* tempted— I have been *so* tempted to write a book without a single footnote in it. My wife just thinks that's a terrible idea. The most important chapter I ever wrote had no footnotes in it when I wrote it. And it's my wife's fault that it's now riddled with footnotes because she says, "You can't do that. They won't.... You'll get in trouble. You won't.... It's not...." And she's right. She's right because the reader, the typical reader, is not at a point where the typical reader will simply relax and say, "Is it true? Does it resonate with light? Is there something about this that is fulfilling?"

I have been able to put more information about God and man into ten short parables than I'm able to put into 170,000 words in *The Second Comforter,* simply because parables don't require you to vindicate or justify. But what it does impose upon the reader is the obligation, then, to open themselves up and say, "Well, how do we do that?"

Well, there was a time— There was a time, and it was back here in your life, there was a time when you did *not* need to go down to the firing range and have a skeet machine firing off a clay pigeon and a 12-gauge loaded with birdshot in it to be able to enjoy yourself if you had a stick. If you had a stick, it was enough because your mind was *alive* with the kinds of things that allowed you to have just as much, if not more, *joy pretending*, as does the adult with the gun and the ammunition and the skeet range and the machine and the clay pigeon and the thing blowing up in the air, and Oooo, isn't *that* fun? Don't you wish there was more of *that* from Hollywood? Too bad we can't load blood in clay pigeons. Then we'd all be at the firing range.

The idea of *submissiveness* is another way of reckoning into the idea of *openness* —the same with *meekness*; the same with *humility* and being *humble*; the same with *patience*. And we ought to clarify the point about a child and patience because at first blush, you look at a child, and you say there is nothing *less* patient than a child—"Can we...? Can we...? Are we there yet? Are we there yet? Can I, can I, can I...? Please! Please! Please! Are you sure? [speaking as a child crying] Aaaahhhh!"

[Internal thoughts of the child]: "Crap, how does this work? Can I? Can I? Can I...? Okay, what if I give *this*? Can I get *that*?" See, they go through all of the tantrum stuff until they begin to negotiate; and sometimes that negotiation thing works, particularly if the kids are bright. (And we've been plagued with really bright kids, so they tend to go and negotiate everything.) They are not patient in *that* sense. They are— Children are patient in the sense that relentlessly, endlessly, they are studying to learn more. They *want* to know more.

I write a blog, and on it I ask more questions than I give answers because what people need are not a bunch of answers. And answers end the discussion. Once you've got the answer, that's the end of that. What you need is a question, and you need a question so that you'll open your mind. And you need to open your mind so you can become like a child. And you need to become like a child so that you're a suitable environment in which revelation can take place. And you need to have revelation take place in order for you to reconnect with heaven. And you need to reconnect with heaven so that you get to know who God is. And you need to get to know who God is so that He can, in turn, make you a member of His own household and redeem you from this current plight in which you find yourself—in darkness and distrust. And what people want from me are answers, and I can hand you an answer and cripple you. Or I can teach you to ask and turn you into, potentially, someone that can make this trek backward, that can make this climb.

When you take the symbols and overlay them upon one another, you wind up with the symbol that was adopted by David as one of the symbols of ancient Israel, United Kingdom, priesthood, Star of David. When you place them side by side, if you read the account given by Lucy Mack Smith of the Urim and Thummim, the Urim and Thummim were similarly these two triangular-shaped— (And this is in the stuff that's gonna be published; you can find the site and description in there.) set in the bow that he would look through. And you gotta ask yourself again the question of, If the Urim and Thummim has *that* symbol contained with it, again the question becomes, Why? Why would we wind up with, embedded in the Urim itself, an instrument in which the contact between God and man is to take place— Why would it bear the symbol that appears there?

The Urim and Thummim becomes another interesting issue to think about as a device, as a mechanism. Joseph Smith, when he began the process of translating the Book of Mormon, in using the Urim and Thummim, found that it was so filled with light—his comment was that "I can see everything in looking through it"—was so filled with light that he wound up having headaches because it was physically painful using the device. Later, Joseph would use a seer stone, and he would block out light because it was less painful to make the process. And later still, towards the end of the translation process, the book wasn't even open. The seer stone wasn't even used because *this prop* had resulted in Joseph acquiring this capacity. At the time that we get Joseph in the section 76 revelation, Joseph's just sitting in an upper room dictating the transcript from heaven while in open vision (without possession of any instrumentality) because the process has *changed* the *person* into being in contact with the heavens—which was the purpose behind it all.

Well, there is another statement made by King Benjamin that I want to suggest, too, as another way to look into the same meaning. Mosiah chapter 2, verses 20 and 21: *I say unto you, my brethren, that*— Oh, that's right; we're not in sacrament meeting. You can actually open your scriptures if you have them. By that I mean no disrespect. I'm honoring the letter from the First Presidency that says, Stop opening your scriptures in sacrament meeting.

> *I say unto you, my brethren, that if you should render all the thanks and*
> *praise which your whole soul has power to possess, to that God who has*
> *created you, and has kept and preserved you, and has caused that ye*
> *should rejoice, and has granted that ye should live in peace one with*

another— I say unto you that if ye should serve him who has created you from the beginning, and is preserving you from day to day, by lending you breath, that ye may live and move and do according to your own will, and even supporting you from one moment to another— (Mosiah 2:20-21; see also Mosiah 1:8 RE)

Then he goes on to say that you're still unprofitable after all of that.

So, if you find yourself out here at the extremity of the mortal condition, you are still supported from moment to moment. The breath that you are taking in is loaned to you by God who gives you the power to live and breathe and move and sustain you from moment to moment. So, if that's where you find yourself, then the deeper you look inside yourself, the farther in you go, the closer you will come to the point of contact between yourself and God.

We have a very coarse kind of intellect in the West. We have a give-us-a-rule; give-us-a formula. If I follow the steps, then as a result of following the steps, I will produce the relevant gas, explosion, fire, compound, cake, cookie— *whatever.* So, if all I want from you, therefore, is a list, and if I follow my list, I will produce, at the end, the fire I want, the taste I'm looking for, the whatever-it-is-I'm-trying-to-build.

And so, when *we* pick up the scriptures, it ceases to be for us a Urim and Thummim, and it turns into a rule book. It ceases to be a contact point between God and us in which God Himself can be speaking—and the manner of revelation that He gives to us are the words contained by other prophets elsewhere. It ceases to be that, and it turns into a bibliography for our behavior; a justification for what we're all about; a way to say, "I'm right; you're wrong." It becomes clutter and noise and nonsense—and useless.

What is inside you, sustaining you from moment to moment, *is God.* What organized you and keeps you intact moment to moment *is God.* What lies at the *deepest core* inside you *is God.* What you should be trying to regress back to and find within yourself *is God.*

The kingdom of heaven is *within* you, said Christ. Well, if the kingdom of heaven is within you—if in your *core*—there is a contact between you and God. Then our rule books don't do us a whole lot of good.

There's another way of looking at the mangled mess that we find in the minds that we have with us. And by the way, the vision of Daniel where it was necessary in the last days to grind up Babylon to dust—despite the fact that

Babylon has been gone for 2,500 years—is because Babylon's still alive and well and running around inside your head. That's the manner in which you think. You're the product of Babylon; you're the product of the Medes and Persians; you're the product of the Greeks; you're the product of the Romans. You're the product of all those things as they've accumulated and been handed down. Therefore, *it* must be ground to dust in a regression back to a point where, within you, you find that simplicity.

There's another tradition. It hails from the East. It is, in fact, the tradition out of which Christ Himself came, and *that* was one that focused upon the transcendence. The gospel of John was written by someone who fully bought into the notion of transcendence—that there is this great, and powerful, and over-governing word (or *order* or *truth* or *light*). And that the greatest embodiment of that word (or *notion* or *truth* or *light*) finds itself embodied fully in the person of Jesus Christ. And that great light, that great truth, came down here in the person of Jesus Christ and dwelt among us.

See, there's a statement rather on point with that in the scriptures as well. Doctrine and Covenants section 88, beginning at verse 6:

> *He that ascended up on high, as also he descended below all things, in that he comprehended all things, that he might be in...and through all things, the light of truth; Which truth shineth. This is the light of Christ. As also he is in the sun, and the light of the sun, and the power thereof by which it was made. As also he is in the moon, and is the light of the moon, and the power thereof by which it was made; [And] the light of the stars, and the power thereof by which they were made; And the earth also, and the power thereof, even the earth upon which you stand. And the light which shineth, which giveth...life, is through him who enlighteneth your eyes, which is the same light that quickeneth your understandings; Which light proceedeth forth from the presence of God to fill the immensity of space—The light which is in **all things**, which giveth life to **all things**, which is the law by which all things are governed, even the power of God who sitteth upon his throne, who is in the bosom of eternity, who is in the midst of all things.* (D&C 88:6-13, emphasis added; see also T&C 86:1 RE)

When we read that, we say, "Cool. Wonder how that science works. Wonder what rules we've got to learn in order to have *that* happen." But an Eastern mystic would say, "Yeah, I have seen that. Yes, I have felt that."

I have stepped outside the door of a house on a perfectly still day when there was no wind, and the temperature outside was the same temperature as what was in my body, and there was no difference in the feel between myself and the air all around me. And I was, at that moment, connected by my body and by my mind to all that is and all that ever was. And I felt behind me a bird flying because the pressure of the wings of the bird in flight touched me—though it was distant from me—because *I* was *it*, and *it* was *me*; and the light in it and the light in me were all one. And I could feel the freedom of flight. And in *that*, I saw God.

And we would say, "Oh, I get it! It's poetry! Okay, so now, let's see. That's probably *free verse*" [audience laughter]. And we miss what is going on. We miss the divine connection that exists.

To stand in the presence of God results in people feeling inadequate and ashamed. Isaiah's words were, *Woe is me!...I am undone;...I am a man of unclean lips, and I dwell [among] a people of unclean lips* (Isaiah 6:5; see also Isaiah 2:2 RE). Well, why is that? [It's] because of the accumulation of junk that exists inside the clutter of our minds and the inability to see in the simplest of things.

I'm sitting at the baseball game, and my son is playing on the Alta Hawks; and there's a bird overhead making a relentless noise, and it's distracting. And I'm the scorekeeper, and I don't spend much time paying attention to those things. But I finally look up between innings, and it's a hawk. And there aren't many hawks that fly in Sandy, Utah around a baseball diamond. And I think, "Huh! That's strange." Then I thought, "What are you doing? This might be a message. There might be something to this." So, I thought, "Well what on earth could the meaning of the hawk be? If it's a message, what is it?" And I came up with nothing, as is almost invariably the case. When I come up with a good question, I usually have to get a lot of help to get a good answer.

Well, the next time I look up, there are two hawks circling the ball field at the Jordan baseball field—so we're on hostile territory—this is being a [BYU] Cougar up at Utah State, [inaudible] and we're on *evil* ground here. And there are two hawks circling the field above going in a clockwise fashion. So, it occurs to me I know *clockwise* generally means *blessing*; *counterclockwise* generally means *cursing*. So, two hawks circling the field—a blessing of some sort." And I think, "Well, what on earth— What on earth could that mean?"

We make it a regular habit to pray for our kids, no matter what they're doing, and on this particular occasion, we'd been praying. And my son's involved in a baseball game, and there's a hawk overhead (which is the symbol of his team, and there were two of them); and my kid comes up to bat, and I look up, and the hawks are gone. And I think, "Huh! Well, that's strange." But we'd been praying about everything, including our kid. My son hit a double. And I thought to myself, "Okay. *So* that I would not miss the point that God answers prayer— *So* that I might not miss the point that God's hand is in *everything*—"

One of the greatest baseball movies ever made is *The Last Samurai,* which all you good Mormons have not seen because it's rated R. It is a terrific baseball movie because when this Western, alcoholic, Civil War veteran soldier gets immersed into the Eastern culture and tries to assimilate to their method of warfare, he's completely unable to master the art; and he's beaten every time he goes up against the fellow who is his chief nemesis until finally, the kid with whom he had been residing comes up to him and says, "Too many minds. Too many minds. One mind." And so, the character, the soldier— He finally gets it, and he ceases to worry about anything other than the reaction to the moment in which he finds himself.

One of the reasons why skiing is appealing—snow skiing—is appealing to people is because you can't plan tomorrow, and you can't worry about yesterday because if you take your mind off this moment, if you're anywhere other than the *now*, you're going to go down, and you're going to get hurt. Riding a motorcycle's rather the same way. If you take your mind off— Skiing and riding a motorcycle are both very childlike experiences.

God is in everything. He's absolutely everywhere. It's necessary for you to pay attention to that in order to open yourself up to that because the process of revelation—

In the East, what people would do to try and get a revelation would be to ponder, to meditate, and to open themselves up. In the West, what we would do to get a revelation is to fast and pray and offer God commitments of 50 different things if He—

"*Please*, please, please, please, *please*, please, please, please, please…! Just this one time…! Just… Oh, please, please… Ever so much… This! And I'll do that! I'll do that! I'll agree to do this. And okay, what am I not doing? And why… What else could… I didn't wear a white shirt to sacrament last… I'll *always* wear a white shirt every time I go! And I believe they ask for dads to volunteer to bless the sacrament with their sons, but I know it's something I need to do. I'm gonna bless the sacrament...! I'm gonna..." And there's a list of 50 things: "I think... I think I can... I think I can... I think I can..."

And God's up there saying, "Hey, I put the answer to the prayer right there. It's in the front yard, ya know?"

"Oh, *oh*! I have to bake some bread! Am gonna make some bread, and take it to the neighbor and welcome him to the neighborhood. And this next-door neighbor who's got this attitude problem... I'll go over and tell them how *wonderful* sacrament meeting is. I'll get it...! I'll get it done! I'll get it done! I'll get it done! Give me the revelation, will ya?!"

And the revelation was sitting right in your front yard waiting for you to come out and to notice.

And we look upon those things, and we keep ourselves distracted from, disconnected with, and incapable of opening ourselves up to the revelation which God, at all points, is offering to us. *The world is filled with revelation.* And our problem is that the manner in which we choose to go about asking for and opening ourselves up to it is so limited in scope, so poor in quality, so alien to the teachings of Christ that it doesn't matter that the Lord is shouting at us all around. We simply won't pay any attention or give any heed to what it is that He has been offering all along.

Full of love— By the way, *patience* of the child is the relentless openness that a child has to instruction, to receiving more, the perpetual walking about with the empty cup. I would like my cup to be filled. It is always— The child is *always* standing with the cupped hand asking for you to fill it.

And *we* go about saying, "Ah! I'm gonna offer a prayer now. What's that formula? Oh, we thank Thee; we ask Thee." We close ourselves off when the child would open themselves up and extend a hand in a petition asking for God to give them something. And it doesn't matter how many different ways the Lord goes about trying to teach us that—either with scriptures or a symbol or a sign. It doesn't matter. We, nevertheless, remain committed to closing ourselves off from and refusing to open up and receive what things the Lord would offer if we simply would be patient, humble, submissive, and come to Him with an open recognition that we lack.

Full of love: Full of love is one of those things which— It's really a reflection of how close you've drawn to the center point. John, whom we call Beloved, seems to have had his eyes opened as to the Savior because at one point, he defines the Lord as *love. God is Love.* You draw nearer to that—and it's not a process of drawing nearer without difficulties. When you read, in particular, the strugglings that Enos had in the Book of Mormon, the closer you draw to the center point, the closer it is you reach to the point of love. And you begin to realize that there are people you don't love; indeed, there are people you despise. But the nearer you approach to God, the more you realize that despite the fact that you have legitimate reasons for harboring resentments or grudges or attitudes about others, it is, nevertheless, the case that if you love, you can't hold onto those things. And you could say, "I hate it. I just hate this love that I have to show to other people [audience laughter], but I can't resist it. You know, that guy— He deserves to get what's coming to him, and here I have no more disposition to give it to him. I can actually look upon him with compassion. And yet, in my rational mind, I sure hope the Lord doesn't because he deserves to get stomped on at some point. I'm not going to do it. You know, live and let live. Let him go. I bring no accusation against him."

And then the phrase, *Willing to submit to all things which the Lord seeth fit to inflict upon him, even as a child doth submit to his father* (Mosiah 3:19; see also Mosiah 1:16 RE). That's a long phrase that's capturing one idea, and that is that—from the vantage point at which the connection is made between the two; at the *moment* in which the *clarity* comes; at the *moment* when you realize what it is God would have you do—it *ceases* to be a question of whether or not you're willing to do it.

If you knew God wanted you to do—choose the thing—sell all you have and give it to the poor? That was what was asked of the rich young man, and he didn't do it. But I commented on that fellow in *Come, Let Us Adore Him* and what he would have been involved with had he sold all he had and gone with the Lord. He would have been there for that final trek into and all of the events that occurred at Jerusalem. And He said, "Come follow me. I mean, sell all you have, give it to the poor, and come. In essence, You're gonna be right there for the greatest moments in history. You're going to ride alongside of me." Now, we look at that as kind of a fool's bargain because he went away mourning because he had great riches, and he didn't want to give them up. But what he didn't know was this was the last opportunity he had to see Christ alive, and he would have and could have been there for everything—all the way from there through the resurrection—had he been on board and done what he was invited to do.

Well, I'm running out of time.

There are portions of the endowment (if you've been through the endowment) that suggests this chiasmic pattern. But the biggest problem is that as adults, we don't see things that children *can* see because our minds are cluttered with craftiness, cunning. We are suspicious of other people; we can be mean; we can be manipulative; we can be jealous; we can be skeptical. Much of the clutter that's in our mind, we learned as we entered into and participate in adulthood and adult services. In order to go forward, we need to go back. In order to get back in contact with God, the regression that was shown in the symbol of chiasmus is part of the process of going back to both an earlier point in time (that is, your childlike attitude) and a more open and a more spiritually welcoming portion that lies only deep, deep inside you at this point.

You know, I think enough of what I've said is what I would be willing to stand on in the presence of God and defend. And so, let me end by bearing testimony to you that this stuff and this symbol and this meaning and this process is, in fact, the path back to God. When you go all the way out to the farthest reach of the universe and you find God sitting upon His throne, one of the shocking realizations that you'll make when you meet God is that God has *always* been with you and that He is as close to you as the very next breath you take.

————

The foregoing excerpts are taken from:

- Denver's *Christian Reformation Lecture Series* Talk #7, given in Boise, Idaho, on November 3, 2018;
- Denver's *40 Years in Mormonism Series* Talk #7 titled "Christ, Prototype of the Saved Man," given in Ephraim, Utah, on June 28, 2014;
- A fireside talk on "The Temple," given in Ogden, Utah, on October 28, 2012;
- Denver's *40 Years in Mormonism Series* Talk #10 titled "Preserving the Restoration," given in Mesa, Arizona, on September 9, 2014;
- His talk titled "Other Sheep Indeed," given at the Sunstone Symposium in Salt Lake City, Utah, on July 29, 2017;
- His remarks given at the Joseph Smith Restoration Conference in Boise, Idaho, on June 24, 2018;
- Denver's *40 Years in Mormonism Series* Talk #9 titled "Marriage and Family," given in St. George, Utah, on July 26, 2014; and

- Denver's talk given at the Chiasmus Conference in American Fork, Utah on September 18, 2010.

In addition, Denver has written extensively about this topic. If you are interested in learning more, please review the following blog posts, among others:

3rd Nephi 11:37-38, posted September 29, 2010;
Mosiah 3:19, posted June 8, 2012; and
Tradition's Grip, posted February 21, 2013.

73. Good Questions

QUESTION: How do we formulate and ask good questions?

———

DENVER: The opening of the book of Enos has some interesting language that describes what Enos went through in order for him to receive revelations and confirmations and blessings from God. The way in which he opens his book is a pretty good description of what it takes to prepare your mind and your heart in order to *get* answers from God. The challenge is not merely to know how to ask a good question, it's also to prepare yourself to receive a good answer.

Enos wrote: *Behold, it came to pass that I, Enos, knowing my father that he was a just man—for he taught me in his language, and also in the nurture and admonition of the Lord* (Enos 1:1). It's important that Enos had been taught in the language of his father because it was in another language that the plates were written; therefore, for him to be able to read and ultimately write upon them, he had to have the competency and command of a foreign language to the one that was commonly spoken. So, he was taught in the language and also in the nurture and admonition of the Lord.

Nurture is an interesting word, and you ought to ask yourself what that looks like to be 'nurtured' and 'admonished' of the Lord—because that suggests to *my* mind that he was trying to incorporate into his life things that he'd been taught by accepting what he got out of the scriptures to nurture (that is, fortify, strengthen, inform him) and to admonish him. We sometimes view the whole thing as a one-way street, where God bestows upon us endless blessings, instead of looking at it as a two-way street ,where God's also in the process of rehabilitating us and correcting us and sometimes disapproving of us, in order for us to be admonished and nurtured in the Lord. I think those two things go together.

And blessed be the name of God for it (ibid), meaning he praises God that his father taught him the language so he could read the scriptures, and then he took seriously enough what he found in the scriptures to let it inform him and to correct him and to point out to him his faults. Therefore, he accepted that admonition *and blessed be the name of the Lord for it.*

And I will tell you of the wrestle which I had before God, before I received...remission of my sins (ibid, vs.2; Enos 1:1 RE). See, the **wrestle** that he had with God is a really apt way to put what's necessary in order to get from where you are to where you want to be in obtaining answers from God to questions that you pose. 'Wrestle' is not complacent. It's not reclining and meditating. It's not sitting back, impatiently tapping your fingers, and waiting for God to do something. It's a wrestle—*actively* working, *actively* searching, *actively* trying to find what it is that you're looking to gain from God.

So Oliver Cowdery wanted to be able to work on and translate—'cuz he saw what Joseph was able to do; he wanted to do the same thing—he wanted to translate. In April of 1829, as he was acting as Joseph's scribe, he wanted to switch roles; and they switched roles temporarily, but his attempt failed. And in the failed attempt, we learn a few things that are applicable not merely to Oliver, but to **everyone** who's going to inquire of the Lord.

> *Even so [sure] shall you receive a knowledge of whatsoever things [ye] shall ask in faith, with an honest heart, believing that you shall receive a knowledge concerning the engravings…* [okay, so "whatsoever things you…ask in faith" almost seems limitless, doesn't it? "With an honest heart, believing…you shall receive a knowledge…." So, that— the breadth of that language seems really loose, really wide, but then it tightens up a bit], *which contain those parts of my scripture of which have been spoken by the manifestation of my Spirit* [meaning that it is through the Spirit that he's gonna be able to obtain what he asks for, in faith, believing that he can receive it]. *Yea, behold, I will tell you in your mind and in your heart, by the Holy Ghost, which shall come upon you and which shall dwell in your heart. Now, behold, **this** is the spirit of revelation; behold, **this** is the spirit by which Moses brought the children of Israel through the Red Sea on dry ground.* (D&C 8:1-3; see also T&C 3:1, emphasis added)

Okay, so first he tells them: whatever you ask for, you're gonna be able to get that—if you ask in faith, with an honest heart, believing that you can receive; and the **manner** in which the answer will come to you is to be told in your mind and in your heart.

There's one time when I was teaching Elders Quorum many years ago, and we were on the topic of the heart, and I was posing the question for discussion: What does "heart" mean? And someone said, "Oh, the heart—the heart is just part of your mind." And so, in response to that answer, I said, "Okay, if the heart is part of your mind, what part of your mind *is* your heart?" Because the heart and the mind are discussed **separately** in scripture; they both have a function. Oliver's being told that in his *mind* he's going to be told something, and in his *heart* he is going to be told something *by the Holy Ghost, which shall come upon you... which shall dwell in your heart.* Well, what part of the human consciousness is the heart?

Joseph defined pure revelation as intelligence, not emotions. **We** tend to view the heart as if it were entirely emotions:

- "Oh, she touched my heart; therefore, I'm in love with her."

- "My heart reaches out to the puppy, to the kitten."

- We tend to view "heart" as if it were merely sentiment, but if you accept Joseph's definition of the Holy Ghost, then the heart is not **necessarily** a place where mere sentiment exists.

Your mind (which might be knowledge) and your heart (which might be wisdom)—in other words, I will tell you in your mind (I'll give you information) and in your heart (I'll give you the wisdom by which you know how to apply the knowledge that you're given), which comes to you by the mind of God, the Holy Ghost, which includes both the Father and His Companion and the Son.

Now, behold, this is the spirit of revelation...this is the spirit by which Moses brought the children of Israel through the Red Sea on dry ground (ibid). So, Moses (we tend to think) had a whole lot of heavenly guidance and advantages that are awesome to behold and greater than what **we** have. But this definition suggests that Moses was relying upon the thoughts that came to him and the wisdom to apply the understanding that he was given; and that it was through **that** mechanism that Moses proceeded in **faith**—and **that** delivered him, and **that** delivered the children of Israel who followed him, also.

Well, then—as we get further into the revelation to Oliver Cowdery—things tighten considerably. Whereas it starts out, *a knowledge of whatsoever things you shall ask in faith, with an honest heart,* it then goes on to say,

> *Trifle not with these things; do not ask for that which you ought not. Ask* [in other words, there are things about which you can make an inquiry, and you just shouldn't be asking; and if you're asking about things that you shouldn't be inquiring about then "whatsoever things you shall ask in faith" doesn't apply. *Do not ask for that which you ought not. Ask that*—here's the first thing:] *that you may know the*

mysteries of God, and [in the case of Oliver] *that you may translate and receive knowledge from all those ancient records which have been hid up, that are sacred; and according to your faith shall it be done unto you.* (D&C 8:10-11; see also T&C 3:3)

So the limit on asking and getting an answer includes: do not/don't/it is not appropriate to ask for things that are inappropriate. So what **is** appropriate to ask about?

- "know the mysteries of God"—that would apply not just to Oliver, but to any inquiring soul.

- "that you may translate and receive knowledge"—okay, it's been translated; we don't need to re-translate it. But **all** of us need to receive knowledge from all those ancient records which had been hid up that are sacred.

- In other words, one appropriate subject for almost limitless inquiry to understanding (for which we have a promise that we can ask and receive an answer—if we ask in faith, with an honest heart, believing that we'll receive knowledge) is inquiring about an understanding of those ancient records that had been hid up that are sacred—or in this case, the Book of Mormon, and (although it wasn't on the horizon in April of 1829) we would also later get (through the translation that Joseph Smith made of the Bible) a record of—a more complete record of—the account of Moses, which includes within it a record of Enoch, and later still, it would include the Book of Abraham.

So if you want to know what **is** within bounds and what **is** appropriate for inquiry, questions:

- About the scriptures,

- About the meaning of scriptures,

- About an understanding of how the scriptures apply.

Those are all things that are appropriate for an inquiry, in particular the Book of Mormon; because used in that manner, the Book of Mormon becomes a great Urim and Thummin, revealing to us things that we would not otherwise be able to comprehend.

Then, later in that same month, there's another revelation that—the same revelation, but it's a revelation that's worded differently, dealing with Joseph's instruction: "Remember that without faith you can do nothing; trifle not with these things. Do not ask for that which you had not ought; ask that you may know the mysteries of God." So the admonition to ask that you might know the mysteries of God—

Mysteries of God consist of things that are important for salvation/are part of the Gospel/ are part of the message/are part of the scriptures, but we just don't get 'em yet. We haven't noticed 'em yet. We don't understand them yet; and therefore, to us, they consist of a mystery. The greatest mysteries are always embodied within ceremonial rites, in which God symbolically teaches us a great deal of things using ritual and symbol (just as He used parables during His mortal ministry to hide things and to require people to be initiated and capable of understanding what He's really talking about); that's what ritual mysteries of God also contain: embedded within them are multiple meanings that are told in story-form, requiring that **we** use the skill, the aptitude, the knowledge (or the "key") to understand why the mystery's so.

The other thing that you have to keep in mind is that Enos wrestled, and Oliver was admonished that he took no thought except to ask and that he need[ed] to study it out in his own mind. Even if you've got a great question, that doesn't mean that you're automatically entitled to an effortless answer.

There was an issue that I struggled with in the scriptures that I'll use as an example. It's one of those things that creates a paradox, if you take the wrong answer. Jesus promised the twelve apostles, at one point—and it was early enough that the twelve apostles included Judas, that would betray Him—He gave to the twelve, including Judas, the promise that when He came in His kingdom, that the twelve of them would sit on thrones, judging the twelve tribes of Israel. And so, if the answer is that the twelve would sit on thrones, judging the twelve tribes of Israel, and Judas is **included**, then there's a paradox of why someone that would betray the Lord would have been found worthy to sit on a throne. So the question presented itself as to how would those twelve thrones be occupied; because Judas—it seems self-evident—should not be qualified to occupy one of them.

It was an issue that comes from reading the scriptures. It's an issue that, to me, seemed incongruent. And the question presented itself in a way that I would like an answer to it. But I didn't just take no thought save to ask; I studied it out. And it seemed to me that shortly after His resurrection, He called an apostle that wrote two-thirds of the books of the New Testament—

the apostle Paul. Even though Paul was not with Him during His mortal ministry, Paul met the Lord on the road to Damascus, and the Lord called him. And Paul would later self-identify as an apostle of the Lord—meaning a messenger that was sent by the Lord. And so Paul claimed the role that would apparently make him a candidate for replacing Judas, assuming Judas fell. And I thought it was safe to conclude that Judas did fall.

But the other eleven, likewise, took a vote, and based upon the criteria of faithfulness and understanding in having been with Him throughout the ministry of the Lord, they drew lots—and the lot fell upon Matthias. Now, Matthias is mentioned in the book of Acts, but we don't have a testimony from him; we don't have letters from him; we don't have any basis upon which to conclude that Matthias would be a better candidate to sit upon the vacant throne than would Paul, other than, clearly, the Eleven felt some considerable confidence in the man. But **we** have no basis upon which to **ratify** their confidence in him. We don't know anything about the man.

Well, I studied it out. I looked at all the verses I could find that might help tip it one way or another, and I came up with my answer and concluded that it had to be the apostle Paul. And so, having worked my way through and reached a conclusion, and believing that I could get an answer from God, I inquired to know about this (that I consider a mystery—an unknown-but-perhaps-important question because the day of judgment holds meaning for all of us, for all mankind), and therefore, will it be Paul that we have to confront, or will it be Matthias? And I concluded it was Paul.

Prayerfully asking the Lord, taking my answer to Him, I got an answer. And the answer was: I was wrong. It was neither Paul, nor was it Matthias—because there was never ~~eleven~~ [twelve] vacancies for the princes of Israel. There were eleven who betrayed their brother (and one about whom we know not enough to determine righteousness or not). But there was one of the sons of Jacob (Joseph) who clearly deserved to sit upon a throne— who, in fact, had visions that told him that others would bow down: the wheat stalks would bow down to him; the stars would bow down to him. The life of Joseph was exemplary. He was prophetic. We have prophecies of his that are preserved in the Book of Mormon and **not** in the Old Testament—which, again, tells us that Joseph the Patriarch was a worthy man and a prophetic man. And therefore, there's no reason to ever remove him from the throne upon which he should sit as the **real** patriarch—who never left his position at the head of his tribe, because there was only eleven vacancies. Judas fell, and therefore, all of the other thrones were available for assignment; and the Lord assigned those to the remaining eleven. But the twelfth—the twelfth was never vacated by the patriarch and prophet— Joseph—who was sold into Egypt.

Very often, if you come up with a great question, the key to getting the answer is to then study it out—unlike Oliver. You don't take no thought save to ask. You study it out. You reach your best conclusion—not profunctorially; not quickly. The objective is to try and get it right. And then, when you think you've reached the very best answer and you've studied it out in your own mind, God'll give you an answer. And if you're in error, He'll give you an understanding that will exceed where you were before. But if you're right, you'll get the confirmation—in your mind and in your heart—to understand (by knowledge and by wisdom) that you have reached the right conclusion, and you have, in fact, gained understanding of one of the mysteries of God.

Good questions **come** from scripture study. The experiences of peoples' lives in scripture give us analogies for every difficulty, every circumstance, every health challenge, every mental challenge, every broken heart, every loss and every gain, and every blessing, and every undeserved gift from God that's bestowed upon us. Everyone that has gone before, in the process of living the Gospel, have been exposed to the challenges of this world. Sometimes it's a bigger challenge to deal with blessings than it is to deal with adversity. But the scriptures tell us how to deal with both.

Study out the thing that is troubling you in your life by going to the scriptures to get guidance. We need to plunge deep into them. There's no reason why you can't get recordings and listen to scripture as you drive, as you find spare moments. There's no reason not to become acquainted with the scriptures by listening to them over and over.

I had—when I was teaching Gospel Doctrine—I had recordings of the Book of Mormon. And the chapters that I would teach, I would listen to on a CD while I'm driving places. I tried to listen to the same chapters—if I was teaching three chapters in Alma, I'd try to listen to those three chapters at least **ten** times all the way through during the week before the lesson. Then I would try to read it—physically reading it from paper—at least **three** times during that week. And then, if I could find commentary or other information, I'd look at that.

We're supposed to plunge deep into the scriptures. That's where you will find your good questions. Good questions reckon from understanding, studying, and comprehending the scriptures. And in the case of the Book of Mormon, in the case of the Teachings & Commandments, they were written originally in English that most of us speak. As to the Bible, there are varying qualities of translations, but the scriptures we adopted in a conference in Boise are the Joseph Smith Translation. It's a whole new root of scripture, and Joseph Smith spoke English as his native tongue. So using the Old and New Testaments— Old and New Covenants that we have in the scriptures that we have accepted by covenant—you also have an English-based version from which to study and from which to discover your questions.

————

The foregoing was recorded by Denver Snuffer in Sandy, Utah on June 15th, 2019.

74. Hyrum Smith

In this episode, Denver addresses the question: What was Hyrum Smith's role in the Restoration?

———

DENVER: Doctrine and Covenants Section 124 has a revelation given in January of 1841 to the saints at that point in Nauvoo, offering something to the saints in that day that is relevant to the history that unfolded thereafter. Beginning at verse 28, the Lord says through Joseph: *For there is not a place on earth that he* ["he" here being the Lord God—*that he*] *may come to and restore again that which was lost unto you, or which he hath taken away, even the Fulness of the Priesthood* (see also T&C 141:10).

Skipping to verse 31: *But I command you, all ye my saints, to build a house unto me...* (see also T&C 141:11).

See, this commandment was unto everyone who at that point claimed to be a saint. All of them, every one of them, was put under the equal burden: *to build a house unto me.*

> *...and I grant unto you, all of you, a sufficient time to build a house unto me; and during this time your baptisms shall be acceptable unto me. But behold, at the end of this appointment your baptisms for your dead shall not be acceptable unto me; and if you do not these things at the end of the appointment, ye shall be rejected as a church, with your dead, saith the Lord your God.* (D&C 124:31-32; see also T&C 141:11)

It's interesting that in verse 31, it says *your baptisms,* and in verse 32 it says *your baptisms for your dead,* which suggests that after verse 31, if we fail in verse 32, that our baptisms will continue to be acceptable, but our vicarious work would not, and the Church would then be rejected.

If you skip to 34, talking about this proposed temple to be constructed: *For therein are the keys of the Holy Priesthood ordained, that you may receive honor and glory*—"honor" being the promise from God into the afterlife, respecting what you can expect to receive from God as an oath and as a covenant; "glory" being intelligence, or knowledge and understanding, light and truth —things that were not comprehended but which God hoped to have the saints at that point comprehend.

Well, he gives to us in this same revelation a measuring stick by which we can determine if we satisfy the requirements that the Lord has set forth. And the measuring stick is this, beginning in verse 44 (well, verse 43 probably we should begin): *And ye shall build it on the place where you have contemplated building it, for that is the spot which I have chosen for you to build it.* So they contemplated it, the Lord approved it, and this would become a spot where the Nauvoo Temple was to be constructed.

> *If you labor with all your might, I will consecrate that spot that it shall be made Holy. And if my people will hearken unto my voice and unto the voice of my servants whom I have appointed to lead my people, behold, verily I say unto you, They shall not be moved out of their place.*
> (D&C 124:44-45; see also T&C 141:13, emphasis added)

"They" being the people; "they" being those that he had chosen to lead them. "They" being, in this instance, the Prophet Joseph Smith and the one who would be appointed to receive priesthood and be appointed to hold the sealing power in this revelation, Hyrum Smith—the one who was designated to be the successor to Joseph Smith in the event of Joseph's death, and the one whom the Lord would take first, Hyrum. Joseph died knowing that his successor had first fallen.

Joseph was the only one who could appoint a successor. He first designated David Whitmer. In 1835, Joseph organized the complementary presidency in Zion. The president was David Whitmer, with counselors: W.W. Phelps and John Whitmer. This made David Whitmer the backup church president if Joseph died. Four days after organizing the Missouri Zion presidency, Joseph explained "if he should now be taken away that he had accomplished the great work which the Lord had laid before him" (*The Joseph Smith Papers, Documents, Volume 4: April 1834-September 1835,* pp. 90-96).

He wrote in his journal the following year, 1835, that the church's permanent foundation was assured because of the Missouri president, who would take over if he, Joseph, were taken. Unfortunately, in 1838 Whitmer resigned as president in Zion, joined the dissenters, and contributed to the agitation that resulted in the Mormon War. Whitmer later organized his own competing church. Presumably, an active dissenter who refused to participate in the church for six years was disqualified as Joseph's successor when Joseph was killed.

A second successor was appointed in 1841. Hyrum Smith was given the same status as Joseph by revelation. Although Hyrum was faithful, he died moments before Joseph, and that left the successor unidentified. This is all the more unfortunate, because Joseph alone had the power to appoint a successor.

There's a revelation that was given in January of 1841, the last lengthy revelation given while Joseph was alive. His last vision that's a second-hand account (still reliable because it was recorded so quickly after) and that contains William Smith is going to replace Hyrum as a counselor to Joseph. And the revelation in January 1841 records:

> And again, verily I say unto you, let my servant William be appointed, ordained, and anointed as counselor unto my servant Joseph, in the room of my servant Hyrum, that my servant Hyrum may take the office of Priesthood and Patriarch, which was appointed unto him by his father, by blessing and also by right, that from henceforth he shall hold the keys of the Patriarchal blessings upon the heads of all my people, that whosoever he blesses shall be blessed and whosoever he curses shall be cursed, that whatsoever he shall bind on earth shall be bound in Heaven; whatsoever he shall loose on Earth shall be loosed in Heaven. And from this time forth I appoint unto him that he may be a prophet, and a seer, and a revelator unto my church, as well as my servant Joseph, that he may act in concert also with my servant Joseph, and that he shall receive counsel from my servant Joseph, **who shall show unto him the keys whereby he may ask and receive**, and be crowned with the same blessing, and glory, and honor, and Priesthood and gifts of the Priesthood, that were once put upon him that was my servant Oliver Cowdery, that my servant Hyrum may bear record of the things which I shall show unto him, that his name may be had in honorable remembrance from generation to generation forever and ever. (D&C 124:91-96; see also T&C 141:32, emphasis added)

So Hyrum was put into a position that was once occupied by Oliver, to stand with Joseph, possessing the ability to ask and receive, so that the channel through which you can know and understand what God wants or intends for people is open as the mechanism to save souls. Because at the end of this, its sole purpose is to save souls. It talks about him and his name had in honorable remembrance from generation to generation. Only descendants of Hyrum occupied the position of the Presiding Patriarch of the Church until 1979, when Eldred G. Smith was made emeritus; but he still signed everything as Patriarch to the Church, and he still kept an office in the Church Office Building.

There's some eagerness that father Hyrum had to get busy—before the Book of Mormon was even done—preaching repentance, because he believed it. And the Lord held Hyrum back. If you go to Doctrine and Covenants section 11, beginning at verse 13, there's a revelation given to Hyrum:

> *Verily, verily, I say unto you, I will impart unto you of my Spirit, which shall enlighten your mind, which shall fill your soul with joy; And then shall ye know, or by this you shall know, all things whatsoever you desire of me, which are pertaining unto things of righteousness, in faith believing in me that you shall receive. But I command you, that you need not suppose that you are called to preach until you are called. Wait a little longer, until you shall have my word, my rock, my church, and my gospel, that you may know of a surety my doctrine.* (See also JSH 14:13-14 RE)

See Hyrum was being told, 'It's good to be eager, but don't go out and try to preach something because you're not yet qualified. You don't have enough knowledge in order to do so.' Likewise, Adam and Eve—not because the Lord held back and told them, 'Don't do it. Don't do it,' but because the circumstances of their lives did not prepare them to do it, until there were generations already alive on the earth. Then they were given the gifts that were necessary in order to begin their preaching.

Hyrum was told in verse 21:

> *Seek not to declare my word, but first seek to obtain my word, and then shall your tongue be loosed; then, if you desire, you shall have my Spirit and my word, yea, the power of God unto the convincing of men. But now hold your peace; study my word which hath gone forth among the children of men, and also study my word which shall come forth among the children of men, or that which is now translating, yea, until you have obtained all that which I grant unto the children of men in this generation, and then shall all things be added thereto.* (ibid, vs. 15 RE)

- Hyrum Smith, who would eventually become co-president with Joseph.

- Hyrum Smith, to whom the Lord would command that he be ordained, not only to priesthood, but to become the one possessing the sealing power over the Church.

- Hyrum Smith, who would be the successor to Joseph, though he was killed before Joseph.

- Hyrum Smith, who was the Prophet of the Church, and Joseph rebuked the Church because they weren't giving heed to Hyrum's words.

- Hyrum Smith, whose letter to the Church ought to be in the Doctrine and Covenants because he was a President, and he issued a general epistle admonishing people.

- Hyrum Smith, whose name is omitted from the list of Church Presidents, even though it should be there.

- Hyrum Smith is told by the Lord, 'Don't go out and start preaching yet. You need to learn something first. You need to be qualified first.' In the revelation to Hyrum given in 1829, and in the lives of Adam and Eve, God is in no great hurry to get people running around preaching before they are qualified.

There's this comment that Joseph Smith made. He said, "I am learned, and know more than all the world put together. The Holy Ghost does, anyhow, and He is within me, and comprehends more than all the world: and I will associate myself with Him." That's in the *Teachings of the Prophet Joseph Smith*, page 350. This is what qualified Adam and Eve to go declare repentance to their children. This is what qualified them to know the truth of all things and have the wisdom of which to impart it, so that they could persuade their children to believe in Christ. This is the fullness of the Gospel of Jesus Christ.

You, to be competent in teaching your children, must first have the Holy Ghost as your guide. Then once you have that, you ought to have command of the scriptures, just as Hyrum was told, to learn what's in them. Then you're qualified to go and to teach your children, and you have an obligation to do that. Children are the means to preserve Zion. Without the conversion of children, Zion has no chance of surviving.

When you go to the story in Moses chapter 5 (see also Genesis 3 RE) and you read about Adam and Eve and their posterity, Adam and Eve have children, and the children are seduced by Satan and persuaded to be led astray. Then they have a son to whom the birthright was going to be granted because he appeared to be interested in the things of God, so much so that he was willing to offer sacrifice. That son, the older one, was named Cain, and the next son born was Abel. But Abel was more attentive to the things of God. Both Cain and Abel offered sacrifices to the Lord. However, the Lord approved the sacrifice of Abel.

At this point in the history of man, if that right of priesthood passed from Adam to Abel, it would have displaced Cain. Cain sought for the right whereunto he would be the one to hold that priesthood. He was the one who wanted it. And the first murder that was committed, was committed against the one who would inherit the birthright, **done precisely for the purpose of eliminating the posterity of Abel**—so that Abel, having no posterity, could not be the one through whom the birthright would be perpetuated. When Cain sought to take what God had instead appointed his younger brother to receive, Cain was deprived of the right of priesthood, and it passed over him and his descendants, so that Cain did not obtain the birthright. And Eve conceived, and she bore a replacement son; and that son, Seth, became the one through whom the promises would be given. And Cain was driven out from the people.

Now you have to understand that (this is in Moses chapter 6): *Adam lived one hundred and thirty years, and begat a son in his own likeness, after his own image, and called his name Seth. And the days of Adam after he had begotten Seth were eight hundred years, and he begat many sons and daughters* (Moses 6:10-11; see also Genesis 3:15 RE). Adam begat **many** sons and daughters, but the son named Seth was the one to whom this priesthood went because there is only one appointed.

> *Seth lived one hundred and five years, and he begat Enos, and prophesied in all his days, and taught his son Enos in the ways of God; wherefore Enos prophesied also. And Seth lived after he begat Enos, eight hundred and seven years, and begat many sons and daughters.* (Moses 6:13-14; see also Genesis 3:16 RE)

So Seth begat Enos and many sons and daughters, but the right of the lineage and the priesthood went from Adam to Seth to Enos.

This is a description of that priesthood (which was briefly restored in one person—Joseph) to be given to Hyrum, because it goes to the oldest righteous descendent. And when it was restored through Joseph Smith, Hyrum was not yet qualified. But when Hyrum became qualified by January of 1841, in the revelation given then, Hyrum is the one to whom the birthright went, being the eldest and being the one who was qualified. This is why it was necessary for Hyrum to die before Joseph—so that in this dispensation, Joseph and Hyrum can stand at the head. Because if Hyrum had not died first, but Joseph had died first, Joseph would have died without having had the passing.

Well, notice that Seth had many sons and daughters. And then you get to the next, Enos. He lived and begat Canaan. Enos also has many sons and daughters, but Canaan was the one upon whom the birthright—

And this follows all the way down, all the way down. You can read it in Moses chapter 6 (see also Genesis 3 RE), how it descends through the line. This pattern repeats over and over again.

(As I'm talking about this, I'm making reference to a diagram that appeared first in *The Millennial Star* on January the 15th of 1847. But what you can see in *The Joseph Smith Papers* on page 298, where they reproduce the same diagram of the Kingdom of God, the only difference being that I have filled in the names on this chart, so that you can see where the names go.)

Now, we get to the point in the history of the world in which, after the days of Shem (who was renamed Melchizedek), people fell into iniquity. They fell into iniquity, and they lost the birthright. There was no continuation of this. It was broken by an apostasy, and it had to be restored again, which ought to give all of us great hope, because Abraham sought for this. He sought for a restoration of the Kingdom of God. He sought for a restoration of this, which only one man on the earth can hold at a time. Abraham chapter 1, verse 2:

> *Finding there was greater happiness and peace and rest for me, I sought for the blessings of the fathers, and the right whereunto I should be ordained to administer the same; having been myself a follower of righteousness, desiring also to be one who possessed great knowledge, and to be a greater follower of righteousness, and possess a greater knowledge, and to be a father of many nations, a prince of peace, desiring to receive instructions, and keep the commandments of God, I became a rightful heir, a High Priest, holding the right belonging to the fathers.* (See also Abraham 1:1 RE)

When you are in possession of **that**, you have no problem asking God and getting an answer. It is the right belonging to the fathers. After a period of apostasy and the break of this line, Abraham received it by adoption. Therefore, this power has the ability to cure the break. This covenant-making through God has the ability to restore the family of God—even when wicked men kill in order to destroy it; even when a substitute needs to be made; even when the fathers turn from their righteousness—yet God is able to cause it to persist. And Joseph Smith was doing something which no one else either understood or had the right to perpetuate. This continued through 10 generations from Adam to Melchizedek, but through Abraham it continued five generations. And it appeared again once on the earth, in a single generation that included Joseph and his brother, Hyrum.

Now, even the mockery of it has come to an end, because there is no such thing as a perpetuation in honorable mention of the descendants of Hyrum Smith in the office of Patriarch in the Church. There have been many signs that have been given by God that He was about to do something new, from the time of the death of Joseph Smith till today. All that was left at the end was for a witness to be appointed, to come, and to say, 'It now has come to an end.' In the last talk that I gave in the 10 lecture series, I said a witness has now come, and I am him. It has come to an end. One of the signs of it having come to an end was the passing of Eldred Smith. There are many other signs that have been given if you are looking for them. You can see them all along the line.

QUESTION: In a recent talk back in March [March 22, 2015] in your home —I believe it was on plural marriage—you said (on page 39 of the transcription):

> There have been many signs given by God that He was about to do something new from the time of the death of Joseph Smith till today. All that was left at the end was for a witness to be appointed, to come [to declare], "[Now it] has come to an end." In the last talk...in the 10 lecture series [quoting you] I said, the witness has now come, and I am he. It has come to an end [with something new now begun]. One of the signs of it having come to an end was the passing of Eldred Smith. (*Plural Marriage*, page 25)

Question: Will you elaborate on the significance of the passing of Patriarch Eldred G. Smith on April 4th, 2013 and how or why we should take this as a sign that something has come to an end? In particular, what has come to an end? You are declaring you are a witness of an end-time event. That seems vital. What is this event? How are you a witness? Why is it important for us to recognize this event? How should we (or how do you think God expects us to) acknowledge such an event in our own lives?

DENVER: Well, in a word, the fullness of the Gentiles ending. One of the last signs of that was the passing of Eldred Smith in 2013, and with him, the office of Patriarch to the Church. That office was never well understood. And I've never been told it was necessary to fully explain the significance, so I've left most of the details unexplained. But to what I've said already I would add the following: The LDS Church makes enthusiastic claims about their priesthood, and those claims would be much more accurate if they were dialed back some; if they were considerably more modest. They claim to have Melchizedek priesthood, which has the following list of things associated with it, when it is described for us the first time in scripture in Genesis chapter 14 of the Joseph Smith Translation (Genesis 7:19 RE), the authority to:

- break mountains,

- divide the seas,

- dry up waters,

- turn waters out of their course,

- put at defiance the armies of nations,

- divide the earth,

- break every band,

- stand in the presence of God.

I pointed out that it's not necessary to do all these things, but any one of them is enough to show that the authority is present. But this priesthood does have signs. The ordination of Hyrum in 1841 was (and I'm reading from the scripture) to *the office of Priesthood and Patriarch.* That's in section 124 verse 91 (see also T&C 141:32). What was intended with that ordination was so that (and again, I'm reading from the same revelation) *His name may be had in honorable remembrance from generation to generation, forever and ever.* That's in 124 verse 96 (see also ibid, RE).

There was a colorable claim to priesthood while Hyrum and his descendants remained in office. That ended. So far as the LDS Church was concerned, it was good riddance—because they found the office was troublesome. It was not part of the Twelve yet claimed the status of Prophet, Seer, and Revelator while it was part of the General Authorities. It was uncontrollable because only the descendants of Hyrum were the holders; that gave them independence, and leaders wanted the office to be discarded, and it has been.

There are many prophecies that foretell the Gentiles will reject their invitation to have the fullness of the gospel. Christ said this would happen in 3 Nephi 16:10 (see also 3 Nephi 7:5 RE). There have been many signs Christ's prophecies were fulfilled. Only one thing now remained to be done. God needed to send a witness to be the final required sign, sent by God to declare His intention to begin something new. The signs include, but are not limited to:

- The condemnation of the church in 1832, which was D&C 84:54-58 (see also T&C 82:20);

- The expulsion from Missouri that happened and was explained in D&C 101:1&2 (see also T&C 101:1-2);

- The forced winter exodus from Nauvoo;

- The suffering during and following the exodus;

- The afflictions, judgments, and wrath of God at the saints, all of which was foretold in D&C 124:44&45 (see also T&C 141:13-14);

- Their pride, lying, deceit, hypocrisy, **murders**, priestcrafts, and whoredoms—all of which Christ foretold in that 3rd Nephi 16:10 verse.

- There has been inquisitorial abuse of the saints once they were isolated in the wilderness. As part of the Mormon Reformation, the population was interrogated to root out heresy, sin, and to root out disbelief with the threat of Blood Atonement, which was slaying the sinner to save them from hell, then being taught.

- There were mass murders. Over 200 non-Mormons were executed at Mountain Meadows to vindicate an oath to avenge the death of the prophets. Originally, that was aimed at those who slew Joseph and Hyrum, but Parley Pratt's death (news of Parley Pratt's death and slaying arrived just at the time that the Mountain Meadows crew was going through Utah, and since Parley Pratt was regarded as a prophet by the saints, it included him, also). Brigham Young traditionally has not been directly implicated, but everyone (including the LDS Church Assistant Historian, Richard Turley) admits that his rhetoric during the Mormon Reformation coupled with the Temple Oath of Vengeance that Brigham Young added to the rites of the Temple—

- (And just as an aside, an Oath of Vengeance for slaying the prophets could not have been put there by Joseph Smith because he and Hyrum Smith had not yet been slain. And so the Oath of Vengeance was necessarily the product of the mind of Brigham Young. But it was part of the Temple rhetoric; and everyone admits that the Blood Atonement and the Oath of Vengeance and the Mormon Reformation and Brigham Young's fiery rhetoric and Jedediah Grant's fiery additions on top of that were responsible for creating the environment in which the slaying took place.)

Other signs are:

- Contradictions in what are called "fundamental teachings." For example, plural marriage was once required for exaltation; now it will result in excommunication. Ordaining blacks would once forfeit all church priesthood; now it is unequivocally condemned as false.

- Adopting a well-paid professional ministerial class—in Alma, the Nehor incident included priests; Nehor advocated priests should not labor with their own hands, but they should get supported with the believers' money, and this was something the Book of Mormon condemned of being guilty of priestcraft. Alma, on the other hand, ordained priests in Mosiah 18:18, and he instructed them that they must labor with their own hands for their own support. In Mosiah 18:24: *And he commanded them that the priests whom he had ordained should labor with their own hands for their support* (see also Mosiah 9:10 RE).

King Mosiah adopted this standard as the **law**. In Mosiah 27:4-5:

> *That they should let no pride nor haughtiness disturb their peace; that every man should esteem his neighbor as himself, laboring with their own hands for their support. Yea, and all their priests and teachers should labor with their own hands for their support, in all cases save it were in sickness, or in much want; and doing these things, they did abound in the grace of God.* (See also Mosiah 11:24 RE)

See, I could raise money if I wanted to. I could raise a lot of money, if I wanted to. And if I raised money off the religion I preach, I could get a lot more done. Instead, I labor with my own hands, and I work nights, evenings, weekends. The amount of work that is going into the book that will come out next, that includes not just me but my wife and practically every spare moment that we have—involves enormous sacrifice. But it has exactly the effect—

We should esteem our neighbor as ourself, laboring with our own hands. We should not think that we are better than anyone.

If you take money from someone in order to advance your religious purpose, the mere act of doing that creates an inequality. It creates an arrogance. It creates—it removes the burden of sacrifice. It removes the humiliation of having to lose sleep and to fret and to worry about things and to face an uphill battle in everything that you do in order to please God. But you can't please God by taking advantage of your fellowman.

There have been changes to the ordinance. Isaiah 24:5 warned: *That the earth also is defiled under the inhabitants thereof; because they have transgressed the laws, changed the ordinances, broken the everlasting covenant* (see also Isaiah 7:1 RE). Those changes include the most single radical change to the temple endowment in 1990. In 2005, they eliminated washings and anointings. Before the January 2005 changes, washings and anointings were literal. The change made them only symbolic thereafter. That has significance, and I leave it to people to query why it has significance. I mean, there was a reason why Christ was anointed preliminary to his death by the woman that blessed and anointed him, and it was to preserve him into the resurrection. Now we don't do that.

There's a quest for popularity. Gordon B. Hinkley was the original employee and secretary for the (what was then called) Radio, Publicity, and Missionary Literature Committee in 1934, the predecessor to the Public Communications Department. By the time he became the 15th LDS Church President, his work had hardwired Public Relations into the institution.

Another problem has been the centrally-controlled, tightly-correlated rejection of teachings, which David O. McKay predicted would lead the church into apostasy. And I discuss this in *Passing the Heavenly Gift*; you can read about it there, if anyone's interested.

The history of gentile Mormonism has been a long downward path. I laid that out in *Passing the Heavenly Gift*. The Gentiles have walked away from the light and increasingly embraced darkness and foolish trust in men. All Mormon sects are now ruled by traditions contrary to the scriptures and commandments of God. They are asleep and cannot be awakened. God is now leading something new and left the leaders of all the various Mormon sects to find their own way.

Emma Smith, Sidney Rigdon, and William Marks said that without Joseph Smith there was no church. That comment was preserved by William Clayton in his diary in August of 1844, because to William Clayton that was offensive. The election had taken place on August the 8th, and so when Emma Smith, Sidney Rigdon, and William Marks said without Joseph Smith there is no church, he recorded it in his journal because he thought that was inappropriate and offensive. But they were right.

Following Joseph's death there was a complete overthrow of the church by the Quorum of the Twelve. The Quorum of the Twelve substituted themselves in the place of the equal distribution of power established by revelation. The First Presidency and the Quorum of the Twelve are supposed to be equal in authority. That's in 107 verse 24.

Joseph never moved a single apostle into the first presidency. They were independently equal bodies. Likewise, the Quorum of Seventy was equal with the Twelve (that's in 107:25-26) and, therefore, should be equal with the First Presidency, also.

The standing High Councils of Zion were also equal in authority. That's in 107:36&37. All the keys, to the extent that there were any, were and are held a hundred percent by the First Presidency, a hundred percent by the Twelve, a hundred percent by the Quorum of the Seventy, and a hundred percent by the High Councils. There was no primacy in the Twelve when originally organized by Joseph Smith according to revelation. In the years before Joseph's death, the Twelve were away from Nauvoo doing missionary work, as their calling required. Joseph spent his final three years in close association with the Nauvoo High Council, as the Nauvoo High Council minutes reflect.

Following Joseph's and Hyrum's deaths Emma remarked:

> Now as the twelve have no power with regard to the government of the church and the stakes of Zion; but the high council have all power, so it follows that on removal of the first president the office would devolve upon the president of the high council in Zion. The twelve were aware of these facts, but acted differently.

Emma was the wife of Joseph Smith, and I know that she's taken a lot of bad press from LDS Mormonism. And at one time, I enjoyed that same opinion, but these are comments that she made in the immediate aftermath of Joseph Smith's death.

None of the equality of these four different bodies survived Brigham Young. When Brigham Young assumed control, all equality was destroyed, and the church became an oligarchy run by the Twelve. This continues from Young until today. Now, the senior Apostle automatically becomes the Church President, an unscriptural and unwise system for consolidating power.

Equality among many has been replaced with the dictatorship of one. Here's another quote:

> *"Emma bore testimony to Lucy Massur that Mormonism was true as it came forth from the servant of the Lord, Joseph Smith, but said the twelve had made bogus of it."*

Bogus is another word for counterfeit. Bogus was always a reference to counterfeit money. Joseph cautioned the saints about violating God's trust. As he put it:

> *His word will go forth in these last days in purity. For if Zion will not purify herself, so as to be approved in all things in his sight, he will seek another people. For his work will go on until Israel is gathered. And they who will not hear his voice must expect to feel his wrath.*

That's in the *Teachings [of the Prophet Joseph Smith]*, page 18.

To the same effect, during the Mormon Reformation, Heber C. Kimball said: "We receive this priesthood and power and authority—if we make a bad use of the priesthood do you not see that the day will come when God will reckon with us and he will take it from us and give it to those who will make better use of it." That's in the *Journal of Discourses, Volume 6*, page 125.

George Albert Smith said essentially the same thing. Brigham Young said essentially the same thing.

We should expect God's house to be ordered around only one principle—repentance. When the pride of a great organization replaces repentance, the heavens withdraw; and when they do, amen to that portion of God's house.

The restoration through Joseph Smith will always remain, even if God chooses to order it differently before His return. It is His to do with as He determines best. He's now sent me as a witness.

The passing of Eldred Smith was a moment in time that reflects the cumulative effect of a lot of decisions, including and beginning with the initial overthrow of the government of the Church by the Twelve at the passing of Joseph and Hyrum; culminating in the final overthrow of the priesthood itself by the death of the discarded Eldred Smith and the discontinuation of the authority that was supposed to have been kept in honorable remembrance from generation to generation. God will bestow that authority again, and it will go forward, but it will go forward without these organizational pretenders that amass wealth and practice priestcraft.

At the beginning of the restoration, while Joseph was still alive, there was an abortive attempt to get founded what would necessarily need to be reestablished in order for there to be Zion. In a sermon that he delivered in August of 1843, he said that the fullness did not exist in the church; if it did, he wasn't aware of it, because the fullness required a man to become a king and a priest. Joseph Smith was made a king, by anointing, the following month on September 28th of 1843. The month before his anointing, he explained "no one in the Church held the fullness of the priesthood; for any person to have the fullness of that priesthood must be a king and a priest. A person may be anointed king and priest before they receive their kingdom." Wilford Woodruff recorded that in his journal on August the 6th of 1843.

The following month then, 28th of September 1843, Joseph was anointed a king and a priest; and the month after that, on October 8th [Internet sources suggest this happened on the 28th],1843, Hyrum Smith was likewise ordained to be a king unto God.

———————

The foregoing excerpts are taken from:

- Denver's *40 Years in Mormonism Series*, Talk #8 titled "A Broken Heart," given in Las Vegas, NV on July 25, 2014;
- The presentation of Denver's paper titled "Was There an Original," given at the Sunstone Symposium on July 29, 2016;
- A fireside talk titled "The Holy Order," given in Bountiful, UT on October 29, 2017;
- Denver's *40 Years in Mormonism Series*, Talk #9 titled "Marriage and Family," given in St. George, UT on July 26, 2014;
- A fireside talk on "Plural Marriage," given in Sandy, UT on March 22, 2015;

- A Q&A session titled "A Visit with Denver Snuffer," held on May 13, 2015; and
- His talk titled "Zion Will Come," given near Moab, UT on April 10, 2016.

In addition, Denver has written extensively about this topic. If you are interested in learning more, please review the following blog posts, among others:

Hyrum Smith, posted July 17th, 2012
Hyrum Smith, Part 2, posted July 18th, 2012
Hyrum Smith, Part 3, posted July 19th, 2012
Things Now Underway, posted December 25th, 2014
All or Nothing, 4, posted November 2nd, 2016
Cursed: Denied Priesthood, posted January 7th, 2018

75. Ministry of the Fathers

In this episode, Denver addresses the question: What is the ministry of the Fathers? What is their role in the restoration, both in heaven and on the earth?

———

DENVER: Now I tell that as background because I recently had another experience in which I spent, as it turned out once again, 40 days in pain. And while in a great agony, I could not take pity on myself. I couldn't. What I thought about was the suffering of our Lord in Gethsemane. And I found myself measuring my own physical misery against what I know our Lord went through there. And I lay in bed praying and thanking the Lord for what He had done on our behalf; thanking the Father for sending His Son and standing down to permit it to go forward. And while in prayer (quoting from his journal):

> I saw a great mountain and upon the top thereof was the glory of the Fathers. To reach the top, all were required to enter through a narrow pass. In the pass was a great beast, cruel and pitiless. The Lord brought people whom he had chosen to the mouth of the pass, and there He told them to wait for him, and He went away. The people did not wait for Him, but began to move forward into the narrow pass. The beast killed some and injured others, and none were able to pass through.
>
> After great losses, many deaths, and terrible suffering, the people chosen by the Lord withdrew and departed from the mountain. After four and five generations, the Lord again brought some few back to the pass, and again told them to stay at the mouth of the pass and wait on Him. But again, there were those who tired of waiting, for they could see in the distance the glory of the Fathers, and they desired to be there. These, being overtaken by their zeal, did not wait but moved into the pass where again the beast killed some or hurt them.
>
> Among those who waited, however, was a man who knelt and prayed, and waited patiently for his Lord. After a great time, the Lord came to this man and took him by the hand, and led him into the pass where the great beast guarded the way. As the Lord led, however, the beast was ever occupied with attacking others, and therefore its

back was turned to the Lord and the man. And so they passed by unnoticed, safely to the top.

The Lord sent the man to the Fathers, who when they saw the man inquired of him, "How came you to be here and yet mortal; for the last who came here were brothers who had been slain, and you are yet alive?" And the man answered, "I waited on the Lord, and He brought me here safely."

Well, for some reason, that was given in time to be read here this evening. And I can't say who the man is—maybe it's President Thomas Monson, maybe it's President Packer, maybe it's one of you. I just can't say. But the fact of the matter is that it is the glory of the Fathers, which Joseph was trying to explain in the last two talks he gave in Nauvoo.

The promise made by Elijah is about reconnecting us to the Fathers. Joseph called them the Fathers in heaven. These are not our kindred dead, because our kindred dead are required to be redeemed by us. These are the Fathers in heaven. Among them would be Abraham, Isaac, and Jacob; and because of this dispensation being what it is, Peter, James, and John.

The purpose of the Holy Ghost is to allow you to see things in their true light, with the underlying intent behind them, and to allow you to do that without distortion and without confusion. The temple is a ceremony designed to teach you about the path back to God; the very same thing that the Book of Mormon teaches repeatedly. The path back to God is so that you can meet with and be instructed by our Savior. The purpose of our Savior is to prepare us in all things so that we can, at last, become Zion. Because if your heart is right and my heart is right, and if I'm looking to God and God only, and you're looking to God and God only, then the trivial things—of having things in common—are of so little import that they matter not.

"Having been approved of God." It is God, and God's approval alone, that matters. It is what God regards of you. It is what is in your heart because God can detect what is in your heart. God knows why you do what you do. God knows why you say what you say. God knows what is in your thoughts. Therefore, to be approved of God is to be weighed against the standard of righteousness and not the whims of fashion. Fashion will come and go, ideas will be popular or unpopular. Righteousness will endure forever. This is the kind of man upon whom the words get spoken, "My Son." The Fathers, about whom I spoke in Centerville, had this association with God. They had this fellowship with God. They had this *sonship* with God. And they had *this priesthood* from God. And the hearts of the children need to turn to the Fathers—and that, too, because Elijah is coming to plant in the hearts of the children the promises that were made.

Now, I want to take another detour into parsing things in a way that you might not have considered before, and for this I want to go to Doctrine and Covenants section 128 and I want to look at verse 21. This is Joseph writing a letter that got canonized, and he's talking about all the stuff that had gone on in the process of getting the restoration fully established on the earth. And he mentions in this letter that he writes, these things:

> *And again, the voice of God in the chamber of old Father Whitmer, in Fayette, Seneca county, and at sundry times, and in divers places [throughout] all the travels and tribulations of this Church of Jesus Christ of Latter-day Saints!* [So the voice of God has been there throughout all of this, as Joseph presided and as the Church rolled forth.] *And the voice of Michael* [Micha-**el**], *the archangel; the voice of [Gabri-el]* ["El" being the name of God] *and of [Rapha-el], and of divers angels, from Michael or Adam down to the present time, all declaring their dispensation, their rights, their keys, their honors, their majesty and glory, and the power of their priesthood; giving line upon line, precept upon precept; here a little, there a little; giving us consolation by holding forth that which is to come, confirming our hope!* (D&C 128:21; see also T&C 151:15-17 RE)

So, I want to suggest to you that Michael, Gabriel, and Raphael are known to us as those who have come—though they were part of the "El," or in the plural form, the Elohim. They came and they served here. They came and they ministered here. Micha*el* descended, and he came to the earth and he was known as Adam in mortality. Gabri*el* came to the earth and he was known in mortality as Noah. There is a big debate over the identity of Rapha*el*. I'll tell you what I think and you can take it or leave it. Rapha*el* is the name that was given to the man who in mortality we know as Enoch.

Now, there are four angels who preside over the four corners of the earth. And Joseph *surely* knew that. And Joseph mentions the names of three of the four. But he leaves the fourth one out. And I find the absence of the fourth one rather extraordinary. The fourth one's name is Uri*el*, also one of the Elohim. And although there are those who will absolutely cry heresy, throw dirt on their hair, and tear their clothes because they are scholars, and they are *bona fide*, and they know I'm talking out of my hat—but I'd remind you Joseph talked out of his hat, too *[laughs]*. That fourth and missing, unmentioned angel is Uri*el*, who in mortality was known to us as John.

Adam is the one in the East, the angel who is considered the one who presides over and has control of the air; which is apt because unto Adam was given the Breath of Life in the beginning. Rapha*el* is in the South and he is associated with the power of fire; which is apt because of his fiery ascent with his people into Heaven. Gabri*el* is the angel in the West who has the power over water; which is apt because in mortality he managed through the Flood. And Uri*el*, though not mentioned, is the one who in the North has the power over the earth; which is apt because he remains upon the earth and he's the guardian at one gate with Elijah at the other end. But you can take and leave all that, as you will. I find the mention here in this letter by Joseph of these individuals, and these Powers, and these four—three of whom are named; the fourth of whom, potentially, is unnamed—to be interesting; though he does mention *divers angels, from Michael or Adam down to the present time* (ibid).

There has to be an opening that occurs in order to prepare the way. The opening at this end is going to be handled by someone who has remained behind, and the opening at the far end is going to be the one to whom the assignment was given to open the way for His return: Elijah, the one who was promised.

Now, I want to be really clear. I don't expect either of those individuals to have any public ministry *again*. They have a role in Zion, and those who dwell in Zion are going to have some contact with them. The three Nephites are a great example. They, like John, were given a similar ministry to remain around and to minister until the end of the earth. And they did minister. Two of the people to whom they ministered were Mormon and Moroni. They, like ministering angels, ministered to Mormon, who in turn ministered to the public. They ministered to Moroni (and kept his hope up in the waning days of that dispensation), but they did not minister publicly.

John will have a role, but the work of Zion is the work of *flesh and blood*. Men have to extend the invitation for God to return, so that men who extend that invitation are worthy of His return and the Lord can safely come without utterly destroying all who are upon the earth. Therefore you need Zion, among other reasons, in order for there to be a place and a people to whom the Lord can safely return without utterly destroying the earth at His coming. However small, however diminutive it may be, there needs to be a Zion that extends the invitation for the Lord to return.

Zion has been the promise of the Lord since the beginning. Adam foretold it at the great meeting in Adam-ondi-Ahman. I've spoken of that previously. I referred to that in a talk I gave in Centerville. I won't read it again. You can find it in D&C 107:56 (see also T&C 154:20 RE).

Enoch foresaw it. He prophesied concerning it. I've read that to you again today, even though I read it previously. Noah had it revealed to him by covenant—I read that to you today from the Joseph Smith translation of Genesis chapter 9. Moses was shown that it would be accomplished—I read that to you earlier today.

Now I want to change your view of one scripture, if I might. I want to take you to Luke chapter 9. You all think that the Mount of Transfiguration had a whole lot to do with Elijah, Moses, and keys, and the Kirtland Temple, and so on. It didn't have anything to do with that. It had to do with the head of the dispensation, Moses, and the one who brought that dispensation to a close, John the Baptist; appearing to Christ on the Mount, to hand off for the new dispensation.

But it also had— It had the purpose of fulfilling the covenant, the promise, the word of the Lord—*Christ*, who spoke concerning Zion. The Mount of Transfiguration is about Zion, as it turns out. And I can prove it from your scriptures.

Christ, in Luke chapter 9, beginning at verse 27, Christ prophesies: *But I tell you of a truth, there be some standing here, which shall not taste of death, till they see the kingdom of God.* That's the latter-day kingdom. That's the one that Christ said was not of this world, that He's going to come and inherit at the end. So He says some of you who are alive today will not die until you see Zion. The gymnastics that have gone into trying to explain that by both Christian, Catholic, and even Mormon commentators, is rather amusing. Keep reading though:

> *And it came to pass about an eight days after these sayings, he took Peter and John and James, and went up into a mountain to pray. And as he prayed, the fashion of his countenance was altered, and his raiment was white and [glistening]. And, behold, there talked with him two men, which were Moses and Elias: Who appeared in glory, and spake of his decease which he should accomplish at Jerusalem.* (Luke 9:27-31; see also Luke 7:4-5 RE)

So, He says some are living; they're not going to die until they see the Kingdom of Heaven. And then he takes those three up on the Mount, and they see some things. Turn to Doctrine and Covenants section 63, beginning —and He's talking about Zion—beginning at verse 20 of section 63:

> *Nevertheless, he that endureth in faith and doeth my will, the same shall overcome, and shall receive an inheritance upon the earth when the day of transfiguration shall come; When the earth shall be transfigured, even according to the pattern which was shown unto mine apostles upon the mount; of which account the fulness ye have not yet received.* (D&C 63:20; see also T&C 50:5 RE)

He promised them that they would get to see the latter-day triumph. He took three of them up on the mountain and he showed them the latter-day triumph. Therefore, there were those that were standing in that generation who did not die until they had seen the latter-day triumph of the Kingdom of God. He fulfilled His own word, and it was put into the gospel in that fashion for that reason.

It will happen! But it requires an awakening, and it requires an arising. It does not require a leader—a servant, maybe; not a leader. It does not require a president. It requires your common consent **by your deeds**; not only to say, but to do.

It will not be achieved by control. It will not be achieved by coercion. It will not be achieved by force. It will not be achieved because there's some big 'strongman' among you. It will only happen if each of you are strengthened in *your* faith and **know** the Lord. It *will* be achieved by humility. It *will* be achieved through meekness. It *will* be achieved by love which is unfeigned— the real thing.

Question #2: In the talk you gave in California you referenced Matthew 24, the signs of the last days; and that the signs have begun, and that it'll all get wrapped up within one generation. Would you be able to shine more light on the vague description of "one generation?"

Denver: Haha! *[laughs]* See, yeah! There've probably been as many Bible commentaries written on the definition of 'generation' as— One offered definition of generation is 'while the teachings/religion/movement remains in an unaltered state.' Almost invariably, however, the way a new revelation from heaven works is that God will reveal Himself in a generation. And then, when the prophet/prophets of that time (the mortals living, the messengers) die, what survives **cannot** be kept intact. It simply cannot be kept intact. You need another Peter; you need another Paul; you need another Moses; you need another one with that standing, or it falls into immediate disrepair. So, while there are living oracles that are in communication with God, that's the best definition of a generation. But you don't—you don't **add on** to the work of a prophet. It goes downhill.

From the death of Moses until the coming of John the Baptist, the only interruptions you get were when these singular men—Elijah, Isaiah, Ezekiel —came upon the scene; and their work was confined to them in that spot. You don't improve upon what God gives. When God gives something, it is living and it is breathing. It is like a fire that has been lit, and it exists until the flame goes out. But when the visions of heaven are gone because the recipient is no longer on the stage—it's what happened with the death of Joseph Smith. Now, I use his name here, and I say that I accept him as an authentic prophet.

All scriptures are focused on the Lord's ministry and message. They are one; and we err when we fail to see a consistent, overall testimony of the Lord's great plan of happiness for all of us within it. Christ's apparent defeat and death were but a prelude to His great triumph over death itself. For those who follow Him, defeat while alive is irrelevant, and ultimate defeat in death itself is irrelevant; because if you follow Him here below you'll be invited to follow Him to greater things above.

Well, ought not Christ to have suffered these things and to have entered into His glory? The answer is: of course. Everything that He did was according to a plan. Every step He took and everything that He taught was intended to bear witness of the ministry and the mission that He had. He satisfied all of the requirements; not only of the Law of Moses but of the Law of the Gospel as well, which He was in the process of introducing to them.

I find it always amusing to consider what was going on, on Mars Hill, when Paul arrived there; and they were always interested in hearing some new thing. When in fact, what Christ on the road to Emmaus wanted was not some *new* thing, but a clearer understanding of the things that had already been given—a clearer understanding of the testimonies that mankind had entrusted to them already; a clearer understanding that His work and His glory was intended to encompass not only Himself, as the Father of all those who will receive Him, but also intended to encompass our own immortality and eternal life.

Then in March of 1844, he picks up the subject again—the 10th of March, 1844. And this time, when he's talking about Elijah, he says:

> "The spirit...and calling of Elijah is...[to] have [the] power to hold the [keys] of the [revelations], ordinances, oracles, powers and endowments of the fulness of the Melchisedeck Priesthood and of the kingdom of God on the Earth; and to receive, obtain, and perform all the ordinances belonging to the kingdom of God, even unto the [sealing] of the hearts of the fathers unto the children, and the hearts of the children unto the fathers, **even those who are in heaven.**" (*History of the Church* 6:251)

The hearts of the **Fathers who are in heaven**; *that's* the mission of Elijah. If you will receive it, this is the spirit of Elijah: that we redeem our **dead** and connect **ourselves with our Fathers which are in heaven**—our dead through us; us to our Fathers in heaven. Who are our Fathers in heaven? Who are our Fathers in heaven to whom we are to be connected? We want the power of Elijah to seal those who dwell on earth to those which dwell in heaven. Those who are in the spirit world—our dead, the ones that need redemption from us—are not redeemed. They cannot be in heaven because they need **us** to be redeemed. **We** need to be redeemed by **our** connecting to the **Fathers who are in heaven**. The **dead** have to be redeemed; the **Fathers are in heaven**. Joseph understood this doctrine.

It is my view that the notion that you go to the temple and do genealogical work, to answer the coming of Elijah, does not conform to the description we're reading here from Joseph Smith. Our ancestors, our kindred dead, they need to be redeemed. They all have an interest in you and your life. And the work that is being done needs to be done. But the gulf that needs to be bridged through the work of Elijah, in the words of Joseph Smith, is to form a bond or a connection.

And of course, now, who was the last one who lived on the earth—not to hold the sealing power, but to ascend to heaven; and to draw together heaven and earth by his ascent—representing the opening of that way through which Zion above and Zion below will be connected with one another? Who was the last guide, as a mortal man, to have walked this path? Because when the Lord comes, He's coming with an entourage; and the path needs to be opened beforehand. And the path, once it's opened, allows men on the earth to be prepared for the coming again of those who are Zion above. Well, Elijah answers. Because Elijah is the one who made that connection.

Again, the doctrin of sealing power of Elijah is as follows if you have power to seal on earth & in heaven then we should be Crafty...first thing you do [is you] go...seal on earth your sons and daughters unto yourself, & yourself unto your **fathers in eternal glory**. (Ehat, Andrew F. and Cook, Lyndon W., *The Words of Joseph Smith*, pg. 331; emphasis added)

"Unto your fathers in eternal glory." That is not your kindred dead. They are relying upon you to be redeemed. The connection that needs to be formed is between you and the Fathers who dwell in glory. And who are the Fathers who dwell in glory? Well, if we go back to the revelation in which Joseph Smith received the sealing power—and he received the sealing power some time before 1831—in that portion of the revelation known as Doctrine and Covenants section 132, verse 49:

> *I am the Lord thy God...will be with thee even unto the end of the world, and through all eternity; for verily I seal upon...your exaltation...prepare [you] a throne for you in the kingdom of my Father, with Abraham your father. I say unto you...whatsoever you seal on earth shall be sealed in heaven...whatsoever you bind on earth, in my name by my word, saith the Lord, it shall be eternally bound in the heavens...whosoever sins you remit on earth shall be remitted eternally in...[heaven];* and so on. (D&C 132:49,46)

Just before that portion of the revelation, in verse 37, he talks about Abraham, he talks about Isaac, and he talks about Jacob. And then concerning those three, the Lord says to Joseph: *Because they did none other things than that which they were commanded, they have entered into their exaltation, according to the promises, and sit upon thrones, and are not angels but are gods* (D&C 132:37).

This is Abraham, Isaac, and Jacob. These are the ones who are gods. And so when Christ—and I think Christ is deliberate about everything He says about the analogies that He uses, and about the stories that He tells. When Christ takes occasion in a parable to tell someone about the status of heaven, the story that He tells is about Lazarus and a rich man. And it says concerning the beggar, Lazarus, when he died he was carried by the angels into Abraham's bosom. So, the dead man Lazarus, with an angelic accompaniment, is taken to Abraham's bosom when he dies. And so the definition of a reward in the afterlife is to go to the bosom of Abraham.

And see, the rich man is dead and he cries. And the rich man, who is now in a state of torment, he cries out. He does not cry out, in Jesus' story, to God. He cries out to Abraham. So when Jesus is describing positions of authority in the afterlife, a person He puts into a position of authority in the afterlife—to answer the petition of the dead rich man for relief from his torment—is Abraham.

> *Father Abraham, have mercy on me, and send Lazarus, that he may dip the tip of his finger in water, and cool my tongue; for I am tormented in this flame. But Abraham said, Son, remember that thou in thy lifetime receivedst thy good things, and likewise Lazarus evil things: but now he is comforted, and thou are tormented.* (Luke 16:34-35; see also Luke 9:20 RE)

There is an equation. Everything will balance. The things that you suffer from —it is the Lord's intention to wipe away every tear. And, if you are one that chooses to inflict tears, then that will be recompensed as well. Because what will be restored unto you is exactly, as we began with Alma, what you send out. It is an equation, after all. Then the rich man cried out:

> *I pray thee therefore, father, that thou wouldest send him to my father's house* [Send Lazarus to my father's house]...*I have five brethren;* [he can] *testify* [to] *them, lest they also come into this place of torment. Abraham* [said] *unto him, They have Moses and the prophets; let them hear them. And he said, Nay, father Abraham: but if one went unto them from the dead, they will repent...said unto him...they hear not Moses and the prophets, neither will they be persuaded, though one rose from the dead.* (Luke 16:27-31; see also Luke 9:20)

Foreshadowing, of course, rejection of the Lord's resurrection and testimony as well.

Understand, I assumed God, and angels, and the heavens themselves were wide open to all of you. I assumed it was a common experience for people to have angelic ministrants. I had every expectation that sooner or later, you're just going to find yourself in the presence of angels, because that's what the restoration is all about. So I had no doubt that that would happen.

I had an experience in which I did encounter an angel. He had very little to say, but he certainly would've answered a question if I'd put one. The words that he said to me were, "On the first day of the third month, in nine years, your ministry will begin, and so you must prepare." And then he waited.

Now, some things that ought to be obvious, if that's a statement that's made, is, "Okay, how does one prepare? What is this ministry? What are you talking about? How am I to do what you just suggested I ought do?" But I wasn't doing *that*. I was looking at him; I was looking at the clothing; I was looking at the scene. I was trying to take in— And there were things that were visible that were odd to me: art, for example. And I thought, Why would you have artwork in the afterlife or in the eternities, or...? I was like a tourist. If I'd had spray paint, I might have sprayed 'Denver was here.' I may have behaved really poorly, but I did not ask a question. So, he leaves. I am left thinking about that scene, and I can conjure it back up into my mind. I can see that moment right now, and it's been decades.

Well, I didn't, at that time, know that you ought to keep a journal. I didn't, at that time, know that you ought to keep a record and know dates. But I kept it in my mind, and I did what I thought was a calculation. And I calculated out when the first day of the third month, in the ninth year, had arrived. And on that date I'm expecting, Hey, hey! Something big! And the date comes, and the date goes, and nothing happens—just another day in school. It's just nothing at all. So I thought, "Okay, 'and so you must prepare' is how heaven gets out of this. I didn't prepare, so it's my fault. I blew it. Not worthy, not prepared. Shoot! I wish I had known what I should have done." Because obviously, I had not done it.

The next year, on the first day of the third month, on my door comes a LDS bishop and Sunday School president to call me to be the new Gospel Doctrine teacher for the ward. It was actually a few days *after* they had extended to me the request that I teach gospel doctrine, that I went back and realized it was the first day of the third month. And then I went back and recalculated everything. And because I had not kept a record, I had assumed that the nine year calculation began from the year in which I was baptized, which was 1973. But it had been some time, apparently months later in '74, so I was off by a year in my calculation.

I hope you realize that God is real, and that He is as concerned about you and *your* day, and in *your* life, as He was concerned about Peter, or Paul, or John, or Mary, or Elizabeth, or Abraham, or Sarah. Every one of you matter to Him. And if He were to speak to you out of heaven today, He would call you by name, just as He has done with everyone to whom He's ever spoken. And if the Lord calls you by name, it's not going to be by your full legal name, it's not going to be by what's on your birth certificate. He will call you by that name your best friend knows you. Because God is intimate with every one of us. He knows everything, including the desires of your heart.

And even though we are all rough customers, the fact is the only reason you're here is because your heart is inclined to follow Him. Your aspirations, your desires, and your hopes can be perfect. And your conduct can be reprehensible. God takes into account the perfection of your hope, and He evaluates you based upon your most noble aspirations. And He's cheering you on to try and get you to move a little closer throughout your life to that ideal, that perfection that you would like to have. We get hungry, we get tired, we get ill, we get weak; and so we excuse ourselves. But through it all we can maintain the aspiration, the hope, the love of Christ. If you do that, He will take that into account as He deals with you.

In the name of Jesus Christ. Amen.

————

The foregoing excerpts are taken from:

- A fireside talk on "The Temple," given in Ogden, Utah on October 28th, 2012;
- Denver's *40 Years in Mormonism Series*, Talk #5 titled "Priesthood," given in Orem, Utah on November 2nd, 2013;
- His talk titled "Zion Will Come," given near Moab, Utah on April 10th, 2016;
- Denver's *40 Years in Mormonism Series*, Talk #6 titled "Zion," given in Grand Junction, Colorado on April 12th, 2014;
- Denver's *Christian Reformation Lecture Series*, Talk #2, given in Dallas, Texas on October 19th, 2017;
- His talk titled "Christ's Discourse on the Road to Emmaus," given in Fairview, Utah on April 14, 2007;
- His talk titled "The Mission of Elijah Reconsidered," given in Spanish Fork, Utah on October 14th, 2011;
- His remarks titled "Remember the New Covenant," given at Graceland University in Lamoni, IA on November 10, 2018; and
- Denver's *Christian Reformation Lecture Series*, Talk #3, given in Atlanta, Georgia on November 16, 2017.

76. Patriarchs

In this episode, Denver addresses the question: What can you tell us about Patriarchs and the Patriarchal Priesthood? Is it on the earth now, and how can we learn more about it?

————

DENVER: Everything about what it is that Abraham was seeking— All of this ties together because there is *only* one gospel.

In the Lectures on Faith, the second lecture, paragraphs 37 to 53, there is a chronology given. I'm not gonna go through the chronology, and you needn't have brought it with you tonight. But that chronology is listed in the Lectures on Faith in order to save you the trouble of going through and tracking it yourself. But, it was important enough to Joseph Smith to put it into the Lectures on Faith so that you know how to reconstruct the Fathers, who they were.

Noah was 502 years old when Shem was born. Ninety-eight years later, the flood came. Noah was 600 years old when the flood came. Shem was 98. (You can see that in paragraph 45 of the second lecture.) Shem lived to be 600. Shem was 448 years old when Noah died. Shem was acquainted with both Noah and Abraham. Abraham lived to be 175 years old (and Shem was alive) and [was] a contemporary *with* Shem for 150 of the 175 years of the life of Abraham. Shem knew Noah, and Shem knew those on the other side of the flood, having lived with them for 98 years before the flood.

Abraham had the records of the Fathers. Look at Abraham chapter 1, verse 31:

> But the records of the fathers, even the patriarchs, concerning the right of
> Priesthood, the Lord my God preserved in mine own hands; therefore a
> knowledge of the beginning of the creation, and also of the planets, and of
> the stars, as they were made known unto the fathers, have I kept even
> unto this day, and I shall endeavor to write some of these things upon this
> record, for the benefit of my posterity that shall come after me. (See also
> Abraham 2:4 RE)

Since Abraham was acquainted with the priesthood that belonged to the Fathers; and since Abraham had a knowledge that was reckoned from priesthood that goes back to the time of the Patriarchs, he, as a consequence of possessing that, knew about the beginning of creation, knew about the planets, knew about the stars *as* they were made known unto the Fathers. Go back to Doctrine and Covenants section 121. It's talking about our dispensation. I want to look at it beginning about verse 28:

> *A time to come in the which nothing shall be withheld, whether there be one God or many gods, they shall be manifest* [because that's included within the knowledge that the first Fathers had. That's included with what was here at one time]. *All thrones and dominions, principalities and powers, shall be revealed and set forth upon all who have endured valiantly for the gospel of Jesus Christ. And also, if there be bounds set to the heavens or...the seas, and to the dry land, [and] to the sun, moon, or stars—All the times of their revolutions, all the appointed days, months, and years, and all the days of their days, months, and years, and all their glories, laws...set times,* **shall** *be revealed in the days of the dispensation of the fulness of times—According to that which was ordained in the midst of the Council of the Eternal God of all other gods before this world was, that should be reserved unto the finishing and the end thereof, when every man shall enter into* **his** *eternal presence and into* **his** *immortal rest.* (D&C 121:28-32; see also T&C 138:21 RE, emphasis added)

Abraham is not merely talking about something both in this verse, Abraham 1:31, as well as what we encounter later on in the Book of Abraham about the various stars that were shown to him and the relationship between them and his Facsimile No. 2, as I recollect, that is an effort to lay out a relationship in the heavens between certain positions of glory and authority. But Abraham is testifying that it was part of the original gospel that was entrusted to the Fathers and that those records were handed down to him.

In Doctrine and Covenants section 121, we find out that that's part of what is supposed to have been included within and is ultimately scheduled for revelation to those that will receive the restoration of the gospel when it is fully upon the earth in the dispensation of the fullness of times.

Abraham's record is a testimony about this knowledge of the heavens. Such knowledge was part of the original gospel that was entrusted to the Fathers. The records of the first Fathers were handed down to him.

We are told likewise in Doctrine and Covenants section 121 *that* knowledge is part of what is supposed to be included within and is ultimately scheduled for revelation *to* those who will receive the restoration of the gospel when it is fully upon the earth in the dispensation of the fullness of times. This knowledge can only return to us through revelation. When it does return, then we, like Abraham, will be at last in possession of the gospel Abraham knew, studied, and taught.

Though the Egyptians tried to preserve the things that came down from the beginning— As we read in the Book of Abraham, the Pharaoh sought *earnestly to imitate [the] order* (Abraham 1:26; see also Abraham 2:3 RE) that came down from the beginning, and the Pharaoh succeeded in large measure in doing that. And he was a righteous man.

> *Pharaoh, being a righteous man, established his kingdom… judged his people wisely…justly all his days, seeking earnestly to imitate that order established by the fathers in the first generations, in the days of the first patriarchal reign, even…the reign of Adam, as also Noah, his father.* (ibid, vs. 26; vs. 3 RE)

Pharaoh was not out there freelancing. He was trying to imitate something, and Egypt did a good job of preserving some things that had fallen into decay elsewhere, but—

The restoration through Joseph Smith and the promises that were made to the Fathers and the statement that was made by Moroni to Joseph on the evening that he came to him and talked about and reworded the promise given through Malachi— All of these are pointing to something that is at this moment still incomplete; a work that is at this moment still undone; a project that remains for *us* if we will receive it to finally *receive*. This points to a work that at this moment is still undone, a project that remains for *us* if we will receive it. But it will require revelation from heaven to be able to restore it. Therefore, it will require people willing to receive new revelation.

Because the way in which Zion is going to come about is going to necessarily be something that is *so* comfortable and *so* familiar on the earth—as a pattern reflecting what it is that exists in the heavens—*that* they who come not only do not burn them up, but they fall upon them, and they kiss their necks (because at last, they have a sister and a brother on the earth united by belief, united by covenant, united by knowledge, united by light and truth or, in other words, the glory of God which is intelligence)—because the purpose of the gospel has always been to inform, to edify, to raise up, to instruct. It was never meant to be reduced to something that is merely repetitious. It was intended to challenge you to your very core in what you do and what you think and how you act. It's intended to make you *godlike* in your understanding.

If you view priesthood as a *brotherhood* or an *association*, then I want to suggest that the way in which you should parse the three orders of priesthood is to parse them this way: As among men, it's merely a brotherhood of men. As between mankind and the heavens, the first order is an order in which there is an association between men and angels. The second order is an order in which there is an association between mankind and the Son of God. And the third order, the highest order—the *Patriarchal Order*—brings one into contact with the Patriarch who, of all the names that He could choose to be called by, chooses to have us call Him *our Father who art in heaven*—the third grand order being Sonship to the Father and association with Him who sits in the bosom of eternity and sustains all the creation.

The highest priesthood is an association with the Father brought about as a consequence of the Father calling, *My son.* It is the Holy Order after the Son of God because those who inherit that become, by definition, His sons. They are the Church of the Firstborn because they are in association with and made by the Father equal to all those who rise up to be Firstborn.

The other reason why I think Patriarchal ought to be viewed as the highest form is because the priesthood which began with Adam was priesthood which was after the Order of the Son of God.

That Priesthood after the Order of the Son of God descended from Adam down to the time of Enoch, and then it got renamed the Priesthood after the Order of Enoch. These are the Patriarchs, and therefore, their priesthood, in the original form of the Holy Order, can rightly be named Patriarchal Priesthood because it was the priesthood of the original Patriarchs of mankind.

When Adam promises that the priesthood that was in the beginning is going to return at the end of the world, also (Moses 6:7-8; see also T&C 154:21 RE), he is talking about a return at the end of the world of that priesthood which was held by the original Patriarchs—a time when, for generations, it was unitary; there was only one. And the designation, the correct designation, of that priesthood is the Holy Priesthood or the Holy Order after the Order of the Son of God. It's a long name, but it was that priesthood that was held by the Patriarchs.

As a consequence of it being that priesthood held by the original Patriarchs (which *was* in the beginning of the world and is to return at the end of the world, also), I prefer to regard the highest order under the name designation of Patriarchal Priesthood.

If you go to Doctrine and Covenants section 84, verse 6: *And the sons of Moses, according to the Holy Priesthood which he received under the hand of his father–in–law, Jethro* (See also T&C 82:3 RE)— Now, just to remind you about this: Jethro was a Midianite; he was a descendent of Midian; Midian was the son of Keturah; Keturah was the wife of Abraham after Sarah. After Sarah died, Keturah bore him children, one of whom was Midian. The birthright had already been given to Isaac.

See, there is so much— There is so much about the priesthood that has yet to be clarified, and I think that is a good thing, and I'm not going to clarify enough for mischief to ensue.

But the fact of the matter is that *that* priesthood which Abraham handed to Midian which then descended down and came to Moses did not possess the birthright—didn't possess that. Therefore, it was not the same thing as the priesthood that had belonged previously to the Patriarchs. It was something less, and it was something different.

But Moses obtained *that* priesthood through Jethro, a Midianite—not even an Israelite—because Midian was named at the same time genealogically as Isaac. And it would be Isaac's son Jacob who would be named Israel, and it was Israel who possessed the birthright that descended down. And so, Moses inherited a *form* of priesthood that was, by its very nature, lesser. It's one of the reasons why the prophets of the Old Testament all had to be ordained directly by heaven in order to obtain what they obtained.

Because of apostasy by the overwhelming majority of Adam's posterity, Abraham was born into apostasy. Abraham's struggle to overcome an apostate world qualified him to be the Father of the righteous. His struggle to return and reclaim faith is the model mankind would see, with very few exceptions, forever after. He was the prototype of *everyman* in a post-deluge world, cut off from God, the Patriarchs, and cut off from the Garden.

Abraham's chosen son with whom the covenant would continue was Isaac. God renewed the covenant with Isaac and again with Jacob and again with Joseph.

But Abraham married after the death of Sarah. His wife, Keturah, bore him sons, also. Among these was Midian. Generations later, the chosen line was devoid of priesthood, but through Midian, a descendant named Jethro was still a priest whose line of authority reckoned back generations. This priest (who had seven daughters) ordained Moses to the very priesthood that allowed him to enter God's presence.

From this we know the house of God extended beyond the Biblical narrative involving Abraham's lineage. God's house included generations of righteous, priesthood-empowered, independently functioning families lost to the scriptural record in our memory.

Anciently, it was by descent through a family line. In Adam's day the eldest worthy, surviving son—Abel was replaced by Seth—held the priesthood in each generation. The accounts in Moses 6:10-23 (See also: Genesis 3:15-23 RE) and in D&C 107:41-53 (See also T&C 154:9-19 RE) are both preserving the priesthood lineage during the era of the Patriarchs. Abraham reconnected to that line and reestablished Patriarchal authority for himself and four generations that followed. Following Moses, the tribe of Levi and the family of Aaron held *an* office.

In the LDS Church, common consent has been used for all but one office, the Patriarch to the Church. *It* was filled through patrilineal succession. Hyrum, as the older brother, held this right, and that's according to D&C 124:91 (see also T&C 141:32 RE), which would continue *from generation to generation, forever and ever*—D&C 124:96 (ibid, vs. 32 RE).

That office has been discarded, and its last occupant, Eldred G. Smith, was made emeritus by President Kimball October 6, 1979, and later died on April 4, 2013, at which point that line came to an end. That also will require a new restoration which will be part of the dispensation completion in this day.

QUESTION: As a second witness then, which you have proclaimed you are, how is the Savior working through you to continue the restoration He began through Joseph Smith?

DENVER: God could, does, and will work through anyone who awakens and then pays attention. There's an army of witnesses and awakened individuals that are being assembled by God.

It's required to know Him, and I know Him. I've been taught and understand His gospel.

The first task is to assure people that He lives, and His gospel exists as an authentic method for saving souls. The second task is to remember the restoration Joseph gave his life to begin. We're ungrateful when we fail to remember and practice *it*.

At the moment, there is almost no clear understanding of that gospel. I'm working to set that up in a comprehensive way. It's never been completed. There's a great deal prophesied to roll out as part of the restoration that has not even commenced! Do we have Zion? What about the lost teachings of the brass plates? Do we have the rest of the Book of Mormon? Do we have the Testimony of John? Do we have restored knowledge of the Jaredites? The list could be very long. But the fact that there *is* a list *tells* us that the restoration *must resume* at some point in order to be completed. We don't have it on the table—but we've forgotten what we once had.

So, the first job is to show that we're grateful enough to remember and to remember it in a fulsome, comprehensive way before God is going to say, "Now, I will permit it to move forward." We haven't gotten to the point of remembering yet which is why we ought to be studying a lot more diligently the material we got in the restoration. We ignore it at our peril.

QUESTION: In the Phoenix or Mesa lecture (or whatever you want to call it —it's called different things by different people) back in September of last year [September 9, 2014], a very powerful moment in time, in my opinion, both personally in my family and among many people who were there because they related it to me, you stated: "The Lord has said to me in His own voice, 'I will bless those who bless you and curse those who curse you.' Therefore..."—just continuing quoting you:

> I want to caution those who disagree with me...feel free,...feel absolutely free to make the case against what I say. Feel free to disagree [to] make your contrary arguments. If you believe I err, then expose the error...denounce it. But take care; take care about what you say concerning me for your sake, not for mine. I live with constant criticism. I can take it. But I do not want you provoking Divine ire by unfortunately chosen words if I can persuade you against it. (Talk 10, Preserving the Restoration, p. 4)

My question: In Genesis 12:3, the Lord said to Abraham essentially the same thing. *I will bless them that bless thee,...curse [them] that [curse] thee* (see also Genesis 7:1 RE). Abraham was further blessed to be the Father of many nations, that in him *shall all families of the earth be blessed* (ibid, vs. 3; vs. 1 RE). Abraham was a prophet. Isaac, Jacob— They were prophets. Abraham referred to the Fathers going all the way back to Adam. (You spoke about that in your talk on plural marriage and elsewhere.) It seems that there is something significant about connecting to the Fathers. Abraham was a Patriarch. The LDS Church no longer has a presiding Patriarch, as we've discussed, or even such an office anymore. Is there a Patriarch on the earth today who can connect us to the Fathers?

DENVER: Well, the simple answer is that there is *always* one on the earth. That has been true from Adam to the present time, yeah. Remember that in Nauvoo, the Lord offered to reconnect the saints but clearly defined the condition for that to happen was necessarily an acceptable temple where He could come and restore the connection. The reconnection is ordinance-based and will require an acceptable temple before it goes beyond the single representative.

Well, the notion that Christ has a mission, has a destiny for mankind; the idea that His glory necessarily encompasses us; the idea that the temple anciently divided things into three levels of holiness; and the idea that His plan is robust enough—that His glory is robust enough—to provide for both the immortality on the one hand and eternal life on the other hand of mankind suggests a Lord who is collegial, who is friendly, who is social, who is as interested in you as you may be curious about Him; a person who, in describing His own glory necessarily includes within it others, is the kind of being worthy of worship and worthy of admiration.

In January of 1844— Now this is some eight years post-Kirtland Temple. This is in January of 1844. Joseph is talking about Elijah, and he says: "The Bible says, 'I will—'" This is taken from [a talk] in front of Robert D. Foster's hotel nearby the Nauvoo Temple, then under construction, in Wilford Woodruff's journal. "The Bible says, 'I will send you Elijah—'" Boy, he put quotes in it, too. Good for Wilford! Man, he's better than my transcription machine in that respect.

> The Bible says, "I will send you Elijah before the great & dredful day of the Lord [of course, he misspelled *dreadful*. He spells it like *dredlocks*, instead of like—] day of the Lord Come that he shall turn the hearts of the fathers to the Children...the hearts of the Children to their fathers lest I Come...smite the whole earth with a Curse," Now the word turn here should be translated (bind or seal) But what is the object of this important mission or how is it to be fulfilled, The keys are to be delivered the spirit of Elijah is to Come, *to* be delivered, *to* come, The gospel *to* be esstablished. Saints of God gatherd Zion built up, & the Saints to Come up as Saviors on Mount

Zion. How are they to become Saviors on Mount Zion by building...temples erecting Baptismal fonts & going...& receiving ordinances, Baptisms, Confirmations, washings anointings ordinations & sealing powers upon our heads in behalf of all our Progenitors who are dead & redeem them that they may come forth in the first resurrection & be exhalted to thrones [and so on]. (*The Mission of Elijah Reconsidered*, p. 16, Transcript, emphasis added; see also *Wilford Woodruff Diary*, January 1844)

And then Joseph laments. This is the only guy— This is an important talk, and this is the only guy that records this—Wilford Woodruff. And Woodruff records Joseph saying:

I would to God that this temple was now done that we might go into it & [get] to work & improve [on] our time & make use of the seals while they are on the earth...the Saints have none [too] much time to save & redeem their dead,...together [with] their living relatives that they may be saved also, before the earth will be smitten. (ibid, p. 16; see also *Wilford Woodruff Diary*, January 1844)

And then this is the place where Joseph says— He's talking about Elijah. He's talking about the seals being on the earth, and he's talking about preparing for Zion. And in this context in January of 1844, this is where Joseph says:

[There's] been a great difficulty in getting anything into the heads of this generation. [It's] been like splitting hemlock knots with a Corn doger for a wedge & a pumpkin for a beetle. Even the Saints are slow to understand [I've] tried for a number of years to get the minds of the Saints prepared to receive the things of God, but we frequently see some of them after suffering all they have for the work of God, will fly to peaces *like glass* as soon as anything Comes [that's] contrary to their traditions, *they cannot stand the fire at all* How many will be able to abide a Celestial law & go through & receive their exhaltation, I am unable to say, [but] many are called & few are chosen. (ibid, p.17; see also *Wilford Woodruff Journal*, January 1844, emphasis added)

But in March of 1844, he picks up the subject again—the 10th of March, 1844—and this time, when he is talking about Elijah, he says:

The spirit...and calling of Elijah is...[to] have [the] power to hold the keys of the revelations ordinances, oricles powers & endowments of the fullness of the Melchizedek Priesthood & of the Kingdom of God on the earth &...receive, obtain & perform all the ordinances belonging to the Kingdom of God...even unto the [sealing] of the hearts of the fathers unto the children & the hearts of the children unto the fathers *even those who are in heaven.* (ibid, p.17; see also *Wilford Woodruff Journal,* March 1844, emphasis added)

The hearts of the *Fathers who are in heaven*— That's the mission of Elijah. If you will receive it, this is the spirit of Elijah: that we redeem our *dead* and connect *ourselves* with our *Fathers* which are in heaven.

"Go to and finish the temple, and God will fill it with power, and you will then receive more knowledge concerning this priesthood." (*Teachings of the Prophet Joseph Smith,* p. 323)

This statement is another reason I suggest the third or highest form of the priesthood should be called Patriarchal Priesthood. Joseph's words suggest *that* ordination to what I call the middle Melchizedek Priesthood could occur outside the temple. He had given those ordinations to others. But for what he calls the Patriarchal Priesthood, it required something which, by its *nature,* necessitated the completion of the temple and required the presence of God.

To restore this fullness, as the revelation given in January 1841 recounts, *it* needed God to come to accomplish. *For there is not a place found on the earth that He may come to and restore again that which was lost unto you or which he hath taken away, even the fullness of the priesthood* (D&C 124:28; see also T&C 141:10 RE). It requires *Him, God,* to come *to* that place, and for *Him, God,* to restore *to* you that which has been taken away—the fullness.

"Go to [you] finish the temple,...God will fill it with power...you will then receive more knowledge concerning this priesthood." (*Teachings of the Prophet Joseph Smith,* p. 323)

The foregoing excerpts are taken from:

- Denver's *40 Years in Mormonism Series,* Talk 4, titled "Covenants," given in Centerville, Utah on October 6, 2013;
- Denver's *40 Years in Mormonism Series,* Talk 5, titled "Priesthood," given in Orem, Utah on November 2, 2013;

- Denver's *40 Years in Mormonism Series*, Talk 10, titled "Preserving the Restoration," given in Mesa, Arizona on September 9, 2014, including footnote 51 found on page 10;
- A Q&A session titled "A Visit with Denver Snuffer," held on May 13, 2015;
- His talk titled "Christ's Discourse on the Road to Emmaus," given in Fairview, Utah on April 14, 2007; and
- His talk titled "The Mission of Elijah Reconsidered," given in Spanish Fork, Utah on October 14, 2011.

77. Authentic Christianity, Part 1

This is the first part of a special series titled "Authentic Christianity," in which Denver addresses the questions: What is Authentic Christianity? How does it differ from Historic or Modern Christianity? Why are there so many divisions between denominations? What is God up to today regarding Christianity?

———

DENVER: I want to talk about religion, but I don't want the topic to be what it usually is, and that's a source of unease, and friction, and conflict, and debate, and discomfort, and—

I mean, religion is one of those things where we find it really easy to do two completely contradictory things: love religion (because we want to be close with God), and take offense at our neighbor (because their religious views differ somewhat from our own), when in fact, the Author of the religion is telling us all to love one another. If we've got Christ in common, we ought to be able to de-emphasize our dissimilarities and emphasize our similarities to find peace in Him.

If you study the events that occurred following the New Testament—that immediate generation following the New Testament; you can see it in the book of Acts; you can see it in the letters of the New Testament—Christ commissioned twelve apostles, and He sent them out with a message to bear about Him. But Christianity in the immediate aftermath of Christ's life had various kinds of Christianity. We had a Matthean Christianity that was based upon the teachings of Matthew. We had a Pauline Christianity that was based upon the teachings of Paul. We had a Petrine Christianity, and it was based upon the teachings of Peter. It was the Petrine version of Christianity that ultimately got the broadest sweep that resulted in the formation of the Catholic Church. But Christianity did not start out centralized. It started out diffused. It's almost as if what Christ wanted to do was to get the word out and let everyone have in common some very basic things in which we could find peace, and love, and harmony with one another—but outside of that, to explore, perhaps, the depths of what the message could be and not to have it insular, rigid, and one-size-fits-all.

We had during that very earliest period—you had obviously commissioned companions that had walked with Jesus, had been witnesses of his teachings, he had brought them aboard, they had heard the sermon on the mount, they had witnessed miracles. John in his gospel makes it clear that they weren't really up to speed with what Christ was doing and what he was about, because he would say things and they wouldn't understand him. From John's gospel, what happened was it was retrospective. It was post-resurrection—when they knew now that Christ was going to come, he was going to die, and he was going to be resurrected, and then he was going to ascend into heaven to be in a position of glory—that they looked back retrospectively and they say, 'Ok, now I get it. Now I understand what he was talking about.' Now those statements about the necessity that he suffer come full circle and we get it. But walking with him during this time period, they were really not tuned in to comprehending what the Savior was intending to do and ultimately would do.

For a millennium-and-a-half the Christian church had a hierarchy, professional clergy, cathedrals, icons, pageantry, and provided social structure. Anything like Christianity's original, independently functioning groups, meeting in homes, and using donated resources as charity for their poor was long forgotten. The Reformation did not attempt to restore an original Christianity. The Reformers were victims of a structure that confined even their imagination. Their aim was much lower. It sought only to reform an admittedly corrupt institution into something marginally better. The rebellion of Martin Luther lead to the establishment of a new Christian institution that mimicked its mother. The Lutheran church bears striking similarities to its Catholic mother. To a casual observer of a Sunday service in both of these churches they can seem identical. The differences are not particularly cosmetic but are based on Lutheran rejection of the pope's authority.

There are three great Lutheran principals: first, grace alone; second, faith alone; third, scriptures alone. These deprive the Catholic pope of religious significance and the Catholic rites of any claim to be the exclusive way to obtain salvation. But none of these were part of original Christianity.

As to grace alone: in original Christianity baptism is *required* for salvation. Christ's simple command to "follow me" was given repeatedly; three times it's recorded in Matthew, twice it's recorded in Mark, once in Luke, and twice in John. Christ showed the way and as part of that he was baptized to—according to his own mouth—*fulfill all righteousness* (Matthew 3:15; see also Matthew 2:4 RE). It was only *after* Christ was baptized that the Father commended Jesus and said He was well pleased.

Christ also had his disciples baptize his followers—you can read about that in John chapter 4 (see also John 3:4 RE). Christ spoke to Saul of Tarsus on the road to Damascus and converted him by that contact. Following his conversion, Saul was healed of blindness, renamed Paul, and immediately baptized. Paul tied baptism to resurrection in Romans chapter 6 (see also Romans 1:25-28 RE). He declared that to be baptized is to put on Christ, in Galatians 3 (see also Galatians 1:7-12 RE). There is only one faith and it is in only the one Lord whom we worship and it requires one baptism to be included in the body of believers, according to Ephesians 4 (see also Ephesians 1:12-16 RE). Peter explained that baptism saves us, in 1 Peter chapter 3 (see also 1 Peer 1:2 RE).

Christians who follow Christ will all be baptized. (If you've not been baptized, or would like to be baptized again, there are those who have authority to administer the ordinance, who will travel to you, or there are some locally who are available to perform the ordinance. The ordinance is free. The service is provided without any charge or expectation of any gift or donation. If you're interested, you can make a request on the website that's identified in things that are around here (learnofchrist.org).

Accordingly, original Christianity believed and taught that baptism was essential to salvation, not merely grace. As to faith alone, the original Christians not only believed in baptism but they also believed they could progress in knowledge, obedience, and virtue. Paul denounced the idea that Christians could sin and follow God: *Shall we continue in sin, that grace may abound? God forbid. How shall we, that are dead to sin, live any longer therein?* (Romans 6:1-2; see also Romans 1:25 RE). Paul envisioned the Christian as becoming a new creation through baptism, after which we walk in Christ's path with sin destroyed: *We are buried with him by baptism unto death: that like as Christ was raised up from the dead by the glory of the Father, even so we also should walk in newness of life.* That's in Romans chapter 6 (Romans 6:4; see also Romans 1:25 RE).

Peter taught that Christians would progress in godliness until the Christian has his or her calling and election made sure:

> *That by these things ye might be partakers of the divine nature, having escaped the corruption that is in the world through lust. [And] beside this, giving all diligence, add to your faith virtue; and to virtue knowledge; and to knowledge temperance; and to temperance patience; and to patience godliness; and to godliness brotherly kindness; and to brotherly kindness charity. For if these things be in you, and abound, they make you that ye shall neither be barren nor unfruitful in the knowledge of our Lord Jesus Christ. But he that lacketh these things is blind, and cannot see afar of, and hath forgotten that he was purged from his old*

sins. Wherefore the rather, brethren, give diligence to make your calling and election sure: for if ye do these things, ye shall never fall. (2 Peter 1:4-10; see also 2 Peter 1:1-3)

As to scripture alone, Luther translated the Bible from a second language that was not commonly spoken—that is, Latin—into the common language of Germany, in order for the common man to read it. If scripture alone defined faith, given the illiteracy that had gone on for a millennium-and-a-half before Martin Luther's day, and given the fact that even the literate would have had to have been bilingual, (whatever country or language they spoke, Latin had become a dead language; they would have to be able to read and understand a dead language) then, by definition, if that's one of the keys to defining Christianity, Martin Luther just defined the overwhelming majority—practically all of the Christian world was incapable of salvation because scripture alone was unavailable to them as one of the required premises of Christianity.

There was no New Testament during the era of original Christianity. The idea of compiling a New Testament originated with a second century heretic who was excommunicated for apostasy. The only scriptures used or cited during the time of original Christianity was the Old Testament, containing none of the teachings of Christ, none of the letters of Paul, Peter, James, or Jude, and none of the four Gospels. It took until the fourth century for a New Testament canon to be settled. By that time many of the writings had been altered. Further, neither Christ nor his apostles handed out a New Testament. They testified of what they knew to be true and administered baptism as a sign of faith and repentance.

Despite this, Martin Luther was entirely correct in condemning Catholicism for its errors and excesses. Following Luther's example, other Protestant churches reformed Christianity in marginal ways. But reconsidering institutional Christianity, in attempting to return to its original form, was not even attempted in the Protestant Reformation. Therefore, Protestantism is only a marginal improvement from its corrupt mother church. It has never been, nor attempted to become, original Christianity.

A return to original Christianity would require a restoration. That did not begin until God spoke to Joseph Smith in 1820. But Joseph's followers also wanted an institution, and now have one of the most wealthy and self-interested institutions claiming to be a church. (They are undertaking approximately a trillion dollar real estate development as part of the Church's enterprise in the state of Florida, constructing everything that it will be necessary, from schools and streets to fire stations and homes, to house over half a million people just outside of Disney World, on what used to be 133,000 acre cattle ranch. That church owns about 3% of the state of Florida.)

Unlike the institutional Christianity of the 1500s, early Christians were called the *ecclesia*— meaning "a congregation or an assembly." But early Christians were not institutional and certainly not hierarchical. The first century of Christianity had no formal organization and no central control. Christians met informally in small groups and worshiped together in homes or public places. In this earliest form, small groups led by both men and women, who were called *deaconoisse*, a word that's translated into English as either "deacon" or "deaconess"; that Greek word means "servant." It was in these home meetings where original Christians worshiped and learned of Christ and Christianity.

Original Christians had no professional clergy. They operated in a way akin to a method described in the Book of Mormon:

> And when the priests left their labor to impart the word of God unto the people, the people also left their labors to hear the word of God. And when the priest had imparted unto them the word of God they all returned again diligently unto their labors; and the priest, not esteeming himself above his hearers, for the preacher was no better than the hearer, neither was the teacher any better than the learner; and thus they were all equal, and they did all labor, every man according to his strength. And they did impart of their substance, every man according to that which he had, to the poor, and the needy, and the sick, and the afflicted. (Alma 1:26-27; see also Alma 1:5 RE)

This is how I believe Christianity ought to be practiced today: without a professional clergy, diverting tithes and offerings that ought to be used to help the poor, needy, sick, and afflicted. We need to—and can return—to those early days of Christianity.

Justin Martyr lived from 110-165 A.D., and he wrote in the Sub-Apostolic Age. His writings give us a glimpse into how Christianity functioned in its earliest days. In his *First Apology* he describes Christian worship. They met in homes, having no church buildings.

Before being considered a Christian, a candidate was baptized "in the name of God, the Father and Lord of the universe, and of our Savior Jesus Christ, and of the Holy Spirit" (*First Apology*, Chapter LXI-Christian Baptism).

Meetings began with a prayer and "saluting one another with a kiss." Then sacrament was prepared and administered using a "cup of wine mixed with water" and bread, which is blessed by "giving praise and glory to the Father of the universe, through the name of the Son and of the Holy Ghost, and offers thanks at considerable length for our being counted worthy to receive these things at His hands" (ibid, Chapter LXV-Administration of the Sacraments).

The early Christians recognized there was an obligation for "the wealthy among us to help the needy." Therefore, after reading scripture and "the memoirs of the apostles or the writings of the prophets" donations were collected (ibid, Chapter LXVII-Weekly Worship of the Christians). Then the donations were distributed to help those who were poor or needy among that group of Christians.

These simple observances were resilient enough to preserve Christianity after the death of the apostles and before any great hierarchical magisterium arose. It was the power of baptism, the sacrament, scripture study and financial aid among believers that gave Christianity its power. But it was diffused, and therefore incapable of destruction. When Justin Martyr was slain, the scattered Christians continued unaffected. It was just like when Peter and Paul were slain, and before them, James was killed. The power of Christianity reckoned from the vitality of its original roots. These roots were in Christ, His message, His teachings, which were employed to relieve one another by the alms shared from rich to poor.

When a centralized hierarchy took control over Christianity, the money that was used for the poor, the widows and orphans, was diverted to build churches, cathedrals, basilicas, and palaces. Ultimately, the wealth generated by the generosity of Christian believers became the tool used by the hierarchy to buy up armies, kings, lands and treasures, which were used to rule and reign as a cruel master over a subjugated population made miserable by the abuse heaped on them from Rome.

Even after the Protestant Reformation, Christianity continued to be ruled by hierarchies. Cathedrals and church buildings consumed and consume resources that are to be used to help the poor. Christ built no building, although He accepted the temple in Jerusalem as His Father's house. Peter built no church building, nor Paul, nor James, nor John. Christianity in the hands of the Lord and His apostles needed no brick and mortar for its foundation. It was built on the hearts of believers, brought together by the charity and assistance shared between them.

Today Christianity is not benefited but weakened by hierarchies, cathedrals, edifices, and basilicas housing opulence, wealth and art. Although the prophecies foretell of a temple to God to be built in Zion, and another to be built in Jerusalem, there are no other structures foretold to be built by Christians or latter-day Israel. How much stronger would Christianity be today if wealth were reserved for the poor and hierarchies were stripped of their wealth?

We would not be undervaluing the gospel and overvaluing the churches if all donations went to aid the poor and none went to support the institutions. We have a hard time even imagining the earliest generation of Christians. We also have a tendency to use what we're familiar with as our guide and standard in trying to understand early Christianity. It affects even how we read our scriptures. I'd like you to try to abandon the picture that you have in your head and imagine a new picture in its place.

About 1,900 years ago the ministry of that generation of believers and witnesses drew to an end and the apostles then had their voices silenced. It would take until 1,675 years ago before there was an attempt to stabilize and define what it meant to be a Christian. Between the time of the death of the apostles and the council at Nicaea there's an interlude in which Christianity assumed extraordinarily divergent forms of Christian belief, many of which were completely contradictory of one another. If you read the ante-Nicene—the prior to Nicaea—fathers of Christianity, the debates, the contradictions, the descriptions—the content of Christian belief was remarkably unstable, unsteady, and very different irreconcilable versions. And 1,675 years ago now the Nicean council made an attempt to redefine what it meant to be Christian, and to stabilize the conflicting Christianities into something that would be singular, and therefore, define what it would mean to be an orthodox Christian. Coming out of Nicaea is a creed—the Nicean Creed—but it would take until about 1550 before the efforts to suppress divergent forms of Christianity succeeded far enough so that we had our orthodox Christian faith in a reasonably stable form.

It was about a 1,000 years ago now, when what is called the Great Schism occurred in which the east and the west divided between the church centered in Rome—the Roman Catholic, or Universal Church, and the Eastern Orthodox Church—divided from one another and no longer shared communion, hierarchy, or their faith in Christ together. It was 500 years ago when Martin Luther posted the *95 Theses* and set in motion the series of events that were discussed in the videos that we were showing just beforehand.

I assume all of you regard yourselves as Christians. I regard myself as a Christian. Today there are approximately 40,000 different Christian denominations. If you go back only 500 years, most of what you regard as Christianity—and in all probability the form of Christianity in which you believe—would not have existed. If you go back earlier still, whatever it is that you hold as your Christian belief—even the current form of Catholicism that's practiced—would be regarded as heretical by the Roman Catholic hierarchy itself. Only 500 years ago the only authorized forms of the Bible were printed in Latin and they were the exclusive property of a Catholic clergy that taught in Latin—a group of people who were told what to do and how to regard Christianity. Unfortunately for almost every one of us, the form of Christianity that we hold in our hearts and that we look to in faith, believing that it has the power to save us, would be regarded throughout almost all of Christian history as heresy, as false, as damnable.

Today—and I say these words advisedly, and I want you to take them seriously—today all Christian churches have become corrupt. They love money more and acquiring financial security and church buildings more than caring for the poor and the needy, the sick and the afflicted. The institutions claiming to be the church of God are all polluted by the cares of the world. I want you to understand what I mean by that. During the Apostolic Era there was no such thing as a Christian church building. Christians met in homes. They did not collect and compensate ministers. They gathered money and they used it to help the poor and the needy among them.

As soon as you get a church building, I regret to inform you, you'll have to hire a lawyer. In what name are you going to take title to your building? How are you going to hide title or hold title and deal with succession? What form will the organization take? Do you intend to qualify for tax deductibility? If so, do you intend to file as a charitable institution, as an eleemosynary institution, as an educational institution? Those are all words that you find in 501(c) of the Internal Revenue Code. And what do you do if you want to hire and fire a minister, and you want to dispossess the one you fired and put into possession the successor in the building, what rights, and who's on the board, and who possesses the right to deal with that? As soon as you own property, the cares of this world invade. It's unavoidable.

If you meet in homes as the early Christians did, and if you gather your tithing—one tenth of your surplus after you have taken care of all your responsibilities, all your needs, whatever's left over—one tenth of that is your tithe. After you gather your tithe then you ought to look at your brothers and your sisters who are there in your meeting, and you ought to help those who have needs, who have health needs, who have education needs, who have transportation needs, who have food needs, who have children that need care. Christians should take care of the poor among them, and no one should be looking at the flock and saying, 'I need your money to support myself.' Christian charities should be used to take care of the poor among you and not to engage in acquiring the cares of this world. This is why all Christian churches have become corrupt. They love money and acquiring financial security and church buildings more than caring for the poor and the needy, the sick and the afflicted.

I speak as part of a very tiny movement, but we're worldwide. We're a very small group of people scattered from Japan to Europe, scattered from Australia to Canada—small group of people, but we are trying to practice authentic Christianity in the form that it was originally intended to be practiced: meeting in homes. I met earlier today with a group of people from this local area, and there are a number in this local area who believe as I do. We celebrated the sacrament as a group together and we reaffirmed one another in our faith.

Jesus Christ taught many principals, truths, precepts, and commandments, but He only taught one doctrine. I'm going to read you Christ's doctrine:

> *Behold, verily, verily, I say unto you, I will declare unto you my doctrine. And this is my doctrine, and it is the doctrine which the Father hath given unto me; and I bear record of the Father, and the Father beareth record of me, and the Holy Ghost beareth record of the Father and me; and I bear record that the Father commandeth all men, everywhere, to repent and believe in me. And whoso believeth in me, and is baptized, the same shall be saved; and they are they who shall inherit the kingdom of God. And whoso believeth not in me, and is not baptized, shall be damned. Verily, verily, I say unto you, that this is my doctrine, and I bear record of it from the Father; and whoso believeth in me believeth in the Father also; and unto him will the Father bear record of me, for he will visit him with fire and the Holy Ghost. And thus will the Father bear record of me, and the Holy Ghost will bear record unto him of the Father and me; for the Father, and I, and the Holy Ghost are one. And again I say unto you, ye must repent, and become as a little child, and be*

baptized in my name, or ye can in nowise receive these things. And again I say unto you, ye must repent, and be baptized in my name, and become as a little child, or ye can in nowise inherit the kingdom of God. Verily, verily, I say unto you, that this is my doctrine, and whoso buildeth upon this buildeth upon my rock, and the gates of hell shall not prevail against them. And whoso shall declare more or less than this, and establish it for my doctrine, the same cometh of evil, and is not built upon my rock; but he buildeth upon a sandy foundation, and the gates of hell stand open to receive such when the floods come and the winds beat upon them. (3 Nephi 11:31-40; see also 3 Nephi 5:9 RE)

We believe and practice this doctrine of Christ. We practice baptism by immersion in living waters—meaning lakes, rivers, streams, and oceans: where there is life. We prefer living waters for a living ordinance. We have authority from God to perform baptism and other ordinances, such as the sacrament, but we are not jealous with our authority and are willing to share it with any man who is willing to accept and follow the doctrine of Christ.

As to the commandment to be baptized, even Jesus Christ went to be baptized by John *to fulfil all righteousness* (Matthew 3:15; see also Matthew 3:4 RE). *And now, if the Lamb of God, he being holy, should have need to be baptized by water, to fulfil all righteousness, O then how much more need have we, being unholy, to be baptized, even by water* (2 Nephi 31:5; see also 2 Nephi 13:2 RE).

If any of you want to be baptized you can request it through our website and someone local will respond. Baptism is an ordinance between you and Christ and does not mean you are joining a formal institution, because we have no institution. We are all equal believers accountable to God. We do try to fellowship with one another and you would be welcome to fellowship with the few believers in this area. We own no buildings; like the early Christians we meet in homes. We ask for tithes, or 10% of what you have left over after you've taken care of all your needs, but anything collected is then used to help anyone in the fellowship meet their needs. We hope for there to be no poor among us because we use donations to help one another.

We cannot bear one another's burdens without fellowshipping with one another, and bearing one another's burdens presumes that you know what the burdens are that someone else carries. Which means that I have been patient enough, I have been attentive enough, I have been friendly enough, and I have been trusted enough that I can find out what the burden is that they bear.

I have a very good friend—went to elementary, junior high, high school with him—and I've kept in touch with him for many years and he has recently contracted a terminal form of cancer. He called me to talk about that without telling his family, without telling his neighbors, without telling his friends because he and I have a friendship that is built upon the kind of trust that allows me to share that burden with him because of the relationship.

We're supposed to help one another get through this ordeal of mortality. And it is an ordeal. It is not easy. Even the people that you think you envy, if you were living inside their world you'd find out that they have burdens they are carrying as well.

Fellowshipping allows us to bear one another's burdens, and bearing one another's burdens implies a whole universe of connectivity, trust, confidence, friendship, and affection between one another before you get to the point that you even know what their burdens are. But *that* is supposed to be a blessing and part of what it means to worship together. Worshipping together, by assisting one another, allows all of us to feel a great part of what it is that Christ is and does. It allows us to know *who* we worship, and it allows us to know *how* to worship Him, and it allows us to know *what* makes us one with one another. Now, it's really hard to accomplish that across state lines, but it still can be done.

The example I use of that friend—he and I have spent a lot of time on the phone since I learned of the illness about a month ago, and that's because I care, and that's because he needs to talk to someone, and because he finds it a relief to be able to do that with me. It can be done. It can be done across any barriers.

All of us are victims of institutional abuse. Many of us can sense it when the slightest hint of abuse appears. One recent writer on your blog has identified it as 'paternalism' and that's not an inappropriate designation for it. We should learn how to be loving and equal with one another. The idea of equality is resisted by a lot of skeptics, who accuse me of wanting authority and control, when I despise control, but I absolutely welcome fellowship, equality, and worship with one another. This isn't easy, but it is godly to pursue and we're going to make mistakes and there are going to be a lot of institutional habits that we walk in and we want to 'whip this into shape.' The idea of a whip—when Christ resorted to the scourge to drive them out—he didn't drive them out to organize them. He drove them out to cleanse the place. If we're going to whip anything, we're going to drive them out. We would be better off practicing the kind of patience, and kindness—and to realize that in terms of Mormonism, almost everyone is a refugee suffering post religious trauma syndrome, and they're going to think you're abusive. They're going to think they want to be used as a tool for someone else's power base; someone wants to use you. The idea that there's someone that doesn't want to use them, or abuse them, but wants to fellowship with them, and help them bear a burden—that's the idea of Christianity at its core and *that's* what's really alien in this world. We need to bring *that* back again.

———

The foregoing excerpts were taken from:

- Denver's *Christian Reformation Lecture Series*, Talk #8, given in Montgomery, Alabama on May 18, 2019;
- Denver's *Christian Reformation Lecture Series*, Talk #2, given in Dallas, TX on October 19th, 2017;
- Denver's *Christian Reformation Lecture Series*, Talk #1, given in Cerritos, CA on September 21st, 2017; and
- A Q&A session titled *A Visit with Denver Snuffer*, held on May 13, 2015.

Today's podcast addresses important questions about authentic Christianity, but is only an introduction to ideas that listeners of any denomination may find important and relevant. These topics are more fully addressed in Denver's eight talks addressed to all Christians of every denomination, which are available to watch, listen, or download for free at learnofchrist.org.

78. Authentic Christianity, Part 2

This is the final part of a special series titled "Authentic Christianity", in which Denver addresses the questions: What is Authentic Christianity? How does it differ from Historic or Modern Christianity? Why are there so many divisions between denominations? What is God up to today regarding Christianity?

————

DENVER: People that have power tend not to be respectful of those that lack power. And if you can treat people as your servants, your slaves, your serfs, then you treat them accordingly. And so, Christianity developed into a monolithic and very abusive control, centered in the Roman clergy, headquartered in Rome. For a whole variety of reasons, including ambitious, local kings who wanted to declare their own independence from the Roman hegemony and who wanted their own ability to waylay the money that was being aggregated through the church and getting exported. They wanted to keep that money locally and get their own hands on it.

A moment came in 1517, when it was possible for Martin Luther, pricked as he was in his conscience, because he believed what Paul had written. He believed what Matthew, Mark, and Luke had recorded. He believed in the faith. And he saw that what was acting itself out on the stage of life bore no resemblance to the lofty perfection that is spoken of in the teachings of the New Testament. He simply had had enough, but his life was spared because politically there was a political leader who saw some advantage in providing protection to Martin Luther. And so, Martin Luther was spared from what had happened to others who had rebelled against Rome. He wasn't burned at the stake. He was instead allowed to post his disagreement. And ultimately found a new brand of Christianity, in which he believed it would be more authentically Christian, and less inauthentically autocratic and authoritarian. But just like what happened in the New Testament with the 12 apostles, immediately upon the emergence of Lutheranism, we get in the same generation—these people met and spoke with one another—John Knox, John Calvin, Zwingli, Martin Luther.

Not only did the fracturing of Roman hegemony cause Protestantism, but Protestantism immediately began to say, We disagree with you about... (choose your topic), and you have multiple Protestant denominations immediately springing into existence. And what had been coercive unity through Roman dictatorship and artificial unification of Christianity for a millennium and a half, immediately upon the first fissure showing up, you have fracture after fracture and disunity after disunity, because Christianity simply disagreed about so many things. And it was inconceivable, inconceivable to them that Christianity did not require you to divide up into mutually exclusive camps in which your brand of Christianity ought to be, at least claimed to be, superior to their brand of Christianity. And if heaven is only for those who have the truest form of Christianity, then those people really need to go to hell, because they aren't quite Christian enough in the truest way, in the most meaningful way, in the most correct way.

So, let's go back and read that verse again: *That in the dispensation of the fulness of times He might gather together in* **one** *all things in Christ, both which are in heaven, and which are on earth, in Him* (Ephesians 1:10, emphasis added; see also Ephesians 1:1 RE). All things. I don't know how many of you sitting here today hearing those who have spoken about Buddhism, or speaking about the Native American tradition, or speaking about Messianic Judaism, I don't know how many of you sitting here today have thought, That speaker has said something true, and I believe that. Whether you think that may be part of Christianity or the teachings of Christ or not, when you hear truth—The dispensation of the fulness of times, which has to occur before the return of the Lord, has to gather together in one *all things*. If that thing to be gathered has been fractured and lost to Christianity, but preserved in Hinduism; if that thing to be gathered is a truth lost to Christianity, broken away and preserved in Buddhism; if that thing to be gathered into one appears anywhere, then in the dispensation of the fulness of times, it all must be brought back and gathered into one.

If you take a piece of art, sculpture, and you fracture the sculpture into bits, and then you gather the bits and you reassemble them, you will not have the unity and the perfection of the original until every piece has been found, every piece has been gathered, and every piece has been put into its proper perspective. Only when they've all been gathered, and only when they've all been put in their proper place—because the sculpture ought not look like Picasso and the Cubists. It ought to look like what it was when originally formed. When that happens, so that you can now see the beauty that's there, then you've completed the gathering. But the prediction is that it will be gathered together in **one**—in Christ, so it doesn't matter if you're a Hindu, and you think Christ is outside—he is other than our tradition. Your tradition must be gathered home also into Christ, because it fits there. And if you're Buddhist and you say, 'Ours is not a religion, but a philosophy, a way of thinking, a way of disciplining the mind,' that way of thinking, that way of disciplining the mind, likewise must be gathered together in Christ for it to find its home. Because the purpose is the salvation and eternal life of every being, of every person. Until we gather all the parts, it is not possible to gather in one, all things that belong with Christ. The search must be global, the search and the invitation must cross cultures, traditions, religions.

You see, the philosophy that motivated Constantine in coercing Christian unity was the desire to see Christians not fight with one another. If you say fighting with one another is the evil end to be avoided, there are really only two ways to approach conquering that evil end to be avoided. One of them is to do what Constantine and the Popes have attempted and what some other centrally-controlled religious organizations, likewise attempt today; and that is by coercion and exclusion and punishment to discipline the adherents, so that they fall in line. That is a compressive, coercive, and dictatorial way of trying to achieve the Christian unity that we seek after.

Another more benign way of attempting exactly the same thing is to say, 'You are free in all your thinking, in all your beliefs. We require very little of you. We believe in the Doctrine of Christ, which was read to us here today. It's very short. Belief in Christ, belief in His Father, acceptance of the Holy Ghost, being baptized in faith, and then allowing that Holy Spirit, that Holy Ghost, to animate you in your search for truth.' And if we begin with diversity, then we begin with appreciation for that diversity, because coming together in the unity that Paul speaks of, in the dispensation of the fulness of times, is not because someone beat you into submission. It's because someone had something to say that resonated as truth to you in such a compelling way that you found yourself persuaded. You found yourself enticed to accept it, you found yourself prizing it, and you welcomed it, and you embraced it. And if someone has not yet embraced it, you explain to them why it's delicious to you. And if they reject it for a season, that's okay too.

There's a revelation that talks about how there are those people who will not taste death, because it shall be sweet unto them. Why do they not taste death? Because death means bitterness. And if, in the authentic Christian's life, the final moments that they spend here are caught up with the testimony of Jesus confirming that they have part with Him in his Kingdom, like Stephen in the very act of being stoned to death, they part this life rejoicing, because whatever they're going through, it doesn't matter. It's joyful to be reunited with that person who represents perfection itself.

The highest aspirations, the highest ideals of Buddhism are present in the Gospel of Christ. The highest ideals of Hinduism are present in the Gospel of Christ. The problem is that in that disunity, in the fracturing, some of the bits of the sculpture that left Christian awareness and departed into the East but were retained by the Hindus, are understood by them, are practiced and accepted by them, but they're outside of the typical Christian awareness. You will not understand the sayings of Jesus the same, if you could put on Hindu eyes for a moment and read what is in the sayings and the teachings of Jesus Christ and of His followers. You'll not understand the teachings of Christ as well, until you've put on Buddhist eyes and you've relooked at the gospel of Christ through that prism, because part of the picture will be missing. Christianity may be disciplined and have its story down. But it lacks the depth, the richness, the kindness, the texture. It lacks the meditative power that you find in Buddhism and Hinduism. As you heard from the people practicing those philosophies, religions, viewpoints today, the fact is that they're fractured too. Part of reunifying everything in Christ is going to reunify the Hindu world as well, reunify the Buddhist world as well.

The title that my talk was given is "What is God up to Today?" He's up to the work and the challenge of reuniting all things in one, in Christ; not by exclusion, and subtraction, and coercion, but by openness, and by addition, and by tolerance.

Jesus Christ had a group of witnesses in a single generation—in a single generation—this isn't a work of fiction. You have four different gospel accounts that come into being in a single generation of time, in which they all agree on the massive truth that this was the Son of God, who came into the world to be the sacrificial lamb, who died—he was rejected and died, and he was resurrected and ascended into heaven. All four of them agree on that. And yet, only Matthew has the sermon on the mount. Some of them mention feeding five thousand, some of them mention feeding seven thousand, and some of them mention both. But not all of them mention everything. There are differences. It's what you would expect if you're dealing with an authentic account of a real person, that lived a real life, and left behind people who were so astonished by what they witnessed from this man that they wrote accounts; and whereas before, they were cowering, and they were running, and they were denying that they knew that man. After his resurrection and they witnessed that, they went forth boldly and proclaimed who he was, performing miracles themselves, based upon the name of Jesus Christ. Something actually happened. And that something was the life of Jesus Christ. And these men went willingly; whereas before they ran and hid, after his resurrection, after they became acquainted with him, they went willingly to their deaths as witnesses of him.

So, I believed that there was something authentic about Christianity. I just wasn't quite sure about the brand of Christianity that my mom, a Baptist, was teaching me in my youth. I also, going down to the Catholic Church, was skeptical—Pope John VI was the Pope back then—seemed like a decent enough chap. The first Catholic Pope that impressed me was Pope John Paul I. That guy was—he was a fan of Mark Twains, ok? Pope John Paul I was the greatest pope that ever lived as far as I'm concerned. I thought there was something missing from the Baptist faith. I thought there was something theatrical and hollow, even inauthentic about what I saw in Catholicism. Not because the pageantry wasn't depicting something noble, and great, and wonderful, but because the players weren't always up to the job of carrying off the pageantry. There were times when it appeared to me that the last thing the priest in Mountain Home, Idaho was interested in was celebrating the service —the mass. He did it anyway, and it was lifeless. His heart wasn't in it. And so, it seemed to me hard for that to drive religious conviction, if the heart of the priest is not in the celebration of the mass. The Baptists were always into the celebration of what they do, because it's based upon a sort of charismatic movement in which enthusiasm is an expected part of it. But I remember the pious gestures, the things from the pageantry of Catholicism, that depicted things—that depicted holiness, and I believe there is holiness. I honestly believe there to be holiness. But I think it is hard to imitate it instead of authentically be it. That's why a "Mother Theresa" stands out as a global figure, because she didn't imitate it. And Mother Theresa stands as evidence that there is such a thing as Catholic holiness.

Another one that stands out in history, as an authentic evidence of Catholicism having holiness, is St. Francis. St. Francis believed and accepted the sermon on the mount. He lived the sermon on the mount. He went to Rome to get an order commissioned by the pope, and the pope laughed at him and said, 'You can't get anyone to live the sermon on the mount.' He said, 'I would give you an order if you could come back here and bring with you twelve men who would be willing to live the sermon on the mount.' St. Francis was the guy that if you saw him in the cold in winter and you gave him a coat, he would wear that coat until he ran into someone that had a greater need than he, and then he would give away his coat to a person in need. When he decided that he was going to become a priest, his father who was a wealthy man, went and intervened and said, 'You can't do this. Everything about you I paid for! You are utterly dependent upon me, and I refuse to let you go do this.' St. Francis took off all his clothes, handed it to his father, and came to the clergy a poor and naked man, literally. He was a devout man. When he came back to the pope with twelve believers, the Franciscans were commissioned, and the Order of the Franciscans came into being. The current pope is named after St. Francis. I think St. Francis was an authentic Christian.

In the last two months of St. Francis' life, he reported that angels were visiting with him. There are a lot of people that dismiss that end-of-life spiritual experience, and telling tales of angels and visits, and such things as, you know, the frailties of a dying body. I don't think so in the case of St. Francis. I think that he was ministered to by angels.

There's an expression—it's found in places some of you would find dubious, but there's an expression about how some people do not taste death. The statement that they do not taste death doesn't mean they don't die. It just means that their death is sweet, because they die in companionship with those on the other side, who bring them through that veil of death in a joyful experience. There are a handful of people who have reported that as they were dying, angels came and ministered to them. I think all authentic Christians, in any age, belonging to any denomination—I don't care what the denomination is—I think all authentic Christians who depart this world find that death is sweet to them, and that they are in the company of angels as they leave this world. And I don't think it matters that the brand that you swore allegiance to, and you contributed your resources to support, matter anywhere near as much as whether you believe in Christ, whether you accept the notions that he advances about the sermon on the mount, and whether you try to incorporate and live them in your life.

Jesus took the law of Moses as the standard. What the sermon on the mount does is say, Here is the standard, but your conduct should not be merely *this*. Thou shalt not kill is not enough. You must avoid being angry with your brother. You must forgive those who offend you. You must pray for those who despitefully use you. Just refraining from murdering one another, with a reluctant heart, bearing malice at them, Well I didn't kill the guy, but I got even! That's not enough. That's not the standard that Christ is advancing. Thou shalt not commit adultery is not good enough. Don't look upon a woman to lust after her in your heart. Jesus is saying, Here's the law, and you can do all of those things and be malevolent. You can be angry. You can be bitter. You can be contemptible. You can hold each other out as objects of ridicule. Its purpose is to make you something more lovely, more wonderful, more kindly, more Christian.

Christ says, to be like him. The sermon on the mount is an explanation of what it's like to be like him. St. Francis made the effort of trying that, of doing that. I suspect that the first time St. Francis gave away a coat in the middle of winter to someone else, that it pained him; he probably felt the biting sting of the cold and thought, How wise is this that I'm doing? Because it's always hard to accept a higher standard and to implement it for the first time. But I suspect by the hundredth time he'd done that, he didn't feel the cold anymore; he felt the warmth in his heart of having relieved the suffering of another person. Because the practice of Christian faith involves the development of Christian skill and the development of Christian charity in a way that changes you. You don't remain the same character that you were when you began the journey. You become someone absolutely and fundamentally different.

So, while I was in the Air Force away from home, I was attending a University of New Hampshire night class, some kind of organizational behavior class. Having grown up in Idaho I knew what Mormons were, and this professor, Cal Colby—he's from Brandeis University, but he was teaching a night class for the University of New Hampshire—just gratuitously started attacking Mormons. And my honest reaction was, What the hell are you talking about Mormons in New Hampshire for? That's a local infestation somewhere out in the West, and there's no—there's none of that going on here. And in the middle of his diatribe a guy raised his hand, Colby called on him, and a fellow named Steve Klaproth defended—because he was a Mormon, defended Mormons. I made the mistake afterwards of saying to the fellow—I didn't know his name at the time, but I know him now—Steve, "Good job." I always hate it when a person in a position of strength picks on someone in a position of weakness, and so I went to the guy that was weak and said, you know, good job. He mistook this for interest in his religion. And I wound up, trying to be polite, I wound up being hounded—literally pamphleteered—missionaries coming. It was gosh awful.

Well, I left New Hampshire on what's called Operation Bootstrap, where they send you to college. I went to Boise State University. The Air Force paid for me to go to school. I came back. When I came back there was this camp out; the camp out was at the birthplace of Joseph Smith in Sharon, Vermont. And I went to the camp out. There was a book that was in the Visitor's Center, and they gave me a copy of that book for free. Steve says, "You should read this." I read that. And at that moment I was surprised, because my reaction to Mormonism had been very, very negative, but the ideals that were expressed in this one statement were lofty and noble, and Christian, and charitable, and I wanted to know, where did this come from? It was something that Joseph Smith had written; a revelation that Joseph Smith had received.

Well, I got baptized for the first time in my life on September the 10th of 1973, into the Mormon church. I was a Mormon until September the 10th of 2013, forty years to the day. And on the 40th anniversary of becoming a Mormon, I was excommunicated from the Mormon church. So, I don't say this to sound like I'm bragging or exaggerating, but I do not know anyone alive today that knows as much about Mormon history as I do. Because while I was part of that, and then afterwards, still, I've read every historical document that I can get my hands on. I've read everything that Joseph Smith said that got recorded, wrote, or transcribed when he had a scribe writing for him. My understanding of Mormon history is encyclopedic.

There's a thing that goes on in Salt Lake City called the Sunstone Symposium. It's run by people who are basically renegade Mormons, intellectuals, and it started out being friendly to the Mormon church, it grew into outright hostility and anger towards the Mormon church, and then it converted into a mixed bag. And some of it is pro, and some of it is con. And I've spoken at the Sunstone Symposium. One of the things I've presented was a paper about Brigham Young, in which Brigham Young's megalomaniacal presiding over Mormonism, during the late 1840s into the early 1850s, and the excesses that went on during that time period, including murders that occurred on Brigham Young's watch, were laid out. Sunstone asked the Dean of Mormon History, the guy that is most respected, Thomas Alexander, to respond to my paper. And Thomas Alexander came and responded to my paper. I was talking about Brigham Young's literal regarding of himself as an actual king from the time they got out of the valley in 1847, until the time he was deposed by the Army of the United States as the territorial governor in 1857. I was talking about that period of time. Thomas Alexander got up and said, No, Brigham Young didn't believe those things, because he said things in 1860 and in 1870, and he read the quotes from 1860 and 1870. Well, as soon as he was deposed as governor, he *knew* he wasn't king. All 1860 and 1870 have to contribute is the fact that Brigham Young ultimately managed to grapple with reality because he had been deposed. But what he was saying in that early time period is exactly what he meant. So, after Thomas Alexander got through with his rebuttal paper, I got up and for five minutes dismantled the Dean of Mormon History's view.

The Mormon church is a cult. It is not an authentic Christian organization. But I believe that you can find Christians who are Mormons. I believe that you can find Christians in every denomination that are out there. I believe that there is an authenticity to belief in Christ that transcends every denomination that's out there. I wrote books about the history of Mormonism that expose many of the things that the Mormon church represents to be true; I show to be false, including their authority claims, including their consistent following of what the founder of Mormonism stood for, believed in, and practiced himself. Joseph Smith raised the largest army. The largest standing army in the United States in 1844 was under the command of Major General Joseph Smith in Nauvoo, Illinois. Literally, he could have taken on the United States Army and defeated them. And do you know what Joseph Smith did with a standing army larger than anyone else in the United States—larger than the Federal Government, larger than any of the state militias—do you know what he did? He disarmed his soldiers, he turned the cannons over to the state of Illinois, he surrendered to the governor of the state of Illinois, and three days later he was murdered while he was in jail. He would rather personally die or give up his life, than to have people on both sides of a fight die as a consequence of a religious dispute.

In 1837, Joseph Smith was in Missouri, and while he was in Missouri hostilities broke out between Mormons and Missourians. Part of the problem with the hostilities was that leaders around Joseph Smith were spoiling for a fight. Literally, spoiling for a fight. Guy named Sidney Rigdon, who was a counselor to Joseph Smith, gave a speech in which he said, If you people show any more aggression towards us, we're going to wage a war of extermination, and we will wipe all you Missourians out. It's called the salt speech; it was delivered on July the fourth of that year. It's an incendiary talk.

There was a Mormon named Sampson Avard, who went about provoking hostilities with the Missourians. Sampson Avard was a Mormon and he had a group that he called the Danites, based upon the tribe of Dan. The blessing that was given to Dan in the 49th chapter of Genesis talks about Dan being an asp in the way that bites the horses. It's a preamble of the violence that the tribe of Dan would render in the posterity of Dan. So, Sampson Avard took the name Danites as his group, and they began to retaliate by burning houses, burning fields, stealing cattle, stealing hogs, bringing them back. Joseph Smith found out about it and he demoted Samson Avard. He was relieved of all responsibility, and Joseph made him a cook. So, the guy who was the militant leader is now a cook.

Hostilities ultimately did break out. It was inevitable that there be retaliations. Each side were saying that they were the victim and the governor of Missouri said, We're going to wage a war of extermination, quoting what the Mormons had said in that July 4th talk. And so Mormons were expelled from the state of Missouri. The militia was outside Far West Missouri, a town called Far West. Joseph Smith and his family, friends, and Mormons were inside Far West. They had a defensive position from which they literally could have caused so many casualties that the militia could never have overrun the town; the cost in blood would have been too high. Joseph Smith surrendered, and told his people to surrender their arms, and he deflated the tension.

He was taken into custody by the state of Missouri, he was charged with treason against the state for fomenting rebellion. And they had a series of hearings, trying to get witnesses to prove that Joseph Smith should be held for trial on the charge of treason. And no one, no one could prove that Joseph Smith was involved with any of the hostilities, until the guy who actually caused the hostilities, Sampson Avard, came to the courthouse to testify, to blame Joseph Smith for everything he had done. And so Joseph Smith was held over on the charge of treason based upon the testimony of the guy who knew what cattle were stolen, what hogs were stolen, what fields were burned —that he was responsible for—and he simply said all that, that Joseph engineered that. And so, based upon the testimony of traitors, Joseph Smith was held in prison for a period of six months over a—over a winter time period in an unheated dungeon, that had bars but no glass on the windows, and they suffered for six months in a Missouri prison.

He was allowed to escape and get back to his people, all of whom had been driven out of Missouri. But while he was in prison, and while he had the opportunity to think about everything, Joseph Smith composed a letter from Liberty Jail that breathes with the spirit of Christian compassion, forgiveness, love, kindness, and refraining from abusing others. This is a man who got betrayed by his friends, and he turns around and shows for his friends, compassion. One of the books that I've written is called *A Man Without Doubt*. In it I set up the historical context out of which Joseph Smith produced the three longest writings of his own, in his life. It's a letter from Liberty Jail; it's Lectures on Faith; and it's a statement of his own history— because the church historian had stolen all the manuscripts. Time and time again the worst enemies of Joseph Smith were Mormons, people that claimed to follow the religion that he was developing. Joseph Smith in my view is authentically Christian, the same way as Saint Francis is authentically Christian. The problem is—and it is an enormous problem—the problem is that everyone outside of the Mormon world looks at him as the property of the LDS Church. They look at him as if he were accurately represented by a group of people that time and time again, he condemned, and time and time again, betrayed him. *A Man Without Doubt* is an attempt to let people see Joseph Smith as a Christian divorced from the LDS Church, or any of the splinter Mormon groups. And to see him, potentially, as an authentic Christian in the same way that I think Martin Luther and John Wesley; even

John Calvin, although Calvin was so militant; he's kind of a drum beater that scares me a little, nevertheless he was authentically Christian.

I think that everyone who sacrifices for the cause of Christ can help contribute to my understanding of what it means to follow Christ. Because people who follow Christ bear the evidence of that discipleship in the way in which they walk, and the things that they do, and the things that they give up, in how they discipline their heart and how they discipline their mind, in how they treat one another. When you find someone whose life bears evidence that they are authentically Christian because of what they do, they are authentically Christian because of what they say. Christ said, 'It's not what goes into the mouth that proves you're unclean, it's what comes out.' What do you say? How do you display the grace of God in your life? I can tell you one way you don't display the grace of God, and that's by condemning, merely because of their affiliation with one Christian group or another, condemning them, as being inauthentically Christian.

Christ looks upon the inner person. All of his parables, all of his parables suggest there's something very different about authenticity and inauthenticity. There are 10 virgins. Well, what are virgins a symbol of? If Christ is using the virgin as a symbol, he's talking about good people. These are, these are good religious people; they have to be. And of that group, only five were allowed in. There's a wedding feast and at the wedding feast he invites friends and they don't come. Well who are the friends of Christ that are invited to come to his wedding feast? And they don't come. They don't come because their hearts aren't right, their words aren't right, their mind isn't right, they are not authentically what Christ is trying to have us be. But he invites and they don't come, because they will not be His. And so, he goes out on the highways and the byways to try and find anyone that will come. And anyone that will come suggests that, well, they could be a Samaritan. Think about the parable of the Good Samaritan from the perspective of a Jewish audience. They were nothing but apostates, and yet he uses the apostate as the illustration of authentic Christian discipleship. They invite in off the highways and the byways, strangers. People that you don't expect to be invited because they're not at your church every week. They're going to some other place or perhaps no place at all. And yet they're invited in, and they're allowed to remain, so long as they have on the wedding garment. In other words, if they come having donned the mantle of authentic Christianity, they're welcome, they're welcomed. We care and we fight about religious issues that are of no moment at all to Christ. And we do that because we're paying clergymen every week to rile us up so that we'll stay loyal to them and their congregation. And we'll contribute and we will view one another with fear and non-acceptance.

You take the money out of Christianity; most ministers would go into politics. They would not hang around. I'm not lying. They have done polls of Christian ministers, to ask them if they believe Jesus Christ is the Son of God who was resurrected. The majority of Christian ministers do not have faith; what they have is a career. And they can't abandon their career. 'If I leave your employ, what's going to become of me? Because I'll be a poor man.' And so they stay employed preaching what they don't believe. It's one of the reasons why I think Father Ordway, in Mountain Home, Idaho, made the gestures and his countenance was devoid of the holiness that should be expressed, of the joy that should be expressed. I saw that in my friend Rick's mother, Mary. I saw in her that, that fire of belief, that devotion. I didn't see it in Father Ordway.

Well, I'm trying to get people to consider the possibility that authentic Christians could come from anywhere, among any people. And that we can fellowship with one another. And that it is even possible to fellowship with one another, even independent of an employee-hireling priest, in which we study together; we worship together; we rejoice in Christ together; we try to figure out how to be more authentically Christian in what we do, and what we say, and how we treat one another, and how we view one another.

And then to take the next step and to contribute our tithes and our offerings to a group of believers, to help believers, to help each other. So that it's not just the support of the clergy and the support of the buildings, the support of the programs, but it's also helping the fatherless and helping the mother who has no one to help her. And to have Christianity, not just theoretically modeled in feel-good sermons, but actively part of life and part of how we deal with and treat one another; in which we all say, 'We've all sinned. We've all fallen short of the glory of God, but let's not let that cause me to condemn you. Let's not let that stop me from trying, in as authentic a way as I can, to be charitable and kind to you, and you to me, and us to the people in need among us.' Because if they were ever an authentic group of people who are Christian, who were helping one another, the appeal of that would cause everyone who comes into their midst to have a change of heart. They'd want to be part of that, they'd want to live that kind of life. Because there's no better life than the one that Christ taught us to model in the sermon on the mount.

Anyway, I've talked for an hour and my experience teaches me that when you've had people sitting and listening to you for an hour, you're a wicked and despicable man if you make them sit and listen to you any longer. So, unless there's anything that someone wants to talk about, ask about—I really do know a lot about Mormon history and it's, it's not at all what the Mormon persona is represented to be, either by the church itself or by its critics. In some ways its history is much worse than the critics tell you. And in some ways, the very beginning of it was much different and much better than what they represent.

I believe Brigham Young introduced the practice of plural wives. I believe that Joseph Smith was an ardent opponent of that. I believe that Joseph Smith has been falsely portrayed because Brigham Young didn't think he could bring that into the practice unless he laid it at the feet of Joseph Smith. And I think there's been a lot of history in Mormonism that tries to lay at the feet of Joseph Smith responsibility for the things that traitors and treacherous and evil men did. And escape responsibility for it by saying, 'Joseph taught it. Oh, he taught it in private. Oh, he lied to the public. He lied to the public about it, but in private he practiced it and he taught it.' And I have to tell you, Joseph Smith was not that kind of man. I read the letters between Joseph Smith and his wife Emma. Emma was a stronger personality than Joseph. Emma was his trusted counselor and guide. Joseph deferred to her, he took advice from her, he took counsel from her, she was better educated than him. The stories that have been attributed to Joseph Smith—you should read *A Man Without Doubt*. You should go back and reconsider whether what you think Joseph was, is it all supportable by a true telling of history? Because I don't think it is, and that's one of the reasons why I'm an excommunicated Mormon, because—because I think the truth is valuable and it's worth searching out.

Let me end by saying that I do believe in the potential for the unity of Christians coming together in one faith. I suspect that sitting here in this room, if every one of you were asked, 'Are you a Christian?,' every one of you would respond, 'Yes.' And I suspect, if I asked you to explain what denomination you were, that probably every one but you would tell you what's wrong with your particular version of Christianity. I don't think the measure of your Christianity is determined by whether or not I want to judge, condemn, dismiss, belittle, complain about your version. The authenticity of your Christianity is reckoned in your heart and in your relationship with God, and if that's authentic and if that's sincere, how dare anyone question that? If I think I know more than you and I have a better view of Jesus Christ and his atonement than do you, then I ought to assume the burden of persuading you. I ought to meekly tell you why you ought to have greater faith in something else; but to demand, and to insist, and to belittle, and to complain—quite frankly that's exactly where early Christianity wound up when Christians were killing Christians because of doctrinal disputes. What kind of nonsense is that? Let's not go there. Let's accept one another as Christians, if any one of us says that they are a Christian, and then if you think you can improve their understanding, have at it, but let's not dismiss, belittle, or discard.

We believe we are approaching a moment in which the Lord is about to return. Read that chapter, Matthew 24. All of the signs that He speaks of will occur in one single generation. If you've not noticed, the signs have begun to appear. It means you are living within a generation in which a great deal is to occur. As it was in the days of Noah so is it about to be. That means dreadful things are coming on the one hand, and it means prophets are going to be among us again—people with messages that come from the Lord.

I'm not here on my own volition. I've not done anything that I've done, throughout the last number of years, on my own volition. I do what I do, I preach what I preach, I testify to what I testify to because, like Paul, I've been sent.

I would rather understate than overstate the case, but let me end by telling you—Christ lives! He died and He was resurrected. I know this to be true because, like Paul, I have seen Him. I don't tell you that to make this seem sensational. I tell you that to give you cause to believe in Him. He is real.

Encountering Him as a resurrected being changed the course of history. It turned cowards into courageous, willing, and enthusiastic witnesses, who faced down the Roman empire to their death. They died willingly. They died as evidence of the truth, that they were testifying to. That kind of faith needs to return again to the earth. That kind of faith is possible again in our day.

Christianity has taken so many turns and so many different forms from the death of the apostles until now. But however you may regard yourself to be a Christian, what every one of us needs is for Heaven itself to reaffirm to us what it is that Heaven would like us, as Christians, to be and to do.

I mention that Christ gave many commandments, precepts, teachings. He also gave a law. His law can be found in Matthew chapters 5, 6, and 7. That is how you and I should practice our Christianity.

The foregoing excerpts are taken from:

- Denver's *Christian Reformation Lecture Series*, Talk #7, given in Boise, Idaho on November 3, 2018;
- Denver's *Christian Reformation Lecture Series*, Talk #8, given in Montgomery, Alabama on May 18, 2019;
- Denver's *Christian Reformation Lecture Series*, Talk #2, given in Dallas, TX on October 19th, 2017; and
- Denver's *Christian Reformation Lecture Series*, Talk #1, given in Cerritos, CA on September 21st, 2017.

Today's podcast addresses important questions about authentic Christianity, but is only an introduction to ideas that listeners of any denomination may find important and relevant. These topics are more fully addressed in Denver's Eight talks addressed to all Christians of every denomination, which are available to watch, listen or download for free at learnofchrist.org.

79. Hope, Part 1

This is the first part of a special series on "Hope," in which Denver addresses the questions: What is hope? How can hope be an anchor for the soul in times of tribulation?

———

DENVER: There's this interesting set of verses beginning in verse eight of D&C 1:

> And verily I say unto you, that they who go forth, bearing these tidings unto the inhabitants of the earth, to them is power given to seal both on earth and in heaven, the unbelieving and rebellious; Yea, verily, to seal them up unto the day when the wrath of God shall be poured out upon the wicked without measure—Unto the day when the Lord shall come to recompense unto every man according to his work, and measure to every man according to the measure which he has measured to his fellow man. (see also T&C 54:2 RE)

These are all negative. These are all sealing up unto destruction. These are all condemnations. These are all, in a word, Aaronic. But, bear in mind, the Aaronic priesthood is not without hope because within it is the power to baptize, which is an ordinance of hope.

I want to go to Doctrine and Covenants section 128 and I want to look at verse 21. This is Joseph writing a letter that got canonized and he's talking about all of the stuff that had gone on in the process of getting the Restoration fully established on the earth. And he mentions in this letter that he writes these things: *And again, the voice of God in the chamber of old Father Whitmer, in Fayette, Seneca county, and at sundry times, and in divers places [throughout] all the travels and tribulations of this Church of Jesus Christ of Latter-day Saints!* (see also T&C 151:15 RE). So the voice of God has been there throughout all of this as Joseph presided and as the Church rolled forth.

> And the voice of Michael, [Mich-a-**el**] the archangel; the voice of Gabri-**el**, ["El" being the name of God] and of Rapha-**el**, and of divers angels, from Michael or Adam down to the present time, all declaring their dispensation, their rights, their keys, their honors, their majesty and glory, and the power of their priesthood; giving line upon line, precept upon precept; here a little, there a little; giving us consolation by holding forth that which is to come, confirming our hope!

So, I want to suggest to you that Michael, Gabriel, and Raphael are known to us as those who have come, though they were part of the El—or in the plural form, the Elohim; they came and they served here. They came and they ministered here. Michael descended and he came to the earth, and he was known as Adam in mortality. Gabriel came to the earth and he was known in mortality as Noah. There is a big debate over the identity of Raphael. I'll tell you what I think and you can take it or leave it. Raphael is the name that was given to the man who, in mortality, we know as Enoch.

Now, there are four angels who preside over the four corners of the earth. And Joseph surely knew that. And Joseph mentions the names of three of the four, but he leaves the fourth one out. And I find the absence of the fourth one rather extraordinary. The fourth one's name is Uriel, also one of the Elohim. And although there are those who will absolutely cry heresy, throw dirt on their hair, and tear their clothes; because they're scholars, and they're *bona fide*, and they know I'm talking out of my hat—but I'd remind you, Joseph talked out of his hat too [laughs]. That fourth and missing, unmentioned angel is Uriel, who in mortality was known to us as John.

Adam is the one in the East—the angel who is considered the one who presides over and has control of the air—which is apt, because unto Adam was given the breath of life in the beginning. Raphael is in the South, and he is associated with the power of fire—which is apt, because of his fiery ascent with his people into heaven. Gabriel is the angel in the West who has the power over water—which is apt, because in mortality, he managed through the Flood. And Uriel, though not mentioned, is the one who, in the North, has the power over the earth—which is apt, because he remains upon the earth; and he's the guardian at one gate with Elijah at the other end. But you can take and leave all that as you will. I find the mention here in this letter by Joseph, of these individuals, and these Powers, and these four (three of whom are named—the fourth of whom, potentially, is unnamed) to be interesting. Though he does mention "divers angels from Michael or Adam down to the present time."

And what did Joseph say about all of the prophets of the Old Testament? He said they *all* held Melchizedek priesthood, and they were *all* ordained by God Himself, because they functioned inside a society that was defective, limited, excluded from the presence of God. But not *those* who received and entertained angels. They were brought up to where they need to be and God *Himself* ordained them. Should you not have hope? Should you not rise up above the level of those who are content to have less? Should you not be willing to mount up on that fiery mountain despite the thunderings and lightnings, despite the earthquakes; despite the fact that you do not believe yourself to be worthy. You're still capable of coming aboard.

Look at Moroni chapter 7 beginning at verse 29:

> *Because he had done this, my beloved brethren, have miracles ceased? Behold I say unto you, Nay; neither have angels ceased to minister unto the children of men. For behold,* **they** *[the angels] are subject unto him, to minister according to the word of **his** command, showing themselves unto them of strong faith and a firm mind in every form of godliness. And the office of their ministry is to call men to repentance, [repentance], to fulfil and to do the work of the **covenants** of the Father...* (see also Moroni 7:6 RE)

Because when you move from repentance, you move into covenants (which is why we needed to speak about that in Centerville), which is why this process has been undergoing for the last year—unfolding how you get back into the presence of God. Because it surely is necessary for there to be a rescue mission; and the rescue mission is designed to raise you, to elevate you, to redeem you.

> *The work of the covenants of the Father, which he hath made unto the children of men, to prepare the way among the children of men, by declaring the word of Christ unto the chosen vessels of the Lord, that they may bear testimony of him. And by so doing, the Lord God prepareth the way that the residue of men may have faith in Christ, that the Holy Ghost may have place in their hearts, according to the power thereof; and after this manner bringeth to pass the Father, the covenants which he hath made unto the children of men.* (ibid. RE)

In a word, those who receive and entertain angels have an obligation then, to declare the words so that others might likewise have faith in Him. That word, having been declared unto you, gives you the hope, the faith, the confidence that you likewise can do so—so that the covenants that are made by the Father can be brought to pass.

Fortunately, fortunately, Aaronic priesthood is exceptionally durable. Fortunately, unlike Melchizedek priesthood, which can only be exercised with extraordinary care and delicacy. The purpose of Melchizedek priesthood being (as I talked about in Orem) to bless. The purpose of Aaronic priesthood being to condemn, and to judge, and to set a law by which men can condemn themselves. Having the authority to do that to yourself is remarkably durable, and used with great regularity. And those that have it generally abide by so lesser a law that they wind up judging and condemning one another; and parading before God as a march of fools—yelling and yammering, pointing and blaming, complaining and bitching about what everyone else's inadequacies are. The purpose of Melchizedek priesthood is to sound the signal, "Know ye the Lord." And eventually, that sermon will be heard by enough that there will be none left who need to be told, "Know ye the Lord," for they shall all know Him. And everyone will take up with Him their concerns and not with one another.

Romans chapter 4: He's talking about father Abraham, and in verse 3 he talks about Abraham believed God. It was accounted unto him for righteousness—faith was reckoned to Abraham for righteousness. Verse 13, it promised that he should be an heir of the world (was not to Abraham or to his seed through the law, but through the righteousness of faith) because Abraham believed in God; he trusted in Him. Therefore, he inherited—he inherited it all—the world. He's the father of the righteous.

Beginning at verse 17:

> *(As it is written, I have made thee a father of many nations,) before him whom he believed, even God, who quickeneth the dead, and calleth those things which [were] not as though they were. Who against hope believed in hope, that he might become the father of many nations, according to that which was spoken, So shall thy seed be. And being not weak in faith, he considered not his own body now dead, when he was about an hundred years old, neither yet the deadness of Sara's womb: He staggered not at the promise of God through unbelief; but was strong in faith, giving glory to God; And being fully persuaded that, what he had promised, he was able also to perform.* (see also Romans 1:20 RE)

There was no proof that an aged, dead (that is now impotent), old man could sire a child with a barren, post-menopausal, Sarah. But Abraham doubted not, and you have before you promises spoken by the voice of an angel concerning the things God has in store for your day, and you doubt? And you question? And you think God not able to bring about what He has said He intends to do? The very day that they have looked forward to, from the beginning of the days of Adam down till now (as we looked at in Centerville) —you doubt that God can bring this to pass? You doubt that what I have been talking about since we began in Boise, and have now arrived here? If God can send someone to declare these things to you, in the confidence and the faith and the knowledge that I'm speaking to you **on His errand**, and I can do it in this room, in this building, in this city *[note added for context: this section of this particular talk was given in a casino building in Las Vegas, NV]*, **salvation comes to you today by the word of God**. And you doubt that God cannot make a holy place somewhere that has not been trodden under the foot of the Gentiles? You doubt that God cannot bring to pass His work in culminating the ages? Have the faith of a grain of mustard seed, because it is coming, it is going to happen, and if you lack the faith, you will not be invited.

If we're required to develop the attributes of Christ, how is it possible for us to do so unless God *patiently* tries to persuade us to *voluntarily* be like Him? And how can you hope to be like Him, if you refuse to be persuaded? God came as one of the weak things of this world. The only way He's ever going to invite you is through one of the weak things of this world, speaking in weakness, asking you to be persuaded. It doesn't matter how earnest I am. I know my standing before God. What matters is your willingness *to be persuaded*. Over that I have no control, and want no control. Over that I simply put the case as the Lord has put it to me, in the hopes that what He has to offer, and what He says needs to be said, will get through to you. But your relationship and your accountability is not to me, it's to Him. Therefore, be persuaded; be persuaded.

The notion that you are going to succeed in acquiring the glory that is likened to God, in a separate and single state, is nowhere found as a promise in scripture. It's not a reasonable expectation. It's a non-scriptural expectation. It is a foolish hope because it does not reckon to the things God created. Understand, those verses that we read in Genesis—those verses were before the Fall. In the condition in which Adam and Eve found themselves at the time that those incidents took place, they were immortal, they had not yet fallen. The marriage and the union of the two of them was intended to last forever, because death had not yet entered into the world. And, as God put it, "It was good."

Marry a wife, sealed, Holy Spirit of Promise, pass by the angels, enter into exaltation, glory, fullness; all of these words are applicable only to the man and the woman together as one. It's only applicable to the exalted state of a marriage that is worthy of preservation into eternity.

Now, instead of focusing on this as something you may receive in the great hereafter as some great reward because you qualified for glory in a parade in the afterlife; why not think about whether the conditions that are being described in the verses that we look at, are themselves, a reward. Think about this as something to be had now, not something to be postponed and hoped for in the afterlife. Not in eternity—but today.

So, the subject about which someone inquires in going to the Lord does not necessarily control the content of what the Lord is going to reveal. Likewise, Joseph made an inquiry to find out about the plurality of wives. What the Lord wanted to talk about was eternal marriage. The Lord's priority is what you see first in section 132.

He's talking about the eternal duration of the marriage covenant. He answers the question, beginning very late in the original revelation, as an afterthought, concerning the issue of the plurality of wives. But it is first and foremost a revelation about the eternity of the marriage covenant. You do not get to an answer about the subject of plural marriage until verse 34. Beginning at verse 1 and going through verse 33, all of that is about the eternity of the marriage covenant. All of that is about marriage of *a man* and *a woman*, like the marriage of Adam to Eve, and like the children of Adam and Eve who went off two by two to create their families.

All of the blessings concerning what you hope to inherit in eternity are tied to the first 33 verses of section 132, dealing with the marriage of *a* man and *a* woman. Therefore, when you read section 132, don't leap to verse 34 and then read retrospectively back into the earlier text that what it's talking about in the earlier text is something other than the marriage of *a* man and *a* woman. The subject matter changes, and the question that was asked begins in verse 34.

So, what was on the Lord's mind and what the Lord inspired an inquiry to produce, is in the beginning of section 132. Look at verse 7:

> *The conditions of this law are these: All covenants, contracts, bonds, obligations, oaths, vows, performances, connections, associations, or expectations that are not made and entered into and sealed by the Holy Spirit of promise, of him who is anointed, both as well for time and for all eternity, and that too most holy, by revelation and commandment... (and I have appointed unto my servant Joseph to hold this power in the last days, and there is never but one on the earth at a time on whom this power and the keys of this priesthood are conferred), are of no efficacy, virtue, or force in and after the resurrection from the dead; for all contracts that are not made unto this end have an end when men are dead.*

So, everything that you hope to receive into the next life, even your *expectations*, all of that has to be obtained from God by covenant.

I mentioned in an answer to a question in Ephraim that the role of the woman was significant, even in the life of Christ. I mentioned that she anointed Him preliminary to His death and burial. One of the things that gave Him the *expectation* of coming forth out of the grave, was the anointing that promised to Him… Why do you think in the temple, the rites include preserving some of the functions of the body? It's not to make you healthy here and now. It's so that you can lay claim upon this as an expectation in the eternities, because if you do not have the expectation conferred upon you by the Holy Spirit of Promise, you'll have to get that in some other cycle; because the only thing you will be able to take with you into eternity, you obtain in this manner. Everything has to be obtained by a covenant.

This is the day in which, at long last, it is possible for what God intended to happen before His return, to actually begin. The Gospel is not supposed to be merely a record of how God dealt with other people at another time. Joseph Smith talked about how we can't read the words of an old book, and then apply those words in an old book—that were meant for someone else at some other time—to us. And then restore ourselves back to God's grace. That is just as true of the revelations given in the days of Joseph Smith as it is true of the revelations given in the New Testament.

Now, we get to the point in the history of the world in which, after the days of Shem (who is renamed Melchizedek), people fell into iniquity. They fell into iniquity and they lost the birthright. There was no continuation of this. It was broken by an apostasy and it had to be restored again; which ought to give all of us great hope, because Abraham sought for *this*. He sought for a restoration of the kingdom of God. He sought for a restoration of this, which only one man on the earth can hold at a time.

Abraham 1:2

> Finding there was greater happiness and peace and rest for me, **I sought for the blessings of the fathers**, and the right whereunto I should be ordained to administer the same; having been myself a follower of righteousness, desiring also to be one who possessed great knowledge, and to be a greater follower of righteousness, and possess a greater knowledge, and to be **a father of many nations**, a prince of peace, desiring to receive instructions, and keep the commandments of God, **I became a**

rightful heir, a High Priest, holding the right belonging to the fathers. (emphasis added)

When you are in possession of *that*, you have no problem asking God and getting an answer. It is the right belonging to the fathers. After a period of apostasy and the break of this line, Abraham received it *by adoption*. Therefore, this power has the ability to cure "the break." This covenant-making, through God, has the ability to restore the family of God even when wicked men kill in order to destroy it; even when a substitute needs to be made; even when the fathers turn from their righteousness. Yet God is able to cause it to persist!

Remember, that in Nauvoo, the Lord offered to reconnect the saints; but clearly defined a condition, for that to happen, was necessarily an acceptable temple, where he could come and restore the connection. The reconnection is ordinance-based and will require an acceptable temple before it goes beyond the single representative.

First, ideas need to be advanced and accepted. Then second, we need to act on the ideas, primarily, by repenting and opening ourselves to the influence of God. Third, we have to be humble and patient and willing to practice the religion before we can have any hope of God deciding to gather us. Practical experience is absolutely necessary. Theories and pretensions are not gonna get us anywhere. Everyone can theorize the virtues that are necessary to gather people together and live in harmony. Everyone can envision *themselves* as one of the residents of a city of peace. But the practical experiences required to iron out our selfishness and competitiveness so we can actually live in peace is another order of magnitude harder.

See, individual salvation and promises of eternal life are just that—they are individual. A restoration of the family of Israel requires more, including cooperation and interrelationships that will be formed by God himself. Promises made to individuals give the individual hope.

If you take the vision of the redemption of the dead, that we find in D&C 138, he saw a vision where there were gathered together, in one place, an innumerable company of the spirits of the just; who'd been faithful in the testimony of Jesus while they lived in mortality, and who had offered sacrifice in the similitude of the great sacrifice of the Son of God, and had suffered tribulation in the Redeemer's name. *All these* had departed the mortal life, firm in the hope of a glorious resurrection through the grace of God the Father and his Only Begotten Son, Jesus Christ. All of them. These were the righteous. They were in Paradise and all of them were worthy. They had hope. And not only did the Savior give them hope before death, He visited with them in the spirit world during the time between His death and His resurrection. But *that* did not get them reconnected to the Fathers in Heaven. Nor did it even get them resurrected because it goes on to say in the same vision:

> *From among the righteous, he organized his forces and appointed messengers clothed with power and authority, and commissioned them to go forth and carry the light of the gospel to them that were in darkness, even to all the spirits of men; and thus was the gospel preached to the dead.* (D&C 138:30)

So the righteous who departed this life firm in the hope of a glorious resurrection, who had offered sacrifice in the similitude—many of whom had seen Him in the flesh, who witnessed Him and were ministered to by Him, and given authority by Him in the spirit world—remained in the world of the dead to *preach* to the dead.

Only the organization, through a temple and associated rites, results in finishing the family of God in the house of order—following the results achieved, or allowing the results achieved by Abraham, Isaac and Jacob— which are described in D&C 132:37. Abraham, Isaac and Jacob—*they did none other things than that which they were commanded, they have entered into their exaltation according to the promises, and they sit upon thrones and are not angels, but are gods.*

In D&C 138 verse 41, *Abraham, the father of the faithful; Isaac and Jacob* were also there. In verses 41, 42 of 138; Abraham, Isaac, and Jacob were there. But in the revelation given in 1843, they're sitting on thrones. They're not in the spirit world proselytizing. They're sitting on thrones. The difference between these two categories are the differences between individual salvation (which can come) and reorganizing the family of God (which must occur by an ordinance, in a temple, to be acceptable to God).

This was why the command was given to build the temple in Nauvoo, and why God offered to restore to them the fullness—that they did not achieve. We need to let God take the lead and then we need to patiently await each step along the way. This is the stuff of which the prophecies speak. And it is the stuff that will be fulfilled. But the rites, and the ordinances necessary to accomplish that... People in this generation don't even have a clue how that necessarily has to roll forth. But rest assured, it will, it will.

Well there's a parable. It's just one verse. It's a very short parable. It moves along, but it's a response that Christ gave to the question that was put to Him by His disciples asking Him: "Tell us what the signs of your return is going to be." And he goes through a list of things but He ends with a little parable at the end. And our translation makes it seem kind of morbid. So I'm gonna substitute "body" for "carcass" because it sounds like what you're dealing with in the current King James version is morbid—not a living body. But He says one of the signs that is going to be of His return is; *Where the body is, that's where the eagles will gather.* The "body" is the New Jerusalem. The "eagles" are going to be angelic ministrants who are going to come.

There has to be an opening that occurs in order to prepare the way. The opening at this end is going to be handled by someone who has remained behind; and the opening at the far end is going to be the one to whom the assignment was given to open the way for His return—Elijah, the one who was promised.

Now, I want to be really clear. I don't expect either of those individuals to have any public ministry again. They have a role in Zion, and those who dwell in Zion are going to have some contact with them. The three Nephites are a great example. They, like John, were given a similar ministry to remain around and to minister until the end of the earth. And they did minister. Two of the people to whom they ministered were Mormon and Moroni. They, like ministering angels, ministered to Mormon who in turn ministered to the public. They ministered to Moroni, (and kept his hope up in the waning days of that dispensation) but they did not minister publicly. John will have a role, but the work of Zion is the work of *flesh and blood.*

Men have to extend the invitation for God to return so that men, who extend that invitation, are worthy of His return, and the Lord can safely come without utterly destroying all who are upon the earth. Therefore you need Zion, among other reasons, in order for there to be a place and a people to whom the Lord can safely return without utterly destroying the earth at His coming. However small, however diminutive it may be, there needs to be a Zion that extends the invitation for the Lord to return.

The Lord does everything according to His higher way of teaching. By beginning with a vision of His return, He set out the foundation for understanding His course, which is one eternal round. Since His first appearance, He has sent divers angels, from Adam or Michael to Hyrum and Joseph Smith, giving line upon line, to confirm my hope in Christ.

In a letter written August 16, 1834, Joseph Smith expected Zion could be established very soon. He wrote, "We have a great work to do but little time to do it in, and if we don't exert ourselves to the utmost in gathering up the strength of the Lord's house, there remaineth a scourge." In the same letter he reminded people in his day that, "So long as unrighteous acts are suffered in the church, it cannot be sanctified neither Zion be redeemed." At the time, he considered the church to be in a "languid, cold, disconsolate state." It was the opposite of the lively, confident, and happy state accompanying righteousness —even when worldly circumstances are direful and the wicked seem to triumph. When doing what the Lord asks, we can be lively, because He will accompany our efforts and add His strength to our labor. If we have a hope in Christ, we can be confident. If our sins have been forgiven, we have every reason to be happy.

In your language you use the name Lucifer for an angel who was in authority before God, who rebelled, fought against the work of the Father, and was cast down to the earth. His name means *holder of light*, or *light bearer*, for he gathered light by his heed and diligence before he rebelled. He has become a vessel containing only wrath and seeks to destroy all who will hearken to him. He is now enslaved to his own hatred.

Satan is a title and means *accuser, opponent, and adversary*. Hence, once he fell, Lucifer became—or in other words was called—Satan, because he accuses others and opposes the Father. I rebuked Peter and called him Satan because he was wrong in opposing the Father's will for me. And Peter understood and repented.

In the work you have performed, there are those who have been Satan, accusing one another, wounding hearts, and causing jarring, contention, and strife by their accusations. Rather than loving one another, even among you who desire a good thing, some have dealt unkindly as if they were opponents, accusers, and adversaries. In this they were wrong.

You have sought to recover the scriptures because you hope to obtain the covenant for my protective hand to be over you, but you cannot be Satan and be mine. If you take upon you my covenant, you must abide it, as a people, to gain what I promise. You think Satan will be bound a thousand years, and it will be so, but do not understand your own duty to bind that spirit within you so that you give no heed to accuse others. It is not enough to say you love God; you must also love your fellow man. Nor is it enough to say you love your fellow man while you, as Satan, divide, contend, and dispute against any person who labors on an errand seeking to do my will. How you proceed must be as noble as the cause you seek. You have become your own adversaries, and you cannot be Satan and also be mine. Repent, therefore, like Peter and end your unkind and untrue accusations against one another, and make peace. How shall there ever come a thousand years of peace if the people who are mine do not love one another? How shall Satan be bound if there are no people of one heart and one mind?

On the third day of April 1836, Joseph and Oliver were in the temple in Kirtland, Ohio. The veil was taken from their minds, and the eyes of their understanding were opened. They saw the Lord in his glory standing above them and the breastwork of the pulpit; and under his feet appeared as it were a paved work of pure gold, in color like amber. His eyes were as a flame of fire; the hair of his head was white like the pure snow; his countenance shone above the brightness of the sun; and his voice was as the sound of the rushing of great waters, even the voice of Jehovah, saying:

I am the Alpha and the Omega; I am he who was slain, I am he who lives; I am your advocate with the Father.

Behold, your sins are forgiven you; you are clean before me; therefore, lift up your heads and rejoice. Let the hearts of your brethren also rejoice, and let the hearts of all my people rejoice, who have, with their might, built this house to my name. For behold, I have accepted this house, and my name shall be here; and I will manifest myself to my people in mercy in this house. Yea, I will appear unto my servants, and speak unto them with mine own voice, if my people will keep my commandments, and do not pollute this holy house.

Behold and see: the hearts of thousands and tens of thousands shall greatly rejoice in consequence of the blessings that shall be poured out, and the endowment with which my servants will be endowed in this house. Behold: the fame of this house shall spread to foreign lands; and this is the beginning of the blessings I shall pour out upon my people. Even so. Amen.

As this vision closed, the heavens were again opened to their view, and they saw and beheld, and were endowed with knowledge from the beginning of this creation to the ends thereof. And they were shown unspeakable things from the sealed record of Heaven which man is not capable of making known but must be revealed by the Powers of Heaven. They beheld Michael, the archangel; Gabriel and Raphael, and divers angels, from Michael or Adam down to the end of time, showing in turns their dispensations, their rights, their keys, their honors, their majesty and glory, and the Powers of their Priesthood; giving line upon line, precept upon precept; endowing them with knowledge, even here a little, and there a little; holding forth hope for the work God was yet to perform, even the revelation of all things which are to come upon the earth until the return of the Lord in glory with His holy angels—to pour out judgment upon the world, and to reward the righteous. And they were unable to take it in; therefore they were commanded to pray and ask to comprehend by the power of the Spirit, to bring all things to their remembrance, even the Record of Heaven which would abide in them. Amen and Amen.

If there was anything more I could do or say that I thought would convince or persuade you to believe in Him, I would do it or I would say it. But despite it all, I realize some of you are going to walk out of here thinking that I'm just another one of these latter-day blowhards, and that's all good and well. Please, however, give heed to the scriptures I've read, the words of Joseph I've quoted, and the fact that I do have a witness that He's approachable. And that He's every bit as much alive today as He was when He walked on the road to Emmaus. And He's every bit as much willing to come and redeem you from the Fall as He is willing to redeem anyone. His work and His glory is culminated in you. His success is redeeming you.

If you think that, well, He's aloof; He's distant; and this is an impossibly high thing to achieve—the fact of the matter is—it is a greater achievement on His end to redeem you, than it is at your end to be redeemed. There's more anxiety, there's more desire, there's more rejoicing in Heaven, when He redeems someone from the Fall than there is here.

He came. He suffered. He lived. He died. He did what He did in order to lift all of Creation, and you are inextricably connected to Him. Therefore, trust that. Receive Him. It may start very slow, very small, very distant. Act on that. Hearken to that. It gets louder. You will never wind up in the company of Gods and angels if you're not willing to have faith in those preliminary things, that you receive, that ask you to go and to do.

————

The foregoing excerpts are taken from:

- Denver's *40 Years in Mormonism Series*, Talk #5 titled "Priesthood" given in Orem, UT on November 2nd, 2013
- Denver's *40 Years in Mormonism Series*, Talk #8 titled "A Broken Heart" given in Las Vegas, NV on July 25th, 2014;

- Denver's *40 Years in Mormonism Series*, Talk #9 titled "Marriage and Family" given in St. George, UT on July 26th, 2014
- Denver's *40 Years in Mormonism Series*, Talk #10 titled "Preserving the Restoration" given in Mesa, AZ on September 9th, 2014
- A fireside talk on "Plural Marriage", given in Sandy, UT on March 22, 2015
- A Q&A session titled "A Visit with Denver Snuffer" held on May 13, 2015
- His talk titled "Zion Will Come" given near Moab, UT on April 10th, 2016
- His conference talk titled "The Doctrine of Christ", given in Boise, ID on September 11th, 2016
- The presentation of "Answer and Covenant", given at the Covenant of Christ Conference in Boise, ID on September 3rd, 2017; and
- Denver's *40 Years in Mormonism Series*, Talk #7 titled "Christ, Prototype of the Saved Man" given in Ephraim, UT on June 28, 2014

PLEASE NOTE: This transcript includes additional material added later by Denver Snuffer, not found in the original recorded audio.

Today's podcast addresses important questions about Hope, but is only an introduction to ideas that listeners of any denomination may find important and relevant. These topics are more fully addressed in Denver's blog, including the entry titled "Alma 13:29" posted June 20, 2010, and in chapter 4 of his book Eighteen Verses.

80. Hope, Part 2

This is the second part of a series on "Hope," in which Denver addresses the questions: What is hope? How can hope be an anchor for the soul in times of tribulation?

———

DENVER: Before the creation, Christ was the great high priest of heaven who would redeem the creation by his sacrifice. The strength of their teaching was focusing on the individuals' relationship with Christ and no organization could replace that individual relationship.

The idea of the love of Christ was preserved in Johannine Christianity. Spirit, knowledge, and ritual were designed to preserve knowledge of Christ. Although lost to western Christianity, John taught that man would become divinitized—or ascend in stages of progression—to become just like God. His teachings have been lost, but two passages in the New Testament writings of John preserve that teaching still. First John 3, beginning at verse 1:

> Behold, what manner of love the Father hath bestowed upon us, that we should be called the sons of God: therefore the world knoweth us not, because it knew him not. Beloved, now are we the sons of God, and it doth not yet appear what we shall be: but we know that, when he shall appear, we shall be like him; for we shall see him as he is. And every man that hath this hope . . . purifieth himself, even as he is pure. (1 John 3:1-3; see also 1 John:13 RE).

And then in Revelation chapter 3, beginning in verse 20, it is Christ who is speaking:

> Behold, I stand at the door, and knock: if any man hear my voice, and open the door, I will come in to him, and will sup with him, and he with me. To him that overcometh will I grant to sit with me in my throne, even as I also overcame, and am set down with my Father in his throne.

Paul was a strict pharisee who followed the law. Paul persecuted Jesus' followers, even assisting when Stephen was killed for his testimony of Christ. He had a great many things to regret. Everything in his life, before his conversion to Christ, gave him a context for understanding Christ and Christ's message. Paul wanted grace, reconciliation, and justification because he needed these to have hope.

As the Lord knelt in prayer, His vicarious suffering began. He was overcome by pain and anguish. He felt within Him, not just the pains of sin, but also the illnesses men suffer as a result of the Fall and their foolish and evil choices. The suffering was long and the challenge difficult. The Lord suffered the afflictions. He was healed from the sickness. He overcame the pains, and patiently bore the infirmities until, finally, He returned to peace of mind and strength of body. It took an act of will and hope for Him to overcome the affliction which had been poured upon Him. He overcame the separation caused by these afflictions and reconciled with His Father. He was at peace with all mankind.

The Lord's suffering progressed from a lesser to a greater portion of affliction; for as one would be overcome by Him, the next, greater affliction would then be poured out. Each wave of suffering was only preparation for the next, greater wave.

The pains of mortality, disease, injury and infirmity, together with the sufferings of sin, transgression, guilt of mind, and unease of soul, the horrors of recognition of the evils men had inflicted upon others, were all poured out upon Him, with confusion and perplexity multiplied upon Him.

He longed for it to be over, and thought it would end long before it finally ended. With each wave He thought it would be the last, but then another came upon Him, and then yet another.

But the Lord was determined to suffer the Father's will and not His own. Therefore, a final wave came upon Him with such violence as to cut Him at every pore. It seemed for a moment that He was torn apart, and that blood came out of every pore. The Lord writhed in pain upon the ground as this final torment was poured upon Him.

All virtue was taken from Him. All the great life force in Him was stricken and afflicted. All the light turned to darkness. He was humbled, drained and left with nothing. It is not possible for a man to bear such pains and live, but with nothing more than will, hope in His Father, and charity toward all men, He emerged from the final wave of torment, knowing He had suffered all this for His Father and His brethren. By His hope and great charity, trusting in the Father, the Lord returned from this dark abyss and found grace again, His heart being filled with love toward the Father and all men. (T&C 161:3, 7-9, 11-12 RE)

Every night as the sun sets, God does something on the mountains that is never the same, always beautiful, and greater in beauty and splendor than anything Monet ever put on canvas.

We ought to love life, and we ought to love one another, and we ought to pursue our education; and we shouldn't bunker down with guns and ammo, fearfully waiting for a direful end to things. Of all people, Christians should have the most hope, the most optimism, the most vitality, and greatest amount of joy in life. We ought to celebrate every day.

Be like Christ—hopeful, and helpful, and positive. He went about doing good. That's who we're supposed to follow, and that's what we're supposed to do. That's how we're supposed to live. Be hopeful. Be helpful.

I hope you realize that God is real, and that He is as concerned about you, and your day, and in your life, as He was concerned about Peter, or Paul, or John, or Mary, or Elizabeth, or Abraham, or Sarah. Every one of you matter to Him. And if He were to speak to you out of heaven today, He would call you by name; just as He has done with everyone to whom He's ever spoken. And if the Lord calls you by name, it's not going to be by your full legal name. It's not going to be by what's on your birth certificate. He will call you by that name your best friend knows you, because God is intimate with every one of us. He knows everything, including the desires of your heart. And even though we are all rough customers, the fact is, the only reason you're here is because your heart is inclined to follow Him. Your aspirations, your desires, and your hopes can be perfect and your conduct can be reprehensible. God takes into account the perfection of your hope, and He evaluates you based upon your most noble aspirations. And he's cheering you on to try and get you to move a little closer, throughout your life, to that ideal—that perfection that you would like to have. We get hungry, we get tired, we get ill, we get weak, and so we excuse ourselves. But through it all, we can maintain the aspiration, the hope, the love of Christ. If you do that, He will take that into account as He deals with you.

When the apostle John wrote his epistle, he described those who had come in by way of conversion through him, and received from him what the Lord had given to him; and he says:

> Behold, what manner of love the Father hath bestowed upon us, that we should be called the sons of God: therefore the world knoweth us not, because it knew him not. Beloved, now are we the sons of God, and it doth not yet appear what we shall be: but we know that, when he shall

appear, we shall be like him; for we shall see him as he is. And every man that hath this hope in him purifieth himself, even as he is pure. (1 John 3:1-3; see also 1 John:13 RE)

I would like to suggest that the Holy Order after the Order of the Son of God includes the fact that those who inherit the Holy Order *are* sons of God. Therefore, in a way, calling it the Holy Order after the Order of the Son of God, is a way of identifying the recipient as someone who has become one of God's sons. Now I think it's appropriate to regard the primary identifier— that is the subject of who the Son of God is—to be Jesus Christ and Jesus Christ alone. Because quite frankly, He's the only one that attained to the resurrection, and it is through the power of the resurrection that we're going to come forth. We do not have the power in ourselves to rise from the dead. The wages of sin are death. We've earned those wages. We will die—we all will die. The Savior did not earn those wages. He died and therefore, His death was unjust; and the law of justice got broken when He died. And therefore, whenever justice makes a claim on any of us, He can point to the fact that justice extracted from Him eternal life—and that is an infinite price for Him to have paid. Therefore, He has compensated for all of mankind's shortcomings, failures; and Christ is the means by which we lay hold upon the promises, but it is His intention to make, of us all, sons of God. Therefore, the Holy Order after the Son of God is when the name is announced, self-identifying the person holding such a Holy Order as one of God's sons; even though they may be mortal; even though they may be in the flesh—the Holy Order is for that very purpose and is after the Order of the Son of God...

> "And all other priesthoods are only parts, ramifications, powers and blessings belonging to the same, and are held, controlled and directed by it. It is the channel through which the Almighty commenced revealing His glory at the beginning of the creation of this earth, and through which He has continued to reveal Himself to the children of men to the present time, and through which He will make known His purposes to the end of time." (Joseph Smith)

Therefore, among other things, the purpose of the Holy Order is to put in place a mechanism by which God can reveal, from heaven, what is necessary for the salvation of man on earth, in every generation; in order to fix what is broken; in order to restore what has been lost; in order to repair, heal, forgive, and reconnect those who are willing to give heed to the message sent from heaven, so that they can rise up to become sons of God.

Joseph Smith writes a letter while he's in exile in Nauvoo, and the letter also tracks what he did in his histories; but he mentions something that is not mentioned in the histories:

> *And again, what do we hear? Glad tidings from Cumorah! Moroni, an angel from heaven, declaring the fulfilment of the prophets—the book to be revealed. A voice of the Lord in the wilderness of Fayette, Seneca county, declaring the three witnesses to bear record of the book! The voice of Michael on the banks of the Susquehanna, [directing] the devil when he appeared as an angel of light! [...or detecting.] The voice of Peter, James, and John in the wilderness between Harmony, Susquehanna county, and Colesville, Broome county, on the Susquehanna river, declaring themselves as possessing the keys of the kingdom, ... of the dispensation of the fulness of times!* (D&C 128:20; see also T&C 151:15 RE)

I have the keys to my dodge truck. Do you have the keys to my dodge truck? Well, they declared themselves as possessing the keys.

> *And again, the Father of God in the chamber of old Father Whitmer...and at sundry times, and in divers places throughout all the travels and tribulations of the Church of Jesus Christ of Latter-day Saints! And the voice of Michael, the archangel; the voice of Gabriel, and of Raphael, and of divers angels, from Michael or Adam down to the present time, all declaring their dispensation, their rights, their keys, their honors, their majesty and glory, and the power of their priesthood; giving line upon line, precept upon precept; here a little, and there a little; giving us consolation by holding forth that which is to come, confirming our hope!* (D&C 128:21; see also T&C 151:15-17 RE)

So Joseph Smith is saying that he was in possession of great knowledge, but he also came into possession of greater knowledge; because Joseph was going to be called upon, in a very serious role, to achieve something that involved trying to bring back nations into the Holy Order that makes sons of God. Therefore, Joseph could not accomplish what needed to be accomplished without having greater knowledge than existed on the earth. And despite the discovery of Dead Sea scrolls, and Nag Hammadi, and research, and translation of texts that were not available in English at the time of Joseph Smith's lifetime, the fact remains that much of that material was simply corrupted. If you are going to try and understand the truth, the way in which that is brought about is by having possession of a *channel through which all knowledge, doctrine, the plan of salvation, and every important matter is revealed from Heaven* (T&C 140:2 RE). Joseph needed to not only be in possession of that channel, but the channel, therefore, needed to respond to—and did respond to—Joseph's petitions and inquiries, in order for him to be able to function in the position that he held.

Just like Joseph, we have perpetual conundrums and contradictions. We all face them. Some are of our own making, but others are just inherent in living in this existence. When we thoughtfully consider the challenges, just like Joseph, it seizes the mind; and like Joseph in Liberty Jail, makes us reflect upon so many things with the "avidity of lightning." That was Joseph's word. The mind is in this frenzied state, and with the avidity of lightning, he's jumping from subject to subject, offence to offence; from things that console, to things that outrage you. From things you know to be true, to things that offend you. Back and forth, and back and forth until, as Joseph puts it: "...finally all enmity, malice and hatred, and past differences, misunderstandings and mismanagement are slain victorious at the feet of hope; and when the heart is sufficiently contrite, then the voice of inspiration steals along and whispers[.]" It's almost poetry the way Joseph describes what he went through there. But it is poetry describing the actual bona fides of Joseph receiving answers from God.

I am certain we will see Zion, because it's been promised, and it's been prophesied from the beginning of time. When father Adam prophesied, being overcome by the Spirit in the valley of Adam-ondi-Ahman, and foretold what would happen to his posterity down to the latest generations, Zion was pointed to. And therefore, from the days of Adam on, all the holy prophets have looked forward to that as the essential moment in the history of the world, because Christ will come and will redeem the world. It will be the end of the wicked; it will be the beginning of something far better. That's been the hope. That's been the promise. That's been what they've looked forward to. I wonder how many of us share that same longing, that same hope, that same desire that originated in the beginning; because if we don't subdue our desires, appetites, and passions enough to try and deal peaceably one with another— choosing deliberately to not contend, even when we know people are wrong. When Christ was confronted and he corrected the error, he corrected only that error. He didn't go on with a list of other weaknesses, failings and challenges. He only addressed the one that was put to him.

We have an opportunity. We have a bona fide, actual offer from God to allow us to be that generation in which the promises get fulfilled. But we have the freedom of choice that allows us to elect to be severed, to be contentious, to be agents of disruption; and to discourage and break the hearts of those who would willingly accept the challenge to repent and follow God.

Accordingly, we must all decide what to make of Joseph Smith. All our fear, wonder and hope rests on resolving what to make of the life of Joseph. This frames the dichotomy in the legacy of that man. With hope in his authenticity, we see him as God's messenger. With doubts about him, we see him as a charlatan. These polar opposites are inherent in his life, and were foretold at the beginning and reconfirmed toward the end of his life.

The angel who appeared to Joseph in September 1823 said:

> "He called me by name, and said unto me that he was a messenger sent from the presence of God to me and that his name was Nephi, that God had a work for me to do, and that my name should be had for good and evil among all nations, kindreds, and tongues, or that it should be both good and evil spoken of among all people." (Times & Seasons, 15 April 1842, p.753)

My mother taught me to hold Joseph for evil. I've studied his life carefully, read what his critics and admirers have claimed for and about him. I've tried not to be hasty in reaching a conclusion. After four-and-a-half decades I've decided to hold Joseph for good. I'm all in. To me he is the real thing—a messenger sent from God to deliver a message that we reject at our peril and accept for our blessing. He had a great soul that searched, stretched, believed, hoped, fought fiercely, defied pain and persecution; and bore the hallmarks we should expect from a prophet messenger from God. He was a brilliant light—rough; cut; homespun; and rustic—but he was ablaze with insight, keen and penetrating; able to capture, with a phrase, a glimpse of the infinite.

Learn from these words Joseph wrote, while in Liberty Jail, about how to set aside all that distracts us to hear God's voice:

> *We received some letters last evening: one from Emma, one from Don C[arlos] Smith, … one from bishop … Partridge, all breathing a kind and consoling spirit. We were much gratified with their contents. We had been a long time without information, and when we read those letters, they were to our souls as the gentle air is refreshing. But our joy was mingled with grief because of the suffering of the poor and much injured saints, and we need not say to you that the floodgates of our hearts were hoisted, and our eyes were a fountain of tears. But those who have not been enclosed in the walls of a prison without cause or provocation can*

have but little idea how sweet the voice of a friend is. One token of
friendship from any source whatever awakens and calls into action every
sympathetic feeling. It brings up in an instant everything that is passed. It
seizes the present with a vivacity of lightning. It grasps after the future
with the fierceness of a tiger. It retrogrades from one thing to another,
until finally all enmity, malice, and hatred, and past differences,
misunderstandings, and mismanagements, lie slain victims at the feet of
hope. And when the heart is sufficiently contrite, then the voice of
inspiration steals along and whispers, My son, peace be unto your soul,
your adversity and your afflictions shall be but a small moment, and
then, if you endure it well, God shall exalt you on high[.] (T&C
138:11)

This world is a place of trial and testing. Before creation, it was planned that
when we came here we would be *proven* by what we experience. That happens
now. Prove yourself by listening to God, hearing His voice, and obeying.
Sometimes we are like Alma and want to do greater things to help God's
work; but the greatest work of all is to respond to God's voice, and prove you
are willing to listen and obey Him.

Take all that you know about nature, take all that you know about this world
and the majesty of it all. Take all that you know that informs you that there is
hope, there is joy, there is love. Why do you love your children? Why do your
children love you? These kinds of things exist. They're real. They're tangible.
And they're important. And they're part of what God did when He created
this world. Keep that in mind when you're studying. And search the scriptures
to try and help inform you how you can better appreciate; how you can better
enjoy; how you can better love; how you can better have hope. What do they
have to say that can bring you closer to God? Not, can I find a way to dismiss
something that Joseph said or did? As soon as Joseph was gone off the scene,
people that envied the position that he occupied took over custody of
everything, including the documents. And what we got, as a consequence of
that, is a legacy that allowed a trillion dollar empire to be constructed.
Religion should require our sacrifice. It should not be here to benefit us. We
should have to give—not get. And in the giving of ourselves, what we get is in
the interior; it's in the heart. It's the things of enduring beauty and value. If
your study takes you away from an appreciation of the love, the charity, the
things that matter most, reorient your study.

The voice of God came to Joseph in Liberty jail when his mind came to
peace.

Finally, hope and peace, and then comes the answer. We have a lot of reasons to be anxious in every one of our lives. There is so much that troubles us, but the voice of inspiration steals along and whispers—when we finally are calm enough. Be still, and know that I am God, gets read as: Be Still!! And know that I am God!! When what it's really saying is: "If you would like to know that I am God, quiet it all down, because whatever pavilion I may occupy, I also occupy part of you." You live and breathe and move because God is sustaining you from moment to moment by lending you breath. He's in you, and He's with everyone of us.

In Jacob chapter 3 verse 2 there's another reference: *We obtain a hope and our faith becometh unshaken, insomuch that we truly can command in the name of Jesus and the very trees obey us, or the mountains, or the waves of the sea.*

That's Jacob illustrating that the faith they have has this effect. He doesn't describe that effect having occurred, simply that it's there. Nephi explained, this is the power that God entrusted him with in Helaman:

> *For behold, the dust of the earth moveth hither and thither, to the dividing asunder, at the command of our great and everlasting God. Yea, behold, at his voice doth the hills and the mountains tremble and quake, and by the power of his voice are broken up and become smooth, yea, even like unto a valley.* (Helaman 4:10 RE)

He was given the sealing power. He was told that the earth will obey you—because he knew that he would not do anything with that power other than what God willed. And shortly after being entrusted by God to this, Nephi prays to God and asks God to send a famine to stop the people from killing one another. So here is someone who can speak the word of God, and the earth itself will obey him, and he uses that to get on his knees and pray and ask God. He doesn't command anything.

That kind of endowment of priestly authority is done because God expressed His faith in the man. Can God have faith in you? Can God trust you?

————

The foregoing excerpts were taken from:

- Denver's *Christian Reformation Lecture Series*, Talk #2 given in Dallas, TX on October 19th, 2017

- Denver's *Christian Reformation Lecture Series*, Talk #3 given in Atlanta, Georgia on November 16, 2017
- A fireside talk titled "The Holy Order", given in Bountiful, UT on October 19, 2017
- A fireside talk titled "That We Might Become One", given in Clinton, UT on January 14th, 2017
- The presentation of Denver's paper titled "The Restoration's Shattered Promises and Great Hope", given at the Sunstone Symposium in Salt Lake City, UT on July 28, 2018
- Denver's remarks titled "Keep the Covenant: Do the Work" given at the Remembering the Covenants Conference in Layton, UT on August 4, 2018
- Denver's remarks titled "Book of Mormon as Covenant" given at the Book of Mormon Covenant Conference in Columbia, SC on January 13, 2019; and
- Denver's lecture titled "Signs Follow Faith" given in Centerville, UT on March 3, 2019

Today's podcast addresses important questions about Hope, but is only an introduction to ideas that listeners of any denomination may find important and relevant. These topics are more fully addressed in Denver's blog, including the entry titled "Alma 13:29" posted June 20, 2010, and in chapter 4 of his book Eighteen Verses.

81. Peter

In this episode, Denver addresses topics connected with the apostle Peter, including keys, practices of early Christians, the Mount of Transfiguration, and more.

———

DENVER: There's a difference between belief and unbelief. Belief means that you have a body of correct information from which to draw in reaching your conviction concerning the gospel of Jesus Christ. Unbelief simply means that you're drawing upon information that is either incomplete, inaccurate, or outright false.

So, with those questions in mind— How shall they call on Him in whom they have not believed? How shall they believe in Him of whom they have not heard? How shall they hear without a preacher? And how shall they preach except they be sent? **Who** can send? In the Apostle Paul's series of declarations— WHO? Who can send? HOW can they be sent? There were no theological seminaries. There were no doctorates of theology. There was no doctorate of divinity.

It's the Catholics who believe and rely on Paul's questions to justify *their* claims. They claim to have an unbroken line of authority, traceable to Peter, to whom the keys of the kingdom were given by Christ. If you are a Protestant, do the keys of the kingdom matter? If you are a Catholic, *what are* the keys of the kingdom given Peter; and how confident are you that those can be transferred *at all*, since Peter got them from Christ directly? And if they can be transferred, how confident are you that they have survived, intact, today?

Protestants and Catholics must both face the question of whether salvation can be obtained apart from the Roman Catholic Church. But Paul asserts a different point, and asks a different question. Catholics and Protestants alike recognize Paul's authority and right to claim that he represented Christ. Paul's conversion, however, was not based on Peter. It was not based on a preacher who was sent to him. It was not dependent upon the keys of the kingdom given to Peter. Paul asserted he was an apostle, but his calling did not come because of a transfer of authority to him by Peter. He was called by God. He begins the first few words of his epistle to the Galatians: *Paul, an apostle, (not of men, neither by man, but by Jesus Christ, and God the Father, who raised him from the dead;)* (Galatians 1:1; see also Galatians 1:1RE).

Was Paul therefore sent? By whom was he sent? You think it obvious, no doubt, but the principle is critical to finding true faith in Jesus Christ. *He is the same* yesterday, today, and forever. If Paul was an apostle because Christ sent him—not men, or man—then for a preacher to be sent to preach the truth, the same should be required today as then. If Christ does not require the same, then Christ has changed, and we know that cannot be true for He is the same forever. If, therefore, a preacher must be sent, then Christ must do the sending. Then the *only* preacher you should heed must be one who declares plainly that he has been sent by God. That *was* the claim of Joseph Smith. It was a claim that ultimately cost his life. It was a claim that, given the hardship through which he passed, and the perils that he faced, and the betrayals that happened, and the lies that have been told by people who have profited by using his name, it is a claim that I believe and I accept.

Another example of one who was sent by God is John the Baptist, who is clearly identified in these words: *There was a man sent from God, whose name was John* (John 1:6; see also John 1:2 RE). Christ's apostles likewise were sent by Him, according to the New Testament. Christ said, *I have chosen you, and ordained you, that ye should go forth bringing forth fruit, and that your fruit should remain* (John 15:16; see also John 9:11 RE). Everyone sent by Christ to preach in the New Testament were given their message from Him. They were sent by Him. Joseph Smith declared he was likewise sent. I would invite you to investigate his claim and see whether it persuades you.

Today—and I say these words advisedly, and I want you to take them seriously— Today all Christian churches have become corrupt. They love money more, and acquiring financial security and church buildings more, than caring for the poor and the needy, the sick and the afflicted. The institutions claiming to be the church of God are all polluted by the cares of the world. I want you to understand what I mean by that. During the apostolic era, there was no such thing as a Christian church building. Christians met in homes. They did not collect and compensate ministers. They gathered money and they used it to help the poor and the needy among them.

Peter taught that Christians would progress in godliness until the Christian has his or her calling and election made sure:

> *That by these [things] ye might be partakers of the divine nature, having escaped the corruption that is in the world through lust. [Besides] this, giving all diligence, add to your faith virtue; and to virtue knowledge; And to knowledge temperance; and to temperance patience; and to*

patience godliness; And to godliness brotherly kindness; and to brotherly kindness charity. For if these things be in you, and abound, they make you that ye shall [be neither] barren nor unfruitful in the knowledge of our Lord Jesus Christ. But he that lacketh these things is blind, and cannot see afar off, and hath forgotten that he was purged from his old sins. Wherefore the rather, brethren, give diligence to make your calling and election sure: for if ye do these things, ye shall never fall. (2 Peter 1:4-10; see also 2 Peter 1:1-3 RE)

Justin Martyr lived from 110-165 A.D. and he wrote in the Sub-apostolic Age. His writings give us a glimpse into how Christianity functioned in its earliest days. In his *First Apology* he describes Christian worship. They met in homes, having no church buildings. Before being considered a Christian, a candidate was baptized "In the name of God, the Father and Lord of the universe, and...our Savior Jesus Christ, and of the Holy Spirit" (*First Apology*, Chapter LXI, Christian Baptism).

Meetings began with a prayer and "[saluting] one another with a kiss." Then sacrament was prepared and administered using a "cup of wine mixed with water" and bread, which is blessed by "[giving] praise and glory to the Father of the universe, through the name of the Son and of the Holy Ghost, and offers thanks at considerable length for our being counted worthy to receive these things at His hands" (Ibid., Chapter LXV, Administration of the Sacraments).

The early Christians recognized there was an obligation for "the wealthy among us [to] help the needy." Therefore, after reading scripture and "the memoirs of the apostles or the writings of the prophets," donations were collected (Ibid., Chapter LXVII, Weekly Worship of the Christians). Then the donations were distributed to help those who were poor or needy among that group of Christians.

These simple observances were resilient enough to preserve Christianity after the death of the apostles and before any great hierarchical magisterium arose. It was the power of baptism, the sacrament, scripture study, and financial aid among believers that gave Christianity its power. But it was diffused, and therefore incapable of destruction.

When Justin Martyr was slain, the scattered Christians continued, unaffected. It was just like when Peter and Paul were slain, and before them, James was killed. The power of Christianity reckoned from the vitality of its original roots. These roots were in Christ, His message, His teachings; which were employed to relieve one another by the alms shared from rich to poor.

When a centralized hierarchy took control over Christianity, the money that was used for the poor, the widows, and orphans was diverted to build churches, cathedrals, basilicas and palaces. Ultimately, the wealth generated by the generosity of Christian believers became the tool used by the hierarchy to buy up armies, kings, lands, and treasures, which were used to rule and reign as a cruel master over a subjugated population—made miserable by the abuse heaped on them from Rome.

Even after the Protestant Reformation, Christianity continued to be ruled by hierarchies. Cathedrals and church buildings consumed—and consume—resources that are to be used to help the poor. Christ built no building, although He accepted the temple in Jerusalem as His Father's house. Peter built no church building, nor Paul, nor James, nor John. Christianity in the hands of the Lord and His apostles needed no brick and mortar for its foundation. It was built on the hearts of believers, brought together by the charity and assistance shared between them.

Petrine Christians: These were followers of a tradition that could be traced to Peter. These Christians emphasized authority and viewed their leaders as shepherds over exiles from heaven. It was the Petrine tradition that led to hierarchical control, as a central feature of the later kind of Christianity that survived. Peter's original teachings evolved and changed, and Peter can't be held accountable for what occurred in a corrupted system. As it evolved, sheep—that is, believers—followed bishops, who were the successors to the apostles. These bishops were believed to hold a commission to lead the flock.

Because original Christianity was peacefully diverse, the differences found in the earliest forms are somewhat preserved in our New Testament. I got a question from the website; I'm reading you the question that came in: "Is it possible Paul and Jesus taught two different gospel messages? There is debate: such *is* the case, *or is it* Paul expressed the message differently than Jesus did? In other words, did Jesus elaborate more content and less terminology, justification, reconciliation, grace, et cetera, and Paul did the opposite? It seems Christ, Peter, James, and John's messages were sublime and easy to understand, whereas Paul's letters are difficult to understand and require fitting the pieces together."

So let's take a look at those two witnesses. Paul was a strict pharisee who followed the law. Paul persecuted Jesus' followers, even assisting when

Stephen was killed for his testimony of Christ. He had a great many things to regret. Everything in his life before his conversion to Christ gave him a context for understanding Christ and Christ's message. Paul wanted grace, reconciliation, and justification because he needed these to have hope.

Peter was a fisherman, but he walked alongside Christ for years. He saw Christ heal the sick, heard Him bless the children, saw Him walk on water. He knew that storms were quieted by Christ's word. He saw the dead rise, and stood on the Mount of Transfiguration when the Father declared Christ was His Son.

Peter was as qualified a witness as Paul to testify Christ was the promised Messiah, but we cannot expect two witnesses with such different experiences, and from such different backgrounds as Peter's and Paul's, to provide us identical testimonies of Christ. Both Paul and Peter understood and explained Christianity according to their background experiences, training, and culture. So long as they agreed on Christ's doctrine and accepted Christ's law, that was enough. They were both Christian and provided us with truth.

I believe Christ has spent the last 500 years inspiring mankind to restore a more correct form of Christianity. He declared He would return again in glory to judge the world, but before His return many prophecies remain to be fulfilled. Almost the entire burden of prophecy focuses on two events: the First Coming of Christ and the Second Coming of Christ. And a great deal about the Second Coming of Christ will require that there be things that occur, prior to His return in glory, that will involve the restoration and the presence of those who speak in His name with authority—testimonies to be born. The world cannot be judged without an adequate prior warning being given. Even if the world is ignoring the message, it doesn't matter. God assumes the obligation to making clear His plans. He assumes the obligation of having the warning voice sound, and whether the world gives any heed or not, it doesn't matter. They've been warned and they will be judged.

One of the prophecies came through Peter. He declared:

> Repent ye therefore, and be converted, that your sins may be blotted out, when the times of refreshing shall come from the presence of the Lord; And he shall send Jesus Christ, which before was preached unto you: Whom the heaven must receive until the times of restitution of all things, which God hath spoken by the mouth of all his holy prophets since the world began. (Acts 3:19-21; see also Acts 2:3 RE)

The time of refreshing—or restoring—promised to come from the presence of the Lord has, in fact, begun. Jesus Christ has been sent again to prepare for His return. I believe that Joseph Smith was an authentic messenger, called by Christ, to help *us* become more Christian. One message sent by Christ in 1829 explains more of what He, Christ, accomplished as the sacrificial Lamb who atoned for our sins. We know from Isaiah that by His stripes we are healed. God laid on Him the iniquity of us all. He bore our griefs, carried our sorrows, and the chastisement *we* earned was put upon Him. (See Isaiah 53:1-6 and Mosiah 14:1-5; see also Isaiah 19:2 RE and Mosiah 8:1-3 RE).

Traditionally, Christians have understood *that* to have been accomplished in the Roman beating, scourging, and crucifixion of Christ. However, many men suffered similarly at the hands of Rome. Christ suffered to remove our sins and repair the *fall* of mankind. Isaiah's description suggests that this was cosmic, and that Christ took the entire burden of mankind's sins upon Himself. Only Luke gives a glimpse into Christ's suffering in Gethsemane. Luke describes it in these words: *And being in an agony he prayed more earnestly: and his sweat was as it were great drops of blood falling down to the ground* (Luke 22:44; see also Luke 13:9 RE).

The way in which the blessings of Peter, James, and John, and the naming of Peter, James, and John, occurs on the Mount of Transfiguration— They went up and they were on the Holy Mount. They were endowed with knowledge. They saw the history of the world, right down to the end of time. They were given an insight into things. We learn about that in Doctrine and Covenants —I think it's 67, but it's in there, you can read it. (See D&C 63:20-21; see also T&C 50:5 RE). They were shown essentially everything because they saw what they saw. This was the reason why Peter negotiated a rapid resurrection. He didn't want to camp in the spirit world. And this is why John said, "Well, I don't want to go there, let me just stay here and I'll minister here." And they made choices as a result of the knowledge that they got on the Mount about what was going to happen down to the end of time. (See D&C 7:1-8; see also T&C Joseph Smith History 13:17-19 RE).

But, this is an order. Peter, and James, and John are symbols of Abraham, Isaac, and Jacob: grandfather, father, and son. And it was Jacob through whom the nations—the twelve tribes, the twelve nations of Israel—were established. And so John, he produced a righteous son. I don't know about the children of Katura, but Ishmael and Jacob have continued their bloodshed right down to this minute. Esau sold his birthright and the garment to Jacob, who presented it to Joseph. And he's the one through whom a great progeny developed.

Peter, James, and John— John is the one who remained to create, as a ministering angel, an analogous progeny—by his ministrations as a ministering angel through the ages. So, when you get to the names of Peter, James, and John in the restoration story, we don't have enough details of what happened to be able to correctly construct *exactly how* Peter, James, and John fit within the restoration of the gospel in the last days. So, if we're going to put them into a context, I would not say that the reason that they came was in order to ordain someone, when that has a really good account provided to us in the account of the conference that happened in June of 1831. I described that in *A Man Without Doubt*, beginning on about page 19 and going through, well, the end of that section.

The folks that got ordained at that conference included five that Joseph Smith ordained: Lyman White, who was excommunicated in 1848; Harvey Whitlock, excommunicated in 1835; Thomas Marsh—who left the Church in 1838, signed an affidavit against Joseph which contributed to his imprisonment in Missouri—he was excommunicated in 1839; Parley Pratt, who apostatized and was excommunicated in 1842, but then reinstated in 1843. Those are the ones Joseph ordained.

The ones Lyman White ordained: John Whitmer, excommunicated 1838; Rigdon, excommunicated in 1844; Partridge, died in 1840; Ezra Thayer, refused to follow the Twelve after Joseph and Hyrum were martyred. (Well, that guy has some potential. [Laughs.]) Joseph Wakefield was excommunicated in January 1834. Ezra Boothe apostatized within months and went on to write anti-Mormon and anti-Joseph publications— And it just goes on; you can read it in there. It didn't work out as well as had been hoped.

The way in which, I would suggest, it would be best to understand is that they came, not for purposes of conferring priesthood—that would occur in June of 1831—but for reconnecting the genealogical line that required someone to be designated as descendants from "the Fathers".

The promise made by Elijah is about reconnecting us to the Fathers. Joseph called them the Fathers in heaven. These are *not* our kindred dead because our kindred dead are required to be redeemed by us. These are the Fathers in heaven. Among them would be Abraham, Isaac, and Jacob; and because of this dispensation being what it is, Peter, James, and John.

The purpose of the Holy Ghost is to allow you to see things in their true light, with the underlying intent behind them, and to allow you to do that without distortion and without confusion. The temple is a ceremony designed to teach you about the path back to God; the very same thing that the Book of Mormon teaches repeatedly. The path back to God is so that you can meet with and be instructed by our Savior. The purpose of our Savior is to prepare us in all things so that we can, at last, become Zion. Because if *your* heart is right and *my* heart is right, and if I'm looking to God and God only, and you're looking to God and God only, then the trivial things of having things in common are of *so little import* that they matter not.

If you're faithful to the Lord, you have no reason to pick a fight with anyone else. Our Lord was a peacemaker. We ought to be peacemakers as well. I have nothing but appreciation for The Church of Jesus Christ of Latter-day Saints. They publish the scriptures that make me wise to salvation. They build the temples in which we can go and learn about the mysteries of God. They delivered to me, through the voice of some Utah boys—I mean they were about the same age as I was, but they were so young and naïve in my universe that I considered them boys—a testimony about the restoration of the gospel through the prophet Joseph Smith. And I have a stronger testimony of the restoration today than I did the day I was baptized. I believe it more fervently, and I know a great deal more about the mysteries of God than I ever thought possible.

I don't think I'm special. If you really knew enough about me to realize that this preaching is not the full definition of who I am, you would probably agree that you're better people than I am. But, I wanted to know *Him*. And I was willing to give away anything and everything; and I am still willing to give away anything and everything. There is *nothing* that I value above the Lord. And I hope that everyone here understands that statement.

If you want to know what one can accomplish without faith, but with an ordination to the priesthood, there's a whole discussion of that in *A Man without Doubt*—about the first attempt to distribute the highest order of priesthood in Joseph's day. There's a description of what an utter failure that was. In fact, it was so great a failure that what Joseph did was he backed up, and he started over again with trying to solve the problem. And the problem did not consist of priesthood, it consisted of the lack of faith. The Lectures on Faith are an attempt to create faith that will have power—which is separate from priesthood.

Men, women, and children can have faith. There was a time when the Mary Fielding story had *her* anointing her oxen and healing them. In the world of the correlated LDS model, she's now calling for the equivalent of Home Teachers to come anoint her oxen. Mary Fielding's *faith* was what healed the oxen.

Would you rather have priesthood without faith, or faith without priesthood? If you have faith, *everything else is possible*. Faith is what is lacking. It is the more important—and *not* this priesthood envy. (Oh, the trouble I could get into by going too far.)

Look, at the end of the day, Peter did not hold any greater or different authority when he came back from a mission and said, "We couldn't cast out any devils. We're bringing this person to you, Lord. Whatever it was you gave us, whatever that ordination thing was, it's just not working." And then Christ said, "Well, this kind come not out except by fasting and prayer." (See Matthew 17:14-21; see also Matthew 9:6-7 RE). Meaning that there is a work to be done to subordinate the body, in order to give the strength to your faith—*necessary* to achieve something.

Peter had absolutely no different ordination than when he entered the temple following the Lord's resurrection, and said, *Silver and gold have I none; but such as I have give I [unto you]: In the name of Jesus Christ...[arise, take up your bed] and walk* (Acts 3:1-8; see also Acts 2:1 RE). What Peter had that was *different* was faith. His ordination amounted to no power, but his faith in Christ healed the sick. And that is not controlled by institutions. That is not controlled by ordination. If you want to know how it's controlled, study the Lectures on Faith, and then listen to what Lisa had to say this morning because she was right on the money.

Zion will require a worthy people. There's a second general epistle as we've got it preserved for us in Peter 2—Second Peter—in which he talks about what he would like to see. I am going to begin at verse 5:

> [Besides] this, giving all diligence, add to your faith virtue; and to virtue knowledge; And to knowledge temperance; and to temperance patience; and to patience godliness; And to godliness brotherly kindness; and to brotherly kindness charity. For if these things be in you, and abound, they [shall] make you that ye shall neither be barren nor unfruitful in the knowledge of our Lord Jesus Christ. (2 Peter 1:5-7; see also 2 Peter 1:2 RE)

This was a great admonition, and this is a great path. And I think Peter thought this through because he knew that this was a progression, that actually follows in almost this order, in almost every life. However, those Saints of that day did not have Zion despite this admonition. Therefore, if you are going to see it in your day, you have to do something more. We have to be more holy than were they. We have to be more disciplined than were they. You see, the word 'discipline' and the word 'disciple' come from the same word. We need to have *greater* virtue than they did.

The Savior is extraordinarily positive; and when He speaks negatively, it's at those moments that I want to pay particular attention and give some careful consideration. One of the spots in which—in 3rd Nephi, in His visit with the Nephites at Bountiful—He spoke quite negatively, He attributed the content of His pessimistic prophecy to the Father; and noted that the reason why He was stating it was because the Father had told Him to. This is in 3rd Nephi chapter 16, verse 10:

> *And thus commandeth the Father that I should say unto you:* [is how He prefaces His direful assessment of the latter-day gentiles]. *At that day when the Gentiles* **shall** *sin against my gospel, and* **shall** *reject the fulness of my gospel, and* **shall** *be lifted up in the pride of their hearts above all nations...above all the people of the whole earth, and* **shall** *be filled with all manner of lyings, and of deceits, and of mischiefs, and [of] all manner of hypocrisy, and murders, and priestcrafts* [and then He goes on from there]...*and shall reject...behold, saith the Father* [this is Christ attributing what the Father has told Him as the source for His message], *I will bring the fulness of my gospel from among them.* (3 Nephi 16:10; see also 3 Nephi 7:5 RE; emphasis added)

In that list, we all can make a self-assessment about a variety of things. But the fact that He included, within the list of the defects of the last-day gentiles, the word 'priestcrafts,' ought to alarm every one of us. Because priestcraft, when it gets defined in the Book of Mormon, is something that I think all are tempted to engage in. Peter was equally concerned, and in his first Epistle [chapter] 5, verses 2 and 3, he wrote: *Feed the flock of God which is among you, taking the oversight thereof, not by constraint, but willingly;* **not for filthy lucre,** *but of a ready mind; Neither as being lords over the [Lord's] heritage, but being ensamples [unto] the flock* (1 Peter 5:2-3; see also 1 Peter 1:19 RE; emphasis added).

It is not appropriate that someone should collect money from the flock, nor "lord it over the flock." Priestcraft is one of those toxic failures of the last-day gentiles—that we have to guard against it appearing among us, as well.

QUESTION FROM AUDIENCE: What's your stance on multiple mortal probations or reincarnation?

DENVER: Dude... [audience laughs]. Multiple mortal probations is probably (let me put it this way)—even if true—a distraction from the test that is presently underway. There are living today, that I've encountered, at least a dozen Peters; I mean like Peter, New Testament Peter, back here again doing his thing. None of *those* fish, though [laughs]. I've met a handful of Johns. I've met four or five Mary Magdalenes. I've met at least three Mother Marys. Okay, so, assuming one of them actually nailed it and they *are* that, what's that got to do with the price of cheese in Wisconsin? How is it going to help you? Are you honest, are you kind, are you charitable? "No, dude, I'm Peter! I mean, once, long ago and far away, I walked on water briefly and I sank. But dude, I did it—and you haven't. So okay, watch me sprint into a pool and I'll accomplish kind of the same thing. I'll stay up for a little—" What's it got to do with anything? Yes, maybe there's something to it; probably not in the form in which most people, who believe in it, believe in it.

What's the definition of a creation? How often in a creation does one appear? If you look carefully at the scriptures, the disciples on the Mount of Transfiguration talking with Christ are given a fulsome vision of everything that is now going to unfold, on into the future. And, these are the disciples; this is Peter, James, and John standing there on the Mount. They look at this, and they look upon the long absence of their spirit from their bodies and they regard it as a form of prison, and so they figure out an escape route. I mean, it's in the scriptures. John says, "Don't send me there, let me stay in this arena and do battle here." And Peter and James—it's actually Jacob—James say, "Let us come speedily into your kingdom," meaning, don't leave us there; resurrect us. They will miss the resurrection because the first resurrection was when Christ came out of the grave, and they were going to die *after* that. Therefore, they were left there. They said, "No, don't leave us there." And so, they secured an early resurrection; so they're not in the spirit world. (See D&C 7:1-8; see also T&C Joseph Smith History 13:17-19 RE).

If a long time in the spirit world is not part of the agenda, then they had no reason to take that up as an issue and have that discussion with the Lord, and make the choices they did. Therefore, if multiple mortalities is like, you know, on Wednesday I die and on Monday I'll be resurrected or reborn as someone else, then there is no long absence of the spirit from the body—there is a continual return. But then you get into the definition of creation, and how many creations have there been for this world, and topics about which even Joseph kept his mouth shut; and so, I'll put a cork in it.

————

The foregoing excerpts are taken from:

- Denver's *Christian Reformation Lecture Series*, Talk #1, given in Cerritos, California on September 21, 2017;
- Denver's *Christian Reformation Lecture Series*, Talk #2, given in Dallas, Texas on October 19, 2017;
- Denver's *Christian Reformation Lecture Series*, Talk #3, given in Atlanta, Georgia on November 16, 2017;
- A fireside talk titled "The Holy Order," given in Bountiful, Utah on October 29, 2017;
- A fireside talk on "The Temple," given in Ogden, Utah on October 28th, 2012;
- Denver's conference talk titled "The Doctrine of Christ," given in Boise, Idaho on September 11, 2016;
- Denver's *40 Years in Mormonism Series*, Talk #10, titled "Preserving the Restoration," given in Mesa, Arizona on September 9, 2014;
- His talk titled "Zion Will Come," given near Moab, Utah on April 10th, 2016; and
- His talk titled "Other Sheep Indeed," given at the Sunstone Symposium in Salt Lake City, Utah on July 29th, 2017.

Today's podcast addresses important questions about Peter and keys, but is only an introduction to ideas that listeners of any denomination may find important and relevant. These topics are more fully addressed in Denver's talk titled "Authority, Keys and Kingdom," given in Sandy, Utah on July 14, 2019.

82. Hope, Part 3

This is the final part of a special series on "Hope," in which Denver addresses the questions: What is hope? How can hope be an anchor for the soul in times of tribulation?

———

DENVER: This is a discussion of hope. It's based upon material that I've previously written as a chapter—chapter 4—in the book *Eighteen Verses*. That chapter is titled "Hope and Mansions." The chapter begins with a quote from the book of Ether. The quote states,

> *And I also remember that thou hast said that thou hast prepared a house for man, yea, even among the mansions of thy Father, in which man might have a more excellent hope. Wherefore, man must hope, or he cannot receive an inheritance in the place which thou hast prepared.* (Ether 12:32; see also Ether 5:6 RE)

That comment is part of an interruption in the book of Ether. The book of Ether was taken from 24 plates. During his abridgment of the Book of Mormon, Mormon (the abridger) mentioned that he intended to include a translation of those 24 plates as part of his translation of the Book of Mormon, but he died before completing that process. The plates were given to his son. His son finished out the record. And after finishing out his father's book, he then added the book of Ether as a translation to fulfill his father's commitment.

In the middle of doing the translation, Moroni didn't feel that his effort was adequate. And he complained to the Lord about his own inability and how the Gentiles would mock that inability as they read his version of the translation of the book of Ether—contrasting the greatness of the words that were contained in the writings from the Jaredites with his own weakness as a translator. And in the middle of his complaining to the Lord, there's this dialogue that happened between Christ and Moroni, and **this** is part of that interruption of the book of Ether and reflects a dialogue that happened between Christ and Moroni.

So when he says, *And I also remember that thou hast said that thou hast prepared a house for man, yea, even among the mansions of thy Father* (ibid), Moroni is saying that he remembers that Christ told him that Christ had prepared a house for man among the mansions of the Father of Christ, *in which man might have a more excellent hope. Wherefore, man must hope, or he cannot receive an inheritance in the place which thou hast prepared* (ibid). This statement is rather profound, connecting hope to mankind's eternal inheritance. We're going to look at that as part of this summary, and it's examined in that chapter 4 of *Eighteen Verses*.

Christ is the one who prepares this house for man in the afterlife. And **Christ** links the concept of hope and the afterlife-inheritance-of-a-house clearly, in this statement in the dialogue between Him and Moroni. We are able to inherit an afterlife-house or -existence because it's made possible through our return to life by the resurrection that was brought about by Christ. We receive that house in the afterlife in order to rise up from the grave and return again into the Heavens to be where the Gods are and to renew a status there. We're going to have a place or a habitation or a resurrection provided by Christ after this life; and that, of course, is the great promise of the atonement.

But the house, says in the verse, that there's something else called "mansions" that belong to the Father (*among the mansions of thy Father*). We tend to think of mansions as some kind of a large, rolling estate that has a lot of servants taking care of it 'cause it's too large for a simple husband and wife to occupy and take care of. But the word "mansion" (in the Greek version, where the word is used in the New Testament), implies a temporary stopping point—or a hotel, in our modern language, or a hostel—someplace where you come, you stay temporarily, and you move on.

If the implication is some "great estate," then what the verse is communicating is that we'll get a house, and that house will be among a place where there are also mansions that had been created by the Father in the hopes that eventually we may likewise inherit a mansion. If, instead, it's a temporary, stopping place, then what we're being promised is an opportunity to rise up and continue on in the process of progression, rising from exaltation to exaltation, until ultimately we receive the resurrection as a right, as an achievement of our own.

A house for man and mansions—there are many of these things, and it suggests that there's going to be different kinds of inheritances in the afterlife, meaning what you choose here and how you behave here has an affect upon there. The purpose of the plan of salvation is not just to have man rise from the grave in some kind of resurrected body (whether it's telestial, terrestrial, or celestial), but the purpose is to permit man to continue on in the journey to exaltation. Everything in the plan of salvation is designed, ultimately, to bring about the celestial exaltation of **all** of the Father's descendants.

When we think of the Father in eternity, that word/that statement/that title is associated with power, glory, and dominion. He's often mentioned in connection with a throne. He presides over everything. He made possible the creation itself. He continues to use that same creative power to sustain us, to prevent us from dissolving back into chaos by preserving us from moment to moment. As King Benjamin put it, the Father *created you from the beginning, [and has preserved] you from day to day by lending you breath that [you] may live, and move, and do according to your own will, and even supporting you from one moment to another* (Mosiah 1:8 RE). Christ, when He was here in the mortal condition said, *I can of my own self do nothing* (TSJ 5:5). When we see the Father mentioned in scripture, we should think of Him who makes all things possible. It is He whose glory, might, and dominion defy all description. The use of "mansions" for mankind (which will be alongside or among the dwelling place of the Father) suggests that we can ultimately be welcomed to live with Him or, as He says in the Book of Revelation, *to sit [on] my throne even as I [have sat down upon] my Father['s]...throne* (Revelation 1:20 RE). And that opportunity is the purpose to preserve us.

But overarching the process of inheritance is the language that Christ uses in His promise about hope—*more excellent hope*. Hope is one of the three bedrock virtues: faith, hope, and charity. A *more excellent hope* suggests a qualitative hopefulness, something of a higher sort. We need to determine how anyone can gain hope which is "more excellent."

The verse includes this wonderful phrase on hope: *Man must hope, or he cannot receive* (Ether 12:32; see also Ether 5:6 RE). That phrase is filled with a great deal of significance. The term "hope," particularly as it's used here, is not that well understood. We sometimes view it as a weak virtue—something of a wisp, a phantom; something that we emote that we would like or desire. But in this context, the word "hope" is much more. It's a **concrete assurance based upon a promise or a covenant**. Hope comes from knowing the Lord has promised a person something. As the Lord has assured us, He does not make (and then break) promises. When He promises something, He **will deliver** it. He does not excuse Himself; even *though the heavens and the earth [may] pass away, [His word] shall not pass away but shall [all] be fulfilled* (T&C 43:3). Anyone who receives a promise from Him has an absolute certainty.

However, the promises of the Lord are invariably about the future, even if it's about the immediate future:

- To Abraham, the promise of a son preceded Isaac's birth by many years.

- To Joseph, the promise of his brothers and father bowing to him was given in a dream many years before he was actually sitting in power in Egypt.

- From the time of the promise to Moses (that Israel would be delivered by his hand) to the time Israel was delivered out of Egypt, there were many months, trials, confrontations, and difficulties.

Between the promise given and the realization of the promise—in every one of these instances—there was only **hope**. It was hope, linked to faith—but hope, nonetheless.

This is the kind of hope spoken of in this verse. It is not a vague notion or a whimsical possibility. **It's trust and confidence springing from a promise given to a person by God.** It is something far greater, more profound, more strongly-felt, more firmly-based than just "expectancy from vague desire."

The word "hope" is commonly used to describe unlikely things. We use "hope" to describe what we want the outcome of a contest between the underdog team and the favored team to be. Hope, in that context, is more of a preference for the outcome. Used in that sense, hope is not based upon anything more than our desire to see the weaker side triumph. Such a preference or desire is not how the word is used in this scripture. As used here, **hope comes from a promise given by God and describes the state of mind of the recipient during the time interval *after* the promise but *before* its realization.** He or she is in the same position as:

- Abraham was *after* God's promise to him, *prior* to Isaac's birth.

- They're like Moses *after* the encounter with the mountainside menorah, where God promised him Israel was to be delivered, but *before* Israel's actual deliverance had taken place.

- They're like Joseph when serving Potiphar, knowing God's promises to him *had not yet happened but certainly would* come to pass.

- This kind of hope relies upon the promise as an anchor to their soul. Hope means "the waiting period." Faith is being tried, but there is every reason to have confidence in the promise because it came from God. Anyone who has the faith to *obtain* such a promise from God can surely have the faith to *trust* the promise will be obtained.

Joseph uses "hope" in a letter which is part of the Teachings & Commandments. As it appears there, Joseph's letter is speaking of that very same kind of hope. He wrote,

> And again, what do we hear? Glad tidings from Cumorah! Moroni, an angel from Heaven, declaring the fulfillment of the prophets, the book to be revealed! A voice of the Lord in the wilderness of Fayette, Seneca County, declaring the three witnesses to bear record of the book. The voice of Michael on the banks of the Susquehanna, detecting the Devil when he appeared as an angel of light. The voice of Peter, James...and John in the wilderness between Harmony, Susquehanna County, and Colesville, Broome County, on the Susquehanna River, declaring themselves as possessing the keys of the kingdom and of the dispensation of the fullness of times. And again, the voice of God in the chamber of old father Whitmer's...in Fayette, Seneca County, and at sundry times and in diverse places, [through] all the trials and tribulations of [the] Church of Jesus Christ of Latter Day Saints. And the voice of Michael the archangel, the voice of Gabriel, and of Raphael, and of diverse angels from Michael, or Adam, down to the present time, all declaring...
>
> Their dispensation, their rights, their keys, their honors, their majesty and glory, and the power of their Priesthood.
>
> [Giving] line upon line, precept upon precept, here a little and there a little, giving us consolation by holding forth that which is to come...**confirming our hope.** (T&C 151:15-17, emphasis added)

Joseph uses "hope" in exactly the same way as Moroni does in his commentary in the middle of the book of Ether. The hope spoken of here has arisen from a multitude of miraculous events pointing to the **reason** for hope. He mentions the prior miraculous visits from angelic visitors; the voice of Christ to the three witnesses; Michael, the archangel, detecting the Devil; Peter, James, and John; God the Father's voice; Gabriel (another archangel); and an unnamed host of angels who were prophets during their mortality and possessed keys during their mortal existence. From among all these were passed to Joseph the understanding that was necessary from the **prior** dispensation, in order for him to be able to discharge his responsibility in **this** dispensation. These various angelic and divine visitors caused Joseph to be consoled *by holding forth that which is to come*—meaning they had given him reason to believe in the promises which had been given. **These experiences had the effect of confirming his hope.** This is the concept in which hope is used in both Joseph's letter and by Moroni. It is a lively expectation based upon the witness from Heaven, promising a thing shall surely be. It is because of a person's confidence in God's promise to them that they have this kind of hope. Joseph wrote of hope because he had had so many witnesses to him from beyond the veil that his faith was unshakable in the expectation of all the promises to be realized.

Hope involves unshakable faith or confidence. It is the thing Jacob writes about when he records in his book,

> Wherefore, we search the prophets, and we have many revelations and the spirit of prophecy. And having all these witnesses, we **obtain a hope** and our faith becometh unshaken, insomuch that we truly can command in the name of Jesus and the very trees obey us, or the mountains, or the waves of the sea. (Jacob 3:2 RE, emphasis added)

The hope comes from many **revelations** in the spirit of prophecy. It's based upon **witnesses** coming from beyond the veil to confirm the expectations. It causes **faith**, which is unshakable, and can cause mountains to move. It is a **power within**, confirmed by Heaven itself, which causes the person to know, through their very being, that a thing shall surely come to pass. It is hope which is **powerful, controlling, and causes a thing to come to pass because it is now their right to receive the thing promised**. God has conferred that right upon them. This is not simply a virtue; it's powerful, even controlling. It bends reality as we know it because it permits a higher power to intervene in the lives of people holding such hope. They have the power to seize upon blessings promised to them and bring them down into their lives. It is godly because it originates in trust, faith, and confidence in God who made the promise.

Hope also involves the afterlife. Our expectations for the afterlife are controlled by the faith we acquire here. Some depart this life with the firm hope of a glorious resurrection. They have this hope because they've made a suitable sacrifice while in this life to obtain the promises *here* which control the hope *there*. The account that was written of Christ's visit to the spirit world (by Joseph F. Smith) talks or mentions those who departed the mortal life firm in the hope of a glorious resurrection.

"Firm in the hope of a glorious resurrection" comes as a result of knowing before you depart from mortality that you have a promise that gives you the **right** to lay claim upon a glorious resurrection. Those who know this, know it because God promised it to them. They got this hope by the kind of lives they lived. They are the ones who have been faithful in the testimony of Jesus while they lived in mortality and have offered an acceptable sacrifice in similitude of the great sacrifice of the Son of God. From this they acquire hope.

It is clear the "hope which controls destiny" is a power. It is something greater than vague desire. It seizes upon and opens up opportunities from God. It is a power from Heaven, merited from obedience, given by the grace of God, and gives rise to a covenant which is assured to the recipient. All those having this firm hope also have a covenant, which they can seize upon to deliver themselves and obtain blessings from Heaven.

Whatever we hope to receive in the next life must come to us through this process. Whether it is something as concrete as a family relationship or as vague as an expectation, all things in the next life are secured to us only through this kind of promise or hope. Hope comes—or is delivered to us—by the Holy Spirit of Promise, when promises are made to us from the other side of the veil.

We all hope for things based upon promises made in scripture. But some hope for things precisely because they have been delivered to them by the voice of God from beyond the veil, securing for them the right to inherit something.

The heirs of exaltation are identified in the Vision of the Three Degrees of Glory: those *who overcome by faith and are sealed by [the] Holy Spirit of Promise, which the Father shed[s] forth upon all those who are just and true* (T&C 69:10), are the ones that depart this life with hope. Faith, in that sense, is related to hope and is based upon knowledge. It's the kind of knowledge that is only obtained through faith great enough for the person to personally receive a promise from God, confirmed through the Holy Spirit of Promise, assuring them they are to receive what has been promised them.

The Sixth Lecture on Faith tells us how this kind of faith (that leads to hope) is gained:

> *Having treated, in the preceding lectures, of the ideas of the character, perfections, and attributes of God, we next proceed to treat of the knowledge which persons must have that the course of life which they pursue is according to the will of God, in order that they may be enabled to exercise faith in him unto life and salvation.*

This knowledge supplies an important place in revealed religion, for it was by reason of it that the ancients were enabled to endure as seeing him who is invisible. An actual knowledge to any person that the course of life which he pursues is according to the will of God is essentially necessary to enable him to have that confidence in God, without which no person can obtain eternal life. It was this that enabled the ancient saints to endure all their afflictions and persecutions and to take joyfully the spoiling of their goods, knowing (not [merely believing]) that they had a more enduring substance...

Having the assurance that they were pursuing a course which was agreeable to the will of God, they were enabled to take not only the spoiling of their goods and the wasting of their substance joyfully, but also to suffer death in its most horrid forms, knowing (not merely believing) that when this earthly house of their tabernacle was dissolved, they had a building of God, a house not made with hands, eternal in the Heavens...

Such was and always will be the situation of the saints of God: that unless they have an actual knowledge that the course...they are pursuing is according to the will of God, they will grow weary in their minds and faint, for such has been and always will be the opposition in the hearts of unbelievers and those that know not God, against the pure...unadulterated religion of Heaven (the only thing which ensures eternal life), that they will persecute to the utmost all that worship God according to His revelations, receive the truth in...love of it, and submit themselves to be guided and directed by His will...

For a man to lay down his all, his character...reputation, his honor and applause, his good name among men, his houses, ...lands, his brothers and sisters, ...wife and children, ...even his own life also, counting all things but filth and dross for the excellency of the knowledge of Jesus Christ, requires more than mere belief, or supposition that he's doing the will of God, but actual knowledge, realizing that when these sufferings are ended he will enter into Eternal rest and be a partaker of the glory of God.

For unless a person does know that he is walking according to the will of God, it would be offering an insult to the dignity of the Creator were he to say that he would be a partaker of his glory when he should be done with the things of this life. But when he has this knowledge, and most assuredly knows that he is doing the will of God, his confidence can be equally strong that he will be a partaker of the glory of God.

Let us here observe that a religion that does not require the sacrifice of all things never has power sufficient to produce the faith necessary unto life and salvation. For from the first existence of man, the faith necessary unto the enjoyment of life and salvation never could be obtained without the sacrifice of all earthly things: it was through this sacrifice, and this only, that God has ordained that men should enjoy eternal life, and it is through the medium of the sacrifice of all earthly things that men do actually know that they are doing the things that are well pleasing in the sight of God. When a man has offered in sacrifice all that he has for the truth's sake, not even withholding his life, and believing before God that he has been called to make this sacrifice because he seeks to do his will, he does know most assuredly that God does and will accept his sacrifice and offering, and that he has not nor will not seek his face in vain. Under these circumstances, then, he can obtain the faith necessary for him to lay hold on eternal life.

It is in vain for persons to fancy to themselves that they are heirs with those, or can be heirs with them, who have offered their all in sacrifice, and by this means obtained faith in God and favor with him so as to obtain eternal life, unless they in like manner offer unto him the same sacrifice, and through that offering obtain the knowledge that they are accepted of him. (LoF 6:1-8)

This description is a description of hope. This is how people are faithful in the testimony of Jesus while they live in mortality and, therefore, can depart this life firm in the hope or expectation of a glorious resurrection.

There's a direct relationship between faith, hope, and charity. Faith comes from obedience and sacrifice. Hope comes from the promise given to a person, by God, which their faith has secured for them. And charity comes as those holding faith and receiving hope, seek to have all others share in the same promises. The greatest gift you can give to another is eternal life. All those who have such a promise from God want everyone else to have a similar promise for themselves. They teach, preach, exhort, and write to share with everyone that same opportunity to gain hope in God. They understand how rare a thing it is to bring a soul to salvation. But they're not interested in merely making a bad-person good or a good-person better, nor are they content to move souls from a Telestial destiny to a Terrestrial destiny. Those who have such promises for themselves long, hope, pray, and preach to bring every other soul back to God to dwell with Him in Celestial glory. They seek the eternal life of all mankind. They participate with God in His great work. They join Christ in His declaration:

For behold, the Lord your Redeemer suffered death in the flesh; wherefore, he suffered the pain of all men that all men might repent and come unto him. And he ha[th] risen again from the dead that he might bring all men unto him on conditions of repentance. And how great is his joy in the soul that repent[eth]. Wherefore, you are called to cry repentance unto this people. And if it so be that you should labor all your days in crying repentance unto this people and bring save it be one soul unto me, how great shall be your joy with him in the kingdom of my Father? And now if your joy will be great with one soul that you have brought unto me in the kingdom of my Father, how great will be your joy if you should bring many souls unto me? (JSH 15:31 RE)

It's a rare thing when any person acquires the firm hope of a glorious resurrection, secured through the voice of the Father, declared by the Holy Spirit of Promise. The wonder is that it happens at all. But it does. And for those to whom such hope has come, they want all others to receive the same promise. Joseph Smith, who had such a hope in him, spoke openly of these things. He wanted all mankind to be exalted. To some extent, we have quieted our voices on this subject. And we need to raise them again.

We are not part of historic Christianity. Nor are we part of a dying Restoration. We have a better hope. We can offer a far greater understanding of God's plan for mankind. We can offer to people words that God has spoken now, in our day. We cannot be content in merely becoming part of mainstream Christianity or part of the dying Restoration movement.

The Restoration was not intended only to create a denomination or an institution. It was intended to redeem souls. It was intended to shout the glorious message that men are able to obtain hope in God, for a glorious resurrection, in which God promises to them that they will receive a house in the next life that will equip them to dwell among the mansions of the Father.

The restored Gospel requires too high a price to ever succeed as a popular, mainstream denomination. But it offers too great a reward to merely be another Christian denomination. We cannot be content with just being a religion. We have to be the work of God in the last days. We have to be the act of God in bringing to pass the completion and fulfillment of His promises and His covenants with the Fathers. All the volumes of scriptures refer to turning the hearts of the children to the Fathers and the Fathers to the children. Promises and hope are tied to them, also.

We need to lay hold upon hope. MAN MUST HOPE! Or he cannot receive.

Hope comes from faith. When men have obtained hope for themselves, they want that hope to be shared by men and women everywhere. Concern for the salvation of others lies at the foundation of charity. If you do not have a firm hope within you, secured by the Holy Spirit of Promise, given you by God, then this verse should awaken you to have this desire. It should rally you. Jacob hoped his preaching would cause us to arouse the faculties of our souls, to shake ourselves that we might awake from the slumber of death and repent. Joseph Smith was similarly hoping to exalt others. We cannot be content with less. The commandments from God are given to us to exalt us, to lead us back. May we all receive such hope for the next life.

Man must hope, or he cannot receive an inheritance with the Father (Ether 5:6 RE). This verse is a shout of joy for all who are willing to hear it.

———

The foregoing was recorded by Denver Snuffer in Sandy, Utah on August 18, 2019.

83. Fasting

In this episode, Denver addresses the question: What is the proper way to fast?

––––––––

But first from the Old Covenants, Isaiah 20:7 RE:

> *Cry aloud, spare not, lift up your voice like a trumpet, and show my people their transgression and the house of Jacob their sins. Yet they seek me daily and delight to know my ways, as a nation that did righteousness and forsook not the ordinance of their God. They ask of me the ordinances of justice, they take delight in approaching to God. Why have we fasted, say they, and you see not? Why have we afflicted our soul and you take no knowledge? Behold, in the day of your fast, you find pleasure and exact all your labors. Behold, you fast for strife and debate, and to smite with the fist of wickedness. You shall not fast as you do this day to make your voice to be heard on high. Is it such a fast that I have chosen? A day for a man to afflict his soul? Is it to bow down his head as a bulrush, and to spread sackcloth and ashes under him? Will you call this a fast and an acceptable day to the Lord? Is not this the fast that I have chosen: to remove the bands of wickedness, to undo the heavy burdens, and to let the oppressed go free, and that you break every yoke? Is it not to deal your bread to the hungry, and that you bring the poor that are cast out to your house? When you see the naked, that you cover him, and that you hide not yourself from your own flesh? Then shall your light break forth as the morning, and your health shall spring forth speedily, and your righteousness shall go before you; the glory of the Lord shall be your rear guard. Then shall you call and the Lord shall answer, you shall cry and he shall say, Here I am. If you take away from your midst the yoke, the putting forth of the finger, and speaking vanity, and if you draw out your soul to the hungry, and satisfy the afflicted soul, then shall your light rise in obscurity and your darkness be as the noonday. And the Lord shall guide you continually, and satisfy your soul in drought, and make fat your bones; and you shall be like a watered garden, and like a spring of water whose waters fail not. And they that shall be of you shall build the old waste places. You shall raise up the foundations of many generations, and you shall be called the repairer of the breach, the restorer of paths to dwell in. If you turn away your foot from the Sabbath — from doing your pleasure on my holy day — and call the Sabbath a delight, the holy of the Lord honorable, and shall honor him, not doing your own ways,*

nor finding your own pleasure, nor speaking your own words, then shall you delight yourself in the Lord. And I will cause you to ride upon the high places of the earth, and feed you with the heritage of Jacob your father; for the mouth of the Lord has spoken it.

DENVER: When it's talking about this— They would invoke a ceremony inside the Kirtland temple to actually wash feet, but it is a symbol of the cleansing and the abandonment of sin. Do you want to have clean feet? We can wash all your feet, but it is not going to take any greater effect upon you than what you already received in the LDS temple. If you want your feet clean, walk in the paths of righteousness and stay in there:

> *That I may make you clean;* [See, that is the cleanliness we seek for.] *That I may testify unto your Father, and your God, and my God, that you are clean from the blood of this wicked generation; that I may fulfil (the) promise, this great and last promise, which I have made unto you, when I will. Also, I give unto you a commandment that ye shall continue in prayer and fasting from this time forth.* (D&C 88:74-76; see also T&C 86:13-14 RE)

You know, *let your food be prepared with singleness of heart that your fasting may be...* (D&C 59:13; see also T&C 46:13 RE). You can fast more effectively by shutting off the things of this world, and tuning in the things of God, than you can by simply going hungry. Some people go hungry and they get grouchy. They don't get closer to the Lord, they get more irritating to their neighbor. (Comment from Stephanie Snuffer: "It is called 'hangry'." Audience laughing.)

God is in everything. He's absolutely everywhere. It is necessary for you to pay attention to that, in order to open yourself up to that, because the process of revelation— In the East, what people would do to try and get a revelation would be to ponder, to meditate, and to open themselves up. In the West, what we would do to get a revelation is to fast and pray, and offer to God commitments of 50 different things if He—

Please, please, please, *please*... Please, please, please, *please*, just this one time, just... Oh, please, please, ever so much— This, and I'll do that. I'll do that, and I'll agree to do this. And okay, what am I not doing and why... What else could... I didn't wear a white shirt to sacrament last hour. I'll *always* wear a white shirt every time I go... I believe they ask for dads to volunteer to bless the sacrament with their sons, but I know it's something I need to do... I'm gonna bless the sacrament... And there's a list of 50 things. I think... I think I can, I think I can, I think I can...

And God's up there saying, "Hey, I put the answer to the prayer right there— it's in the front yard, ya know."

Oh, ooooh! I gotta bake some bread...and go make some bread and take it to the neighbor and welcome him to the neighborhood... And this next door neighbor who's got this attitude problem, I'll go over and tell them how wonderful sacrament meeting is... I'll get it done, I'll get it done, I'll get it done... Give me the revelation, will ya! [audience laughter]

And the revelation was sitting right in your front yard, waiting for you to come out and to notice.

And we look upon those things and we keep ourselves distracted from, disconnected with, and incapable of opening ourselves up to the revelation which God, at all points, is offering to us. *The world is filled with revelation.* And our problem is that the manner, in which we choose to go about asking for and opening ourselves up to it, is so limited in scope, so poor in quality, so alien to the teachings of Christ, that it doesn't matter that the Lord is shouting at us—all around. We simply won't pay any attention or give any heed to what it is that He has been offering all along.

BLOG POST from August 11, 2015, "answer to an email:"

I know of no way to receive light and truth from heaven but by patient, obedient, and disciplined living by everything God has said, commanded, or instructed. It is as the Lord told His disciples, some things are not overcome "but by fasting and prayer." A haphazard inquiry from a proud and hard-hearted soul will not likely receive an answer from the same Lord who spent entire nights alone in solitary prayer. Our Lord's prayers were so private that His own disciples needed to ask Him to teach them how to pray, because He did not display it for them to learn from by overhearing. He went alone, apart, and in private, and then prayed for hours, oftentimes overnight. This was Christ. This was He who is "more intelligent than them all." Yet people expect they can ask in haste about something that shatters their paradigm and, in their pride, expect to have everything they always believed be ratified to their satisfaction, and what annoys them to be denounced. Until the heart is broken and willing to accept the sad news that they are wrong, and God is going to correct them, they are not likely to get an answer other than—they are right. In fact, they've been right all along. Answers from a meek and lowly

Lord come with the greatest accuracy to the meek and lowly inquirer. There are but few of those living.

DENVER: Look, go to D&C section 88. I want to read this and take a slightly different view of it. Beginning at verse 119 of Doctrine and Covenants section 88:

> *Organize yourselves; prepare every needful thing; and establish a house, even a house of prayer, a house of fasting, a house of faith, a house of learning, a house of glory, a house of order, a house of God;*
>
> *That your incomings may be in the name of the Lord; that your outgoings may be in the name of the Lord; that all your salutations may be in the name of the Lord, with uplifted hands unto the Most High.*
>
> *Therefore, cease from all your light speeches, from all laughter, from all your lustful desires, from all your pride and light-mindedness, and from all your wicked doings. Appoint among yourselves a teacher, and let not all be spokesmen at once; but let one speak at a time and let all listen unto his sayings, that when all have spoken that all may be edified of all, and that every man may have an equal privilege.*
>
> *See that ye love one another; cease to be covetous; learn to impart one to another as the gospel requires.*
>
> *Cease to be idle; cease to be unclean; cease to find fault one with another; cease to sleep longer than is needful; retire to (your) bed early, that ye may not be weary; arise early, that your bodies and your minds may be invigorated.*
>
> *And above all things, clothe yourselves with the bond of charity, as with a mantle, which is the bond of perfectness and peace.*
>
> *Pray always, that ye may not faint, until I come. Behold, and lo, I will come quickly, and receive you unto myself. Amen.* (D&C 88:199-126; See also T&C 86:29-30 RE)

Think of this as a description of you as husband, you as wife, and your children. And make your house *this* house. Make this your family—a family of prayer, a family of fasting, a family of faith, a family of learning—therefore a family of glory, which will bring about a family of order; and therefore, a house of God.

Turn to Luke chapter 18, because there the Lord pretty much tells you how it is He evaluates whether someone has purified themselves before Him. This is a story that the Lord makes up, in chapter 18 of Luke, telling a parable to those who trusted in themselves—that they were righteous. Beginning at verse 10:

> *Two men went into the temple to pray; the one a Pharisee, and the other a publican. The Pharisee stood and prayed thus with himself, God, I thank thee, that I am not as other men are, extortioners, unjust, adulterers, or even as this publican. I fast twice in the week, I give tithes of all that I possess. And the publican, standing afar off, would not lift so much as his eyes unto heaven, but smote upon his breast, saying, God be merciful to me a sinner. I tell you, this man went down to his house justified rather than the other: for every one that exalteth himself shall be abased; and he that humbleth himself shall be exalted.* (Luke 18:10-14; see also Luke 10:7 RE)

God can *only exalt the meek*, because only the meek can be trusted. This is what it means to sanctify yourself. Our idea of purity and Christ's idea are entirely based on different criteria. Why is meekness required *of* a God, *by* a God? What would happen if God Himself were not patient, willing to suffer abuse, and be rejected? What would happen if God were egotistical? What would happen if God did not return blessings for cursings? What would happen if God were not exactly what He preached in the Sermon on the Mount? What if God did not bless those who despitefully used and abused Him? What would happen if God did not submit Himself to fall into the hands of wicked men, to be despised and rejected? And then to be killed in shame: hanging naked on a cross in full view of the world, while people spit upon Him, and while they mocked Him, and they ridiculed Him, saying, "If you really are what you say you are, come down from the cross, *then* we will believe."

Woe unto all those who say, "If you really are who you say you are…" when the voice of God is sounding in their ears. *They* would have rejected the Lord as well. *They* would have crucified the Lord as well. They are not His sheep because they do not hear His voice. If they were His sheep, they would hear His voice.

But these people who have been separated from our common fare, there could not be a happier people than among *all* the children of God because, you know what? There comes a point when you have separated yourself from the crap, that your capacity to incorporate more and more truth and light allows you to say, "Well, this is more interesting than that was anyway." There's something more engaging about truth and light, and there's something more fascinating about the things of eternity than there is about any of this stuff.

We are all weak, we are all vulnerable, we are all carbon-based mud piles at the moment. And this carbon-based pile of mud around which my spirit has been wrapped into—it gets tired, it has appetites, it has weaknesses. But the reason why they threw fasting in there was to subordinate that body, and to teach it that the spirit is something that ought to be in control. There comes a point at which, if you've allowed the spirit to have its way, you'll find that the things that are fascinating to this pile of mud that you walk around in are far less interesting than the things of the spirit. And whatever principle of intelligence you attain to in this life is going to rise with you, and if it does, then you're going to have so much the advantage in the world to come. And why is that? Because in the world to come, the crap that's here has no utility, it has no value. It's here to test you, it's here to try you, and it's here to give you an opportunity to overcome it. But it's not here for you to revel in—it's for you to dig yourself out from.

The Lord tells a story in Mark—this is Mark chapter 9. Beginning at verse 17, there's this fellow who comes to Christ and says,

> *Master, I have brought thee my son, which hath a dumb spirit;* [The spirit overtakes him, he foams at the mouth, and gnashes his teeth.] *I spake to thy disciples that they should cast him out...they could not. (And Christ says,) O faithless generation, how long shall I be with you? how long shall I suffer you? ...they brought (the boy) unto him...he saw him, straightway the spirit (tore) him...he fell on the ground...wallowed foaming...he asked his father, How long (has it been) since this came (into) him? And he said, Of a child. And oftimes it (casteth) him into the fire, and into the waters, to destroy him: but if thou canst do any thing, have compassion on (him)...help us. Jesus said unto him, If thou canst believe, all things are possible to him that believeth...straightway the father of the child cried out, [cried out,] and said with tears, Lord, I believe; help thou mine unbelief [help thou mine unbelief].* (Mark 9:17-24; see also Mark 5:8-9 RE)

You don't need more of what you already have. Why are you here? Well, most of you. Some have come only to criticize and gather information. Some of you in the hardness of your heart are going to come to the point where, in the day of judgment, you will look back on this moment and realize, "I damned myself by the hardness of my heart and the bitterness of my soul, because I came to judge a man whose heart was right before God, and mine was not." Your heart will be broken in that day.

But look at *this* man whose heart was broken on *this* day. He cried out, *"Lord I believe; help thou mine unbelief."* "I have a desire, I have a willingness, but it is so fragile! It is so frail that I don't think it's enough!" *That's* not the problem. Cry out! Ask Him!

Remember His disciples who had been following Him, His disciples who were His faithful followers— His disciples couldn't fix this boy. And they had given up everything to come and follow Him. Jesus healed him. After the incident, the disciples came to Him and said, "Why could we not cast him out?" Christ answered them, *This kind can come forth by nothing, but...prayer and fasting* (Mark 9:29; see also Mark 5:11 RE).

Why do you have to be afflicted by prayer and fasting, if you're a follower of the Lord, in order to get to the point that you can accomplish this? Because *you* don't fall prostate, crying out with tears. If this man, in this condition, can say, *"I believe; help thou mine unbelief."* If this man can do this and have the Lord, on his behalf, work a miracle, *you too* can believe enough, *you too* can accomplish what you desire, *you too* can come to Him.

Matthew covers the same incident. But in Matthew he picks up— This is Matthew chapter 17, beginning at verse 19:

> *Then came the disciples to Jesus apart, and said, Why could not we cast him out? ...Jesus said unto them, Because of your unbelief: for verily I say unto you, If ye have faith as a grain of mustard seed, ye shall say unto this mountain, Remove hence to yonder place; and it shall remove; and nothing shall be impossible unto you. Howbeit this kind (come) not out but by prayer and fasting.* (Matthew 17:19-21; see also Matthew 9:7 RE)

Look, at the end of the day, Peter did not hold any greater or different authority when he came back from a mission and said, "We couldn't cast out any devils. We're bringing this person to you, Lord. Whatever it was you gave us, whatever that ordination thing was, it's just not working." And then Christ said, "Well, this kind come not out except by fasting and prayer." Meaning that there is a work to be done to subordinate the body, in order to give the strength to your faith, necessary to achieve something.

Peter had absolutely no different ordination than when he entered the temple following the Lord's resurrection, and said, "Silver and gold have I none; but such as I have give I unto you. In the name of Jesus Christ, arise, take up your bed and walk." (See Acts 3:1-7; see also Acts 2:1 RE.) What Peter had, that was different, was faith. His ordination amounted to no power, but his faith in Christ healed the sick.

———

The foregoing excerpts are taken from:

- Denver's comments during an assembly on "Missionary Work" in Eden, Utah on July 2, 2016;
- Denver's talk given at the Chiasmus Conference in American Fork, Utah on September 18, 2010;
- Denver's blog post of August 11, 2015, titled "answer to an email:";
- Denver's *40 Years in Mormonism Series*, Talk #9 titled "Marriage and Family," given in St. George, Utah on July 26, 2014;
- Denver's *40 Years in Mormonism Series*, Talk #8 titled "A Broken Heart," given in Las Vegas, Nevada on July 25, 2014;
- His talk given at the "Zion Symposium" in Provo, Utah on February 23rd, 2008; and
- His conference talk titled "The Doctrine of Christ", given in Boise, Idaho on September 11, 2016.

Today's podcast addresses important questions about Fasting, but is only an introduction to ideas that listeners of any denomination may find important and relevant. These topics are more fully addressed in Denver's blog, including but not limited to these entries:

Last Week's Comments, May 19, 2012
3rd Nephi 13:16-18, October 21, 2010
Sacrifice, July 1, 2018
3rd Nephi 12:6, October 5, 2010
3rd Nephi 20:12, September 15, 2010

84. Zion's Return, Part 1

This is part 1 of a special series on the much anticipated, and much prophesied, return of Zion.

———

DENVER: In the beginning, there was a unitary priesthood. It was the Holy Order after the Order of the Son of God. But in order to prevent the too frequent repetition of the name of the Son of God it got renamed, first after Enoch and then later after Melchizedek. But it is referring to one original, unitary priesthood which is the Holy Order after the Order of the Son of God. Yet Joseph spoke about three great divisions. In the beginning, because the first patriarchs had that original, unitary fullness of the priesthood after the Order of the Son of God, and because Abraham acquired the rights of the fathers or the first father, Adam, and therefore, like Adam, held the Holy Order after the Order of the Son of God, I use the term Patriarchal Priesthood to refer to that original fullness and to nothing else, and I divide them up into three categories and three nomenclatures using those terms.

There is the Spirit of Elias, there is the Spirit of Elijah, and there is the Spirit of Messiah. These three great spirits unfolded in the work of God in the generations of man in a steady *de*scent, and they will be likewise inverted like a chiasm and return in an *a*scent so that at the end it will be as it was in the beginning—*[that] same Priesthood which was in the beginning shall [be] in the end of the [earth] also* (Moses 6:7; see also Genesis 3:14 RE) was the prophecy that Father Adam gave—Enoch quoting Adam, Moses quoting Enoch; the prophecy being contained in the Book of Moses or soon, in the Book of Genesis.

The first spirit was the Spirit of Messiah. Adam dwelt in the presence of God. Adam represents that original fullness. Adam was the first man. Adam received instructions and spoke to God face-to-face. He dwelt in a temple—from which he was cast out—but he dwelt in a temple and therefore, Adam represents the Spirit of Messiah.

The Spirit of Elijah is represented by Enoch who, when the earth was threatened with violence and men were to be destroyed because of the wickedness upon the face of the earth, was able to gather a people into a city of peace, and to have the Lord come to their city of peace and remove them from the coming violence and destruction. He is a type of the Spirit of Elijah because Elijah would likewise later ascend in the fiery chariot into heaven. He

426		The Denver Snuffer Podcast, Volume 2: 2019

is a type of the Spirit of Elijah because it is the Spirit of Elijah and that ascent into heaven that must prefigure the return of the Spirit of Messiah in the last days in order to gather a people to a place that God will acknowledge, will visit, and will shield from the coming violence that will involve the destruction of the world. And so Enoch becomes the great type of the Spirit of Elijah, although the name "Elijah" is associated with a man who lived later still but who duplicated, among a hardened people, in a fallen world, the same achievement as Enoch had accomplished; albeit Enoch did so with a city, and Elijah did it as a solitary ascending figure. Yet it will be Elijah and his Spirit which, in the last days, will likewise prepare a city for salvation and preservation.

And then there is the Spirit of Elias, which is represented by Noah, in which everything that had gone on before was lost, things begin anew, and Noah begins a ministry of attempting to preserve what was before by preaching repentance. And so Noah, as the messenger or the Elias, bears testimony of what once was.

Well, in the end, before the Lord's return, these same three spirits need to have been brought into the world in order for the completion of the plan that Adam prophesied about and that was in the heart of the Lord from before the foundation of the world. The Spirit of Elias declaring the gospel has to come again into the world, and it did in the person of Joseph Smith, and in the message that he brought, and in the scriptures that he restored, and in the message and the practices that he was able to bring about, however short-lived that success may have been. Elias and the Spirit of Elias came through Joseph Smith into the world.

We have yet to take the Spirit of Elias seriously enough to move on to receive something further. *But* we are now facing a crossroads in which it may be possible to restore again, and continue the work, and move forward. Moving forward successfully however, will require the Spirit of Elijah. This time the Spirit of Elijah is not to prepare a people so that they might ascend into heaven, but instead to prepare a people so that those who come will not utterly destroy them. There must be a people prepared to endure the burning that is to come. Just as Enoch's people were prepared, shielded, and brought worthy to ascend so as not to be destroyed by the flood, the Spirit of Elijah must prepare people in order for them to endure the day that is coming that shall burn the wicked as stubble. That will be people living in a place of peace, and they will be the only people who are not at war one with another. They will be people who accept a body of teachings and allow them to govern their daily walk—both with each other and with God, so that they receive *commandments, not a few* and *revelations in their day*, because that is what the people of Zion must necessarily be willing to do.

We are promised that one will come who will be part of Jesse and part of Ephraim, who will set in order, whose identity will be established by the work accomplished and not by the foolishness of prideful claims made by someone who's done nothing. If the work is done, once it's completed, you might be able to guess. But any fool can run around claiming themselves to be whatever their peculiar schizophrenia allows them to claim.

The third spirit that is to return is that spirit which was in the beginning. It is the Spirit of Messiah—this time the Messiah Himself. This time He will come to His house. He will dwell there. Everything must be prepared in order for Messiah to return. And so in the end, as it was in the beginning—Adam being a type who represents dwelling in the presence of God, or the Spirit of Messiah—in the end it will be Messiah Himself who returns to dwell among a people who are prepared. This is a chiasm. It's a returning to the beginning as the work of the last days walks backward in time to the point where it all began.

Elias goes before to prepare for a greater work that is coming after, just as the Aaronic ordinances go before. Joseph Smith said the Spirit of Elias was revealed to him, but "the Spirit of Elijah holds something more. It holds the revelations, ordinances, endowments and sealings necessary to accomplish turning the hearts of the fathers to the children by securing an unbroken thread between the living and the fathers in heaven. This can only be done in a temple prepared for that purpose. [I'm reading Joseph.] Without sealing of living children to the fathers in heaven, who dwell in glory and who sit upon thrones, the return of the Lord with Enoch and the other thousands who will accompany him would result in none escaping the judgments to come. (Teachings of the Prophet Joseph Smith, pp. 336-337)

Isaiah prophesied in Isaiah chapter two, verses two and three: *And it shall come to pass in the last days, [that] the mountain of the LORD's house shall be established in the top of the mountains, and shall be exalted above the hills, and all nations shall flow unto it* (ibid; see also Isaiah 1:5 RE). In this context, in this prophecy, *all nations* is not Russia, and China, and Ethiopia, and Uzbekistan, and Turk-crap-istan and I'm-a-nut-istan. *All nations*, in this context, means all the 12 tribes of Israel. The nations are the 12 tribes of Israel. Period. That's it. That's who is going to flow unto it. So you won't need an international airport. Nor will you need to host the Olympics.

The mountain of the LORD's house shall be established in the top of the mountains, and shall be exalted above the hills; and all nations shall flow unto it and many people shall go and say, Come [ye] let us go up to [the mountain of the Lord, to] the house of the God of Jacob, and he will teach us of his ways and we will walk in his paths. (ibid)

The paths of God lie in the heavens. So if you're going to learn to walk in his paths you're going to have to learn how to walk in the heavens.

For out of Zion shall go forth the law, and the word of the Lord from Jerusalem (ibid). The *ensign* that is prophesied to be established (Isaiah 11:12; see also Isaiah 5:5 RE), in the context, in the meaning of that day, had reference to a zodiacal, a constellation, a depiction of the heavens themselves. So when an "ensign" is going to be reared—and it's going to tell you about how to walk in the paths of God—this is talking about something very, very different than what most of us today would envision.

Zion is going to be a connection between heaven and earth, and *at* that place you will learn of the God of Jacob's *ways* and you will walk in His *paths*, because heaven and earth will be connected, and the stairway connecting the two will be opened, and the heavens and the earth will be reunited again, and this is going to happen in the top of the mountains.

In March of 1831, there was a revelation given that we can read in D&C 49, verses 24 and 25: *But before the great day of the Lord shall come, Jacob shall flourish in the wilderness, and the Lamanites shall blossom as the rose. Zion shall flourish upon the hills and rejoice upon the mountains, and shall be assembled together unto the place which I have appointed* (see also T&C 35:8 RE). *The mountains*—these were the prophecies at the beginning, as the restoration was starting to roll forth.

Joseph Smith said this: "Our Western tribe of Indians are descendents from that Joseph that was sold into Egypt, and that the land of America is a promised land unto them, and unto it, all the tribes of Israel will come with as many of the Gentiles as shall comply with the requirements of the new covenant." That's a letter that Joseph Smith wrote to N. C. Saxton that can be found in *The Personal Writings of Joseph Smith*, compiled by Dean C. Jesse, at page 273. He's talking about the Western tribes of Indians in that comment which will make more sense as we get further into this material. But it really did mean 'out West.'

Having been approved of God. It is God and God's approval alone that matters. It is what God regards of you. It is what is in your heart, because God can detect what is in your heart. God knows why you do what you do. God knows why you say what you say. God knows what is in your thoughts. Therefore, to be approved of God is to be weighed against the standard of righteousness, and not the whims of fashion. Fashion will come and go. Ideas will be popular or unpopular. Righteousness will endure forever. This, this— this is the kind of man upon whom the words get spoken, *My Son.* The fathers, about whom I spoke in Centerville, had this association with God. They had this fellowship with God. They had this sonship with God. And they had this priesthood from God. And the hearts of the children need to turn to the fathers, and that too, because Elijah is coming to plant in the hearts of the children the promises that were made.

Now, I want to take another detour into parsing things in a way that you might not have considered before, and for this I want to go to Doctrine and Covenants section 128 and I want to look at verse 21. This is Joseph writing a letter that got canonized and he's talking about all of the stuff that had gone on in the process of getting the restoration fully established on the earth, and he mentions, in this letter that he writes, these things:

> *And again, the voice of God in the chamber of old Father Whitmer, in Fayette, Seneca county, and at sundry times, and in divers places through[out] all the travels and tribulations of this Church of Jesus Christ of Latter-day Saints!* [So the voice of God has been there throughout all of this, as Joseph presided and as the Church rolled forth.] *And the voice of Michael, the archangel; the voice of Gabriel,* ["El" being the name of God] *and of Raphael, and of divers angels, from Michael or Adam down to the present time, all declaring their dispensation, their rights, their keys, their honors, their majesty and glory, and the power of their priesthood; giving line upon line, precept upon precept; here a little, [and] there a little; giving us consolation by holding forth that which is to come, confirming our hope!* (D&C 128:21; see also T&C 151:15-17 RE)

So, I want to suggest to you that Michael, Gabriel, and Raphael are known to us as those who have come, though they were part of the El, or in the plural form, the Elohim, they came and they served here. They came and they ministered here. Michael descended, and he came to the earth and he was known as Adam in mortality. Gabriel came to the earth and he was known in mortality as Noah. There is a big debate over the identity of Raphael. I'll tell you what I think and you can take it or leave it. Rapha*el* is the name that was given to the man who in mortality we know as Enoch.

Now there are four angels who preside over the four corners of the earth and Joseph surely knew that. And Joseph mentions the names of three of the four. But he leaves the fourth one out. And I find the absence of the fourth one rather extraordinary. The fourth one's name is Uri*el*, also one of the Elohim. And, although there are those who will absolutely cry heresy, throw dirt on their hair, and tear their clothes because they are scholars, and they are *bona fide*, and they know I'm talking out of my hat—but I'd remind you Joseph talked out of his hat too. That fourth and missing, unmentioned angel is Uri*el*, who in mortality was known to us as John.

Adam is the one in the East, the angel who is considered the one who presides over and has control of the air. Which is apt because unto Adam was given the breath of life in the beginning. Raphael is in the South, and he is associated with the power of fire, which is apt because of his fiery ascent with his people into heaven. Gabriel is the angel in the West who has the power over water, which is apt because in mortality, he managed through the Flood. And Uriel, though not mentioned, is the one who in the North has the power over the earth, which is apt because he remains upon the earth and he is the guardian at one gate with Elijah at the other end. But you can take and leave all that as you will. I find the mention here in this letter by Joseph, of these individuals and these powers, and these four, three of whom are named, the fourth of whom, potentially is unnamed, to be interesting. Though he does mention *divers angels for Michael or Adam down to the present time* (ibid).

There is so much more that has to go on and be understood if you are going to save yourself and any soul in this generation, in that kingdom which we claim we would like to inherit. We claim we'd like to inherit it without any idea of the consequences of what it would take in order to ascend there, or without any regard to the fact that you don't take one of the El and bring them down into mortality pain-free. You say that the Son of God condescended to come and be here, and I say so did Micha*el*, and so did Rapha*el*, and so the Gabri*el*. Because coming down and condescending to be here on a rescue mission, by those who dwell in glory, is an act of service and sacrifice that we simply take for granted out of the abundance of our ignorance.

If you go to and you look at Doctrine and Covenants section 76, beginning at verse 50, and you read through the list of things that are descriptors of those that are going to inherit celestial glory—beginning at verse 50, and we don't have time to go through all of the things that are there, but in 51 it says that these are people

> ...*who received the testimony of Jesus* [that is, Christ testifying to them that they're saved], ...*believed on his name* [these are people who] *were baptized after the manner of his burial, being buried in water in his name, this according to the commandment which he has given—That by keeping the commandments they might be washed and cleansed from all their sins, ... receive the Holy Spirit by the laying on of the hands of him who is ordained and sealed unto this power;* [that sounds a little different than what we do] *And who overcome by faith, and are sealed by the Holy Spirit of promise, which the Father sheds forth on all those who are just and true. These are they who are the church of the Firstborn. These are they into whose hands the Father has given all things—These are they who are priests and kings, who have received of his fulness, and of his glory;* [I hope you read those words now with a little different meaning than you did before 9:30 today.] *And are priests of the Most High, after the order of Melchizedek, which was after the order of Enoch, which was after the order of the Only Begotten Son. Wherefore, as it is written, they are gods, ...all things are theirs, whether life or death, or things present, or things to come, all are theirs...they are Christ's, and Christ is God's. They shall overcome all things.* (That's in the future.) *Let no man glory in man, but rather let him glory in God, who shall subdue all enemies under his feet. These shall dwell in the presence of God and his Christ forever and ever. These are they whom he shall bring with him, when he shall come in the clouds of heaven to reign on the earth over his people. These are they who shall have part in the first resurrection. These are they who shall come forth in the resurrection of the just. These are they who are come unto Mount Zion, and unto the city of the living God, the heavenly place, the holiest of all. These are they who have come to an innumerable company of angels, to the general assembly and Church of Enoch, and of the Firstborn. These are they whose names are written in heaven, where God and Christ are the judge of all. Just men made perfect through Jesus the mediator of the new covenant, ...whose bodies are celestial, whose glory is that of the sun.* (D&C 76: 51-70; see also T&C 69:10-22 RE)

Those who inherit everlasting burnings. These are those who are referred to as the "El." These are those that were referred to when Moroni said Elijah will come to plant in the hearts of the children the promises made to the father, and when Joseph spoke in August the 27th of 1843, that Elijah *will* come— he *will* come. I've written a paper on this and I'm not going to repeat that.

Therefore, when I consider these things, I reach a different conclusion than the Elijah narrative that we generally talk about, and the conclusion that I reach is that when it comes to Elijah's role and Elijah's mission—the purpose was, in the last days on the cusp of the Lord's return, in order to open the channel through which the Zion that has been taken above can return, there will be a ministry, just as Joseph put it, still future in 1844 (March, April, May, June—three months before the death of the Prophet, yet future)—the purpose of which is to make possible the reuniting of those that dwell above with those that dwell below, formed by a people who are capable of bearing the presence of the Lord; coming back into His presence and not withering at the sight; coming back into His presence and being able to dwell at peace. And I would suggest that the peace of Zion has much less to do with whether or not the outward hostilities of those who will be burned at His coming are fighting with one another and those inside the city are not taking up arms, but it is rather the peace that comes as a consequence of having shed your sins and being able to endure the presence of the Lord. Because these are those people who have *let virtue garnish their thoughts unceasingly* because *their bowels have been full of charity towards all men, and to the household of faith* (D&C 121:45; see also T&C 139:6 RE). Imagine that. Can you imagine that it's necessary that you have charity for those who are within your own household of faith? Can you imagine that I need to tolerate and even love those inside my own community of belief who think me an emissary of the devil? Who think me an apostate? Toward *them* I must show charity?

And let virtue garnish thy thoughts unceasingly (ibid). Because you see, if you are not so constituted within your own heart—where there can't be any lies— if within your heart you are not at peace in charity toward those who would in the name of your own religion despitefully use you, then your *confidence* cannot *wax strong in the presence of God* (ibid). And all of this is connected to "the doctrine of the priesthood."

Can it be said concerning your own marriage, that it is not good for the man to be alone? Are the two of you together, better than what each of you are alone? Is your marriage a source of joy, of happiness, of contentment, of companionship? The Lord told them to multiply and replenish the earth. Do you find within your family relationship that there's joy and rejoicing and happiness as a consequence of the environment that you and your wife put together?

Is your relationship—as a woman—is your relationship in the image of God? Is there godliness about the way in which you and your husband interact? If you had to reckon whether or not someone, looking at the two of you, would see within you the image of God, would they do so? These aren't just happy notions for the afterlife. These ought to be descriptions of what your marriage could and should look like. Can you sense the glory of God in your marriage? Remember, we looked at this in D&C 93:36. *The glory of God is intelligence, or in other words Light and Truth* (see also T&C 93:11 RE). The glory of God being light, the glory of God being truth. Is that something that is present within the marriage that you have? Is your marriage filled with life? With light? With truth? With understanding?

Turn back to D&C section 121. There's a couple verses there that I want to suggest, particularly if you view the man and the woman together as one. Read these verses as if it's descriptive of "the one," which is you and your wife. This is beginning at verse 40 of section 121:

> *Many are called, but few are chosen. No power or influence can or ought to be maintained by virtue of the priesthood, only by persuasion, by long-suffering, by gentleness and meekness, and by love unfeigned; by kindness, and pure knowledge, which shall greatly enlarge the soul without hypocrisy, and without guile.* (D&C 121:40-42; see also T&C 139:5-6 RE)

Within your family, within your marriage, are you and your wife learning to use persuasion? Within your marriage, are you and your husband learning to use gentleness in dealing with one another? Are the two of you together, facing one another, in all the difficulties that come as a result of being married, are you facing that together in meekness? Do you find that, in all the relationship troubles, turmoils, and challenges, what predominates is kindness? Is there a search for understanding that results in pure knowledge when it comes to a dilemma? Look at verse 37:

> *That they may be conferred upon us, it is true; but when we undertake to cover our sins, or to gratify our pride, our vain ambition, or to exercise control or dominion or compulsion upon the souls of the children of men, in any degree of unrighteousness, behold, the heavens withdraw themselves; the Spirit of the Lord is grieved; and when it is withdrawn, Amen to the priesthood or the authority of that man.* (D&C 121:37; see also T&C 139:5 RE)

It's been my observation that so soon as the Spirit of the Lord withdraws, that quickly will another spirit step in to assure you that you're right, you should be vindicated, that you ought to proceed on in the arrogance of your heart to feel yourself justified and vindicated. There are false spirits that go about, but they're no better an audience to receive the whisperings of those false spirits, than it is the abusers who, having grieved the Spirit and caused it to withdraw, accept then counsel from yet another spirit that says, "You're right, press on! Well done! You're good! You're right! You'll be vindicated. This is all God's work, and you're a great man because you're engaged in God's work! Do not back down, do not relent. Forget about persuasion, you should never be long-suffering, you should make those under your rule suffer. They should yield to your rule. There is no place for meekness. We believe in a God of strength, a God of power, a God whose work can be done despite the frailties of man! There is no need for men to be meek. And it's kind in the end, afterall, to punish, and to force, and to coerce, because we have a good objective in mind."

All of the lies and all of the deceit that led in turn to Catholicism falling into the abyss that it fell into are presently in play with spirits—that worked this out long ago—taking the Restoration of the Gospel as yet another opportunity in which to whisper in, once the spirit is withdrawn.

So, does your marriage help you avoid covering your sins? Does your marriage —because you're never going to solve this problem in the community until you first begin to solve it within the walls of your own home. You're never going to have Zion that exists somewhere among a community, until first that community is composed of those who have a marriage that is in the image of God.

Does your marriage help you avoid gratifying your pride? Does it help hold down your vain ambition? Is your ambition to exalt the two of you, rather than the one of you? Does it bring you time and time again to not exercise control, but to respect the freedom to choose?

Well, Enoch launches his ministry, and at some point in his ministry he does do what the Lord said he would do some hundreds of years earlier. In Moses, Chapter 7 now, we've moved a whole chapter later, and this is verse 13:

> And so great was the faith of Enoch that he led the people of God, and their enemies came to battle against them; and he spake the word of the Lord, and the earth trembled, and the mountains fled, even according to his command; and the rivers of water were turned out of their course; [and] the roar of the lions was heard out of the wilderness; and all nations feared greatly, so powerful was the word of Enoch, so great was the power of the language which God had given him. (Moses 7:13; see also Genesis 4:13 RE)

You see, that's one of the unique attributes about the existence of Zion when you have it. When you have Zion in place then it is the Lord that fights the battles against it. You do not need to have a weapons budget in the Zion camp. It doesn't happen. The battle to be fought is fought by the Lord, and in the descriptions given through the Prophet Joseph Smith about the last days the people decide that they will not take on Zion, because Zion is too terrible because of the Lord. It is not their munitions. In fact, the description includes a statement that those that will not take up arms against their neighbor are the only ones that flee to Zion and the only ones that aren't out killing.

Which then raises the conundrum of: Then why does the remnant, which will build Zion, *tear in pieces and trample under foot* the gentiles? Why do they do that? Oh! Oh, stop thinking with a damn howitzer in your hand, and start thinking about the image of Babylon that is going to be torn in pieces and trodden under foot. You do not need anything other than the *truth* to tear in pieces the Gentile's kingdom. And it *will* be trodden under foot by the truth.

Now, Zion's final development says: *The fear of the Lord was upon all nations, so great was the glory of the Lord, which was upon his people. And the Lord blessed the land, and they were blessed upon the mountains, and upon the high places, and did flourish* (Moses 7:17; see also Genesis 4:14 RE). That's where you'll find Zion. Not on a plain and not in a valley. You will find it in the high places on the mount, not merely symbolically. No one will have a height from which to peek down into the goings-on in Zion. They will be beneath, and Zion will be above. And Zion's presence will be terrible. I'm not going up there. You going up there? I mean, I've got a flak vest and I'm not going up there. It's the same problem Israel had before the mountain when Moses was up on the mountain communing with the Lord.

Mountaintops are acceptable substitutes for temples. I doubt the people of Zion are going to have a budget with which to build what needs to be built. Well, the Lord has a way of making do. *The Lord called his people Zion, because they were of one heart, and one mind, and dwelt in righteousness; and there was no poor among them* (Moses 7:18; see also Genesis 4:14). There were no poor among them physically; there were no poor among them spiritually. They did not compete; they cooperated. They did not envy; they shared. They did not look to pass a zoning law. I'll tell you how to ruin Zion, how to keep it from coming—pass a zoning law. Let's police the neighborhood. Let's get some restrictive covenants. The instant you start to regulate Zion it's gone; it's slipped right between your fingers. No man need say to another: know ye the Lord; for they're all going to know him who dwell in Zion (Jeremiah 31:34; see also Jeremiah 12:9 RE).

I've thought about writing a fictional account of this curious city in which people who have children live in big houses, and people who have no children live in small houses, and no one has a job or a schedule but everyone works. And one day the lead character gets up, walks outside, and notices that the lawn could use mowing and so he goes and finds a lawn mower and he starts mowing. And he mows from one place in his house across the city to the other side, and everywhere he goes, that he finds grass, he mows. And when he finishes after a couple of weeks he returns to his house and says, "Huh, the grass has grown," and so he starts mowing again, and he does this because he feels like mowing the grass for the time being.

And then after a season he notices that there's only one person working in the bakery. Well, he's never worked in a bakery, but he decides he'll go see what it's like to work in a bakery. And he rather likes that, and so he spends a year in the bakery doing that. And he wonders whatever happened to the lawns. They've been cut, but he doesn't know who's been cutting them, and on his way to try and find someone who's cutting the yards, because he liked doing that, he has something in common with them. He would like to know how they liked it and what their pattern was. 'How did you do that?' But on his way, he gets distracted by the orchard that needs harvesting, so he spends the fall harvesting that.

And the story just ends with complete chaos. A total ungoverned society, in which everyone's at peace, and no one has a job, and everyone works, and the only thing that motivates is what needs doing. 'Hey, let's go do it. And let's do it for as long as we feel like doing it, and then let's do something else.'

———

The foregoing excerpts are taken from:

- Denver's conference talk titled "Things to Keep Us Awake at Night" given in St. George, UT on March 19th, 2017
- Denver's *40 Years in Mormonism Series*, Talk #6 titled "Zion" given in Grand Junction, CO on April 12th, 2014
- Denver's *40 Years in Mormonism Series*, Talk #5 titled "Priesthood" given in Orem, UT on November 2nd, 2013
- His talk titled "The Mission of Elijah Reconsidered", given in Spanish Fork, UT on October 14th, 2011; and
- Denver's *40 Years in Mormonism Series*, Talk #9 titled "Marriage and Family" given in St. George, UT on July 26th, 2014

85. Zion's Return, Part 2

This is part 2 of a special series on the much anticipated, and much prophesied return of Zion.

———

DENVER: So let's go back to Joel in the 2nd chapter, begin at the 28th verse and look at that. This is what has not yet been fulfilled, but is soon to come.

> *And it came to pass— And it shall come to pass afterward* [beginning at verse 28, of chapter 2 of Joel], *that I will pour out my spirit upon all flesh; and your sons and your daughters shall prophesy, your old men shall dream dreams, your young men shall see visions. And also upon the servants and upon the handmaids in those days will I pour out my spirit. ...I will shew wonders in the heavens and in the earth, blood, and fire, and pillars of smoke. The sun shall be turned into darkness, ...the moon into blood, before the great and the terrible day of the Lord.... And it shall come to pass, that whosoever shall call on the name of the Lord shall be delivered: for in mount Zion and in Jerusalem shall be deliverance, as the Lord hath said, and in the remnant whom the Lord shall call.* (Joel 2:28-32; see also Joel 1:12 RE)

Now one of the things that we perhaps take for granted (but we have to give credit to Joseph Smith for doing) is distinguishing between all of these references to Jerusalem and these references to Zion. Until Joseph spoke, it was assumed that that was the same thing. It's not. And we know that there will be Zion on the one hand, and we know that there will be Jerusalem, a gathering there, on the other hand. And we know that this prophecy concerning your sons, your daughters, prophesy, dreams, visions, all of this being poured out; this is something that is yet to happen, but it is soon to come to pass. We have a great deal to look forward to that the angel Moroni —instructing Joseph Smith—covered with him on that night when he first appeared to him; promising that these things were going to come to pass, and they still have not yet come in.

Think about all the ways that there are to err. In the warnings that are given in Section 121 of the Doctrine and Covenants concerning priesthood: *It can be conferred upon us, [it's] true; but when we undertake to cover our sins, or... gratify our pride, our vain ambition, or to exercise control or dominion or compulsion upon the souls of the children of men, in any degree of unrighteousness...*(D&C 121:37; see also T&C 139:5 RE). And by the way, any degree of unrighteousness—it tells you (in verse 41) how power or influence is to be affected, and it is not by virtue of the priesthood. It is *only by persuasion, ...longsuffering, ...gentleness and meekness, and by love unfeigned. By kindness and pure knowledge which shall greatly enlarge the soul without hypocrisy* (D&C 121:41-42; see also T&C 139:5 RE).

This presents an opportunity for everyone, every time, to fail. In addition to all of this, if you go to second Nephi chapter 26, at verse 29: *He commandeth ... there shall be no priestcrafts; for, behold, priestcrafts are that men preach and set themselves up for a light unto the world, that they may get gain and praise of the world; but they seek not the welfare of Zion* (see also 2 Nephi 11:17 RE). Zion can only come about as a consequence of consecration and sacrifice, and not as a result of seeking to get gain. In fact, when you are in the employ of the Lord, you ought to be sacrificing; it should'nt be gainful. It should cost you in order to serve.

To accomplish purity, there are absolutes that are necessary. Sacrifice is absolutely necessary, and equality is necessary as well. Or at least, there be no poor among us. My guess is, that among us sitting in this room here today, there are those who have significant issues with financial needs; and there are some sitting here today who could help in solving those.

In Alma chapter 1 it talks about a circumstance in which the priests served. Alma 1, beginning at verse 26.

> And when the priests left their labor to impart the word of God unto the people, the people also left their labors to hear the word of God. And when the priest had imparted unto them the word of God they all returned again diligently unto their labors; and the priest, not esteeming himself above his hearers, for the preacher was no better than the hearer, neither was the teacher any better than the learner; and thus they were all equal, and they did...labor, every man according to his strength. And they did impart of their substance, every man according to that which he had, to the poor, and the needy, and the sick, and the afflicted; and they did not wear costly apparel, yea they were neat and— yet they were neat and comely. (Alma 1:26-27; see also Alma 1:5 RE)

You see they prospered in this, and they were blessed because of it. We should learn from their example when they were prospering, about what it was that they did that was right that brought it about. The ideal is not to have a professional class of clergyman. The ideal is to have every one of us be equal.

There has to be an opening that occurs in order to prepare the way. The opening at this end is going to be handled by someone who has remained behind, and the opening at the far end is going to be the one to whom the assignment was given to open the way for His return—Elijah, the one who was promised.

Now, I want to be really clear. I don't expect either of those individuals to have any public ministry again. They have a role in Zion, and those who dwell in Zion are going to have some contact with them. The three Nephites are a great example. They, like John, were given a similar ministry to remain around and to minister until the end of the earth. And they did minister. Two of the people to whom they ministered were Mormon and Moroni. They, like ministering angels, ministered to Mormon who, in turn, ministered to the public. They ministered to Moroni and kept his hope up in the waning days of that dispensation, but they did not minister publicly. John will have a role, but the work of Zion is the work of flesh and blood. Men have to extend the invitation for God to return; so that men, who extend that invitation, are worthy of His return, and the Lord can safely come without utterly destroying all who are upon the earth. Therefore, you need Zion, among other reasons, in order for there to be a place and a people to whom the Lord can safely return without utterly destroying the earth at His coming. However small, however diminutive it may be, there needs to be a Zion that extends the invitation for the Lord to return. Now the good news is that Zion will be preserved. And the even better news is that all of those good people of the earth, who live in ignorance, but who would've accepted the truth if it were brought to them; they will be preserved also. There will be a mission field into the millennium.

But the really, really bad news is in the laundry list of those whom the Lord intends to destroy at His coming—that is the description of those who are Telestial, and therefore cannot endure His presence when He shall come—all of the liars, all of whoremongers, all of the people who have taken our Lord's name in vain *having not authority*, all of those who have preached for hire and practiced priestcraft— (One of the reasons it needs to be eradicated, before you get to Zion is so you're not ignited like a torch head to the amusement of everyone else that is in Zion); there has to be an end of all that nonsense. Our Lord was and is meek. When He said: "I am more intelligent than them all," when He said: "I am the greatest of all;" there wasn't one whit of arrogance in His announcement of that. What He was saying is: "Please have confidence in me. Please trust what I say to be true. Please recognize I've paid a price in order to be able to minister." You needn't respect the messenger, but you must respect the message, because salvation is limited in every generation, to those who are authorized to preach repentance and to baptize. And if they're not authorized, then it is powerlessness. However good it may make you feel, it is powerlessness.

Moses chapter 7; this is the Lord speaking to Enoch in a vision recorded subsequently by Moses by revelation, but it is a restoration of the Book of Enoch and the conversational speaker is the Lord, beginning in Moses chapter 7 verse 60. *And the Lord said unto Enoch: As I live, even so will I come in the last days, in the days of wickedness and vengeance, to fulfil the oath which I have made unto you concerning the children of Noah* (see also Genesis 4:22 RE).

This is the Lord's oath to Enoch. He's going to come, he's going to come in the last days.

> *And the day shall come that the earth shall rest, but before that day the heavens shall be darkened, and a veil of darkness shall cover the earth; and the heavens shall shake, [and the earth,] and also the earth; and great tribulations shall be [had] among the children of men, but my people will I preserve; And righteousness will I send down out of heaven; and truth will I send forth out of the earth, to bear testimony of mine Only Begotten; his resurrection from the dead; yea, and also the resurrection of all men; and righteousness and truth will I cause to sweep the earth as with a flood.* (Moses 7:61-62; see also ibid. 4:22 RE)

The thing that is possible now by you sitting at a keyboard anywhere in the world. You can cause the truth to flood the earth.

> *To gather out mine elect from the four quarters of the earth, unto a place which I shall prepare, an Holy City, that my people may gird up their loins, and be looking forth for the time of my coming; for there shall be my tabernacle* [in this context the tabernacle to be built is His house], *and it shall be called Zion, a New Jerusalem. And the Lord said unto Enoch: Then shalt thou and all thy city meet them there, and we will receive them into our bosom, and they shall see us; and we will fall upon their necks, and they shall fall upon our necks, and we will kiss each other;* (ibid. vs. 62-63; see also ibid. vs. 22 RE)

This is the second return of Enoch, as well. First His house, then Enoch.

> *And there shall be mine abode, and it shall be Zion, which shall come forth out of all the creations which I have made; and for the space of a thousand years the earth shall rest. And it came to pass that Enoch saw*

the day of the coming of the Son of Man, in the last days, to dwell on the
earth in righteousness for the space of a thousand years; (ibid. vs. 64-65;
see also ibid. vs. 22-23 RE)

Zion exists before these things can happen. If Zion does not exist, these
things will be delayed. They will not be prevented; because the Lord has, by a
covenant, ensured that they will happen. But the fact that the Lord has, by a
covenant, ensured that it will happen is no guarantee that we will see it,
because we will only see it, if we undertake to abide the conditions by which
He can accomplish His work.

This is the Joseph Smith Translation of Genesis chapter 9.

> *And the bow shall be in the cloud; and I will look upon it, that I may*
> *remember the everlasting covenant, which I made unto thy father Enoch;*
> *[yea] that, when men should keep all my commandments, Zion should*
> *again come on the earth, the city of Enoch which I have caught up unto*
> *myself. And this is mine everlasting covenant, that when thy posterity*
> *shall embrace the truth and look upward, then shall Zion look*
> *downward, and all the heavens shall shake with gladness and the earth*
> *shall tremble with joy. And the general assembly of the church of the*
> *First-Born shall come down out of heaven, and possess the earth, and*
> *shall have place until the end come. And this is mine everlasting*
> *covenant, which I made with thy father Enoch.* (Genesis JST 9:21-23;
> see also ibid. vs. 22 RE)

The covenant that God made again with Noah. The covenant that he made
originally with Adam. The covenant which *some* generation will rise up to
receive, whether that's you, or whether you go to the grave without realizing it
or not, is entirely up to you.

Now I need to read you something. This is Ezekiel beginning in chapter 33,
at verse 25.

> *Wherefore say unto them, Thus saith the Lord GOD; Ye eat with the*
> *blood, and ye lift up your eyes toward your idols, and shed blood: and*
> *shall ye possess the land? Ye stand upon your sword, ye work abomination,*
> *and ye defile every one his neighbour's wife: and shall ye possess the land?*
> *Say thou thus unto them, Thus saith the Lord GOD; As I live, surely they*
> *that are in the wastes shall fall by the sword, and him that is in the open*
> *field will I give to the beasts to be devoured, and they that be in the forts*
> *and in the caves shall die of the pestilence. For I will lay the land most*

desolate, and the pomp of her strength shall cease; and the mountains of Israel shall be desolate, that none shall pass through. Then shall they know that I am the LORD, when I have laid the land most desolate because of all their abominations which they have committed. Also, thou son of man, the children of thy people still are talking against thee by the walls and in the doors of the houses, and speak ye one to another, every one to his brother, saying, Come, I pray you, and hear what is the word that cometh forth from the LORD. And they come unto thee as the people cometh, and they sit before thee as my people, and they hear thy words, but they will not do them: for with their mouth they shew much love, but their heart goeth after their covetousness. And, lo, thou art unto them as a very lovely song of one that hath a pleasant voice, and can play well on an instrument: for they hear thy words, but they do them not.

And when this cometh to pass, (lo, it will come,) then shall they know that a prophet hath been among them. And the word of the LORD came unto me, saying, Son of man, prophesy against the shepherds of Israel, prophesy, ... say unto them, Thus saith the Lord GOD unto the shepherds; Woe be unto to the shepherds of Israel that do feed themselves! Should not the shepherds feed the flock? Ye eat the fat, and ye clothe you with the wool, ye kill them that are fed: but ye feed not the flock. The diseased have ye not strengthened, neither have ye healed that which was sick, neither have ye bound up that which was broken, neither have ye brought again that which was driven away, neither have ye sought that which was lost; but with force and with cruelty ye have ruled them. And they were scattered, because there is no shepherd: and they became meat to all the beasts of the field, when they were scattered. My sheep wandered through all the mountains, and upon every high hill: yea, my flock was scattered upon all the face of the earth, and none did search or seek after them. Therefore, ye shepherds, hear the word of the LORD; As I live, saith the Lord GOD, surely because my flock became a prey, and my flock became meat to every beast of the field, because there was no shepherd, neither did my shepherds search for my flock, but the shepherds fed themselves, and fed not my flock; Therefore, O ye shepherds, hear the word of the LORD; Thus saith the Lord GOD; Behold, I am against the shepherds; and I will require my flock at their hand, and cause them to cease from feeding the flock; neither shall the shepherds feed themselves anymore; for I will deliver my flock from their mouth, that they may not be meat for them. For thus saith the Lord GOD; Behold, I, even I, will both search my sheep, and seek them out. As a shepherd seeketh out his flock in the day that he is among his sheep that are scattered; so will I seek out my sheep, where they have been scattered in the cloudy and dark day.

And I will bring them out from the people, and gather them from the countries, and will bring them to their own land, and feed them upon the mountains of Israel by the rivers, and in all the inhabited places of the country. I will feed them in a good pasture, and upon the high mountains of Israel shall their fold be: there shall they lie down in a good fold, and in a fat pasture and they shall feed upon the mountains of Israel. I will feed my flock, and I will cause them to lie down, saith the Lord GOD. I will seek that which was lost, and bring again that which was driven away, and will bind up that which was broken, and will strengthen that which was sick: but I will destroy the fat and the strong; I will feed them with judgment. And as for thou, O my flock, thus saith the Lord GOD; Behold, I will judge between cattle and cattle, between the rams and the he goats. Seemeth it a small thing unto you to have eaten up the good pasture, but ye must tread down with your feet the residue of your pastures? And you've drunk from the deep waters, but ye must foul the residue with your feet?

And as for my flock, they eat that which ye have trodden with your feet; and they drink that which ye have fouled with your feet. Therefore thus saith the Lord GOD unto them; Behold, I, even I, will judge between the fat cattle and between the lean cattle. Because ye have thrust with [the] side and with [the] shoulder, and pushed all the diseased with your horns, till ye have scattered them abroad; Therefore will I save my flock, and they shall no more be a prey; and I will judge between cattle and cattle. And I will set up one shepherd over them, and he shall feed them, even my servant David; he shall feed them, and he shall be their shepherd. And I the LORD will be their God, and my servant David a prince among them; for I the LORD have spoken it. And I will make with them a covenant of peace, and will cause the evil beasts to cease out of the land: and they shall dwell safely in the wilderness, and sleep in the woods. And I will make them and the places round about my hill a blessing; and I will cause the shower to come down in his season; there shall be showers of blessing. And the tree of the field shall yield her fruit, and the earth shall yield her increase, and they shall be safe in their land, and shall know that I am the LORD, when I have broken the bands of their yoke, and delivered them out of the [hands] of those that served themselves of them. And they shall no more be a prey to the heathen, neither shall the beast of the land devour them; but they shall dwell safely, and none shall make them afraid. And I will raise up for them a plant of renown, and they shall be no more consumed with hunger in the land, neither bear the shame of the heathen any more. Thus shall they know that I am the LORD their God, am with them, and that they, even

> *the house of Israel, are my people, saith the Lord GOD. And ye my flock, the flock of my pasture, are men, and I am your God, saith the Lord GOD.* (Ezekiel 33:25-33, 34:1-31; see also Ezekiel 17: 2-11 RE)

I was required to read that, but I am not required and therefore will not comment on that.

So now we should realize, I hope, that that city which Melchizedek, the King of Peace was able to teach righteousness sufficiently so that it was taken up from the earth; reserved to the last days and the end of the world. The next time we have such an event on the earth; the next time there is this kind of a gathering and this kind of a population anywhere, it will not be for the purpose of going up. It will be for the purpose of permitting those who have gone up, to come back down. It will be for the purpose of having those who can endure the presence of those who come— because those who come will burn up all those who are unworthy, and therefore, some few need to be gathered so that the earth is not utterly wasted at His coming. *As it was in the days of Noah, so also shall it be at the time of the coming of the Son of Man* (Matthew JST 1:41; see also Matthew 1:11 RE). How many people were required in order to have the Ark be an acceptable place in which God could preserve all of humanity? It was a portable Ark of the Covenant, in which the family was preserved.

And so, if it's going to be as it was in the days of Noah, there is this net that has been cast out to gather together all manner of fish. But as the Lord tells the parable, the angels are going to come, and they're going to pick through all manner of fish; and they're going to keep the good, and the rest are going to be scheduled for burning. And so, the question is, how diligent ought the search be into the things of God? How carefully ought we to consider the things that have been restored to us through the Prophet Joseph Smith? The fact is that this stuff is assigned to our dispensation. And I'm reading from the Book of Mormon—which the world does not have or accept. I'm reading from the book of Abraham—which the world does not have or accept. I'm reading from the Joseph Smith Translation—which the world does not have and accept. All of you have this information in front of you. All of this material has been restored through someone that we claim we honor and regard as a Prophet. Well, they who come will burn up those who are unprepared. And therefore, what should we be doing in order to make sure that we are included among those who *are* prepared?

I want to look more into Enoch. So let's go back to the book of Abraham— opps excuse me, the book of Moses. Moses chapter 7, beginning at verse 60.

And the Lord said unto Enoch: As I live, [This is covenant language. This is God swearing by his own life. This is God promising that if He lives, so shall this word live. If He's alive, He shall vindicate what He's about to say.] *As I live, even so will I come in the last days, in the days of wickedness and vengeance, to fulfil the oath which I have made unto you concerning the children of Noah; And the day shall come that the earth shall rest, but before that day the heavens shall be darkened, and a veil of darkness shall cover the earth; and the heavens shall shake, and also the earth; and great tribulations shall be among the children of men, but my people will I preserve; And righteousness will I send down out of heaven; and truth will I send forth out of the earth, to bear testimony of mine Only Begotten; his resurrection from the dead; yea, and also the resurrection of all men; and righteousness and truth will I cause to sweep the earth as with a flood, to gather out mine elect from the four quarters of the earth, even unto a place which I shall prepare, an Holy City, that my people may gird up their loins, and be looking forth for the time of my coming; for there shall be my tabernacle, and it shall be called Zion, a New Jerusalem. And the Lord said unto Enoch: Then shalt thou and all thy city meet them there.* [These are they who, when they come, will burn up those unprepared for their coming, so that it leaves neither root nor branch.] *We will receive them into our bosom, and they shall see us; and we will fall upon their necks, and they shall fall upon our necks, and we will kiss each other; And there shall be mine abode, and it shall be called Zion, which shall come forth out of all the creations which I have made; and for the space of a thousand years the earth shall rest. And it came to pass that Enoch saw the day of the coming of the Son of Man, in the last days, to dwell on the earth in righteousness for the space of a thousand years; But before that day he saw great tribulations among the wicked; and he also saw the sea, that it was troubled, and men's hearts failing them, looking forth with fear for the judgments of the Almighty God, which should come upon the wicked.* (Moses 7: 60-66; see also Genesis 4:23 RE)

This is the Lord, describing to Enoch what would happen by way of covenant —the Lord swearing: *"As I live, even so will...,"* and He tells him what's going to come to pass in the last days. This is among the promises that were made to one of the fathers (and this is one of the fathers) and these are the covenants whose time is now upon us. This is the day in which we need to be prepared so that those who went before and ascended up the ladder, can return and fall upon your neck and kiss you; and you fall upon their neck and kiss them. A sacred embrace, through the veil, evidencing fellowship between you *here*, and them *there*. The Lord promising and covenanting these things are going to happen. But notice, there has to be a tabernacle. He has to come and take up His abode. There has to be preparation made. These things require some effort to be made *here*, in order to prepare for His return. If there is no one here who is willing to engage in what's necessary to bring this to pass (because everyone looks around and expects someone else to do it), then you're neglecting the duty that's devolving upon you—as one of those who was assigned to come down in this day, in order to honor the fathers, and honor the Lord; by allowing the covenants that have been made to be fulfilled.

It's a good thing that we forfeit the power to make authoritative covenants from time to time; because if we had everything that we claim we had, and if we lived under an obligation that God would honor, and if we chose to violate that (as will be the case when we have Zion), you cannot endure a Terrestrial glory in a Telestial state—lying, and stealing, and deceiving, and adultery, and whoremongering, (all of the abominations that people prize in this generation), your lusts, your ambitions, your desires to lord it over one another, (the common affliction of the Gentile); all of those things are a level below what Zion requires. And so, if one happily strolls into Zion, while profaning the conditions upon which it will be established, they subject themselves to the penalty of being where they should not be, in a condition in which they cannot endure. The destruction that occurred at Christ's death on the Americas was the destruction of the wicked only. If you look at 3rd Nephi chapter 10, verse 12 (see also 3 Nephi 4:10 RE), you find out that the more righteous were saved. Those who live a Telestial law will be destroyed.

Turn to Doctrine and Covenants section 76. I want to begin at— well, I may as well back up. I was going to begin a little later on. I want you to remember the chant "Follow the Prophet, Follow the Prophet," which we can drill in mindlessly to the youth with the drumbeat cadence that sounds rather like [Indian chant]. You know, Follow the Prophet, follow the Prophet," you do that, "Follow the brethren, Follow the brethren".

> *The glory of the telestial is one, even as the glory of the stars is one; for as one star differs from another star in glory, even so differs one from another in glory in the telestial world; For these are they who are of Paul, and of Apollos, and of Cephas. These are they who say they are some of one, and some of another—some of Christ...some of John, ...some of Moses, ...some of Elias, ...some of Esaias, ...some of Isaiah, and some of Enoch; But received not the gospel, neither the testimony of Jesus, neither the prophets, neither the everlasting covenant* [yet to be established]. *Last of all,* [and this is a general description of those who have telestial behavior] *these...are they who will not be gathered with the*

saints, to be caught up unto the church of the Firstborn, and received into the cloud. These are they who are liars, and sorcerers, and adulterers, and whoremongers, and whosoever loves and makes a lie. These are they who suffer the wrath of God on earth. These are they who suffer the vengeance of eternal fire. (D&C 76: 98-105; see also T&C 69:26)

That is a broad description of those who *cannot* be in Zion. And notably, it begins with a list of those who *follow the prophets!* Almost as if the Lord, in the revelation to Joseph Smith, anticipated your day and warned you: "Do not go thither! Do not partake of that! Receive the testimony of Jesus! Prepare when He offers the Everlasting Covenant! Do that!" To the extent that a church or an organization worships or trusts a man in lieu of Christ, it will lead you to telestial destruction. It will not— Those who believe in it will not survive the destruction of the wicked that precedes the Lord's return.

The purpose of the temple is not merely to inspire you with the conviction that it is possible to rend the veil, to pass through the veil, to see and meet with our Lord—who has promised us repeatedly, that the stories in the Book of Mormon are stories designed to tell you over, and over, and over again about coming back into the presence of the Lord. Even wicked Lamanite converts—many of them have what we, in our scholarly language, would call a throne theophany; and they did so upon conversion, because their conversion was with real intent. Therefore, the Book of Mormon is a text about the Second Comforter. But what is being talked about in this verse, in Moses chapter 6, is about dwelling in His presence. And when it comes in verse— again this is Moses 6, verse 57 (see also Genesis 4:9 RE), it says when it comes to dwelling there, no unclean thing can dwell there, because He's the man of holiness. This presents the real message, or the real meaning of what the temple is trying to convey to us in our day. And we're just about running out of time to accomplish that in our day. And if we don't, then you know He passes on and maybe starts this up with another people in another day, as he's so often done before.

To come to the veil and to meet with the Savior—He can clean you up. He, through His grace, can give you all that you lack. To dwell in the presence of God requires something more, something different. It requires that you grow from where you are now, to the place where the Lord intends to lead you. He intends to have you *be* true and faithful in all things. Because in the ceremony in the temple, once you go through the veil you don't come back— you stay there. And the purpose of going there in this day, in this setting, is to enable the return of Zion. We don't need a profoundly new and far reaching economic system to make us have all things in common in order to bring again Zion—and we don't need possession of the real estate in Jackson County, Missouri to bring again Zion. We don't need any of the implements, or locations, or infrastructure, to have Zion return. We need one thing and that's *you*. You to be clean. You to be holy. To leave behind you, not only the door, but the house in which you dwell, that you established that door to bar Him through. You need to come and live with Him. It is possible. These are not cunningly devised fables, as the apostle Paul put it. This is the gospel of Jesus Christ.

Look at the definition that the Lord gives of salvation in Ether chapter 3. This is the definition that the Lord gives, *Behold, the Lord showed himself unto him, and said: Because thou knowest these things ye are redeemed from the fall; therefore ye are brought back into my presence; therefore I show myself unto you* (Ether 3:13; see also Ether 1:13 RE). This is the meaning of salvation. This is the fullness of the gospel of Jesus Christ. This is contained in the Book of Mormon, which has the fullness of Jesus Christ in it. The Lord showed himself unto Him and said, *Because thou knowest these things ye are redeemed from the fall; therefore ye are brought back into my presence; therefore I show myself unto you.* (ibid.)

The character, and the nature of God is probably better understood by what we have in the Book of Mormon—and it is perfectly consistent with the testimony of the gospel writers who knew Christ in mortality. And if you take what we've got in a fairly battered New Testament record and the Book of Mormon together, and what happened in the life of Joseph Smith, and you weave them all together; you begin to understand that God is a very patient, loving, kindly being. And that the mysteries of God, largely consist in developing the attributes of godliness in us. The things that matter the most are the things that make us more like Him—better people, more kindly. You want to know more of the mysteries of God? Serve your fellow man, and be of more value to them. In the process of blessing the lives of others, you find out that you know more of the character of God as a consequence of that.

Let me end by bearing testimony that God really is up to a work right now. And the work that is underway can culminate in Zion. Covenants were made. Promises were given. God has an obligation to the covenant fathers that He *will* vindicate. God's words will be fulfilled—all of them! None of them are going to fall to the ground unfulfilled. The question is not, will God bring about the culmination of all His purposes? The question is, are we willing to cooperate with Him to bring those purposes to pass in our day? It could— The offer that God makes— (This appears in scripture nearly as often as the promise in Malachi.) God says, *How oft would I have gathered you as a hen gathers her chicks under her wings, and ye would not?* (3 Nephi 10:5; see also 3 Nephi 4:9 RE). Could God have brought about His purposes and vindicated His promises in the days of Moses? Could He have done what He had promised to do, when Christ was here on the earth? Could He have done it in the days of Peter? Could He have done it in the days of Joseph Smith? The question is never whether God will vindicate His promises. The question is, will there ever come a people who will respond to the Lord's willingness to gather them as a hen gathers her chicks under her wings, and be gathered, and be content with being gathered, and being at peace with one another? We have that opportunity, but so many generations before us have had the same opportunity, and they would not. The question isn't whether God is going to do it, or whether God is willing to do it now. The question is, are we willing to cooperate with Him in that process to do our part? We get really petty with one another, and we shouldn't be. We ought to value one another so highly that we'll do anything we can to support one another and to assist in bringing about the purposes of God. At the end of the day, obedience to God is simply blessing one another by the way we conduct ourselves. I like the Lamanite King's prayer, *I will give away all my sins to know you* (Alma 22:18; Alma 13:10 RE). We tend not to be willing to give away our sins. We want to harbour 'em and cultivate 'em and celebrate 'em. We ought to be more— We ought to love God more and our sins less. God can fulfill His promises, in our day, before we leave this stage of the action. It can happen. Whether it happens or not, is up to us and how interested we are in doing as He bids us. Of that, I bear testimony, in the name of Jesus Christ, Amen.

———

The foregoing excerpts are taken from:

- Denver's *40 Years in Mormonism Series*, Talk #10 titled "Preserving the Restoration" given in Mesa, AZ on September 9th, 2014
- His talk titled "Zion Will Come" given near Moab, UT on April 10th, 2016
- Denver's *40 Years in Mormonism Series*, Talk #2 titled "Faith" given in Idaho Falls, ID on September 28th, 2013
- Denver's *40 Years in Mormonism Series*, Talk #6 titled "Zion" given in Grand Junction, CO on April 12, 2014
- *Denver's 40 Years in Mormonism Series*, Talk #4 titled "Covenants" given in Centerville, UT on October 6, 2013
- A fireside talk on "The Temple", given in Ogden, UT on October 28th, 2012; and

- Denver's remarks titled "Book of Mormon as Covenant" given at the Book of Mormon Covenant Conference in Columbia, SC on January 13, 2019

86. Endure It Well

DENVER: How can you know if the boils you receive in life are due to being like unto Job or because you are more akin to Pharoah?

It's a great question; I love the question. First, there's an interesting exercise that I would commend to any of you. Go to the account of Exodus, the early events, and only read the words of Moses. Just read Moses' responses—his reactions, his complaints, his fear, his doubts—and what you will realize is that it doesn't matter if someone occupies a great position, as Moses did, or the lives that each of us are now living. No one fits easily, or comfortably, or without anxiety into the work of the Lord. There's a measure that you take of yourself in which you look inward and say, "I'm not adequate to what needs to be done; I don't have the faith required," and you'll see that that's exactly what Moses was telling God—that looking inward he did not think himself equal to it.

In the Book of Mormon, Nephi gives us an account of their journey—after they had been delivered from Jerusalem, which was about to be destroyed, and they were migrating—here are some comments that he makes about their experience:

- *We have suffered much afflictions, hunger, thirst, and fatigue* (1 Nephi 5:10 RE);

- *...we did travel and wade through much affliction in the wilderness* (vs. 11);

- *...we had suffered many afflictions and much difficulty, yea even so much that we cannot write them all* (vs. 14).

This is Nephi explaining his experience in the wilderness. Afflictions, hunger, thirst, fatigue—so many afflictions that they can't even talk about 'em. We don't look at those words; we pass over them as if Nephi were somehow being modest, or Nephi were being self-deprecating. We pass over what Moses says when he's getting the responsibilities imposed upon him by the Lord, as if it's just common sense that he's heroic, and larger than life, and greater than the common man. When you read his reaction, he sounds like us; he sounds common; he sounds ordinary. And when you read the lamentation—we suffer because we are, because we're mortal, because we're here, because that's the common lot that is designed to be experienced as a consequence of the Fall. And there's no escaping that.

The question isn't: Are we going to suffer while we are here? The only question is: To what degree do we bear up under the troubles of this life, graciously and humbly? And acknowledging that God rules in the heavens above, He rules in the earth beneath, and He rules in your life, too. And that everything that you experience is designed to make you be added upon by the things that you suffer and the things that you experience here.

I was asked, verbally, if I would comment on some of the challenges that people of faith have in defending the Book of Abraham. And that's probably a subject that's worth writing about, rather than just talking off the cuff, but here's, generally, my observation: The people want to know what Joseph did and how he did it, in order for them to understand maybe how **they** can do it.

So there's this relentless inquiry into: How did that process take place? What went on? When, in fact, the gifts of God are almost entirely incapable of being transferred from one to another. Each person has to come to God on their own.

Oliver Cowdery was a man of faith, and he believed in Christ and the possibility of the Second Coming of Christ being proximate (or in close proximity) to his life. He believed in and he got answers from God. And then he hears about what Joseph is doing, and he goes to become his scribe.

One of the early revelations that were given to Oliver talked about his own— Oliver's own— gift; that he had this gift in which Oliver could get yes or no answers by using the—what we would call a "divining rod"—or a stick that would respond positively or negatively to inquiry. And so he had this, and the revelation does not call it anything other than *a gift*. May seem like a peculiar gift to you and I, but it's nevertheless a gift, and it came from God.

Joseph had a gift in which he was capable of receiving revelation—sometimes through instrumentalities, sometimes by study, sometimes simply by God speaking through him in the first person in a spontaneous way. How he went about doing that is unique to him. The way in which you relate to God is unique to you. Running out and trying to replicate something in order for you to know the process by which God involved Himself in revelation in Joseph Smith's experience is not gonna teach you what Joseph Smith experienced.

The fact that I have concluded that Joseph Smith was a restrained man, in many respects a very modest man, whose defense of what he believed to be the truth was fierce, but who recognized that there were a lot of people, including his own wife, Emma Smith, who had a better education than did he—

Joseph was like a sponge when he thought he could get truth or help from others, and he was meek and humble in that respect. But if God had revealed something to him, he was an iron-fisted, immovable man for the truth, personally and privately, just as the scriptures say concerning Moses. Moses was the meekest of all men. If you just read the dialogue from Moses in Exodus, you'll see nothing but meekness in that man. If you'll read Joseph Smith's three documents in *A Man Without Doubt,* you'll see a meek man— **unbelievably frustrated** by some of the circumstances into which he was put, **searching** to find the right way out of the dilemma, **trying** to get God aroused to anger in the same way that the circumstances aroused Joseph to anger, but **submitting always** to whatever the will of God was for him. Ultimately, Joseph Smith left to go to be imprisoned in Carthage knowing he would not come back from there, or at least expecting that he would not, and commenting about how his life was no value to his friends, as he returned and he went back for the slaying.

Say what you want about those final moments in the life of Joseph Smith. He put himself in harm's way to prove his fidelity to his friends. He would not forsake **them**, as they claimed he was doing in **their** hour of need, and ultimately gave his life up. That's not the conduct of a con-man. That's not the way in which someone who's going to lie and cheat and steal and behave as an immoral exploiter of others would conduct their lives. Joseph, in my view, was not just a virtuous man but he qualified as one of those who hath no greater love, because he went back and surrendered at the behest of his brethren—in part, with the hope that by losing his life, Nauvoo would be spared the slaughter that had gone on at Far West, and Haun's Mill, and elsewhere.

And so, when you ask about the translation issues and the controversy over the Book of Abraham, the bottom line/the real issue is: However the mind of Joseph was set on fire with the restoration text of father Abraham's account of his search, you have to decide that the content either is from heaven or it's a lie.

There was a series (it's now been abandoned), but it's a series that was begun at Brigham Young University. The first volume of it—the Book of Abraham series—the first volume of it was pretty good. What they did was take concepts that are included in the text of the Book of Abraham which were completely unknown in the Christian world at the time that the Book of Abraham was put into print. They had to be **unique** concepts. If you could already find them in the Bible, or if you could already find them in what was available to the Christian world generally, then those weren't included. They had to be **unique** ideas. They took and gathered the unique ideas that come out in the Book of Abraham, about which Joseph Smith would have known nothing, and then they looked into other material that exists from diverse places about legends or stories concerning the life of Abraham. And what they found is that there were **Hindu** traditions that talked about Abraham, that preserved some of the very same incidents that are only found in the Book of Abraham at the time Joseph published the Book of Abraham. They found there were **Islamic** texts that were similarly describing the same kind of event, the same incident that's unique to the Book of Abraham. They found sources that were in **Coptic Egyptian** texts. They amalgamated into one volume (it's a pretty big volume) all of the parallel accounts from the life of Abraham in cultures from around the world or religious traditions from around the world that Joseph Smith nailed on the head in his account of the Book of Abraham.

That approach does not defend Joseph Smith as a translator of Egyptian, because it has nothing to do with the papyri, but it does a pretty good job of defending Joseph Smith as a **revelator**—as someone to whom God could reveal light and truth, and he could accurately record it—because echoes of the unique material in the Book of Abraham show up in the ancient world and in other cultures that date back nearly to the time of Abraham. So, the real question is, Do you trust Joseph?

I know of no more cheerful a Being in the universe than Christ. When He says, *Be of good cheer*, we ought to all accept that as the mantra. There is nothing that any of us will ever go through that He hasn't gone through with a considerable greater degree of difficulty. He lived with a higher 'specific gravity' than any of us had to ever fight against. And He won for each of us a prize that is potentially eternal. It will be eternal, one way or the other; but if you take full measure of what He offers, it will be delightfully eternal.

Cowardice is largely predicated upon fear. Don't be cowardly. Don't be fearful. Fear is the opposite of faith. For goodness sake, you're already in the battle! You're already going to be overtaken. The fact of the matter is that no one gets out of here alive. Live this life nobly, fearlessly. When you take the wounds that come your way, you make sure that they come to your front! Don't let 'em shoot you in the back. Go about your life boldly, nobly, valiantly. Because it is only through valiance in the testimony of Jesus Christ that you can hope to secure anything—not valiance in your fidelity to anything other than Jesus Christ. The fact of the matter is that faith must be based in Him, and Him alone.

Turn back to Doctrine and Covenants section 121. This is a letter Joseph composed while he was in the Liberty Jail—mind you the Liberty Jail, and he'd been there suffering through wintertime. It was now in the spring when Joseph had no date in mind in which he would go free or even if he would go free, or whether the original order of execution would be carried out, even though he'd been kept in jail for many years without it having been carried out.

In these circumstances, verse seven and eight of D&C 121: *My son,* [that alone ought to be reassuring to Joseph of course] *My son, peace be unto thy soul; thine adversity and thine afflictions shall be but a moment; And then, if thou endure it well, God shall exalt thee on high; thou shalt triumph over all thy foes* (See also T&C 139: 9 RE). *Endure it well.* Joseph, in the extremity of Liberty jail being told, *endure it well.* You think you have challenges, you think you have difficulties, you think you face dilemmas in your life—*endure it well.* Your adversity and your afflictions are gonna be for a small moment, and then if you endure it well, something better is going to come.

And then, as if it weren't enough reason, turn to 122, verse eight: *The Son of Man hath descended below them all. Art thou greater than he* (See also T&C 139:10 RE)?

If you think that your burdens that you carry are great, remember the burdens that were carried by the Son. He faced burdens that were inordinately greater than yours. All of us should be tested to our limits. All of us should be **proven** by the experiences that we endure. The only way to test some things is to destroy them. The only way to test you through mortality is to cause mortality itself, with the eventual coming of death. That's the way it works.

Look at verse 4 of Ether chapter 3.

> *And I know, O Lord, that thou hast all power, and can do whatsoever thou wilt for the benefit of man; therefore touch these stones, O Lord, with thy finger, and prepare them that they may shine forth in darkness; and they shall shine forth unto us in the vessels which we have prepared, that we may have light while we shall cross the sea. Behold, O Lord, thou*

canst do this. We know that thou art able to show forth great power,
which looks small unto the understanding of men. (Ether 3:4-5; see also
Ether 1:11 RE)

He's not asking for this in order to have a light show. He's asking for this out
of pity and concern, charity and intercession for others who will be left in the
dark. He is trying to do something to bless and benefit others in a very
practical way. He hopes to make the lives of others better. He's not doing this
for himself. He's doing it on behalf of his people.

Therein also lies something very important about the attitude of this man that
tells you why it is that God had respect for this man.

Think about what it means to have the power of God. Think about what it
means for God to be able to do all things, including sustaining you from
moment to moment by lending you breath. And then for God to say you are
free to choose to do, with what he's lending to you, whatever it is that you
choose to do. Think of the patience of our God. Think of the meekness of our
God. And think about the test that you are presently taking to prove who and
what you are. And whether or not, in the circumstances of this test, you are
proving that you can be trusted to have the meekness, to have the patience, to
endure in humility what will be done. To endure the abuses that God allows
to take place in order to permit His children to gain experience. So that in the
long run they can ultimately know the difference between good and evil and
on their own choose to love the good and to stay away from the evil.

Think about that. And think about this record, and think about the test that
is currently underway, and think about what it is that you in your life should
be choosing, and doing, desiring and holding to your breast.

And it came to pass that when the brother of Jared had said these words, behold,
the Lord stretched forth his hand and touched the stones one by one with his finger
(Ether 3:6; see also Ether 1:12). Now I want to pause because the only thing
that the brother of Jared ever sees at this point, the only thing that comes—
the Lord may stretch forth his hand—but the only thing that is seen is His
finger.

It's not—I mean I really love Catherine Thomas. I love her books. I own
them, I've read them, and I like what she did with the brother of Jared at the
veil—but it's simply based upon a fanciful connection between the dialogue
at the veil in the temple ceremony and this incident here. But the hand of
God never emerges. What emerges—and you can read it, it's in this verse six;

it's again in verse nine—the Lord asks him, 'Did you see more than this?' He says, 'No, it's the finger.' However, I put one of the stones in my hand. Let's assume for a moment that I have eight and eight, and let's assume that you touch it. It's impossible to touch the stone that's in your hand without feeling that the stone has been touched.

We read this record and we don't notice what's really going on. Here they are in my hands, eight and eight, and the finger of the Lord touches the stones one by one with his finger. Now, there is nothing in this record that suggests that after the last stone gets touched, or after the stone the Lord was touching at the moment that the finger is seen that there are any more stones left to be touched. One, two, three, four, five, six, seven, eight, nine, ten, eleven, twelve, thirteen, fourteen, fifteen, sixteen. This record read in fairness suggests to me that the brother of Jared stood there and witnessed 15 of the 16 stones, felt the touch on 15 of the 16 stones, before on the last stone he saw the finger of the Lord. Think about that for a moment. Think about coming into contact, admittedly through a stone, but coming into contact with the Lord when He manifests Himself for the first time to man physically. Think about that.

And the veil was taken from off the eyes of the brother of Jared, and he saw the finger of the Lord; and it was as the finger of a man, like unto flesh and blood.... [That's the way in which the Lord chose to manifest Himself because he came into contact with sixteen stones.]

> *And the brother of Jared fell down before the Lord, for he was struck with fear. And the Lord saw that the brother of Jared had fallen to the earth; and the Lord said unto him: Arise, why hast thou fallen? And he saith unto the Lord: I saw the finger of the Lord, and I feared lest he should smite me; for I knew not that the Lord had flesh and blood. (Ether 3:6; see also Ether 1:12 RE)*

It frightened him to realize that the God who controls all things had flesh and blood. This was a great secret that ought not get out, and now he knows it, and knowing it, it frightened him. He's intruding into space that he didn't want to intrude into and he felt convicted that somehow that was something he ought not know.

> *The Lord said unto him: Because of thy faith thou hast seen that I shall take upon me flesh and blood; and never has man come before me with such exceeding faith as thou hast; for were it not so ye could not have seen my finger. Sawest thou more than this? [My finger. Sawest thou*

more than this?] And he answered: Nay. [Didn't see the hand, saw the finger, and he didn't see more than this.] Nay; Lord, show thyself unto me. The Lord said unto him: Believest thou the words which I shall speak? (Ether 3:9-10; see also Ether 1:12 RE)

This is a necessary prerequisite, because what the Lord is about to speak to him will be covenantal. When it comes to prophecy, covenants, commitments by God, what He's about to do requires that the brother of Jared have faith in what's going to happen. He's going to show him all things.

He answered: Yea, Lord, I know that thou speakest the truth, for thou art a God of truth, and canst not lie. And when he had said these words, behold, the Lord showed himself unto him, and said: Because thou knowest these things ye are redeemed from the fall; therefore ye are brought back into my presence; therefore I show myself unto you. Behold, I am he who was prepared from the foundation of the world to redeem my people. I am Jesus Christ. I'm the Father and the Son. In me shall all mankind have life, and that eternally, even they who shall believe on my name; and they shall become my sons and daughters. And never have I shown myself unto man whom I have created, for never has man believed in me as thou hast. Seest thou that ye are created after mine own image? Yea, even all men were created in the beginning after mine own image. Behold this body, which ye now behold, is the body of my spirit; and man have I created after the body of my spirit; and even as I appear to thee to be in the spirit will I appear unto my people in the flesh. And now, as I, Moroni, said I could not make a full account of these things which are written, therefore it sufficeth me to say that Jesus showed himself unto this man in the spirit, even after the manner and in the same likeness of the same body even as he showed himself unto the Nephites. (Ether 3:12-17; see also Ether 1:12-14 RE)

What was the body that Jesus showed Himself unto the Nephites in? What is the difference between water as a solid, water as a liquid, and water as a gas? The difference between that, if you want to take a scriptural word, is temperature. Excuse me, that's a scientific word. Scriptural word is "quickened". In one condition it is *quickened*, in another condition it is less quick but in science the difference between the two is temperature.

God dwells in everlasting burnings. In order to be with or near Him, a man must be *quickened* in order to endure the presence. Does that mean that in a *quickened* state, it is impossible for a *quickened* being to manifest itself in a solid form? Well, take a look at Doctrine and Covenants section 131 verse 7:

There is no such thing as immaterial matter. All spirit is matter, but it is more fine or pure, and can only be discerned by purer eyes; We cannot see it; but when our bodies are purified we shall see that it is all matter.

Doctrine and Covenants section 77:2 includes this statement: *That which is spiritual being in the likeness of that which is temporal; that which is temporal in the likeness of that which is spiritual* (See also T&C 74:2 RE).

D&C 88 verses 15 to 16*: The spirit and the body are the soul of man. And the resurrection from the dead is the redemption of the soul* (T&C 86:2 RE). This definition was given by revelation to Joseph Smith in 1832. Three years later in 1835, Chandler came through and sold the mummies to Joseph Smith. He did not bother translating the end part of the Book of Abraham as we have it, until the 1840's in Kirtland; excuse me, in Nauvoo. But when he translated it in Nauvoo, he knew the definition of what a *soul* was, that is a spirit and a body. When he translated the Book of Abraham, in Abraham chapter 3 verse 23, speaking of those in the pre-existence, he says: *God saw these souls that they were good, and he stood in the midst of them, and he said: These will I make my rulers; for he stood among those that were spirits* (See also Abraham 6:1 RE). They were souls, possessing therefore a spirit and a body. And they were spirits because they had not come down yet, in the beginning, to be in this condition. And it's speaking about *the noble and great.*

And by the way, I talked before about the definition of rulers in the Gentile world, and that's someone who exercises authority over them. In the vernacular of both the Book of Mormon and in the vernacular found here, *rulers* in the house of God have nothing to do with dominion over someone else. A ruler is someone who teaches. A ruler is someone who is able to give an accurate gauge by which to measure things. A ruler is someone who teaches the truth. If you would want to be a ruler in the house of God, then you have to be someone who declares and teaches the truth.

Take a look at Alma chapter 13 because this is where it becomes very important for us. Alma chapter 13 beginning at verse 17:

> *Now this Melchizedek was a king over the land of Salem; and his people had waxed strong in iniquity and abomination; yea, they had all gone astray; they were full of all manner of wickedness.* [This is his audience.] *But Melchizedek having exercised mighty faith, received the office of the high priesthood according to the holy order of God, did preach repentance unto his people. And behold, they did repent; and Melchizedek did establish peace in the land in his days; therefore he was called the prince*

> *of peace, for he was a king of Salem; and he did reign under his father.*
> (See also Alma 10:2 RE)

First, he received this priesthood. Second, he preached repentance. But nothing would have happened except for, third, the people who heard him did repent. And because of that people who are described as having waxed strong in iniquity, people who are described as being captivated by abominations, people who have all gone astray turned out to be the very people among whom this City of Peace got established. But they did it. They did it by repentance. This isn't something Melchizedek pulled off. This is something that the people accomplished, and they accomplished it because of their repentance.

I want you to contrast that with another group. This group is in Mosiah chapter 12. Mosiah chapter 12 beginning halfway through verse 12. This is people reacting to the message that Abinadi was delivering to them. They're accusing Abinadi, and they're saying,

> *And he* [Abinadi] *pretendeth the Lord hath spoken it. And he saith all this shall come upon thee except thou repent, and this because of thine iniquities. And now, O king, what great evil hast thou done, or what great sins have thy people committed, that we should be condemned of God or judged by this man? Now, O king, behold, we're guiltless, and thou, O king, hast not sinned; therefore, this man has lied concerning you, and he has prophesied in vain. Behold, we are strong, we shall not come into bondage, or be taken captive by our enemies; yea, and thou hast prospered in the land, and thou shalt also prosper.* (See also Mosiah 7:14-15 RE)

Here is the pride. Here is the vanity. Here is the very thing which, had the people to whom Melchizedek spoken, had they done this, there would have been no City of Peace, there would have been no Salem, there would have been no second Zion.

You generally hail from a tradition that assures you that you're in the right way. You generally come from a tradition that says you're better than others. You're able to look down your nose at other people who stumble about in the dark, because they don't have all the great truths that you have. The fact of the matter is, you generally, not specifically, because there are some to whom this absolutely does not apply, your hearts are right before God. But there aren't many.

You've been handed this tradition and the wicked one cometh, and he takes away Light and Truth, and he does it because of the false traditions you've been handed. The greatest among us is wholly inadequate. The greatest among us can't be trusted with the power of God, not yet anyway. The greatest among us is still in need of repentance. Every one of us should walk fearfully before God, not because God isn't generous, but because what He offers can turn you into a devil. The only way to be prepared and not fall is to realize the enormous peril that you present potentially to the universe. Before you get in a position to enjoy the status that God offers to us all, you need to work out your salvation with fear and trembling, exactly like Paul said. You need to purge, remove, reprove. This attitude we see in this man in this account, this is the man of God! Christ may be the prototype of the saved man, but I know of no record anywhere in scripture that exposes the heart of the real disciple of Christ as well as does this chapter expose the heart of this man. This is what we should become. This is why the Lord could open up to him. This is why this man became, in the history of the world coming up to this moment, despite the fact the Lord came to Adam-ondi-Ahman and administered comfort to Adam in the Valley of Adam-ondi-Ahman, here He came and showed Himself as He truly was—as a pre-existent spirit, possessing a soul as tangible as man's—and ministered to him in a way which, if you understood what it takes for a *quickened* being to condescend into the presence and make himself known as He does here, was an enormous sacrifice by our Lord.

———

The foregoing excerpts are taken from:

- Denver's Q&A session at the Keeping the Covenant Conference in Boise, ID on September 22, 2019
- Denver's *40 Years in Mormonism Series*, Talk #1 titled "Be of Good Cheer" given in Boise, ID on September 10th, 2013; and
- Denver's *40 Years in Mormonism Series*, Talk #8 titled "A Broken Heart" given in Las Vegas, NV on July 25th, 2014

87. Prototypes of the Saved Woman

In this episode, Denver discusses Mary (the Mother of Christ), Mary Magdalene, and Eve as prototypes of the saved woman.

————

DENVER: John wrote that Mary Magdalene saw, even embraced the risen Lord, and related to the others her testimony of having seen Him returned to life, resurrected from the dead!

> "[These] accounts differ in details. [They have]...similarities and differences. They are universal in the fact that Christ was seen by the women (or a woman) first, and not by His Apostles. [John's account]...records that Christ told Mary: "Touch me not." In the Joseph Smith Translation the words are changed to read: "Hold me not" (JST John 20: 17). Joseph's change of the text was warranted.

> [I tell you that] when Mary realized it was Jesus, she embraced Him joyfully. She did not timidly reach out her hand, but she readily greeted Him with open arms, and He, in turn, embraced her. [It's] difficult to describe what I saw of the incident, apart from saying that the Lord was triumphant, exultant, overjoyed at His return from the grave! She shared His joy. I was shown the scene and do not have words to adequately communicate how complete the feelings of joy and gratitude were which were felt by our Lord that morning. As dark and terrible [as] were the sufferings through which He passed, the magnitude of which is impossible for man to put into words, these feelings of triumph were, on the other hand, of equal magnitude in their joy and gratitude. [He had attained to the resurrection of the dead! Just as He had seen His Father do, He likewise held the keys of death and hell!] I do not think it possible for a mortal to feel a fullness of either. And having felt some of what He shares with His witnesses, I know words are inadequate to capture His feelings on the morning of His resurrection. He had the deep satisfaction of having accomplished the most difficult assignment [to be] given by the Father, knowing it was a benefit to all of His Father's children, and it had been done perfectly.

> Mary and Christ embraced. There was nothing timid about the warm encounter she had with Him. Then He said to her, "Hold me not"

because He had to ascend, return and report to His Father. Joseph Smith was correct when he changed the language.

I then saw Him ascend to heaven. I saw the golden heavenly light glowing down upon Mary as she watched His ascent. All this happened while it was yet dark on the morning He rose from the dead. He has shown this to me and I can testify to it as a witness." (See, *Come, Let Us Adore Him*, pp. 256-7.)

QUESTION: In the beginning, you said that there was a woman, first, who saw Christ had risen. Was there any special reason you did not give her name?

DENVER: No, it was Mary. Yeah, yeah. Any reason why I didn't use the name of the woman? The reason I use the category is because we are categorical. Our defect and our impairment is we have the brilliant, the ingenious capacity for looking out over people and filtering out all the females. It's a gift. I don't know how we manage that, but we do—we do manage that. And the scriptures plainly tell a different story. And it's that different story that's our problem (not the personal identity of the woman involved; or her relation to the Lord; or her obvious reaction to Him); and Joseph altering the text to say, "don't hold me" as opposed to "don't touch me," which means that he removed "don't touch me" from the text. She was touching Him, and tells you something else potentially about their relationship; because if she was embracing and attempting to hold Him, and He was saying: "I've got another appointment to keep, I'll be back, but don't hold me;" it suggests something else about what was going on there. Why was she there at that point in the morning? Why was it still dark? And why did He elect that moment to come and rejoin her?

The notion that you are going to succeed in acquiring the glory that is likened to God, in a separate and single state, is nowhere found as a promise in scripture. It's not a reasonable expectation. It's a non-scriptural expectation. It is a foolish hope, because it does not reckon to the things God created. Understand, those verses that we read in Genesis—those verses were before the Fall. And the condition in which Adam and Eve found themselves at the time that those incidents took place, they were immortal—they had not yet fallen. The marriage and the union of the two of them was intended to last forever, because death had not yet entered into the world. And as God put it: *it was good*.

Marry a wife, sealed, Holy Spirit of Promise, pass by the angels, enter into exaltation, glory, fullness—all of these words are applicable only to the man and the woman together as one. It's only applicable to the exalted state of a marriage that is worthy of preservation into eternity.

READING FROM TALK 7: The role of the woman is to become wisdom, because creation will only move forward if guided by wise counsel and prudent adaptations. Only together do they become complete and, therefore, "one." Alone, they are sterile; but joined, they are infinite because they continue. Knowledge, alone, may provide the spark of creation, but it is potentially dangerous when merely energetic. Creation must be wisely assisted to avoid peril. Wisdom, alone, is not an agent of action. Knowledge can initiate action, but wisdom is necessary to guide and counsel. The physical is a mirror of the spiritual. The seed of man provides the spark of life, but it is the womb of women in which life is developed to become viable. Likewise, the role of the woman in nurturing new life here, is akin to the role of wisdom in eternity. Together, these become whole—capable of both producing and then guiding creation. The woman sacrifices her blood to bring new life here. This physical world reflects the spiritual. This is the best I can think of to differentiate their eternal roles. In scripture, wisdom is feminine. In Hebrew, it is called "chokmah" (phonetically khok- maw'), which is a feminine noun. In Greek it is "sophia" which is, likewise, a feminine noun.

Without stating something inappropriate, Christ could not have done what He did, if He had not had a woman to fulfill a role in relation to Him. She anointed Him preliminary to His death, burial, and resurrection. She was the first one to greet Him when resurrected. It was not possible, under the process required for salvation of a God, for Him to accomplish all that was needed without the presence of the woman. There is no Father without a Mother. There is no God without a Divine Consort at His side. She has a distinct role, to accomplish some needful things, in connection with finishing the path to godhood.

DENVER: The account continues and describes the creation of the woman. Here, the parable distinguishes between the process of creating the man, Adam; and creating his spouse, the woman, Eve. *And I, the Lord God, said unto mine Only Begotten, that it was not good that the man should be alone, Wherefore, I will make an helpmeet for him* (Gen. 2:11 RE).

God the Father said to the Only Begotten that He (God the Father), will be the one to make Adam's "helpmeet." It was not good for Adam to be alone because he was not complete without a suitable companion to help him progress and develop. The creation parable continues:

And I, the Lord God, caused a deep sleep to fall upon Adam, and he slept, and I took one of his ribs, closed up the flesh in the stead thereof, and the rib, which I, the Lord God had taken from man, I made a woman, and brought her unto the man. And Adam said, This I know now is bone of my bones, and flesh of my flesh. She shall be called woman, because she was taken out of man. (Gen. 2:12 RE)

The parable of the creation of the woman, therefore, differs from the creation of the man. She was not formed from the dust of the ground. She was formed from a rib—from an already existing part of the man. She was born from something equal to him and able to stand beside him in all things.

But the parable about the woman, Eve, means a great deal more. She was at Adam's side before the creation of this world. They were united as "one" in a prior estate when they progressed to become living "souls" with both bodies and spirits. They were sealed, before this world, by the Holy Spirit of Promise, and proved to be true and faithful. They once sat upon a throne in God the Father's Kingdom. In that state, they were equal and eternally joined together. She sat beside him and was a necessary part of his enthronement. Her introduction into this world, to join her companion, was needed to complete Adam. It was not good for him to be alone. They were "one" and therefore, Adam, without Eve, was not complete—or in the words of the parable: "not good to be alone."

Like the man, Adam, the woman, Eve, was the spirit offspring of the Heavenly Father and the Heavenly Mother. But unlike the man Adam, who was the physical offspring of Christ, the woman Eve needed to be the physical offspring of God the Father and God the Mother. Eve was Adam's sister in spirit. She was also his biological aunt. She had to be the direct descendant of the Heavenly Mother in order to endow her with her Mother's creative abilities. That power belongs to the Mother. The fertility of Eve and, thereafter, of all the daughters of Eve, came because of the power given from direct descent from the Heavenly Mother.

Women descend from mother Eve, who was born the biological daughter of Heavenly Mother. Women descend from Heavenly Mother to endow them with Her creative power of fertility to bear the souls of men. Eve was not beneath Adam, nor subject to his rule when first created. Eve was put beside him to complete him and to be his helpmeet.

There was another condition required to enable Christ to lawfully redeem the daughters of Eve as well as the sons of Adam. The parable of the creation includes this step to put Eve under Adam's responsibility. The account explains that Eve (and by extension her daughters) was put under Adam's rule. Adam was handed responsibility and accountability for Eve. These are the words in the parable: *Thy desire shall be to thy husband, and he shall rule over thee* (Gen. 2:15 RE).

Adam was made accountable to "rule" in the fallen world. All the mistakes, mismanagements, failings, wars, and difficulties of mortality are the responsibility of the appointed "ruler." Adam would not have been accountable for Eve unless she was made subject to his "rule." Once under Adam's rule, the redemption of Adam also became the redemption of Eve. Therefore, Adam and the sons of Adam, and Eve and the daughters of Eve, were all rescued through Christ's atonement for mankind.

Adam and Eve declared and cried repentance together: they labored side-by-side: they received the garment at the same moment: they were instructed on sacrifice at the same time: they were taught and received the Holy Ghost at the same moment: they experienced the baptism of fire; and Adam prophesied at the same moment that Eve (overcome by the Spirit, and the Spirit of Wisdom) was able to interpret and define what was going on; and how all of this was suitable and appropriate. They two were one.

You hear those who say, "The Church has all the keys but we do not yet have the keys of the resurrection." That's because even when you are resurrected, you will not have the keys of resurrection until you, like Christ, have gone from exaltation to exaltation; until you likewise attain to the power to resurrect all that depends upon you. John 5:19, *The Son can do nothing of himself, but what he seeth the Father do: for what things soever [the Father] doeth, these also doeth the Son likewise.* And the Father went before, and the Son follows after. And if you think that you can, at some point, like Him, attain to the status of godhood, then you're going to have to do precisely what it is that the Gods do. Therefore, to understand Christ is to understand the challenging destiny about which Joseph Smith is speaking in this last Conference talk given in 1844. "Until you attain to the resurrection of the dead and are able to dwell in everlasting burnings, and to sit in glory, as do those who sit enthroned in everlasting power." (*History of the Church*, 6:306; from a discourse given by Joseph Smith on Apr. 7, 1844, in Nauvoo, Illinois)

The best way to explain it without saying something inappropriate would be this: Christ could not, COULD NOT, have done what he did if he had not had a woman who fulfilled a role in relation to him. She anointed Him preliminary to His death and His burial. She was the first one to encounter

Him in the resurrection. You do not get Him through what he needed to go through without the presence of the woman taking care of some needful things in connection with that.

READING FROM TALK 7: God's patience for us is infinite. It will require going "from exaltation to exaltation" before we ascent to the place of Christ, "the prototype of the saved man." But we have all eternity to work out our salvation.

Those who think it is enough to merely "get into heaven" are really talking about "the deaths" and not what God offers His children. God offers eternal lives. Those who will endure to the end, worlds without end, will receive eternal life and obtain the resurrection.

We must be exactly and precisely like Christ to receive all power in heaven and earth, including the power of the resurrection. It was only after His resurrection Christ claimed this power.

DENVER: I want to mention that beyond there being a fellowship of man or males, and a brotherhood, there is also a fellowship that is extended, as well, to women. If you find a woman in scripture who has had the ministry of angels, you have a sister who has joined in that association. I won't take time to do so, but if you look in Judges chapter 13, verses 2 to 5, you have Samson's mother being ministered to by an angel—promising the coming of the one would be a judge in Israel. You have in Genesis chapter 18, verses 9 to 15, Abraham's wife with angelic ministrants. And the most obvious case being Mary, in the book of Luke chapter 1, verses 26 to 31, in which Mary is ministered to by Gabriel, one of the Elohim, who came to announce that she would conceive and bear a child, though she knew no man.

Take note that there are on a number of occasions, women, who conceive and bear children, but the births are miraculous. In the case of Mary, the child that was born was conceived in a miraculous way, as was Samson, as was John. Whether it's infertility and barrenness, whether it's being past the age of menopause, or whether it's not having had intercourse; there are these beings who come into the world as a consequence of something other than the normal manner of conception. And yet, everything else unfolds biologically the same as a normal birth. And the child that is born obviously inherits mortality and blood from the mother.

Who would you reasonably expect to be the woman chosen, before the world was organized, to become the mortal mother of the Lord? Who would you expect Heavenly Father would want to bear His child, if not His Spouse? Together, God the Father and Mary can be acknowledged as the Parents of Christ. The scriptures shift the focus of the "condescension" from Christ, to His Mother, and then back to Her Son—the seed of the woman.

Lectures on Faith describe Christ as "the prototype of the saved man." Lecture 7 focuses attention on Christ as the Savior and Redeemer. But the lecture extends the requirement met by Jesus Christ to also apply for every saved man. In other words, for any man to be saved, they must "attain to the resurrection," like Christ. Shifting attention for a moment from Jesus Christ, as our Redeemer and Savior, to His Mother; we could acknowledge Her as "the prototype of the saved woman." In other words, we can consider what *She* did, a Divine pattern to be followed by women.

If God the Father obeys the same commandments He imposes upon His children, then for Him to father a child with any woman, other than His wife, would violate His decrees about adultery and chastity. Marian theology is largely absent from Mormonism, other than to suggest that because the Father impregnated her, she is destined to be added to His eternal harem as an additional spouse. Traditional Mormon teachings have been crudely fixated on the mechanics of Mary's conception. There is almost no interest in whether she has any pre-earth role with the Father; or whether she was the Mother in Heaven—the Divine Spouse of the Father, who condescended to come to earth to bear Their Only Begotten in the flesh. If She were to be acknowledged in that role, it would require a complete re-envisioning of Her. It would raise the issues of why or how She, an immortal and exalted God, could return from that exalted state back to mortality to bring our Redeemer and Savior into this world. It would draw a contrast between the Father's involvement with this creation and the Mother's.

The Father can, and does, acknowledge others as His. But, unlike the Son who has repeatedly visited this earth, walked upon it, been handled by people, eaten here; the Father does not come into contact with this earth in its fallen state. The only time the Father had contact with this earth was before the Fall, in the Paradisiacal setting of Eden—which was a Temple at the time. Whenever there has been contact with the Father thereafter, He has been at a distance from this earth.

There is a formality with the Father that does not exist with the Son. For example, the Son has eaten with mortal man while He was immortal, both before His ministry in the flesh and after. As our Redeemer, He is directly responsible for us, and has contact with us to perform His redemptive service.

The Father, on the other hand, is different in status, responsibility, glory, and dominion. The Son can appear to mortal man without showing His glory or requiring any alteration of the mortal, who beholds Him. To behold the Father, to endure His presence, one must be transfigured. Mortal man cannot behold the Father's works while mortal, for if you comprehend them, you cannot afterward remain mortal in the flesh.

That's taken from pages 383-387 of Removing the Condemnation, and there are a lot of footnotes to that, which will be in the paper I put up. Like this description of the Son, the same description should apply to His Mother.

The Father is the source of glory, and likened to the sun. The Mother reflects and shares this glory, and is likened to the moon. She reflects God's glory, endures within it, and is empowered by it. She can participate with Him in all that is done, wielding that glory. "Knowledge" is the initiator or force, and "wisdom" is the regulator, guide, apportioner, and weaver of that power. If not tempered and guided by wisdom, knowledge can be destructive. Wisdom makes the prudent adaptations required for order. The Father and Mother are One. But the Mother bridges the gulf between the Throne of the Father and fallen man. She made it possible for the Son of God to enter this fallen world for the salvation of everything in it.

If Christ is the prototype of the saved man, is Mary the prototype of the saved woman? Yes.

How did she earn her place on the throne without having atoned?

Because she sacrificed and led the lamb to the slaughter. She had a lamb whose fleece was white as snow, and she led that lamb everywhere she wanted it to go. And she gave up her son, and attained to the resurrection, and laid claim upon her body; because she condescended to come here and to fulfill that work.

———

The foregoing excerpts are taken from:

- Denver's conference talk titled "The Doctrine of Christ," given in Boise, ID on September 11th, 2016
- His talk titled "Christ's Discourse on the Road to Emmaus," given in Fairview Utah on April 14, 2007

- Denver's *40 Years in Mormonism Series*, Talk #9 titled "Marriage and Family," given in St. George, UT on July 26th, 2014
- Denver's *40 Years in Mormonism Series*, Talk #7 titled "Christ, Prototype of the Saved Man," given in Ephraim, UT on June 28, 2014
- Denver's conference talk titled "Our Divine Parents," given in Gilbert, AZ on March 25th, 2018
- Denver's *40 Years in Mormonism Series*, Talk #5 titled "Priesthood," given in Orem, UT on November 2nd, 2013; and
- Denver's Q&A session at the Keeping the Covenant Conference in Boise, ID on September 22, 2019

88. Interview with Denver, Part 1

This is the first part of Shawn McCraney's interview of Denver Snuffer for the Gospel Tangents podcast, which was recorded on October 8th, 2019 in front of a live audience.

————

Shawn: Denver Snuffer.

Denver: Shawn.

Shawn: It's good to meet you. I've heard many things about you. I have not followed up to confirm any of it. I've heard about you for years. I'm glad you finally agreed to come on. I've tried to get you a couple times.

Denver: [Laughs]

Shawn: You're camera shy. You prefer the radio.

Denver: Or writing.

Shawn: Or writing, yeah. But let me explain, kind of, to you and our audience if you're not familiar with the approach we take. We do this with every guest. I don't do research at all. I've just *heard* things. I don't do inquiries. People have told me things over the years, but they're not really that significant. The purpose I want people to come on the show is to have *them* tell *us* everything they want to say, and then we'll do some— I'll do some, "Stop for a second; explain that a little bit," if you want. If you say, "I don't want to," you don't have to, and it won't be an inquisition of any sort, and you're free to— And it's so that people who watch the show (many of them who have come out of Mormonism) can say, "Is this a viable alternative for me?"

Denver: Mmmhmm.

Shawn: We've had atheists; we've had transhumanists; we've had every type on the earth. But years ago—a couple years ago—we were doing a show [background rattling] (yeah, that happens sometimes), and I said on the show, "I think the only true religious leaders in the state of Utah are John Dehlin, Denver Snuffer, and myself." And the reason I said that is, John Dehlin— He is leading the "I wanna be me: free; I wanna be what I am: gay, straight, no

God, any god, and I just don't even care." And John is kind of the Pied Piper of that group.

I am: Forget relig—organized material—religion altogether. I trust in the Lord Jesus Christ "with all your heart." Forget about priesthood; forget about sacrament, communion. And I base that off my eschatology.

Denver: Mmmhmmm.

Shawn: *You* are unique because you have been LDS.

Denver: Mmmhmmm.

Shawn: And you are continuing on what—the only thing I can say now, not *knowing*—is, it seems to be, a form of Mormonism. Is that proper?

Denver: It's fair.

Shawn: Fair?

Denver: I think— Yeah, I think I would say that.

Shawn: So what we try to do is—in the first part (which lasts a little less than an hour)—is we want to know all about you: Grandma and Grandpa; Mom and Dad; upbringing; education; what you were like as a kid; when you were baptized; how active were you?— siblings; thoughts. And that usually takes us, even with people who don't think they have much to say, up to the first hour. You probably will fill it easily.

Denver: Hmmm.

Shawn: After that, we'll come back, and we'll see if— I wanna go— I want you to kind of end up, if you can, Denver, with when you started to say, "Wait a second," and then, "I'm gonna to do something about my view of Mormonism myself." And we'll do Part 2 about what you've done, where you're at, what's happening. And then in Part 3, I wanna do some word association. And there's 40 words, and I'll say it, and then you respond, and we'll use that as a platform to talk back and forth. And in that one, we'll be a little bit—not combative. I could sit here and fight with you on everything you say.

Denver: Sure.

Shawn: I'm not gonna do that. I don't care. I respect your rights to believe whatever you want, teach whatever you want. I really do because I believe you're responsible for what you believe and teach, and your ways may be better than mine as far as I'm concerned. So it's not to attack. But in Part 3, I might say, "Well what about this or what about that?" And you can explain, and we'll go from there. Does that sound all right with you?

Denver: That sounds fine.

Shawn: Okay. So, Denver Snuffer: the man, the myth, the legend. Take it away—about you.

Denver: Well, you mentioned parents. I'm Junior. I was named after my father. My father was a twin. I'm grateful for the fact that he got the name Denver because his twin brother was named Dempsey [audience laughter]. That may have been really problematic, but Denver is okay as a name.

My father is a World War II veteran. He joined the military after Pearl Harbor. As he explained it to me, everyone was pissed off when Pearl Harbor happened, and everyone wanted to go fight the Japanese, himself included. So, he joined to go fight the Japanese, and he wound up going to fight Hitler. And at the beginning of the war, his comment was he had no beef with Hitler. The war was fought without any appreciation for what Hitler was really up to inside the camps.

But he landed on Omaha Beach on June 6, 1944. He got through as a combat engineer. He was one of the first people on the beach, and his assignment was to blow up the tank traps. But as it turned out, first of all, the water was so rough that morning that none of the tanks made it to shore; and second of all, the tank traps were the only things that were keeping the bullets from killing all of them. So, when the mess unfolded, he wound up as a combat engineer, not blowing up tank traps but blowing up some of the fencing that was preventing them from getting up to combat with the pillboxes.

And he was a very modest man about all that he had been through during World War II. He was also in the Battle of the Bulge but he didn't like to talk about it, so we had to pry it out of him with questions and very often the answers would deflect, but he might give you a sentence here, and he might give you a phrase there, and it was up to you to put it all together over time.

One of the things that shocked me, and I wish he had—well, maybe it was a good thing he didn't live long enough—but one of the things that shocked me was the details of the Omaha landing in *Saving Private Ryan* because some of the things that were depicted in that Omaha Beach scene, I had heard from my father, you know, while he was still living, but they were details that I'd never heard anyone else talk about.

Turns out Spielberg had interviewed whoever he could find that had survived to get the details. There really *was* a GI on that beach whose arm had been blown off who was holding his severed arm with his other arm, and he was walking around in shock. And people saw him. Spielberg picked it up; he put it in the show.

But to me, you know, they made World War II movies (John Wayne and *The Longest Day*). They made a lot of movies in which that generation was depicted in a heroic way.

And I always respected my dad, even when we butted heads. He seemed to me to be a historic figure, larger than life—didn't mean we agreed with one another.

I recall after I had finished law school, I was kind of full of myself. I graduated from Brigham Young University's law school, J. Reuben Clark Law School. And after I graduated, I went back to my hometown to visit my parents and let them bask in the glory of their law- school-graduated son. I was sort of full of myself, as law school tends to make one. And while I was there visiting, my dad took me down to—don't remember which bar it was (I don't think it was the Rendezvous), but it was one of the bars in Mountain Home, Idaho—to visit with his friends. He wanted to show me off. And while we're there at the bar, you know, he introduced me, proud as he was, law school graduate, and I viewed them as my intellectual inferiors. You know, none of them had the equivalent of a doctor's degree.

We'd sat around and we talked, and over the course of the conversation, what dawned on me was I was talking to people who had lived through more history and had a greater grasp on life and everything that's going on here than I could hope to have because the stress of difficulty. I mean, these people had been through the depression. They'd been through World War II. They'd been through the Korean conflict. They'd seen a popular president assassinated. They'd been through a lot.

And here I was, full of myself because I had a piece of paper. And it was one of those sobering moments that I really thank my dad for because there are people whose lives live in the trenches of this world who rise to greater levels of kindness, understanding, charity towards others, humility, than some of us who enjoy simply the benefit of the environment that they made possible by the sacrifices that they made. It sobered me. It was another one of those moments with my father that I look back on and think, you know, those few moments in a bar in downtown Mountain Home, Idaho probably were the corrective experience necessary to take a law school graduate, full of himself, and put his feet back on the ground.

My father believed in God and was a Mason and tolerated my mother's Baptist faith—even let the Baptist minister come over and eat dinner at our house, as she was wont to invite him over to do. And he was devout in his own way, but he was not churchy. My mom, on the other hand, was churchy. She taught Vacation Bible School. I was enlisted in Vacation Bible School. I got all the indoctrination that one gets as a Baptist.

We were in Idaho. Idaho has an infestation of Mormonism and, therefore, throughout my youth, I was inoculated against the cult of Mormonism. And I knew that if Jesus and Santa Claus are the good guys in the universe, the devil and Joseph Smith are the bad guys, and so I had very little respect for the idea of Mormonism.

I had one sibling, my sister. She embraced the Baptist religion. They always put that call out at the end of the service, you know, while everyone's singing *Just As I Am*. They invite you to come forward and be saved and be baptized, and I felt the tug a time or two, but I always managed successfully to resist the impulse, and I grew up without ever having joined a church. The only church I ever joined was the LDS Church. And we can talk about the process that got me there, but I was an incredibly content kid.

I had a Schwinn Stingray. I could put that thing on its back wheel, and I could ride it like a unicycle in a wheelie all through town. We were a safe community, and the kids were allowed to do what the kids wanted to do, and I spent my childhood roaming free. There were practically no violent crimes that percolated to the attention of kids in my hometown.

There was a guy, though. We were sitting in Carl Miller Park, and someone came riding their bike through the park yelling, "Tom Lynn just killed a Mexican at the Rendezvous!" Well, Rick Beck (who was my next-door neighbor and my buddy growing up)— Rick Beck's father owned the

Rendezvous. The Rendezvous was a bar. Carl Miller Park is not that far from the Rendezvous bar, and someone just got killed by Tom Lynn. We knew who Tom Lynn was, too. So we hopped on our bikes, and we rode down to the Rendezvous to see what the crap's going on.

There's a crowd. There's wailing. But we're kids, you know. We don't know any better. We elbow our way to the front, and sure enough, Tom Lynn blew the head off a fellow at the Rendezvous.

My father was chosen for jury duty on the trial of Tom Lynn, and Tom Lynn was convicted, and he went off to the penitentiary. And he finally came home, and he became one of the poker players in the weekly poker game that my dad participated in. Well, so a juror who had sent the guy off to the penitentiary and the guy who had been convicted played poker every week. And one evening at the poker table, Tom Lynn leaned over and put his head on the table, and they thought he was tired, so they dealt him out. He died playing poker with my dad at the poker table.

That was the kind of thing that, oddly enough, you remember from your youth and from the things that went on. But I never felt endangered by that. We rode our bikes off in the morning. We floated canals on tubes. We had our fistfights. We had our pranks. We started fires. We escaped liability for what we'd done in Idaho at that point.

They had a law. Because there were so many kids that were helping farmers, you could get a driver's license at age 14. So at 14 years old (it was daylight only, so you'd only drive during the day), you could get a driver's license, and kids started driving at age 14. And there was no difference between a driver's license and a motorcycle license. So, if you had a driver's license, you could ride a motorcycle, and we did. But I mean, you're looking back on it, you think, no one wore helmets; we rode in shorts; we did stuff that should have killed us, and we survived; but it was, in its own way, idyllic. It was a lot of fun.

Shawn: Fantastic.

Denver: So anyway, there's that.

Shawn: Has anyone written *The Ballad of Old Tom Lynn*?—because that is a story!

Denver: No, that's a country western song.

Shawn: Absolutely! You've heard of old Tom Jones. Well, let's get old Tom Lynn. That is fascinating.

You're quite a storyteller. You're good at that.

Denver: Well, he was convicted. He got beat up by the guy he killed. He left the bar, went home and got the shotgun, came back, called the guy out. When the guy came out, he blew his head off. It was the fact that he left the bar and went home instead of responding in the moment that got him ultimately convicted for...

Shawn: Wow!

Denver: ...for what he'd done wrong.

Shawn: Well, Mountain Home.

Denver: Yes.

Shawn: And you were there through high school?

Denver: I was. Then I went in the military.

Shawn: What branch?

Denver: Air Force. They were peaceable, you know, compared to the Marines. They had a (Gibb Wheeler's older brother, and I want to say it was Tom Wheeler, but it was Gibb's older brother)— He got drafted, and he went to Nam. And he wound up Marine and in the trenches, and very often they'd encounter those tunnels; and he was a tunnel rat. He went in. He came back weirded up. He had some—well, today we'd call it PTSD. But he'd also— He had a lot of battle injuries and what have you, and he was sort of the walking example of why one in Mountain Home does not want to be a Marine and go to Vietnam. And so, he helped inspire a lot of enlistments in the Air Force.

Shawn: I see.

Denver: Myself being one of them.

Shawn: And where were you stationed?

Denver: New Hampshire.

Shawn: Was that eye-opening to an Idaho boy?

Denver: I rather liked New Hampshire. I was surprised, though, that there was a Mormon out there. That's part of the later story, but I spent two and a half years in New Hampshire and then a year and a half in Texas. And then I left and ultimately got admitted to law school shortly thereafter—never returned to Idaho although that *was* the plan. I got a job offer out of law school that kept me in Utah. I'd never planned to remain in Utah. But yeah, the Air Force and in New Hampshire was an interesting time and an interesting experience.

Shawn: Was that where you were introduced—because you went to law school at BYU—so, you either converted at BYU or...

Denver: No, it was earlier. It was actually while I was on active duty.

Shawn: Oh, tell us about it.

Denver: I was attending night classes at the University of New Hampshire, and a professor who was on loan from Brandeis University, Cal Colby (in the middle of a—it was a business management class), was talking about corporate ethics and corruption and just went off on the Mormon Church which, to the ears of someone that had grown up in Mountain Home, Idaho, and was now safely thousands of miles away from the Mormon infestation, thought the whole idea of bringing up Mormonism in a class seemed so superfluous. It was silly. I mean, okay, Cal—Professor Colby—we'll stipulate the Mormon Church is corrupt. If it exists, it's gotta be corrupt. It was founded by, you know, the devil's best friend. So, I took no exception to the professor's position.

But there was a fellow in the class who raised his hand and took on the professor and defended the Mormon Church, and I thought that was, first of all, bizarre. I mean, what the hell? Are you kidding me? And he got the better of him. He did a fabulous job of defending the faith against the charge of corruption specifically being addressed in the management class.

I made the mistake afterwards— I didn't know the fellow from Adam at that point, but he became a good friend. I made the mistake afterwards of saying that I thought he'd done a great job and, you know, good for him because he'd had the courage to speak up. Undergraduates are very vulnerable to the predilections of your professors, so, to defend and to be contrary, that's fairly remarkable.

The fellow's name is Steve Claproth, and he and I became good friends, but he mistook that for interest, and then they sic these missionaries who pamphleteer and filmstrip you—you probably did that.

Shawn: I did.

Denver: Did you use the filmstrips and the felt board?

Shawn: Oh yeah.

Denver: Yeah, they did all that. And they mistook politeness for interest. I was not interested. If being raised by a Baptist mother and not heeding the call to come forward and be saved had been successfully resisted over the course of 18 years, pamphleteering and filmstripping was not at all likely to excite my interest in Mormonism.

But these guys were so *nice* and so *clean-cut*, unlike you now. I mean, look at you!

Shawn: [Laughing] Look at *you*!

Denver: You're a refugee from the Mormon mission. I never went on a mission.

Shawn: I know.

Denver: Okay, but you did. Anyway, you know how [audience laughter]— You know how that was.

Shawn: I do.

Denver: They were clean-cut. They wore white shirts and ties and suits. And their sincerity just— It *clung* to you; it was so earnest. I hated to break their hearts and tell 'em, "Dude, I think your faith is full of crap!" So, I refrained from that. It was at least interesting.

But I was a long, long, *looonnggg* investigator. It's because of the scarcity of interest in Mormonism in New England that the missionaries persisted for as long as they did. It was nice.

They asked me to read some Book of Mormon stuff. I did as they asked, being polite. They wanted to know the next time we got together, "What did you think? What did you think of what you'd read?" I don't think they were calling me "Brother" yet then. And my response, literally, and I meant it (it seems funny now, but I meant it at the time)— I said, "It's gotta be scripture. It's every bit as boring as the Bible." It had all that, you know, King Jamesian antiquity about it, and it did not grip me.

But by the same token, the things that had gripped me are the kinds of things that I see in here. It's the stories that are told about Daniel in the lion's den, and you've got a picture of David holding the head of Goliath, and you've got Christ with the storm. It's the Bible stories that you learn in your youth that, you know, tug at your heart. Reading the actual scriptural canon, at least at *that* point in my life, was not connecting in the same way that the stories or the interpretation based upon what the scriptures contain meant to me.

So, reading the Book of Mormon was rather the same kind of experience. It's arm's length and not appealing.

Shawn: I'm going to jump in real quick. How about the Gadianton robbers story, or the 2,000 stripling warriors story, or Alma the Younger story? Did they affect you the way those stories on the wall affected you?

Denver: They would eventually, but they didn't at the time because the problem is it's clothed in the scriptural, canonical, off-putting verbiage that, at that point, I did not relate to. I do relate to that kind of language today, but at that point, I had not acquired yet the tongue for that other language, and it is another language.

But Steve Claproth invited me to a— I don't know if it's called a young men's camp-out or called an Aaronic Priesthood camp-out. I don't know what they were calling it at the time.

But as it turns out, Joseph Smith was born in Sharon, Vermont, which is about as far away from where we are now to Nephi as where we were in New Hampshire was, away from Joseph's birthplace.

So, he invited me to camp out, and hey, camping's fun. So, I went up to the Joseph Smith [Birthplace] Memorial [in Sharon, Vermont]. They've got an obelisk there, 38½ feet tall, a foot for every year of the life of Joseph. They pointed out the obelisk and its height and the reason for its height. And I was surprised because I hadn't realized that Joseph Smith had lived so short a lifetime.

There was a— Back at that time, the stake encompassed states, so the stake president was the stake president over Maine, Vermont, New Hampshire, parts of Massachusetts—*big* stake. I think the fellow was from Boston. His predecessor stake president had been L. Tom Perry. (There's a story about him, too, eventually, if we get there.)

Anyway, the stake president got up and gave a talk, and it was about David and Goliath, one of those old favorite stories from back when. And he filled in details, and he talked about things that made the story come alive even better than had Vacation Bible School. And it surprised me to have Mormons talking about that kind of content in a getaway with the—you know—the young skulls full of mush, being indoctrinated into the vagaries of the cult that I viewed them as. And the talk was actually quite good and touching and held a good moral story.

We spent the night. The next morning the visitors' center was open. As you are looking at the obelisk, it's the visitors' center on the right, not the one on the left. On that one they had a counter back in those days. (They renovate everything, so it's probably now a mega-mall of some kind, probably selling trinkets that are profitable.) But back in those days, there was a counter.

There was a couple of old people behind the counter, what I would now say is a *missionary couple*, but they were manning the desk, and they had literature and pamphlets and crap that I'd been given by missionaries as they were filmstripping and all the rest of that. And there was a red volume called the Doctrine and Covenants and Pearl of Great Price, and I hadn't seen that thing, and I asked them what that was. They started to tell me, and then Steve, who was— I was his golden contact. Steve elbowed his way in between, and he proceeded to talk it all up, and he dog-eared the Joseph Smith History (which I had previously gotten in a pamphlet), and he dog-eared Doctrine and Covenants section 76.

I wanted the elderly couple behind the counter to tell me how much it cost to buy one of these things, and they said it was free, and so I got out with my book before they changed their mind and wanted to charge me because I expected all religions want your money.

Anyway, it was actually after the camp-out, after we got back, and after I had taken the time to look at the book that I went to that dog-eared section 76 of the D&C, and I was struck by that. It was not the missionaries; it was not the camp-out; it was not the clean-cutness of them all. It was the *incongruence* between everything I thought I knew about Joseph Smith being raised and the content of D&C section 76 that seemed to resonate with good things, virtuous things, answering questions about the afterlife. It just seemed incongruent, and it struck me at that moment.

I'd been an investigator, probably half a year or more. I'd been through all kinds of missionary companions that had come and gone. But the actual investigation of Mormonism in a sincere way commenced then. Everything else had been wasted time. And it was a matter of overcoming a lot of presumptions and prejudice that I'd been raised with that required, you know, sober reflection and taking time, and careful, solemn thoughts which, in a 19–year-old now, was something new for me.

I have to admit that one of the barriers for me was the fact that, however unchurched my father may have been, he seemed to be aligned with my mother in the opinion about Mormonism, and so I didn't want to disappoint him or enrage my mom or piss off my sister. And growing up, my friends were universally aligned in their viewpoint about Mormonism. And everyone looked down on the religion, although there were a handful of Mormon kids that were accepted at school. The religion itself was not well-regarded.

One of the things that Mormons tend to do is to be politically active, and Idaho is no exception. So, the legislature in Idaho, which had a very large LDS presence and, therefore, very large LDS influence, on occasion boiled up into political conflict with Mormonism being one of the issues that divided people into camps. And so, you know, the concern crossed my mind as I was investigating Mormonism that one of the things that would be lost in the transition would be all the friends I valued, family members, my past history.

I mean, Dude, I was *cool*. I was sophomore class vice-president; junior class president; I was a drummer in a rock band. I was *cool*. If you had a party in Mountain Home, you needed to invite me, or it wasn't a *thing*. I mean, and now, white-shirt-clad nerds are to become my compadres, and I'm gonna leave the cabal that I grew up with, and I'm gonna sit among the nerdly? This is the destiny that the religion brings you to? You know, I don't want to be sacrilegious, but you know, *"if it be possible, take this cup from me"*— It's not a lamentation I couldn't identify with. This seemed like a horrible, *horrible* exchange to be made.

In the context of everything in life that you like, enjoy, you find to be desirable, fun, Mormonism was a form of death to everything that had gone before. It required— The enormity of the sacrifice in the mind of a 19–year-old was practically incalculable. It was— The barrier to entry for me was like trying to leap across the Grand Canyon. *I just did not see myself doing that.*

In fact, one of the things that I concluded was that even if I were to become a Mormon, there was no way I could become a very good one. I hated the idea of being a bad one, but I didn't think I could become like them. They were better than me. They were living cleaner lives, doing cleaner things, and enjoying hokey stuff. And, you know, they hadn't been to the places I'd been; they hadn't seen the things I'd seen; they hadn't done the stuff I'd done.

And, you know, a lot of my Air Force buddies— Coming out of boot camp, it was rare. In the Army they try to keep units together. In the Air Force they just scatter you to the four winds. I got assigned in a squadron in a barracks in which another guy from my flight (that's what they called it in boot camp) was also assigned at the same time, so they made us roommates.

Well, my roommate, Mike, was a— He was a black fellow from Watts. I mean, he'd lived through the riots in Watts. One of the reasons he was in the Air Force was not because he was afraid of the draft. He was in the Air Force because he wanted to get off the streets, and his mama wanted him somewhere safe. And so, he's a refugee from Watts, and I'm from Mountain Home, Idaho, but the two of us really got along well in spite of what you would view as an insurmountable cultural gap between where we reckoned from. Hell, he was just a guy like me, and we had a lot of fun doing the same things. And some of the same things that we did are the kinds of things that they denounce in General Conference.

For some reason (I guess it was because of the streets of Watts), one of the things that Mike liked was cheap wine. You know, you can go down and get a bottle of—there was Ripple, and—

Shawn: Ripple [laughs]!

Denver: And Annie Green Springs and all that crap.

Shawn: Strawberry Hill.

Denver: Yes, Strawberry Hill. They made all that crap for kids, really, and, you know.

So, me and Mike, Jimmy Givens— Jimmy was a black kid, also, from Detroit, kind of a refugee himself. My friends, my buddies in the context, primarily were black fellows. And there was a *serious, serious* racial tension nationally and conflict—racial tension and conflict. And Martin Luther King got murdered. There was just a— There was a problem, and the Air Force was trying to address that at the time by having race relations classes. The race relation class that was being taught, in my view, only made things worse. I mean, it sort of pointed out what in everyday life could be just ignored. It pointed it out, and I thought they were doing a terrible job.

Well, the squadron had a command in the barracks, and the command in the barracks had a young—oh, he was a lieutenant of either first or second, but who was in charge of that race-relations thing—and he called me down. I was required to go down and report in to the fellow in charge of the squadron, and I thought, *What have they found? I mean, what contraband had they managed to locate up in the room during inspection? How much trouble was I in?* They called me in, shut the door, sat me down. He was very personable. He came around the desk. He sat like we were buddies. He was chatting me up. And the reason he wanted to talk to me was to find out how come I got along with the black guys in the squadron the way I did. I mean, I didn't even think about it. I mean, Summers and me played chess, and we hung out. There was no "getting along." I am; they are; it's a— I didn't know what to tell them.

I mean, here they are, dealing with this crisis. Here they are, trying to help with the crisis. Their attempts at help are only making it worse, and this guy wants me? I'm a *teenager* from Mountain Home, Idaho, hanging out with guys from Mississippi and Watts and Detroit and New York, and we're not *in* any of those places. I can't take them down to the canal and inflate a tube and hop on the tube and go down. And we're not in Mississippi. We can't go catchin,' you know, catfish. And we're not in New York, so we can't, you know, run through the projects. And we're not in Watts, and we can't burn something. We're in New Hampshire, and all we're doing in New Hampshire is hanging out, doing what you do in New Hampshire when you're bored, and you're getting paid by the military, and there's time on your hands.

Shawn: And this was all prior to being—

Denver: Yeah, yeah, yeah. I mean, Jimmy Givens would subsequently become a black Muslim, and I would subsequently become a Mormon.

We used to go drink beer at the bowling alley and get pizza. The pizza was gosh-awful. It was like cardboard with cheese on it—and bad cheese at that—and drink Budweiser. So, we'd been reassigned to different places. We ran into each other after I had joined, and I said, "Well, let's go to the bowling alley," because that's what we used to do.

We went over to the bowling alley, and I was trying to warm up to the fact that I didn't drink. And as I'm about to tell him that I didn't drink beer anymore, he tells me he doesn't drink beer anymore. And I asked him what that was all about, and he said he'd become Muslim, and they don't drink. I said, "You're kidding!" I said, "I've become Mormon, and Mormons don't drink." And he said, "Well, in my religion, you're a blue-eyed devil" because I have blue eyes. And I said, "In my religion you can't hold the priesthood!" And we had a laugh about our respective religions, had a pizza, and drank a Pepsi because they only had Pepsi on base for some reason, but you know— sugar rush. Everyone liked Pepsi back then.

So, are we out of time? Is that...?

Shawn: Well, we're getting close.

Denver: Okay.

Shawn: But— And because we're getting close, I'm gonna jump in and move us forward. So, then what was it that got you, having hung out with some black guys and their friends, and you joined the church then, later, that *banned* the blacks from having the priesthood?

Denver: Yeah, that was weird. That was one of those— Again, it's just one of those—

Shawn: Was there any conflict there?

Denver: Oh, sure. There's conflict in all of this. I did not want *that* to be *my* destiny. In fact, joining Mormonism to me was a form of death. It was literally— The only thing that I consoled myself with was that I wouldn't be a very good one, and it probably wouldn't last, but I felt like I needed to join.

I happened to be alone, which was odd in a military barracks. I was alone. It was quiet, which, again, is odd in a military barracks, and I decided to pray about this whole thing. I'd been asked to do it. I'd been cajoled and harangued and pamphleteered and taught to do it, but I hadn't really taken the opportunity to do it. The story they tell about Joseph Smith praying vocally for the first time struck me as something—well, I hadn't done that yet. And so, alone in the barracks on a quiet weekend evening, I got down and prayed and asked God (over an army blanket, kneeling in the barracks) about the whole of it and whether or not there was anything to this; and if so, whether I could be excused, or I needed to, you know, to rally to the call—what ought I do; and finished praying—and nothing. There was no conduit from heaven that opened up, and there was no, you know, earthquake.

I sat on the bed and just reflected on it all, thought about what had gone on. And I thought about the reasons why Mormonism could not be true from what I knew. I came up with reasons why it could not be true, and as I thought about each reason, in turn, I got an answer to—I *thought* of an answer—to the dilemma, to the problem.

There cannot be any more scripture because whosoever adds to the book, God will add to his condemnation. Whoever takes away from the book, God will take away his part in the Book of Life, so there can't be more scripture which is what Mormonism is predicated upon—except that book happened to have been written chronologically before much of the rest of the New Testament canon. So, that's really not a barrier.

Beware of prophets, you know, false prophets. They come to you in sheep's clothing, but inwardly they're ravening wolves. So, can't I dismiss him as a false prophet? And the solution is, well, there's no statement that there will never be another prophet. In fact, there are prophets referred to in the Book of Acts.

Shawn: Okay.

Denver: There are unnamed prophetesses in the Book of Acts, and, therefore, the end of the ministry of Christ is not the end of the presence of prophets or the gift of prophecy. In fact, the gift of prophecy is named in one of Paul's letters to the Corinthians, so, you know, you can't dismiss it on that basis.

Shawn: But because of time, Denver, the— Doctrinally, I'm getting that in terms of prophets and added scripture and whatever. But did you have any queries and qualms about polygamy? Certainly growing up, if Mormonism was the— If Joseph Smith was the brother of the devil, or whatever that saying was...

Denver: Yeah, yeah.

Shawn: ...certainly you'd heard all the dirt. So the polygamy, the blacks and the priesthood, the misogyny that historically has been there, all of that.

Denver: All that stuff, yeah, all that.

Shawn: You had answers for that as well?

Denver: I didn't ask necessarily those specific questions. I asked questions on a big picture about the foundation of the possibility of a new revelation itself. And literally, I spent a couple of hours doing that—question and then thought of an answer, question and thought of an answer. After a couple of hours of that alone, meditatively, in my room, the last query that I came up with was: *Well, how do I even know there is a God? And that's the ultimate question, and how do I know that?* And the thought came in response to that, *Who do you think you've been talking to for the last two hours?* And that brought me up cold because my conclusion was: If that is how God communicates, and if God communicated with me, then I had the responsibility to respond to that communication because I would like it to continue. I would like it not to end.

But the price that would be required to have that continue seemed to be far greater than was reasonable or rational. It seemed like I was literally giving up my world in order to respond to that. But my conclusion was: If that's an answer from God, and He's made Himself known now to me in the context of this inquiry, then I need to respond favorably to that answer and go ahead and become baptized. And so, feeling like I literally was giving everything I had on the altar, I went ahead and got baptized in the Atlantic Ocean on October the 10th, 1973. Oh, excuse me, I said October—September the 10th of 1973, September 10th. We're in October now. And that is also a significant date, and we can talk about that eventually.

Shawn: And with that final thought from Denver, we're going to pick it up in Part 2 next week where we're going to hear about what his—briefly, what his membership and his activity and marriage and kids (I don't know if he has them; I know he has a wife)— And then we're going to see when that changed and what started happening. And so, join us then. Remember, put your comments down below. Let us know what you think, questions you might have. We'll pick them up on the phone and talk about those when you look and watch tomorrow.

––––––––––

The forgoing interview is rebroadcast here with permission from Shawn McCraney, host of the *Heart of the Matter* YouTube channel.

89. Interview with Denver, Part 2

This is the second part of Shawn McCraney's interview of Denver Snuffer for the Gospel Tangents podcast, which was recorded on October 8th, 2019 in front of a live audience.

———

Shawn: Denver Snuffer. Last week we heard about your life in story form. It was a great prose, it was narrative; it flowed from one interesting tale to another and brought us to the point where he was baptized in September of… '72?

Denver: '73.

Shawn: '73. East Coast, Atlantic Ocean.

Denver: Atlantic Ocean.

Shawn: What I want to do on this part, if we can, is I'm going to try to— When you interview someone you don't know, you learn how to approach that person in the second part and third part, and so I'm going to kind of move us along at a pace where we can get to more information because we've got a lot to cover.

Denver: We do!

Shawn: We do. All right, so you were baptized. Tell us about how long it was until you met your wife, and what you did between that time.

Denver: Well, one of the differences after baptism was— Where before, reading scripture had very little appeal or connection to me, after baptism the scriptures came alive to me. It seemed to me that what the New Testament was talking about as history…

Shawn: I want to ask you again about your wife, though.

Denver: …was living.

Shawn: You're not answering—you know you're not answering.

Denver: No, no…

Shawn: We need to keep this thing so people will watch it.

Denver: These two go together.

Shawn: I know, but...

Denver: My zeal...

Shawn: Yeah...

Denver: My zeal turned me into a golden-contact-generation facilitator for the missionaries. Where the entire New England States mission had been relatively dead, I had the missionaries teaching *everyone*. I had dozens of people who they were teaching. *And* they were baptizing. And one of the people that I got interested in the church, interested enough to ultimately be baptized, was a gal that I wound up later marrying.

Shawn: Yes!!

Denver: I baptized her.

Shawn: Excellent!!

Denver: Yeah.

Shawn: That is a beautiful story!

Denver: She's not my present wife.

Shawn: Oh, dang it!!

Denver: Yeah.

Shawn: Come on, man! Okay. No, it's okay.

Denver: So, yeah.

Shawn: So, you've been married twice?

Denver: Yes. She subsequently divorced me and left the church.

Shawn: Okay.

Denver: Yeah, left me.

Shawn: So she never had the truth?

Denver: Well…

Shawn: I'm just kidding.

Denver: Yeah, but I baptized her. I got orders transferring me to Texas, away from New Hampshire, and I knew that if I left— She's my, you know, my product, my conversion evidence. And about that time Spencer Kimball gave a talk that said any two people can be married if they'll live the gospel. So really, it doesn't matter who the hell you marry if you live the gospel. That was bad advice, but I took it in my zeal.

I got a fellow who was Jewish to join the church. I got a number of people, that subsequently I stayed in contact with, to join the church. The ward in Portsmouth, New Hampshire, visibly grew as a result of the zeal. I was obnoxious. I was just **on fire!**

Shawn: But we know that early converts to *any* group are always the ones they put in for recruitment because you're most on fire, and so that's normal.

Denver: It is.

Shawn: We get that, right? So, move us along. You got married, you got divorced—quote, within a 'short period of time?'

Denver: Yeah. I wound up in Texas. We had our first daughter in Texas. We had two daughters, two sons. And she ultimately— After law school, she divorced me and she left the church—and I had four kids. I married my current wife. She and I have had five more children.

Shawn: Wow!

Denver: But she raised nine, so…

Shawn: Wow!

Denver: So yeah, she's the mother of nine. She grew up in the LDS Church and lived in Sandy—grew up in the town we currently live in.

Shawn: You're kidding?

Denver: Yeah.

Shawn: Nine kids.

Denver: Yeah!

Shawn: So when you met—what's her first name?

Denver: Stephanie.

Shawn: Stephanie.

Denver: Yeah.

Shawn: When you met Stephanie, your oldest child was how old?

Denver: Oh, see *now* you're requiring me to remember things that only mothers…

Shawn: You're remembering the name of guys in bars who said hello to you!

Denver: But ages?!

Shawn: Okay.

Denver: Ages?!!!

Shawn: All right, around…

Denver: Really!

Shawn: Around— Were they still in high school?

Denver: Yeah. She was she was in junior high and she was the oldest. And then the youngest was Benjamin. He was in kindergarten.

Shawn: How'd you meet Stephanie?

Denver: She had worked at my law office. We were growing and we were hiring. And there was an office management class that was taught in the local

— It was a high school program, but they drew students from a variety of high schools and she was one of the hires from that program. Another hire out of that program is still working for me—Lisa. She came in and has been with me for like— I've been practicing law 38 years, and I think about 35 of those I've had Lisa with me. Anyway, Stephanie was a University of Utah student. She was a year away from graduating, and she'd been talking about going on an LDS mission when she graduated. One of the jokes was that she had had 1,500 first dates, but she didn't have a second date. She rather intimidated...

Shawn: Oh, wow!

Denver: ...boys.

Shawn: But not men.

Denver: But she didn't intimidate me. Anyway, I found myself divorced. She invited me to a Thanksgiving dinner with her family, took pity on me. You know, that was nice. She was the only person I had known for *years*. And dating after divorce is a— It's all phony. I mean whoever you're...

Shawn: Dating's all phony from *any* age.

Denver: Yeah, but they're going to put on something...

Shawn: But you can start at 13!!!

Denver: Yeah, well, there's that. But...

Shawn: It's the same game!!

Denver: She'd been at the office for three/three-and-a-half years at the time.

Shawn: Yeah.

Denver: And so I knew her. I knew her on a good day, I knew her on a bad day. And why not date someone you know instead of dating someone that's going to, you know, do their best to fool you.

Shawn: It sounds like you got a gem.

Denver: Yeah.

Shawn: Any woman who would take on four kids, raise them, and then another five…

Denver: Yes.

Shawn: Hats off!

Denver: Yeah, yeah.

Shawn: Great! Fantastic! I should be interviewing Stephanie too.

Denver: She would be a better candidate for a whole lot of reasons.

Shawn: So you raised your nine children. You're an appellate attorney. Is that…

Denver: I just finished arguing before the Tenth Circuit, but I do trial work as well.

Shawn: Okay.

Denver: Yeah.

Shawn: So, and you're raising them. Does she work with you while raising the kids? Are you active in the ward? What jobs are you holding?

Denver: Well, okay, there's that. You know I'm not Mormon *now*.

Shawn: Yeah, I know.

Denver: Yeah, okay.

Shawn: But you were when you married Stephanie.

Denver: I was.

Shawn: And she was too.

Denver: And we got married in the Salt Lake Temple.

Shawn: Salt Lake Temple.

Denver: Yes, yes!

Shawn: Did you have the four kids sealed to you?

Denver: They were sealed to me from the prior, you know…

Shawn: Right.

Denver: No reason to have them sealed to her that we could think of. I suppose there was a time when we could have done that. I can't get in a temple these days.

Shawn: Yeah, yeah. I bet.

Denver: Persona non grata.

Shawn: Yeah. So, you're raising the family. How was— Were you active, you and Stephanie? Are you going to the temple monthly, or quarterly, or like that?

Denver: Yeah, we were. We were active, faithful. I think I was a hundred percent home teacher for the last 15 years of membership. I taught gospel doctrine. I was a ward mission leader in Sandy, Utah, which is tantamount to a do-nothing job because no one joins the church in Sandy, Utah. They made me the ward mission leader, and for the first time in seven years, they had baptisms while I was on that assignment.

Shawn: So your zeal continued on?

Denver: Well, I'm not sure that it was— It was contemplative. If you're going to believe in a faith, then that faith ought to be as carefully and continuously examined as you can. I taught gospel doctrine for about 25 years. I never taught the same lesson twice. I wanted to get into the material deeper, each time that you go round. And so the lesson that I would teach—the fourth time you go through the material—was considerably more in-depth than what it was taught, you know, four cycles earlier when you were going through that material. To me, it was always a matter of trying to understand more deeply, more profoundly, more carefully. And in that regard, you need to be willing to find things that you don't want to find. You need to confront things that you don't want to confront.

The exploration into Mormonism has been exhilarating and disappointing, challenging and reassuring. It's been a bundle of conflicts, and it's been marvelous throughout. And I enjoyed immensely the entire time that I was active in the church. I was *thrown* out; I didn't leave voluntarily. The current president of the LDS Church came to my stake and called a new stake president—because the old one defended me—called a new stake president, handed him my membership records, and said, "This man needs to be dealt with. The committee's decided that this man needs to be dealt with."

Shawn: Before you go forward on that, Denver, take us back to the one of the — Give us a main thing, for our audience who doesn't know you, of one of those things that was difficult to find in the constant teaching, and searching, and preparing that you were doing—one of the first things that was really brutal to see the reality of it, and you said, "Wait a second."

Denver: There are a number of them. There was a disconnect, across the board, at the end of the life of Joseph Smith and then when the election was held in Winter Quarters in December of '47. There was a disconnect between those. When I became a Mormon, I read everything I could get my hands on —all the biographies, all of the histories, everything there was from early church history, everything B.H. Roberts put out there, all of the biographies.

I had a command of Mormon history—in the way that the church presented its history and the apologists presented the history. But D. Michael Quinn wrote about early Mormon history in a way that was, to me, heretical and contradictory. He was telling a different narrative than the narrative that the church was telling, and he made me mad. But because I was always searching, I read his book. And then I looked at his bibliography and his footnotes. And then I searched to find the source material to try and show, to myself, why Michael Quinn was being *unfair* and *biased* in the way he was presenting this material. That he was not— He was a critic, he was not a historian; *this is unfair.* But the more I looked, the more I found I agreed with what Michael Quinn was saying and the more problematic the orthodox histories were. And I have taken some of those issues farther than I think Michael Quinn has taken the issues, and so he and I have some disagreements about things that I probably have disagreements with most Mormons about. I just did not think that the church was truthful. For a whole lot of reasons, the church was not being truthful about its history. Now understand, I'm not trying to rock anyone's boat.

Shawn: Yeah.

Denver: I'm not trying to say, "Hey, let me come bitch-slap you because you ain't right and I am!" That was not my objective. I had approached, I took— We rented a motorhome. We went back to the Nauvoo temple dedication— well, it was the open house. We didn't stay for the dedication. You had to have tickets for that and I didn't have the pull to get them. We went back— rented a motorhome, took my kids, we parked on, is it Mulberry? The Main Street there? Mulholland. We parked on Mulholland, and one of the evangelical folks had rented a shop and they were giving out anti-Mormon stuff in the shop on Main Street. And I sent my kids in and I said, "You kids go in and you get every bit of anti-Mormon stuff you can find in there, and and bring it in here in the motorhome." So they went in and they harvested what they could. They brought it back, and I said, "You go through all this stuff, each one of ya, and you find where they've made mistakes. And if you can't find they've made a mistake, bring it to my attention and I'll go over it." Because I wanted them to see.

We drove down as a family during General Conference, to drive through and look at the signs of the protesters during General Conference. You grew up in Utah; you're insulated. I joined the church in New Hampshire. I believed, in Texas that was another— There's a lot of stories out of Texas about Mormons and how we interface down there. I *wanted* my kids to encounter the opposition, the push back, because if you've got a faith that you haven't examined— I would rather have a child awaken to some truths and depart from the faith, at least temporarily, and come back to it, than I would have a kid that simply salutes and says, "Yes, sir!" to an unexamined faith. And so I wanted them— I want to struggle with it; I want them to struggle with it.

So, as an aid— I have one son who went on a mission. The one son who went on a mission came home from his mission and fell away from the church. And I wrote a book that was designed to help him understand the value of the faith that he'd been raised in, as an exercise in pure, religious devotion as opposed to respect for an institution. In some respects, you have to destroy the respect for the institution in order to penetrate to the level where there's value, there's truth, there's holiness. And so I wrote a book that was intended to heal the broken Mormon heart, and to allow them to say, "Yeah, there's problems in this institution, but there's no reason to throw away those things of value, and truth, and goodness that you can find within it." So, the book was written primarily for a struggling son, and then for whomever else there may be out there that could benefit from it.

Shawn: What's the name of the book?

Denver: *Passing the Heavenly Gift.*

Shawn: I think I've seen it. Was that part of the reason Nelson said…

Denver: Yes, that was *the* reason I got kicked out. They wanted that book suppressed; they wanted it taken off the market. Well, the book percolated for a bit and it had an effect on my son—it was very positive. It also had an effect on those who were troubled that was very positive.

The stake president, who was given the assignment to get rid of me, took that book and gave it to 20— He bought 20 copies and he gave it to 20 men inside our stake, none of whom were at all an appropriate audience to read that thing. None of them knows there are problems in Mormon history. They're just going along fat, dumb, and happy with whatever's being dispensed each Sunday. And to find out that there's trouble in paradise, I mean, it shook them to the core. And so these people, unprepared to hear anything about this, are given a book that's shaking to the core. And they find out about murders, and they find out about deceit, and they found out about treachery, and they find out about dishonesty, and they find out about lies. They find out about things that you will only find if you go search for it, or if you happen to wind up in a position where someone's trying to proselytize you away and they want to present you the problem; so now it's dumped in your lap. None of these were candidates for that book. All of them read and all of them came back with the same consensus, "Oh, this book is horrible. Oh, this is terrible."

Well yeah, if you think that what you're getting is pure and undefiled, that book will upset you. But if you think what you've got is something you're prepared to walk away from and abandon, because you feel betrayed, that book will help you. It will provide you with a way to have faith in spite of failure, to have hope in spite of setback.

Brigham Young turned Utah Mormonism into a trap. It was a horrible period of time. The Mormon Reformation and the Home Missionary Program was literally designed to determine whether or not the church should kill you. Brigham Young did not believe that the failure was at the leadership level, he believed the failure was at the rank and file. And that the reason all of the cattle died when they took them to Cache County, and the winter was so bad, was because the members were sinning. And as a consequence of the members sinning, God had punished them by destroying the cattle. It never occurred to him that maybe his leadership was flawed. He never questioned that. I think Brigham Young had a mental breakdown when the 'Battle Axe of the

Lord' didn't respond to Johnston's Army, and he was actually dispossessed to the governorship.

I presented a paper on that, and I did that at Sunstone; and one of those papers I presented at Sunstone is in a book called *Eight Essays*. I just want to make sure... no... "Other Sheep Indeed," no... it's not it. It's called "Brigham Young's Telestial Kingdom." It's not in this book of essays, but I brought you this book that includes several of my Sunstone presentations and a couple of other things that I've written. Chapter 8, which is the eighth essay in this book, is called "Problems in Restoration History." And I brought you three books.

Shawn: Thank you.

Denver: This one is a series of essays that has been recently published, gathering together things I've written over the years.

This one's called *A Man Without Doubt*. *A Man Without Doubt* presents three failures that Joseph Smith confronted. And in response to each of the three (he wrote his lengthiest three efforts to try and help people), I give an introduction and a set up to describe why the document got written, and then I get out of the way and let Joseph talk. And it goes to show that Joseph Smith's biggest nemesis were his own followers.

And then this book is called *Come Let Us Adore Him*. The cover of this book is a sketch by Leonardo Da Vinci, incomplete, but a drawing that he made of the Nativity. And I thought, "What a perfect cover," because this book is an incomplete sketch of the Savior. But you can tell the subject matter of the Nativity from what Da Vinci *had* done, and you can make it out in rough form. I took, in *Come Let Us Adore Him* (a book that was written while I was still an active member), and I selected from the life of the Savior those incidents in the Gospels that have never been adequately addressed, in order to understand the personality of the Lord—the ministry of the Lord, the meaning of things that he had done. And so while it is incomplete, it really does—in my attempt—try to introduce the Lord to people in a way that that makes Him seem a far more resilient, far more firm minded, far more authentic character, that really did respond to the burden of prophecy and fulfilling the burden of prophecy.

I got into a lot of trouble because I tried to deal honestly with problems in Mormonism. I know that there are people who want to dismiss Mormonism altogether, for a whole host of reasons. But there are people that want to dismiss evangelical Christianity, Catholicism, Islam. What I found is that if you take all of the the disagreements, the level at which we argue back and forth about issues, and you say, "Okay, that exists and that's true enough," *but* what is it when evangelical Christianity approaches the idea of holiness, of goodness, of God and man's relation to one another? What is it that evangelical Christianity has to offer that is the highest, and best, and most pure, and most desirable? What you'll find is that in Catholicism—what is highest, most noble, what is best, what is most desirable—and in evangelical Christianity, it's the same. The same is true of Mormonism, and the same is even true of the deepest Islamic thinkers. In fact, at its highest level in the search for light and truth and goodness, you can find it in the Bhagavad Gita. You can find it in Buddhism.

Shawn: And what is it? What's that common thread?

Denver: Christ said to His disciples—and it was in a harrowing moment: He had just announced that one of them was going to betray Him, and He had just sent Judas on his task. And in *that* moment, before He goes out in the Garden to suffer, He says, "By this shall men know that you are my disciples, that you have love for one another." Okay? So, is it an act of love for me to search for and to find the things that I can agree with and that I treasure, that *you* believe in and that *you* treasure? Is it an act of love for me to come and argue and denounce?

I understand that people defend the idea that by denouncing, we're really helping to save because we need to rebuke them. But Christ's interface with the critics that *He* had was almost uniformly tolerant, and benign, kindly, and attempting to get them to see something higher and better—right up until *He* chose the moment (I defend that in this book, that Christ chose the moment) for His sacrifice. He went in to cause, at the Passover, the sacrifice of the Paschal Lamb by His "Woe unto you scribes and Pharisees, hypocrites!" by comparing them to whited sepulchers. He went in and He controlled the moment of sacrifice because it was necessary that the Paschal Lamb be slain on the Passover.

And so, His provocation controlled timing. But up until the moment of the provocation, you know, we found someone that was taken in adultery. Well, He doesn't deal with that other than in a kindly way, to force them to look into their own conscience. And looking into their own conscience, they back down. Is it lawful to give tribute to Caesar? Well, show me a coin. Whose image is on this coin? Well, give to Caesar the things that belong to Caesar, and give to God the things that belong to God. Those are not the words of a hostile, street-preaching evangelical with a fist in your face, those are the words of someone that actually is trying, in a loving and kindly way, to reclaim someone from from error.

And I love to be corrected from error, but many times people trying to correct me have not done the work I've done. I would venture to say, if anyone has written or read a history of Mormonism that was written before 2010, they're way behind in understanding what the current state of Mormon history is. Most people read and rely on second and third-hand sources. I have devoted the last decades to looking for original journals, original diaries, original content, contemporaneous newspaper accounts; searching for the source material.

Historians write fiction. They try to smooth over the events to try and make a narrative, to try and give you the moral of the story. When lives are lived without a storyline, they're lived without the plot being developed. They set out to achieve something headed in this direction, and that's their goal. But through a bunch of missteps, misfortunes, oppositions, failures, they wind up over there. So the historian comes along and says, "Here's the story of their glorious trip there," when the life that was lived was frustrated; it was hedged up. They lived their lives with blinders on, stumbling through circumstance-and-predicament after circumstance-and-predicament. And to ignore the reality of what they went through is to ignore what, really, the lessons are.

I suggested in a talk I gave a couple weeks ago at a conference that people read the account in Exodus and only look at Moses' words. Just read what Moses says—ignore the rest of the story and isolate what Moses has to say. This is a man overwhelmed, intimidated, frightened—judging his own inadequacy, protesting to God about his unfitness, his unsuitability—about the difficulty of the challenge; about his own reluctance. *That's life.* The problem is we pick up the scriptures and we do to the scriptures exactly what has been done to Mormon history.

When you and I talked about doing this interview, I said, "I think every Christian should study Mormon history, every Christian should get deep into Mormon history." Because they'll realize there's an institution, a *trillion*-dollar institution—a political powerhouse, an economic engine, a social force in the entire world—sitting here, built upon a whole bunch of misrepresentations, falsehoods, and skewing of the events. If you were to study carefully the content, in order to be able to see the difference of that, a Christian (if they're being fair) would then have the problem of going back, and saying, "What might I learn, if I had available to me the source material to do the same thing to the evolution of the Christian Church? And how might I reconsider, a little more humbly, my own dogmatism about my state?"

And if you're Jewish and you go back to the period of Ezra and Nehemiah—the incidents immediately preceding the Babylonian captivity, the discovery of the scroll, the reading of the law—what you realize is that Judaism was in tatters at the end of the first temple period, and it got rebuilt and reconstructed. And it doesn't matter, *it doesn't matter* how many of the scholars' tools get applied to try and ferret out, from the clues that we have left, the content of the the the old canon and the veracity of the new canon. The fact is you can't do with those what I am able to do with Mormon history because I have far more available, first-hand resources from which to conduct my reconstruction of the Mormon experience. But by analogy, every lesson you learn along that reconstructive effort should lead to the humble acceptance of the fact that the form of Christianity currently believed, by the entire Protestant world, *did not exist* in any form for 1,500 years. It's an invention, a relatively recent one, that is the fruit of the effort that was made by Martin Luther in putting his life on the line to rebel. And ultimately, much of evangelical Christianity is the product of that founder, Roger Williams of Rhode Island.

But in Mormonism, I have the ability to look and see where the fingerprints are. I still have access to source material from which I can actually say, "I know what's going on down there is based on myth and dishonesty." And I can somewhat reconstruct a more accurate version, and vision of what it began as, from the available source material.

I've got the Ante-Nicene and Pre-Nicene fathers' works; they're a valuable resource. We've got the lectures that were done by Martin Luther; we know what drove him. We don't have access to the papal archives; we don't know what they have suppressed. We do know that there were early teachings that divided, at about 1,000 A.D., the Eastern Orthodox from the Catholic world; and that they represent a preservation, in part, on the eastern side, the things that were neglected and lost on the western side, and vice versa. But we come onto the scene at a point in history in which it's *arrogant* to say, "I can tell you what pure Christianity looks and feels like," because we've come so late to the party.

The one thing I can know for certain is that one of the evidences of actual Christianity is the *love* that people can have for one another, across *all* the rubble, across *all* the ruin, across *all* the disagreements. And if we can begin with the highest, most noble aspirations of loving and caring for one another

— Christ chose, deliberately, a character that would be considered odious in the Good Samaritan. He was not only odious socially and politically, in the story he would have been odious economically. And here you've got someone that the Jews had this religious disconnect, and yet, the one who helped him overlooked his Samaritanism, overlooked his predicament.

"What was he doing on the road if... He should have been smart enough to travel in a pack... He should never... It's his own fault to fall among thieves! He's a foolish man, he got what he deserved!" There's none of that. There's no, "You're a foolish man, you shouldn't be Jehovah's Witness!" "You're a foolish man, you shouldn't be Catholic!" "The ministry and Catholicism has turned into rampant pedophilia: you should be *anything but* Catholic!" "How can you be *that*?!"

Why am I trying to inflict pain upon a Catholic who's doing his best to hold on to his faith, instead of inspiring him to look for something noble and good and virtuous that's exemplified in his faith—like praising Mother Teresa, and saying, "She deserves the sainthood that your church is going to visit upon her?"—because *he* exemplifies the kind of human caring for one another that Christ came to deliver. *And* Saint Francis, I mean the current Pope—everything the current Pope is doing or not doing (notwithstanding, he chose a name for which I have abiding respect; and he earned my respect as a consequence).

Shawn: I could personally listen to you. And I understand why you have people who listen to you and follow, because you have a great perspective—which, I agree with everything you said. I have no problem.

Denver: No.

Shawn: The show is called *Heart of the Matter* and I need to get, for our audience, to the *heart* of what this all means. And you're a great teacher, and you're laying out principles here that are established in the history of Christianity and Mormonism. But what does that mean? Because on one hand, you're saying we're wasting our time poking on the Catholics, and this and that, but *you are* poking on the North Temple Mormons. You do go after *them*. So the love thing, it seems to be, apparently, somewhat lost between you and North Temple. And so I agree with you that, look, let's just let people believe what they're going to believe, let's point out the positives—all that you said—but what are you about now? What are you doing? What is happening? What's the threat? Why do they consider you a *threat*, besides the obvious?

Denver: Yeah. When I— Most of what I have written was written at a time that I was a faithful member of the church, therefore, most of what I've written reflects the viewpoint from inside faithful Mormonism.

Shawn: Can you tell our audience what you've written? I'm sorry to interrupt your thought.

Denver: The first...

Shawn: How many books?

Denver: Well, seventeen volumes of material, but in addition there's— They asked for, and I gave permission, to gather collected works of blog posts and other things. And so, there's a number of those volumes that are... I think five of those, so if you count them, like 22 volumes.

Shawn: And how do people get those?

Denver: Oh, you can buy them on Amazon.

Shawn: Just look up Denver?

Denver: Yeah.

Shawn: Twenty-two volumes on Amazon.

Denver: Yeah, they're all there.

Shawn: All right.

Denver: The breach came when *Passing the Heavenly Gift* was written. Again, it was still written *inside* the Mormon world. It was *after that* (and I got kicked out) that I felt no need at all to pull punches, and so what was written after that— I've been asked, "Why don't you go back to that first book, *The Second Comforter* (which is the short name. The long name is *The Second Comforter: Conversing with the Lord Through the Veil*—which as a former Mormon should should mean something to you)."

Shawn: It rings a bell.

Denver: It rings a bell. Or at least three knocks. (Audience laughter.)

So *that* book was written to try and inspire people to seek for, and obtain for themselves, revelation. Look, the Joseph Smith story, the Book of Mormon, the testimonies of the missionaries— When I came into Mormonism, I thought all those good people were visited by angels and experiencing miracles; and my expectation was that that was commonplace. I thought that's what Mormonism was: it was a revival of the original New Testament religion with all of the accouterments that occur in that New Testament religion.

Shawn: Road to Damascus. You're waiting for it.

Denver: The whole thing.

So, when it was within the first year of being baptized and the scriptures were opening before my mind, that having an angelic visit—which happened—I thought that was commonplace, that happened to everyone. That's, you know, that's what Mormonism is. It's, you know, the veil gets thin, you go through, they come through, you have fellowship on the other side.

It was really not until I got out of Texas to Utah, into the Brigham Young University Law School, that associating weekly with, you know, the hometown crop of Mormonism out of the mission field, that it began to dawn on me that extraordinary experiences were not expected—and actually weren't even welcomed. The miraculous was deferred to the hierarchy; and the hierarchy was responsible for dispensing that to you and me. And so, what *The Second Comforter* (the first book I wrote) was attempting to do was to testify and to suggest the miraculous—the thinness of the veil, the proximity of angels—needs to become commonplace in Mormonism.

Shawn: Let me stop, just for a second.

Denver: Yeah.

Shawn: You just dropped a *huge* bomb.

Denver: Oh.

Shawn: *Gigantic* bomb.

Denver: Which was?

Shawn: That you were visited by an angel. You went like *this* to respond to that.

Denver: Oh.

Shawn: *But,* maybe it's that to you, "Oh yeah, of course. I visit with them weekly, you know." *But,* to most people— That's not a reality for most people. I'm not saying it should or shouldn't be, I'm just saying most people don't seem to have that reality. So, can you explain a little bit about that? Or do you— Maybe what the North Temple guys say, "It's a little too sacred, I don't discuss that?"

Denver: No. I've never bought in to that idea. But there is an idea that I do buy into, and the idea is that Christ did a variety of miraculous things— always charging those to whom the miracle had been given to tell no one about it. There's another comment that He makes...

Shawn: But we know that was because He was, like you said, orchestrating His death, and had that...

Denver: He was, He was. But there's another comment that He makes, and I put these two together, not— (It's a long story why I put them together, but I put these two together), He says it is a wicked and an adulterous generation that seeks after a sign. I believe that the more you talk about the miraculous, the more you attract a certain personality. That is, in Paul's words, they have itching ears. They really want a tale; they really want the fantastic. When the burden of Christianity is the daily life, it's treating one another kindly; it's loving those that are in need; it's doing things for others. And so, I tend not to speak about the miraculous, primarily because I don't want people that are eager for *only* the miraculous, because it's the wrong sort, and it's not the burden...

Shawn: But Denver, the first book you wrote is about...

Denver: Yes, the miraculous—in an effort to try and get others to experience it, not to boast of myself.

Shawn: Right. I know. I'm not finding you boastful, I just want to know...

Denver: But I'll tell you what happened in that first visit, because it really reflects poorly on me. And I have no problem telling the story because it shows what a poor candidate I am for doing any kind of work on an errand from God. I can still close my eyes and see everything about it. It made *that* indelible of an impression upon me at the time. I was caught up— I know that the scriptures speak using a phrase, 'I was caught up to an exceedingly high mountain.' I think I understand what that phrase means because I was, in fact, caught up. I could see the circle of the horizon of the earth in the distance.

Shawn: So you just crushed the flat-earthers right there!

Denver: Yeah. I could see, and I was standing on an actual surface.

Shawn: Okay.

Denver: And there were actual walls, and there were paintings on the walls, okay? And I'm taking this in. And there's a personage there. I could sketch him if you gave me— Well, I'm not going to do that. (I thought she was going to hand me a pen.)

Shawn: (He thought you were bringing him a pallet!)

Denver: Yeah, I could sketch him 'cause I can still picture him. Okay, he had a beard, he had hair, but it was not, like, long and flowing. It was reasonably well groomed, and, you know, not shoulder length but not collar length either—white hair, white beard, elderly, as somber a personage as you would ever encounter. And he said to me exactly this: "On the first day, of the third month, in nine years, your ministry will begin; and so, you must prepare."

Shawn: Wow.

Denver: That's exactly what he said. Okay, so, here's *my* attention span—I hear that and I think, "I wonder why the walls are transparent? Why would you have a wall if you can see right through the thing? And why are they painting? Don't they have photography? And why is it that I know *that* painting I'm looking at is Moses? Because I *know that face is the face of Moses!* And no one's ever shown me a picture, but that's Moses—and he's bald. I had no idea Moses was bald. Because one of the criteria for the high priest— A defect included baldness. That's weird! And where are we?"

So, this is where *my* head is at, and I've just had an angel give me— I didn't ask, "Prepare? Wh...what? How? Mini...ministry? Wh...whaat?" And the man literally waited. He wasn't going to force anything. He had a message, he had the content, and he gave it to me. It was up to me then to inquire, and I didn't inquire. I'm acting like a tourist. It's only weeks later, I mean— Then I was dismissed, I mean, and as I was dismissed I noticed, as I departed, that there was someone arriving. And I thought, "Does heaven operate like, you know, a bus terminal where there are people coming and going all the time? 'Cause that's interesting." And I believe that as I departed, that the direction that someone arriving came from was earthward, and therefore, coming up.

But the whole thing was singular. I didn't talk about it, but I did write down an account of that. And it was only weeks later that it occurred to me that that was an opportunity to learn a whole lot, but I didn't ask a single question. In fact, I was so distracted that I didn't— I got out of it a message that I didn't understand, that deserved inquiry, that deserved *some* amplification, explanation, elucidation—*something* other than those words because I didn't know what to make of those words. And as I thought about it in the weeks that followed, all I had were questions. So when I had questions then I made it a matter of prayer—and I got nothing.

Shawn: We're out of time.

Denver: Yeah.

Shawn: Nine years, three months, first day of the third month…

Denver: Yeah.

Shawn: What date? What date—what is that, or what was that?

Denver: Oh, it's a good story, but we'll…

Shawn: But I just want to know that day to whet our audience's appetite.

Denver: Oh, it was the day—after the year I thought it was—in which the Sunday School president, the bishop, came to my house and called me to be the Gospel Doctrine teacher for the first time. And I taught gospel doctrine for 25 years after that. Yeah.

Shawn: So that gives us some idea.

When we come back with Denver, we're going to have more exchange on some *words* that I want to throw at him, and just let him say what he thinks about these words. And then we're going to hear him tell about what he's— What's really happening now with what he's doing *today* within the faith—

and I'll call it the faith of all faiths—within the faith. What is he doing? And what does it mean to people who are seeking?

Really appreciate you taking the time. Appreciate your audience's respect. We've had some audiences not respectful. These guys are good, so that best reflects well on you in some ways.

Denver: That's good. That's good.

Shawn: Yeah, it is good. And so let's keep going, and we'll come back and see you next week here on *Heart of the Matter.*

———

The foregoing interview is rebroadcast here with permission from Shawn McCraney, host of the *Heart of the Matter* YouTube channel.

90. Interview with Denver, Part 3

This is the third and final part of Shawn McCraney's interview of Denver Snuffer for the Gospel Tangents podcast, which was recorded on October 8th, 2019 in front of a live audience.

————

Shawn: All right, welcome back. We were just talking, Denver and I. One thing we have in common (we have a lot of things in common, actually), but one thing is we never change our clothes! Thank you for that joke, Denver.

Part 3— Part 1: We heard about Denver's life through story, really. It was a lot of different, sort of chronological, a little bit disparate—but stories that led up to his conversion and baptism in 1973 and into the Mormon Church.

And then we talked a little about (in Part 2) about his getting married to his wife of all these years, nine kids between them and together. And then we talked about Mormonism and about sort of how he got the hook and yanked offstage a little bit. We talked about that in Part 2, so if you're just catching up with us today, we're—or tonight—we're gonna talk a little bit more specifically. And I am *begging* for truncated, succinct answers.

Now, this is a man of words, and he's eloquent and intelligent, so intelligent that the empty— He just says things in a way that really paints the picture, but our low- attention-span audience doesn't necessarily always get that. So, I'm hoping we can do this:

Now, I have four categories. These are the categories, Denver: *social issues, Mormonism, doctrinal basics, and Denver Snuffer.* 'K? So, you choose the category. I have about ten questions in each. That shows you how short you have to be, and I want to hear what you believe, think, teach, share on the concept presented.

Denver: Okay, what were the categories again?

Shawn: *Social issues?*

Denver: Nah.

Shawn: *Mor*—that would be last then—*Mormonism?*

Denver: Sure, let's do that.

Shawn: Thoughts on, first of all, *Joseph Smith.*

Denver: Misunderstood, far more personally insecure than people make him out to be; far more respectful and dependent upon Emma than the LDS tradition would ever acknowledge; and in many respects never felt comfortable with the role that he was assigned.

Shawn: Excellent, and the brevity almost makes me cry.

Denver: Yeah, I know. It does me, too. [Laughter]

Shawn: *Brigham Young.*

Denver: An ambitious man who managed to see, in the construct that Joseph bequeathed him, the potential for monetizing it (in what we would call today *monetization*); who successfully developed it into an empire of control and dominion that today reflects *far more* the Brigham Young version of Mormonism than does it reflect the Joseph Smith version.

Shawn: Translation for our audience: He's a dude that's fallen off a tree to make money.

Denver: Yeah, he's the first multi-millionaire west of the Mississippi.

Shawn: Excellent.

Denver: And he was a carpenter from New England!

Shawn: Right.

Denver: It's like you elect someone to Congress, and they come back—22 million in their pocket.

Shawn: Yeah.

Denver: How'd that happen? You make him church president, and he becomes a multimillionaire. How'd that happen?

Shawn: So, it's obvious, between Joseph Smith and Brigham Young, you see a lot going on.

Denver: Joseph Smith had a pending petition in bankruptcy when he died. Brigham Young died a wealthy man. Yeah.

Shawn: *Priesthood.*

Denver: *Fabulously* misunderstood. *Completely* misused by the Catholic precedent to subjugate and to control that left so indelible an impression upon the minds of the Christian world that that abusive view echoed down right to today. Priesthood in the form that Christ exemplified it is a call to *service* and *subservience* and not a call to...

Shawn: Be served?

Denver: Yeah, what we've turned it into. It (priesthood) is synonymous, in my mind, with abuse and, primarily, male abuse.

Shawn: Okay, so just curious— Just to take that out a little farther, do you believe in *a* priesthood which is based or exemplified in *service* that both men and women bear?

Denver: I've redefined the concept, and I—you don't read what I've written, so you wouldn't know this—but I've redefined the concept of priesthood as *fellowship.*

Shawn: Okay.

Denver: I think women can have fellowship with one another, and that's a form of *priestesshood.* Men can have fellowship with men; that's a form of priesthood. Men can have associations with angels; that's a form of priesthood. And I think the way to conceptualize priesthood in its best form is as an *association* between sisters or an association between brethren.

Shawn: Fascinating, fascinating. *Water baptism.* (I have heard, just to let you know, that you do perform these, and I've heard, *often.*) So, water baptism.

Denver: Water baptism— And I've said that I think having a living ordinance should be done in living water, that you ought to go out into a river or a lake, a stream, a body of living water in which nature created it, not going inside a building in a tile font and be baptized. I think living ordinances should be by immersion in living water, and it ought to be in a facility that God created— to *remind* us that this is something intended to draw us closer to God, to be born again. Anytime you find living water, as you come out of the *water* from baptism, you see new *life*. You see the animal kingdom and the plant kingdom. I believe in baptism by immersion, and I think it ought best be done in living water.

Shawn: Okay. A couple things—one, I'm sure you know that the *earliest* church fathers believed in living water. In fact, that was one of the main things, but the question I have is can anyone do these? You believe in immersion. Can a teenager baptize a woman or...

Denver: Yeah, one of the things that I have recommended— In the Book of Mormon, there's this example of Alma who had been a servant in an unrighteous king's court. They're called *the wicked priests of King Noah*. He was one of the wicked priests. He gets converted by Abinadi, as you know. He goes out, and he starts his own thing. Well, before he performs a baptism, he prays, and he asks God for the authority to baptize, and he gets an answer that gives him the authority, in answer to prayer, to baptize.

I've recommended before you baptize anyone, pray and ask God to give you the right to baptize and get from God, as Alma did, the *yea*, the *yes*, and then perform baptism—and yeah, anyone.

Shawn: So, authorize it. So, what you have done there, and I love this— C.A.M.P.U.S. stands for Christian Anarchists [Christian Anarchists Meeting to Prayerfully Understand Scripture], and I won't go into it, but I love the fact that you leave it in the hands of the person who says, *The Lord has said I can.*

Denver: Yeah.

Shawn: And you let them take that responsibility on because ultimately, it's between them anyway.

Denver: Yeah. In fact, the more you can push responsibility onto the individual, and the less you try to aggregate power to yourself— It's a toxin. It's a toxin to the person getting it, and it's a toxin to the person that is giving it. People need to be responsible to God directly.

Shawn: I love that.

Denver: Man.

Shawn: I love that. That's beautiful. *Sabbath day.*

Denver: Yeah. Dude, that would require an hour of talk to…

Shawn: Come on, you can summarize it!

Denver: We're commanded to keep the Sabbath day holy. I recommend that you do something on the Sabbath day always to remember God. If you find yourself in a predicament where, due to the circumstances of life, you're doing things that you would rather not do on the Sabbath, then do them cognizant in remembering God. You can serve God even if what you do on the Sabbath is work as a mechanic. Just do what you do for the benefit and the glory of God.

Shawn: Is the Sabbath day—and I don't want to belabor this— Are we talking about Friday night to Saturday night, or are we talking about Sunday?

Denver: That's the problem because that requires a long explanation, but…

Shawn: In you, does it matter?

Denver: I'm content with Sunday Sabbath. I understand why some would say it ought to be on Saturday. I believe that the answer to the question goes all the way back to the Fall and how everything got pushed forward. And I think Christ's resurrection on what had become the *first* day of the week was really restoring the early Fall…

Shawn: Okay.

Denver: …because they didn't have the Sabbath at the beginning. They were kicked out of the garden. And then Christ's resurrection authorizes the celebration of the Sabbath on Sunday as opposed to Saturday. But look, keep *a* Sabbath day holy. Yeah.

Shawn: So, we could say you're Sabbath fluid.

Denver: I'm Sabbath fluid. [Laughter]

Shawn: Okay.

Denver: That sounds cultish.

Shawn: Yeah, well, we have gender fluidity. I figure we can have Sabbath fluidity.

Denver: Sabbath fluidity.

Shawn: All right. *Tithing.* Gotta give it to me straight, Brother.

Denver: I believe that you have a responsibility to care for yourself, to care for your children, to care for your wife and that the payment of tithings is not to be done before taking care of everything that's necessary for food, shelter, clothing, medical care, education; that whatever is left *over*, you tithe on that.

Shawn: Okay.

Denver: You don't tithe on your gross.

Shawn: Got it.

Denver: Yeah.

Shawn: Appreciate that approach *far* better than the evangelicals in this valley who pitch the old LDS struggle: *And the Lord will bless you. Give us the money you would have paid on your electric bill.*

Denver: Yeah! Yeah! And God gave you the money to use for your *electric* bill!

Shawn: Yeah.

Denver: And you're using it to support... Yeah, it just— It makes no sense.

Shawn: *Word of Wisdom.*

Denver: Okay. The Word of Wisdom was not given in defined terms. It was given in colloquial language. The Word of Wisdom had no meaning until the high council at Far West interpreted what they thought the Word of Wisdom meant. At a *later* time, Hyrum Smith was asked about the meaning of the Word of Wisdom, and Hyrum Smith, respectful of the order of things, repeated what the high council at Far West had said.

I believe the Word of Wisdom actually *recommends* beer—barley drinks.

Shawn: Sure.

Denver: Mild barley drinks—what's it talking about? At that point, it meant beer. I believe that hot drinks are *not* coffee, tea. I believe hot drinks are what people at the time—we now identify this as an Indian word, *firewater*—I believe that what it's talking about are those drinks that when you take bourbon, or you take some hard liquor, and you drink it, it burns your throat.

Shawn: I've never heard of that.

Denver: I think the hot drinks is referring to hard alcohol. Wine in the sacrament is *commended*. It's the only liquid that's mentioned for use in scripture—wine for the sacrament; and I believe that beer is just fine. I think hard liquor is probably hazardous. (And a good friend of ours died from liver failure.)

Shawn: Sure.

Denver: And it would be very hard to accomplish that with beer, but you can certainly achieve that with vodka.

Shawn: So, would it be safe to say that you really don't appreciate hard alcohol based off the Word of Wisdom? But do you give the liberality of people who are participating?

Denver: It's a *word* of *wisdom*…

Shawn: Okay.

Denver: …that is given, not by commandment or constraint. I think it's unwise, and I think I know from personal experience in my youth that hard liquor tends to make one act foolishly.

Shawn: Yeah.

Denver: Yeah. My father…

Shawn: Not me, but everybody else, it does.

Denver: My father and Wayne Water's father met for the first time after the two of us had been picked up. He, Wayne, was guilty of a DUI. I was just along for the ride, but, yeah, hard liquor will make one behave foolishly.

Shawn: *Russell M. Nelson.* And I have to put a rule on this. You don't get to say, "Quick!"

Denver: Yeah. No, look. I think he's the victim of a system that he inherited that he does not see any way to execute his role other than in conformity to the system that he inherited, and he would be *far, far* better off if he said the *system* is not the *gospel.*

The gospel is not necessarily confined. We do not need to be slavishly following an *order* of things. The truth will set you *free,* and tradition— In the Book of Mormon, tradition is a negative. *Every time* the word *tradition* is used in the Book of Mormon, it is used in a negative way except on, I think, two (and it may be three) occasions where it specifically identifies the tradition as being good. Otherwise, the default for tradition is always evil.

Russell Nelson is leading an organization that has been out of control, probably since 1890. And I picked that day because that was when the lawyer wrote Official Declaration 1 that Wilford Woodruff published in order to satisfy the Tucker-Edmonds Act [Edmonds-Tucker Act] and to extract the church from the loss of their property.

You can't serve God and Mammon, and right now a lot of hard choices *ought* to be made. Mormonism would thrive if they made the right choices, if they were willing to lay aside the traditions and the things that cultivate and curate the wealth. Forget about the world; the world's headed for destruction anyway.

Shawn: Ooh, we'll have to talk about that.

Denver: The more you hold on to that, the more disappointed you're gonna be at the outcome. But the things of eternal life—they'll be with you forever.

Shawn: Last one: *Communion.*

Denver: Oh! In the sense of the sacrament, *sacramental communion,* I believe that that ought to be celebrated every Sabbath (but as often as someone feels inclined to do so) and that it ought to be breaking of bread, the taking of wine. And I think that wine was intended to be part of the sacramental observance because a little bit of wine, for most people, will put you in a more meditative state, in a more reflective state.

We're very harried in our every day. Our minds are busy running from place to place. We have short attention spans. Wine has a way of slowing you down a little and letting your attention span expand a little, and your reflection become a little more deep. I think communion in that sense— I see no problem if someone wants to have communion celebrated as a sacrament every day. But I also think there's a communion between people, a fellowship.

Shawn: Okay, yeah.

Denver: Yeah, a sharing of ideas. There are a lot of things that everyone holds in common, and there are so many things that we can fight about. I don't think we please God when we decide, Ah, what we're going to talk about today is what we fight about. There ought to be a lot more (used to be!)—They invited ministers to come to the tabernacle and to preach in the tabernacle to a Mormon audience.

Shawn: D. L. Moody!

Denver: Yeah! Van Der Donckt, the chaplain of the United States Senate.

Shawn: Wow.

Denver: And B. H. Roberts!

Shawn: Wow.

Denver: They gave lectures...

Shawn: Did that happen there?

Denver: Yeah!

Shawn: That's where we get the...

Denver: Yes!

Shawn: ...Van Der Donckt?

Denver: Yes! That's from the tabernacle!

Shawn: On materialism?

Denver: Yes!

Shawn: Wow!

Denver: That's tabernacle! Yeah.

There was a time when Mormonism was confident enough that it would allow someone to come in and criticize. Mormonism today has no confidence to let a critic come in and criticize 'cause it *scares* them.

Shawn: This is an aside. I don't know your age; you look young but gray. But the question I have is: Do you remember the days when priesthood meeting (I was really— I was a kid, about eight), opening priesthood meeting was like a debate! *I don't like that candidate!* Another person would say, *Oh I…*

Denver: Yeah.

Shawn: …*I think he's great!*

Denver: Yeah.

Shawn: They were *open!*

Denver: It was lively. See, what happened is that Joseph Fielding Smith and Bruce R. McConkie, his son-in-law, *wanted* to stabilize Mormonism. I think they were far less concerned with getting it right and far more concerned with just stabilizing it. They were opponents of that, and I loved that era.

Shawn: That was a great era.

Denver: That was fun.

Shawn: That *ends* your first category, Mr. Denver Snuffer! We have the *basics in doctrine, yourself,* or *social issues.*

Denver: Wait a minute. Are we going through all of them?

Shawn: Yes!

Denver: I chose one...

Shawn: This is interesting!

Denver: ...I chose one in the expectation that that would be it.

Shawn: Your expectations were incorrect, sir. [Laughter]

Denver: So, this is all double jeopardy. This is all— Yeah, we don't ring the bell and say, *Okay, you've made it to the end.*

Shawn: No, we knock three times, remember?

Denver: Yeah. Man. So, what was the first one 'cause we may as well do…

Shawn: *Social issues.*

Denver: That's the one I like least, so, yeah, let's go there.

Shawn: *Marijuana.*

Denver: It's funny. One of the fellows who was going to meet me here is not here because he has to harvest his marijuana crop. He has a license (this is weird, okay?). He lives in Utah. He's been licensed by the state of Utah to grow a crop of marijuana, which he has grown and is now harvesting because it's supposed to snow tomorrow, and he's gonna turn it into CBD oil that's legal. And how weird is that?

Shawn: It's weird.

Denver: I mean, seriously. Look, I…

Shawn: Herbs?

Denver: …I think—yeah, I get all that—but I think smoking stuff is ill-advised to your lungs. (You know, edibles over in Colorado might be an answer for some people.)

I do think that there's therapeutic uses of a whole variety of things. I learned from a fellow whose daughter's in med school that one of the very first heart medications that they developed for blood thinning came from using a poisonous snake venom to adjust it for dosage that will allow the blood to be thinned in order to help heart patients prevent further damage. If snake venom can have a therapeutic use, then it's likely that just about everything in the hands of someone that knows what they're doing can have a therapeutic use. We react hysterically because someone abuses something without ever considering that maybe further use ought to be experimented with to find out where it fits.

This creation was fine-tuned by God who put man as the culmination of that creation, and everything—*everything*—was given for the use and benefit of man in the Garden of Eden. Now, he was kicked out. The *kind* of environment became progressively more hostile, but that doesn't mean that everything in the garden didn't exist for the use and benefit of man. We just abuse stuff.

Shawn: Like your views; I really do! *Government.*

Denver: The United States has one of the greatest governmental structures ever created, and it is populated, at present, by scoundrels and knaves and dishonest and just wretched individuals. *Fortunately*, we have egomaniacal leaders occupying all three branches of government which is exactly what the Founding Fathers anticipated would happen, and so, we get a daily vaudeville show.

Shawn: Yeah.

Denver: I mean, it's slapstick humor what's going on back in Washington.

Shawn: Yeah.

Denver: Are you telling me that that both political parties don't realize there's an immigration problem that could be solved? Why are we ignoring a problem when we're importing disease? Why can't someone that has a disease that would like to come here go through a system that welcomes them but cures their disease before they set them loose in the general public? Some people say, Well, we want to welcome them, and some people say, Oh, this is a danger; we have to have it regulated. Why can't we both welcome them and regulate it and do it in a way that protects the people that are here and aids the actual people that are coming in?

Our government right now is utterly dysfunctional, and we're the beneficiaries of that because they leave us alone.

Shawn: So, you have obvious ideas. Let me get more to the point on that one, government. *What is your thought on the separation of church and state?*

Denver: It was always intended that the state not be allowed to meddle in the church, but I think that churches were always expected to speak up and to have a voice. I think churches *ought* to speak up.

I think there are a lot of issues that affect churches and the values of the churches. And when you say that you have to gag the churches, then are the only voices that are permitted in the public discourse the secular voice, the atheist voice? Why is the atheist voice more pure and worthy of being heard than the religious voice if you're going to open up the First Amendment for everyone to speak? It just— It makes no sense. We've skewed it. Churches should be as vocal as they want to be. Atheists should likewise be as vocal as they want to be.

The only thing that shouldn't happen is that a government should not say, This religion is destined to prosper and succeed, but that one is destined to ruin in taxation. They should be hands off. The government shouldn't control that.

Shawn: Got it.

Denver: But if churches have the ability to win the political argument and to elect people to Congress that represent their views, churches should have the right to rally and to elect.

Shawn: With the continued support of tax-exempt status?

Denver: I think so because anytime you say you will forfeit your taxes in… The power— Oliver Wendell Holmes said the power to tax is the power to destroy. The power to destroy when it comes to churches— You really have to take a tax-free approach.

Shawn: Got it.

Denver: You just have to.

Shawn: Got it.

Denver: Otherwise, government can destroy it.

Shawn: I see. Excellent. *Abortion.*

I think I know what you're gonna say on most of these, but let's just get it on the record.

Denver: Yeah. I think you're taking a life.

Shawn: Okay. *Homosexuality.*

Denver: I think it is the— Ultimately, anyone who does not have children— I don't care what their orientation is. Having a sexual union between the man and the woman that produces a child, no matter what it is that drives your libido, is part of what it means to be human, made in the image of God, and to experience, in this life, part of what is our destiny.

Shawn: Okay.

Denver: And, therefore, I understand that there may be people who find that challenging. Nevertheless, I think they will find greater joy and happiness in having and raising a child than they can in a union that will deprive them of that.

Shawn: Got it.

Denver: So, I mean, I don't want to throw rocks at anyone. What I would like to do is encourage them to contemplate the value and the godliness of the union of the man and the woman and the product of progeny.

Shawn: Got it.

Denver: Yeah.

Shawn: *Capital punishment.*

Denver: Because I have been a lawyer and seen innocent people be convicted, some— At least one fellow is in jail right now for a crime he did not commit that we're doing what we can to try and change that. I hate to have finality like execution when you have the potential for error. If you *know;* if the person confesses, I don't have a problem with an execution although if there's no proof to support his confession, and all he's doing is using you to commit suicide, I got a problem with that.

But there's a serial killer I heard about driving into work today. He's confessed to...

Shawn: Ninety-four.

Denver: ...ninety— Yeah, and he's got proof, and they found bodies where he said they'd find them. I don't have any problem with execution.

Shawn: That's no connection to blood atonement.

Denver: Oh, gol!

Shawn: I just have to ask! You got to clear up the mystique, Brother.

Denver: Yeah, Yeah. I think the whole notion of blood atonement is asinine. The Apostle Paul said he was guilty of murder.

Shawn: Yeah.

Denver: I mean, the whole concept was he committed a sin, but most...

Shawn: Yeah.

Denver: Christ's blood can't reach, so we gotta shed your blood.

Shawn: Right.

Denver: Ah, yeah, that's nonsense.

Shawn: I'll just throw this one out there. We'll end it with that one. *Evangelicalism.*

Denver: A recent innovation, largely dependent upon the constructural framework that Martin Luther came up with, which itself was, in a way, to escape Roman Catholicism without, you know, trusting that Catholicism's excommunication of you will consign you to hell. I mean, evangelical views were inevitable, and I think they are supportable by the biblical text, but they are really recent. Here, the evangelicals are the only ones that got it right?

Shawn: Yeah.

Denver: Then we've got like 1750 years of Christians that are consigned to hell because it didn't *exist.* I mean, look, given the chaos of what Christianity came to in the wake of Catholicism and Martin Luther and Knox and Calvin, evangelicals are probably putting a better face on the ruling of Christianity than most. And I have a lot— I harmonize with a lot of what the evangelical world has to say.

Shawn: Not on my list, but just between, you know, you and I, have you done much reading of Erasmus?

Denver: No! I should do that.

Shawn: Yeah, really interesting.

Denver: Okay.

Shawn: We have two categories left, my friend, and I know the one you're *not* gonna pick unless you want to get the pain out of the way. We can do *Denver Snuffer*, or we can do *the basics of doctrine*.

Denver: Well, let's do *the basics of doctrine*, and then— Aren't we out of time? [Laughter]

Shawn: No. I know you're hoping for that. We're not letting that happen.

Denver: I need to... [Denver gestures *stretching out* space between his hands. Laughter.]

Shawn: Yeah, you're good at that! All right. *God the Father.*

Denver: God the Father is clearly cross-culturally recognized as an existent male deity that, in Jewish tradition and in Egyptological depiction and in Hinduism, offered the promise of a redemptive God-Son who would come to rescue mankind from a predicament. P

And I think that God the Father in our current scriptures, biblical and Mormon, seems distant and disconnected; and yet, God the Son comes in and says, I do what the Father tells me to do. I'm a reflection of Him. I'm here as His, essentially, His surrogate. When you see me, you've seen the Father. P

And so, we have this disconnect between us and the Father that Christ was trying to disabuse us of to try and make the Father seem just as loving, just as sacrificial, just as kindly as is the Son. And we've lost that. P

One of the fascinating things that Mormonism has is that Christ in the Book of Mormon repeatedly refers to things He's doing as what the Father told Him to do; and in dialogue in the first books of Nephi (First and Second Nephi), the Father's voice is actually heard. I mean, Bruce R. McConkie, when trying to stabilize Mormonism, says that God the Father never talks to mankind except to introduce His Son. P

This is [imitating B. R. McConkie]... Actually, I think I can do that voice. *This is my beloved Son...*

Shawn: It's called... [copies Denver's gesture, *stretching out* the space between his hands].

Denver: *...in whom I am well pleased; hear [ye] him*—Bruce R. McConkie (Matthew 17:5; Matthew 9:4 RE). But he's *wrong* because the Book of Mormon says,...

Shawn: Right.

Denver: ...in the first-person voice of the Father, a lot of things that aren't *This is my beloved Son; hear him* (Luke 9:35; Mark 5:5 RE).

Now, I could go on...

Shawn: You can.

Denver: ...about that, but they seem to be growing increase...

Shawn: Yes and no, quick yes or no. *A body of flesh and bones?*

Denver: Glorified body...

Shawn: Okay. Glorified body of flesh and bones?

Denver: Yeah, within...yeah! Look, when you talk about that...

Shawn: Denver, yes or *damn no*! [Laughter]

Denver: In order to know the biology of a resurrected being...

Shawn: You're killing me...

Denver: Yeah, okay. Yes.

Shawn: Okay, thank you. *King Follett Discourse. Once a man?* Yes or no.

Denver: Well, if you define Christ as God, absolutely, God was once a man.

Shawn: No, I'm not talking about incarnation through Christ. I'm talking about the Father. Yes or no, darn it! Come on! My mom is waiting for me for dinner! [Laughter]

Denver: Is your Mom still— Are you still living in a basement? What's up with you, Man? [Laughter] Is this religious gig so poorly paid?

Shawn: You think I would live in a basement? I live *here*!

Denver: Oh. Well, I hope they shut down the...

Shawn: It's the only time I get sleep.

Denver: ...the cabinet plant next door.

Shawn: Are you gonna give me one on that? *God the Father, once a man.* Yes, no?

Denver: I believe that God has made it possible for people, as is stated in Revelation, chapter 3, to sit on a throne as Christ sits on a throne with His Father; and that, as a consequence, the deification of man (which is an Eastern Orthodox preserved doctrine) is true.

In terms of the genealogy of God the Father, you know, we can go round and round on that without ever getting an answer...

Shawn: I don't want to go round and round.

Denver: ...in the King Follett discourse.

Shawn: Okay.

Denver: But yeah.

Shawn: Okay. You're too wily of an attorney to know how to just manipulate the hell out of me, so I'm jumping categories, and we're going like this down the thing. *Are you a prophet?*

Denver: The testimony of Jesus is the spirit of prophecy, so everyone ought to be a prophet.

Shawn: So, that would be a yes.

Denver: Everyone ought to be a prophet.

Shawn: Are you a prophet in the sense of the missionaries going door to door in, say, like unto Moses?

Denver: No, I don't have a podium, and I don't have a tabernacle, and I don't have a temple, and I don't have an organization.

Shawn: Less specifically. Do you receive revelation for people?

Denver: I receive revelation.

Shawn: For others.

Denver: Some people have thought what I had to say significant enough that they use it in their own lives.

Shawn: Okay.

Denver: Do I have the ambition of trying to lead a group of people? If so, my ambition is to lead them to become prophets in their own right.

Shawn: Okay.

Denver: Yeah.

Shawn: All right, fair enough. The next one: *Satan.*

Denver: Because of a revelation, I happen to know that *Satan* is a title, and what it means is *accuser.* And we can be Satan, as Christ said to Peter, *Get thee behind me, Satan* [See Matthew 16:23], when Peter was trying to convince the Lord that he didn't need to go undertake the sacrifice; and I think Satan is a role any one of us can occupy as soon as we want to become accusers of one another. And you know that— The opposite of that is what Christ talked about, loving one another.

Shawn: Okay, so, it's more of a principle, concept, rather than an entity.

Denver: I think anyone can become an accuser...

Shawn: Okay.

Denver: …and an adversary, and many people do.

Shawn: *Hell.*

Denver: I think there is such a thing as torment and regret, but I think that the inflictor of that torment is ourselves.

Shawn: So, not literal flames.

Denver: No, no, no, no, no, no pitchforks, no horned heads and pointy tails and…

Shawn: That's only the Mormons.

Denver: Yeah.

Shawn: Just kidding—total joke because people used to say we had horns. Geez, you guys at home— I know what you're thinking. Anyway, *have you seen Jesus?*

Denver: Well, yeah, and a little bit of a description of that is given in the book that I gave to you.

Shawn: Okay, good.

Denver: Yeah.

Shawn: All right.

Denver: Yeah.

Shawn: *Different from the angel or the angel…?*

Denver: Oh yes, yes, yes, yeah.

Shawn: Okay.

Denver: Yeah.

Shawn: *Are you the head of this dispensation?*

Denver: Well, the way you define *dispensation* requires that you understand the term. Do I have a dispensation? Has the gospel been dispensed to me from heaven so that I'm not dependent upon something including the words of an old book to know God? Yes.

Shawn: Okay.

Denver: Does that mean that now I get to run a multi-national corporation? No. I'm doing my best to try and preserve faith in Christ at a time when, because of everything that's going on in our current environment that is so corrosive, it is increasingly more difficult for people to have faith in Christ. P

But I know He's real; and I know that He died for the salvation of a fallen world; and I know that He's going to come to judge it and redeem it; and that between now and then, faith is going to be increasingly more difficult to hold on to. And I hope to do what I can to have people preserve their faith in Him and stop squabbling with our fellow believers. Yeah.

Shawn: In the context of asking that question, Denver, ...that Joseph was the head of that dispensation, you know, where we have to pass through the sentinels, and you got to see him, Brigham Young, and all that. The question is: Can people enter into—and we're going to get to heaven next—but enter into heaven without your approval?

Denver: Yeah. Well, I would hope, yeah. I would *hope*.

Shawn: So would I, but you never know on this day. Some people might say, *No they've got to come through me.* I just want to know.

Denver: Yeah, yeah, that— To me, that's kind of a silly notion.

Shawn: Is it?

Denver: So, I mentioned before, Saint Francis...

Shawn: Yeah.

Denver: ...and that the current pope took the name of Saint Francis, and that endeared him to me. Saint Francis believed in the Sermon on the Mount, and he wanted to start a Catholic order in which they *lived* the Sermon on the Mount. He was initially turned down because the pope didn't think anyone could do that. And so, he went out, and he got a group of followers, and they lived the Sermon on the Mount; and they came back, and he got his order.

When Saint Francis was dying in his final illness in the last weeks of his life, he said angels came and ministered to him, okay? Joseph Smith's older brother Alvin died. As Alvin lay dying, he was talking about the angels that had come into the room and were ministering to him.

Those two illustrations are what I believe happens with the Christian journey and the Christian redemption. There are a lot of people who live very good lives who, in the waning— When they were stoning Stephen (in the Book of Acts), Stephen is standing there in the final moments of his life being brutally slain, and he says, *The heavens opened to me, and I see the Son of man on the right hand of power* [See Acts 4:10 RE]. He beholds the heavens open.

These are the kinds of people that died with a firm expectancy that they have salvation because something occurred before they departed. A lot of people think that that's an event that needs to occur in the life of a Christian soul when they're 14 years old or 12 or 50 years. P

I think for most people, they *do* have that experience, but it's in the waning moments of life, and I think that a lot of people experience that here in order to have the right to inherit it there. And some of that last-minute babbling that you hear from the dying souls or the mentally-impaired that are talking about babblings that sound religious, there's something more going on. And I think God's mercy extends far and wide and is experienced by many, many souls outside of the confines of denominationalism.

Shawn: Totally agreed, and that's a beautiful hopeful thought that you have. *Second Coming.*

Denver: Ooh! An absolutely...

Shawn: That's a thumbs-up?

Denver: Yeah! It's an absolutely firmly predicted, inevitable event. If everything that was said in scripture concerning our Lord and concerning the prophecies that have been and are being fulfilled are true, then, without any doubt, there will be a Second Coming; and Christ will come to take possession of this world that He created—*belongs* to Him!

Shawn: Right!

Denver: He'll reclaim it!

Shawn: Right! *Do you subscribe to the highest degree of the celestial kingdom? Are the three kingdoms part of your theological makeup?*

Denver: I believe in the idea of progression.

Shawn: Okay.

Denver: I believe in the idea of being *added upon.* Yeah. There's a lot more to that story than just— And the idea that you're gonna finish this world; and you're gonna depart; you're gonna arrive somewhere; and that that's where you get to, you know, build your condo on the beach and remain forever...

Have you ever read Mark Twain's short story and act, An Extract from Captain Stormfields Visit to Heaven?

Shawn: I don't believe so.

Denver: It's freakin' hilarious, and it's pretty good.

Shawn: I'll have to read it.

Denver: It's pretty good, yeah!

Shawn: A couple more, and we're done. *Are you a cult leader?* You have to have heard that from somebody.

Denver: Well, it's actually kind of silly when you think about it. Yeah. Look. I say what I say openly. I advocate in favor of faith. I advocate in favor of truth. I don't think that history should be skewed in order to prop up a false proposition. I think that sometimes the study of history is painful and requires you to come to a reckoning about what's going on or what went on. And I don't doubt that you can (if you define the term carefully enough) say that I lead a cult, or that you lead a cult, or that Mormonism is a cult, or that the Roman Catholic Church is a cult. But, in the sense that there's some kind of secretive...

Shawn: Right!

Denver: ...you know, sexually aberrant...

Shawn: Right.

Denver: ...criminally deviant—all of those things usually go with the idea of cultism—no, I try to be as open and as forthright and as forthcoming as I possibly can be.

I do speak very little about the miraculous and the otherworldly because I think it attracts the wrong kind of people. I would rather teach in order to have people have their own experience and to enjoy their own communion with the heaven. And then, they've got it for themselves. They don't need me talking that stuff up. I think talking that stuff up— It really skews people's perception of you, the way they interact with you, and it limits their own growth. *They* need to grow. Everyone needs to become prophets in their own right.

Shawn: Yeah.

Denver: Yeah.

Shawn: One last question with...it tags onto that last one 'cause...and then...thank you for answering it. It's— I *hate* it because you get called a cult leader if you do anything, *anything*! They just... *You're a cult leader!*

But, the question is: Typically and historically, we see that leaders of groups— They fall for gold, glory, or girls. That's, you know— We've seen that historically through almost *every* group, *almost* everyone. They fall for one of those.

And I don't think you're having a problem with the girls, and I don't think you're having a problem with the gold (at least as far as I know), but the *glory* — Are people allowed, that are in your group, to disagree with you and remain loved, and can someone— Like here, we have people who say, *You know, Shawn, you're crazy; I don't believe that.* You say, *So what, stay here.* You have that same approach?

Denver: Yeah! And, in fact, there are a lot of things that go on that I disagree with, and I just hold my tongue. There are things that get discussed that I know if I weigh in, I can get my way, and I think that's bad for me, and I think that's bad for them.

Shawn: Yeah!

Denver: I have a very different view of what Joseph Smith was, and what he accomplished than most ex-Mormons. I think the trajectory of Joseph Smith's life— He died at age 38 and a half. He was still a young man. When you go back to— One of the letters that you'll find in here is the one he wrote from Liberty Jail. You have this priesthood structure, control, hierarchy. You have all of this stuff being constructed in the religious development that Joseph Smith undertook.

Then you have things literally fall all apart at Far West. Three witnesses abandoned him; members of the Quorum of the Twelve abandoned him; members of the Quorum of the Twelve signed affidavits that helped put him in jail. The hierarchy had been decimated by opposition and infighting, and he wound up in jail because of that.

He's in jail, and he's writing a letter, and in his letter, he puts something that completely reverses everything that had gone on before. *No power or influence can or ought to be maintained by virtue of the priesthood, only by gentleness and persuasion and pure knowledge* (See T&C 175:31; 139:6 RE).

Joseph Smith's ark, which tended towards the authoritarianism, began to be dramatically reconsidered during the imprisonment in Liberty Jail. What he wrote in there absolutely eviscerated hierarchical control, and when he gets to Nauvoo, and he gives the talk to the Relief Society in Nauvoo, he says, *You are depending too much upon the prophet, and you are darkened in your minds because you're neglecting the duties that devolve upon yourselves.*

Well, if we're students, and we're careful students of history, and we can see what's going on in downtown Salt Lake right now; and we know that *that's not going to yield* the kind of righteous, self-sufficient, self-confident Christian souls converted to a living faith that would go to their death because in their hearts, they harbor the conviction that what they're doing and what they're living is, in fact, pleasing to God—then you *can't*—you can't take away from people and aggregate to yourself the authority or the control.

The thing I try consciously (and that I've asked my wife, and *she* tries constantly to remind me of) is it is not a virtue or an advantage to be the one in charge. It's a virtue, and it's an advantage to be down laboring alongside and helping lift others. It's an advantage to try and teach and preach in a way that will make them better people for your having been there. And if you've managed to move people along so that *they* can reach a state of harmony that we would call Zion (or City of Peace), and you're not there, but you helped facilitate it, then you've done something for which God will give you what you're due, whatever that may be. You trust Him. You leave it in His hands. But to say, *I need to be the mayor of Zion* is— It's Nauvoo all over again.

Shawn: Sure!

Denver: Joseph Smith's experiment in restoration efforts to try and bring about the kingdom of God (the Lord's Prayer asks that His kingdom return) didn't work! It didn't work.

And the Book of Mormon says *this* land shall not have kings on it. I don't want to be a king. I would love to be a servant in the service of the Lord and to elevate others.

Shawn: I've really enjoyed this. I have a new appreciation for you as a person. And your thoughts—I think they're great. I think they're— If they are what you claim them to be— I always have to have that caveat 'cause I don't know you personally, but in terms of what you've communicated, it's been excellent. And I think you give people hope, and you seem to want to help them to stand on their own two feet, to know the Lord and walk with Him in that way. And I really appreciate you taking the time, all this time, to do this. Thank you for...

Denver: You bet, and yeah, you'll probably figure a lot more out about me in those, particularly the essay books. And let's *not do* this again!

Shawn: All right! [Laughter] We will *not*. But I do have *one* favor: a message for the audience. That's the camera. They really want to see you, what you have to say.

Denver: Yeah. Look, there is absolutely no reason to be afraid of the truth. The truth will not harm whatever you're doing, and that includes what's going on in downtown Salt Lake. It may require that you change the nature of the message. But the truth will not harm you. The more of it that you can deal with...

We tend to think that the opposite of faith is hatred. It's not. The opposite of faith is fear. Fear is what produces a lack of confidence that produces evil and hatred—*fear*.

Stop being afraid of the truth! Christ said the truth shall make you free, and He meant that. It's true. You don't need to carry the burden around of trying to hide or conceal or mislead. Just be forthright, honest. And the fact that you're a weak man— All of the heroes of the Old Testament were weak men.

We don't lose our faith in God because David betrayed one of his generals, ultimately sending him off to be murdered in order to hide his adultery. We don't hide that. Our opinion of David is altered as a consequence, but our faith in God is not; the same of Peter denying the Lord— That is *not* evidence that Peter wasn't commissioned and sent forth with a message. It just meant that he wasn't as strong as he would like to have been, or perhaps that we would like to have seen him be. But none of us are, either.

None of us have ever been strong enough to carry the burden that was necessary for our own redemption. That's what Christ did for us. So, confessing your own inadequacy is simply another way of reminding us that we're all dependent upon the Lord. So be truthful!

Shawn: Praise God! Denver Snuffer, we will see you next week here on Heart of the Matter.

———

The foregoing interview is rebroadcast here with permission from Shawn McCraney, host of the Heart of the Matter YouTube channel.

91. Garments, Part 1

This is part 1 of a series about garments, where Denver discusses temple garments, wedding garments, and other clothing as mentioned in the scriptures.

———

DENVER: Marriage was the first ordinance; it was introduced before the Fall; it was introduced before man was instructed on sacrifice. Go back to the Book of Moses in chapter 4, in verse 27—after they had transgressed, but before they had been sent out of the Garden—we learn in verse 27 of Moses chapter 4: *Unto Adam, and also unto his wife, did I, the Lord God, make coats of skins, and clothed them* (See also Genesis 2:18 RE). Now, it's important that while the account sometimes refers to Adam by meaning both Adam and Eve, in this case, it was necessary for a clarification to be made. The garment that was given unto them to clothe their nakedness is also referred to in the temple as the garment of the Holy Priesthood. And God wants the record to be clear: *Unto Adam, and also unto his wife, did I, the Lord God, make coats of skins, and clothed them.* Therefore, Adam was not clothed and then told, 'You go and do this and clothe your wife;' God clothed them both. God did not expect Adam to intercede when it comes to the clothing of the woman. God treated her as if she too were about to embark upon a journey into mortality that would require her likewise to understand the principle of sacrifice. Because think about it for one moment. You learn (we'll look at this just in a moment), you learn that they practiced sacrifice thereafter, but when were they taught the principle of sacrifice? They were taught at this moment.

There are legends about—and they show up in a variety of ways; they even show up in mythical characters—but there are legends about the animal that was chosen by God to slay and to offer as a sacrifice, in order to clothe them with the skins of an animal. I rather like the theme of many of those. The theme is that when the animals were brought to Adam and Adam named the animals, there were some that he really liked more than others; but there was one particular animal he liked above all the rest. It was that animal, and that animal's consort, who were slain in order to provide the clothing for Adam and Eve; so that Adam and his wife Eve could understand that the principle of sacrifice came at an enormous price. And so the animal was no longer able to exist in this sphere, having been used originally while yet in the Garden to provide the coats, and to drive home the point about the sacrifice that's required in order to clothe the nakedness of the man and the woman. [I'm thinking in a room this warm some of you might envy the nakedness of Adam and Eve. I'm hoping that you refrain though.]

So, if you turn over to Moses chapter 5, beginning at verse 5—this is talking about after they had been expelled from the Garden—it says:

> *He gave unto them commandments that they should worship the Lord their God and should offer the firstlings of their flocks for an offering unto the Lord, and Adam was obedient unto the commandments of the Lord. And after many days an angel of the Lord appeared unto Adam saying. Why doest thou offer sacrifices unto the Lord? And Adam said unto him, I know not save the Lord commanded me. Then the angel spake saying, this thing is a similitude of the sacrifice of the Only Begotten of the Father which is full of grace and truth.* (See also Genesis 3:2-3 RE)

So, that sacrifice that was performed that brought such sadness in verse 27 of chapter 4, that occurred before they were driven out of the Garden, was simply a commandment to do, which Adam and Eve then did. And it was some time later, *many days* later—and *many days* is not defined. It appears to me, from the context as we go further, that *many days* in this context means "many years." In fact, it means more than "many years;" it means "many generations." There were many generations of men alive on the earth while Adam and Eve were there before the explanation of why they were offering sacrifice is finally given to them. And you're impatient. And you want to know more, and you want to know it now. And you don't think that God tries the patience of all those to whom He will eventually come.

So, reading between the lines of the Old Testament (because the record doesn't make it clear), we can assume that the garment that was given to Adam in the beginning was handed down through each of those, just like the records were handed down through each of those; and it was that garment that came into the possession of Joseph that the jealous brothers took and destroyed—well, damaged; a remnant of it remained—all of which proved to be an allegory to what history would show about that family.

We don't know if, at the time of destroying the relic of the garment, they destroyed the relic of the records of the fathers, because the record is silent about that. But it's pretty clear that if they couldn't share in the prize, if they couldn't share in the artifact, if they couldn't share (and from their perspective, this is probably the correct way to categorize it) in the talisman—

See, when Abraham received the records of the fathers, he got it from his father, who was an idolater. He regarded those records as nothing more than a talisman, a good luck charm. Abraham regarded it as something different, and he worshipped the God of Heaven, and through them he connected to the God of Heaven. Well, the brothers who were jealous of this passing down of a relic, that's more "talisman" than "meaningful source of inspiration and knowledge about God," may well have destroyed it. They may have copied it. There may have been other versions of it that were made available, or parts of it, if they were interested in it; but I think the original of that may, just like the garment that was given to Adam, have been destroyed at that point.

We're reading in the Joseph Smith Testimony [History], look at the next verse: *While I was thus **in the act** of calling upon God... . In the act of calling upon God!* If you're in the right way, with the right faith, looking for the right answers, you don't even get to finish the sentence. God knows what ye have need of even before you ask. It's in the Sermon on the Mount. Christ tells you that. That horrible aching, that longing, that hollowness, that emptiness within you—is what Christ was designed to fill; that's His purpose in coming to His temple.

So while he was *in the act of calling upon God, [he] discovered a light appearing in [his] room, which continued to increase until the room was lighter than at noonday, when immediately a personage appeared at my bedside, standing in the air, for his feet did not touch the [ground]* (JS-H 1:30; see also JSH 3:2 RE). As an interesting aside, I want to ask the question: Why? Why did Moroni stand in the air, his feet not touching the ground? It's an interesting topic we're not going to talk about here. It's off subject; it won't get us Zion anyway, but there's stuff here.

Oh, and look at this:

> *He had on a loose robe of most exquisite whiteness. It was a whiteness beyond anything earthly I had ever seen; nor do I believe that any earthly thing could be made to appear so exceedingly white and brilliant. His hands were naked, ...his arms also, a little above the wrist; so, also, were his feet naked, as were his legs, a little above the ankles. His head and neck were also bare. I could discover that he had no other clothing on but this robe, ...it was open, so that I could see into his bosom.* (Ibid.)

Notice this. This is not ceremonial garb; as a consequence of which I can tell you that it's okay to be buried without temple regalia; because you're not going to be wearing that stuff in the resurrection anyway, if you inherit what the angels of God, including Moroni—who is certainly exalted—wear.

You can read about the description of what Christ wears in the scriptures, as well. Ceremonial garb is just that—it is ceremonial garb. It is designed to teach you about the creation, to endow you with certain knowledge about the process of being exalted; but it is not the attire that you'll see on the streets of heaven. I actually think—I think they look Egyptian. I think their attire looks Egyptian, but that's neither here nor there.

This is a guy who was wearing only a robe. It's not ceremonial. He doesn't have shoes on his feet. He doesn't have a bonnet on. He doesn't have a variety of things that we would associate with ceremonial dress. You can read a description of Christ's attire in Third Nephi, chapter 11, verse 8. And the description there is very much like the description that we have here—Christ and Moroni wearing the same kind of thing. And then, hey, just for the fun of it, let's go back to Exodus 28.

Exodus 28. (I want to revert back to my Cecil B. Demille-esque stuff):

> And these are the garments which they shall make; a breastplate, and an ephod, and a robe, and a broidered coat, a mitre, and a girdle: and they shall make holy garments for Aaron thy brother, and his sons, that he may minister unto me in the priest's office. And they shall take gold, and blue, and purple, and scarlet, and fine linen... (Exodus 28: 4-5; see also Exodus 15:1 RE)

...and yellow and green and purple and orange and mauve and...I'm sorry. You can read it; it's in here. Ooh, *the ouches of gold and the chains of pure gold* (at the end) *of wreathen work*...(ibid, vs. 13-14; para. 4). I mean, he dresses you in funny attire, okay? God goes through the ceremonial attire, and he dresses you up, and the purpose of the dress is ceremonial to communicate to you, through symbolism, knowledge about certain things. But they are not an end; they are a symbol. Six days of creation: six articles of clothing, each one of which can be associated with one of the days of creation. Therefore, as you enter through the veil, it is as if the entirety of all creation is redeemed in your person. You represent salvation for the entirety of creation, because in you, should you be able to be rescued, creation itself continues. These are symbols. They communicate to the mind ideas—ideas that are eternal. They are not ends in themselves.

Well, keep that in mind, because you're here to be trained. You're here to learn something. You're here to learn about the power of godliness. And by "here," I don't mean this room tonight, although I think that is certainly true. I'm talking about this lifetime in which you find yourself—this place, this terrible fallen world, this glorious opportunity in which sacrifice is actually possible. You don't avoid it, and you don't necessarily seek it out. But when it comes upon you, you face it down bravely. And you stand where God places you. And you don't let any man move you from where it is that God would have you be, because therein lies salvation. You're obeying a law ordained before the foundation of the world. You can't lay hold upon such blessings unless you obey the law upon which it is predicated. There will always be, in absolute numbers, only a few who will find that straight and narrow path. There will be an overflowing abundance of those who will fight against it, because they serve their master. You don't have time to worry about them. You serve yours. And that Master needs to be Christ.

In D&C 45, verse 16, let's look at that one. He says:

> *...I will show it plainly, as I showed it unto my disciples as He stood* [This is verse 16 of D&C 45, I'm sorry; verse 16.] *I will show it plainly as I showed it unto my disciples as I stood before them in the flesh, and spake unto them, saying: As ye have asked of me concerning the signs of my coming, in the day when I shall come in my glory in the clouds of heaven, to fulfil the promises that I have made unto your fathers.* (See also T&C 31:4)

This is a description of how He intends to return.

Go to D&C 49, beginning at verse 22 He says:

> *Verily I say unto you the Son of Man cometh not in the form of a woman, neither a man traveling on the earth. Wherefore, be not deceived, but continue in steadfastness, looking forth for the heavens to be shaken, and the earth to tremble and reel to and fro as a drunken man, for the valleys to be exalted, and for the mountains to be made low, and for the rough places to become smooth—and all this when the angel shall sound his trump.* (See also T&C 35:7)

This is how He intends to come. He may send people who are messengers. He may send people who have things to say from Him, but when He returns He's going to return in glory.

Section 133, if you go there and you read, beginning at 46:

> And it shall be said: Who is this that cometh down from God in heaven
> with dyed garments; yea, from the regions which are not known, clothed
> in his glorious apparel, traveling in the greatness of his strength? And he
> shall say: I am he who spake in righteousness, mighty to save. And the
> Lord shall be red in his apparel, and his garments like him that treadeth
> in the wine–vat. (See also T&C 58:6)

I just add parenthetically that His apparel is red. Period. Period. He will be
clothed in red. And if someone offers you a vision in which they vary from
this, I'll add my voice to Joseph's and bare testimony that when He appears
His apparel—apparel, will be red.

Now I want to refer to a verse, and refer to this verse in the context of the
temple. Apply these words solely and exclusively for a moment to the temple:
Do not expect to eat the bread or wear the garment of the laborer in Zion. If
you oppose the work, if you stay your hand, if you refuse, and others do the
labor, don't expect to eat the bread or wear the garment. (D&C 42:42; see
also T&C 26:12)

Now here's a sober moment that I want to remind you about, which need not
continue. Go to Ether, chapter 12. This is Moroni as he's completing the
translation of the record that his father said would be included within his
father's book, the Book of Mormon, but his father did not translate. So,
Moroni translated it and included it within the Book of Mormon. And as he's
wrapping up his translation he includes a dialogue. It's a very sobering
dialogue in Ether, chapter 12, beginning at verse 36:

> And it came to pass that I prayed [this is I, Moroni, the translator. This
> isn't Ether. This is Moroni's interlude.] I prayed unto the Lord that he
> would give unto the Gentiles grace, that they might have charity. And it
> came to pass the Lord said unto me: If they have not charity it mattereth
> not unto thee, thou hast been faithful; wherefore, thy garments shall be
> made clean. And because thou hast seen thy weakness thou shalt be made
> strong, even unto the sitting down in the place which I have prepared in
> the mansions of my Father. And now I, Moroni, bid farewell unto the
> Gentiles. (Ether 12:36-38; see also Ether 5:7-8 RE)

Did you see what just happened? Moroni begged the Lord to give unto the
Gentiles grace. And the Lord says, 'It doesn't matter to you.' He did not give
Moroni what he asked for! He did not promise the Gentiles would receive

grace! The Lord could not do that, because it would abrogate both the law (grace for grace), and our agency, because we are free to choose. Therefore, the Gentiles inherited the Restoration with no promise from Christ to Moroni that those who would receive this record would be given the grace of God. That is dependent upon you.

> *Now I, Moroni, bid farewell unto the Gentiles, yea, and also unto my brethren whom I love, until we shall meet before the judgment–seat of Christ, where all men shall know that my garments are not spotted with your blood. And then shall ye know that I have seen Jesus, and that he hath talked with me face to face, and that he told me in plain humility, even as a man telleth another in mine own language, concerning these things.* (ibid, vs. 39)

This is that Lord who, when you pass through the thunderings and lightnings, you'll speak with. He talks in plain humility. It is not His position to cause fear in your heart, but to bring to you comfort. His purpose is not to leave you comfortless, but to come and comfort you. It's you that presents the barrier. It's you that presents the fear. And that rightly so, because we ought to fear. And what we should fear is our own weakness and our own sins, because our greatest sin is our ignorance.

> *And only a few have I written, because of my weakness in writing. And now, I would commend you* [this is Moroni commending you, the Gentiles, who are going to receive this book] *I would commend you to seek this Jesus of whom the prophets and apostles have written, that the grace of God the Father, and also the Lord Jesus Christ, and the Holy Ghost, which beareth record of them, may be and abide in you forever.* (ibid, vs. 40-41)

He asked for grace to be given. God cannot give it. Then he turns and he says, 'You Gentiles, please, seek for His grace; it cannot otherwise be given you.' The Book of Mormon's assessment of us is sober indeed, and the arrogance with which we read that book blinds us to our predicament in which we find ourselves.

The plea: seek for grace. It is through grace that we obtain charity. It is through charity we are able to bless others. Because the fact of the matter is you can't bless anyone, or hold that priesthood that is primarily designed to administer blessings and not cursings, unless you have charity for others; unless you are willing to do things you would rather not do; unless you are willing to subordinate your will to the will of the Father. Because it is the purpose of the Father to bless all of His offspring. Therefore, it is only through grace you acquire what you need to be of use to God the Father and his Son, Jesus Christ.

So when Christ begins his planting He's actually a restorer of an earlier religion. Instead of this being something altogether revolutionary and new, Christ was a restorer. He was an antiquarian. He was bringing back something which once had been. He was trying to get people to understand. See, the religion that Moses was trying to restore was originally significantly greater than the one that he wound up restoring because the people were unwilling to accept the earlier version so those things were broken, destroyed, discarded, and a new innovation was established through Moses, the great law giver, who gave a law of lesser performances, observances, rites in order to point forward to something else that would be coming so that maybe when that something else, when it came, could explain to them what the law was intended to have them observe. The paschal lamb that occurs where the blood on the lentil and the door post saves you from the destroying angel is a type of Christ because Christ's blood will save you from destruction. The rites involving the shedding of blood in the courtyard, of either the tabernacle or later the temple, was designed to be a propitiation, a form of paying the debt for sin. The wages of sin are death. Therefore, it's necessary that death be demonstrated through the sacrifice of animals in order to have your mind pointed forward to some great sacrifice whose effect will be saving you from sin. In the courtyard, of either the tabernacle or in the temple, when you sacrifice animals and you spill their blood by cutting the neck and letting the blood flow out, blood gets all over the ground; it gets tracked; it gets splashed; it gets upon you. And prophets use this analogy of blood and sins, and blood on your garments, and shaking the blood off of your garments as an analogy that's based upon the effect of performing the law of Moses, which itself is intended to point you to Christ. And Christ demonstrated, by His teachings and actions, that He fully understood that was what was happening, and that was who He was and what His role was. When Christ knelt to wash the feet of the disciples, one of the things that washing feet in that culture accomplished was cleansing the blood off the feet, that was tracked everywhere when you got near the courtyards of the temple, in order to show that they were unaccountable for sin. He was removing from them the guilt that the blood was intended to exhibit.

Question: This is decidedly limited in what is appropriate to be said, but the question is about: Since Christ came to fulfill the law, and the practice of animal sacrifice was done away with, and what we're to offer is a broken heart and a contrite spirit as a sacrifice, and animal sacrifice was a type to teach the people of the coming Messiah—He fulfilled that. Why would animal sacrifice be reinstated?

Answer: OK, as—I don't want to get out ahead of where we are at this point, but let me say, it will be done for entirely appropriate purposes that will be perfectly satisfactory to the understanding of those that are involved. It's not gonna be some kind of temple-turned- slaughterhouse. It's not gonna be a production line in which the hems of your garments, and the blood shaking from the hems of your garment, becomes a cliché because of the abundance of the flowing of blood in the courtyards of the temple of Solomon and later the temple of Herod. It will be decidedly confined, limited, for purposes that will be adequately understood by those who, on the rare occasions when that practice is reinstated, participate, witness. But I think that's all that can be said. You won't be disappointed.

The Gospel is delicious. Get rid of that stale, wretched stuff that you consume and go on to find the Life, the Light, and the vigor that is contained in the words that we have in scripture. This stuff is delicious. If you'll partake of it and prepare yourself, you can improve this estate in a way that will reflect credit in the next estate. Don't forfeit the opportunity.

Thus they become high priests forever. They become high priests forever. They had it before the foundation of the world. They come here, they have authority here, and that authority began there and it will continue into the next life. Therefore, they can bless, and you're blessed indeed.

> *Thus they become high priests forever, after the order of the Son, the Only Begotten of the Father, who is without beginning of days or end of years, who is full of grace, equity, and truth. And thus it is. Amen. Now, as I said concerning the holy order, or this high priesthood, there were many who were ordained and became high priests of God; and it was on account of their exceeding faith and repentance, and their righteousness before God, they choosing to repent and work righteousness rather than to perish; Therefore they were called after this holy order, and were sanctified, and their garments were washed white through the blood of the Lamb.* (Alma 13:9-10; see also Alma 9:10 RE)

You say you want to be baptized and to be cleansed from all sin? I say have at it! But in addition, this prototype of the saved man requires that you do something in addition. You may only achieve a limited amount of grace in this life, but that limited amount of grace you must hold fast to. You cannot receive more if you will not receive what's offered now. And if you will receive what's offered now, you'll be added upon.

None of us is spared from mutual failure. We are not Zion. We will never be Zion if we do not repent. All of us must repent, turn to face God with full purpose of heart, acting no hypocrisy, or we will not establish godly peace among us.

The "Answer to the Prayer for Covenant" and the Covenant are the beginning blueprint. That blueprint teaches the need to be better people. Following it is more challenging than reciting it. No one can learn what is required without doing. Working together is the only way a society can grow together. No isolated spiritual mystic is going to be prepared for Zion through his solitary personal devotions. Personal devotion is necessary, of course, but the most pious hermit will collide with the next pious hermit when they're required to share and work together in a society of equals having all things in common. Do not pretend it will be otherwise. Failing to do the hard work outlined in the Covenant is failing to prepare for Zion. It's failing to have oil in the lamp. It's failing to put upon you the wedding garment.

If you think you are one of the five virgins who will be invited in when the bridegroom arrives and have never attempted to obey the Lord's commandments, you will find yourself left outside when the door is shut. If you come from the highways and byways without a wedding garment because you failed to keep the covenant, you'll be excluded.

There is work to be done. Almost all of it is internal to us. The five prepared virgins and the strangers who brought a wedding garment will be those who keep the Covenant. It is designed to give birth to a new society, new culture, and permit a new civilization to be founded.

———

The foregoing excerpts are taken from:

- Denver's 40 Years in Mormonism Series, Talk #9 titled "Marriage and Family" given in St. George, UT on July 26th, 2014
- The Denver Snuffer Podcast, episode 60 titled "The Third Root," released March 10, 2019
- Denver's 40 Years in Mormonism Series, Talk #1 titled "Be of Good Cheer" given in Boise, ID on September 10th, 2013

- Denver's 40 Years in Mormonism Series, Talk #7 titled "Christ, Prototype of the Saved Man" given in Ephraim, UT on June 28, 2014
- Denver's conference talk titled "Things to Keep Us Awake at Night" given in St. George, UT on March 19th, 2017
- Denver's 40 Years in Mormonism Series, Talk #8 titled "A Broken Heart" given in Las Vegas, NV on July 25th, 2014
- Denver's Christian Reformation Lecture Series, Talk #4 given in Sandy, Utah on September 7, 2018
- Denver's conference talk titled "Civilization", given in Grand Junction, CO on April 21, 2019; and
- The Q&A Session following that talk on the same day.

92. Garments, Part 2

This is part 2 of a series about garments, where Denver discusses temple garments, wedding garments, and other clothing as mentioned in the scriptures.

––––––

DENVER: One of the things that I was reminded about this week by a friend (I coined it, but he suggested the idea) is that it's important that you not get the misimpression that before you wind up in the presence of the Lord, *you* have the responsibility of making yourself absolutely spick-and-span. In terms of connecting with the Lord, it is essentially a come-as-you-are party because you're never going to be able to do the heavy lifting required to be clean in His presence. He does that; you don't. He extends the invitation; you accept it. It's a come-as-you-are party.

There are two parables that the Lord told that I want to put together to help illustrate the point. One of them is in Matthew chapter 22 (see also Matthew 10:17-19 RE). It's a parable about a wedding feast. And the Lord, in that parable, talks about how the folks that were invited wouldn't show up. And because the folks that were invited would not show up, an invitation was extended, essentially, to whoever was out on the streets. And the folks that were out on the streets were brought in. Begin at verse 8 of chapter 22: *Then saith he to his servants, The wedding is ready, but they which were bidden were not worthy* (Matthew 8:22; see also Matthew 10:18 RE).

You know, he's telling a story, largely about a condition that persists whenever you find a religious organization functioning, because institutions have a way of having their own cares. Joseph Smith was a disastrous businessman. He created financial debacle after financial debacle. The most notorious one was the failure of the Kirtland Safety Society Anti-Banking Group—*Anti*, because they couldn't get the bank charter. But if you file for bankruptcy in the state of Utah, one of the things that they do at the discharge hearing—in order to help people feel better about themselves—is they remind people that at the time of his death, Joseph Smith had a pending petition in bankruptcy. And that is supposed to salve the conscience of those who find themselves in that extremity.

The fact is that Joseph was not a particularly good businessman because he didn't care for business. He wound up giving away his inventory to the needy folks, rather than trying to profit off of the needs of the Saints. There was some exasperation about that. Well, we fixed that. We have, managing the church and attending to the financial interests of the kingdom (as we call it now), those that are more than qualified financially. I suspect a profligate like Joseph Smith would be unsuitable for management today. But in any event, the parable starts with the Lord, who's trying to get people to come to the wedding, telling the servants the wedding's ready but those that I've asked are not worthy:

> *Go...into the highways, and as many as ye shall find, bid [them] to the marriage. So those servants went out into the highways* [always the servants, always angels do this work; they do the gathering], *and gathered together all as many as they found, both bad and good: and the wedding was furnished with guests. ...when the king came in to see the guests, he saw there [was] a man which had not...a wedding garment...Saith unto him, Friend, how camest thou...hither not having a wedding garment?...He was speechless...The king [said], Bind him hand and foot...take him away...cast him into outer darkness. There shall be weeping [and wailing] and gnashing of teeth.* (Matthew 22:9-13; see also Matthew 10:18-19 RE)

So, I won't put that on the table, because in this part of this parable you have anyone who will come being invited, because the people that were targeted for attendance simply aren't worthy to come. So anyone gets to come. And now you have among them someone who doesn't have on a wedding garment. And for that I want to refer you to Luke chapter 15, because in Luke chapter 15 we run into the Lord talking about a robe being supplied. This is the son who found himself, having been in a far-off land, filling *his belly with the husks that the swine did eat...no man gave unto him.* He comes to himself, says: *How many hired servants of my father's have bread enough and to spare, and I perish with hunger?* So when he goes back to see his father, look at what happens in verse 22 of Luke chapter 15: *But the father said to his servants* [again, it's the angels that do this], *Bring forth the best robe and put it on him; ...put a ring on his hand, and shoes on his feet* (Luke 15:16,17,22; see also Luke 9:13-14 RE).

You see, this, I think, has to be kept in mind whenever you're looking at someone who's arrived at the feast, bidden from the highway, who arrives and doesn't have on the robe. The Master is the one that wants you to wear it. The Master is the one that will furnish it. Don't think that the purpose of the Lord is to judge. The purpose of the Lord is to redeem, and for that purpose He is infinitely patient and willing, if you will respond, with forgiveness of your sins, as He does consistently throughout the Book of Mormon.

If we are going to begin again, it must be in conformity with the Doctrine of Christ; it must be taught by the spirit of truth, and it must follow the pattern that was given in Kirtland for us to follow.

Now, having said all that, let me read to you some things which the Lord said concerning *this* moment, because He's talking about an event that will happen. This is from Matthew chapter 22, beginning at verse 2:

> *The kingdom of heaven is like unto a certain king, which made a marriage for his son, And sent forth his servants to call them that were bidden to the wedding; and they would not come. Again, he sent forth other servants, saying, Tell them which are bidden, Behold, I have prepared my dinner: my oxen and my fatlings are killed, and all things are ready: come unto the marriage. But they made light of it, and went their ways, one to his farm, another to his merchandise. And the remnant took his servants, and entreated them spitefully, and slew them. But when the king heard thereof, he was wroth: and he sent forth his armies, and destroyed those murderers, and burned up their city. Then saith he to his servants, The wedding is ready, but they which were bidden were not worthy. Go...therefore into the highways, and as many as ye shall find, bid to the marriage. So [the] servants went out into the highways and gathered together all as many as they found, both bad and good: and the wedding was furnished with guests. And when the king came in to see the guests, he saw there a man which had not on a wedding garment: And he saith unto him, Friend, how camest thou in hither not having a wedding garment? And he was speechless. Then said the king to the servants, Bind him hand and foot, and take him away, and cast him into outer darkness; there shall be weeping and gnashing of teeth. For many are called, but few are chosen.* (see also Matthew 10:17-19 RE)

Now, several things about this: This is one of those places in scripture in which "remnant" is used in a negative way. A remnant. God invites *all* to come to the wedding feast of his Son. This is when the kingdom is going to be established in the last days. He invites all to come. And from among all of those people who had been invited, there's a remnant of those who still hold onto the Restoration, and they are the worst of all. They have the hardest hearts. They are the ones who will not come.

And after the Lord deals with them, then He goes out and invites *everyone* to come. Everyone! Come in! And included among those that are invited in, are *as many as they found, both bad and good* (ibid). They're all invited to come in, and there's no excluding the bad—speaking after the judgments of this world.

Bad people get invited in and when they come, and when they arrive, it's not whether they're a bad person or a good person that determines whether they get to stay or not. It's the presence or absence of a wedding garment.

Well, turn to Luke chapter 18. This is Luke chapter 18, beginning at verse 10:

> *Two men went up into the temple to pray; the one a Pharisee, the other a publican. The Pharisee stood and prayed thus with himself, God, I thank thee, that I am not as other men are, extortioners, unjust, adulterers, or even as this publican. I fast twice in the week, I give tithes of all that I possess. And the publican, standing afar off, would not lift up so much as his eyes unto Heaven, but smote upon his breast, saying, God be merciful to me a sinner. I tell you, this man went down to his house justified rather than the other: for everyone that exalteth himself shall be abased; and he that humbleth himself shall be exalted.* (Luke 18:10-14; see also Luke 10:7 RE)

Didn't matter that he was a "bad man." Didn't matter that the other was a "good man." I tell you at the wedding feast, it would be the publican who wore the "wedding garment." The first wedding garment—if you want to call it that—is the original garment that was given to Adam and Eve in the Garden to cover their nakedness, and to cover their shame before God. All of which is an allegory.

The covering required the sacrifice of an animal to teach them the principle of sacrifice, and to foreshadow the death of our Lord that would be required in order to restore us back to a state before God. And so, what the covering given to Adam and Eve in the Garden represented was the sacrifice of our Lord. It was our Lord's atoning sacrifice which makes it possible for us to be covered, so that our shame is no longer there. Instead, God looks upon the righteousness of His Son, who has clothed us; and not upon our own guilt, and our own weakness, and our own shortcomings. He beholds the image of His Son in the garment that we have put on.

And so it is, that in the wedding feast to which people are invited, the first who got invited would not come. But even the "bad ones"—even the "bad ones" who are out in the byways, even the ones... There's about 13 million inactive Latter-day Saints. There's a lot of "bad ones" out there, who are only kept from the truth because they haven't heard it yet.

If I had the means, I'd buy an ad space in the *Los Angeles Times* and I'd say: "Here's the Doctrine of Christ," and I would quote 3rd Nephi. And I would say afterwards: "If you believe this doctrine and you want to be baptized and get the Holy Ghost, meet me at…," and I would put a location; and I would hope that included among those who came would be gang members—inner-city people who live lives of desperation and violence—who want a way out. Can you imagine what would happen if you sent someone back into an abusive neighborhood, clothed with the power of repentance and the Holy Ghost?

We can't fix this world by legislating, but we can fix *anything* by changing hearts. Those that are invited will not come. They'll even abuse those who try to take them in. But there are plenty of folks in the byways who are only kept from the truth because they don't know where to find it. This is your responsibility. This is your work to do. This is the day in which these things need to be done.

Oddly enough, in our own day—in our own day—the Lord tells a slightly different version of exactly the same stuff, prophesying how it's going to happen among *us* in our day.

Go to Doctrine and Covenants section 58. This is talking about—well, I'm going to begin at verse 7: *And also that you might be honored in laying the foundation and in bearing record of the land upon which the Zion of God shall stand* (see also T&C 45:2 RE).

I am going to put this into some footnotes when I finally get around to publishing in a book form the talk that was given in Grand Junction. But I'll stick it in here because we've touched on the words, *the land upon which the Zion of God shall stand* (ibid). I pointed out there all of the historical reasons why Zion could exist somewhere other than in property owned in Jackson County, Missouri, and could, in fact, be constructed elsewhere.

Joseph Smith and Sidney Rigdon, in their first trip out to Jackson County, Missouri, came there in order to confirm and ratify that this was the place where Zion would be built, and they got language and revelation that said this was "the land of Zion." And so everyone since then till now, are all relying upon that language saying, "it's going to be Jackson County, Missouri." That same month that Joseph and Sidney went out, Sidney Rigdon gave an explanation of what the geography of that "land of Zion" was. He said it began at Kirtland, Ohio, and it ran to the Pacific Ocean. So the land of Zion is rather flexible in where the Lord might choose ultimately to locate it.

So there's going to be some land where Zion will stand. *And also, that a feast of fat things might be prepared for the poor* (ibid, vs. 8). So the feast—the feast that is being prepared—has a highly specific audience in mind in the revelation. It's the poor.

> *Yea, a feast of fat things, of wine on the lees well refined, that the earth may know that the mouths of the prophets shall not fail; yea, a supper of the House of the Lord, well prepared, unto which all nations shall be invited. First, the rich and the learned, the wise and the noble; And after that cometh the day of my power; then shall the poor, the lame, and the blind, and the deaf, come in unto the marriage of the Lamb, and partake of the supper of the Lord, prepared for the great day to come. Behold, I, the Lord, have spoken it.* (ibid, vs. 8-12)

Did you get that? First they invite "the rich," and then "the learned;" and the nations shall all be invited—"the wise, the noble." Doesn't say they enter in. Doesn't say they'll partake. It was prepared, after all, for "the poor"—and the people who will enter in—who do finally make it into Zion where they get to partake. *Then shall the poor* [that's who it was prepared for] *the lame, the blind, and the deaf, come in unto the marriage of the Lamb, and partake of the supper of the Lord, prepared for the great day to come* (ibid).

Every time you partake of the Sacrament, it's a reminder of the promise that there will, at last, be some great wedding feast. It's not just in remembrance of the blood and of the body, but it's also a preliminary to the final feast that the Lord intends to offer.

Well, who are "the rich"? Who are "the learned"? Who are those that are presently considered "wise"? And who are those who make the claim that they are "the noble, the elect"? They do not enter into the wedding feast in Zion.

And who is it that is "the poor"? Who is it that is derided, even in today's vocabulary, and accused of being "lame"? Who is it that is considered to be "blind" and "misled"? Who is it that is referred to as being "deaf," because they cannot hear and respect all the great wisdom that pours forth from these empty cisterns, having nothing but drivel to offer? Quoting one another endlessly, as if one misled man on a false path can offer light to a fool following after him.

I hope we are "the poor." I hope I am speaking to "the lame." I hope you are counted among those that are considered "blind," and I hope that you have ears not for what any man has to say, but for what the Spirit alone has to confirm to you. I hope you're "deaf" to everything in this world, but have ears for what our Lord has to say.

This is the day in which, at long last, it is possible for what God intended to happen before His return, to actually begin. The Gospel is not supposed to be merely a record of how God dealt with other people at another time. Joseph Smith talked about how we can't read the words of an old book, and then apply those words in an old book—that were meant for someone else at some other time—to us; and then restore ourselves back to God's grace. That is just as true of the revelations given in the days of Joseph Smith, as it is true of the revelations given in the New Testament.

It becomes really apparent when you read them out of the scriptures, because all our footnotes, and all of our chapter headings, and all our cross referencing —it sort of gives you an impression that this stuff is talking about *us*. Right here. Right now. When you read them as they were written in *the Joseph Smith Papers*, it really becomes clear that when God is talking about how the church is "living" and "alive" and "approved," it's because He's talking to Joseph Smith. And the church is listening to what Joseph Smith had to say. And "rolling forth" is the voice of God in *that* day. And Joseph Smith commissioned people to go out and to take it; and they took it, and they went out and preached it; and when they preached it, others were converted. And the people that were converted actually had experiences and came to know God. But that's because God acted to set it in motion in the person of Joseph Smith. Joseph had a covenant given to him by God. Therefore, Joseph could testify to these words, and they were true, and God owned them; and people who follow them received the wages of those who follow God. It worked! We can't mimic that and have the same effect.

God has to say: "This is what I want to do." And if no one else will say it to you, I'm saying it to you. Everything that has been said in this talk—which began in Boise and concludes here today—everything that has been said is, in fact, exactly what happened when God offered something through Joseph. He's offering something again, right now, in our day, to you, to any that will hear, to any that will listen. The work is beginning again.

I suppose it was necessary that what began in Joseph's time had to run down to the condition that it's in at present. That it had to become a leaky ruin of a farm, that Joseph himself no longer even wanted, before it was possible for the Lord to say, "At this moment we turn a new leaf." But my word, can't you see the signs of the times? Can't you look about and see that the whole world is waxing old like a garment? Can't you see that there is, right now, a balance of things that are kept at bay only to preserve the possibility that a remnant might be claimed? God promised He would do this.

Well, all things testify of what is currently getting, at last, underway. And make no mistake about it, it *is* getting underway. And I don't care where you look; I don't care what society you look at; I don't care what economy you observe, what culture you observe—the earth and all of the people on her are waxing old like a garment. And do you know what they do with garments that are old? They're burned. The way to preserve yourself consists in having faith in God. And the conditions upon which faith in God is obtained are exactly the same for you as they were for Moses, and Abraham, and all of those who have ever had faith; Joseph Smith being the latest, great example of that.

––––––

The foregoing excerpts are taken from:

- Denver's *40 Years in Mormonism Series*, Talk #2 titled "Faith" given in Idaho Falls, ID on September 28th, 2013; and
- Denver's *40 Years in Mormonism Series*, Talk #10 titled "Preserving the Restoration" given in Mesa, AZ on September 9th, 2014

Today's podcast addresses important questions about garments, but is only an introduction to ideas that listeners of any denomination may find important and relevant. These topics are more fully addressed in Denver's blog, including but not limited to these entries:

1 Nephi 14:3-4, posted July 6, 2010
"This" and "that", posted January 5, 2019

93. Meekness and Humility, Part 1

This is the first part of a series on "Meekness and Humility," which is intended to go deeper than mere words and definitions. The hope is to give you the chance to get a feel for the underlying state-of-being associated with meekness and humility, so you can resonate with these attributes and bring them into your life. We encourage you to pause and ponder on any examples of meekness and humility that come to mind as you listen, including nature, scriptures, and/or examples from your own life. We hope these episodes are meaningful and relevant to everyone's hope and desire for Zion.

———

DENVER: Meekness is a difficult attribute to recognize. It's found in the relationship between man and God, not between man and man. To be meek is to follow the Lord's will, even when one doesn't want to do so, even when it brings one into conflict with friends, family, or community. Meekness is measured as between the servant and the Lord, not as between the servant and his critics. Meekness, among other things, involves a conscious effort to avoid harming or offending others. It requires an absence of pride or self-will. It is *not* insistent upon being recognized or applauded. It denotes a willingness to suffer without complaint.

Others may never recognize the meek because meekness does not vaunt itself nor demand notice. There's great freedom in meekness; it relieves the meek from the burden of seeking their acclaim. It gives them the security of feeling God's approval for the course of their living. It's private.

Meekness means a person voluntarily restrains himself and uses the absolute minimum control or authority over others. It is related to humility. Humility is voluntarily submitting to the control or power of God—in other words, obedience. Meekness affects a person's relationship with his fellow man. There's nothing showy or attention-grabbing about the meek; instead, they are content to know they have a relationship and power with God. Unless God requires something to be done or revealed, the meek do not voluntarily put this authority on display.

Our Lord was, and is meek. When He said, "I am more intelligent than them all" (see Abraham 3:19; see also T&C 145, Abraham 5:4 RE), when He said, I am "the greatest of all" (see D&C 50:25-27; see also T&C 36:5 RE), there wasn't one whit of arrogance in His announcement of that. What He was saying is, "*Please*, have confidence in me. *Please*, trust what I say to be true. *Please*, recognize I've paid a price in order to be able to minister."

Christ— In Luke chapter 9, beginning at verse 27, Christ prophesies: *But I tell you of a truth, there be some standing here, which shall not taste of death, till they see the kingdom of God* (Luke 9:27; see also Luke 7:4 RE). That's the latter-day kingdom. That's the one that Christ said was not of this world, but He's going to come and inherit at the end. So, He says, "Some of you who are alive today will not die until you see Zion." The gymnastics that have gone into trying to explain that, by both Christian—both Catholic and even Mormon commentators—is rather amusing. Keep reading though:

> *And it came to pass about an eight days after these sayings, he took Peter and John and James, and went up into a mountain to pray. And as he prayed, the fashion of his countenance was altered, and his raiment was white and [glistening]. And, behold, there talked with him two men, which were Moses and Elias: Who appeared in glory, and spake of his decease which he should accomplish at Jerusalem.* (Luke 9:28-31; see also Luke 7:5 RE)

So, He says some are living; they're not going to die until they see the Kingdom of Heaven. And then He takes those three up on the Mount and they see some things. Turn to Doctrine and Covenants section 63, beginning —and He's talking about Zion—beginning at verse 20 of section 63:

> *Nevertheless, he that endureth in faith and doeth my will, the same shall overcome, and shall receive an inheritance upon the earth when the day of transfiguration shall come; When the earth shall be transfigured, even according to the pattern which was shown unto mine apostles upon the mount; of which account the fulness ye have not yet received.* (D&C 63:20-21; see also T&C 50:5 RE)

He promised them that they would get to see the latter-day triumph. He took three of them up on the mount and then He showed them the latter-day triumph. Therefore, there were those that were standing in that generation who did not die until they had seen the latter-day triumph of the Kingdom of God. He fulfilled His own word, and it was put into the gospel in that fashion for that reason.

It will happen! But it requires an awakening, and it requires an arising. It does not require a leader—a servant maybe, *not* a leader. It does *not* require a president. It requires your common consent *by your deeds*, not only to say, but to do. It will *not* be achieved by control. It will *not* be achieved by coercion. It will *not* be achieved by force. It will *not* be achieved because there is some big 'strongman' among you. It *will* only happen if each of you are strengthened in *your* faith and *know the Lord.* It *will* be achieved by humility. It *will* be achieved through meekness. It *will* be achieved by love, which is unfeigned— the real thing.

I don't need or want, or even welcome, your admiration or your praise. You're probably more admirable than am I. I'm not telling you these things because I can *do* these things. I'm telling you these things because *this* is what the Lord would have *us* do. He's told us what was on His mind, and here it is; it's laid out for us. The question is not, "Who's great and noble and going to stroll in there?" The question is, "Who's meek; who's humble; who's appreciative of their inadequacies?" Who's willing to say, "When I count up all my foibles and failings, and I look at them, I don't think I have any ground upon which to criticize anyone else."

King Benjamin had something to say about the character of a child, and he gives this in his big talk, beginning in Mosiah where they're all together for his farewell address. This is Mosiah chapter 3, verse 19:

> *The natural man is an enemy to God, and has been from the fall of Adam...will be, forever and ever, unless he yields to the enticings of the Holy Spirit, and putteth off the natural man and becometh a saint through the atonement of Christ the Lord, and becometh as a child* (Mosiah 3:19; see also Mosiah 1:16 RE).

Then he elaborates what it is about the child that is so useful in yielding to the enticings of the Holy Spirit: putting off the natural man, becoming a saint through the atonement of Christ. All of those are driven by these kinds of characteristics, which are childlike:

> *Submissive, meek, humble, patient, full of love, willing to submit to all things which the Lord seeth fit to inflict upon him, even as a child doth submit to his father* (Ibid).

Those are the characteristics of a child that manages to change their mind, or to facilitate their development.

Well, there was a time— There was a time, and it was back here in your life— there was a time when you did not need to go down to the firing range and have a skeet machine firing off a clay pigeon, and a 12-gauge loaded with birdshot in it, to be able to enjoy yourself. If you had a stick— If you had a stick, it was enough because your mind was alive with the kinds of things that allowed you to have just as much (if not more) joy pretending as does the adult with the gun, and the ammunition, and the skeet range, and the machine, and the clay pigeon, and the thing blowing up in the air— And, "Oooo, isn't that fun?" And, "Don't you wish there was more of that from Hollywood?!" Too bad we can't load blood in clay pigeons; then we'd all be at the firing range.

The idea of submissiveness is another way of reckoning into the idea of openness—the same with meekness, the same with humility and being humble, the same with patience. And we ought to clarify the point about the child and patience because at first blush, you look at a child and you say there is nothing less patient than a child: "Can we...?! Can we...?! Are we there yet?! Are we there yet?! Can I, can I, can I...?! Please! Please! Please! Are you sure?! Aaaahhhh!!!! Crap, how does this work?! Can I?! Can I?! Can I...?! Okay, what if I give *this*, can I get *that*?!"

See, they go through all of the tantrum stuff until they begin to negotiate, and sometimes that negotiation thing works—particularly if the kids are bright. And we've been playing with really bright kids, so they tend to go and negotiate *everything*. They are not patient in *that* sense. They are— Children are patient in the sense that relentlessly, endlessly, they are studying to learn more. They *want* to know more.

I write a blog, and on it I ask more questions than I give answers because what people need are not a bunch of answers; and answers end the discussion. Once you've got the answer, that's the end of that. What you need is a question, and you need a question so that you'll open your mind. And you need to open your mind so you can become like a child. And you need to become like a child so that you're a suitable environment in which revelation can take place. And you need to have revelation take place in order for you to reconnect with Heaven. And you need to reconnect with Heaven so that you get to know who God is. And you need to get to know who God is so that He can, in turn, make you a member of His own household, and redeem you from this current plight in which you find yourself in darkness and distrust. And what people want from me are answers—and I can hand you an answer and cripple you *or* I can teach you to ask and turn you into, potentially, someone that can make this trek backwards, that can make this climb.

Look, strip yourselves of jealousies and fears, humble yourselves before Me. You're not sufficiently humble! Let's learn from their failure! Let's not repeat it! Why do we need to keep plowing the same line over and over, through the same rocky soil, when no fruit has *ever* yielded from that particular furrow? Strip yourselves! Don't envy those who sit in the chief seats; they are, rather, to be pitied. Gain your own grace with God as Moroni asked you to do. God alone decides when, where, and how He will reveal Himself to you.

Look at D&C 88, verse 68: *Therefore, sanctify yourselves...* You have to rise up to accomplish that. *Sanctify yourselves...* by your stripping of jealousies and envies, by your humility before Him. *That* sanctifies yourself because you become disconnected from *this* place. *That your minds become single to God...* (D&C 88:68; see also T&C 86:12). *Single to God*—meaning that He occupies a place of priority in which He is central to you. Not that you neglect your family, you can't do that; not that you neglect your labors, you cannot do that.

But I have to tell you, some of the people that are driven in desperation try and improve their circumstances—that are sitting downstairs. If ministered to in a kindly way, some of those people have a heart that is better prepared for receiving the truth, more tender and poignant because of the circumstances of their life, than are the hearts of many of us who, in our plenty and in our conceit about our own goodness, think ourselves better than them. When the truth of the matter is, more than anything else, it is our humility that qualifies us. More than anything else, it is our sincere apprehension of just how weak, how vulnerable, how easily distracted we are.

Think about what it means to have the *power of God.* Think about what it means for God to be able to do *all* things, including sustaining you from moment to moment by lending you breath. And then for God to say, "You are free to choose to do (with what He's lending to you) whatever it is that *you* choose to do." Think of the patience of our God. Think of the meekness of our God. And think about the test that you are presently taking to prove who and what you are, and whether or not in the circumstances of this test, *you* are proving that *you* can be trusted—to have the meekness, to have the patience, to endure in humility what will be done—to endure the abuses that God allows to take place in order to permit His children to gain experience, so that in the long run they can ultimately know the difference between good and evil; and on their own *choose* to love the good and to stay away from the evil.

You, generally, hail from a tradition that assures you that you're in the right way. You, generally, come from a tradition that says you're better than others. You are able to look down your nose at other people, who stumble about in the dark because they don't have all the great truths that you have. The fact of the matter is you, generally—not specifically because there are some to whom this absolutely does not apply—your hearts are right before God; but there aren't many.

You've been handed this tradition, *and [the] wicked one cometh and [he takes] away light and truth* (D&C 93:39; see also T&C 93:11 RE), and he does it because of the false traditions you have been handed. The greatest among us is *wholly* inadequate. The greatest among us can't be trusted with the power of God—not yet, anyway. The greatest among us is *still* in need of repentance. *Every one* of us should walk fearfully before God, not because God isn't generous but because what He offers can turn you into a devil. The only way to be prepared and not fall is to realize the enormous peril that *you* present, potentially, to the universe.

Before you get in a position to enjoy the status that God offers to us all, you need to work out your salvation—with fear and trembling, exactly like Paul said. You need to purge, remove, reprove. *This* attitude we see in *this* man, in *this* account (the brother of Jared)—*this is* the man of God! Christ may be the prototype of the saved man, but I know of no record anywhere in scripture that exposes the heart of the real disciple of Christ as well as does this chapter expose the heart of this man. *This* is what *we* should become. This is why the Lord could open up to him. This is why this man *became*, in the history of the world, coming up to this moment—despite the fact the Lord came to Adam-ondi-Ahman and administered comfort to Adam in the valley of Adam-ondi-Ahman. *Here,* He came and showed Himself, as He truly was—as a pre-existent spirit possessing a soul as tangible as man's—and ministered to him in a way which, if you understood what it takes for a quickened being to condescend into the presence and make Himself known as He does here, was an enormous sacrifice by our Lord. Verse 18:

> *He ministered unto him even as he ministered unto the Nephites; and all this, that this man might* know *that he was God, because of the many great works which the Lord had shown unto him.* (Ether 3:18; see also Ether 1:14 RE)

This is how God is known—by His works! It's not the lightning show, it's not the shaking on the mountain; it's the great works that proceed forth from Him. Think about what He did when He appeared unto the Nephites: God introduces Him *three times* before the people who were there were finally able to listen with their ears and hear the introduction. And then after the introduction is given, they still see Him descend, and He descends dressed in white and stands before them. Despite the introduction, despite the descent, despite Him standing in front of them, what the people think is "This must be an angel."

Clearly, He has arrived in a way that is extra-human. He's manifested Himself, being able to use the law of gravity in a way that we can't. He descends, He stands there; but none of them are overwhelmed. None of them fall down and worship Him. None of them do anything but look at Him! He's so plain, so ordinary, so commonplace in the appearance that He makes, that when they see Him, they stand there and they look rather like tourists at this man dressed in white who has now appeared to them. And He says, "Here's who I am." He introduces Himself (in 3 Nephi chapter 11, verse 11) three times in order to tell you who He is. Three times He talks about obeying the will of the Father, suffering the will of the Father in all things, glorifying the Father by taking upon Himself the sins of the world. Even standing in front of them, He bears testimony of Someone greater than Him.

It is the humility of the individual standing in front of them and His introduction of Himself, in 3 Nephi, that brings them to their knees. They fall down at that point and worship Him because when He opens His mouth and you see *what* He is, and *who* He is, and what proceeded forth out of the heart of that Man, you know you are listening and looking at God indeed. And they fall down and they worship Him.

Turn to chapter 4, verse 7:

> *And in that day that they shall exercise faith in me, saith the Lord, even as the brother of Jared did, that they may become sanctified in me, then will I manifest unto them the things which the brother of Jared saw, even to the unfolding unto them all my revelations, saith Jesus Christ, the Son of God the Father of...[heaven] and of...earth, and all things that in them are.* (Ether 4:7; see also Ether 1:17 RE)

This is the ministry of the Lord. This is the comfort that he (the brother of Jared) would have, that He promises to bring to us. This text, that we're looking at in Ether chapter 3, is probably the best, single text in existence to study about gaining the knowledge of God and the process by which it is gained. But most importantly, it exposes the attitude that is possessed by the person who comes back to be redeemed. It tells you—not directly, it tells you indirectly—by telling you what he did. 'Go thou and do likewise' (see Luke 10:25-37; see also Luke 8:7-8 RE). Everything that you have been put through, and every challenge that you have been given, and every weakness that you possess have been given to you in a *studied way* to bring you, hopefully, to your knees. To bring you, hopefully, to feel the chastening hand of God so that you, in your day, in your circumstance, can look upon that as a gift because it surely is.

'I give unto men weakness that they may come unto me, and if they'll humble themselves and come unto me, I'll make weak things strong.' That's also in the book of Ether, and that's in an aside in which Moroni is complaining that the Gentiles aren't going to believe this book; the Gentiles aren't going to believe this record. They're going to say, "This stinks!" They're— Ether chapter 12, verse 26:

> When I had said this, the Lord [God] spake unto me, saying: Fools mock, but they shall mourn...my grace is sufficient for the meek, that they shall take no advantage of your weakness; And if men come unto me I will show unto them their weakness. (Ether 12:26-27; see also Ether 5:5 RE)

That's an unavoidability! That's an inevitability! You stand in the presence of a just and holy Being, you're going to realize your weaknesses. You're going to recognize what you lack.

> I give unto men weakness that they may be humble; and my grace is sufficient for all men that humble themselves before me; for if they humble themselves before me, and have faith in me, then will I make weak things become strong unto them. (Ibid.)

How do weak things become strong? Not by fighting the battle that you're going to lose. It's by appreciating, as the brother of Jared did, the fact that none of us can come into the presence of God without feeling keenly this scripture. But it is given unto— Fools mock...they shall mourn. I (this is Christ speaking) *I give unto men weakness* [for one purpose], *I give unto them weakness that they may be strong*. (Ibid.)

The anvil that you're dragging around? That anvil was given to you. Don't curse it. Pray for God to come and lift it. You're never going to be able to get far carrying it anyway. You may not even be able to lift it, but in the economy of God, *that* is a gift. It's a gift. Not for you to act upon and surrender to, but for you to fight against in humility and meekness, and to say, "I'm not winning. I haven't won. It goes on and on, and yet *still*, I fight against it."

When will you finally come to Him and cry out? When, in the bitter anguish of your soul, like Joseph Smith in Liberty jail, "How long must I endure this? How long do I have to suffer from the abuse of the guards? How long do I have to sit inside a gated room, in a dungeon, to hear stories about the rape of the people who followed me? And the murder of the people that believed what I was teaching?" (See D&C 121; see also T&C 138 RE. Also see Parley Pratt Autobiography (1985), p.179-180.)

How long did Joseph's heart break in Liberty Jail? He emerged from that ordeal a fundamentally different man than the man who went in. People who say, "Oh yeah, in Nauvoo he got carried away with all kinds of things"— We'll talk more about that tomorrow. We'll talk more about this whole idea of marriage, and we'll touch upon the notion of plurality of wives. We'll brush up against that tomorrow.

Look, these scriptures, these invitations, these prophecies, *and this message* (that began in Boise and will conclude in Phoenix), this message is inviting you to do what was originally prophesied as this dispensation began (that we looked at, at the beginning in Boise, Idaho). The game's afoot. The challenge is underway. The opportunity is here. There was a price that had to be paid; it involved several generations. You do not kill a man like Joseph, by the conspiracy of his followers, without forfeiting an opportunity—but that moment has come to an end and a new moment is upon us. And if you'll hear it, I can declare to you in the name of our Lord that the day of salvation has once again arrived. Have faith! Be believing! He's real! I gave you a description of His demeanor. I gave that last time and I'm reiterating again, here, some of the things about His attributes. Come to Him! Seek for Him! Have faith in Him! You have more reason to have faith and confidence in Him, right now, than the brother of Jared did in his day to have faith and confidence in Him.

There's an incident that I think— One word, one word in this incident really explains a great deal of what I have been talking about in this last installment. This is an event that occurs within the Book of Mormon, that may seem otherwise quite puzzling. But now that we've looked at the Ether chapter 3 material, and we go back and we look at this incident, it suddenly begins to have a connection to it. This is in Alma chapter 22. It involves Lamoni's father, the king. I want you to look at the father, beginning in verse 17 of Alma chapter 22:

> *And it came to pass that when Aaron had said these words, the king did bow down before the Lord, upon his knees; yea, even did he prostrate*

himself upon the earth, and cried [...and cried] *mightily, saying.* ([emphasis added] Alma 22:17; see also Alma 13:10 RE)

It's not the words of the prayer that provoked or gathered the attention of Heaven, though the prayer is in fact needed, relevant, and exactly what the Lord answered. It's what came before.

This is the king! This is the king that can have people killed, if he chooses to do so! This is the one who, like God, among his people exercises the power of life and death. This is the one who could exact from them taxes. This is the one who has absolutely no reason to do what he's doing here, but look what he does: he prostrates himself upon the ground, and he *cries out mightily*. He doesn't pray. He mirrors exactly what the brother of Jared did when *he* approached God, in the depths of humility and in the sincerity of his heart, showing absolutely his appreciation for the difference between himself, on the one hand, and God, on the other.

Don't mistake me—I do not think it is necessary to physically engage in this kind of display. When the display is an extension of what is in the heart, that is absolutely fine. But when what is in the heart is right, it doesn't matter how it's displayed because God looketh on the inner man. This king was so overtaken by what he had heard that he was *not* ashamed to prostrate himself in front of the missionaries. He was *not* ashamed to cry out in the depths of humility. He didn't care who saw it. He didn't do this for to be seen. He didn't care that he was being seen. He did this because at that moment, that was what he was. He was seeking grace from the throne of Grace. *O God, Aaron hath told me that there is a God; and* if *there is a God, and* if *thou art God...* ([emphasis added] Ibid., vs 18).

Do you see this? This isn't someone who's certain. This is someone who is convicted of his own inadequacy. It may not be that you don't know enough, it may actually be that you know too much that's wrong. It may be that what you lack— It's all going to be erased and started over anyway. If you could gaze into Heaven for five minutes, you realize that people that have been writing about this stuff since the beginning of time, who haven't gazed into Heaven, don't know what they're talking about. The suppositions, and the connections, and the ideas that get floated around are not only false, many of them are offensive to God. They're not right. The board's going to be erased. God's going to re-order it. You're going to see things in a completely different light when it happens.

It's not that you're brilliant and a shining light of knowledge. It's what's in your heart, and how has your heart been prepared? And if your heart is open to receive: *I will give away all my sins to know thee...that I may be raised from the dead, and be saved at the last day. And now when the king had said these words, he was struck as if he were dead* (Ibid.). And then look what happens when he recovers, because as he was struck as if he were dead, he's converted. The Lord ministers to him.

And in verse 23: *The king stood forth, and began to minister unto them. And he did minister unto them, insomuch that his whole household were converted unto the Lord.* This is what happens when converted to the Lord—you can't stand to look about you and see other people who are left in the dark. You want to invite them, rather, as Nathanael was invited: "Come, and see for yourself" (see John 1:46; see also John 1:7 RE). You come to the Lord; you come and see for yourself. This little bit of skeptical praying, "If there's a God, if thou art God, will you make yourself known to me?" *That* worked—not because this is a magic incantation.

Those folks who go through ceremonies think that ceremonies have some powerful mojo, some compelling voodoo, but the purpose of the ceremony is to teach you a precept. The precept is what you ought to find within your heart. Rites and ordinances are intended to testify to a greater truth—it was anciently among the Jews. It is an Aaronic priesthood function to turn around and look at the ordinance as if it were an end in itself. It is *not* an end in itself, it is intended to be a symbol reminding you of some great truth concerning our God.

The capstone of the ceremonies that were restored through Joseph, involving a dialogue between you and the Lord in which you're brought back into His presence, and then following that, you're taken away and you're sealed for eternity—those are *lofty* concepts. They are powerfully portrayed in the ordinances and the rites. They are intended to convey to you the reality that all of this is possible because God does, in fact, intend to preserve *you* and all those associations that you prize, so long as they are worthy.

Don't think that you lack the faith! If *this* king, with *this* prayer, can go to God and can ask and get an answer— *That's not the impediment.* The impediment is the pride of your heart, the hardness of your heart, the self-reliance that you think that you own, the traditions that bind you down, the arrogance of your heart, the unwillingness to *cry out mightily* to God and then to be open to receiving an answer. This was enough; and you too can do enough.

The Lord tells a story in Mark. This is Mark chapter 9. Beginning at verse 17, there's this fellow who comes to Christ and says,

> *Master, I...brought...thee my son, which hath a dumb spirit.* [The spirit overtakes him, he foams at the mouth and gnashes his teeth.] *I spake to thy disciples that they should cast him out...they could not.* [And Christ says,] *O faithless generation, how long shall I be with you? how long shall I suffer you?...they brought [the boy] unto Him...*[he foams]...*straightway the spirit [tore] him...he fell on the ground...wallowed foaming...he asked [the] father, How long [has it been] since this came unto him? And he said, Of a child. And oftimes it [casteth] him into the fire, and into the waters, to destroy him: but if thou canst do any thing, have compassion on [him]...help us. Jesus said unto him, if thou canst believe, all things are possible to him that believeth...straightway the father of the child cried out [cried out], and said with tears, Lord, I believe; help thou mine unbelief. [Help thou mine unbelief.]* (Mark 9:17-24; see also Mark 5:8-9 RE)

You don't need more of what you already have. Why are you here? Well, most of you. Some have come only to criticize and to gather information. Some of you in the hardness of your heart are going to come to the point where, in the day of judgment, you will look back on this moment and realize, "I damned myself by the hardness of my heart and the bitterness of my soul because I came to judge a man whose heart was right before God, and mine was not." Your heart will be broken in *that* day.

But look at this man whose heart was broken on this day. He cried out, *Lord, I believe; help thou mine unbelief.* "I have a desire, I have a willingness, but it is so fragile! It is so frail. I don't think it's enough." *That's* not the problem. Cry out! Ask Him!

Remember, His disciples who'd been following Him, His disciples who were His faithful followers, His disciples couldn't fix this boy. And they'd given up everything to come and follow Him. Jesus healed him. After the incident the disciples came to Him and said, *Why could [we not] cast him out?* Christ answered them, *This kind can come forth by nothing, but prayer and fasting* (Mark 9:29; see also Mark 5:11 RE).

Why do you have to be afflicted by prayer and fasting, if you're a follower of the Lord, in order to get to the point that you can accomplish this? Because *you* don't fall prostate, crying out with tears. If this man, in this condition, can say, *I believe; help thou mine unbelief;* if this man can do this and have the

Lord, on his behalf, work a miracle, *you too* can believe enough, *you too* can accomplish what you desire, *you too* can come to Him. Matthew covers the same incident, but in Matthew he picks up— This is Matthew chapter 17, beginning at verse 19:

> *Then came the disciples to Jesus apart, and said, Why could not we cast him out?...Jesus said unto them, Because of your unbelief: for verily I say unto you, If ye have faith as a grain of mustard seed, ye shall say unto this mountain, Remove hence to yonder place; and it shall remove; and nothing shall be impossible unto you. Howbeit this kind [come] not out but by prayer and fasting. (Matthew 17:19-21; see also Matthew 9:7 RE)*

Faith as a grain of mustard seed was what the Lord said they needed. The defect does not consist in the absence of faith in the Lord. The defect consists in the arrogance and hardness of the heart, that prevents you from crying out in the realistic and anguish of your heart, looking to God who is trying to bring you to Him. *That* depth of humility, *that* status of being someone who is utterly harmless, *that* condition in which you present no threat to the righteous— You are harmless as a dove, you seek only the betterment of others. That is who God is, and what you must become in order for God to be able to redeem you *to be like Him.* That's you voluntarily changing to be that person by your submission to Him—because there is no reason to give to the proud, the vain, and the warlike the ability to torment and to afflict others. There is every reason to give to someone—who would ultimately be willing to give the rain to fall on the righteous and the wicked, and make the sun shine on both the righteous and the wicked—the power of God because the power of godliness consists in this kind of a heart. And in this kind of a heart, God can accomplish anything.

Turn to Luke chapter 18, because there the Lord pretty much tells you how it is He evaluates whether someone has purified themselves before Him. This is a story that the Lord makes up, in chapter 18 of Luke, telling a parable to those who trusted in themselves that they were righteous. Beginning at verse 10:

> *Two men went up into the temple to pray; the one a Pharisee...the other a publican. The Pharisee stood and prayed thus with himself, God, I thank thee, that I am not as other men are, extortioners, unjust, adulterers, or even as this publican. I fast twice in the week, I give tithes of all that I possess. And the publican, standing afar off, would not lift...so much as his eyes unto heaven, but smote upon his breast, saying,*

God be merciful to me a sinner. I tell you, this man went down to his house justified rather than the other: for every one that exalteth himself shall be abased; and he that humbleth himself shall be exalted. ([emphasis added]Luke 18:10-14; see also Luke 10:7 RE)

God can only exalt the meek because only the meek can be trusted. This is what it means to sanctify yourself. Our idea of purity and Christ's idea are entirely based on different criteria. Why is meekness required *of* a God, *by* a God? What would happen if God Himself were not patient, willing to suffer abuse and be rejected? What would happen if God were egotistical? What would happen if God did not return blessings for cursings? What would happen if God were not *exactly* what He preached in the Sermon on the Mount? What if God did not bless those who despitefully used and abused Him? What would happen if God did not submit Himself to fall into the hands of wicked men, to be despised and rejected? And then to be killed in shame, hanging naked on a cross in full view of the world while people spit upon Him, while they mocked Him, and they ridiculed Him, saying, "If you really are what you say you are, come down from the cross, *then* we will believe."

Woe unto all those who say, "If you really are who you say you are," when the voice of God is sounding in their ears. *They* would have rejected the Lord as well. *They* would have crucified the Lord as well. *They* are not His sheep because they do not hear His voice. If they *were* His sheep, they *would* hear His voice.

In a letter written August 16, 1834, Joseph Smith expected Zion could be established very soon. He wrote:

> "we have a great work to do...but little time to do it in and if we dont exert ourselves to the utmost in gathering up the strength of the Lords house, there remaineth a scorge" ([spelling as in original], JS Papers, Documents Vol. 4, p. 106.)

In the same letter he reminded people in his day that:

> "so long as unrighteousness acts are suffered in the church it can not [be] sanctified neither Zion be redeemed." ([spelling as in original], Ibid., p. 107.)

At the time, he considered the church to be "in a languid cold disconsolate state." (Ibid.) It was the opposite of the lively, confident, and happy state accompanying righteousness, even when worldly circumstances are direful and the wicked seem to triumph. When doing what the Lord *asks*, we *can* be lively because He will accompany *our* efforts and add His strength to our labor. If we have a hope in Christ, we can be confident. If our sins have been forgiven, we have every reason to be happy.

Virtue and patience are required of us, every bit as much as it has been required in *every* age. We cannot wallow in sin, nor be prideful, and expect to do *any better* than those who have already failed. The best guard against our failure is humility, meekness, long-suffering, and patience. We must not charge ahead when the Lord has not prepared the way for us to proceed safely. There's much still to be done, but it must be done when, where, and how the Lord directs; and that also not in haste because haste brings confusion, resulting in pestilence—including violence and jarring contentions.

From emails and phone calls I've received since my talk in Moab, it's clear that there are those who want to move *now*, in haste. There are ambitious men who offer to lead others hastily into new paths, claiming to be so mighty and strong that they can offer great rewards in the afterlife—in exchange for following *them* here. I offer you no such thing. You must look to Christ for forgiveness of your sins, and follow His example of self-sacrifice, patience, obedience, and virtue.

I can only urge you to patiently allow the *true Shepherd* to guide us all into *His* pastures, showing Him the respect due to a Redeemer. I mentioned the idea of kingship in Moab. Remember the great King, Christ, came—not to *be* served but *to* serve. He did not lord it over others, but *He knelt* to elevate them. He came as a meek and lowly servant, and went about doing good. He died to save the lives of others. When He arose from the dead, He went to the Father and advocated forgiveness for those who despised and abused Him!

What kind of king would God send? Even if his bowels are a fountain of light and truth, and even if he were to hold the scepter of power in his hand, I doubt a king sent by the Lord would be markedly different than our True King. He would endure the abuse of misunderstanding, criticism, and mockery from those who refuse to understand. He would serve patiently, never asserting any claim to greatness. Joseph said, In this world, "the more a man is exalted, the more humble he will be, if actuated by the Spirit of the Lord." *(JS Papers, Documents, Vol. 4, p. 198.)* When such a king dies, and returns to God to report, he will have only kindness for those who opposed him as he served God. *We* should *all* be like *that. We* should *all be* like *our Lord.*

Christ's greatest commandments were simple, and given to every one of us:

- *Thou shalt love the Lord thy God with all thy heart, and with all thy soul, and with all thy mind* (Matthew 22:37; see also Matthew 10:23 RE).

- *Thou shalt love thy neighbour as thyself* (Matthew 22:39-40; see also Matthew 10:23 RE).

- *Therefore all things whatsoever ye would that men should do to you, do ye even so to them: for this is the law and the prophets* (Matthew 7:12; see also Matthew 3:44 RE).

- If we do these things, there's no time to proclaim our greatness, to assert the right to be a leader, or to command others. Servants do not strut, but behave meekly. They only take such acts as the true Master commands.

Turn back to D&C section 121. There's a couple verses there that I want to suggest, particularly *if* you view the man and the woman together as one. Read these verses as if it's descriptive of '*the one,*' which is you and your wife:

> *Many are called, but few are chosen.* [This is beginning at verse 40 of section 121.] *No power or influence can or ought to be maintained by virtue of the priesthood, only by persuasion, by long-suffering, by gentleness and meekness, and by love unfeigned; By kindness, and pure knowledge, which shall greatly enlarge the soul without hypocrisy, and without guile* (D&C 121:40-42; see also T&C 139:5 RE).

Within your family, within your marriage, are you and your wife learning to use persuasion? Within your marriage, are you and your husband learning to use gentleness in dealing with one another? Are the two of you, together, facing one another in all the difficulties that come as a result of being married? Are you facing that together in meekness? Do you find that in all the relationship troubles, turmoils, and challenges, what predominates is kindness? Is there a search for understanding that results in pure knowledge, when it comes to a dilemma? Look at verse 37:

> *That they may be conferred upon us, it is true; but when we undertake to cover our sins, or to gratify our pride, our vain ambition, or to exercise control or dominion or compulsion upon the souls of the children of men, in any degree of unrighteousness, behold, the heavens withdraw*

themselves; the Spirit of the Lord is grieved; and when it is withdrawn, Amen to the priesthood or the authority of that man. (D&C 121:37; see also T&C 139:5)

It's been my observation that so soon as the Spirit of the Lord withdraws, *that quickly* will another spirit step in to assure you that you're right, you should be vindicated; that you ought to proceed on in the arrogance of your heart to feel yourself justified and vindicated. There are false spirits that go about, but there are no better an audience to receive the whisperings of those false spirits than it is the abusers who, having grieved the spirit and caused it to withdraw, accept the counsel from yet another spirit that says, "You're right, press on! Well done! You're good! You're right! You'll be vindicated! This is all God's work, and you're a great man because you're engaged in God's work! Do not back down, do not relent. Forget about persuasion; you should never be long-suffering, you should make those under your rule suffer. They *should* yield to your rule. There is no place for meekness: we believe in a God of strength, a God of power, a God whose work can be done despite the frailties of man. There is no need for men to be meek—and it's kind in the end, after all, to punish, and to force, and to coerce because we have a good objective in mind!"

All the lies and all of the deceit that led, in turn, to Catholicism falling into the abyss that *it* fell into, are presently in play with spirits that worked this out long ago—taking the Restoration of the Gospel as yet another opportunity in which to whisper in, once the spirit is withdrawn.

So, does your marriage help you avoid covering your sins? Does your marriage, because you're never going to solve this problem in the community until you first begin to solve it within the walls of your own home— You're never going to have Zion that exists somewhere among a community until, *first,* that community is composed of those who have a marriage that is in the image of God. Does your marriage help you avoid gratifying your pride? Does it help pull down your vain ambition? Is your ambition to exalt the two of you, rather than the one of you? Does it bring you, time and time again, to not exercise control but to respect the freedom to choose?

Your kids are going to make mistakes. It's not your job to force them to *not* make the mistake. It's your job to counsel them, and to let them have the experience by which your counsel makes sense and is vindicated. You hope the mistakes that they make are not too serious, but even if they're serious and they involve lifelong struggles, it's their right to choose; and it's your obligation to teach and to persuade, and then to *rejoice* when they return after they are tired of filling their bellies with the husks that the pigs are fed. It's your job to go and greet them, and put a robe on their shoulder, and put a ring on their hand, and to kill the fatted calf.

It's *not* your job to beat them and to chain them to the farm, so they can't go away and behave foolishly. They need to know that your bonds of love towards them are stronger than death itself. They need to know that they will endure in your heart into eternity. And not only your children, but one another because we *all* make mistakes. *Do not* exercise dominion, *do not* exercise compulsion; exercise long-suffering, gentleness, meekness, and kindness. Some of the biggest disasters come when you do not give people the right to choose freely, and you attempt to coerce them. Be wise, be prudent, be someone that they would respect and they would listen to.

Now, it's clear when it comes to the gospel that the gospel has, as its standard, absolutes. Doctrine and Covenants 1, section 31, says, *For I the Lord cannot look upon sin with the least degree of allowance (D&C 1:31; see also T&C 54:5 RE).*

And if that's not a troubling enough idea, then if you go to King Benjamin in Mosiah 4, verse 29, it says (this is King Benjamin talking): *And finally, I cannot tell you all the things whereby ye may commit sin; for there are divers ways and means, even so many that I cannot number them (Mosiah 4:29; see also Mosiah 2:6 RE).*

So, there's an infinite supply of opportunities with which to commit sin, *and* God cannot look upon that with any degree of allowance. It's sort of a formidable challenge for us to look at, but there is a divine purpose underlying that. And that divine purpose is to bring us in humility to God, recognizing that there's a gulf between who and what we are, and what it is that is expected of us in order to be truly holy.

————

The foregoing excerpts are taken from:

- A Glossary of Gospel Terms, *Meekness*, Restoration Edition p.160,
- Denver's talk titled "Zion Will Come," given near Moab, Utah, on April 10th, 2016,
- Denver's *40 Years in Mormonism Series*, Talk #6, titled "Zion," given in Grand Junction, Colorado, on April 12th, 2014,

- Denver's talk given at the Chiasmus Conference in American Fork, Utah, on September 18, 2010,
- Denver's *40 Years in Mormonism Series*, Talk #8, titled "A Broken Heart," given in Las Vegas, Nevada, on July 25th, 2014,
- His conference talk titled "The Doctrine of Christ," given in Boise, Idaho, on September 11th, 2016,
- Denver's *40 Years in Mormonism Series*, Talk #9, titled "Marriage and Family," given in St. George, Utah, on July 26th, 2014, and
- Denver's *40 Years in Mormonism Series*, Talk #10, titled "Preserving the Restoration," given in Mesa, Arizona, on September 9th, 2014.

94. Meekness and Humility, Part 2

This is the final part of a series on meekness and humility which is intended to go deeper than mere words and definitions. The hope is to give you the chance to get a feel for the underlying state of being associated with meekness and humility so you can resonate with these attributes and bring them into your life. We encourage you to pause and ponder on any examples of meekness and humility that come to mind as you listen, including nature, scriptures, and/or examples from your own life. We hope these episodes are meaningful and relevant to everyone's hope and desire for Zion.

———

DENVER: The Protestant Reformation was two things: First, it was a protest against the corruption of Roman Catholicism (hence the term *Protestant*) because the protestors rejected the corrupt Roman hierarchy then in charge of western European Christianity. Second, it was an attempt to reform corrupted Christianity into something better (hence the term *Reformation*) because the protestors hoped to recover and establish something marginally better than the institution headquartered in Rome.

They hoped to reform Christianity into something better representing the *actual* commandments and teachings of Jesus Christ. None of the Protestant fathers hoped to reestablish the original Christian church (or what is referred to as the *primitive* church) which once existed when Peter, James, John, Matthew, Luke, and other New Testament figures lived. When Emperor Constantine made Christianity the state religion of the Roman Empire, it did not improve Christianity; it compromised it.

Christianity is best understood and practiced by the meek and the humble.

Christ came as a lowly servant, kneeling to wash the feet of others. He held no office, no rank, commanded no fortune, submitted to Jewish and Roman authorities. He was abused and rejected. His only tool was the truth. He was born in a stable and continually regarded by the leaders as unimportant. There was nothing about His position that commanded respect.

When those who claimed to follow Him acquired the rank of official Roman Empire state religion, Christianity could not have become more alienated from how Christ lived. Silk robes and gold headpieces worn by church leaders replaced the rough clothing and crown of thorns worn by Christ. This was a tragedy, not a triumph. Christianity was utterly broken. It has not been fixed, even by the Reformation.

I believe that there is tension, if not outright hostility, between charity as a priority on one hand and knowledge as priority on the other hand; and that as between the two, it is more important to acquire the capacity for charity or love of your fellow man than it is to gain understanding. It's like what Paul said, "If I have all gifts and know all mysteries but have not charity, I'm nothing." (See 1 Corinthians 1:51) Charity, or the love of your fellow man, is the greater challenge and the more relevant one, and when you've acquired that, you can add to it knowledge.

But knowledge has the ability to render the possessor arrogant and haughty, whereas charity renders the possessor humble. If you want the greatest challenge in life, try loving your fellow man unconditionally and viewing them as God would view them and then behaving according to that view. And out of that, you will learn a great deal more about Christ than you can simply by studying. Walking in His path is a greater revelation of who He is than anything else that's provided.

Well, the more I began to take in the truths of the content in the Book of Mormon, the greater the gap grew between the lip service paid to the Restoration by the Mormon Church (the LDS Church) and the *practice* of the institution itself. In fact, the Book of Mormon, used as a guide or measuring stick, condemns *all* of the institutions of Christianity. In fact, it condemns everyone except the few who are the humble followers of Christ and points out (despite *that* few being humble followers of Christ)— nevertheless, *they* are led that in many instances, they do err because they're taught by the precepts of men.

If you want precepts that come from God, the best place to look at this point is the Book of Mormon text. The closer you look, the more you'll see. The more you see, the more you'll find that right now, the religion of Jesus Christ is hardly practiced anywhere on this earth. If it's going to be practiced at all, it needs to be done by you, by someone who is eagerly searching for and trying to find words that come from Jesus Christ as your guide, as something to lead you back to Him, as the message intended for the last days, and as the means by which you can interpret the *earlier* New Testament, the *earlier* Old Testament, to find out exactly what *they* mean—because the key to unlocking *all* of what God has been, is presently, and will ultimately be involved with to fulfill all the prophecies is contained primarily in the text of the Book of Mormon.

And so, if you want to escape before the ultimate destruction of that great image with the head of gold *beforehand*, to be prepared for the coming of the Lord; if you're a sincere Christian, you don't need to go and join another denominational institution. But you *better* take seriously the Book of Mormon and study *it* and take *its* interpretations, *its* meaning, *its* guidance seriously because it *is* the standard that has been planted in the last days as the ensign of truth to which all Christians, if they believe in Christ, need to rally in order to be part of His great latter-day work.

Mormonism is compelling. It's a very big religion, at least when it began. Since it's beginning, it has diminished considerably. Joseph Smith asserted:

> "The first and fundamental principle of our holy religion is, that we believe [that] we have a right to embrace all, and every item of truth, without limitation or without being circumscribed or prohibited by the creeds or superstitious notions of men, or by the dominations of one another, when that truth is clearly demonstrated to our minds. " (Letter from Joseph Smith to Isaac Galland, Mar. 22, 1839, Liberty Jail, Liberty, Missouri, published in *Times and Seasons*, Feb. 1840, pp. 53–54; spelling and grammar modernized.)

Everything that's true, lovely, or of good report was intended to be part of original Mormonism.

Joseph's original Mormonism was inclusive, not exclusive. All truth belonged to Mormonism, but it never pretended to have it all. Mormonism was the search for truth. It was originally the search to discover truth without fear of finding something new. To Joseph, Mormonism did not possess all truth. His religion was not based on *conceit* but on *humility*—the willingness to continue to search, pray, study, and hope for newly revealed additions. It was understood there was a great deal more yet to be discovered. The claim that Mormonism was the *only true and living church* presumed the willingness to hear God's voice and receive new truth. It was not because it already had all truth. It was *living* during Joseph's life because it continued to grow and expand. Living organisms grow; dead ones decay.

Opposition in scripture seems clear, but when we struggle in our environment, it becomes much more difficult to make decisions about what is right, what is wrong, what is good, what is bad, what is of God, what is deception, what is truth, what is false. But that's not a correct understanding because the scriptures may reveal the conflict in sharp contrast, but it was no different in that day than it is today. Deciding between the opposing sides was not any more clear to those living at the time the scriptures were written than the opposition you encounter every day of your life.

The scriptures were written by or about prophets who took clearly opposing positions from those who were deceived. The clarity you read in scripture is because the views and opinions of prophets were used to *tell* about the events. But as the events happened, those living at the time had to have faith to distinguish between truth and error, to believe or to ignore a message from the Lord.

It is no different for them than it is for the dilemma that we face today. Does the message invite or entice you to believe in Christ and to do His works? Does it get presented in a way that displays patience, long-suffering? Does it use gentleness and persuasion, meekness and love, and consistency with the revelations and commandments found previously in scripture? Or does it appeal to your vanity, to your arrogance? Does it make you proud of yourself, or does it make you, instead, wish that you were a better person?

Humility is absolutely required to progress. The more we think we understand, the less willing we can become to receive more. Joseph said, "It is the constitutional disposition of mankind to set up stakes and bounds to the works and ways of the Almighty (TPJS, p. 320)." He also said, "I never heard of a man being damned for believing too much, but they are damned for unbelief (ibid, p. 374)." James 4:6 says, *God resisteth the proud but giveth grace unto the humble.*

Damnation is limiting progress or stopping progress. Setting up boundaries to what the Lord can do is *voluntary damnation.* No matter how much you believe you know, if you will be humble, then you will learn a great deal more. We must continue progression, *or*, if we don't, we accept damnation and that, too, voluntarily.

And then there is Moses, who is called in scripture, *the meekest of all men* (See Numbers 7:22), and gentiles depict him as a bully and a strongman. And yet, Moses saw no reason to be jealous when others were out prophesying—would that all men would do that. Moses, like Adam, like Christ, is an example of how the word *dominion* should be understood.

All three [were] gardeners, responsible for trying to make their garden thrive, grow, and bear fruit. In reality, those who have held the greatest dominion given by God have all lived lives of meekness and service. They were the opposite of what gentiles regard as a strongman, the *opposite*.

Mormonism cannot (or at least, should not) consider itself the exclusive possessor of *the* sacred canon, or that there is only one canon containing Gods' teachings—*the* God's teachings. There are words from heaven spread throughout our world by deliberate planting of the Gods.

Continuing: *For out of the books [that] shall be written I will judge the world, every man according to their works, according to that which is written* (2 Nephi 12:10).

These *books* hold terrible importance for Mormons because we are going to be judged by the Gods based on a comparison between *our works* and that which is written. With such a warning, we Mormons ought to be humble about our claims to know more than other faiths. We should be modest in thinking we are especially graced by the Gods' words and should be anxious to scour the globe to discover the sacred texts of other cultures. In humility, we should invite *them* to share the truths *they* value most with us because we've shown that we will respect what *they* regard as sacred.

It's really hard to sit inside your own life and to be realistic about your own personal failings. We always tend to apply tests that are given in scripture outwardly and to say, "As long as I use persuasion and pure knowledge, then I can beat you into submission and never yield the argument because I'm doing what was said is the criteria—*gentleness*: Okay, I won't yell at you; *meekness*: Okay, I'll be polite enough to let you say what you have to say before I— I won't interrupt; *love unfeigned*: Okay, I love you, brother; I *love* you, brother; and *Persuasion*: Okay, when I get my opportunity to present mine, I'm going for the brass ring. I'm gonna…"

Wait a minute! What if that's God trying to get through to you? What if the way in which God is trying to persuade you is by the meekness of the humble Lord who speaks to us in plain humility; who comes to us, not to try and overawe us, but comes to us saying: *You are me in embryo. I know what it took for me to become the Son of God, and I know you can do it, too.* What if the Lord is your greatest cheerleader, and He wants nothing more than to try and get you to be more like Him? You can't be more like Him when the center of everything is yourself, and you never self-examine. We all deserve criticism.

It requires humility to approach God and ask Him for His answer and yet more humility to know it is from Him and not my own ego, presumptions, hopes, desires, wants, and conceit. It is for me as it was for Joseph. Only *when the heart is sufficiently contrite, then the voice of inspiration steals along and whispers* (T&C 138:11) the truth. *That* comes from a purer source, higher than myself and more filled with light than any man—*certainly* greater light than I have.

This was once a temple text and has become somewhat corrupted. I'll not make any corrections or clarifications. This is from Proverbs 8 in the King James Version. The version we have has additional passages about the foolish woman at the beginning and again at the end. I am going to discard those words attributed so that the words that are attributed to the Heavenly Mother alone can be isolated and looked at to be considered. She states:

> *Hear, for I will speak of excellent things, and the opening of my lips shall be right things. For my mouth shall speak truth, and wickedness is an abomination to my lips. All the words of my mouth are in righteousness, there is nothing froward or perverse in them.* (Proverbs 8:6-8; see also Proverbs 1:35 RE)

She proclaims Herself as the reliable source of truth, righteousness, and plain (meaning *clear*) understanding. She is opposed to wickedness, frowardness (meaning *stubbornness* or *contrariness*), and perversity.

If *we* are *froward*, we are stubborn or contrary with one another. We dispute. We find it difficult to agree. How much debate and anger are produced by frowardness?

Jacob (called James in the King James Bible) mentioned *wisdom* in his letter. In contemplating Her, Jacob suggested we should be *easy to be entreated*.

> *Who is a wise man, and endowed with knowledge, among you? Let him show out of good conduct his works with meekness of wisdom. But if you have bitter envying and strife in your hearts, glory not and lie not against the truth. This wisdom descends not from above, but is earthly, sensual, devilish; for where envying and strife are, there [is] confusion and every evil work. But the wisdom that is from above is first pure, then peaceable, gentle and easy to be entreated, full of mercy and good fruits, without partiality and without hypocrisy. And the fruit of righteousness is sown in peace, of them that make peace.* (Ep Jacob 1:14)

Wisdom from above can endow us with the kindly demeanor of brothers and sisters who seek what is good for one another. How often are the words of our mouths froward and perverse? The Divine Mother refuses to speak wickedness and abominations, and Her influence brings others to depart from such failures.

Continuing:

> *They are all plain to him that understandeth and right to them that find knowledge. Receive my instruction and not silver, and knowledge rather than choice gold. For wisdom is better than rubies and all the things that may be desired are not to be compared to it* (Proverbs 1:25).

Proclaiming *wisdom is better than rubies*, She asks us to receive Her instruction rather than seek silver and gold. Nothing else is to be compared with Her wisdom. She instructs in virtues that would make *any* person better. But Her instruction will also make living in peace with others *possible*. Nothing in this world is more desirable than acquiring wisdom (understanding and putting knowledge to wise use). Zion will require the wisdom to use pure knowledge in meekness, humility, and charity. Zion will require *Her* influence.

Frowardness is a really old English word, so old that Microsoft Word incessantly corrects it to *forwardness*, because *forwardness* we use. *Frowardness* is old, and we don't have a good word for it, but it means exactly what's defined in the talk—being contrary, being stubborn, being difficult to get along with.

Froward people are continuously nagging other people because they either think the other person is wrong, or they think themselves right, and therefore, they agitate rather than become meek and submissive and humble and patient and kindly.

I suspect that that part of the talk had something to do with the activities that have gone on, although I haven't looked to see. I've heard from a couple of people that there was some head-butting. Head-butting is not a bad thing so long as it's not done in a way so as to break hearts, create divisions, and make people hold ill will toward one another.

People are very different one from another. Not only are men and women different from one another, women are different from each other, and men are different from each other; and personalities are *always* going to be ill-fitted. Getting people to mesh together?— That's not going to result in, somehow, this universal similarity of personality. It's important that people preserve their differences. It's important that people have the gifts that have been given to them by God preserved intact and not suppressed because someone doesn't like the way that their gift gets expressed.

I've mentioned it before—I just find the artwork that Monet does with his version of impressionism the highest and greatest use of the paintbrush. But I think Van Gogh's impressionism is crude and elementary; and quite frankly, I mean, his suicide stopped the outpouring of that stuff; and in some ways, you know, maybe the art world is benefitted by that.

When he was a realist in the early stages, some of what Van Gogh did was rather lovely, but his impressionism— I see that when my wife substitutes in fourth grade, and she brings presents home from her kids. But there are people who love Van Gogh. *Sunflowers* sold for 44 million last time it sold. You know, some people really love Van Gogh. I assume that in the resurrection, they'll figure out that they were duped. But for here and now, in this fallen world with its perverse set of priorities, that's all good and well; and if they've got the money, and they want to use it that way, that's fine.

Zion is going to have people whose artistic outpouring is going to be *fabulously* different from one another. You look at the totem pole artistry of the Alouettes, and you look at the carved artistry of the Hawaiian Islands, and you look at the sculpture of Michelangelo—and these are *radically, radically* different, one from the other, so much so that you're bridging these enormous cultural divides to look at these different kinds of sculpture.

Why would we ever want to have a studied school of artistic discipline that produces nothing more than some uniform product when beauty and artistry can find so many unique forms of expression? Why would we ever want that?

And the brother of Jared is asked, "Did you see more than this?" "No." "Will you believe me if I show myself to you?" "Yea, I know you're a God of truth, and you cannot lie. I'll believe all your words." (See Ether 1:12)

Why do you think the Lord posed the question, "If I show myself to you, will you believe in me?" Why do you think that Mormon writes about how he's spoken face-to-face in plain humility as one man speaks to another? We want the thundering and the lightning and the ground shaking on Sinai.

And when the Lord appeared to the brother of Jared, before appearing, He asked him, "Now when you see me, are you going to believe me?" (ibid, vs 12)

He loveth all who will have him to be their God.

"Well, I knew not that God was a man. You seemed— You seemed so much bigger and better when you were the burly thunderer from behind the curtain announcing that you are the great and powerful Oz. But now that the curtain's drawn aside, and you're like— Man was created in your image, and it's literally— It literally means that." (It takes some of the varnish off it all.)

God's greatness does not consist in striking awe in the eye of the beholder because of glory. It consists in the humility, the virtue, the goodness, the purity of the being. We worship God not because He is powerful. We worship God because He represents everything that is pure and holy and good, everything that is desirable above all else. The purity of that fruit that was delicious that Father Lehi talked about and Nephi wrote about, it is so because of its goodness. Because it is exactly what the highest and the best and the most noble should be. That's who God is.

If I can help you envision our Lord a little more, let me describe Him in terms of His characteristics. Our Lord was and is affable, but He is not gregarious. He was approachable, and He is approachable, and He's not aloof. He's patient. He's willing to guide, and He's willing to teach. He is intelligent, but He is not overbearing. He's humble in His demeanor even though the power that he possessed and possesses is undeniable. He is, therefore, both a Lamb and a Lion.

I want you to entertain three truths about Him in your mind as we begin the subject today. Those three truths are:

• He is quick to forgive sin;

• He allows all to come unto Him;

• And He is no respecter of persons.

In some respects, our own respect for or our disrespect for ourselves is the impediment in coming to Him because we tend to think that we aren't good enough. Because He is quick to forgive sins, it really doesn't matter if you're not good enough because one of the first orders of business when you come into His presence is He forgives you. He cannot look upon sin with the *least* degree of allowance, but He has the capacity and the ability to forgive sin. Therefore, although your sins may be as scarlet, He can, He will, and He does make you white as snow, no longer accountable. Therefore, you needn't fear, but you can approach boldly our Lord.

The simple answer is that there is always one [temple] on the earth. That has been true from Adam to the present time, yeah. Remember that in Nauvoo, the Lord offered to reconnect the saints but clearly defined the condition for that to happen was necessarily an acceptable temple where He could come and restore the connection. The reconnection is ordinance-based and will require an acceptable temple before it goes beyond the single representative.

First, ideas need to be advanced and accepted, and, second, we need to act on the ideas primarily by repenting and opening ourselves to the influence of God. Third, we have to be humble and patient and willing to practice the religion before we can have any hope of God deciding to gather us.

Practical experience is absolutely necessary. Theories and pretensions are not going to get us anywhere. Everyone can theorize the virtues that are necessary to gather people together and live in harmony. Everyone can envision *themselves* as one of the residents of the city of peace. But the practical experiences required to iron out our selfishness and competitiveness so we can actually live in peace is another order of magnitude harder.

In the Nauvoo City Council minutes, you see them grappling with a society that is trying to be composed of Saints, and the practical problem solving goes on. There are moments when I'm reading the Nauvoo City Council minutes that I'm laughing because they go to solve one problem, but the solution creates another. Basically, people are discourteous of one another, and because they're discourteous of one another, they adopt an ordinance in order to end one discourtesy only to create yet another discourtesy on top of that.

For example, one of the problems that they had was that Nauvoo was organized as a city in which everyone had a garden plot. But because the garden plots were not fenced, horses and foot traffic would go through the gardens, and the result of that was the destruction of needed food stuffs. So, they couldn't get people to build fences around their gardens. The solution to the problem was to turn the hogs loose because when the hogs are loose, the hogs are going to go into the gardens. And so, they adopted an ordinance, and the ordinance let the hogs in Nauvoo go free, and that produced the required fences that they wanted at the expense of hog wallows in the middle of the streets in the middle of Nauvoo until finally some guy, tired of the hog problem, went out and killed and butchered and ate a couple of hogs that another guy said belonged to him; and he sued him, and they had the public fight over it.

The point of all this isn't hogs and the Nauvoo City High Council. The point of all this is we need practical experience, not theory. And the way in which the practical experience can be had is in gathering in fellowships or societies, collecting our own tithing, and then grappling with the fact that there is a pile of money sitting there which is *ever* a temptation and to deal with that in a responsible way that forces individuals to confront their own self-will, their own pride, their own desire, their own jealousy, their own envy, their own ambition, their own covetousness.

In the fellowships that have been organized, there have been moments of profound breakthroughs in the kind of attributes that you would want for Zion. One group, when they begin their meeting, they gather all of the needs, and they put all of the needs together. Then, they gather the money, and the money is always cash and in a container that they don't know how much cash there is. Without opening the cash then, they open the needs, and as a group, they reason together and agree on what the priority of the needs are so that they have a list of the most compelling and on down. Once they know what the most compelling, the second, the third, the fourth are, they open it up, and they count the money.

There have been occasions— On one occasion, the person whose need could be satisfied (because there was enough money there) looked at the person next in line in priority behind them and concluded that in *their* heart, they thought *that* need greater than their own. If they satisfied that need, there would be nothing left for them. So, they voluntarily passed on their priority and took none of the money and allowed it all go to the next person behind them. That is a person that I would willingly add to a community because they've learned self-sacrifice.

Someone who advocates incessantly, we've *got* to live the United Order; we've *got* to have consecration—because they intend to benefit from that—is unfit to be gathered. They would destroy Zion. Someone who says, "What can I give at the cost of my own self-sacrifice?" and who is willing to live the law of consecration in order to bless and benefit others (not expecting themselves to be blessed or benefitted but, instead, for themselves to carry a burden), those people can be gathered, and they present no threat. But the way in which those people get identified is by practical experience which is what the fellowshipping communities are designed, by the inspiration of God, to allow to take place.

Every one of us theorizes that we are a great candidate for Zion. Go out and get some practical experience and see how great of a candidate you truly are. You'll be disappointed in yourself. Most of us would be, anyway.

Alma taught a lesson that we accepted by covenant as a statement of our faith:

> *And now, my beloved brethren, I have said these things unto you that I might awaken you to a sense of your duty to God, that ye may walk blameless before him, that ye may walk after the Holy Order of God after which ye have been received. And now I would that ye should be humble, and be submissive and gentle, easy to be entreated, full of patience and longsuffering, being temperate in all things, being diligent in keeping the commandments of God at all times, asking for whatsoever things ye stand in need, both spiritual and temporal, always returning thanks unto God for whatsoever things ye do receive. (Alma 5:6)*

The greatness of a soul is defined by how easily they are entreated to follow the truth. The greatest of those who have ever lived have been submissive and gentle souls. In a day when Satan accuses and rages in the hearts of men, it requires *extraordinary* will and *steely* determination to remain easily entreated by truth.

The new scriptures is a historical event that throughout the entirety of history, going back to the time of Moses, has only happened three times. It happened with Moses; it happened with Ezra; it happened through the prophet Joseph Smith and through the faithful diligence of a remnant of the people who sought to reconnect in our day and to honor that third Restoration through Joseph Smith. *It is beyond historic.* It is something designed to alter the course of history.

But some people look upon signs like that as inconsequential and easy to dismiss. I can testify to you that the heavens themselves rejoiced at what happened there. Even if you're dismissive; even if you're nonchalant about it, it is, nevertheless, one of the greatest developments to occur in history, and it happened in your lifetime.

The saints were rejected in 1844. Nothing has been done to repair the condemnation in 1831 [1832] or to reclaim people since the rejection in 1844. No one has attempted to repent and remember the former commandments—not only to *say*, but to *do*—until today.

Stop your damn squabbling! Don't go back and revert to pre-1820 Christian conduct that aroused God's ire. I use the word *damned* in the scriptural sense because that's exactly what it is. Stop squabbling! Stop disagreeing! Surrender your pride! If you think you're right; if you think someone needs to be corrected; if you think you have a higher, holier, better way, stay and persuade. Be meek. Be humble. Solicit other people and appeal to their heart.

We should welcome everyone. We should welcome Latter-day Saints. We should welcome Community of Christ. We should welcome Catholics. We should welcome Presbyterians. We should welcome *every* kind of person and then treat them with respect and kindness and understanding. Let them bring their ideas, and let you teach them those truths that you presently understand. The religion of Joseph Smith which is—it's in that video that was shown just before the opening prayer—the religion of Joseph Smith is to accept all truth.

Just because it hasn't entered into your hard heart and your closed mind yet doesn't make it untrue. There are truths in rich abundance that hail from all quarters of the earth. As religions have discarded truths, many of them have sought and fought to retain the most important core; and the most important core of many faiths and the highest aspiration and the highest ideal. It doesn't matter if you're talking the Cherokee tradition, the Hindu tradition, the Islamic tradition, the Polynesian, the Hawaiian tradition. It doesn't matter. The highest aspiration remains for the individual to connect to God and for God to recognize and connect with the individual.

There's really no difference if we welcome one another, and we treat each other kindly. Someone that may have a religion that is very strange to us— If they bring with them the aspiration to know God, and we can persuade them that God has done a work among us through Joseph Smith (through the labor that has been done to recover that Restoration), maybe they'll labor alongside us as the Restoration wraps up.

It is a great deal left to be done. And there is no one seriously entertaining the possibility of constructing a city of holiness, a city of peace, a people that are fruit-worthy to be laid up against the harvest. No one has made the effort until now. And while you may look at us and say, "You've done a crude job. You've done a rudimentary job. It needs improvement." Then help us improve it! Stop sitting back and throwing rocks! This is a time to gather, not to disperse. The same garbage that existed at the beginning (when Joseph looked around and saw confusion and disharmony) *wants to creep in* among us.

Recognize that's a false spirit. If you'll cast it out of yourself, and if you'll look at the words of the covenant that was offered in September of 2017, what you'll find is that Christ wants us—like the Book of Mormon explains—to be meek, to be humble, and to be easily entreated. And therefore, entreat one another to honor God and recognize that all of us aspire to be equal, whether you're at the top or at the root. The aspiration is the same: *to be equal.*

> *But remember that without the fruit of repentance and a broken heart and a contrite spirit, you cannot keep my covenant, for I, your Lord, am meek and lowly of heart. Be like me. You have all been wounded, your hearts pierced through with sorrows because of how the world has treated you. But you have also scarred one another by your unkind treatment of each other, and you do not notice your misconduct towards others because you think yourself justified in this. You bear the scars on your countenances from the soles of your feet to the head, and every heart is faint. Your visages have been so marred that your hardness, mistrust, suspicions, resentments, fear, jealousies, and anger toward your fellow man bear outward witness of your inner self; you cannot hide it. When I appear to you, instead of confidence, you feel shame. You fear and withdraw from me because you bear the blood and sins of your treatment of brothers and sisters. Come to me, and I will make sins as scarlet become white as snow, and I will make you stand boldly before me, confident of my love. (Answer and Covenant, T&C 157:49)*

The fact that I have concluded that Joseph Smith was a restrained man (in many respects, a very modest man) whose defense of what he believed to be the truth was fierce, but who recognized that there were a lot of people (including his own wife, Emma Smith) who had a better education than did he, Joseph was like a sponge when he thought he could get truth or help from others. And he was meek and humble in that respect. But if God had revealed something to him, he was—he was an iron-fisted, immovable man for the truth.

Personally and privately (just as the scriptures say concerning Moses), Moses was the meekest of all men. If you just read the dialogue from Moses in Exodus, you'll see nothing but meekness in that man.

If you'll read Joseph Smith's three documents in *A Man Without Doubt,* you'll see a meek man, *unbelievably* frustrated by some of the circumstances into which he was put, *searching* to find the right way out of the dilemma, trying to get God aroused to anger in the same way that the circumstances aroused

Joseph to anger, but submitting *always* to whatever the will of God was for him.

Ultimately, Joseph Smith left to go to be imprisoned in Carthage knowing he would not come back from there or, at least, expecting that he would not; and commenting about how his life was of no value to his friends, as he returned —and he went back for the slaying.

Say what you want about those final moments in the life of Joseph Smith. He put himself in harm's way to prove his fidelity to his friends. He would not forsake *them* (as they claimed he was doing in *their* hour of need) and ultimately gave his life up. That's not the conduct of a con man. That's not the way in which someone who's going to lie and cheat and steal and behave as an immoral exploiter of others would conduct their lives. Joseph, in my view, was not just a virtuous man, but he qualified as one of those who *hath no greater love* (See John 9:11) because he went back and surrendered at the behest of his brethren—in part, with the hope that by losing his life, Nauvoo would be spared the slaughter that had gone on at Far West and Haun's Mill and elsewhere.

And if ye...say unto this mountain, Be thou cast down and become smooth, it shall be done. And behold, if ye [shalt] say that God shall smite this people, it shall come to pass (Helaman 3:19).

And then, because He knows the nature and the character of the man [Nephi] involved in giving this authority, God commands him. He has to go out and deliver the message, *Except ye repent ye shall be smitten, even unto destruction* (ibid). He didn't want to do that because that's not the character of the person who, with unwearyingness, would go out and declare the word of God because such people have in their heart one and only one objective, and that is the salvation of the souls of men. But now, this troubling message has to be given, and when he goes, and he delivers it, he doesn't even use the authority that he's been given. He simply asks the Lord if the Lord will smite.

Imagine how different things are when you know that there is no power or authority *in the priesthood itself.* But the power to influence others comes only by persuasion, long-suffering, gentleness, meekness, love unfeigned, and by kindly presenting pure knowledge. Imagine that a teacher must greatly enlarge your soul to actually claim priesthood. How different would that be for you? You would be drawn to attend a meeting for what great light it could provide you. You would no longer endure those meetings, conferences, and conversations that are low, mean, vulgar, and condescending. *Leave* if they do if you're not edified, and your soul is not enlightened. Religion classes and meetings that bore us are an obscenity. Discussions filled with a myriad of unenlightened personal opinion are the real pornography of today's Mormonism.

I know of no way to receive light and truth from heaven but by patient, obedient, and disciplined living by everything God has said, commanded, or instructed. It is as the Lord told His disciples, some things are not overcome but by *fasting and prayer* (See Matthew 9:7). A haphazard inquiry from a proud and hard-hearted soul will not likely receive an answer from the same Lord who spent entire nights alone in solitary prayer.

Our Lord's prayers were so private that His own disciples needed to ask Him to teach them how to pray because He did not display it for them to learn by overhearing. He went alone, apart, and in private, and then prayed for hours, oftentimes overnight. This was Christ. This was He who is *more intelligent than [them] all* (Abraham 5:4).

Yet, people expect they can ask in haste about something that shatters their paradigm and in their pride expect to have everything they always believed to be ratified to their satisfaction, and what annoys them to be denounced. Until the heart is broken and willing to accept the sad news that they are wrong, and God is going to correct them, they are not likely to get an answer other than they are right. In fact, they've been right all along. The answers from a meek and lowly Lord come with the greatest accuracy to the meek and lowly inquirer. There are but few of those living.

This is my focus: I try to do what I have been asked, when asked to do it, in exactly the manner it's told me to accomplish and leave the results entirely to the Lord. If I do only what He asks, then the outcome is His alone. I cannot take credit or blame. I cannot be flattered or criticized because it has but little to do with me. If the result is something great, then I do not own it and can take no credit for it. If it results in something terrible, then I cannot blame myself for failure or take upon myself the disappointment. If I respect man's agency and allow them to choose, then I have discovered that I ought to likewise respect God's agency and allow Him to lead. Given my limitations, I may suggest, petition, give observations, protest, and complain to the Lord, but I have no right to reject His direction and fail to follow His instructions.

There is no such thing as a *spiritual accomplishment*. As soon as we think *we've* achieved, our hearts are off-track. There is only humility and meekness. These two virtues allow God to accomplish something because it removes our own vanity and pride from the equation. No matter how well-intended, we are *not* God, we are *not* wise, and we do not have at our disposal enough intelligence to outthink our adversaries. God can. We cannot. If we want to fail, then we just need to take the initiative. If we wish to succeed, then we kneel before God and do as He asks.

————

The foregoing excerpts are taken from:

- Denver's *Christian Reformation Lecture Series*, Talk #3 given in Atlanta, Georgia on November 16, 2017;
- Denver's *Christian Reformation Lecture Series*, Talk #5 given in Sandy, Utah on September 7, 2018;
- The presentation of Denver's paper titled "Was There an Original" given at the Sunstone Symposium on July 29, 2016;
- Denver's conference talk titled "Things to Keep Us Awake at Night" given in St. George, Utah on March 19, 2017;
- His talk titled "Other Sheep Indeed" given at the Sunstone Symposium in Salt Lake City, Utah on July 29, 2017;
- His comments at the Unity in Christ Conference in Utah County, Utah on July 30, 2017;
- A fireside talk titled "That We Might Become One" given in Clinton, Utah on January 14, 2018;
- Denver's conference talk titled "Our Divine Parents" given in Gilbert, Arizona on March 25, 2018;
- Denver's remarks titled "Book of Mormon as Covenant" given at the Book of Mormon Covenant Conference in Columbia, South Carolina on January 13, 2019;
- Denver's *40 Years in Mormonism Series*, Talk #7 titled "Christ, Prototype of the Saved Man" given in Ephraim, Utah on June 28, 2014;
- A Q&A session titled "A Visit with Denver Snuffer" held on May 13, 2015;
- Denver's remarks titled "Keep the Covenant: Do the Work" given at the Remembering the Covenants Conference in Layton, Utah on August 4, 2018;
- Denver's lecture titled "Signs Follow Faith" given in Centerville, Utah on March 3, 2019;
- The presentation of "Answer and Covenant" given at the Covenant of Christ Conference in Boise, Idaho on September 3, 2017;

- Denver's Q&A session at the Keeping the Covenant Conference in Boise, Idaho on September 22, 2019;
- Denver's *40 Years in Mormonism Series*, Talk #5 titled "Priesthood" given in Orem, Utah on November 2, 2013;
- The presentation of Denver's paper titled "The Restoration's Shattered Promises and Great Hope" given at the Sunstone Symposium in Salt Lake City, Utah on July 28, 2018;
- Denver's blog entry titled "Answer to an Email" posted August 11, 2015; and
- An email Denver wrote to LDS Freedom Forum user Jesef which was posted on March 8, 2016.

95. Good Cheer

In this episode, Denver addresses the question: How can we be of good cheer, even when we have a broken heart and a contrite spirit?

WOMAN READING FROM DENVER'S BLOG: And behold, I have given you the law and the commandments of my Father, that ye shall believe in me, and that ye shall repent of your sins, and come unto me with a broken heart and a contrite spirit. Behold, ye have the commandments before you, and the law is fulfilled. (3 Nephi 12:19)

This hearkens back to the doctrine of Christ given preliminarily to the audience. Repent. Be baptized. Receive the Holy Ghost. These commandments are the foundation upon which all else is to be built.

To all that He explained before, He has added, *repent of your sins, and come unto me with a broken heart and a contrite spirit* (ibid). Repenting will be accompanied by a broken heart and a contrite spirit. When you turn to Him and see clearly for the first time how dark your ways have been, it should break your heart. You should realize how desperately you stand in need of His grace to cover you, lift you, and heal you. You can then appreciate the great gulf between you and Him (see Moses 1:10).

If you had to bear your sins into His presence it would make you burn with regret and fear (see Mormon 9:3-5). Your own heart must break.

When you behold how little you have to offer Him, your spirit becomes contrite. He offers everything. And we can contribute nothing but our cooperation. And we still reluctantly give that, or if we give a little of our own cooperation, we think we have given something significant. We have not. Indeed, we cannot (Mosiah 2:20-21). He honors us if He permits us to assist. We should proceed with alacrity when given the chance to serve.

How patiently He has proceeded with teaching us all. We have the law. We have the commandments. Still we hesitate. Still He invites and reminds us: Repent. Come to Him. Do what was commanded. The law is fulfilled, and He is its fulfillment. Look to Him and be saved.

The proud spirit is foolish and blind. Our perilous state is such that we can forfeit all that we have ever been by refusing Christ's invitation to repent and turn again to Him.

But we still hesitate. We still hold back.

He really can save you. He has that power. He holds those keys. Even death and hell are conquered by Him (Mosiah 15:7-9). But His victory cannot become ours unless we repent and turn again to Him.

Think of those you have lost to the grave. All those living will likewise be lost unless we come to Christ. We have hope only in Him.

It seems too simple a thing to achieve so great a result. It has always been like that (1 Nephi 17:41). Look to Him and be saved. Keep His commandments. Repent. He can and will lead you from wherever you find yourself at present back into the light. It really does not matter what foolish traps you have surrounding you. So soon as you turn to face Him, He will direct you back safely. Repent and keep His commandments and they will bring *you* to Him. (Denver's blog entry titled "3 Nephi 12:19," posted October 10, 2010)

> *Then will ye longer deny the Christ, or can ye behold the Lamb of God? Do ye suppose that ye shall dwell with him under a consciousness of your guilt? Do ye suppose that ye could be happy to dwell with that holy Being, when your souls are racked with a consciousness of guilt that ye have ever abused his laws? Behold, I say unto you that ye would be more miserable to dwell with a holy and just God, under a consciousness of your filthiness before him, than ye would to dwell with the damned souls in hell. For behold, when ye shall be brought to see your nakedness before God, and also the glory of God, and the holiness of Jesus Christ, it will kindle a flame of unquenchable fire upon you.* (Mormon 9:3-5)

Peter literally experienced the bitterness of hell in that disappointed glance from the Lord. It came from recognizing how great a disappointment he was to the Lord. It was produced by a mere glance from Christ. He who loved all of us the most was the One whom Peter, in return, cursed and denied. When he saw himself through the Lord's disappointment, it made Peter bitter, filled with remorse, and caused him to retreat to weep alone.

We do not want to disappoint the Lord. None of us want to see that same look from the Lord that He showed Peter. We have opportunities to do what He asks us every day. All of us do. Little things, moment to moment, particularly if you look for them. They matter. Every thought, every word, every deed—they matter. Let them reflect credit upon your faith in Him.

I'm not saying be dour, long-faced or stoic. Quite the contrary. "Be of good cheer" was His oft repeated expression, even using it as a greeting on many occasions (see Matt. 14:27; Mark 6:50; John 16:33; Acts 23:11; 3 Ne. 1:13; D&C 68:6, among others). Cheerfully go about doing good, and trust in Him. He will guide you. He was happy. He was cheerful. So are those who know Him best (see, e.g., JS-H 1:28).

There isn't a single thing you do for His sake which He will forget or fail to credit to you. Nor is there a single mistake which He will remember and hold against you, *if* you repent (see D&C 58: 42).

You should let your thoughts be such that you will be confident in His presence (D&C 121: 45). Be of good cheer. (Denver's blog entry titled "Be of Good Cheer," posted May 21, 2010)

DENVER: I know of no more cheerful a being in the universe than Christ. When He says: "Be of good cheer," we ought to all accept that as the mantra. There is nothing that any of us will ever go through that He hasn't gone through, with a considerable greater degree of difficulty. He lived with a higher specific gravity than any of us had to ever fight against. And He won for each of us a prize that is potentially eternal. It will be eternal, one way or the other. But if you take full measure of what He offers, it will be delightfully eternal.

Cowardice is largely predicated upon fear. Don't be cowardly. Don't be fearful. Fear is the opposite of faith. For goodness sake, you're already in the battle! You're already going to be overtaken. The fact of the matter is that no one gets out of here alive. Live this life nobly, fearlessly. When you take the wounds that come your way, you make sure that they come to your front! Don't let 'em shoot you in the back. Go about your life boldly, nobly, valiantly; because it is only through valiance in the testimony of Jesus Christ that you can hope to secure anything—not valiance in your fidelity to anything other than Jesus Christ. The fact of the matter is that faith must be based in Him, and Him alone.

The work of God really is of deep import and the "light-mindedness" issue doesn't have a single thing to do with a sense of humor or laughter. It doesn't have anything to do with that. Light-mindedness has to do with treating lightly things that are really important. Light-mindedness means that you do not assign the correct value to something that comes from God—you treat it lightly. I don't care how much you laugh—and yes, God has a sense of humor—and when I'm all dour, and desperate, and pleading, very often the first response of the Lord is a quip about how inappropriately I'm behaving. The first message in the first talk of the "10 talks" was to be of good cheer because our Lord is of good cheer. He takes seriously the things that will save us, but he really does enjoy our company and wishes that we likewise enjoyed one another's company as we ought to do.

> *It is not enough to receive my covenant, but you must also abide it. And all who abide it, whether on this land or any other land, will be mine and I will watch over them and protect them in the day of harvest, and gather them in as a hen gathers her chicks under her wings. I will number you among the remnant of Jacob, no longer outcasts, and you will inherit the promises of Israel. You shall be my people and I will be your God, and the sword will not devour you. And unto those who will receive will more be given, until they know the mysteries of God in full.*

> *But remember that without the fruit of repentance, and a broken heart and a contrite spirit, you cannot keep my covenant; for I, your Lord, am meek and lowly of heart. Be like me. You have all been wounded, your hearts pierced through with sorrows because of how the world has treated you. But you have also scarred one another by your unkind treatment of each other, and you do not notice your misconduct toward others because you think yourself justified in this. You bear the scars on your countenances, from the soles of your feet to the head, and every heart is faint. Your visages have been so marred that your hardness, mistrust, suspicions, resentments, fear, jealousies, and anger toward your fellow man bear outward witness of your inner self; you cannot hide it. When I appear to you, instead of confidence, you feel shame. You fear and withdraw from me because you bear the blood and sins of your treatment of brothers and sisters. Come to me and I will make sins as scarlet become white as snow, and I will make you stand boldly before me, confident of my love.*

> *I descended below it all, and know the sorrows of you all, and have borne the grief of it all, and I say to you, Forgive one another. Be tender with one another, pursue judgment, bless the oppressed, care for the orphan, and uplift the widow in her need for I have redeemed you from being orphaned and taken you that you are no longer a widowed people. Rejoice in me, and rejoice with your brethren and sisters who are mine also. Be one.* (T&C 157:48-50)

It's almost amusing for people in their arrogance to assume that they know enough to understand what God is doing or has done because the things of

God are of deep import; and careful and solemn and ponderous and prayerful thought can only find them out. Your understanding has to reach into heaven itself and search into and contemplate the darkest abyss, if you're going to save any soul, including your own and that's not accomplished casually, nor is it accomplished without sacrifice. (see *TPJS*, pg 137, March 25, 1839)

A Lord, whose own heart was broken, ultimately requires a great deal to happen to create a broken heart and a contrite spirit, willing to endure, however uncomfortable it may make you feel, all that God requires of you to do in order to be a son of God—and that's not accomplished in an instant suddenly. It's accomplished carefully and over trial after trial, test after test, temptation after temptation; but, ultimately, it will be required before the return of the Lord. It will be mandatory, before the return of the Lord, for the original Holy Order to exist in all of its components. It has to. And there has to be established, on the earth, all of the rites that originally belonged in the days of Adam, because that has to be surrendered back. And it has to go back through those that had possessed it in order for God to have the right to come and claim this world as His own, and to exercise dominion over it; because if the dominion over the world belongs to someone other than Him, His word cannot be broken, and He cannot come and interfere with the right of dominion that exists on the Earth. It has to exist. It has to be fully restored, and it has to be in the possession of those who will not covet it—those who will not, like Cain, attempt to influence the conditions of salvation for the souls of men—those who look upon it merely as a burden to be held, under the authority of God, belonging to Him, to be returned to Him so that He can come and fix this broken world and bring wickedness to an end.

Christ tried to explain what it was that would make us right in the Sermon on the Mount. He says here is the commandment: *Thou shalt not commit adultery,* but I say to you, you can walk around all day not committing adultery and still be a lustful, wretched, perverse, undesirable, unlovely, unbecoming, depraved soul. So don't lust in your heart. You have read and it's been told you: *Thou shalt not kill.* You can do a lot of damage to another human being without killing them. Words can be weapons. You can do a lot of damage with the words you speak, and never inflict a single bruise on another person's body; but you can break their heart, and Christ says: *Love your enemies.* Do good to those that hate you and despitefully abuse you. Don't be angry with your brother. Don't call them names. Return good for evil (see Matthew 5-7; see also Matthew 3 RE).

Christ was saying the problem isn't your conduct, the problem is your heart. And I want to take that heart—Christ telling us—I want to take that heart that you've got and I want to break it. I want you to have a broken heart and I want you to have a contrite spirit, because the only way you're going to let me come in is if what you're doing, to surround yourself, is broken down enough to permit me to come in.

There remains [a] great work yet to be done. Receive my covenant and abide in it, not as in the former time[s] when jarring, jealousy, contention, and backbiting caused anger, broke hearts, and hardened the souls of those claiming to be my saints. But receive it in spirit, in meekness, and in truth. I have given you a former commandment that I, the Lord, will forgive whom I will forgive, but of you it is required to forgive all men. And again, I have taught that if you forgive men their tresspasses, your Heavenly Father will also forgive you; but if you forgive not men their tresspasses, neither will your Heavenly Father forgive your tresspasses. How do I act toward mankind? If men intend no offense, I take no offense, but if they are taught and should have obeyed, then I reprove and correct, and forgive and forget. You cannot be at peace with one another if you take offense when none is intended. But again I say, judge not others except by the rule you want used to weigh yourself.

I will give to you words to speak to the people to accept my covenant, and you shall read [these] words to them. Read first to the people these words I now speak, and then read the words of the covenant, and the people who will receive and do my words and my covenant shall then stand and say, Yes.

Then by my law and my word they will be mine, and I will be with and lead my people onward through the spirit of Truth, the Comforter, the Record of Heaven, the peaceable things of immortal glory, even the holy ghost which will abide with them, and you will be children of the Most High God, fellow servants and numbered with the congregation of the just. Therefore rejoice! And the angels are given charge to watch over and protect my people. My eyes are over the whole earth and all men everywhere are before me. Men conspire to overthrow and oppress, and use violence to control others through fear. My Spirit restrains the destroyer, to allow those who are in the world and willing to give heed to my words time to prepare, but I will not always suffer...the wickedness of man.

The Earth groans under the wickedness of mankind upon her face, and she longs for peace to come. She withholds the abundance of her bounty because of the offenses of men against me, against one another, and against her. But if righteousness returns and my people prove by their actions, words, and thoughts to yield to my Spirit and hearken to my commandments, then will the Earth rejoice, for the feet of those who cry peace upon her mountains are beautiful indeed, and I, the Lord, will bring again Zion, and the earth will rejoice.

In the world, tares are ripening. ...So I ask you, What of the wheat? Let your pride, and your envy, and your fears depart from you. [And] I will come to my tabernacle and dwell with my people in Zion, and none will overtake it.

Cry peace. Proclaim my words. Invite those who will repent to be baptized and forgiven, and they shall obtain my Spirit to guide them. The time is short and I come quickly, therefore open your mouths and warn others to flee the wrath which is to come as men in anger destroy one another. The wicked shall destroy the wicked, and I will hold the peacemakers in the palm of my hand and none can take them from me.

Be comforted, be of good cheer, rejoice, and look up, for I am with you who remember me, and all those who watch for me, always, even unto the end. Amen. (T&C 157:58-66)

———

The foregoing excerpts are taken from:

- Denver's blog entry titled "3 Nephi 12:19," posted October 10, 2010;
- Denver's blog entry titled "Be of Good Cheer," posted May 21, 2010;
- Denver's *40 Years in Mormonism Series*, Talk #1 titled "Be of Good Cheer," given in Boise, ID on September 10th, 2013;
- Denver's conference talk titled "Things to Keep Us Awake at Night," given in St. George, UT on March 19th, 2017;
- The presentation of "Answer and Covenant," given at the Covenant of Christ Conference in Boise, ID on September 3rd, 2017;
- A fireside talk titled "The Holy Order," given in Bountiful, UT on October 29, 2017; and
- His remarks given at the Joseph Smith Restoration Conference in Boise, ID on June 24, 2018

96. One Eternal Round

In this episode, Denver answers the question, "How can God's paths be straight, when his course is one Eternal round?"

———

DENVER: I don't believe it is necessary to reveal any new thing in order to be able to teach in a manner that opens eyes to everything the Lord has, and is doing, other than to expound the scriptures. He didn't think it was necessary.

If you go to verse 19, of the Joseph Smith History, and you read the words that come out of the Lord's mouth when He speaks to Joseph, he quotes or paraphrases Isaiah, Jeremiah, and Paul. In just one short run-on sentence, the Lord talks about the doctrines that they teach for commandments the doctrines of men; *[they have] a form of godliness, but they deny the power thereof.... They draw near to me with their lips, but their hearts are far from me* (JS-H 1:19; see also JS-H 2:5 RE).

Once again, when He appears to Joseph in the First Vision, our Lord is expounding the scriptures. He picks, and puts it together, and says—this is the condition in which you find yourself. This is what the prophets were speaking about. This is that day about which mankind would search the earth and not find the word of God.

When Moroni comes to visit with Joseph Smith, what does Moroni do in order to qualify Joseph for the ministry that he's about to embark upon? Moroni quotes prophecies from Malachi, from Isaiah, from Peter, from Joel. And so, it took a long time for me to be able to see the pattern, but the pattern in which the Lord reveals and discusses new truth is the same in every generation. And so, when He came, in answer to prayer, and spoke to me sitting in a barracks—despite the fact that there were no fireworks, no pillar of fire, no shining man in a robe—He used the scriptures and expounded them to increase my understanding.

So today, I want to use the scriptures in order to bear testimony of who our Lord is, and how significant His example is for us. And I told you before, in Idaho Falls, that, in my view, *The Lectures on Faith* are scripture. They were adopted as such, and I'm to read from the 7th Lecture on Faith, paragraph 9, about Christ.

Where shall we find a saved being? For if we can find a saved being, we may ascertain without much difficulty what all others must be in order to be saved. ... We think that it will not be a matter of dispute that two beings who are unlike each other cannot both be saved, for whatever constitutes the salvation of one will constitute the salvation of every creature which will be saved. And if we find one saved being in all existence, we may see what all others must be or else not be saved. We ask, then: Where is the prototype? Or where is the saved being? We conclude as to the answer of this question there will be no dispute among those who believe the Bible that it is Christ. All will agree [with] this, that he is the prototype or standard of salvation, or in other words, ...he is a saved being. And if we should continue our interrogation, and ask how it is that he is saved, the answer would be, because he is a just and holy being. And if he were anything different from what he is he would not be saved, for his salvation depends on his being precisely what he is and nothing else. For if it were possible for him to change in the least degree, so sure he would fail of salvation and lose all his dominion, power, authority, and glory, which constitutes salvation. For salvation consists in the glory, authority, majesty, power, and dominion which Jehovah possesses, and in nothing else, and no being can possess it but himself [and] one like him. (LoF 7:9 RE)

We read this and then we immediately gloss over it, as if what salvation consists of is Him and fairy dust, which He can distribute to make us like Him. This teaching that appears, this was what Joseph Smith worked on, editing for the months prior to the publication of The Doctrine and Covenants in 1835. He doesn't say in his diaries that he spent anytime on the revelations. That was trusted to a committee, and the committee was responsible for getting those ready for publication. And they did a bunch of freelancing and embellishing and expanding; and some of the stuff they added to the revelations was remarkably more expansive than what Joseph had received—revealed to him. That's not where Joseph spent his time. He spent his time on *The Lectures on Faith*. And this is early in his ministry. This is when he wanted to make sure that the doctrine was correct—and this is the doctrine that came rolling out in that first publication. And yet despite that, we tend to read this and not take it seriously.

If you are going to be saved, you must be **exactly**, you must be **precisely** what Christ is, and **nothing else**... K? You! At that moment, that is when you are saved. As a consequence of that, to speak of Christ is necessarily to speak of salvation. To understand Christ is to understand salvation. Despite how plainly this has been put, we still stop short of comprehending the doctrine.

You say you want to obtain an *expectation* here, that will follow you into the next life. I say if the authority to seal this did not first exist, and was not handed down from before the world was, then it would not last in the after-life. Joseph held up a ring and said, "There's no beginning and there's no end, it's one eternal round". I'm telling you, you're only on part of the cycle here. But, you *are* on part of this endless cycle *here*. *Now*. Today matters a great deal, therefore, what you do here matters infinitely, eternally, everlastingly. It matters! You have your doubts, but you should weigh them in the balance. Why not exercise faith? Why not change your eternal destiny? Why not choose good today?

The Gospel is delicious. Get rid of that stale wretched stuff you consume as part of an organized and stifled herd; and go on to find the life, the light, and the vigor contained in the words of scripture. The doctrine in our scriptures is delicious! Stop putting barriers around the scriptures. Stop forcing them to mean what you have been told they must mean. Let *them* tell *you* what they say about your preconceptions distorting their meaning. There's no rigid "orthodoxy" that governs or correlates their meaning. You will discover they are filled with a new religion altogether. In that religion, God is speaking to you directly. He is alive, and He is involved in your life. If you will partake of it and prepare yourselves, you can improve this estate in a way that will reflect credit into the next estate. Don't forfeit the opportunity.

Thus they become high priests forever. They become high priests when they have exercised faith and show good works that, in that status, lasts forever. They qualified before the foundation of this world. They come here, into this cycle, and they have authority here. But their authority began before the foundation of *this* world, and they can confer blessings that will continue into the *next* life. Therefore, they can bless, and you are blessed indeed.

> *Thus they [have] become high priests forever, after the order of the Son [of God], the Only Begotten of the Father, who is without beginning of days or end of years, who is full of grace, equity, and truth. And thus it is. Amen. Now, as I said concerning the holy order, or this high priesthood, there were many who were ordained and became high priests of God; and it was on account of their exceeding faith and repentance, and their righteousness before God, they choosing to repent and work righteousness rather than to perish; Therefore, they were called after this holy order, and were sanctified, and their garments were washed white through the blood of the Lamb.* (Alma 13:9-11; see also Alma 10:1 RE)

Do you see what's right before you? You say you want to be baptized and to be cleansed from all sin? I say, have at it! But in addition, the *prototype of the saved man* requires you do something more. You may only achieve a limited amount of grace in this life, but to that limited amount of grace, you must hold fast. You cannot receive more, if you will not receive what is offered to you now. But, if you will receive what is offered now, you will be added upon forever and forever. Or, in other words, you move up the ladder by how you conduct yourself in this cycle of creation; and in the next cycle, you will have so much the advantage. You can choose to move upward and to be added upon, or you can choose instead to remain as you are, worlds without end. The scriptures speak of things that happened "before the foundation of the world" or "in the first place" or "from the foundation of the world."

These statements make it clear what went on before *this* creation mattered and affected *who you are now*. In like manner, what you achieve in *this* life, through your heed and diligence, will affect what comes *after*. The course we are on has been ordained by God and is "one eternal round."

God has been at this a long time. Christ has, likewise, been involved for many repeated cycles of creation. Moses was told:

> By the word of my power, have I created them, which is mine Only Begotten Son, who is full of grace and truth. And worlds without number have I created; and I also created them for mine own purpose; and by the Son I created them, which is mine Only Begotten. [It is endless, and it is cyclical.] ...For behold, there are many worlds that have passed away by the word of my power. And there are many that now stand, and innumerable are they unto man; but all things are numbered unto me, for they are mine and I know them. (Moses 1:32-33,35; see also Genesis 1:6 RE)

This is God's great work. It has been going through cycles of creation, fall, redemption, judgment, and re-creation forever. It is endless. The Lord told Moses just how vast this process has grown:

> The heavens, they are many, and they cannot be numbered unto man; but they are numbered unto me, for they are mine. And as one earth shall pass away, and the heavens thereof even so shall another come; and there is no end to my works, neither to my words. (Moses 1:37-38; see also Genesis 1:7 RE)

This is a continual, endless cycle, worlds without end. Man falls into the cold realm of the temporal, but is returned again to the spiritual. The process allows development to occur in increments, as we choose, for our development. When a cycle begins, man is spirit. When it is underway, man is temporal and physical. But when a cycle ends, man is spirit again. We are nearing another turn of the wheel when wickedness will end. As modern revelation describes it:

> For the hour is nigh and the day soon at hand when the earth is ripe; and all the proud and they that do wickedly shall be as stubble; and I will burn them..., saith the Lord of Hosts, that wickedness shall not be upon the earth; For I will reveal myself from heaven with power and great glory, with all the hosts thereof, and dwell in righteousness with men on earth a thousand years, and the wicked shall not stand. [Then] when the thousand years are ended, and men...begin to deny their God, then will I spare the earth for but a little season; And the end shall come, and the heaven and the earth shall be consumed and pass away, and there shall be a new heaven and a new earth. (D&C 29:9,11,22-23; see also T&C 9:3,7)

As one ends, another begins. The cycle repeats, but nothing is lost. The old passes away, but everything is kept to be used again, *both men and beasts, [and] the fowls of the air, and the fishes of the sea; And not one hair, neither mote, shall be lost, for it is the workmanship of mine hand* (ibid. vs. 24 -25). It all continues in one eternal round, worlds without end.

When men are judged and condemned, they are sent away into everlasting fire prepared for the devil and his angels. They go away and cannot ascend to God's presence, because where God is, *they cannot come, for they have no power* (D&C 29:29). But, God cautions us:

> Remember that...my judgments are not given unto men; and as the [worlds], ... as the words have gone forth out of my mouth even so shall they be fulfilled, that the first shall be last, and...the last shall be first in all things whatsoever I have created by the word of my power, which is the power of my Spirit. [God set out how this cycle begins and ends]. For by the power of my Spirit created I them; yea, all things both spiritual and temporal—First spiritual, secondly temporal, which is the beginning of my work; and again, first temporal, and [second] spiritual, which is the last of my work—Speaking unto you that you may naturally understand; but unto myself my works have no end, neither beginning;

but it is given unto you that ye may understand, because ye have asked it of me and are agreed. (D&C 29:30-33; see also T&C 9:9 RE)

So, in the first place, before this world was organized from an already existing and previously used prior creation, the condition was spiritual. But it fell and became the temporal place where we presently reside—though patterned after the earlier world where we used to live, while in its spiritual state. Its present condition will be destroyed and returned again to a spiritual state. It will be quickened, and no longer the cold place it is today.

Have you ever noticed how the descriptions of the pre-earth organization and the Millennium seem alike? Have you ever wondered what *worlds without end* means? Have you ever considered how God's work never ends, and yet it has definite increments separating things from one cycle and the next?

God's works do not end. You are the developmental work God has chosen as His greatest accomplishment. He intends to bring to pass your immortality and eventual eternal life. How long that requires for any given individual depends upon how long it takes *you* to become like the prototype of the saved man. How long *you* will delay attaining to the resurrection is within your own control. I'm hoping to awaken you to the great work lying before you.

The first appearance of the Lord was in the 50th year of my life—an age considered suitable for more than a thousand years for a man to qualify for service in the Holy Order after the Order of the Son of God. The Lord has visited with and taught me on many occasions since then, but never at my insistence. I have never controlled His appearing. My experience is that He cannot be conjured nor controlled. I can petition, but *He* comes when *He* decides. The Lord has never appeared to me in a dream. I've always been awake, fully aware of my surroundings, and with my senses unimpeded. When awakened during the night, sleep has always fled, and following such an encounter, I was always unable to return to sleep.

The Lord does everything according to His higher way of teaching. By beginning with a vision of His return, He set out the foundation for understanding His course, which is one eternal round. Since His first appearance, He has sent divers angels from Adam or Michael to Hyrum and Joseph Smith, giving line upon line, to confirm my hope in Christ. The most important thing for us is to repent, be baptized, and let virtue and righteousness guide our thoughts, deeds, and words. We ought to deal fairly with one another, and to be kind. You may remember abuses from priesthood leaders in your last church. *Do not bring that with you.* Leave behind all the sins and errors found in other organizations and show Christ-like patience and charity to one another.

We follow Christ to become more like Him. He requires faith, repentance, and baptism; and bestows the Holy Ghost to bring all things back to our remembrance. When we hear Christ's message to repent and be baptized, it is our duty to respond, and then warn others so they can escape the coming judgment. The whole world struggles under a burden of sin that we are powerless to remove without Christ. He suffered and overcame the sins of the world so we can avoid the consequences of sin, on condition of repentance and baptism, as He explained in a revelation in 1829:

> *For behold, I, God, have suffered these things for all, that they might not suffer **if** they would repent; But if they would not repent they must suffer even as I; which suffering caused myself, even God, the greatest of all, to tremble because of pain, and to bleed at every pore, and to suffer both body and spirit—and would that I might not drink the bitter cup, and shrink—* [In that context, the word shrink means cower. Christ cowered.] *Nevertheless, glory be to the Father, and I partook and finished my preparations unto the children of men. Wherefore, I command you again to repent, lest I humble you with my almighty power.* (D&C 19:16-20; see also T&C 4:5-6 RE)

When the Lord spoke to Joseph in 1829 about the atonement, He mentioned only suffering in Gethsemane—not His death on the cross; because it was in Gethsemane His greatest work was accomplished. I was shown it, and have given an account in the book *Come, Let Us Adore Him.*

In order for His work to be completed, He had to die. Death allowed Him to attain the resurrection, and break the bonds of death.

> *For the time cometh, saith the Lamb of God, that I will work a great and...marvelous work among the children of men; a work which shall be everlasting, either on the one hand or on the other—either to the convincing of them unto peace and [eternal] life, or unto the deliverance of them to the hardness of their hearts and the blindness of their minds unto their being brought down into captivity, and also into destruction, both temporally and spiritually, according to the captivity of the devil, of which I have spoken.* That's First Nephi 14: 7. (see also 1 Nephi 3:26 RE)

There will be a time when the accounts will all be settled. Everything will become everlasting, and people will either inherit eternal lives and move forward, or they will return to be destroyed both temporally and spiritually again. Joseph Smith commented in the King Follett Discourse about the process of gaining exaltation. He explained:

> "You must begin with the first, and go on until you learn all the principles of exaltation. But it will be a great while after you have passed through the veil before you will have learned them. It is not all to be comprehended in this world; it will be a great work to learn our salvation and exaltation even beyond the grave." (*TPJS*, p. 348)

Death and hell are the devil's domain—he's the god of that world. And since we have death and suffering here, he calls himself the god of this world. Those who come here are subject to his buffeting and his will. They're tormented, tempted, troubled, and then they die. While captive here, they endure the insults of the flesh, and the difficulties of trying to find their way back to God. Those who find *Him*, however, are able to receive peace and life eternal through a higher process. The devil is bound for them, and they are able to be *added upon* by the experiences and the difficulties here.

All of this is called a "great and marvelous work" to occur "among the children of men." Note, it isn't the *remnant,* or the *gentiles,* but *the children of men.* Why so? Is everyone invited? Why, if everyone is invited, will it largely only affect the *remnant,* and the *gentiles,* and the *scattered Israel,* and *Jews*? What about the *heathen,* since they are also *the children of men*? Don't they also have part in the first resurrection? Will even some of them be included among *the children of men,* who belong and behold this *great and marvelous work*?

Why is it *everlasting,* whether it is for *peace and eternal life,* or *captivity and destruction*? Isn't **Everlasting** another of God's names just like **Eternal** and **Endless**? If so, then what does the *everlasting peace and eternal life,* and *everlasting captivity and destruction* really involve?

Why does God want us to respond to His message and get out of this Telestial Kingdom into another higher kingdom? Why does He want us to become like Him? How is this experience able to make us more like Him? If one is involved in the continuation of the lives, is that distant and second-hand? Or does God, or the Gods get involved directly with His or Their children? What causes hardness of heart? What causes blindness of their eyes? Why are those whose hearts are hard, unable to receive Christ? Why are those who are blind unwilling to see Him?

This cycle of inviting people to come to the Lamb of God has been going on for some time now. When mankind generally rejected Him after the time of Noah, there was a chosen people who were given a sacred tradition. Ultimately, they got proud, failed to recognize Him when He came, rejected His message, and killed Him. Gentiles converted and became the inheritors of His teachings. Then the gentiles began to persecute the previously chosen people for generations. In this verse, the gentiles are remembered, sacred materials are entrusted to them with an obligation to spread that sacred material back to the earlier chosen people. However, for the gentiles to be able to accomplish this, they need to hold onto the sacred materials and teachings. You simply can't spread abroad what you've failed to retain.

If the gentiles let the sacred materials and teachings fall into disuse, forfeit their priesthood by draining it of any power, and have nothing to offer the previously chosen people, then the gentiles will be cast off, trodden under foot, and destroyed, as we've seen earlier. This verse reminds us of what is at stake—*Eternity*, or at least God's judgment. It'll be embarrassing to return to Him unimproved, and un-added upon; particularly when His hand was stretched out to us all the day long. Gentiles, who do as they are asked, are given all the blessings of the chosen people. Those who do not are rejected and destroyed.

As a friend and I discussed last week, Hindu's advise us to get off the wheel and return to God. They may be onto something with that thought. One eternal round, indeed.

It is of note that Christ points to the Father in all things, and therefore, points to the Father in this teaching in 3rd Nephi 18:4, as well. The commandments He teaches are those which the Father hath commanded Him, that He should give unto you. In every respect the Son points to the Father. It is always the Father's will and the Father's glory that Christ seeks to uphold.

The Son seeks our glory and exaltation, while giving credit to the Father for all He does. Though the Savior occupies the central role in the process, He serves others. Selflessly, He instructs us on how we may be blessed and glorified. Selflessly, He points to the Father as the one to receive your testimony by obedience. Selflessly, He explains the Father is the one who has commanded these things. But through it all, it is Christ who has been the messenger of salvation. He's the one whose sacrifice made possible our redemption. It is Christ whose body and blood we must partake of for redemption. It is Christ of whom the Father testifies. Christ bears testimony of the Father. The Father bears record of the Son. In one eternal round, they form a circle. It is Christ's work and the Father's commandment which invites us to join in that circle and become one with Them. How simple the ways provided for us in this condescension of God. How plain the way has been given. Yet we find reasons to do more, or less, than what is asked. For that we forfeit blessings, which might otherwise have been ours.

This is a dark world, with so many options for getting it wrong. Like King Benjamin said, I cannot tell you all the ways whereby you may sin, because they are literally infinite. The challenge is not to identify errors, because that can occupy a lifetime and never move you an inch forward. The real challenge is to finally recognize there is only *One*. One Lord, one faith, one baptism, and it is His. He's the keeper of the gate and He employs no servant there. He does send people out from time to time to point to Him as He stands at the gate, but when we come ~~abroad~~ [aboard] with Him, it is through Him alone we find ourselves redeemed and forgiven.

For me there has been repeated reminders that the Lord's path is straight, and does not vary from side to side, nor is there any degree of changeableness for Him. But His course, that is the pathway we find ourselves on, is *one eternal round*. Meaning we are in orbit, so to speak, around Him and His pathway. For us, we move in an upward spiral—sometimes facing in one direction, and sometimes turned around in the opposite direction—as we move upward along His path. We are here to be "added upon," and sometimes that process is so incremental, so slight, and so apparently limited, that we can live a lifetime and only move a single step forward toward God. But for God, who is infinite and eternal, that fulfills His promise, and even His expectations for the most of mankind.

We are here to experience the difference between light and dark, good and bad, and gain knowledge of good and evil. If a man lives without God in the world, and his days are few and mean, he may nevertheless rejoice in eternity for what he gained by experience here. Even the abuse inflicted upon us can turn to God's glory, if we return to Him better able to know the difference between good and evil. The Gospel plan is infinite and holds out promise for every man and woman who ever lived and died. How great a step we gain, in the few years of mortality allotted to us, is not as important as the experience from which we are better able to discern between good and evil.

———

The foregoing excerpts are taken from:

- Denver's *40 Years in Mormonism Series*, Talk #7 titled "Christ, Prototype of the Saved Man" given in Ephraim, UT on June 28, 2014, including additional explanatory comments added later to the transcript and subsequently recorded on December 8, 2019
- Denver's conference talk titled "The Doctrine of Christ", given in Boise, ID on September 11th, 2016
- Denver's blog post titled "1 Nephi 14:7", posted July 7, 2010, and subsequently recorded on December 8, 2019
- Denver's blog post titled "3 Nephi 18:4", posted November 11, 2010, and subsequently recorded on December 8, 2019; and
- Denver's comments included in an email exchange posted March 8, 2016 on LDS Freedom Forum by user Jesef, subsequently recorded by Denver on October 26, 2019

97. God in Our Day, Part 1

This is the first part of a special series on what God is doing in our day.

———

DENVER: Alright, so I want to skip to the time period that is relevant to our day in Jacob chapter 5, beginning at verse 48—because all the rest of that stuff is past history, and what we're trying to do now is to figure out, from where we are, how we get to the spot in which we might not be burned up, root and branch. Beginning at verse 48:

> And it came to pass that the servant said unto his master: Is it not the loftiness of [the] vineyard—have not the branches thereof overcome the roots which are good? [That is to say, the roots, the original covenant, the original stock from which we reckon—they were good. But we've become lofty in the way in which we approach things, and as a consequence of that, we have done something that has so cumbered the construct of where we find ourselves, that we've essentially destroyed the ability of the roots to do us any good.] And because the branches have overcome the roots thereof, behold they grew faster than the strength of the roots, taking strength unto themselves [that is, their pride, their haughtiness; they decided that they were driving this and not the covenants that were originally made in the beginning], Behold, I say, is not this the cause that the trees of thy vineyard have [all] become corrupted? And it came to pass that the Lord of the vineyard said unto the servant: Let us go to and hew down the trees of the vineyard and cast them into the fire, that they shall not cumber the ground of my vineyard, for I have done all. What could I have done more for my vineyard? But, behold, the servant said unto the Lord of the vineyard: Spare it a little longer. And the Lord said: Yea, I will spare it a little longer, for it grieveth me that I should lose the trees of my vineyard. (Jacob 5:48-51; see also Jacob 3:22-23 RE)

See, the Lord, despite the fact that He can't think of anything else that He's left undone in all of His preparations—and it is only that; it is only His preparations—

Go to Doctrine and Covenants section 19, and look at what it is that the Lord did for us in the atonement. In describing what He went through—in verse 19 of section 19 of the Doctrine and Covenants—the Lord says: *Glory be to the Father, I partook and finished **my preparations** unto the children of* *men* (emphasis added; see also T&C 4:5). That's what He did! And He has finished that. He finished His preparations. But 20, now, is us: *Wherefore, I command you again to repent, lest I humble you with my almighty power* (ibid, para. 6). That's us. He's done His part. What more could He do? Well, the only other thing He could do is rob us of our agency, and He's not prepared to do that because our existence then would come to an end—because without the freedom to choose, we don't have existence. Therefore, what more could He have done? But it does grieve Him that He's going to lose the trees of his vineyard.

> *Wherefore* [the Lord says], *let us take of the branches of these which I have planted in the nethermost parts of my vineyard* [that's where we find ourselves], *and let us graft them into the tree from whence they came* [that is, let's restore the covenant—or at least make it possible for it to be so]; *and let us pluck from the tree those branches whose fruit is most bitter* [that's coming], *and graft in the natural branches of the tree in the stead thereof. And this will I do that the tree may not perish, that, perhaps* [perhaps—on the off chance that; that without the ability to control the outcome; that depending upon what you decide to do—perhaps] the Lord *may preserve unto* Himself *the roots thereof for mine own purpose* [that is, some of the promises that were made back to the Fathers that their seed would not be utterly destroyed; might be fulfilled; perhaps]. (Jacob 5:52-53, see also Jacob 3:23 RE)

How great a number is required in order for the Lord to vindicate His promise? It's not numerosity. It's never been about a big volume. It's the quality of the salvation. Because if you can save but one, what you have saved is infinite and eternal. And therefore, it continues on forever.

Behold, the roots of the natural branches of the tree which I planted whithersoever I would are yet alive... (ibid, vs. 54). Those promises remain; they are still in play. What the Father promised—what the covenants that were established did—remain in play. It is yet possible for the Lord to vindicate everything that has been given.

Wherefore, that I may preserve them also for mine own purpose, I will take of the branches of this tree, and I will graft them in unto them (ibid). This is the process by which the house of Israel is restored; not in the way that you mass-produce, but in the way in which some rise up and lay hold upon that original religion that belonged to the Fathers, that came down from the beginning, that existed one time—that is to exist again.

Yea, I will graft [into] them the branches of their mother tree, that I may preserve the roots also unto mine own self [notice the word *mother* appears in there, too —the *mother tree*] *...when they [may] be sufficiently strong perhaps they may bring forth good fruit unto me, [that] I may yet have glory in the fruit of my vineyard* (ibid).

And then they go through things—verse 61: *...call servants, that we may labor diligently with our might in the vineyard, that we may prepare the way, that I may bring forth again the natural fruit...*(see also ibid, para. 25). That's the whole purpose of the endeavor. And when they call servants in order to help them, the labor of the servants is confined to trying to make the vineyard finally produce fruit again.

Verse 62: *Let us go to and labor with our might this last time, for behold the end draweth nigh, and this is for the last time that I shall prune my vineyard* (ibid).

He tells them again in verse 64: *...the last time, for the end draweth nigh. And if it [so be] that these last grafts shall grow, and [shall] bring forth...natural fruit, then [ye shall] prepare the way for them, that they may grow* (ibid).

Again in verse 71:

> *For behold, this is the last time that I shall nourish my vineyard; for the end is nigh... the season speedily cometh; ...if ye labor with your might with me ye shall have joy in the fruit which I shall lay up unto myself against the time which will soon come. And it came to pass...the servants did go and labor with their mights; and the Lord of the vineyard labored also with them.* (See also Jacob 3:26 RE)

Because the Lord in the last effort is not going to leave the servants that He sends unattended to by His ministration. This is why, in the verses we've been reading in every location we've been at, we find the personal ministry of the Lord Jesus Christ direct, immediate, and involved. He continues to remain personally in charge of what is going to happen. But, as it begins to happen they have to sit back and watch. Because the question isn't, 'Is the labor any less, any well prepared, any less capable, any less complete?' The question is, 'What are the branches going to do?'

You can minister all you want to the tree, but the tree has to respond, sometimes to what they view as offensive pruning, offensive digging, offensive conduct, of cutting, moving, and grafting, and saying, 'What you have here is error. What you have here is a bundle of false tradition that will damn you.'

You can plant the doctrine. You can restore the truth. You can have the Prophet Joseph Smith declare to you that he wants to be held to account for every word of the testimony that he delivers to you in a colonized set of scripture. But if you decide that you're going to throw that away and you will not allow it to graft in and inform you about the nature of God and the nature of the religion that God is seeking to deliver to you, then the ministration and the pruning and the care does not result in fruit. It simply results in a rather damaged vineyard continuing to produce precious little other than what is suitable to be gathered into bundles and burned

Okay, let's go back to that 11th chapter of Isaiah (Isaiah 5:3 RE), because man, have we made a mess of that. Okay, this is about to be fulfilled. *There shall come forth*—this is chapter 11 of Isaiah—*There shall come forth a rod out of the stem of Jesse.* The Rod is a servant who is a descendent of Jesse—who is a Levite—and Ephraim, unto whom is rightly belonging the priesthood. Keep your finger there on that chapter 11 of Isaiah, and turn back to Doctrine and Covenants section 113, and you'll see where these words are explained. Who is the Stem...spoken of...

> *Verily thus saith the Lord: It is Christ.* Verse 3: *What is the rod spoken of in the fifth verse of the 11th chapter of Isaiah, that should come of the Stem of Jesse? Behold... saith the Lord: It is a servant* [a servant!] *in the hands of Christ, who is partly a descendant of Jesse... as well as of Ephraim, or of the house of Joseph, on whom there is laid much power.* (See also T&C 129: 1-2)

Well, look. Until you succeed, you've failed. I don't care who comes along, claiming whatever they want to claim. Until the work is done, you can't take credit for it—period. There's all kinds of nonsense that circulates about 'Who has the keys? Button, button, who's got the button?' Look, someone's going to do a work. When the work is done, you will know. Until the work is done, no one can be identified with the role—period. It is arrogance; it is pretentiousness; it is foolishness for anyone to step forward and say: 'I, I, I am that man!' Do the work. Finish the course. Fulfill the covenant. You do that, you can take the name. Until you do the work, it's just noise.

So there's gonna come forth:

> *A rod out of the stem of Jesse...a Branch shall grow out of his roots:...the spirit of the LORD shall rest upon him, the spirit of wisdom and understanding, the spirit of counsel and might, the spirit of knowledge and of the fear of the LORD.* [Oh, thank God! Someone will finally

fear the Lord more than they fear man! I look forward to that moment.] *And shall make him of quick understanding in the fear of the LORD: and he shall not judge after the sight of his eyes, neither reprove after the hearing of his ears: But with righteousness shall he judge the poor, and reprove with equity for the meek of the earth:...he shall smite the earth with the rod of his mouth.* [In this context it is the word of God.] *And with the breath of his lips [he] shall...slay the wicked. And righteousness shall be the girdle of his loins,...faithfulness the girdle of his reins. The wolf...shall dwell with the lamb,...the leopard shall lie down with the kid; and the calf and the young lion and the fatling together; and a little child shall lead them.* [These things are shortly to come to pass.] *And the cow and the bear shall feed; and their young ones shall lie down together: and the lion shall eat straw like the ox. The sucking child shall play on the hole of the asp, and the weaned child shall put his hand on the cockatrice's den. They shall not hurt nor destroy in all my holy mountain: for the earth shall be full of the knowledge of the LORD, as the waters cover the sea.* [You see, it's knowledge, full of knowledge of the Lord. That's what you have to lay hold on.] *And in that day there shall be a root of Jesse, which shall stand for an ensign of the people; to it shall the Gentiles seek: and his rest shall be glorious. And it shall come to pass in that day, that the Lord shall set his hand again the second time to recover the remnant of his people, which shall be left.* (Isaiah 11:1-11; see also Isaiah 5:3-4 RE)

Well, this shall shortly come to pass. Not then, not that day, but by and by.

You know, when a branch is spoken of, if you look at John 15:1-6 (I'm not going to do that because our time is far spent; see also John 9:10 RE), but Christ gives a sermon about Him being the "true vine," about how you cannot bear fruit unless you are connected to the true vine. Once again, that is a genealogical term; that is a "family of God" term; that is a "son of God" term, and He intends to make many sons of God.

Joseph is receiving, in this first interview with the angel Moroni, an announcement about the first indications of the restoration of God's intent to restore a holy family. God is telling us what He wants. He—God—wants to have upon the earth again His family. But we must respond—we. This is your dispensation; this is your time. You came down here with the intent of living and finding the things that will bring you back. This is your opportunity. Don't let some other group claim that it doesn't belong to you. These scriptures are only going to be fulfilled when enough people awake and arise to realize that it is devolving upon you the obligation to find, to heed, to seek, to search, to pray, to obey, and to form what is necessary in order to fulfill the promises and the covenants that were made to the fathers.

Another statement from Joseph makes it clear the Restoration was intended to reintroduce the original religion of the Bible, not the diluted Christianity of his day. The original Faith, in the first dispensations, had more understanding than what we find preserved in the Bible. Joseph was searching back into these beginnings. His heart was *turned to the fathers* of the first generations. He wanted a return of their original as part of the end. It was to be nothing less. Consider this declaration:

> [H]as the day of miracles ceased? Or have angels ceased to appear unto the children of men? Or has he withheld the power of the Holy Ghost from them? Or will he do so, so long as time lasts, or the earth shall stand, or there shall be one man upon the face thereof to be saved? Behold, I say unto you, Nay. For it is by faith that miracles are wrought. It is by faith that angels appear and minister unto men. Wherefore, if these things have ceased, woe be unto the children of men, for it is because of unbelief, and all is vain. For no man can be saved, according to the words of Christ, save they shall have faith on his name. Wherefore, if these things have ceased, then has faith ceased also, and awful is the state of man, for they are as though there had been no redemption made. (Moroni 7:35-38; see also Moroni 7:7 RE)

If the heavens open to us, we have faith. If the heavens are brass, we are faithless. Without faith, it is as if Christ provided us no redemption. These words are as inspiring as they are sobering.

At the conclusion of the vision of the three-heavens, Joseph wrote the following. It clarifies that we are supposed to access heaven, and see for ourselves the glory to be found there:

> But great and marvelous are the works of the Lord, and the mysteries of His Kingdom which He showed unto us, which surpasses all understanding, in glory, and in might, and in dominion, which He commanded us we should not write while we were yet in the Spirit, and are not lawful for men to utter, neither is man capable to make them known, for they are only to be seen and understood by the power of the Holy Ghost, which God bestows on those who love him and purify themselves before Him, to whom He grants this privilege of seeing and knowing for themselves that through the power and manifestation of the

Spirit, while in the flesh, they may be able to bear His presence in the world of glory. (D&C 76:114-118; see also T&C 69:29)

This privilege of seeing and knowing for ourselves is available to us *while in the flesh*. The Restoration aimed to reconnect us to Heaven in a literal way. This is the same that transpired with Enoch and others in earlier Dispensations.

The Book of Mormon is filled with ascension lessons and examples. There is one verse that captures Joseph Smith's ascent theology. That verse compresses it into a single sentence. It explains why the Book of Mormon contains the *fullness of the gospel*. And it's perhaps Joseph's most inspired declaration:

> *Verily thus says the Lord: It shall come to pass that every soul who forsakes their sins, and comes unto me, and calls on my name, and obeys my voice, and keeps my commandments, shall see my face and know that I Am, and that I am the true light that lights every man who comes into the world*[.] (D&C 93:1-2; see also T&C 93:1)

Every soul includes you and me. Every one of us has equal access to the Lord. The conditions are the same for all. Forsake sins; come to Christ; call on His name; obey His voice; keep His commandments. This is far more challenging than obedience to a handful of "thou shalt nots" because so much is required to be done, so much required to be known. A great deal of study and prayer is required to stand in the presence of the Lord. Once done, we shall see His face and know that He is the true light that enlightens every one. He is the God of the whole world.

Immediately after His resurrection, Christ did not minister to gentiles. But after the Book of Mormon came forth, Gentiles are also eligible for Christ's ministry in very deed:

> *And it shall come to pass that if the Gentiles shall hearken unto the Lamb of God in that day that He shall manifest himself unto them in word and also in power, and in very deed, unto the taking away of their stumbling blocks*[.] (1 Nephi 14:1; see also 1Ne 3:25 RE)

His promise to us is predicated on hearkening to the Lamb. Gentiles failed to do so, and upon Joseph's death, a great dearth set upon the Restoration. Until there is Gentile repenting and returning, it will continue to unwind. Since June 27, 1844 we have a Restoration slow moving car wreck. The pace of that decay is accelerating.

We must rage against the fading of that light, *and seek the face of the Lord always, that in patience we may possess our souls, and...have Eternal life* (D&C 101:38; see also T&C 101:6).

Evidence of Christ is everywhere. Joseph used cosmological terms in a passage describing the importance of light coming from Christ and His Father:

> *He is in the sun and the light of the sun, and the power thereof by which it was made. ...He is in the moon and is the light of the moon, and the power thereof by which it was made, as also the light of the stars and the power thereof by which they were made, and the earth also....* (D&C 88:7-10; see also T&C 86:1)

If you are alive, you are connected to Christ. If you detect the light of the sun, you detect a testimony of Christ. If you behold the moon moving in her cycles overhead, you behold a testimony of Christ.

False traditions are as destructive for us as outright disobedience. The result is the same. The difference is that when we know we disobey we feel guilt, but false traditions fool us into thinking we're obedient when we are merely misled.

Joseph also provided us with Christ's personal explanation of what He endured in order to atone for our sins. It is a profound statement, more so I think than anything found in the Four Gospels about the suffering that Christ had. [I'm looking at the time. I'll put this paper up on my website for you to read.]

There are hundreds of potential quotes that could be added to this paper. One final quote will end this part of the paper: *[W]hen ye are in the service of your fellow beings, ye are only in the service of your God* (Mosiah 2:17; see also Mosiah 1:8 RE).

This was how Christ lived His life. He showed forth the glory of God by serving and elevating others. We, too, can serve God by giving comfort to our fellow men and women. There is no end to the opportunities to help others. This life is abundant in opportunity to reflect God's grace, kindness, and help by service to others. If you act that part, you are in God's service. Think Sub-for-Santa and consider joining Sub-for-God. It will add 364 days of opportunity.

The angel who visited Joseph in 1823 said his name would be had for good and evil among all people. A similar message was repeated 16 years later in March 1839 when the voice of the Lord spoke to Joseph in Liberty Jail. God said to Joseph,

> *The ends of the earth shall inquire after your name, and fools shall have you in derision, and Hell shall rage against you, while the pure in heart, and the wise, and the noble, and the virtuous shall seek counsel, and authority, and blessings constantly from under your hand. And your people shall never be turned against you by the testimony of traitors, and although their influence shall cast you into trouble, and into bars and walls, you shall be had in honor.* (D&C 122:1-4; see also T&C 139:9)

Although these two are similar, there is a profound difference between the angel's statement in 1823 and the voice of God in 1839. The angel only said people would speak good and evil of Joseph. But God added a description of those who would speak evil, and those who would speak good of Joseph.

That voice of God said, *fools shall have [Joseph] in derision.* Because I accept this statement as God's, I am led to conclude all who have spoken derisively of Joseph have done so foolishly. We ought to stop our foolishness. We need to end the derision of Joseph.

God also condemned the *testimony of traitors* against Joseph. While alive, Joseph identified some of his contemporary traitors and named them: George Hinkle, John Corrill, Reed Peck, David Whitmer, W. W. Phelps, Sampson Avard, William McLellin, John Whitmer, Oliver Cowdery, Martin Harris, Thomas Marsh, and Orson Hyde. These had been prominent leaders, trusted friends, and one-time believers in Mormonism. It was false testimony from those from within the flock that led to imprisonment of Joseph and other leaders.

The traitors of 1838 were joined by yet more traitors between 1842 and '44. In Missouri, Joseph was accused of treason and inciting violence. In 1842-44, Joseph's traitors accused him of adultery, polygamy and lying. John C. Bennett was a sexual predator who claimed, amidst his secret seductions, that Joseph Smith authorized him to engage in his promiscuity.

When his misconduct came to light, Bennett admitted Joseph authorized no such wickedness. He swore under oath,

"...that he never was taught any thing in the least contrary to the strictest principles of the Gospel, or of virtue, or of the laws of God, or man, under any circumstances, or upon any occasion either directly or indirectly, in word or deed, by Joseph Smith: and that he never knew the said Smith to countenance any improper conduct whatever, either in pubic or private; and that he never did teach me in private that an illicit, illegal intercourse with the females was, under any circumstances, justifiable; and that I never knew him so to teach others." ("To the Church of Jesus Christ of Latter Day Saints, and to all the honorable part of Community." *Times and Seasons*, Vol. 3 (July 1, 1842) pp. 840-41.)

William Law was also involved in secret adultery, and Joseph Smith refused to seal Law's marriage. A conspiracy of traitors in 1844 included William Law, Charles Ivins, Francis Higbee, Chauncey Higbee, Robert Foster and Charles Foster, who published the *Nauvoo Expositor* accusing Joseph Smith of the very evil Joseph had been hunting down and eradicating through high council proceedings since the Bennett affair had become public two years earlier.

Joseph was unequivocal in his opposition to adultery and plural wife taking. About the time Bennett's misconduct was beginning to come to light, Joseph Smith organized the Female Relief Society to encourage moral and chaste conduct in Nauvoo. In addition to the steps he took privately to discipline those involved directly, he made many public declarations against plural wives and in favor of chastity and moral purity. These included, among others, among many others:

"Inasmuch as the public mind has been unjustly abused through the fallacy of Dr. Bennett's letters, we make an extract on the subject of marriage, showing the rule of the church on this important matter. The extract is from the Book of Doctrine and Covenants, and is the only rule allowed by the Church. *'Inasmuch as this church of Christ has been reproached with the crime of fornication, and polygamy; we declare that we believe, that one man should have one wife; and [that] one woman, but one husband, except in case of death, when either is at liberty to marry again."* ("Notice." *Times and Seasons*, Vol. 3 [September 1, 1842], p. 909; "Marriage." *Doctrine and Covenants*, Section C1, 1835, p. 251.)

That was published in the *Times and Seasons*. And then a letter that was also published in the *Times and Seasons*:

"As we have lately been credibly informed, that an Elder of the Church of Jesus Christ, of Latter-day Saints, by the name of Hiram Brown, has been preaching Polygamy, and other false and corrupt doctrines, in the county of Lapeer, state of Michigan. This is to notify him and the Church in general, that he has been cut off from the church, for his iniquity; and he is further notified to appear at the Special Conference, on the 6th of April next, to make answer to these charges." ("Notice." *Times and Seasons*, Vol. 5 [February 1, 1844], p. 423.)

And then in a talk that he gave:

"What a thing it is for a man to be accused of committing adultery, and having seven wives, when I can only find one. I am the same man, and as innocent as I was fourteen years ago; and I can prove them all perjurers." (*History of the Church*, Vol. 6, p. 411.)

He also encouraged the Relief Society to adopt a declaration titled "A Voice of Innocence." It was read publicly by W. W. Phelps on March 7, 1844, then edited by Emma Smith, adopted by the Relief Society, and published in the *Nauvoo Neighbor* on March 20, 1844.

Because of the testimony of traitors, Joseph Smith has been held in derision from 1842 to the present. He is accused of being a sexual predator, liar, and adulterer. Fools have repeated the accusations originally made by the confessed adulterer John C. Bennett, though Bennett testified under oath that Joseph was not responsible and never behaved in any improper way toward women.

In the derision of Joseph today we now have a chorus that includes the LDS Church, which claims him as their founder. It comes from Brian Hales, who claims to be an accurate biographer. It comes from anti-Mormons, and Christian ministers, and fundamentalists who have created a caricature they claim to be Joseph. There is little difference between these people and William Law, Charles Ivins, Francis Higbee, Chauncey Higbee, Robert Foster, and Charles Foster, who published the *Nauvoo Expositor*. There is an immense chorus of fools holding Joseph in derision, even among those who claim to be devout followers of the faith he restored.

I think the voice Joseph heard in Liberty Jail was God's. If I am right, then God's advice to *the pure in heart, wise, noble, and virtuous* is to *seek counsel, authority and blessing* from Joseph. God's advice leads me to adopt a view of

Joseph that is consistent with nobility and virtue. I do not believe you can regard Joseph as a sexual predator, liar, and adulterer without holding him in derision. The chief and unavoidable result of thinking of Joseph in those terms has been a legacy of excusing institutional lying, and promoting adulterous thoughts, and inappropriately entertaining the concept of women as mere breeding stock for the use of men.

It is not possible to harbor lustful, deceitful and adulterous thoughts in your heart and claim to be pure in heart. I do not believe you can conspire to commit bigamy and adultery and claim to be virtuous. I do not believe you can decide to trust the words of traitors and villains who contradict Joseph's account of his marital fidelity to Emma and to claim to seek counsel from Joseph. In short, those who claim to accept the restoration, but believe Joseph was a sexual predator, do not qualify as noble, wise, virtuous, or pure in thought.

All the restorationist groups that descend from the Brighamites are religious polygamists. Whether they think it right to practice that abomination at present, or only think it a true part of their religion, they are polygamists. Their faith descends from a great whore, and her daughters are likewise whores. It's time for those involved to awaken to their awful situation and admit their mother is a whore.

Joseph said and wrote a great deal publicly to condemn plural marriage. He said nothing in public to defend or justify it. Ok? We have an enormous record of Joseph opposing and condemning. We have no public declaration from Joseph Smith advocating or defending it. Clearly he did not want to be known as its advocate. He wanted to be understood as a staunch opponent of it.

It's important to realize the restoration was hijacked by polygamy and has never regained the momentum Joseph envisioned. That abomination has darkened men's hearts and broken women's hearts. It is used to justify looking upon women with lust in men's hearts, contrary to the Lord's command in the sermon on the mount.

I hold Joseph in some considerable esteem. On the lightning-rod issue of plural wives, I've decided the historical record does not convict Joseph of polygamy, lying, deception, sexual improprieties, or exploitation of women. If I thought of Joseph Smith as a man capable of such things I would join his traitors in deriding him. I prefer to think him virtuous and noble. I think it is only possible for any person whose heart is pure, and who prizes virtue, wisdom, and nobility to respect Joseph Smith by regarding him as pure, wise, noble, and virtuous. To me, adultery, promiscuity, and deceit are none of those things.

I reject adultery by any name or description. It's morally wrong if you call it plural wives, polygamy, celestial marriage, or any other misnomer. Adultery is prohibited in the Ten Commandments, and remains an important prohibition for any moral society.

Mormonism should never have been saddled with Brigham Young's program of making adultery a sacrament. But Mormonism should not have been saddled with many institutional accretions. Between June 27, 1844 and today, there have been too many incorrect subtractions, and far too many uninspired additions. Mormonism today requires both dramatic subtractions and necessary additions. No one seems willing to do that with the precision required to *strive to show yourself approved unto God, a workman that need not to be ashamed, rightly dividing the word of truth* (2 Timothy 2:15; see also 2 Timothy 1:6 RE).

Brigham Young was not the only one who betrayed Joseph and caused his memory to be held in derision. David Whitmer betrayed Joseph in 1838, testified against him, and helped cause his Missouri imprisonment. Many years later, Whitmer's testimony as a traitor and accuser was published in "An Address to All Believers in Christ." Though he had been excommunicated in 1838 and never lived in Nauvoo, he accepted and echoed the *Nauvoo Expositor's* claims about Joseph and polygamy.

Bastille posed the question in a song, "Pompeii": "Where do we begin? The rubble or our sins?" I think it begins with our sins. They first have to be set aside through Christ. But afterwards we have a Mormon landscape filled with rubble, out of joint, out of level, out of plumb, collapsed, or collapsing. Mormonism's founding texts tells us this is as it should be for the present. We were never supposed to see Zion before the witnessed Gentile failure and apostasy.

Christ declared to the Nephites a warning to the Gentiles:

> *"And thus commandeth the Father that I should say unto you, At that day when the Gentiles shall sin against my gospel and shall reject the fullness of my gospel and shall be lifted up in the pride of their hearts above all nations and above all the people of the whole earth, and shall be filled with all manner of lyings and of deceits and of mischiefs, and all*

manner of hypocrisy and murders and priestcrafts and whoredoms and of secret abominations, and if they shall do all those things and shall reject the fullness of my gospel, Behold, saith the Father, I will bring the fullness of my gospel from among them." (3 Nephi 16:10; see also 3 Nephi 7:5 RE)

This is not phrased as a possibility, but as an inevitability. It was never a question of "if" the gentiles would reject the fullness. It has always been only a matter of "when" it would take place. The various institutions quarrel over whether it has happened. Some of them deny it can or will happen. The soothing mantra "we will never lead you astray" defies the message Christ was commanded by the Father to declare to us.

Joseph Smith has been held in derision for too long. Even those who claim to follow the commandments from God that came through him, deride his memory. This has gone on unchecked for far too long. The saints fell under condemnation in 1831 for taking lightly the Book of Mormon and former commandments given through Joseph Smith. Then eight years later we're warned it was foolish to hold Joseph in derision. Reclaiming the restoration requires repentance. First, recovering and accepting the text of the Book of Mormon, and restoring the former commandments to what God originally spoke. That's been done by a small group of remnant believers. But second, we need to end the derision of Joseph and acknowledge that he was pure of heart, noble, and virtuous, and to act accordingly. It's foolish to magnify his errors to justify our own. It's wicked to attribute uncommitted sins to him to give ourselves a license to sin. Generations have been cursed for this error. We have been led astray. All of us in every branch of Mormonism err.

We've stumbled, and we've fallen down. We've discarded the expansive theology of Joseph Smith. The earliest dispensations had truth from Heaven as their guide. Joseph began re-assembling what was lost, but was slain before it was completed. We are the offspring of Heaven, and are capable of reuniting with Heaven while mortal. We also have the opportunity, through eons of progression, to become as our Parents, the Gods.

Now is the time to awaken, arise, and shake off the dust.

Some will awaken, arise, shake off the dust, and push forward to recover the restoration. God will set His hand a second time to accomplish His covenants. We're promised that there will be a last-days' Zion established on this, the American continent. We know that when it is here:

> [E]very man that will not take his sword against his neighbor must needs flee unto Zion for safety, and there shall be gathered unto it out of every nation under Heaven, and it shall be the only people that shall not be at war one with another. And it shall be said among the wicked, Let us not go up to battle against Zion, for the inhabitants of Zion are terrible, wherefore we cannot stand. And it shall come to pass that the righteous shall be gathered out from among the nations, and shall come to Zion singing with songs of everlasting joy. (D&C 45:68-71; see also T&C 31:15)

The restoration has indeed squandered many opportunities by those who went before. Most of those who accept Joseph Smith as a founder of their religion are still squandering the opportunity to see the work continue. But God's purposes do not fail and we have the option to proceed now. Some generation, at some point, still has a glorious, promised completion to anticipate. As long as some, even a very few, are willing to walk in God's path, they will see the completion of this glorious, final work.

> This is the purpose that is purposed upon the whole earth, and this is the hand that is stretched out upon all the nations. For the Lord of hosts has purposed, and who shall disannul? And His hand is stretched out, and who shall turn it back? (2 Nephi 24:26-27; see also 2 Nephi 10:8 RE)

Why not now? Why not us? All that's required is to repent and return. The promise we have in exchange for our returning to the path is the stuff all the prophets and righteous from the days of Adam have eagerly anticipated.

––––––

The foregoing excerpts are taken from:

- Denver's *40 Years in Mormonism Series*, Talk #4 titled "Covenants" given in Centerville, UT on October 6th, 2013
- Denver's *40 Years in Mormonism Series*, Talk #1 titled "Be of Good Cheer" given in Boise, ID on September 10th, 2013; and
- The presentation of Denver's paper titled "The Restoration's Shattered Promises and Great Hope," given at the Sunstone Symposium in Salt Lake City, UT on July 28, 2018

98. God in Our Day, Part 2

This is the second part of a special series on what God is doing in our day.

———

DENVER: This is the Lord describing to Enoch what would happen by way of covenant, the Lord swearing, "As I live, even so will..." (Moses 7:60; see also Genesis 4:22 RE). And He tells him what's going to come to pass in the last days. This is among the promises that were made to one of the fathers; and this *is* one of the fathers, and these *are* the covenants—whose time is now upon us. This is the day in which we need to be prepared so that those who went before, and ascended up the ladder, can return and fall upon your neck and kiss you, and you fall upon their neck and kiss them—a sacred embrace through the veil, evidencing fellowship between you here, and them there— the Lord promising and covenanting these things are going to happen.

But notice, there *has* to be a tabernacle; He *has* to come and take up His abode. There *has* to be preparation made. These things require some effort to be made *here*, in order to prepare for His return. If there is no one here who is willing to engage in what's necessary to bring this to pass (because everyone looks around and expects someone else to do it), then you're neglecting a duty that's devolving upon you as one of those who was assigned to come down, in this day, in order to honor the fathers and honor the Lord by allowing the covenants that have been made to be fulfilled. Take a look at Doctrine and Covenants section 107, because in this we see that *first* Zion:

> *Three years previous to the death of Adam, he called Seth* [his son], *Enos* [his grandson], *Cainan* [the son of Enos], *Mahalaleel* [son of Cainan] , *Jared* [son of Mahalaleel], *Enoch* [son of Jared], *and Methuselah* [son of Enoch], *who were all high priests, with the residue of his posterity who were righteous, into the valley of Adam-ondi-Ahman, and there bestowed upon them his last blessing.* (D&C 107:53; see also T&C 154:19 RE)

This is the original, first patriarchal blessing being given by Adam; he having summoned them there. And as he's giving his last blessing, three years previous to his death, the Lord appeared unto them. So the Lord comes to dwell with these seven high priests and Adam:

> *The Lord appeared unto them, and they rose up and blessed Adam, and called him* [Mich-a-el] *Michael, the prince, the archangel. And the Lord*

administered comfort unto Adam [Ask yourself, what comfort is it that the Lord administers?], *[he] said unto him: I have set thee to be at the head; a multitude of nations shall come of thee...thou art a prince over them forever. And Adam stood up in the midst of the congregation; and, notwithstanding he was bowed down with age, being full of the Holy Ghost, predicted whatsoever should befall his posterity unto the latest generation. These things were all written in the book of Enoch, and are to be testified of in due time.* (D&C 107:54-57; see also T&C 154:19-20 RE)

This is the original covenant. *This is* the first father. *This is* what was set in motion before the death of Adam, under the binding influence and ratification of the Holy Ghost—or the mind of God—in which Adam, under the influence of that Spirit, predicted whatsoever should befall his posterity unto the latest generation. This is the original covenant. This is the original *father*. Words spoken as a consequence of the influence of the Holy Spirit *become* the words of God. They will not fall to the ground unfulfilled. The everlasting *covenant* in our day is "new" only as a consequence of it having been restored to *our* attention recently. It is *not* a new thing; it is a very *old* thing, going back to the days of Adam. It was known to him. *You* were known to him. What was going to happen in *your* day was predicted and promised as a consequence of him.

Prophecies (as I've said before) revolve around two, and primarily two events only—one being the first coming of the Lord; the other one being the coming of the Lord in judgment at the end of the world. Now, there are plenty of prophecies that reckon to other events that are intermediate; *however*, the primary focus is the First and the Second Coming of the Lord—the vindication of the promise that the Father made in the beginning that He would redeem us all from the grave; and the vindication of the promise that, at some point, the world would come to an end as to its wickedness and there would be peace again on the earth. Everything revolves around those two prophetic events.

But there will always be 10,000 voices that rise up in opposition to say, "Lo, here; lo, there; come and hearken to *my* precept." (See Joseph Smith History 1:4; see also T&C 1 Joseph Smith History 1:11 RE.) I don't ask you to hearken to anything other than what we find in the scriptures.

But you should ask yourself the same question that Malachi posed:

Who may abide the day of his coming?...who shall stand when he appeareth? for He is like a refiner's fire and like [a] fullers' soap: And he shall sit as a refiner and purifier of silver [Yeah, who shall stand?]...the day [comes that] shall burn them up...[so] that it shall leave them neither root nor branch (Malachi 3:2-3, and 4:1; see also Malachi 1:6,10 RE).

And who shall abide *that* day? Well, we have an answer to that, I guess—3 Nephi chapter 9—which the Book of Mormon was designed as the scripture, as the foundation, the keystone for our day. Go to chapter 9 of 3 Nephi and read what is said there. And this is the Lord speaking, 3 Nephi chapter 9, verse 12 and 13:

Many great destructions have I caused to come upon this land, and upon this people, because of their wickedness and their abominations. O all ye that are spared because ye were more righteous than they, will ye not now return unto me, and repent of your sins, and be converted, that I may heal you? (3 Nephi 9:12-13; see also 3 Nephi 4:6-7 RE)

These people were more righteous—not because they were sin-free. They were more righteous because they hearkened to what the Lord was telling them to hearken to. It didn't mean that they weren't a project, that they weren't a work in process. It simply meant that they did in fact hear His voice, and therefore responded to it! These were the people who were spared. Go to chapter 10, and verse 12:

And it was the more righteous part of the people who were saved, and it was they who received the prophets and stoned them not; and it was they who had not shed the blood of the saints, who were spared. (3 Nephi 10:12; see also 3 Nephi 4:10 RE)

Did you notice that? It's the definition—this is how you get spared; this is how you become "His seed"—*They who received the prophets and stoned them not.* Understand, this is Christ speaking. Therefore, these three things you need to know: God exists; you need to study until you have a correct understanding of His character, perfections, and attributes; and then you have to live your life so that you actually know that the course you're leading in your life conforms to what He would have. Turn to verse 23:

But it is also necessary that men should have an idea that he is no respecter of persons, for with the idea of all the other excellencies in his character, and this one wanting, men could not exercise faith in him;

because if he were a respecter of persons, they could not tell what their privileges were, nor how far they were authorized to exercise faith in him, or whether they were authorized to do it at all, but all must be confusion; but no sooner are the minds of men made acquainted with the truth on this point, that he is no respecter of persons, than they see that they have authority by faith to lay hold on eternal life, the richest boon of heaven, because God is no respecter of persons, and that every man in every nation has an equal privilege. (Lectures on Faith 3:23; see also T&C 110, Lectures on Faith 3:23 RE)

That's you! That's you! God has done nothing for Joseph Smith He will not do for you. I understand all of the doctrinal arguments. I can make them all. I *have* made them all—and I've made them to the Lord. I've argued with Him on every point of doctrine that any of you— I've quoted to Him every scripture that any of you have advanced, and *many* more besides! And the Lord has only borne testimony back, consistently—*this stuff is true.* You're hedging up the way of your own salvation, and of the salvation of others, when you say, "No one has the privilege in our day, yet, to lay hold on salvation." You're hedging up the way, you are damning yourself, and you are damning those that will listen to you when you say, "People in our time are not yet authorized to exercise faith in God unto salvation," because you *are* authorized.

I have done so. I have spoken with Him as a man speaks to another. He speaks *in plain humility*, reasoning, as one man does with another. *He will reason with you.* The first night I got a testimony, I was in the middle of an argument, with God—I thought with myself—until when I got down to the final question in my mind, which was, "How do I even know there *is* a God?" To which the response came, "Who do you think you've been talking to the last two hours?" I didn't realize that that still, small voice, which will talk with any and all of you, was God. When you exercise the required faith to permit Him to step out from behind the veil, like the brother of Jared, He'll do that too. He's no respecter of persons. You should not question what your privileges are, nor how far you are authorized to exercise faith in Him, or whether you're authorized to do it at all. *Don't have doubts about your privileges.*

In the parable that Joseph was given, in the D&C, about the unjust judge and the aggrieved woman, it was a *constant* petitioning. Little children not only don't know a lot of things, they know that they don't know. And they ask persistently, incessantly, because they desire to know what they don't know. They're like sponges; and we're like rocks. You can throw a rock into the water and pull it out again, and it's still a rock. But you throw a sponge in and you pull it out, and it is *greatly* increased. Children are like the sponge; they're porous, and we are not.

Well, Doctrine and Covenants section 93, verse 1—you probably all can recite that in your head (I hope). I'm not going to read it. I'm looking in Mormon—and I'm trying to find a verse in Moses. Moses 6, verse 57:

> *Wherefore teach it unto your children, that all men, everywhere, must repent, or they can in nowise inherit the kingdom of God, for no unclean thing can dwell there, or dwell in his presence; for, in the language of Adam, Man of Holiness is his name, and the name of his Only Begotten is the Son of Man, even Jesus Christ, a righteous Judge, who shall come in the meridian of time.* (Moses 6:57; see also Genesis 4:9 RE)

So, in order to come into the presence of the Lord, we have to be clean. Well, in the ceremony of the temple, the way in which you become ceremonially clean is by borrowing things from the Lord through the ceremony. You are washed; though not quite as vigorously as you may have been in Nauvoo. You are anointed; though not perhaps as thoroughly as you might have been in Nauvoo. You know that strong drinks— Next time you have a Word of Wisdom lesson, and they're talking about strong drinks and the washing of the body— They used cinnamon-flavored or included mixed whiskey to anoint and wash you, rather, in the Kirtland, and then again in Nauvoo. And, as it turns out, for the washing the body, it's really a pretty good antiseptic. One of the things that Joseph talked about in [the] Nauvoo era was about how angels sometimes have a hard time visiting with men because they stink, and that we really ought to clean ourselves up because we'll offend the sensibilities of the angels. There's a notion for you—one of the doors to barring entry is...anyway.

In the temple, you borrow cleanliness through the ceremony itself—which washes you, which anoints you, which dresses you in new and clean clothes, and then progressively confers upon you *symbols* that suggest *all* of creation. Symbolically, the entirety of creation comes through and is redeemed, as a consequence of your own redemption. Because *if* you are redeemed, you *are* infinite and eternal; and creation itself goes on. But *here*, no unclean thing can dwell *there*, or dwell in His presence, which then leads to the reason for the temple.

The purpose of the temple is not merely to inspire you with the conviction that it is possible to rend the veil, to pass through the veil, to see and meet with our Lord who has promised us repeatedly— That the stories in the Book of Mormon are stories designed to tell you, over and over and over again, about coming back into the presence of the Lord. Even wicked Lamanite converts, many of *them* have what we—in our scholarly language—would call a 'throne theophany;' and they did so upon conversion because their conversion was with real intent.

Therefore, the Book of Mormon is a text about the Second Comforter. But what is being talked about in this verse, in Moses chapter 6, is about dwelling in His presence. And when it comes, in verse—again this is Moses 6, verse 57 —it says, when it comes to dwelling there, *no unclean thing* can *dwell there*; because He's the Man of Holiness. This presents the real message or the real meaning of what the temple is trying to convey, to us, in our day. And we're just about running out of time to accomplish that, in our day. And if we don't, then, you know, He passes on and maybe starts this up with another people in another day, as He's so often done before.

To come to the veil and to meet with the Savior— *He* can clean you up. *He*, through His grace, can give you all that you lack. To *dwell* in the presence of God requires something more, something different. It requires that you grow —from where you are now to the place where the Lord intends to lead you. He intends to have you *be* true and faithful in all things. Because in the ceremony in the temple, once you go through the veil, you don't come back; you stay there. And the purpose of going there in *this* day, in *this* setting, is to *enable* the return of Zion.

We don't need a profoundly new and far-reaching economic system to make us have all things in common, in order to bring again Zion. And we don't need possession of the real estate in Jackson County, Missouri, to bring again Zion. We don't need *any* of the implements, or locations, or infrastructure to have Zion return. We need one thing, and that's *you—you* to be clean, *you* to be holy; to leave behind you not only the door but the house in which you dwell, that you established that *door* to bar Him through. You need to come and live with Him. It *is* possible. These are *not* cunningly devised fables, as the apostle Paul put it. This is the gospel of Jesus Christ. Look at the definition that the Lord gives of salvation, in Ether chapter 3. This is the definition that the Lord gives:

> *Behold, the Lord showed himself unto him, and said: Because thou knowest these things [you] are redeemed from the fall; therefore [you] are brought back into my presence; therefore I show myself unto you.* (Ether 3:13; see also Ether 1:13 RE)

This is the meaning of salvation. This is the fullness of the gospel of Jesus Christ. This is contained in the Book of Mormon, which has the fullness of Jesus Christ in it. The Lord showed Himself unto him, and said, *Because thou knowest these things ye are redeemed from the fall; therefore [you're] brought back into my presence; therefore I show myself unto you.*

Every dispensation of the gospel has left only a remnant behind. Christ's work is designed to preserve a remnant, and at the end, gather *all* remnants together again. The Restoration that was given through the Prophet Joseph Smith has likewise put itself in a position where now it can only produce a remnant, but one that will be preserved and not abandoned.

In 3 Nephi chapter 21, the Lord talked about some things that become exceptionally relevant in light of what we've covered today.

> *And verily I say unto you, I give unto you a sign, that ye may know the time when these things shall be about to take place—that I shall gather in, from their long dispersion, my people, O house of Israel, and...establish again among them my Zion;* [This is addressing all of those various remnants, wherever that they may be found, so long as they are some residue of the house of Israel.] *And behold, this is the [sign] which I will give unto you for a sign—for verily I say unto you that when these things which I declare unto you, and which I shall declare unto you hereafter of myself, and by the power of the Holy Ghost which shall be given unto you of the Father, shall be made known unto the Gentiles* [See, the gentiles had to first receive some things] *that they* [the gentiles] *may know concerning this people who are a remnant of the house of Jacob, and concerning this my people who shall be scattered by them* [the gentiles]; *Verily, verily, I say unto you, when these things shall be made known unto them* [some constituent group of gentiles] *of the Father, and shall come forth of the Father, from them unto you.* (3 Nephi 21:1-3; see also 3 Nephi 9:11 RE)

It can't come from any source other than from the Father—the Father and Christ being one. The authority to minister and to deliver it coming from Them. The power to baptize being brought forth from some remnant of the gentiles who care to bear it.

> *For it is wisdom in the Father that they* [the gentiles] *should be established in this land, and be set up as a free people by the power of the Father, that these things might come forth from them unto a remnant of your seed, that the covenant of the Father may be fulfilled which he hath*

covenanted with his people, [with *His* people] *O house of Israel.* (Ibid., vs. 4)

O house of Israel is much more. *O house of Israel* is that same inclusive of all bits and remnants, wherever they may be found. I talked about covenants when we were in Centerville and about the fulfillment of the covenants. *All* of the covenants which apply to people scattered everywhere, *all* of those included within the previous remnants, they need to be gathered into one constituent group.

> *Therefore, when these works and the works which shall be wrought among you hereafter shall come forth from the Gentiles,*

Not their *book,* their *works.* Not their *book,* the *works* bringing to pass the Doctrine of Christ—establishing repentance, declaring and baptizing by the authority of Christ, having people visited by fire and the Holy Ghost. These are the 'works.' *These are the 'works.'*

> *Shall come forth from the Gentiles, unto your seed which shall dwindle in unbelief because of iniquity; For thus it behooveth the Father that it should come forth from the Gentiles, that he may show forth his power unto the Gentiles.* (Ibid., vs. 5-6)

That's what He needs now to do. That's what He intends *to do, if* you will receive it.

> *For this cause that the Gentiles, if they will not harden their hearts, that they may repent and come unto me and be baptized in my name and know of the true points of my doctrine, that they may be numbered among my people, O house of Israel.* (Ibid.)

You can't get there except through the power of the doctrine and the power of the ordinance, that God has given, in the way that it has been given; performed with the exactness, fidelity, and language that has been given to us by Christ Himself.

> *When these things come to pass that thy seed shall begin to know these things—it shall be a sign unto them, that they may know that the work of the Father hath already commenced unto the fulfilling of the covenant which he...made unto the people who are of the house of Israel.* (Ibid., vs. 7)

All of them. It's a witness that His work has commenced.

> *And when that day shall come, it shall come to pass that kings shall shut their mouths; for that which had not been told them shall they see; and that which they had not heard shall they consider. For in that day, for my sake shall the Father work a work, which shall be a great and...marvelous work among them; and there shall be among them those who will not believe it, although a man shall declare it unto them. But behold, the life of my servant shall be in my hand; therefore they shall not hurt him, although he shall be marred because of them. Yet I will heal him, for I will show unto them that my wisdom is greater than the cunning of the devil. Therefore it shall come to pass that whosoever will not believe in my words, who am Jesus Christ, which the Father shall cause him to bring forth unto the Gentiles, and shall give unto him power that he shall bring it forth unto the Gentiles, (it shall be done even as Moses said) they shall be cut off from among my people who are of the covenant.* (3 Nephi 21:8-10; see also 3 Nephi 9:11-12 RE)

[Whoever] will not believe in my words, who am Jesus Christ... These are Christ's words. We touched on these words all the way back in Boise. It was quoted by the angel Moroni, referring to Joseph Smith Acts 3, verses 22 to 23.

> *For Moses truly said unto the fathers, A prophet shall the Lord your God raise up unto you of your brethren, like unto me; him shall ye hear in all things whatsoever he shall say unto you. And it shall come to pass, that every soul, which will not hear that prophet, shall be destroyed from among the people.* (Acts 3:22-23; see also Acts 2:3 RE)

That prophet is Christ. It doesn't say Christ is going to come and deliver His words, it says "His words." Those who *will not believe in my words, who am Jesus Christ...they shall be cut off.*

And the angel Moroni said to Joseph, in verse 40 of the Joseph Smith History, *The day had not yet come when* "they who would not hear his voice should be cut off from among the people," *but soon would come* (Joseph Smith—History 1:40; see also T&C 1, Joseph Smith History 3:4 RE).

That prophet is Christ. His words are what I've spoken to you today.

> *And my people who are a remnant of Jacob shall be among the Gentiles, yea, in the midst of them as a lion among the beasts of the forest, as a*

young lion among the flocks of sheep, who, if he go through both treadeth down and teareth in pieces, and none can deliver. Their hand shall be lifted up upon their adversaries, and all their enemies shall be cut off. Yea, wo be unto the Gentiles except they repent; for it shall come to pass in that day, saith the Father, that I will cut off thy horses out of the midst of thee, and I will destroy thy chariots; And I will cut off the cities of thy [lands], and throw down all thy strongholds; And I will cut off witchcrafts out of [the] land, and thou shalt have no more soothsayers; Thy graven images will I also cut off. (3 Nephi 21:12-17; see also 3 Nephi 9:12 RE)*

Graven images are people you worship. Graven images include men to whom you submit as objects or idols of authority—in whom you trust, thinking that they can deliver you by some magic, using some key that they purport to hold. Whether Catholic, or Mormon, or Fundamentalist, graven images— They're going to be cut off.

Thou shalt no more worship the works of thy hands; And I will pluck up thy groves out of the midst of thee; so will I destroy thy cities. And it shall come to pass that all lyings, and deceivings, and envyings, and strifes, and [priests'crafts], and whoredoms, shall be done away. For it shall come to pass, saith the Father, that at that day whosoever will not repent and come unto my Beloved Son, them will I cut off from among my people, O house of Israel [that's all remnants gathered together]*; And I will execute vengeance and fury upon them, even as upon the heathen, such as they have not heard. But if they* [speaking of the Gentiles, *if they*] *will repent and hearken unto my words, and harden not their hearts, I will establish my church among them, and they shall come in unto the covenant and be numbered among this the remnant of Jacob, unto whom I have given this land for their inheritance.* (Ibid., vs. 17-22)

Because every time there's a covenant, there is always a land; and this is the land that God covenants He will give. And the people to whom he will give it are those that come back and receive the covenant, including the gentiles in whose ears this first shall sound. If they will come, and come in unto the covenant— That is not yet possible. It requires more than has, at present, been given. It *is* possible to come in and become part of His church. It *is* possible if you follow, as you've been instructed today, to become part of the church He recognizes and will preserve. But, coming fully into the covenant, that will require more than has, at present, been given. It will require a covenant. It will require adoption. It will require sealing. It was what Joseph looked forward to have happen at some point in the future, during the days of his prophecy.

> *And they shall assist my people, the remnant of Jacob, and also as many of the house of Israel as shall come, that they may build a city, which shall be called the New Jerusalem. And then shall they assist my people that they may be gathered in, who are scattered upon all the face of the land, in unto the New Jerusalem. And then shall the power of heaven* [In this case it is the singular; it's not the 'powers' because when you have Him present with you, you have all the authority.] *...then shall the power of heaven come down among them; and I also will be in the midst. And then shall the work of the Father commence at that day.* (3 Nephi 21:23-26; see also 3 Nephi 10:1 RE)

Christ will come. Once the covenant has been renewed, the city of Zion will follow. The Lord's presence will come, and then the final stage begins.

> *Even when this gospel shall be preached among the remnant of this people. Verily I say unto you, at that day shall the work of the Father commence among...the dispersed of my people, yea, even the tribes which have been lost, which the Father hath led away out of Jerusalem. Yea, the work shall commence among all the dispersed of my people, with the Father to prepare the way whereby they may come in unto me, that they may call on the Father in my name...then shall the work commence, with the Father among all nations in preparing the way whereby his people may be gathered home to the land of their inheritance. And they shall go out from all nations...they shall not go out in haste, nor...by flight, for I will go before them, saith the Father, and I will be their rearward.* (Ibid., vs. 26-29)

It's not going to happen in haste. And the work of the Father that will commence in those nations, to commence the possibility for the gathering, will involve destroying a great deal of political, social, and military obstructions that *prevent* the gathering—prevent even the *preaching* to those that *would* gather, if they could hear. But the work of the Father? (And it's always masculine when it comes to destruction.) The work of the Father is going to bring this to an end. All the scattered remnants will be brought back again. The original, unified family of God will be restored again. The *fathers* will have our hearts turned to them because in that day, once it's permitted to get that far, we will be part of that family again.

This is the day in which, at long last, it is possible for what God intended to happen before His return to actually begin. The gospel is not supposed to be merely a record of how God dealt with other people at another time. Joseph Smith talked about how we can't read the words of an old book, and then apply those words in an old book—that were meant for someone else, at some other time—to us, and then restore ourselves back to God's grace. That is just as true of the revelations given in the days of Joseph Smith as it is true of the revelations given in the New Testament.

It becomes really apparent when you read them out of the scriptures because all our footnotes, and all of our chapter headings, and all our cross referencing — It sort of gives you an impression that this stuff is talking about *us*, right here, right now. When you read them as they were written in the *Joseph Smith Papers*, it really becomes clear that when God is talking about how the church is living, and alive, and approved, it's because He's talking to Joseph Smith. And the church is listening to what Joseph Smith had to say, and *rolling forth* is the voice of God in *that* day. And Joseph Smith commissioned people to go out and to take it, and they took it and they went out and they preached it. And when they preached it, others were converted. And the people that were converted actually had experiences and came to know God. But that's because God acted, to set it in motion in the person of Joseph Smith. Joseph had a covenant given to him by God, therefore Joseph *could* testify to these words— and they were true, and God owned them, and people who followed them received the wages of those who follow God. It worked!

We can't *mimic* that and have the same effect. God has to say, "This is what I want to do." And if no one else will say it to you, I'm saying it to you. Everything that has been said in this talk (which began in Boise and concludes here today), everything that has been said is, in fact, exactly what happened when God offered something through Joseph. He's offering something again, right now, in our day—to you, to any that will hear, to any that will listen. The work is beginning again.

I suppose it was necessary that what began in Joseph's time *had* to run down to the condition that it's in at present. That it had to become a leaky ruin of a farm, that Joseph himself no longer even wanted, before it was possible for the Lord to say, "At this moment, we turn a new leaf." But, my word, can't you see the signs of the times? Can't you look about and see that the whole world is waxing old like a garment? Can't you see that there is, right now, a balance of things that are kept at bay, only to preserve the possibility that a remnant might be claimed? God promised he would do this.

Until today, I really haven't done anything more than read scriptures and bear testimony to you that they're true. This wasn't my idea, and I can't tell you how happy my wife and I will be when we conclude this, and this project is done. There'll be some— This transcript, and there'll be— I'm going to edit them all and put them into a book; and the book, in order to be readable, has to have run-on sentences, and grammar, and everything fixed. So it has to be readable in its own way. So there's that still left to do, but the project, and the labor, and the work that needs to be done, is you.

If you don't lay hold upon this, if you don't move this forward, if you don't rise up, then I suppose He'll find another people. But you ought to allow yourself to be found, and you ought to allow yourself to be numbered among those who choose to have that gospel *live* again. The gospel shouldn't be the words of an old book. The gospel should be alive in you, rolling forth with new vigor—every day a revelation of His involvement in your life and in the lives of those around you.

———

The foregoing excerpts are taken from:

- Denver's *40 Years in Mormonism Series*, Talk #4, titled "Covenants," given in Centerville, Utah, on October 6th, 2013,
- Denver's *40 Years in Mormonism Series*, Talk #7, titled "Christ, Prototype of the Saved Man," given in Ephraim, Utah, on June 28, 2014,
- Denver's *40 Years in Mormonism Series*, Talk #2, titled "Faith," given in Idaho Falls, Idaho, on September 28th, 2013,
- Denver's fireside talk on "The Temple," given in Ogden, Utah, on October 28th, 2012, and
- Denver's *40 Years in Mormonism Series*, Talk #10, titled "Preserving the Restoration," given in Mesa, Arizona, on September 9th, 2014.

99. A Bag Full of Jesus

In this episode, Denver discusses how the community of Zion will be centered around the temple, and founded upon equality, service, and the words of Christ.

————

DENVER: In all of the Restoration Mormon groups that exist (from the Community of Christ, in its present form, to any of the fundamentlist groups), the way in which the structure of the people has been organized is with a top-down system, in which you have some function that takes place at the very top of this, and that's what radiates down to fill and to control the entirety of whatever group it is. And we know this doesn't work. If this kind of a system could be fixed by putting a righteous man at the top, then we could've fixed Catholicism, and we didn't need a new church. This organization has its inherent flaws. In addition… The fundamental problem with this is that you have an inequality that is structurally built into the system. And you can't escape that. It just is. I mean, to look at that is to know that what you've developed is a model in which there's inequality.

The only way in which you can have equality is if everyone's regarded to be on the same level. There's no higher, and there's no lower. There is only one. If you look at the example of the Savior who came to minister, the way in which the Savior ministered literally was to put himself below and then to labor to raise everyone else. In fact, if you're looking at the model of the Savior, if you're gonna draw a connecting line, the connecting line would turn this entire model upside down. Because He knelt to serve. And He knelt to raise. And He served beneath everyone else. And His objective was to treat them all as if they were those to whom He came to minister. And He didn't assume a different role.

In fact, if you pay close attention to the relics of what we have left over of the post-apostolic era, the Christian churches that got established by the apostles that knew Christ were built like this—they had exactly the same look and feel as the fellowships that we have. They met in homes. On occasion they would go into someone else's synagogue or someone else's facility to teach, but they were a home-based, level community in which everyone was on an equal footing. And the bishops were elected by the common consent to serve temporarily. It would be like electing someone to be president or bishop or grand poobah of the upcoming Boise conference, who then serves in whatever that role is until the conference ends, and at the end of that, they drop back

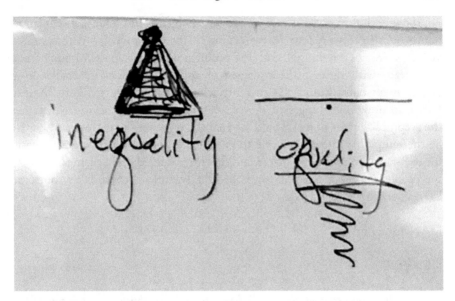

into… And their purpose is simply to facilitate something. Their purpose isn't to "great me, little you."

So, the model of Zion, in my view, has to be a model that assumes the equality of the participants. In my view, at this point in history there can only be one definition of success. And that is the New Jerusalem, Zion, and the return of the Lord. If success is defined as getting a movement going, we have every different flavor of movement. We have Christian Jews. We have gay, Methodist, female bishops. For all I know, somewhere in the world we have a gay Imam issuing fatwah's who may have eaten Mexican food. But the infinite variety of religious errors is inexhaustible. The proof of 'doing, believing, and acting' (in the way that pleases the Lord, satisfies the covenants that got made long ago to other people, and achieves what the fulfillment of all the ages anticipate) is the New Jerusalem, Zion, and the return of the Lord.

If we define success as anything other than that, then we're really looking for the wrong thing—which, again, is one of the reasons why I don't think numbers matter.

Now, if you want to see with clarity what the imagination of mankind gives you for a dystopian future, all you'd have to do is watch TV or go to any movie—because they are propounding a view of a dystopian future that ranges from MadMax to the Mazerunner. But they all have the same theme, and that's that we're all gonna die ugly, horrid deaths, and it's our own fault. That's the theme of our adversary.

So, the question is: given where we are now (which is not Zion), and at some points even in this process, as the scripture—incoming email—demonstrates vividly, we're not anything like it. The problem we have is in envisioning what —I mean, with some realistic degree of appreciation for the challenge— envisioning what it would take to get us from 'where we are' to 'there.' And if I were to draw one thing that represents an indispensable accoutrement for the accomplishment of it, I would say that the one thing that's required has to be the temple. Without a temple to ground the society, to provide the basis for the structure of a new society, a differently ordered one... I mean, this is the prophesy. This is page 600 in your Old Testament, towards the bottom, last paragraph, left hand side.

MAN: One or two?

DENVER:

> *The mountain of the Lord's house shall be established in the top of the mountains, and shall be exalted above the hills and all nations shall flow unto it. And many people shall go and say, Come ye, ...let us go up to the mountain of the Lord, to the house of the God of Jacob; and He will teach us of His ways, and we will walk in His paths:* ***for out of Zion shall go forth the law.*** *(Isaiah 2:2-3, emphasis added; see also Isaiah 1:5 RE)*

See, you have to have this in order to learn something. And what it is that you learn there is so valuable that those who come and receive it regard what they have been given as a law. I don't know how many times in scripture the Lord says, "Eye hath not seen, nor hath ear heard, nor **yet** hath it entered into the heart of man what great things the Lord has prepared for you."

And how often does He tells us that there are things that have been kept hid from the foundation of the world that He would like to give. And then we have the prophecy that says, "The time's gonna come when you're not gonna need to say to me and I'm not gonna need to say to you, 'Know ye the Lord,' for everyone will know Him from the least to the greatest." A temple serves as the basis for orienting a society that gets built around and centered in the temple.

It's a different way of living; it's a different way of thinking; it's a different way that reorients you instead of to this [the inequality triangle], orients you to that [the equality inverted-triangle]. Let's go learn about the path of God. You have to have **this** [equality] in order to structure a society around this [the temple]. And I don't think it's going to be easy. The challenge is right there—the world has never managed to get right there [equality]. Never. And that includes communities of monks, nunneries, that includes ascetic people, Walden Pond. Everyone who has tried Utopia—everyone who has envisioned Utopia—has failed because they haven't had the "seed" [of equality and service] that is constructed around the mountain of the Lord's house with the law that will go forth out of Zion—because Zion is differently situated.

Now, this is on page 82 of **this book** [Doctrine and Covenants, Restoration Edition, Preview], and it's talking about the glory of the Telestial kingdom. If you skip down a little while it says, these people *are liars, and sorcerers, and adulterers, and whoremongers, and whosoever loves and makes a lie.* Okay, so, it's a bad crowd. But earlier when it's talking about the people who merit this Telestial condition: *the glory of the Telestial is one, even as the glory of the stars are one.* You know, you can sit on the surface of the earth and look out into the heavens, and you can pick out the stars instantly, and it doesn't matter that they are visible to the human eye—there are category one stars; there are category… To the human eye, you can pretty well see up to category six stars, sometimes category seven—but you can see them and know and recognize instantly that they are a star because they have this consistently subordinate degree of glory. And yet, they still stand out in contrast to the night sky, because they "shine in the darkness."

> *The glory of the Telestial is one, even as the glory of the stars are one; for as one star differs from another star in glory, even so differs one from another in glory in the Telestial world; for these are they who are of Paul, and of Apollos, and of Cephas, these are they who say they are some of one and some of another: some of Christ…* (D&C, RE Preview, pg. 82; see also T&C 69:26)

Disappointingly, some of the voices that have been raised in opposition to the work of the Lord right now are those who claim to be of Christ. "I am faithful to Jesus, and all I need is a bag full of my Jesus. And if I fetch that bag full of Jesus, well, He tells me everything I need to know. And (hmm…) He tells me not to do this covenant, and He tells me (hmm…) you're creating another Mosaic dispensation. And (hmm…) you're being misled, and (hmm…) and Jesus tells me it's so. And my bonafides is, Look! It's Jesus. See, see… I got my Jesus coat."

When it comes to Zion, it's not "Jesus plus me." This is isolation; this is destruction. This is… Read the Sermon on the Mount. The gist of the Sermon on the Mount was how to make you and you and you [pointing to people in the room] live together in peace. It's not teaching you how to sit on a mountain somewhere and say, "I got Jesus, and you know what? I'm better than you. You know what? I… I fetch revelations, and Jesus likes me. I don't know what's wrong with you people, but as for me, I'm cool. I'm Fonz." (You know. I don't know how many of you remember Happy Days, but…)

That's not the message for the culmination of the work of the Lord. The message for the culmination of the work of the Lord is the unity of His children. "How oft would I have gathered you as a hen gathereth her chicks under my wings, but ye would not." And why would ye not? Well, because one chick looks at another chick and says, That chick really rubs me wrong. And the gist of the Sermon on the Mount is, "Hey, get over it." The problem isn't your fellow chick; the problem is entirely internal to you. Because as soon as you start saying, "I am of Jesus, and that makes me better than you because you're of John. I am of Jesus, and that makes me better than you because you're of Cephus, you're of Paul." Everyone who's doing that has forgotten that what Christ is attempting to do is to make **you** less of a savage and more like Him.

Everyone needs to be on the same line of equality, and if you have anything to do or to contribute, then help raise the line. Help the line love one another. Because as people, Zion can never be done in isolation with Jesus and you. Zion consists of people of one heart and of one mind—not because someone has managed to obtain a following for themselves. That's irrelevant. They're of one heart and of one mind because they respect the Lord, they desire to do what the Lord is telling them to do, and they forgive one another, and they're able to live in peace with one another. The reason we don't live in peace with one another is because we will not accept and do what the Lord asks us to accept and do.

Now, the problem is that if one man lives the Sermon on the Mount and his neighbor is willing to exploit that, he will come and ask for his coat. And then he'll come and ask for his cloak. And then he'll come and ask for his lawn mower. And then you've got Homer Simpson taking everything from Ned [*The Simpsons* TV series]. **That's not Zion**. But in a society that is structured around it, in which everyone has **the same commitment to doing what the Lord asks**, Homer's either gonna change and become acceptable as a neighbor, or Homer will never even be gathered because he will destroy the society. And eventually, if Homer's left outside and he's watching the society from a distance long enough, he may ultimately become persuaded that this and this is valuable enough a thing to have that I'm willing to do this. I'm willing to be no better, no worse. In fact, when I think about it, maybe in order to get that, every one of us have to turn into that [refer back to the photo above of the Lord being the "dot" under the "equality line," where He endeavors to lift the line]. We all have to kneel down and to raise one another. Because we'll never get to the point we need to get to if we don't regard the welfare of others highly enough to sacrifice our own interests for the betterment of everyone else—which is exactly what the Savior did. And He did it all the way to the end, in which he sacrificed everything.

WOMAN: I mentioned to you… I would go so far as to say that, at least as far as I have noticed, all scriptural accounts of the prophets or people "seeking for more"… So, Nephi saying, "Tell me, Lord, what did my father see?" Or… It's all designed for the betterment of the human family. Nephi says over and over and over again, "I seek these things to bring **my people** to the presence of the God of Abraham, Isaac, and Jacob." It is its only purpose. "Jesus and me"—it's just you; it's just you. And I haven't found in the scriptures where people who are seeking for this are seeking for it for any other reason, any other stated reason, than "I wanna bring my brothers and sisters to the presence of the God of Abraham, Isaac, and Jacob." It says over and over and over again. Yeah, if you're doing it for any other purpose, I don't think you'll be stopped up, but I don't think you'll… I don't think you'll get out of it what you're actually intended to get out of it. And eventually, it'll just be a bunch of "me's."

DENVER: You know, there shouldn't be anything flattering about any of this process. And there ought to be a lot of pain going along in the process, because helping other people (particularly when they're as stubborn and obstinate and as abused in their past as refugees from the typical Mormon experience are that come to this; they got a chip on their shoulder)…

Look, let's assume that, for some reason, Jesus comes and sits in your living room tonight and spends the evening talking to you. Okay? Do you think He cares more about you two because He spent the evening talking to you than He does about every other person who's living at this moment? I mean, if He's trying to restore a people and to redeem the offspring of Adam, everyone alive matters. We're not going to be able to change the world until we finally get in a position to have an actual seed planted that measures up to what is required for Zion—and **that** has been attained twice that we know of. It happened once with Enoch. It happened once with Melchizedek.

Now, if you look at the structure that has failed to produce Zion, the structures that have failed to produce Zion always involves this [inequality triangle]. If you separate structure from the content of teaching, Christ may have put together something that turned into this [the inequality triangle] twice now. But the content of what He teaches is this [equality inverted-triangle]. And if you took seriously what Joseph received when he was in Liberty Jail composing the letter from Liberty Jail, you would realize that what the Lord was talking to Joseph about in Liberty was that *no power or influence can or ought to be maintained by virtue of the priesthood* (T&C 139:6). In Liberty Jail, even though this model [inequality triangle] had been erected, the revelation turned it on its ear...except **that** message never survived into practice.

It's on paper, and it's exactly what the Lord taught (in the Sermon that gets repeated twice in the volume of the New Testament and the Book of Mormon)—but it didn't get practiced. And so, because this model [inequality triangle] produces, internal to it (model after model after model as you go from Ward to Stake to Region to Seventy to Twelve to First Presidency—it's just a whole bunch of this, endlessly repeated)... The best way to avoid falling into that trap is what's happening with the new scriptures project, and that is the elimination of this structure. We don't need to know about it, because it won't work.

Begin from this proposition and treat one another as if you are equals (because, in fact, you are), and gather in groups small enough that common consent is a simple thing to achieve.

WOMAN: So, why the two conflicting models? I'm a little bit confused about the fact that they say both in the scriptures. They both seemingly come from the Lord, so that... I think that's where a lot of the hang-up is—is that we seemingly can justify both from Him. So, why the conflicting models?

DENVER: When the world began, the way in which the world was organized was as a family. And it was easy at the beginning to recognize that the Lord had given to Adam dominion over the whole world. His authority and his right to preside was unquestioned. Because of the fall and because of the entry of death into the world, everyone knew that the time would come when Adam would die. Therefore, everyone knew that that right would descend from Adam to someone in the next generation.

Eve was so impressed (over a long enough period of time of observing the conduct of Cain) that after an endless parade of rebellious apostate children, Eve had regard to Cain and said, We've gotten a man of the Lord; therefore, he cannot fail (see Genesis 3:6 RE)—because he had demonstrated a period long enough for Eve to make that observation about him and to feel confident that he was chosen of the Lord. He had a younger brother. And the younger brother imitated the example of his righteous, older brother—except as time went on, as it turned out, Cain became weary in well-doing and **did** get tempted (like all of his peers) and **did** at least contemplate some of the benefits of serving the adversary; and in making an offering, innovated (in order to split the difference between the Lord, whom he wanted to give lip service to, on the one hand, and the rest of what was going on, on the other) in order to have it both ways—whereas his younger brother remained true and faithful, devoted and singularly-minded to the Lord.

And the Lord spoke to both of them. And to Cain He said, "You need to... You need to choose. You need to be either with Me, or you are against Me. This is not a path that allows you to continue to walk in two directions." But there was no such complaint by the Lord to his younger brother. Cain realized, at that point in the world, that through the inheritor would come— through his lineage—the Messiah. And Cain was contemplating the risk of being displaced and losing—forfeiting—that right. And so Cain, accepting council from the adversary, who suggested to him there's an easy way out of this dilemma... "I mean, everyone's gonna die anyway—just move up the time period. Kill him now. You're going to inherit what he might have inherited because if he's not here, he can't inherit it." And so, he commits the first murder.

Take that moment in time and ask yourself: Okay, if Cain was willing to murder his brother in order to gain ascendency in the right of descent from Adam, **why not kill Adam?** (It's an ob... I mean, it's a solution that gets adopted throughout the book of Ether. Kill the king. Kill the older brother. Kill the king.) It was unthinkable. It was unthinkable. Even Cain the murderer would not **dare** kill Adam. And what did Adam do with his son the murderer? He just sent him away.

You realize just how kindly a soul father Adam was when you consider he had to grapple with apostate children. He had to grapple with the first murder. It was fratricide involving his own children, and yet, no one questioned Adam's right.

Well, the Jews respected authority. They had been slaves (I'm saying the Jews; it was really all of us). They had been slaves. They were in a vertically integrated society, and when they came out of it, they were unfit to be what they needed to be as equals. And so the Mosaic dispensation took a problem of slavery and solved the problem by land inheritance (for eleven tribes) and priesthood (by one), and the eldest of the descendants of Aaron becomes a high priest, and he presides. And you get a structure that will work—trying to bring slaves along to become something better, higher, more noble—and you can find a sense of that nobility in the Pentateuch. But they never overcame the impediment that they were given from a couple of hundred years of slavery in order to rise up.

When the Savior structured the New Testament organization, it was essentially a nod in the direction of the family of Abraham with Peter, James, and John; and the twelve princes—the twelve apostles; the seventy and... It was a nod in their direction, because they claimed that they would be saved by reason of their descendancy from Abraham alone. So, He recreates the family of Abraham in order to make it appealing and familiar.

But what He taught was based upon the equality and the unity of all. But again, you're dealing with (initially) Jews, and then (secondarily) you are dealing with the Roman empire. And over the course of 324 years, what Jesus left behind was recast into the Roman Empire with a pontiff or a pope (imitating Caesar Augustus), with a college of Cardinals (imitating the Roman senate), with Archbishops (imitating one of the military levels of regional command), with Bishops (imitating another level of the Roman army)... And so, they rebuild what Christ left behind—which appeared, for all the world, to look like that—into an imitation of the Roman empire.

Joseph started with Americans who, presumably, believed in the equality of all men—the freedom of all men. He began in a Democratic Republic in which anyone could be elected president, assuming they were born here—unless of course you have the press sympathising with you, in which event a foreign birth doesn't matter and...

So, when it comes to the experiment in Joseph's day, particularly with the desires of the... I mean, if the Restoration at the beginning was a snake, the snake looked like this [like a snake that swallowed a rat]—and that's Kirkland filled with Cambellites. It's so distorted, the center of gravity of Mormonism. I mean, you probably had (in total) around seventy-eight people that accepted the Book of Mormon (in three different locations). When the first missionaries were sent out and comes aboard, you know, 275—and then 500 **in Kirkland**. It **is** the church, and they're Cambellites. And the throwaway of that changed the trajectory, and we never landed on our feet again. (Although in Liberty Jail, Joseph was reminded **again** that you're supposed to be a servant, and everyone is supposed to be on a level. And you're supposed to raise them.)

So, now here we are 180 years plus since, and what do we have? I mean, this model works if... If you're evaluating success by the measures that the world uses, this model has created—probably, if you were really given access to the numbers—a trillion dollar empire. I mean, Bezos may be a rank amateur compared to what the Corporation of the President has—if we had the numbers out there. I can tell you that the project that they are undertaking in Florida, over the course of its life, will involve approximately a trillion dollars in today's money in order to complete that project. And they have confidence that they can undertake it.

So, this model really works **if** what you are trying to measure is success the way the world measures it: numbers, dollars, wealth, politics, social influence, the ability to mobilize a vote, the ability to influence politics, state legislatures, congressmen, senators, the ability to publish what they want to publish. We've got this model begun, but I can tell you it's a lot of work to stay below the line; and it's a lot of work to reassure people that they belong on the line together. But you know what? We have people with remarkable talent who have spent a lifetime acquiring skills and developing the ability... And in many respects, what we're able to do (using nothing more than that model and volunteers) **rivals** what this other, much bigger organization does —with as much quality, with as much attention, with as much skill.

At the end of the day, this community is built around a new law that is centered on Christ and makes every one of us no greater, no less; we all become servants; we all become His. And **you** are supposed to **bear** Christ in your countenance—which means you act, you behave, you serve, you kneel, you wash the feet, you do what's necessary to elevate others.

We have an obligation to tell the world what we believe and to tell it plainly. We have an obligation to live it and to demonstrate it—but I don't think we have the obligation to bludgeon people into coming aboard. And if they're not persuaded and they want some "Jesus and them" and to charge up and wallow in their own self righteousness, they would be problematic in this, in any of it. A whole lot of personal pronouns referring to the speaker in teaching about Christ... I mean, the most self-revealing thing I've written with little vignettes in *The Second Comforter,* and they are essentially an illustration of how to do something wrong—how to make an error, how to make a mistake—followed by a chapter explaining how to do it right. If you read that book, by the time you get to the end of the book, you're probably saying, "This guy made a lot of mistakes in his life, and God still worked with him. That gives me hope because I'm not **that** big a screw up."

MAN: Hopefully not to sidetrack... You know, one of the effects of the Second Comforter being kinda the first book you wrote, and sort of the starting point of all this is that there are those who value and claim an experience with the Lord makes you right, makes you an authority, makes you the one to be believed and listened to because you can't possibly be wrong. And in conjunction with that, there is a whole chorus of everybody who's met Jesus and met the Father and met the Mother. And I mean, you name it, all of these experiences and everybody claiming and... I guess my question is, frankly, the nuts and bolts. Is it really that... Well, is it really possible... because I believe these people are having these experiences with entities claiming to be the Lord. Is that more or less what's going on then, you know, when it says there will be false Christs. Is that a literal thing—entities coming and saying, "Congratulations, you made it, and I'm Jesus"?

DENVER: I'd have to... Well, ultimately, I would probably have to have a revelation before I could make my mind up about something. I don't challenge other people's claims. I leave them alone. But it is extraordinarily possible to have met with the Lord and been given an assignment by Him and to be ill-informed, partly-informed, erroneously oriented, and to require correction from the Lord. I'm not gonna give any examples, but time and time again, when I've inquired about something that I really needed to get an answer to, I've been told to study it out and to figure it out and to present the answer to the Lord. And I've done that. I've studied it out, I've figured it out, and I've presented my answer to the Lord—only to have the reaction of this, "Yeah, turn around. Okay? **That's** the answer. You're not only wrong, you're disappointingly wrong." It's like, "You know, I **vouched** for you in the corridors, and they're gonna be laughing. That's the best you've got?" I can't tell you how many times I've been wrong in my conclusions. But if I come and tell a conclusion to the public, **I know** it's right. And it's not me. It's right because I've been corrected.

And so, I can't tell you—I'd have to know a whole lot more about the people involved. And I don't know if people speak from a position of unjustified self-confidence or not. I can tell ya, I don't speak from the position of unjustified self-confidence. In my view, I am probably as error-prone and as wrong about my guesses as the next guy. But if I get corrected by the Lord and He makes a matter clear to me, I will speak with confidence about it—because I know what He just said. I know what His position is on that. Otherwise I'm inclined to... I mean, I hate... Anymore, I hate to even speculate, even casually. And if I do, I try to make it really clear that all I am doing is speculating. That may seem so vague. Let me make one concrete example just so that... This is only an illustration to show you that I'm dumb.

Christ says to His apostles in the New Testament that when the end comes, "You twelve are gonna sit on the throne, judging the twelve tribes of Israel"— then Judas fell, So, Judas fell; the twelve apostles are gonna sit on the twelve thrones; they're gonna be judging the tribes of Israel—and I wanna know what's up with Judas. I mean, clearly, he's a suicidal betrayer; he's a bad guy. Alright? (Maybe I want him judging me. Maybe he'll be extraordinarily liberal about his assessment of me. I mean, I didn't do **that**. I did a lot of bad stuff, but I didn't do **that**.) But I reached a conclusion that he was gonna be replaced. So, I was inquiring somewhat diligently to know the answer to this. (Now, I got an answer to this, but I think the only reason I got an answer to this was because this question has come up repeatedly since then, and I've given the answer.)

But I was curious about it, and in praying about it, the Lord said, "Well, what do you suppose?" So, I had to figure it out. And I figure you can take the entire universe and narrow it down real tight: You either got the apostle Paul, who got called by Him, or you got Matthias, who got selected by lot and replaced Judas. So, it's gotta be one of those two guys, so... Eenie meenie miney... Nah, nah—I'm not gonna do... I think it's Paul; it's gotta be Paul! I mean Paul... Dude, he wrote two thirds of the books of the New Testament. It's gotta be Paul! So, with confidence, I go back to the Lord to get the answer. And I present my answer to the solution: It's Paul. Well, no. It's not Paul.

There were twelve who presided over the tribes, and one of them did not fall, retained his position—and Joseph will **always** be there. There has only been eleven vacancies. And so, the eleven vacancies are filled by the eleven who remained true and faithful, whom He selected. And Joseph retains his position at the head of the tribe, which I would never have supposed. But I can tell you that with confidence. And I can tell you it's not Paul. And it's not Matthias. And it's not Judas. Time and time again, there are those kinds of things that come up. Most of it has to do with what's happening in real time right now. If I talk about it, I talk about it with confidence—not because I'm self-confident, but because I know what the Lord has to say about something.

Now, the Lord doesn't do unnecessary acts. He doesn't just gratuitously accommodate mankind. He has a purpose. And therefore, I assume the purposefulness of that is to give us hope and to confirm that He's going to work with us to get this done. Mankind is so situated that we are always able to destroy, fall short, rebel, and collapse into a heap—and so, you always have to realistically acknowledge that mankind can fail.

We've had Zion here two times. We are promised that it will happen a third time. We know it is going to be accomplished at some point. For that reason, it makes sense—given the time in which we find ourselves living—that we should expect that if we're willing to work with Him that this might come about. But we can always fail. I mean, the rule is "you fail." The exception is… Twice it's succeeded, and it's, you know, gonna be a third exception at some point.

———

The foregoing excerpts are taken from an organizational meeting for the Covenant of Christ Conference, held in Burley, Idaho on May 13, 2017.

Appendix 1: Episodes Containing New Material

The following episodes include all new material that was recorded for the podcast, or material that was previously unreleased to the public, as indicated:

53: Discernment, Part 3	All new material
60: Third Root	All new material
61: Witness in All the World	All new material
62: Every Word, Part 1	All new material
63: Every Word, Part 2	All new material
73: Good Questions	All new material
82: Hope, Part 3	All new material
83: Fasting	Contains some new material
88: Gospel Tangents Interview, Part 1	All new material
89: Gospel Tangents Interview, Part 2	All new material
90: Gospel Tangents Interview, Part 3	All new material
93: Meekness & Humility, Part 1	Contains some new material
94: Meekness & Humility, Part 2	Contains some new material
95: Good Cheer	Contains some new material
96: One Eternal Round	Contains some new material
99: A Bag Full of Jesus	All previously unreleased material

Appendix 2: Index

Index

333–334, 339, 344–345, 348,
366, 370, 373–374, 381–382,
387–388, 396, 398, 408, 410,
412–414, 417, 420, 427,
429–431, 433, 435, 446, 463,
466, 469, 474, 513, 532, 540,
556, 579, 582, 593, 597, 600,
603, 605, 607–608, 610, 612,
615–617, 641

Godliness, 17, 86, 105, 178, 190,
274, 345, 372, 395–396, 402,
432, 448, 522, 540, 567, 599

Good fruit, 188, 579, 612

Good works, 601

Gospel Doctrine, 268, 302, 330,
494, 507

Gospel of Jesus Christ, 53, 100,
102, 106, 225, 237, 253, 308,
333, 394, 448, 630–631

Government, 33–34, 77–79, 93,
96, 120, 173, 176, 316, 318,
363, 520–521

Government of God, 77–78, 93,
96, 120

Grace, 38, 44, 84, 250–251, 314,
344–345, 365, 376–377,
384–385, 397–398, 412, 447,
537, 541–544, 553, 559, 562,
564, 577, 592, 601–602, 617,
630, 636

Grafting, 145, 189, 192, 194, 612

Gratitude, 145, 462

Grave, 73–74, 104, 108, 164, 185,
263, 376, 404, 407, 441, 462,
593, 606, 626

Graven images, 634

Great and abominable church, 129

Great and spacious building, 259

Great Knowledge and Greater
Knowledge, 90

Great Teacher, 502

Great Whore, 119–120, 129, 165,
222, 621

Greece, 34

H

Handmaid, 437

Hardness of Heart, 606

Haughtiness, 15, 187, 314, 610

Heathen, 15, 443, 606, 634

Heavenly Gift, 315, 497, 503

Heavenly Host, 218, 227

Heber J. Grant, 202

Heed and Diligence, 380, 602

Heirs, 193, 412, 414

Hell, 32, 86, 94, 114, 238, 279,
313, 352, 356, 361, 462, 478,
483, 490, 523, 526, 528, 593,
606, 618

Herod, 544

Hierarchy, 115, 155–157, 175,
191, 195–196, 344, 348–350,
397, 504, 533, 574

High priesthood, 459, 544, 601

High priests, 544, 601, 625

Hindu, 176, 356, 358, 454, 586,
607

Historic Christianity, 259, 415

Holiness, 181, 280, 339, 359, 366,
447, 496, 499, 586, 593,
629–630

427–429, 431–441, 443,
445–449, 460, 533–534, 538,
541, 545, 551–552, 555–556,
568, 571–572, 574, 580–581,
584–585, 598, 622–625,
630–631, 635, 638–643, 650